THE OXFORD HANDBOOK OF

U.S. SOCIAL POLICY

THE OXFORD HANDBOOK OF

U.S. SOCIAL POLICY

Edited by

DANIEL BÉLAND, CHRISTOPHER HOWARD

and

KIMBERLY J. MORGAN

OXFORD
UNIVERSITY PRESS

OXFORD
UNIVERSITY PRESS

Oxford University Press is a department of the University of
Oxford. It furthers the University's objective of excellence in research,
scholarship, and education by publishing worldwide.

Oxford   New York
Auckland   Cape Town   Dar es Salaam   Hong Kong   Karachi
Kuala Lumpur   Madrid   Melbourne   Mexico City   Nairobi
New Delhi   Shanghai   Taipei   Toronto

With offices in
Argentina   Austria   Brazil   Chile   Czech Republic   France   Greece
Guatemala   Hungary   Italy   Japan   Poland   Portugal   Singapore
South Korea   Switzerland   Thailand   Turkey   Ukraine   Vietnam

Oxford is a registered trademark of Oxford University Press
in the UK and certain other countries.

Published in the United States of America by
Oxford University Press
198 Madison Avenue, New York, NY 10016

Library of Congress Cataloging-in-Publication Data
The oxford handbook of U.S. social policy / edited by Daniel Béland, Christopher Howard,
Kimberly J. Morgan.
pages cm
ISBN 978-0-19-983850-9 (hardback : alk. paper)
1. United States—Social policy.   2. Public welfare—United States.   3. United States—Social
conditions.   I. Béland, Daniel, editor of compilation   II. Morgan, Kimberly J., 1970 editor of
compilation.   III. Howard, Christopher, 1961 editor of compilation.
HN57.O945 2014
361.6'10973—dc23
2014016381

1 3 5 7 9 8 6 4 2
Printed in the United States of America
on acid-free paper

CONTENTS

PART VI PROGRAMS FOR THE DISABLED

PART VII PROGRAMS FOR WORKERS AND FAMILIES

PART VIII   POLICY OUTCOMES

List of Contributors

Edwin Amenta is a professor of sociology, political science, and history, University of California–Irvine.

Christina M. Andrews is an assistant professor in the College of Social Work, University of South Carolina.

Daniel Béland is a professor and Canada Research Chair in Public Policy at the Johnson-Shoyama Graduate School of Public Policy, University of Saskatchewan.

Edward D. Berkowitz is a professor of history and of public policy and public administration, George Washington University.

Leslie I. Boden is a professor in the Department of Environmental Health, Boston University School of Public Health.

David Brady is director of the Inequality and Social Policy Department at the WZB Berlin Social Science Center.

Andrea Louise Campbell is a professor of political science, Massachusetts Institute of Technology.

Lee A. Craig is the Alumni Distinguished Undergraduate Professor in the Department of Economics, North Carolina State University.

J. Taylor Danielson is a PhD candidate in the School of Sociology, University of Arizona.

Stephanie D'Auria is an assistant professor in the Department of Anthropology and Sociology, Vanguard University.

Lane M. Destro is an assistant professor in the Department of Sociology, Roanoke College.

Larry DeWitt was the official Historian of the Social Security Administration from 1995 to 2012.

Peter Dreier is the Dr. E.P. Clapp Distinguished Professor of Politics and Chair of the Urban and Environmental Policy Department, Occidental College.

Jennifer L. Erkulwater is an associate professor in the Department of Political Science, University of Richmond.

Teresa Ghilarducci is director of the Schwartz Center for Economic Policy Analysis and Chair of the Department of Economics, The New School for Social Research.

Daniel P. Gitterman is the Thomas Willis Lambeth Distinguished Chair in Public Policy, University of North Carolina–Chapel Hill.

Colleen M. Grogan is a professor in the School of Social Service Administration and director of the Graduate Program in Health Policy & Administration, University of Chicago.

Craig Gundersen is the Soybean Industry Endowed Professor of Agricultural Strategy in the Department of Agricultural and Consumer Economics, University of Illinois at Urbana–Champaign.

Madonna Harrington Meyer is a professor of sociology, faculty associate at the Aging Studies Institute, and senior research associate at the Center for Policy Research, Syracuse University.

Jessica Hausauer is a PhD candidate in the Department of Sociology, Syracuse University.

Crosby Hipes is a PhD candidate in the Department of Sociology, University of Maryland–College Park.

Christopher Howard is the Pamela C. Harriman Professor of Government and Public Policy at the College of William and Mary.

Laura S. Jensen is an associate professor in the Center for Public Administration and Policy, School of Public and International Affairs, Virginia Tech.

Jennifer Klein is a professor in the Department of History, Yale University.

Meredith Kleykamp is an associate professor in the Department of Sociology and director of the Center for Research on Military Organization, University of Maryland–College Park.

Robert C. Lieberman is provost and professor of political science, Johns Hopkins University.

Sandra Loughrin is an assistant professor in the Department of Sociology, University of Nebraska–Kearney.

Julia F. Lynch is an associate professor in the Department of Political Science, University of Pennsylvania.

Suzanne Mettler is the Clinton Rossiter Professor of American Institutions in the Department of Government, Cornell University.

Sonya Michel is a professor in the Department of History, University of Maryland–College Park.

Joya Misra is a professor in the Department of Sociology and Center for Public Policy and Administration, University of Massachusetts–Amherst.

Stephanie Moller is an professor in the Department of Sociology, University of North Carolina–Charlotte.

Kimberly J. Morgan is a professor of political science and international affairs, George Washington University.

James A. Morone is the John Hazen White Professor of Political Science, Public Policy and Urban Studies, Brown University.

Andrew Morris is an associate professor in the Department of History, Union College.

Jonathan Oberlander is a professor and vice chair of the Department of Social Medicine, and a professor in the Department of Health Policy and Management, University of North Carolina–Chapel Hill.

Ellen Reese is a professor of sociology and chair of Labor Studies, University of California–Riverside.

David Brian Robertson is the Curators' Teaching Professor of Political Science, University of Missouri–St. Louis.

Tracy Roof is an associate professor of political science at the University of Richmond.

Michael W. Sances is a PhD candidate in the Department of Political Science, Massachusetts Institute of Technology.

Alex Schwartz is a professor of urban policy at the New School.

Emily A. Spieler is the Edwin W. Hadley Professor of Law, Northeastern University.

Jeffrey M. Stonecash is a professor emeritus of political science in the Maxwell School of Citizenship and Public Affairs, Syracuse University.

Robin Stryker is a professor in the School of Sociology, affiliated professor in the Rogers College of Law and the School of Government and Public Policy, and research director of the National Institute for Civil Discourse, University of Arizona.

Amber Celina Tierney is a PhD candidate in the Department of Sociology, University of California–Irvine.

Alex Waddan is Senior Lecturer in American Politics, University of Leicester (UK).

Alexis N. Walker is an assistant professor in the Department of Political Science, Stetson University.

R. Kent Weaver is Distinguished Professor of Public Policy at Georgetown University and a Senior Fellow at the Brookings Institution.

Stephen A. Woodbury is a professor in the Department of Economics, Michigan State University, and a senior economist at the W. E. Upjohn Institute for Employment Research.

Acknowledgments

....

This handbook is the product of several years of work involving the participation of several dozen contributors, whom we thank for their dedication to this project. Collectively, you enriched our understanding of U.S. social policy in many ways. Special thanks to our editor David McBride at Oxford University Press, who believed in this project and enthusiastically supported it from the beginning. At Oxford University Press, we also thank Sarah Rosenthal and the rest of the editorial and production team. Daniel Béland acknowledges support from the Canada Research Chairs Program.

PART I

INTRODUCTION

CHAPTER 1

....

THE FRAGMENTED AMERICAN WELFARE STATE:

Putting the Pieces Together

....

DANIEL BÉLAND, CHRISTOPHER HOWARD,
AND KIMBERLY J. MORGAN

1 INTRODUCTION

....

THE welfare state has long been a source of controversy and struggle in the United States and other advanced industrialized nations. Contemporary politics in this country and others is often dominated by the contentious questions of who gets what from government, and who pays for it. The distributive choices that emerge from these struggles have major consequences for individuals, societies, and politics. Social policy thus offers a crucial window on the workings of government, making it important for scholars and informed citizens alike to understand the origins of social programs, their politics, and their impact on society. In the United States, that means delving into a complex and fragmented system of social provision that has emerged over the past hundred years, but the roots of which reach back to the early American Republic. It also requires us to understand the array of economic, social, and political forces that have produced this fragmented system of social provision and to put the pieces of the jigsaw puzzle together so as to understand its real-world effects. This is the purpose of this volume.

The objective of this chapter is to provide a short, synthetic introduction to the American welfare state while offering an overview of the entire *Oxford Handbook of U.S. Social Policy*. This introduction mirrors the basic structure of our handbook, as it moves from a historical and comparative overview of the American welfare state to a discussion of key theoretical perspectives on social policy development and, finally, to a discussion of current policy issues and challenges.

2 COMPARATIVE AND HISTORICAL PERSPECTIVES

Social policy refers to programs that redistribute resources across society and often seek to cushion people against life's socioeconomic risks. These programs usually take the form of cash transfers or in-kind benefits such as medical care. Taken together, social programs constitute the *welfare state*, a term that implies uniformity and coherence but in fact often conceals a tremendous amount of variation in terms of programmatic design and political dynamics.

In this handbook "social policy" and "welfare state" are used interchangeably. The concept of "welfare regime," which is discussed below, is broader than "welfare state," as it refers to the relationships among governments, markets, and families in the provision of welfare (Esping-Andersen 1990, 1999). Modern social programs span a multitude of policy areas, including programs for the unemployed, retirees, the sick, the disabled, the poor, and families with children (Béland 2010). All of these policy areas are explicitly analyzed in this handbook. Some, such as retirement pensions and health care, are represented by several chapters each, a reflection of the programmatic complexity and fragmentation of the American welfare state.

Importantly, as Esping-Andersen (1990) and many others have recognized, "private" benefits offered by employers play a key role in the world of social policy, which adds to the sheer complexity of social programming. This is particularly true in the United States, where employers and other private providers have long been prominent social policy actors, a situation promoted by large tax subsidies and contracting out for the delivery of social services (Esping-Andersen 1990; Hacker 2002; Howard and Berkowitz 2008; Klein 2003; Morgan and Campbell 2011). Further exacerbating policy complexity, the public and private realms tend to overlap, and the public-private mix is now a major feature of social policy research in the United States and elsewhere (for an overview, see Béland and Gran 2008). Consequently, this handbook pays close attention to both public and private benefits, for example, devoting entire chapters to private health insurance and pension benefits.

Public-private interactions and the above-mentioned policy area fragmentation do not fully account for the complexity of the American welfare state, because the United States is also a federal polity (Finegold 2005). Although more centralized in some respects than countries like Canada and Switzerland (Obinger, Leibfried, and Castles 2005), the United States features major regional inequalities and, especially, jurisdictional and institutional overlaps that exacerbate complexities in policy design and implementation. This level of policy complexity varies from one policy area to another, which becomes clear after reading the chapters devoted to particular programs and policy areas. On the one hand, as the chapters on Social Security and Supplemental Security Income (SSI) make clear, public pensions for the disabled and older people constitute a relatively centralized policy area in which the national government is dominant. As the chapters on Temporary Assistance for Needy Families (TANF) and Unemployment Insurance show, benefits for the unemployed and those on public assistance are much more decentralized because the states are heavily involved. Finally, as the chapters on Medicare and Medicaid suggest, some policy areas like health care feature national social programs (Medicare), which coexist with much more decentralized measures (Medicaid). In a field such as health care, these territorial and political-institutional complexities are exacerbated by the role of nongovernment providers in the allocation of public and private benefits. This is true in the case of Medicare because private intermediaries participate in the delivery of publicly funded benefits (Morgan and Campbell 2011).

Federalism, the public-private mix, and distinctions among policy areas are not the only sources of welfare state complexity and fragmentation in the United States. As far as public social programs are concerned, it is common to draw an analytical line among three main types of programs: social assistance, social insurance, and universal benefits and services (Esping-Andersen 1990; O'Connor 2002; Olsen 2002). Typically financed through general tax revenues, social assistance programs offer means-tested benefits. An example is TANF, which is discussed extensively in one chapter and mentioned in several others. In contrast, social insurance benefits are mainly financed through payroll taxes. Workers become entitled to benefits largely based on their contribution history, rather than on need, as is the case for social assistance provisions. The two most prominent social insurance programs in the United States are Medicare and Social Security, which are each featured in separate chapters and mentioned in several others. Finally, universal benefits and services are derived from citizenship or residency. These benefits and services may be considered social rights and are mostly financed through general tax revenues. Canada's Medicare system is an example, as it covers the entire population as a matter of right (Maioni 1998). In the strict sense of the term, there are no large-scale, national universal benefits in the United States, as public social policy in this country has long been characterized by the institutional and ideological dichotomy between social assistance and social insurance programs (Fraser and Gordon 1992; Steensland 2008).[1]

Discussing these three types of social programs, Gøsta Esping-Andersen (1990, 1999), one of the leading scholars of comparative welfare states, created a well-known typology of "welfare regimes." These regimes overlap, and there is great internal diversity within each regime and even within each country, as social policy arrangements vary from one policy area (or even one specific program) to another (1990, 28). With this in mind, we can turn to his three welfare regime types and see where the United States fits.

First, the social democratic regime (e.g., Denmark, Norway, and Sweden) is characterized by the dominant role of government in the allocation of welfare and the existence of large universal benefits and services, creating strong citizenship rights. Second, the Bismarckian regime (e.g., Belgium, France, and Germany) is grounded in large and fragmented social insurance systems, whose main goal is income and status maintenance rather than citizenship equality. For Esping-Andersen (1990), this regime also places a large welfare burden on the family, especially women, who are traditionally encouraged to stay at home to take care of their children or aging relatives. Finally, the liberal regime (e.g., Canada, the United Kingdom, and the United States) gives a central role to market forces and private benefits, which means that government plays a residual role in the provision of welfare. In other words, government tends to intervene only when the market is perceived to have "failed." Thus, Esping-Andersen (1990) is using "liberal" in the European sense of the term, which refers to promarket and individualistic ideas and institutions. In this context, the liberal regime leaves much room for private benefits, which are a main source of social protection for workers and their families.

Esping-Andersen's work has been widely criticized for his relative neglect of gender (Lewis 1992; Mahon 2001; Orloff 1993; Sainsbury 1999), as well as for the way he classifies specific countries or entire regions of the world, such as Southern Europe (Ferrera 1996) and Oceania (Castles 1993). That said, few scholars would challenge the idea that the United States belongs to the liberal welfare regime, at least as far as its reliance on (government-subsidized) private social benefits is concerned. For instance, unlike Canada and the United Kingdom, the United States does not have a universal, public health-care system. Instead, it relies on a mix of private and public insurance, which has not led to universal coverage (even if fully implemented, the 2010 Patient Protection and Affordable Care Act will leave tens of millions of U.S. residents without coverage). Nor does the United States offer paid parental leave. However, the "liberal" label only goes so far in capturing what is distinctive about the U.S. welfare state. As Lynch notes in her chapter for this volume, the U.S. welfare state is also notable for its wide geographic variability, the degree to which deservingness criteria are employed in awarding benefits, and its tilt towards support for seniors over younger people.

Based on the above discussion about the American welfare regime in comparative context, it is clear that the widespread reliance on private benefits (and on government regulations and tax incentives tied to them) exacerbates policy fragmentation. In fact, programmatic diversity, federalism, and complex public-private interactions have transformed the American welfare state into a complex regime that does not work all that well as far as reducing poverty, insecurity, and inequality, or even controlling costs[2] (Béland 2010; Hacker 2006; Howard 2007). The chapters on poverty, inequality, and social citizenship at the end of our handbook document the successes and flaws of this welfare state.

Although it is relatively easy to describe the key characteristics, and even the main shortcomings, of the American welfare state, explaining why it developed that way is a crucial intellectual challenge. Before we turn to theoretical perspectives directly addressing this challenge, which are discussed in Part II of the handbook, the basic historical narrative offers some insights.

Formulated in Part I, this narrative covers about four centuries, from the colonial era to the present. There are five main periods under study, each of which is the topic of a separate chapter. From the colonial era to the nineteenth century, parishes and later local communities played the most central role in social policy, which focused primarily on the poor, in an institutional environment modeled on the English Poor Law. Even during the nineteenth century the states and the national government had only a limited role in civilian social policy. As noted in Laura Jensen's chapter on the early American Republic, however, the eighteenth and nineteenth centuries witnessed the development of large pension and land grant programs for veterans and their survivors. Since then, military benefits have been a crucial yet understudied aspect of social policy in the United States.

As shown in David Brian Robertson's chapter on the Progressive Era of the 1890s–1920s, the Progressive movement transformed social policy debates in the United States by paying systematic attention to the increasingly widespread social problems related to industrialization, urbanization, and massive immigration. Although political and institutional factors limited the scope of the social reforms enacted during the Progressive Era, this period laid the foundation for a more active government, which would materialize in a bolder and more systematic way during the New Deal.

The New Deal of the 1930s dramatically increased the role of the national government in social policy through the development of large public works programs; the implementation of new grants-in-aid to the states; the adoption of a payroll tax that provided incentives for states to offer Unemployment Insurance; and finally, the creation of old-age insurance (now known as Social Security), the first entirely national social insurance program in the United States. Although some of these programs made it difficult for women and minorities to benefit, and key public works programs were dismantled during World War II in a context of renewed prosperity, the period covered in the chapter by Andrew Morris was a true turning point in welfare state development.

As discussed in Jennifer Klein's chapter, the postwar era witnessed the incremental expansion of old-age insurance and the creation of new social programs like Medicaid and Medicare. But this period also witnessed a massive expansion of private health and pension benefits, which is essential to understanding the complex and fragmented social policy system that remains in place to this day. The War on Poverty in the 1960s placed new emphasis on urban poverty and introduced several new programs such as food stamps and Head Start. It took place in the context of the civil rights movement and attempts to end racial exclusion in the American welfare state, which had long been entrenched.

Since the 1970s we have witnessed the alternation (and sometimes the superimposition) of the politics of austerity and of attempts to expand social benefits to fill gaps in the American welfare state, such as the lack of universal health coverage. Whereas the first decades of the postwar era can easily be categorized as a growth era, more recent decades are hard to classify because of a complicated mixture of expansion and retrenchment. Health care is a key example, as the United States has tried to combine cost control with greater access to health insurance, which were two central objectives of the 2010 Affordable Care Act. While it is tempting, and accurate, to view economic constraints as a source of austerity, polarization among political parties has also played an important role, as shown by Alex Waddan in his chapter on social policy s the 1970s.

3 Theoretical Approaches

As suggested above, the American system of social provision is a peculiar one, given its complexity, fragmentation, and decentralization. How can we explain the development and persistence of such a welfare state? The chapters in this handbook provide individual pieces of the puzzle that, when put together, can help us understand why social provision in the United States looks as it does.

First, social policy-making in the United States takes place in a distinctive institutional environment (Steinmo 1994). The decision-making apparatus is characterized by a remarkable degree of fragmentation, with multiple veto points that render hazardous any policy-making efforts likely to arouse some opposition. Especially unique is the preponderant role of Congress. No other country among the advanced industrialized nations has a parliamentary body that is so powerful yet so fragmented and porous in its institutional setup. Potential laws must maneuver through subcommittees, committees, and two chambers of Congress, before facing the prospect of being vetoed by the president or overturned by the Supreme Court. By contrast, in most of the wealthy democracies, parliamentary systems centralize power in the hands of the government—the prime minister and a small number of cabinet ministers who oversee executive branch agencies and are able to craft and enact important reforms (Weaver and Rockman 1993; Pierson 1994). As some of the historical chapters in this volume show, U.S. presidents have often come into office with similar reform agendas, only to struggle to guide these agendas through a decision-making environment that is laden with barriers.

The majoritarian electoral system, in which members of Congress are elected through winner-take-all elections at the district level, reinforces these tendencies. Scholars have identified a number of ways in which a single-member-district electoral system, as opposed to one based on proportional representation (PR), may undermine redistributive policies. First, PR and the resulting multiparty coalition governments give voice to a wider swath of the electorate (Alesina and Glaeser 2004), ensuring that popular opinion is more closely represented by the parties in power (Huber and Powell 1994). In addition, Iversen and Soskice (2006) argue that as majoritarian electoral systems tend to generate only two parties, middle-class voters have to choose between throwing in their lot with either a party of the working class or the wealthy. The latter is usually seen as a safer bet, bringing at the very least tax reduction and no redistribution for the middle class, whereas voting for the former may lead to both high taxation and redistribution toward the working class and the poor. The result is a party system tilted toward the right: as Edwin Amenta and Amber Celina Tierney note in their contribution to this volume, the United States has never had the socialist or social democratic parties that, in the European context, have been strong champions of the welfare state (Korpi 1983).

Finally, a majoritarian electoral system renders members of Congress more beholden to the interests of their individual districts than to a programmatic party; indeed, political parties in the United States have usually been "big tent" parties—loose coalitions of disparate groups and interests, rather than disciplined organizations that pursue centrally defined policy agendas (see chapters by Stonecash and Gitterman, this volume). Such parties have a limited hold on their members, leaving much room for individual political entrepreneurialism based on the preferences of particular districts. On the one hand, loosely organized parties can produce policy leadership by individuals who have amassed sufficient power in Congress to spearhead such reforms (Zelizer 1998). But it also enables other members of Congress to use one of the levers of veto power available to them to stymie such efforts.

American federalism reinforces many of these tendencies, as the United States is composed of 50 states with similarly porous institutional arrangements. In addition, there is a long-standing commitment—which some argue is constitutionally protected—to a particular form of federalism that leaves much responsibility for social policy to state and local governments. For certain programs, such as Medicaid or TANF, there is some amount of intergovernmental burden sharing through federal-state matching fund arrangements. During the Great Recession that began in 2007, the federal government committed considerably greater resources to state-run supplemental nutrition assistance (food stamps) and unemployment insurance programs. But states also have experienced burden shifting, with the federal government mandating program expansions without sufficient fiscal resources (Posner 1998). Because states are responsible for raising their own revenues, competition among the states has tended to depress the overall level of taxation, undercutting their ability to cover the responsibilities imposed on them by the federal government or favored by their own citizens (Alesina and Glaser 2004).

These political institutions also create opportunities for organized interests to influence the policy-making process, as each veto point can also function as an access point. Here again is an area in which the United States is distinctive from a cross-national standpoint. As Tracy Roof describes in her chapter, the United States has long been characterized by a high degree of societal organization and mobilization and by the strong influence of interest groups over the policy-making process. The latter is enhanced by the porous quality of American political institutions and the imperative for legislators to build and maintain political support within their districts. Moreover, the great frequency of elections, and their rising cost, renders politicians dependent on groups for campaign financing. Whether or not campaign contributions actually buy influence over policy agendas and voting behavior has been difficult to prove definitively (Baumgartner and Leech 1998). At the very least, campaign spending helps groups get past the door of the targeted legislators' offices (Hall and Wayman 1990), where they can make the case for policies they prefer. Not everyone enjoys such access.

The United States is somewhat unique in its lack of corporatist institutional arrangements that might mediate the influence of these groups (Wilson 1982). In much of Western Europe, corporatist bargaining systems have encouraged the formation of peak-level associations and negotiations among them to resolve complicated distributive issues. The result has been a greater degree of redistribution, as business groups have agreed to the expansion of the welfare state in return for labor peace or wage restraint (Crepaz 1998). In the United States, the group with the loudest voice, most money, or savviest lobbying strategy is likely to prevail, generating zero-sum battles among groups to secure their own interests. And although labor unions have at times wielded influence over social policy—the creation of Medicare in 1965 being a key example—they have often been outmaneuvered or outspent by business-backed opponents of the welfare state.

The status quo institutional bias described above also makes it easier for groups to oppose change than to achieve it, impeding the expansion of the welfare state but also preventing efforts to institute major cuts in it. As a number of scholars have shown, policies often generate their own supportive constituencies or may have other feedback effects that influence the subsequent politics of the welfare state (Skocpol 1992; Pierson 1994). The Social Security program, for example, created support among senior citizens while also giving them the economic resources that facilitated greater political participation (Campbell 2003). By contrast, other programs, such as Aid to Families with Dependent Children, have undermined the sense of solidarity and support for the program that might be felt among program recipients (Soss 2000), while also generating a political backlash (see Reese, D'Auria, and Loughrin, this volume). In general, path dependent processes can generate considerable stasis in public policy, although slow-moving developments can also be occurring under the surface and cumulate in significant change (Streeck and Thelen 2005).

Institutional features of American politics go a long way toward explaining the truncated nature of the public and visible welfare state. The creation or expansion of direct social programs must overcome considerable institutional obstacles and is most likely when the same party controls Congress and the presidency, with large majorities in both chambers and a high degree of agreement within the party in power. Such circumstances have been rare, but they enabled the passage of New Deal policies in the 1930s and Great Society programs in the 1960s. Major social spending initiatives that have been attempted in other periods have often failed or been significantly watered down. By the same token, attempts to dramatically overhaul the American system of social provision have hardly fared better. The status quo bias of the American political system has contributed thus to policy stasis and drift (Hacker 2004). Institutional factors also help explain other features of American welfare state politics, such as the late development of many social programs compared to developments in other nations.

However, a focus on political institutions alone will only take us so far in explaining the politics of U.S. social policy. Although there are clear barriers to public policy, some policies do make it through the institutional labyrinth, and not simply in exceptional moments (Howard 2007). For example, as several chapters in this volume show, policy makers have regularly developed and maintained social programs for certain groups that are viewed as deserving (see Erkulwater; Jensen; Kleykamp and Hipes; Mettler and Walker, this volume). Moreover, a focus on institutional barriers may be better at explaining what the United States lacks—a large, direct, public, and visible system of social provision—and less effective at accounting for what it actually has—a submerged or hidden welfare state that is large and delivers social programs through complex public-private arrangements.

To explain some of these aspects of the American welfare state, we might turn to political culture and the values expressed through public opinion. As Andrea Louise Campbell and Michael Sances argue in their chapter, Americans value and support many government programs, but they do not like government. Majorities of Americans say that they would like more spent on senior citizens, children, the homeless, and the poor, but they will assert with equal conviction that they do not want the size of government to grow and would like to pay lower taxes. This contradictory set of opinions shapes a political environment in which politicians often feel pressure to address popular demand for social programs, yet try to do so with as little overt growth of government as possible. One result is the recurring delegation of authority to other actors, shifting responsibilities onto state and local governments and constructing public-private partnerships as a way to meet popular demand for social programs (Morgan and Campbell 2011). Tax expenditures represent another important instrument for addressing social problems without creating large new bureaucracies (Howard 1997). Given the power of antitax sentiment and rhetoric in American politics, reducing taxes in the service of social policy objectives can potentially satisfy the two sides of American public opinion.

Although political institutions may make it more likely that certain actors are able to prevail over others, we also need to know about the kinds of policy ideas these actors bring to the table (Béland and Waddan 2012; Blyth 2002; Danielson and Stryker, this volume; Padamsee 2009; Stryker and Wald 2009). Many of the political actors who have devised solutions to the nation's collective social problems may prefer a "government out of sight," relying on private alternatives and indirect or more localized modes of governance over those that are direct, national, and highly visible (Balogh 2009; Clemens 2006). The emergence and spread of neoliberalism since the 1970s has also been an important source of reform ideas, such as the proposal to convert Social Security into a system of private accounts or to turn Medicare into competing private insurance plans (Béland and Waddan 2012). Although large-scale reforms of this sort have been stymied by both institutional veto points and popular opposition, the commitment to shrinking the size of the welfare state is a central platform of the Republican Party and has been embraced by some centrist Democrats as well.

Americans and their leaders also tend to express certain "cultural categories of worth"—beliefs about who is deserving of social programs (Steensland 2006)—that have shaped the development of the welfare state. As Jensen shows, the use of such categories to justify social entitlement dates back to the early American Republic and influenced social policy throughout the nineteenth century. In the latter half of that century pensions for Civil War veterans valorized those seen as having honorably served the nation, although growth in the pensions was also fueled by the patronage-based system of party politics (Skocpol 1992). Advocates for mothers' pensions and protections for women and children in the late nineteenth and early twentieth centuries sought to draw upon a similar strand of republican thought, holding up mothers as the embodiment of civic virtue by dint of their contribution to the reproduction of the citizenry (Skocpol 1992). Since then, notions of deservingness have shaped the political viability of many social policy initiatives, underpinning programs such as Medicare and Social

Security—the benefits of which are viewed as "earned" due to the contributions that workers made to them—while undercutting social assistance programs—"welfare"—for the able-bodied (e.g., Reese, D'Auria, and Loughrin, this volume). Much of U.S. housing policy reflects a belief that owners deserve more government help than renters (Dreier and Schwartz, this volume).

Overall, Americans express little support for redistribution toward those who have not earned their benefits in some way (see the chapter by Campbell and Sances). Work is an important avenue toward entitlement, for example justifying the creation of the Earned Income Tax Credit, which benefits only those who work for wages, as opposed to a system of guaranteed income that would provide a floor under the incomes of all regardless of their work history (Steensland 2006). Military service to the country also grants entitlement to an array of benefits and services that are more generous and comprehensive than those most ordinary citizens receive (see Kleykamp and Hipes, this volume). For example, while "socialized medicine" has been a recurring bogeyman in American politics, veterans have long benefited from what is essentially socialized medicine—the VA health-care system (Stevens 1991).

Cultural beliefs about gender roles, race, and ethnicity have shaped U.S. social policy in myriad ways. As in most welfare regimes, women's entitlement to social benefits in the United States usually came through relationships of dependence on either male breadwinners or relatives (see chapters by Jensen and Michel, this volume). The rise in women's workforce participation since the 1960s generated pressure in many countries for new policies that would support mothers' employment, such as paid parental leave or subsidies for broad-based access to child care. Such proposals were defeated in the United States, reflecting and reinforcing the view that responsibilities for caregiving are best left to the private sphere. As the chapters by Sonya Michel on work-family policy and Madonna Harrington Meyer and Jessica Hausauer on long-term care argue, public responsibility in these areas remains truncated, leaving people to cobble together caring arrangements from what is available in the private marketplace and a patchwork of tax-based subsidies and means-tested assistance. The growing acceptability of mothers' employment helped undercut support for the AFDC program, which had allowed single mothers of young children to care for children at home. The welfare reform in 1996 thus imposed strict work requirements on poor single mothers and increased spending on work supports as a way to reduce welfare "dependency" (see chapter by Weaver in this volume; Orloff 2006).

Whether or not diversity in general undercuts social solidarity and support for redistribution is a subject of continuing academic debate (see Alesina and Glaeser 2004; Banting 2005), but in the United States, racial antagonisms have mattered in several ways. First, cultural categories of deservingness have clearly been tainted by race, as the conflation of poverty and race in the public mind since the 1960s helped generate antipathy toward the AFDC program (Gilens 2000). Racial diversity has had other consequences for the welfare state, as racial conflict has influenced the structure of political competition and the nature of the party system, as described by Robert Lieberman in this volume. Throughout a good part of the twentieth century, the Democratic Party was divided between northern and southern wings that held fundamentally different interests in social policy. While northerners represented white and immigrant workers and supported redistributive initiatives, southerners represented a racial hierarchy that depended on the formal disenfranchisement of blacks and their economic subordination. These deep divisions hampered the unity of the Democratic Party and frequently gave rise to cross-party coalitions between conservative Republicans and Southern Democrats to either block social reforms or craft them in a way that would prove least empowering to African Americans (Lieberman 1998; Quadagno 1994).

Putting together the findings of this research, one can see how political institutions have shaped and refracted public opinion, interest group mobilization, and social structural forces in a way that has produced a highly distinctive system of social provision. Clearly Americans have a desire for protections against life's risks, and politicians have responded. But they have done so in a way that reflects the great difficulties of passing policy in the United States and that is often responsive to politically powerful interests.

4 POLICY ISSUES AND CHALLENGES

The welfare state is more than a contest among competing ideas, interests, and institutions. It is also a crucial means of relieving hardship and improving lives. A generation ago scholars wrestled with the question of why the United States did so little for its needy citizens. In particular, they tried to understand why, as many European nations were introducing social insurance programs during the late nineteenth and early twentieth centuries, the U.S. government did not (e.g., Lubove 1986; Orloff 1988; Orloff and Skocpol 1984), and why the United States repeatedly failed to enact national health insurance (e.g., Starr 1982).

Those questions remain important, and they still animate the research agenda (e.g., Quadagno 2005). In recent years, however, scholars have noticed other features of the policy terrain. While the American political system does seem almost immune to large, sudden changes, scholars have found instances of incremental changes that ultimately had large cumulative effects. Notable examples include the spread of employment-based retirement and health benefits in the decades after World War II, which was fueled in part by the tax code (Hacker 2002), and sizable increases to Social Security benefits during the late 1960s and early 1970s (Derthick 1979). Scholars also found moderate-sized innovations in social policy such as Section 8 housing vouchers (1974), new tax breaks for families with children in 1975 (the Earned Income Tax Credit) and 1997 (the Child Tax Credit), new regulations to help the disabled find and keep a job (1990), and the addition of a Medicare drug benefit in 2003. Both kinds of changes have implications for the mix of public and private—combining social insurance, public assistance, tax expenditures, social regulations, insurance, direct government provision, and contracting out—and make the American welfare state larger and more dynamic than it was once believed to be. One is reminded of a hydrothermal vent, deep below the ocean's surface, that may be too harsh for many creatures to survive, yet on closer inspection still teems with life.

All this activity could be a positive sign that the American welfare state has been responsive to the needs of its citizens. In some respects, this is true. One of the greatest accomplishments of the U.S. government over the last half century has been the dramatic decrease in poverty among the elderly, and that drop was due largely to Social Security and Medicare (Campbell 2003, ch. 2; Englehardt and Gruber 2004). Senior citizens may be the best-known beneficiaries, but they are not the only ones. The United States has made major strides in providing health insurance to children, especially by enlarging Medicaid. Expansions to the Earned Income Tax Credit have helped millions of low-wage workers and their families live above the poverty line (see Gitterman, this volume). During and after the Great Recession of 2007–2009, the U.S. government spent record sums on unemployment benefits and food stamps. That aid helped millions of Americans keep a roof over their heads and food on the table (on food assistance programs, see Gundersen, this volume). The Affordable Care Act (2010), once fully implemented, will make medical care more available to several million low- and moderate-income citizens. In short, U.S. social policy has helped many, many people over the years, and our society would be very different without the welfare state.

As the chapters in Parts III and IV demonstrate, the American welfare state nevertheless falls short in certain ways, and important challenges remain. Here we wish to highlight a few general problems that cut across social programs and have attracted considerable attention; for more specific problems, readers should consult individual chapters.

A problem that many policy makers worry about is the growing cost of social programs. Anything related to the elderly or health care—e.g., Social Security, Medicare, and Medicaid, as well as workers' compensation; fringe benefits for government workers; and tax expenditures for pensions, housing, and health insurance—usually tops the list of concerns. One might reasonably infer from these debates that the American welfare state is too generous and needs to be cut back. Yet despite this apparent largesse, poverty and inequality are unusually high compared to other affluent democracies. These are classic measures of how well a welfare state is performing, and the signs are not encouraging. In fact, it has been decades since the United States made any significant progress in reducing poverty, and inequality has been growing (Brady and Destro, Moller and Misra this volume). From this perspective, the American welfare state is in trouble because it is too small or badly designed, or both.

The cost problem is not new, nor is it confined to the United States. Since the 1970s policy makers in many nations have worried about whether they can afford to keep all the promises they have made to their citizens. While slower economic growth has limited the revenues available to fund social programs, aging populations and changes in work and family structure have increased the demand for social benefits, while escalating medical costs have boosted the price of key benefits. Less money coming in plus more money going out equals fiscal trouble (Béland 2010; Craig, this volume). It is common, for example, to hear warnings about looming trust fund "crises" for Social Security and Medicare, the two biggest social insurance programs (Berkowitz and DeWitt, Oberlander, this volume). Programs financed by general revenues, such as Medicaid and Food Stamps, are often singled out by those who believe that social spending is largely responsible for the budget deficit and national debt.

Because most parts of the American welfare state are quite popular (Campbell and Sances, this volume) and defended by well-organized groups (Roof, this volume), elected officials have been reluctant to eliminate or substantially retrench social programs. They have instead resorted to periodic trimming. This is a delicate task, for too big a cut could anger voters. When Social Security ran dangerously low on funds in the early 1980s, officials raised the normal retirement age from 65 to 67, which had the dual benefit of bringing in more money and reducing the total benefits paid. Officials also made sure that this change would happen very gradually and would not start for another two decades in order to minimize backlash from senior citizens (Berkowitz and DeWitt, this volume). Trimming Medicare costs has meant adjusting complicated reimbursement schedules for doctors and hospitals rather than curbing eligibility or taking away benefits from seniors (Oberlander, this volume). The biggest cuts to disability insurance came not from legislation, but from administrative actions that were harder for the general public to detect—and many of these cuts were later restored (Erkulwater, this volume). The minimum wage was never explicitly lowered, but was allowed to erode in value as inflation took its toll (Gitterman, this volume). The stock of public housing units gradually diminished in part because Congress failed to set aside enough monies for maintenance and repairs (Schwartz, this volume). In this context, the large, durable, and very public cuts to "welfare" in 1996 (Weaver, this volume) appear to be the exception rather than the rule.

The high priority placed on cost control in this country reflects to some degree the growing power of conservatives. Congressional Republicans, as a group, are more conservative now than at any time since the New Deal (Stonecash, this volume). Since 1980, Republicans have controlled parts of government much more often than they did during the initial growth period of the welfare state, from the 1930s to the 1970s. Conservative think tanks such as the Heritage Foundation and the Cato Institute have become well-established and influential. Many conservatives want to do more than slow the growth of the American welfare state; they want to shrink it (Hacker and Pierson 2006). Thus it has become more common for truly radical changes—such as partially privatizing Social Security, converting Medicare to a voucher system, or changing Medicaid to a block grant—to be proposed by the political Right.

Conservatives have been less interested, however, in cutting the "hidden welfare state" (Howard 1997) of tax expenditures. Cutting tax expenditures would appear equivalent to raising taxes, which Republicans abhor. Moreover, many of these tax expenditures benefit important constituencies such as affluent voters and the housing industry. To be fair, both political parties have been active in defending and even expanding this part of the American welfare state (Howard 2007). As a result, debates over cost control in the United States are focused on some types of social spending more than others.

The main threats to these tax expenditures come instead from the gradual erosion of health and pension benefits in the private sector and from the occasional tax reform (e.g., in 1986) that may have a temporary impact (Patashnik 2008).

Those on the political Left tend to be disturbed more by the millions of Americans who live in poverty and by the growing distance between rich and poor. The cost problems, they argue, can be solved by finding additional revenue, usually from the more affluent, and by wringing waste and inefficiencies out of current programs (especially health care). The greater challenge for them is reducing the number of have-nots in society. Although experts disagree about the best ways to measure poverty and inequality, clear patterns emerge no matter which measure is used. Children, single-mother families, blacks, and Hispanics are among the most disadvantaged groups. Despite the considerable benefits of Social Security, Medicare, and Medicaid, many of the very old still live in poverty, and a sizable fraction of the elderly live just above the poverty line. Inequality is getting worse, largely because of rapid gains at the top of the income distribution. As the chapters in this volume make clear, these trends began well before the latest recession (see Brady and Destro, Moller and Misra, and Weaver, this volume).

What should be done? For some, the answer is to make the American welfare state look more like its European counterparts. This would entail universal health insurance (which the Affordable Care Act does not promise), paid parental leave for all workers, and more support for child care, for example. An alternative approach would be to change the existing distribution of taxes and benefits so that the affluent pay more, receive less, or both. The Affordable Care Act has modified Medicare to impose higher taxes on the rich, and one of the more popular proposed changes to Social Security is to lift the cap on income subject to payroll taxes. Likewise, many analysts have suggested curbing the extent to which tax expenditures help affluent individuals to save for retirement, buy health insurance, and purchase a home (Ghilarducci, this volume). Those tax breaks could be targeted more at middle- and lower-income Americans, or the additional tax revenue could help fund traditional spending programs. Clearly, these two approaches are not mutually exclusive.

What can be done, politically, is the more vexing question. Most U.S. social programs have developed strong constituencies based on some combination of beneficiaries and third-party providers (e.g., doctors, hospitals, nursing homes, insurance companies, pharmaceutical makers, agribusiness, home builders, realtors, and investment firms handling pension funds). They have a vested interest in the status quo and would probably oppose any major cutbacks. The groups most likely to benefit from a bigger welfare state are politically weak. No one expects children or single mothers to influence votes in Congress, much less the next election. The two major political parties, at least at the elite level, have been moving farther apart from each other, making compromise increasingly difficult (Stonecash, this volume). A case in point is the Affordable Care Act, which congressional Republicans overwhelmingly opposed and have repeatedly tried to repeal. In general, anything that looks remotely like a tax increase or income redistribution has been opposed vigorously by conservatives.

These are not exactly ideal conditions for sudden departures in policy. Absent some large and sustained shift in party control of government, it seems reasonable to expect that incremental adjustments to social programs will continue, some pleasing liberals and others more to the liking of conservatives. Some of these adjustments will probably become quite important over time. Yet overall coherence and clear direction will likely be in short supply.

Notes

1. Public education could be seen as an aspect of social citizenship, but we do not consider education policy in this volume, as it is not typically understood as a component of the welfare state.
2. Regarding costs, for instance, OECD data show that in 2007 the United States spent more than 25 percent of its GDP (Gross Domestic Product) on social benefits, when both public and private programs are included. This is higher than for countries such as Canada, Finland, Japan, the United Kingdom, and Spain (Adema, Fron, and Ladaique 2011). See also the contribution of Lynch in this volume.

References

Indicates recommended reading.

Adema, Willem, Pauline Fron, and Maxime Ladaique. 2011. "Is the European Welfare State Really More Expensive? Indicators on Social Spending, 1980–2012; and a Manual to the OECD Social Expenditure Database (SOCX)." *OECD Social, Employment and Migration Working Papers* No. 124. http://dx.doi.org/10.1787/5kg2d2d4pbf0-en.

Alesina, Alberto, and Edward L. Glaeser. 2004. *Fighting Poverty in the US and Europe: A World of Difference.* New York: Oxford University Press.

Balogh, Brian. 2009. *A Government Out of Sight: The Mystery of National Authority in Nineteenth-Century America.* New York: Cambridge University Press.

Banting, Keith. 2005. "The Multicultural Welfare State: International Experience and North American Narratives." *Social Policy & Administration* 39:98–115.

Baumgartner, Frank R., and Beth L. Leech. 1998. *Basic Interests: The Importance of Groups in Politics and in Political Science.* Princeton, NJ: Princeton University Press.

Béland, Daniel. 2010. *What Is Social Policy? Understanding the Welfare State.* Cambridge: Polity Press.

Béland, Daniel, and Brian Gran, eds. 2008. *Public and Private Social Policy: Health and Pensions in a New Era.* Basingstoke, UK: Palgrave Macmillan.

Béland, Daniel, and Alex Waddan. 2012. *The Politics of Policy Change: Welfare, Medicare, and Social Security Reform in the United States.* Washington, DC: Georgetown University Press.

Blyth, Mark. 2002. *Great Transformations: Economic Ideas and Institutional Change in the Twentieth Century.* Cambridge: Cambridge University Press.

Campbell, Andrea Louise. 2003. *How Policies Make Citizens: Senior Political Activism and the American Welfare State.* Princeton, NJ: Princeton University Press.

Castles, Francis G., ed. 1993. *Families of Nations*. Dartmouth, UK: Aldershot.

Clemens, Elisabeth S. 2006. "Lineages of the Rube Goldberg State: Building and Blurring Public Programs, 1900–1940." In *Rethinking Political Institutions: The Art of the State*, edited by Ian Shapiro, Stephen Skowronek, and Daniel Galvin, 187–215. New York: New York University Press.

Crepaz, Markus M. L. 1998. "Inclusion vs. Exclusion: Political Institutions and the Welfare State." *Comparative Politics* 31:61–80.

Derthick, Martha. 1979. *Policymaking for Social Security*. Washington, DC: Brookings Institution.

Englehardt, Gary V., and Jonathan Gruber. 2004. *Social Security and the Evolution of Elderly Poverty*. Working Paper 10466. Cambridge, MA: National Bureau of Economic Research.

Esping-Andersen, Gøsta. 1990. *The Three Worlds of Welfare Capitalism*. Princeton, NJ: Princeton University Press.

Esping-Andersen, Gøsta. 1999. *Social Foundations of Postindustrial Economies*. Oxford: Oxford University Press.

Ferrera, Maurizio. 1996. "The Southern Model of Welfare in Social Europe." *Journal of European Social Policy* 6 (1): 17–37.

Finegold, Kenneth. 2005. "The United States: Federalism and Its Counter-factuals." In *Federalism and the Welfare State*, edited by Herbert Obinger, Stephan Leibfried, and Francis G. Castles, 138–178. Cambridge: Cambridge University Press.

Fraser, Nancy, and Linda Gordon. 1992. "Contract versus Charity: Why Is There No Social Citizenship in the United States?" *Socialist Review* 22 (July): 45–68.

Gilens, Martin. 2000. *Why Americans Hate Welfare: Race, Media, and the Politics of Antipoverty Policy*. Chicago: University of Chicago Press.

Hacker, Jacob S. 2002. *The Divided Welfare State: The Battle over Public and Private Social Benefits in the United States*. New York: Cambridge University Press.

Hacker, Jacob S. 2006. *The Great Risk Shift: The Assault on American Jobs, Families, Health Care, and Retirement and How You Can Fight Back*. New York: Oxford University Press.

Hacker, Jacob S., and Paul Pierson. 2006. *Off-Center: The Republican Revolution and the Erosion of American Democracy*. New Haven, CT: Yale University Press.

Hall, Richard L., and Frank Wayman. 1990. "Buying Time: Moneyed Interests and the Mobilization of Bias in Congressional Committees." *American Political Science Review* 84 (September): 797–820.

Howard, Christopher. 1997. *The Hidden Welfare State: Tax Expenditures and Social Policy in the United States*. Princeton, NJ: Princeton University Press.

Howard, Christopher. 2007. *The Welfare State Nobody Knows: Debunking Myths about U.S. Social Policy*. Princeton, NJ: Princeton University Press.

Howard, Christopher, and Edward D. Berkowitz. 2008. "Extensive but Not Inclusive: Health Care and Pensions in the United States." In *Public and Private Social Policy: Health and Pension Policies in a New Era*, edited by Daniel Béland and Brian Gran, 70–91. Basingstoke, UK: Palgrave Macmillan.

Huber, John D., and G. Bingham Powell Jr. 1994. "Congruence between Citizens and Policymakers in Two Visions of Liberal Democracy." *World Politics* 46 (3): 291–326.

Iversen, Torben, and David Soskice. 2006. "Electoral Institutions, Parties, and the Politics of Class: Why Some Democracies Redistribute More than Others." *American Political Science Review* 100 (2): 165–182.

Klein, Jennifer. 2003. *For All These Rights: Business, Labor, and the Shaping of America's Public-Private Welfare State*. Princeton, NJ: Princeton University Press.

Korpi, Walter. 1983. *The Democratic Class Struggle*. Boston: Routledge & Kegan Paul.

Lewis, Jane. 1992. "Gender and the Development of Welfare Regimes." *Journal of European Social Policy* 2 (3): 159–173.

Lieberman, Robert C. 1998. *Shifting the Color Line: Race and the American Welfare State*. Cambridge, MA: Harvard University Press.

Lubove, Roy. 1986. *The Struggle for Social Security, 1900–1935*. 2nd ed. Pittsburgh: University of Pittsburgh Press.

Mahon, Rianne. 2001. "Theorizing Welfare Regimes: Toward a Dialogue?" *Social Politics* 8 (1): 24–35.

Maioni, Antonia. 1998. *Parting at the Crossroads: The Emergence of Health Insurance in the United States and Canada*. Princeton, NJ: Princeton University Press.

Morgan, Kimberly J., and Andrea Louise Campbell. 2011. *The Delegated Welfare State: Medicare, Markets, and the Governance of Social Policy*. New York: Oxford University Press.

Obinger, Herbert, Stephan Leibfried, and Francis G. Castles. 2005. "Introduction: Federalism and the Welfare State." In *Federalism and the Welfare State*, edited by Herbert Obinger, Stephan Leibfried, and Francis G. Castles, 1–48. Cambridge: Cambridge University Press.

O'Connor, Julia S. 2002. "Understanding the Welfare State and Welfare States: Theoretical Perspectives." In *Political Sociology: Canadian Perspectives*, edited by Douglas Bear, 110–128. Oxford: Oxford University Press.

Olsen, Gregg M. 2002. *The Politics of the Welfare State: Canada, Sweden, and the United States*. Toronto: Oxford University Press.

Orloff, Ann Shola. 1988. "The Political Origins of America's Belated Welfare State." In *The Politics of Social Policy in the United States*, edited by Margaret Weir, Ann Shola Orloff, and Theda Skocpol, 37–80. Princeton, NJ: Princeton University Press.

Orloff, Ann Shola. 1993. "Gender and the Social Rights of Citizenship: The Comparative Analysis of Gender Relations and Welfare States." *American Sociological Review* 58:303–328.

Orloff, Ann Shola 2006. "From Maternalism to 'Employment for All': State Policies to Promote Women's Employment across the Affluent Democracies." In *The State After Statism: New State Activities in the Age of Liberalization*, edited by Jonah Levy, 230–268. Cambridge, MA: Harvard University Press.

Orloff, Ann Shola, and Theda Skocpol. 1984. "Why Not Equal Protection? Explaining the Politics of Public Social Spending in Britain, 1900–1911, and the United States, 1880s–1920." *American Sociological Review* 49:726–750.

Padamsee, Tasleem. 2009. "Culture in Connection: Re-Contextualizing Ideational Processes in the Analysis of Policy Development." *Social Politics* 16 (4): 413–445.

Patashnik, Eric M. 2008. *Reforms at Risk: What Happens after Major Policy Changes Are Enacted*. Princeton, NJ: Princeton University Press.

Pierson, Paul. 1994. *Dismantling the Welfare State? Reagan, Thatcher and the Politics of Retrenchment*. New York: Cambridge University Press.

Posner, Paul L. 1998. *The Politics of Unfunded Mandates: Whither Federalism?* Washington, DC: Georgetown University Press.

Quadagno, Jill. 1994. *The Color of Welfare: How Racism Undermined the War on Poverty*. New York: Oxford University Press.

Quadagno, Jill. 2005. *One Nation Uninsured: Why the U.S. Has No National Health Insurance*. New York: Oxford University Press.

Sainsbury, Diane. 1999. *Gender and Welfare States Regimes*. Oxford: Oxford University Press.

Skocpol, Theda. 1992. *Protecting Soldiers and Mothers: The Political Origins of Social Policy in the United States*. Cambridge, MA: Belknap Press.

Soss, Joe. 2000. *Unwanted Claims: The Politics of Participation in the U.S. Welfare System*. Ann Arbor: University of Michigan Press.

Starr, Paul. 1982. *The Social Transformation of American Medicine*. New York: Basic Books.

Steensland, Brian. 2006. "Cultural Categories and the American Welfare State: The Case of Guaranteed Income Policy." *American Journal of Sociology* 111 (5): 1273–1326.

Steensland, Brian. 2008. *The Failed Welfare Revolution: America's Struggle over Guaranteed Income Policy*. Princeton, NJ: Princeton University Press.

Steinmo, Sven. 1994. "American Exceptionalism Reconsidered: Culture or Institutions?" In *Dynamics of American Politics: Approaches and Interpretations*, edited by Larry Dodd and Calvin Jillson, 106–131. Boulder, CO: Westview.

Stevens, Rosemary. 1991. "Can the Government Govern? Lessons from the Formation of the Veterans Administration." *Journal of Health Politics, Policy and Law* 16 (2): 281–305.

Streeck, Wolfgang, and Kathleen Thelen. 2005. *Beyond Continuity: Institutional Change in Advanced Political Economies*. Oxford: Oxford University Press.

Stryker, Robin, and Pamela Wald. 2009. "Redefining Compassion to Reform Welfare: How Supporters of 1990s US Federal Welfare Reform Aimed for the Moral High Ground." *Social Politics* 16 (4): 519–557.

Weaver, Kent R., and Bert Rockman, eds. 1993. *Do Institutions Matter? Government Capabilities in the U.S. and Abroad*. Washington, DC: Brookings Institution Press.

Wilson, Graham. 1982. "Why There Is No Corporatism in the United States." In *Patterns of Corporatist Policy-Making*, vol. 2, edited by Philippe C. Schmitter and Gerhard Lehmbruch, 219–36. London: Sage.

Zelizer, Julian E. 1998. *Taxing America: Wilbur D. Mills, Congress, and the State, 1945–1975*. New York: Cambridge University Press.

PART II

HISTORICAL DEVELOPMENT

CHAPTER 2

....

SOCIAL PROVISION BEFORE THE TWENTIETH CENTURY

....

LAURA S. JENSEN

1 INTRODUCTION

....

THE origins of modern American social policy commonly are believed to lie in the economic crisis of the Great Depression and the consequent enactment of the Social Security Act of 1935. This focus on the twentieth century is misguided. First and foremost, it is historically inaccurate. Social provision has been a core task of government in the United States since before the American Revolution. Local governments operated an extensive array of relief programs under British colonial rule that remained in place after independence. Colonial and state governments provided pensions and land grants for disabled military veterans and their survivors. They also supplemented local assistance by creating institutional means of care for various classes of dependent citizens and pensions for certain public servants. Major national programs also provided pension and land benefits to military veterans, their survivors, and other citizens, and a burgeoning array of religious and civic organizations established assistance programs that complemented public efforts. Social provision was in fact "big business" (Green 2003, 1) in America long before the concept of the welfare state was invented.

The importance of pre-twentieth-century social benefits lies not simply in their existence or even in their scope, but moreover in the role they played as policy precedents that shaped the evolution of social provision and the American welfare state. Early social benefits established powerful norms about who was deserving of aid, the forms of aid that should be given, which public and private institutions and organizations should provide aid, and why. Viewing contemporary social policy as a product of the twentieth century obscures this path of development, and it blinds us to the ways in which current policy has and has not managed to escape from the legacy of the past. We can better understand the character, dynamics, and limits of contemporary American social policy by attending to its deep historical roots.

The social provision that developed in America over the course of the seventeenth, eighteenth, and nineteenth centuries was distinguished by several key characteristics. These include the provision of social benefits by all levels of government (local, state, and national); considerable subnational control over, and variation in, those benefits; a high degree of selectivity in their distribution; and the use of social benefits to advance policy goals other than social welfare. These characteristics resulted from sociopolitical differences between the colonies and, later, federalism; the logic of the English poor laws; the ambition to establish a new nation of continental proportions; and the discriminatory hierarchies of race, gender, and ethnicity that existed in America in its formative years. This essay details the evolution of U.S. social benefits chronologically, detailing the paths of development followed by local, state, and federal benefits and the aggregate foundation they established for modern American social policy.

2   The Colonial and Revolutionary Periods

Many who chose to immigrate to the American colonies were people of moderate or few means. Some had spent all they had to pay for the journey to America, or sold themselves into indentured servitude in exchange for ocean passage. Others had been abducted and forced into bondage, or were transported convicts, beggars, orphans, vagrants, and political prisoners. The trip across the Atlantic was hazardous and debilitating, and those who survived it frequently reached shore ill or infirm, only to face conditions of deprivation and hardship. Poverty was common in the early years of the colonies, and it grew as European settlement expanded and the colonies matured (Herndon 2004; Trattner 1999). Certain groups were at higher risk of becoming impoverished because they lacked the resources necessary to cope with the vagaries of wars, poor harvests, economic downturns, natural disasters, illness and disability. These included single women, children, the elderly, Native Americans, and free and enslaved blacks (Herndon 2004). Blacks and Native Americans faced particular challenges because the social and economic framework established by and for white settlers severely constrained their opportunities.

Colonial governments promised to care for men who were disabled during the wars against Native Americans and the French and were thus unable to support themselves. In 1636, the Plymouth Colony established the first pension law in America, guaranteeing that any soldier maimed in combat would be "maintained competently" for life by the colony. Similar laws were enacted in Virginia, Maryland, New York, and Rhode Island. Veterans' widows and orphans typically also received pensions, provided that they were poor (Glasson 1918).

2.1 The Poor Law and Poor Relief

Colonial assemblies also acknowledged public responsibility for persons unable to support themselves or be supported by family, but drew on the familiar terms of England's 1601 Poor Law to make localities responsible for poor relief and its cost. New England most closely adhered to the English Poor Law, appointing overseers of the poor to assess and collect taxes for the care of the needy under the direction of town authorities. By contrast, Pennsylvania relied on county government (Katz 1986; Quigley 1996; Trattner 1999). In southern colonies, where the Anglican Church was widely established, the parish originally was the local unit responsible for poor relief, with the church's board of vestry in charge of assessing and collecting the requisite taxes. Similarly, New Amsterdam relied on officers of the Dutch Reformed Church to raise funds through voluntary contributions and distribute aid, an arrangement that lasted until the colony came under English rule in 1664 (Green 2003; Trattner 1999).

Local responsibility for funding and administering poor relief ensured that public assistance under the poor laws would be a solution of last resort, and that membership in a local community would be the first criterion determining eligibility for aid: only "settled," legal residents could claim public support. Cities and towns devised a host of legal safeguards designed to protect their coffers against persons likely to become "chargeable," including time requirements for legal residency, restrictions on transiency and land sales to strangers, and regulations governing the hosting of boarders and travelers. Settlement disputes between towns (conflicts over the jurisdiction poor persons properly belonged to) were common, and often resulted in litigation. Transients (persons who had been living in a town but had not become legal residents) were "warned out" and removed by constables. Those who were expelled and dared to return were subject to harsh penalties, including heavy fines and whippings (Herndon 2001; Katz 1986; Trattner 1999). Warning out was practiced most vigorously during the eighteenth century in New England, where the majority of those removed were women without spouses, children, and persons of color (Herndon 2001). Settlement laws in the South tended to be less strict than in New England, but they still existed for local officials wishing to enforce them (Green 1999).

The forms of aid received by indigent colonists varied. Some assistance was indirect, as when authorities granted tax exemptions to struggling individuals or allowed poor community members to plant gardens or graze cattle on public land. When indirect aid proved insufficient, officials might offer direct help, such as medical care, firewood, food, blankets, clothing, rent money, or small stipends. These "outdoor relief" measures were aimed at sustaining the poor in their own homes, and generally were expected to be temporary (Green 2003; Herndon 2004; Lee 1982; Trattner 1999).

There also were forms of "indoor relief." Local families with adequate means sometimes shared the burden of caring for destitute community members in their homes for portions of the year. The more common practice was to place the poor in private homes at public expense, ordinarily by auctioning them off to the lowest bidder (Katz 1986; Trattner 1999). Pauper, illegitimate, and orphan children typically were bound out in apprenticeship indentures and raised in more prosperous households, where they received basic literacy education and learned domestic skills or a trade. Indentured children were such a critical source of labor for colonial farmers and artisans that in some areas they were actively sought out, relieving local governments of the expense of their care (Green 2003; Katz 1986). Poor children may have been the main source of labor from outside of the family in New England (Nash 2004).

Finally, some group institutions—almshouses or poorhouses and workhouses—were built in the most populous cities to provide indoor relief, anticipating an approach that would become far more prevalent in the nineteenth century. For example, the Virginia Assembly decided in 1646 to establish a workhouse in Jamestown (Green 2003). Charleston erected a workhouse in 1734 (Herndon 2004). A year later, Boston opened the doors of a workhouse on its Common, and in 1750 launched what may have been the nation's first "workfare" program: a linen factory where poor women could work to provide for themselves while reducing the city's poor relief expenditures (Nash 1979, 169; 2004). Almshouses were established in Boston in 1662; New York, 1700; Philadelphia, 1732; Providence, 1753; and Baltimore, 1773 (Katz 1986; Lee 1982; Rothman 2002).

In theory and in law, almshouses were supposed to care for the "worthy" poor (aged, infirm, mentally ill, disabled, and other persons who could not care for themselves), whereas workhouses were intended to incarcerate vagrants, beggars, and other able-bodied "unworthy" paupers and place them at hard labor. In practice, these distinctions often were blurred (Quigley 1996; SenGupta 2009), resulting in mixed or hybrid institutions serving diverse populations. Indigent women and men generally saw almshouses as penitentiaries rather than asylums, places to be avoided at all costs (Nash 2004).

Workhouses and poorhouses resulted from both public and private, philanthropic action. For example, Boston's original almshouse was built in part with bequests and contributions from a number of local citizens (Lee 1982). When Philadelphia's public almshouse (built in 1732) failed to accommodate burgeoning numbers of paupers and local poor taxes escalated, the City turned in 1766 to a private corporation led mostly by Quaker merchants to construct and run a new, larger edifice containing both an almshouse and a workhouse (Nash 2004).

Individuals and voluntary organizations also provided significant aid to the poor during the eighteenth century in both the North and the South. Churches often took up collections for their needy members, and particular faiths spent a major portion of their time, effort, and money to aid the poor. Numerous other associations, including fraternal societies, social organizations, and nationality groups such as Boston's Scots Charitable Society formed to provide relief for the impoverished. Social welfare in the colonial period was essentially a joint venture, and public assistance and private aid were complementary (Green 2003; Trattner 1999).

Ideologies of gender and race shaped both the experience of poverty for men and women and the relief policies that were established in the colonial era (Abramovitz 1996; Trattner 1999; Wulf 2004). Women's differential responsibilities as child bearers and caregivers placed them at a disadvantage when circumstances required them to manage their own households and support their dependents by earning money. Moreover, law and custom severely limited female property ownership, rendering most women dependent on men for their legal settlement status. When their fathers, husbands, or masters failed to provide, or abandoned them, or died, women often became transients and were warned out of their home communities. Women and their children were disproportionately needy in both the North and the South, disproportionately warned out and removed, and disproportionately institutionalized in urban almshouses (Abramovitz 1996; Herndon 2001; Nash 2004).

Public social benefits typically were not available to people of color under the colonial poor laws, which essentially assumed that needy persons would belong to the dominant white, Anglo-American culture. The predicament of Native Americans converted into wandering, poor refugees as they were forced off of their original lands largely was ignored (Quigley 1996; Trattner 1999). Slaves were considered the responsibility of their masters and prohibited from receiving aid in most of the colonies. Escaped slaves and free blacks were also generally denied public aid, and were among those most frequently warned out (Herndon 2001). Left to their own devices, they created programs of care via black churches and mutual assistance associations, a pattern of self-help that would prove enduring (Green 1999; SenGupta 2009).

Despite the existence of significant public relief and private charity, need was unrelenting by the end of the eighteenth century. The poor "were omnipresent" (Nash 2004, 24) in the decade before the Revolution, and their situation worsened significantly during the war and its aftermath. Relief rolls expanded, associated expenditures soared, and local officials began to appeal to colonial assemblies for help in aiding the unfortunate (Trattner 1999).

2.2 Veterans' Benefits

Although social provision was evolving at the local level, it also was becoming the responsibility of the national and state governments. In order to hold together a fighting force sufficient for winning the war for independence, the Continental Congress voted in May 1778 to create pensions of seven years' half pay for officers of the Continental Army and Navy, along with lump-sum, one-time grants for noncommissioned officers and soldiers. Unlike the "invalid" pensions enacted in 1776, which provided half pay for life or during disability to Army and Navy members who lost limbs or otherwise were rendered incapable of earning a living in the service of the United States, these benefits were based on service only, and offered only to Continental officers. They were highly controversial. Opponents argued that they were antithetical to Revolutionary principles, and would bankrupt the nation (Glasson 1918; Jensen 2003).

Army and Navy officers, by contrast, found the measure insufficient, and threatened to quit the war effort unless they received pensions of half pay for life plus benefits for the survivors of those killed. The Continental Congress eventually relented in 1780, creating pensions for the widows and orphans of Continental officers (the first such law in the United States) and half-pay for life for officers. Legislation passed days before the war ended in 1783 promised the Continental officers five years' full pay in lieu of half-pay for life, but because the Confederation government was in default between 1784 and 1789, it could neither redeem the certificates the officers were given nor even pay the interest due on them. By the time the U.S. government enacted a provision for the certificates' redemption in 1790, many were in the hands of speculators; veterans had sold their certificates for a return as low as twelve and a half cents on the dollar (Glasson 1918; Jensen 2003; Resch 2000). They were infuriated by being "cheated twice" (first by the government, when it reneged on its promise of pensions, and then by the speculators who took advantage of them), and continued to press the U.S. government for half pay for life (Resch 2000, 209). Although the U.S. Congress acted promptly after the nation's founding to enact disability pensions, it did not revive the service pension measure. The issue would linger unresolved on the congressional agenda for decades.

In addition to national veterans' pensions, the Continental Congress enacted and extended a program of land entitlements in 1776 and 1780, respectively, promising Continental Army veterans acreage in the western wilderness that was to become the U.S. public domain. The largest land grants were conferred on those of the highest military rank. Problems with Native American and foreign land claims, protracted interstate conflict over the boundaries and disposition of the lands involved, and the payment of the nation's war debt delayed the provision of actual bounty lands until 1796, when a tract in Ohio finally was made available. By then, many veterans, officers, and soldiers alike had sold their land rights for a fraction of what they eventually would have been worth, as had happened with the pension commutation certificates (Jensen 2003).

States also created pensions and land grants for Revolutionary veterans and their survivors, in some cases anticipating the policies of the Continental Congress. For example, the Virginia General Assembly passed a series of laws beginning in 1775 establishing disability and survivors' pensions. In 1779, Virginia promised half pay for life to officers serving until the end of the war, as did Pennsylvania in 1780 (Glasson 1918). Virginia also established land entitlements in present-day Kentucky and Ohio for men serving for at least three years in national or state forces and their survivors (Weisiger 2006). Similarly, North Carolina gave veterans land grants in the Cumberland (now Tennessee) in 1782, their size determined by military rank and length of service (Campbell 2006). Georgia, New York, and North Carolina, also states with extensive western land holdings, likewise offered land bounties to their state veterans; so did the relatively landless Maryland, Massachusetts, and South Carolina (Jansen 1992). Many veterans sold state land bounties to speculators rather than stake their claims in the west (Campbell 2006; Weisiger 2006).

Because Revolutionary pensions and land grants boosted the enlistment and retention of military men, they functioned as forms of pay. Yet, they had much broader significance as an original strain of national social policy that judiciously provided individual-level public benefits to particular groups of American citizens (see Kleykamp and Hipes, this volume). In addition to committing the United States to public expenditures far into the future, they gave rise to military and civilian expectations about national social provision that extended well beyond the confines of the original veterans' programs (Jensen 2003).

3 THE IDENTIFICATION OF DESERVING CITIZENS

The history of U.S. colonial and Revolutionary social benefits illuminates how the determination of qualifying criteria is an essential dimension of social provision. The critical distributive dilemma for all societies, as Deborah Stone (1984) has observed, lies in deciding when the normal rules of production and distributive justice should be suspended and some form of social aid be given (whether by kin, neighbors, church, or government). This dilemma may be framed, as in the case of poverty and public assistance, or wartime injury and disability pensions, as a conflict between work and need. However, as the examples of the Revolutionary veterans' entitlements show, demands for public benefits may be (and indeed often are) based on criteria other than need, such as service to the state (Jensen 2003). Because there is no natural or intrinsic definition of who deserves aid and who does not, every society must invent its own criteria of deservingness, implement them, enforce them, and renew or reinvent them in the face of changing social or economic conditions (Stone 1984).

In colonial and Revolutionary America, poverty was a necessary condition for receiving assistance, but not a sufficient one. As discussed earlier, legal residence in a particular locality also was required, as was the inability to earn a living through manual labor. Evaluations of the poor were deeply gendered, with assessments of need and deservingness hinging on how well men and women conformed to patriarchal, contemporary standards of behavior (Herndon 2001; Wulf 2004). Race was another critical criterion: the fates of those identified as persons "of color" generally were not of public concern (Herndon 2001). Requests for aid were made and considered on an individual basis; local authorities judged the circumstances of individuals asking for public relief and rendered decisions distinguishing between the "deserving" or "worthy" and the "undeserving" or "unworthy" poor. Persons displaying deference toward decision makers were more likely to garner support, and those who received it were expected to be grateful and submissive to their social and economic betters (Herndon 2004).

The legislation granting pensions and land to military veterans also relied on socially constructed criteria of deservingness, including specific military service, class, and gender. However, national pension enactments broke new ground in creating benefits for groups or legal *categories* of persons who were deemed deserving because they met a set of criteria specified in law. So, too, did contemporary federal statutes granting relief to victims of particular disasters (Dauber 2013). This *programmatic* approach to social provision is the hallmark of modern welfare-state organization. Though early national benefits did not create a welfare state *per se*, they established policy precedents both by creating national programs of care and by inventing a mode of policy making (legal entitlement) that would become a standard operating procedure of the U.S. government in the future (Jensen 2003).

4 FROM THE EARLY REPUBLIC TO THE TWENTIETH CENTURY

The U.S. Constitution empowered Congress to tax and expend funds to provide for the nation's common defense and "general welfare" (Article I, Section 8). However, it did not explicitly obligate the U.S. government to care for needy citizens, and neither the concept of local responsibility for poverty nor the poor laws were contested in the Revolution, or in the debates leading up to the new national government's establishment. The poor laws thus continued to organize social provision in the original states (under civil instead of parish jurisdiction in the South), and they progressively were adopted in the West as the frontier expanded and new states were admitted to the union (Rothman 2002; Trattner 1999).

4.1 The Proliferation of the Poorhouse

The social and economic dislocations caused by the American Revolution only exacerbated growing problems of need in the United States, especially on the more densely populated eastern seaboard. In New York, persons removed from their places of settlement due to the war became a new category of dependents known as the "state poor," whose relief was charged to the state. Initially, neither this nor other nascent forms of state-level provision for special needy groups (such as the blind or the deaf) were understood to repudiate the locally based poor law system (Trattner 1999). However, as immigration brought an expanding and more diverse population, market capitalism grew, and wage labor transformed the nature of work and income security, some began to question local relief as well as extant beliefs about poverty and social provision. Authorities increasingly saw the poor less often as unfortunate neighbors than as strangers prone to laziness, vice, and other dangerous tendencies, and criticized public assistance as a threat to character, the work ethic, and private charity (Katz 1986; Rothman 2002). As a consequence, more centralized, institutional means of social provision for the needy began to take hold.

Although poorhouses and workhouses had existed on American soil since the mid- to late 1600s, their use increased significantly in the first half of the nineteenth century. Some states enacted legislation requiring each county to establish at least one poorhouse, with the costs of construction, maintenance, and operations funded by county tax revenues. Other states passed laws enabling, but not requiring, counties to build poorhouses (Katz 1986; Rothman 2002; Trattner 1999). States also began building their own poorhouses, workhouses, and other facilities due to a burgeoning nonresident population. By the end of the Civil War, four out of five persons accepting extended assistance in Massachusetts received indoor relief, and the situation was similar in other states (Trattner 1999).

Proponents believed that poorhouses and workhouses would eliminate settlement disputes between cities and towns and spread the cost of assistance more evenly across local jurisdictions. In their group approach to care, they would also be more economical. Because the poorhouse was less attractive than other forms of outdoor and indoor relief, it was expected to deter many potential paupers from applying for aid. The even less appealing workhouse, or house of corrections, would provide a therapeutic setting, controlling the behavior of those placed in it while encouraging (indeed, requiring) their temperance and industry (Green 2003; Katz 1986; Rothman 2002; SenGupta 2009; Trattner 1999).

Despite the hopes of its advocates, the poorhouse widely was considered an inhumane, failed institution by the mid-nineteenth century (Katz 1986). Although conditions varied from place to place, with some poorhouses providing adequate care, contemporary investigations found the majority of such facilities to be poorly built, poorly administered, unhealthy, miserable, and cruel. New York's poorhouses had glaring problems, for example; heat, ventilation, clean water, decent food, and adequate sanitation were often lacking. Paupers in the Cayuga poorhouse lived in tiny, crowded, often windowless rooms, mixed together regardless of age, sex, illness or disability (Rothman 2002). Poor blacks, whether diseased or healthy, were consigned to live in the filthy, damp cellar of the New York City almshouse (SenGupta 2009).

The situation generally was no better in the South or the Midwest. Local authorities condemned the Richmond, Virginia poorhouse's sleeping accommodations in 1859 as "a disgrace to the city," with bedding "too dirty for a respectable dog kennel" (Green 2003, 63). Illinois's Cook County poorhouse was so unsanitary by the late 1870s that the Board of Public Charities complained to the state governor. This was where individuals were committed if they violated Chicago's "ugly law," an ordinance that barred physically disabled persons from appearing in public (Coco 2010).

The poorhouse nonetheless persisted throughout the nineteenth century and beyond, as did outdoor relief, despite growing efforts to repudiate and replace it. Even as county and state governments consolidated control over the care of dependent and "deviant" populations in poorhouses, workhouses, orphanages, insane asylums, and prisons, cities and towns continued to exert considerable influence over social provision (Katz 1986; Rothman 2002), reflecting the extent of need in the industrializing United States, the persistence of localism, and a lack of competing social policy alternatives.

4.2 Federal Veterans' Benefits

In the afterglow of military victory in the War of 1812, with a hefty surplus in the U.S. treasury, former Revolutionary officer President James Monroe proposed the creation of service pensions for the surviving officers and soldiers of the Continental Army (Glasson 1918; Jensen 2003). Monroe's recommendation garnered strong public and congressional support. However, some congressmen were unsure that the federal spending power (U.S. Constitution, Article I, Section 8) included the ability to establish programmatic benefits for individual citizens. The most heated debate in Congress revolved around the issue of the proposed program's eligibility criteria, since granting pensions to all Revolutionary veterans was not believed to be appropriate or feasible. Which veterans of the nation's original war should qualify for benefits, and on what basis? What criteria should be used to identify the *most* deserving among them and entitle them (but not others) to pensions (Jensen 2003)?

The Pension Act of March 1818 granted benefits exclusively to Continental Army and Navy veterans who had served for a minimum of nine months (or until the end of the war), who continued to be U.S. residents, *and* who, *because of reduced circumstances, were in need of their country's assistance for support.* Poverty and, in effect, old age (due to the passage of time) had been grafted onto national military service as criteria of deservingness. Continental veterans also had to be willing to apply for pensions by declaring and proving their indigence in a court of law. Should their cases be judged affirmatively, officers would be entitled to receive pensions equal to $20.00 per month, and noncommissioned officers, soldiers, mariners, marines, and musicians entitled to pensions of $8.00 per month—provided that they relinquished any federal disability pensions they might have, which paid identical benefits (Glasson 1918; Jensen 2003). This was approximately what contemporary, free nonfarm and farm laborers earned (Lebergott 1960). It is not difficult to see the substantive and procedural influence that the poor law had on the service pensions of veterans of the Continental Army. Nonetheless, selectively entitling citizens to national aid on a categorical basis was a major departure from ongoing law and practice, especially when thousands of other American paupers demanded Congress's attention "in an equal degree" (Senator William Smith of South Carolina, January 29, 1818, cited in Jensen 2003, 76).

The Pension Act stimulated other veterans of the Revolution to ask for benefits. Some petitioned individually for private relief bills, drawing analogies between their military service and that of the men receiving programmatic assistance. Others endeavored to convince Congress to broaden the service pension program's eligibility criteria, typically by arguing that their characteristics and circumstances were not meaningfully different from those of the men chosen to receive benefits. Still other men filed fraudulent pension applications. The push for benefits strained the capacities of Congress, officials in the Departments of War, Treasury, and Justice, and field agents charged with pension administration, and led to additional legislation and administrative regulation (Glasson 1918; Jensen 2003). Problems in implementation and pressures for fiscal retrenchment notwithstanding, pensions eventually were granted to most Revolutionary veterans, including militia members, by 1832, regardless of whether they were indigent, as long as they had served in the war for a minimum of 14 days. Congress also created pensions for the widows and orphans of Revolutionary veterans in 1836. At its peak in the 1830s, the Revolutionary pension system consumed almost 20 percent of the federal budget (Glasson 1918; Jensen 2003).

Some 55,000 to 60,000 veterans received pensions for their service in the Revolution, among them hundreds of African Americans (Van Buskirk 2007). One of the most remarkable aspects of the Act of 1818 was that it was implemented in its early years without respect to color; once applications were forwarded from local jurisdictions to Washington, service and poverty seemingly preempted race as criteria of deservingness. Yet as the pension system was amended to become more inclusive, culminating in the Act of 1832, the Pension Office become less accommodating, and the applications of a disproportionate number of black men were rejected (Van Buskirk 2007). Barred from formal military service, women were never slated to benefit from the Revolutionary pension system except as dependents of men. The pension claims made by the few women who disguised themselves and served in combat confounded contemporary officials, whose responses are a study in contemporary gender norms (Jensen 2003).

Veterans of the War of 1812 also lobbied Congress for benefits, but did not succeed in obtaining pensions for more than five decades after their service. The Act of 1871 granted pensions to all surviving, honorably discharged soldiers and sailors who had served in the War of 1812 for at least 60 days or those who had received personal mention by Congress for specific services in that conflict. Widows of the War of 1812 also received pensions, provided that they had been married prior to the treaty of peace and had not remarried. Neither poverty nor disability was required in order to receive benefits. However, age was a *de facto* criterion, just as it had been in the case of the long-awaited Revolutionary pensions. Additionally, loyalty to the United States during the Civil War was an explicit requirement. Until the law's amendment in 1878, no pension claims were allowed under the Act of 1871 from citizens of the former Confederacy, regardless of whether they or their deceased spouses or fathers had served the nation in its second, decisive war for independence (Jensen 2003). Roughly 23,000 surviving veterans and widows of the War of 1812 received pensions in 1873 and 1874. The 1878 removal of the loyalty criterion and the widows' marriage date restriction caused the rolls to swell to almost 35,000 by 1880, with the majority of claims coming from widows due to the deaths of aged veterans (Glasson 1918).

Established shortly after the end of the Civil War, the War of 1812 pension program reflected the bitter politics of a nation recently divided and only marginally reunited. The program became law during the years of the "radical" Reconstruction, when some Southern members of House and Senate had not yet returned to their seats in Washington. It also was established in the wake of the Pension Act of 1862, which had created the United States' largest and most generous pension program to date—for veterans of *Union* military forces *only*. The Act of 1862 granted benefits to men who served in all Union forces (national or state level) and their survivors, including not only widows and orphans, but also the mothers and sisters of men slain in combat. It also provided pensions for men disabled during the war, those who became disabled later in their lives as a consequence of their service, and, eventually, as amended, any man who became disabled after serving in Union forces. Repeatedly broadened throughout the nineteenth century and into the twentieth to include new categories of Union veterans and survivors, the Civil War pension system provided benefits to almost one million Americans in the years 1893–1908, and utilized over 40% of the federal budget at its peak (Glasson 1918; Skocpol 1992).

Given the policy precedents established in early conflicts, the enactment of the Civil War pension system was a predictable response to the outbreak of the war. So, too, was its expansion to include veterans and dependents who were not covered under the original law. What was remarkable was the extent to which the Civil War pension system became a tool of nineteenth century patronage democracy, used by Republicans in an effort to sway voters in politically competitive states in the Midwest and Northeast (Quadagno 1988; Skocpol 1992). In addition to increasing benefits and liberalizing eligibility, members of Congress actively intervened with a backlogged Pension Bureau and sponsored private bills in an effort to secure benefits for constituents (Orloff 1993). Mugwumps and other middle- and upper-class American reformers decried the pension system as an egregious example of the consequences of patronage politics and the corruption of party machines (Orloff 1993; Skocpol 1992).

The South despised the pension system. No matter how many years passed after the nation's reunification, and no matter how great Southern suffering was in the wake of the war, citizens of the former Confederacy never received any Civil War-related pension benefits from the U.S. government. They resented the pension system's very existence as well as its cost, because it was funded largely by federal tariffs that disproportionately burdened the South, even as the former Confederate states were required to raise taxes to provide benefits for their own disabled and poor veterans (Orloff 1993; Quadagno 1988; Skocpol 1992).

The War of 1812 and Civil War pension laws demonstrated that contemporary federal actors understood the symbolic and substantive power of creating and distributing benefits selectively (Jensen 2003). Although the passage of time effectively converted the Civil War pension system into a program of public assistance for aged and disabled men and their survivors, it served only a preferred portion of the nation—those citizens who had "participated victoriously in a morally fundamental moment of national preservation" (Skocpol 1992, 151). Disgust with the Civil War pension system on a variety of grounds caused many Americans to become skeptical about national social provision at precisely the point in the early twentieth century when local and state social benefits were hitting the limits of their effectiveness, and when other nations were moving in the direction of nationalized social insurance programs (Orloff 1993; Skocpol 1992).

4.3 Federal Land Benefits for Military Veterans and Other Persons

The United States also created a range of national land benefits during the nineteenth century. Some benefits, as previously discussed, were land grants established on the basis of national military service. The land bounty program originally established by the Continental Congress for veterans of the Revolution was carried forward by the U.S. government, which also established land grants for categories of soldiers fighting in the War of 1812.

Army officers were denied War of 1812 land entitlements despite their service and Revolutionary policy precedent, possibly because of the millions of acres needed and the projected cost in lost land-sale revenues. The government's omission of officers from its program of Mexican War veterans' land grants renewed the anger of the War of 1812 officers, who had unsuccessfully been lobbying for land and service pensions for some thirty years. They were joined in pressing Congress by the War of 1812's militiamen and their survivors, a group that included many thousands of voters. Federal statutes enacted in the 1850s progressively proffered more and more land until all men who had served for a minimum of 14 days in any force in any American war since 1775 became entitled to 160 acres of the public domain (Jensen 2003). In contrast, President Franklin Pierce vetoed a contemporary bill to provide the states with 10 million acres of public land to be sold for the support of the "indigent insane," asserting in his 1854 veto message that it was unconstitutional for the federal government to become the provider of charity throughout the United States (Jensen 2003; Trattner 1999). The veto was upheld in Congress.

It is vital to note that much of the land dispensed by the federal government in the late eighteenth and nineteenth centuries was expropriated from America's aboriginal residents. Native Americans had held claim to the land within the United States' borders at the time of the nation's founding, and they still inhabited much of the continent. Most neither considered themselves to have been conquered in the Revolution nor believed that their land claims had been nullified by the European treaties that granted the United States sovereignty over the territory east (and later, west) of the Mississippi River. Moreover, under long-standing European legal doctrine accepted by the U.S. government, they retained the right to use, enjoy, and profit from the land as long as they continued to occupy it. The Removal Act, which in 1830 began a long process of relocating Native Americans to federal reservations in the trans-Mississippi west, was enacted partly (if not primarily) for the purpose of rendering the Native Americans' ancestral lands available to white settlers. Although many people sold their land warrants instead of migrating, policies such as military land bounties accelerated the westward expansion of white property ownership and settlement while simultaneously extending the empire of the United States (Jensen 2003).

Military veterans were not the only Americans who became entitled to federal land benefits during the nineteenth century. Relief statutes enacted in the early national period repeatedly extended credit to persons owing the U.S. government money on western land purchases, waiving interest payments and ignoring forfeiture provisions in a distinct departure from the treatment accorded citizens who were in debt for other reasons. In addition, although people generally were subject to heavy fines and imprisonment for living on the public domain, certain "squatters" who moved into lands within particular regions or who advanced the construction of sawmills or gristmills while squatting were granted preferential purchase or "preemption" rights to lands they illegally occupied. After the Army's efforts in the Seminole Wars were less than successful, the U.S. government promised acreage in Florida to men willing to move there and fight off "marauding" Native Americans and escaped slaves for a minimum of five years. Though such schemes assisted fewer people than other nineteenth-century federal land programs, they nonetheless were forms of social provision where benefits were granted selectively to persons who served the goals of the U.S. government (Jensen 2003).

The Homestead Act, enacted in 1862 by a Union Congress occupied with fighting the Civil War, was far more universal in its provision of land. However, it initially barred white citizens of the Confederacy and all blacks from receiving benefits. (Under the U.S. Supreme Court's 1857 *Dred Scott* decision, blacks were not considered citizens.) Though these exclusions were eliminated from the Homestead Act five years later, they reflect both contemporary struggles to define citizenship and deservingness and the U.S. government's facility in categorizing and selectively entitling particular groups to benefits as a means of accomplishing national policy purposes. The *Southern* Homestead Act, passed in 1866 by a Union-dominated Reconstruction Congress to add former Confederates and freedmen to the subset of the citizenry already entitled to land, was the first piece of national legislation to prohibit discrimination on the basis of race or color in its interpretation or implementation. In contrast to military veterans' expectations and the policy path followed after previous U.S. wars, Union veterans never received land grants greater than those promised to ordinary homesteaders (Jensen 2003).

In 1865, shortly before the Civil War's end, the government established the Bureau of Refugees, Freedmen, and Abandoned Lands within the Department of War. Charged with facilitating the transition from slavery to freedom in the South, the Bureau was the nation's first federal welfare agency (Trattner 1999). In addition to managing the disposition of abandoned and confiscated southern land and property, introducing a system of free labor, paying federal bounties to black soldiers, settling disputes, and enforcing labor contracts between white landowners and black laborers, the agency provided relief to both white and black citizens on an unprecedented scale, supplying needy refugees and former slaves with food, health care, clothes, housing and job search assistance, and legal aid (Bremner 1980; Green 2003; Trattner 1999). The Freedmen's Bureau also encouraged and financed the establishment of schools for black children, including some training schools and colleges, with the assistance of missionary and aid societies (Bremner 1980). As W. E. B. DuBois (1901) observed some four decades after its creation, the Bureau was a public agency of wide significance and vast possibility. Yet, it demonstrated the persistence of poor law norms and racism in condemning pauperism and dependency, and in compelling former slaves to enter into labor contracts binding them to fieldwork and other low-paid wage work (Stanley 1998).

4.4 Beyond Poor Relief and Veterans' Benefits: Municipal and State Social Provision

Social provision for individuals other than dependent persons or military veterans was a tricky matter in nineteenth-century America due to the prerequisites of American federalism. Although communities relied heavily on the efforts of citizens willing to serve the common good, tangible recognition of those efforts had to comport not only with national law, but also with state statutes and constitutional provisions, including those restricting the expenditure of public revenues to "public purposes." As a consequence, when state and municipal governments tried to create pension funds and other benefits for firefighters and policemen in the mid- to late-nineteenth century, they faced lawsuits challenging those benefits' legality (Sterett 2003).

Although the outcomes of litigation varied by place and over time, the validity of municipal and state pension schemes generally hinged on a judicial finding of "public service." Tax revenues could fund pensions for aged and disabled firefighters and police because they performed public functions involving the same kinds of risk and heroism as military service. Providing pensions to the survivors of police and firemen was also a legitimate public purpose because death was not considered to extinguish the claims of those who had sacrificed their lives through hazardous public service (Sterett 2003).

Although framing the legitimacy of disability and old age pensions in this way facilitated the expansion of public social provision to new groups of Americans, it constrained possibilities for including others by reinforcing existing hierarchies of gender and race. Those performing dangerous civic work were presumptively male, and, as a matter of practice, white men of some means (Sterett 2003). Disability and old age pensions for firefighters and police preserved the independence of the "iconic nineteenth century citizen" (SenGupta 2009, 85) and his survivors while leaving most women, children, and persons of color to remain categorized as dependents worthy only of poor relief.

Rooting the validity of pensions in dangerous service also rendered problematic the extension of pensions to teachers and other civil servants who did not risk their lives on the job. Broader provision of pensions to public employees in the twentieth century would depend on changing conceptions of work as well as more progressive understandings of the role of the state (Sterett 2003). The extent to which these conceptions could transcend gendered and racialized constructions of citizens and their needs remained to be seen.

5 Conclusion

By the dawn of the twentieth century, a considerable history of social provision existed in the United States. Although generalizing across almost three hundred years of policy and practice is fraught with challenges and risks, the social provision that existed in America before the twentieth century can be seen to share three distinguishing characteristics. The first of these is a significant degree of subnational control over, and variation in, social benefits. In large part, this was a product of the social, economic, demographic, and political differences that existed between the original thirteen colonies as well as the sheer geographic distance between those colonies and even between localities. Local and regional control and variation in policy and practice was perpetuated by the United States' inauguration of a federally organized system of government in which both the national government and the states were established as sovereigns in their respective "spheres" of authority. That the states could and did govern independent of national authority allowed the U.S. government largely to ignore poverty (except veterans' poverty) as a state or local matter until the late nineteenth century. Subnational discretion was enhanced by the widespread belief that local communities should be responsible for needy citizens, an inheritance of the English poor law.

The second key aspect of pre-twentieth-century American social provision is the high degree of selectivity that characterized the distribution of public and private benefits. This selectivity resulted from resource limitations as well as from adherence to the poor law principle that assistance should only be given to persons who were truly worthy of it. Implementing that principle required the creation of venues in and processes by which judgments could be made about individual citizens' deservingness. The illiberal, ascriptive hierarchies of gender, race, and ethnicity that existed in America in its formative years (Smith 1999) powerfully influenced these judgments. As a consequence, benefits were not granted routinely or universally, even within demographically similar groups of citizens.

The selectivity with which benefits were provided also resulted from the U.S. government's invention of categorical entitlement programs aimed not simply at providing social welfare but, more centrally, at advancing national undertakings including the conduct of war, the expropriation of Native American land, the extermination of people of color, and territorial expansion on an unprecedented, continental scale. The use of targeted national-level benefits for policy purposes other than the enhancement of citizen well-being is the third distinguishing characteristic of pre-twentieth-century American social provision. Unlike social benefits intended to keep citizens quiescent, eighteenth- and nineteenth-century federal benefits were aimed at mobilizing the public both psychically and physically on behalf of the state (Jensen 2003). Thus, those benefits were intimately related to the project of nation building, a goal distinct from those pursued by more established nations during the same time period.

In sum, the convergence of poor-law-based norms, gender and racial discrimination, federally organized governance, and the dynamics of national defense and territorial expansion facilitated the development of a distinctly American approach to social provision over the course of the seventeenth, eighteenth, and nineteenth centuries. This was the foundation on which American social policy would be formulated in the twentieth century. New rationales and criteria of deservingness, cultural and legal, would need to be invented if the United States was to provide more inclusively and comprehensively for the American people.

REFERENCES

*Indicates recommended reading.

Abramovitz, Mimi. 1996. *Regulating the Lives of Women: Social Welfare Policy from Colonial Times to the Present*. Rev. ed. Boston: South End Press.

Bremner, Robert H. 1980. *The Public Good: Philanthropy and Welfare in the Civil War Era*. New York: Knopf.

Bremner, Robert H. 1992. *The Discovery of Poverty in the United States*. Rev. ed. New Brunswick, NJ: Transaction.

Campbell, Wesley Judkins. 2006. "Charles Gerrard: Early Benefactor of the University of North Carolina." *North Carolina Historical Review* 83 (3): 293–321.

Coco, Adrienne Phelps. 2010. "Diseased, Maimed, Mutilated: Categorizations of Disability and an Ugly Law in Late Nineteenth-Century Chicago." *Journal of Social History* 44 (1): 23–37.

Dauber, Michele Landis. 2013. *The Sympathetic State: Disaster Relief and the Origins of the American Welfare State*. Chicago: University of Chicago Press.

Du Bois, W. E. B. 1901. "The Freedmen's Bureau." *Atlantic Monthly* 87 (521): 354–365.

Glasson, William H. 1918. *Federal Military Pensions in the United States*. New York: Oxford University Press.

Green, Elna C. 1999. "Introduction." In Elna C. Green, ed., *Before the New Deal: Social Welfare in the South, 1830–1930, vii–xxvi*. Athens: University of Georgia Press.

*Green, Elna C. 2003. *This Business of Relief: Confronting Poverty in a Southern City, 1740–1940*. Athens: University of Georgia Press.

*Herndon, Ruth Wallis. 2001. *Unwelcome Americans: Living on the Margin in Early New England*. Philadelphia: University of Pennsylvania Press.

Herndon, Ruth Wallis. 2004. "Colonial Period through the Early Republic." In Gwendolyn Mink and Alice O'Connor, eds., *Poverty in the United States: An Encyclopedia of History, Politics, and Policy*, 1:1–8. Santa Barbara, CA: ABC-CLIO.

*Jensen, Laura S. 2003. *Patriots, Settlers, and the Origins of American Social Policy*. Cambridge: Cambridge University Press.

Jansen, Daniel. 1992. "A Case of Fraud and Deception: The Revolutionary War Military Land Bounty Policy in Tennessee." *Journal of East Tennessee History* 64:41–67.

*Katz, Michael B. 1986. *In the Shadow of the Poorhouse: A Social History of Welfare in America*. New York: Basic Books.

Lebergott, Stanley. 1960. "Wage Trends, 1800–1900." In The Conference on Research in Income and Wealth, National Bureau of Economic Research, ed., *Trends in the American Economy in the Nineteenth Century*, 449–500. Cambridge, MA: UMI. Available at http://www.nber.org/chapters/c2486.

Lee, Charles R. 1982. "Public Poor Relief and the Massachusetts Community, 1620–1715." *New England Quarterly* 55 (4): 564–585.

Nash, Gary B. 1979. "The Failure of Female Factory Labor in Boston." *Labor History* 20 (2): 165–188.

*Nash, Gary B. 2004. "Poverty and Politics in Early American History." In Billy G. Smith, ed., *Down and Out in Early America*, 1–37. University Park: Pennsylvania State University Press.

Orloff, Ann Shola. 1993. *The Politics of Pensions: A Comparative Analysis of Britain, Canada, and the United States, 1880–1940*. Madison: University of Wisconsin Press.

Quadagno, Jill. 1988. *The Transformation of Old Age Security: Class and Politics in the American Welfare State*. Chicago: University of Chicago Press.

Quigley, William P. 1996. "Work or Starve: Regulation of the Poor in Colonial America." *University of San Francisco Law Review* 31: 35–83.

Resch, John. 2000. *Suffering Soldiers: Revolutionary War Veterans, Moral Sentiment, and Political Culture in the Early Republic*. Amherst: University of Massachusetts Press.

Rothman, David J. 2002. *The Discovery of the Asylum: Social Order and Disorder in the New Republic*. Rev. ed. New York: Aldine de Gruyter.

SenGupta, Gunja. 2009. *From Slavery to Poverty: The Racial Origins of Welfare in New York, 1840–1918.* New York: New York University Press.

*Skocpol, Theda. 1992. *Protecting Soldiers and Mothers: The Political Origins of Social Policy in the United States.* Cambridge, MA: Belknap Press of Harvard University Press.

Smith, Rogers M. 1999. *Civic Ideals: Conflicting Visions of Citizenship in U.S. History.* New Haven, CT: Yale University Press.

Stanley, Amy Dru. 1998. *From Bondage to Contract: Wage Labor, Marriage, and the Market in the Age of Slave Emancipation.* Cambridge: Cambridge University Press.

Sterett, Susan M. 2003. *Public Pensions: Gender and Civic Service in the States, 1850–1937.* Ithaca, NY: Cornell University Press.

Stone, Deborah A. 1984. *The Disabled State.* Philadelphia: Temple University Press.

*Trattner, Walter I. 1999. *From Poor Law to Welfare State: A History of Social Welfare in America.* 6th ed. New York: Free Press.

Van Buskirk, Judith L. 2007. "Claiming Their Due: African Americans in the Revolutionary War and Its Aftermath." In John Resch and Walter Sargent, eds., *War and Society in the American Revolution: Mobilization and Home Fronts,* 132–160. DeKalb: Northern Illinois University Press.

Weisiger, Minor T. 2006. "Virginia Revolutionary War Records." *Research Notes Number 8.* Library of Virginia, Research and Information Services Division. Available at http://www.lva.virginia.gov/public/guides/rn8_varev.pdf.

Wulf, Karin. 2004. "Gender and the Political Economy of Poor Relief in Colonial Philadelphia." In Billy G. Smith, ed., *Down and Out in Early America,* 163–188. University Park: Pennsylvania State University Press.

CHAPTER 3

....

THE PROGRESSIVE ERA

....

DAVID BRIAN ROBERTSON

1 INTRODUCTION

THE Progressive movement changed the path of American social policy between the 1890s and the early 1920s. Unprecedented changes, novel social problems, innovative ideas, and new political actors fueled the Progressive reform impulse. Progressive reformers confronted many impediments: constraints on state and national government authority, the limited capability of state governments, the impact of interstate economic competition on state government activity, the separation of government powers, and patronage-based political parties. Inventive progressives developed many strategies to overcome these impediments. They built up government capacity, constructed new public bureaus and agencies, and grew the power of elected executives. Leading progressive reformers became innovative policy entrepreneurs and helped construct policy reform networks. They utilized the federal government's revenue and spending powers, pressed for uniform state laws, and sought political reforms that bypassed political parties and legislatures.

These Progressive policy strategies achieved only limited success, for two reasons. First, legal restrictions on federal government authority continued to limit American social policy. The failed campaign to eliminate child labor illustrates how limited federal jurisdiction prevented a national response to one of the conspicuous problems of the period. Second, trade unions' opposition to specific social reforms weakened and fragmented political coalitions essential for social policy innovation. Progressive campaigns for health and unemployment insurance show how trade unions helped defeat ambitions to establish universal social policy. The progressive reformers were most successful in securing maternalist social policy, such as limitations on working hours for women and aid to widows and their families. These impulses, impediments, strategies, and diverse results produced a Progressive Era social policy that expanded chiefly at the state and local levels. This social policy was strikingly uneven across the population, and interstate competition limited experimentation even in the most reform-minded states. Finally, stark gender and racial divisions and social stigma marked American social policy by the 1920s.

2 The Progressive Impulse

Progressivism refers to the widespread reform impulse that originated in the 1890s and altered American social policy in the first two decades of the twentieth century. Progressivism reflected a growing concern about the physical, economic, and moral problems created by industrialization, urbanization, and the concentration of economic power (Hamby 1999). Progressive reformers fought to expand democracy, professionalize government, and make industrial capitalism more humane. Many emphasized that such evils as poverty, unemployment, disease, the inability to work, and alcohol were eating away at the nation. Energetic progressives pressured government at all levels to alleviate these problems (Hofstadter 1956, 185–196; McGerr 2003; Rodgers 1982).

Several streams fed the progressive impulse. First, industrialization spurred a rapid transformation of American society. Dynamic factories in growing cities manufactured products for an expanding national market. By 1920, more than half of Americans lived in towns or cities of at least 2,500 people. At the same time, new techniques of production, transportation, and communication knit the nation and its problems into a much more closely bound fabric (Fishback 2007). These changes most deeply influenced the nation's Eastern and Midwestern industrial core. Most of the South, in contrast, remained a poor, agricultural area. The West, dotted with a few cities, was unevenly settled and dependent on commodity agriculture and extraction.

Second, social change redefined the American social-policy agenda. Industrialization and urbanization disrupted individual lives, snapped family support systems, and made more Americans dependent on the vagaries of industrial capitalism. Urban families often relied on earned wages instead of the support of extended rural support networks. Periodic economic panics and recessions left many urban workers and their families in grinding poverty when jobs dried up. Many who could not work, such as widows, children, the elderly and the disabled, lacked the means to escape destitution. Other problems, such as overcrowded tenements, urban sewerage, garbage and pollution, and crime plagued the most dynamic areas of the economy. Millions of new immigrants flooded into cities, compounding urban challenges. Because a majority of these new immigrants came from Southern and Eastern Europe, and because many were Roman Catholic or Jewish, their arrival made the cities more diverse and aggravated cultural collisions (Haines 2000, 193–203).

Third, changing circumstances and social problems nurtured innovative ideas about reform. Some Protestant intellectuals championed a "Social Gospel" movement that invigorated many reformers. The Social Gospel held that Christian values had to be applied to alleviate social and economic injustice, slums, destructive and immoral behavior, and to protect innocent and vulnerable people (Morone 2003, 219–221, 346–348). The drive to engineer social improvement also informed much of Progressive thinking. Ideas about "scientific charity" and "scientific management" suggested that improved public and private management could manufacture social improvement. New social sciences produced many reform-minded scholars determined to use these tools. New thinking in economics suggested that market flaws, such as public goods and negative externalities, justified more government intervention in the economy (Caporaso and Levine 1992, 79–99).

Educated middle-class reformers, often women, took the lead in formulating and spreading these ideas. Many learned about emerging social problems while working in settlement houses such as Jane Addams' Hull House in Chicago. Settlement houses, established in working-class immigrant neighborhoods, aimed to help assimilate immigrants and improve the worst urban environments. In 1907–1908, social scientists revealed appalling work and living conditions in a systematic survey of Pittsburgh (Greenwald and Anderson 1996). Robert Hunter, the author of *Poverty* (1904), estimated that 10 percent of Americans were poor, victims of the industrial system. Muckraking journalists publicized corporate abuse, disgusting factory conditions, and the exploitation of children. Faith in social engineering motivated some businessmen to join the call for social reforms (Wiebe 1962).

Fourth, rapidly organizing advocacy groups channeled and amplified these reform ideas (Wiebe 1967). Farmers and their agricultural organizations stayed engaged in politics after the eclipse of the Populist movement. Placing "unremitting pressure for public control of private economic power," farm organizations shaped a wide variety of new laws and public agencies (Sanders, 1999, 1). Trade unions grew larger, stronger, and more vocal (Robertson 2000, 69–70). Individual unions, such as the machinists, the miners, and the garment workers, put substantial weight behind coalitions that demanded public worker protections and even social insurance. Women's clubs in cities fought for improved health and housing for children. State and local women's clubs and the National Federation of Women's Clubs pressured lawmakers for a range of reforms. The National Consumers League, founded in 1899, battled for state and federal child labor protections. A National Congress of Mothers (later the PTA) urged improvements in public education (Flexner and Fitzpatrick 1996, 171–172; Muncy 1991; Skocpol 1992, 326, 333). A host of professional and policy organizations—including the National Conference of Charities and Corrections, the American Association for Labor Legislation (AALL), and the settlement houses—also coalesced with other groups to work for more government action. These groups created loosely connected state and national reform networks that shared information, strategies, and successful tactics across state boundaries (Wiebe 1967, 164–195).

3 Impediments and Opportunities

Nineteenth century American institutions provided both obstacles to reform and opportunities for social change. These arrangements included the restricted policy authority of the national government, the fragmentation of social policy authority across the states, the role of interstate competition in discouraging state policy innova-tion, the separation of powers at all levels, and the decentralized patronage party system.

The Constitution severely complicated Progressive reform by limiting federal author-ity and fragmenting state policy across the national landscape. The Constitution gave the national government the powers of sovereignty in defense, trade, and interstate governance, and it provided for broad powers to raise revenues (especially through the tariff), but it did not authorize the national government to administer everyday life or to regulate economic development within states. Federal-court rulings circumscribed both the national and state government's powers to regulate business discretion, creat-ing a "no-man's land" of free market autonomy and hemming in efforts to use any level of government to protect citizens from the uncertainties and hazards of industrializ-ing America (Scheiber, 1975; Bensel 2000, 289–354; Robertson 2011, 80–85). The fed-eral government could collect revenue, but, until the late 1930s, it lacked the regulatory authority essential for nationally uniform social policy.

By 1900, the states bore the chief responsibility for dealing with the challenges caused by industrialization, urbanization, economic risk, and social discontent. Federalism fragmented social policy authority into 48 different state jurisdictions, each with a dif-ferent constituency, culture, history, and institutional capacity. Many state governments were unprepared for the challenge. At the start of the twentieth century, only six state legislatures met annually, and most state legislatures convened once every two years for a limited session. In state legislatures, rural areas were overrepresented, whereas the cities, the strongest supporters of progressive reforms, had fewer representatives than swelling populations would warrant (Teaford 2002, 12–16; Weir 2005, 165).

Moreover, each state government oversaw only a portion of an increasingly national-ized market economy, making it hard for any state to respond effectively to the social problems within its territory. In-state businesses, often exposed to out-of-state eco-nomic competition, had strong incentives to fight unions, tax increases, and other intrusions on business autonomy and profits. The welfare of enterprises, economic entrepreneurs, and speculators weighed very heavily in state and local decisions about public spending, regulations, natural resources, and vulnerable citizens (Scheiber 1975). Opponents of effective factory safety rules, labor laws, and state-managed social insur-ance slammed these ideas as direct threats to state prosperity (Robertson 2000, 17–18).

The result was a patchwork of reform across the nation. The economic gulf that sepa-rated the most industrialized states and the relatively poor Southern states exacerbated the problem. Massachusetts was highly industrialized and pioneered many American social initiatives, but Southern states remained agricultural and could boast of a large pool of very low-wage, unskilled workers. Many Southern landlords provided pater-nalistic protections for their African-American tenant farmers, binding these tenants closely to the landlords and cultivating a strong aversion to public-welfare programs (Alston and Ferrie 1999, 13–33, 53–59). Southern states used their comparative advan-tage in low wages and limited government to lure Northern employers, such as textile manufacturers, to expand in the South.

The separation of government powers further complicated social-reform efforts at all levels. New social legislation had to emerge from a gauntlet of institutions, each rooted in different constituencies, with different calendars and powers. Veto points were abundant, making it relatively easy for one chamber of a legislature, or for an executive, to stop legislation. It was difficult to build the concurrent majorities and institutional cooperation required to make effective laws. The courts in the late nineteenth century had become a veto point of last resort for those opposed to interfering with business. Business used the courts again and again to frustrate opponents like trade unions (Orren 1992; Ernst 1995).

The existing political parties were as much an obstacle as a vehicle for Progressive reform. American mass-based political parties had developed before industrialization, and were relatively strong at the state and local levels because state governments controlled police powers and domestic policy. These parties emphasized patronage and power. National parties were relatively loose, programmatic coalitions of state and local parties bound by a minimal policy agenda. In contrast to industrializing nations in Europe, the American party system did not realign along class lines or produce a socialist party in the early twentieth century (Duverger 1964, 22–23; Robertson 2000, 40–47, 126–139). Political competition evolved differently in each state. With control over many elections laws, states made it difficult for socialist and progressive reform parties to establish a durable electoral base. Progressive politicians such as Robert LaFollette, Hiram Johnson, and Robert Wagner found it easier to run as Democrats or Republicans than to create a new alternative reform party, as the Populists proved in 1892 and Theodore Roosevelt's Progressive Party proved in 1912 (Milkis 2009). The American Federation of Labor rejected both political socialism and an independent labor party distinct from the Democrats and Republicans. Instead, the AFL befriended allies in both major parties, gradually aligning with the Democrats.

4 Progressive Strategies for Reform

By adapting to these impediments and opportunities, Progressive reformers left a distinctive mark on the development of American social policy. These reformers increased the budgetary and administrative capacity of government and enhanced executive authority to bypass some of the separation of powers. They built nationwide policy networks and used both federal grants-in-aid and uniform model laws to advance social policy in all the states.

Progressives built new administrative units aimed at specific social problems. For example, settlement-house leaders and women's clubs lobbied successfully for a U.S. Children's Bureau in 1912 (Lindenmeyer 1997). Members of the Committee of One Hundred on Public Health, including economist Irving Fisher, Jane Addams, Booker T. Washington, and Thomas Edison, pushed for the administrative changes that greatly broadened the mandate of the U.S. Public Health Service in 1912 (Rosen 1972). Trade unions fought for a separate Department of Labor; when it was established in 1913, its first Secretary, William B. Wilson, a mineworker leader and U.S. Representative, made it a bridgehead for labor reform (Robertson, 2000, 10).

Public agencies multiplied and government was strengthened at the state level, where social policy authority was acknowledged. Budget preparation and legislative bill development became more professionalized. Nonpartisan merit selection enhanced the professional capabilities of administrators (Teaford 2002, 11, 59–68, 77–80). Thirteen states implemented a workable income tax by 1922. State income taxes increased state revenue and strengthened state government authority; state and local revenues, spending, and employment all outpaced the federal government between 1902 and 1932 (Teaford 2002, 56–59; Robertson and Judd 1989, 35–36).

Public intellectuals championed social-policy innovation. Florence Kelley became the most influential female public official in the United States when appointed as chief factory inspector for Illinois in 1893 (Sklar 1995). In the first decades of the 1900s, the American Association for Labor Legislation (AALL), an association of reform-minded scholars and leaders influenced by University of Wisconsin economist John R. Commons, publicized employment problems and urged government action. The AALL produced a detailed "Practical Program for the Prevention of Unemployment" that recommended a network of public employment offices and state industrial commissions that could manage the regulation of factories and child labor, unemployment insurance, and other policies (AALL 1915). These laws inspired such progressives as Louis Brandeis to write that states provided the nation with "social laboratories" for improvement (*New State Ice Co. v. Liebmann*, 1932).

Progressives also looked to elected executives to galvanize government action. Reform mayors such as Detroit's Hazen Pingree, Toledo's Samuel "Golden Rule" Jones, and Milwaukee's Daniel Hoan implemented local initiatives on behalf of jobless and impoverished citizens. Reform governors, such as Wisconsin's Robert LaFollette and California's Hiram Johnson, championed a range of statewide reforms. U.S. Presidents Theodore Roosevelt and Woodrow Wilson asserted an activist domestic-policy agenda.

Alliances of social reformers across the levels of government struggled against the obstacles of federalism. Reformers who sought national improvement built networks among state government, municipal government, and nongovernmental groups to strengthen their political influence. Coalitions of women (including the women's clubs, settlement house leaders, the NCL, and the Women's Trade Union League) were among the most effective reform networks (Skocpol 1992, 314–372). These networks brought a new kind of politics of expertise to American policy formation, a politics that sometimes transcended partisan conflicts and even bypassed elected officials. New agencies and the reform-minded executives helped build these networks. According to political scientist Kimberley Johnson (2006, 9), dozens of new Federal policy initiatives "knit together legislators, bureaucrats, interest groups, reformers, and citizens into ever tighter bonds, and raised the bar of what it was possible for American government, whether at the national or state level, to do." A 1909 White House Conference on the Care of Dependent Children, for example, convened 200 prominent social reformers who exchanged ideas and laid plans for local and state action (Crenson 1998, 11–16).

Federal grants-in-aid became a more attractive tool for energizing *all* the states to pursue policies aimed at national results. Although Federal regulatory authority was constrained, Federal power to raise revenue was well-established. The Sixteenth Amendment (1913) specifically authorized a federal income tax and expanded federal revenue capacity. Reformers recognized that the federal government could put its financial and other resources to work by providing cash grants to the states. Under such a grant-in-aid program, the federal government would send money to the states, stipulating that the state establish a specific kind of public program and match federal funds with funds from their own sources. These grants, then, gave every one of the states an incentive to expand into new policy domains. Federal grants could induce a dormant state government to take action in a specific field of national interest, such as building a national highway network. Grants provided a mechanism for national action that evaded Constitutional restrictions on national authority by allowing the states to retain policy authority. States could make significant decisions over how they used their Federal funds (Southern states, for example, could preserve racial segregation). The Progressive Era saw the beginnings of federal grant-in-aid activism through grants for road construction, vocational education, and agriculture improvement (Robertson 2011, 107–110).

Meanwhile, progressive reformers campaigned for uniform state laws, aiming to enact the same, model statute in each of the states. These uniform law campaigns aimed to produce identical policies across the nation. Instead of grants, the federal intervention would support the laws by gathering and disseminating information. However, the uniform law strategy was very difficult. Whenever a proposed reform threatened an economic interest that was influential in a given state, the interest fought against the reform. Reformers bore the burden of proof for showing that such a law would *not* put the state at an economic disadvantage. It was rare, therefore, that *all* the states adopted uniform laws (Nugent 2009, 77–88).

5 THE LIMITED REACH OF PROGRESSIVE SOCIAL POLICY: THE CASE OF CHILD LABOR

Although national conditions favored government action and progressive reformers developed clever strategies to energize government, impediments to active government were stout. Progressive reform thus yielded a series of fragmented, incomplete reform achievements. Nothing better illustrates the way progressive strategies ran into formidable obstacles than the campaign to ban child labor (Trattner 1970; Wood 1968).

The plight of wage-earning children was as widely recognized as any issue of the Progressive Era. Hundreds of thousands of children labored in factories, sweatshops, domestic services, and street occupations. By 1902, a few of the industrialized states had set 14 as a minimum age for workers, an age limit comparable to that in Britain and Germany. However, other states fought government restrictions on child labor. Southeastern states such as North and South Carolina, Georgia, and Alabama resisted child-labor laws because low-wage child workers gave their growing textile industries a comparative advantage over states with more child regulations. One in four textile workers in these southern states were children (Davidson 1939, 55; Wood 1968, 3–8).

Reformers bent on eliminating child labor initially conceded that the Federal government had no legal authority to ban it (Annals 1906, 289–292). Instead, the child- labor reformers battled state by state. Florence Kelley and others organized a National Child Labor Committee (NCLC) that spearheaded a broad coalition for stricter child- labor standards nationwide. In 1904, the NCLC issued a model uniform state child-labor law, and coordinated efforts to win its adoption by all the states, but manufacturers in many states complained that if their state acted, such laws would disadvantage them and state prosperity in interstate competition. In 1912, only nine states had laws that met the standards laid out in the NCLC's model bill. Indeed, state laws were becoming even more varied (Ogburn 1912, 203–205; Trattner 1970, 45–67, 70, 105–107, 115).

Frustrated by the state-by-state strategy, the NCLC put forward a federal child- labor bill. This NCLC bill directly challenged the Constitutional limits on federal government authority. Congress enacted a Federal Child Labor Act (the Keating-Own Bill) in 1916, despite the opposition of textile manufacturers and the National Association of Manufacturers (Wood 1968, 42–45).

Textile mill owners immediately disputed the constitutionality of the Federal Child Labor Act. In *Hammer* v. *Dagenhart* (1918), the U.S. Supreme Court struck down the law, arguing that validating it would end "all freedom of commerce," could eliminate "the power of the States over local matters…" and would "practically" destroy "our system of government" (*Hammer* v. *Dagenhart* 1918). Reformers next tried to use federal revenue powers to achieve their goal. Congress passed a new federal law that imposed a 10 percent tax on employers' net profits for each year that they failed to conform to the national child-labor standards. When the Supreme Court struck down this law, Chief Justice William Howard Taft wrote that, if upheld, the federal law would "break down all constitutional limitation of the powers of Congress and completely wipe out the sovereignty of the States" (*Bailey* v. *Drexel Furniture Company* 1922).

Child-labor reformers next proposed to a Constitutional amendment to ban child labor. Congress passed the amendment, but manufacturers and their allies, including farmers and some Catholic leaders, worked tirelessly against ratification in the states. It was defeated even in states relatively friendly to reform, such as New York and Massachusetts (Trattner 1970, 163–167, 174–176; Wood 1968, 221).

6 TRADE UNIONS' SELECTIVE RESISTANCE TO SOCIAL POLICY

The American Federation of Labor (AFL), the most politically influential American labor organization, joined Progressive campaigns against child labor but refused to support universal labor regulations and social insurance programs. The AFL generally opposed legal protections for male workers because it believed that these laws undermined its own approach to worker protection.

By 1900, the AFL officially dedicated itself to "pure and simple" unionism, seeking material gains for workers by negotiating directly with employers. Years later, this strategy—termed "voluntarism"—seemed narrow, selfish, and conservative. But voluntarism, at least until the end of World War I, should be understood as an ambitious and combative strategy, ultimately aimed at unionizing the entire capitalist workforce. The AFL sought to establish inclusive worker protections and to limit employer discretion without any direct government help. In the words of AFL President Samuel Gompers, "the whole population should be joined in one united federation of labor..." If all workers were unionized, they could negotiate directly with employers to establish economic security through maximum hours, higher wages, and employment security. In principle, voluntarism required the AFL to be forceful and inclusive, and incorporate all female and minority workers (but it did not require the Federation to integrate these groups with white male unions). In its most radical form in the early 1900s, the AFL strategy was essentially syndicalism (Tomlins 1985, 56; Robertson 2000, 66–73).

For Gompers and other Progressive-era AFL leaders, government-provided universal protections for *all* workers, including men, would undermine voluntarism by weakening *unions'* control of material benefits and thus union economic power. An AFL committee rejected public pensions in 1902, for example, on grounds that the "the conditions, wages, and other concerns of the working people should be arranged through the efforts of organized labor" (Kaufman et al 1997, 58–60; Nelson 1969, 65–67, 77). When the U.S. Supreme Court struck down an eight-hour law for bakers, Gompers pointed out that the bakers' union maintained a 10-hour workday themselves despite this government ruling; their labor agreement endured but a law did not (*Lochner* v. *New York*, 1905; *AFL Proceedings* 1905, 32).

Labor leaders often found themselves opposed to progressive reformers on specific social policies. Although the U.S. Commission on Industrial Relations (1913–1915) provided a national forum for the addressing vulnerable workers, members from unions and from reform groups could not agree on the way to move forward. The Commission majority, representing the unions' view, complained that government could not credibly protect workers: "the mass of workers are convinced that laws necessary for their protection against the most grievous wrongs can not be passed except after long and exhausting struggles." A minority report overseen by AALL leader John R. Commons argued that labor market governance would be trustworthy if delegated to industrial commissions run by impartial experts. A national industrial commission would make labor market rules, administer laws, adjudicate disputes, manage employment services, vocational education, workplace regulation, child labor, work insurance, immigration, and statistics (U.S. Commission on Industrial Relations 1915, 38–39, 113–114, 172, 186).

The AFL did not trust the impartiality of these progressive experts, but it did not reject all social policy, either. It joined reform coalitions selectively, when these coalitions aimed to use government to reach those workers that unions could not easily organize and protect. It supported workers' compensation for victims of work accidents, public vocational education for future workers, and public regulations for women and children. This selective union support for social policy helped the campaign for workers' compensation, but it hampered subsequent campaigns for health and unemployment insurance.

Most nations initiated the modern welfare state by establishing public compensation for workplace injuries (Kangas 2010, 91–94). Before workers' compensation, maimed workers or the widows and orphans of fatally injured workers had to seek compensation for their losses by suing employers. Litigation was a long, costly process with unpredictable results. Employers had many defenses that allowed them to escape liability for work injuries. The AALL pressed for workers' compensation and the National Manufacturers Association, representing many employers dissatisfied with the court system, began to support it (Schwedtman and Emery 1911, 259–260; Moss 1996, 121–122). Union leaders joined workers' compensation campaigns, battling to ensure that the new programs would provide generous benefits and limit employers' power over the programs. Unions especially sought state government insurance monopolies, aiming to preclude a role for private insurance companies. Most of the states had enacted such laws by 1920 (Fishback and Kantor 2000).

As workers' compensation spread across the states, the AALL expanded its social insurance agenda to the larger problem of health. The AALL won an early legislative victory when Congress, in 1912, placed a high tax on white phosphorus matches, a source of a terrible industrial disease called "phossy" jaw (Moss 1996, 79–96). Compulsory health-insurance laws aimed at industrial disease constituted "the biggest next step in labor legislation" for the AALL. When the AALL published a model compulsory state health-insurance bill in 1916, its leaders were optimistic. Workers' compensation laws had spread rapidly, and in 1916, both the American Medical Association and the National Association of Manufacturers endorsed public health insurance in principle (Moss 1996, 132, 141). Sympathetic legislators introduced the AALL bill in fifteen state legislatures, and ten states funded commissions to investigate health insurance (AALL 1918).

But AFL leaders decisively opposed public health and other social insurance proposals (*AFL Proceedings* 1914, 66–68). Gompers argued that health insurance gave employers too great a financial stake in employees' health, and that public health insurance would strengthen public bureaucracies that could hamper trade unions. Instead, Gompers argued that the organized power of workers constituted "the most potent and the most direct social insurance of the workers" (U.S. Bureau of Labor Statistics 1917, 846). He supported voluntary public health insurance subsidized by government and run by trade unions (Gompers 1916, 335–336, 350). Despite Gompers' opposition, state labor federations in 29 states supported public health insurance. Ferocious opposition from doctors, insurers, and manufacturers, however, defeated proposals in California in the New York State Assembly (Numbers 1978).

The AALL advanced unemployment insurance as the "final link" in its Practical Program for the Prevention of Unemployment (AALL 1915, 189–190). The AFL preferred shorter hours and public works as a solution for unemployment. Gompers believed that

British social-insurance programs had "taken much of the virility out of the British trade unions" (Gompers, 1916, 677; Nelson 1969, 65–67, 77.). With both manufacturers and AFL leaders aligned against the AALL's model bill, and considered secondary even by its advocates, unemployment insurance received little public debate in the Progressive Era (Nelson 1969, 17–18, 76).

7 THE MATERNALIST WELFARE STATE

Although the AFL fought off social policy for all male and female workers, a "maternalist" welfare state took root (Skocpol 1992, 2, 311–524; Koven and Michel 1993). The network of maternalist reformers, mostly women, believed that women shared an identity based on domestic and family responsibilities, that female reformers played a motherly role toward the poor, and that their experience as mothers "made women uniquely able to lead certain kinds of reform campaigns and made others deserving of help" (Gordon 1994, 51, 55). These reformers' views of the needy (in their view, primarily immigrants) reflected their middle- and upper-class backgrounds. For most of them, immigrants from southern and eastern Europe not only represented a different economic class, but even a different race unlike the Anglo-Saxon Protestant culture that dominated the United States. They devoted relatively little attention to African Americans (Gordon 1994, 84–85).

Neither the AFL nor the courts blocked protective labor legislation for women as they did laws protecting men. Gompers regarded "women workers and minors as particularly the concern of the Government" (Cong. Rec., Feb. 12, 1914, 3406). The states had the right to fix hours for women and children as "wards of State," argued U.S. Representative and United Mineworkers leader William B. Wilson, whereas men, as "a part of the State," should pursue protections through direct negotiation with employers (Cong. Rec., Dec. 14, 1911, 382–385, 389). In *Muller v. Oregon* (1908), the U.S. Supreme Court upheld Oregon's 10-hour law for women's workday, holding that, "…as healthy mothers are essential to vigorous offspring, the physical well-being of woman becomes an object of public interest and care in order to preserve the strength and vigor of the race."

The *Muller* decision fired up the movement to limit women's working hours. Coalitions of trade unions, consumers leagues, and women's clubs spurred state legislatures to act (Skocpol 1992, 373–401). Eighty percent of the states had legislated restrictions on female working hours by the start of World War I (Brandeis 1935, 474–483). These very successes, however, mobilized opponents, and the restriction of women's hours stalled in the 1920s.

A newer proposal, a legal minimum wage for women, had less success. Soon after the *Muller* decision, the National Consumers' League championed a model minimum-wage bill for women and children. The NCL, the Women's Trade Union League, and the AALL campaigned for the bill, but the AFL provided almost no support (some state and local unions did support it). Massachusetts enacted the nation's first minimum wage law in 1912, but it allowed its commission only to publish, and not enforce, minimum-wage rates. Although 16 states passed minimum-wage laws by 1923, they did little to protect industrial workers. The U.S. Supreme Court struck down a minimum-wage law for the District of Columbia in 1923, freezing the campaign until the New Deal (Brandeis 1935, 502–522; Hart 1994).

Maternalist reformers often pressed for laws that would help immigrant families conform to their own views of the proper family structure and gender relationships. Problems such as illegitimacy and desertion, which seemed to affect mainly immigrant families, motivated maternalists to advocate the expansion of social work aimed at building "suitable homes" raised to "American standards" in immigrant communities Often the idea of raising immigrant communities was based on the superiority of Protestant values to those of Catholics and Jews. The white maternalists were committed "to means-testing, 'morals-testing,' and expert supervision and rehabilitation so as to inculcate into the poor the work habits and morals they so often (or so the reformers believed) lacked" (Gordon 1994, 29, 46, 129). Most maternalist reformers (with notable exceptions such as Florence Kelley) did not consider blacks and Mexicans "as objects of reform"; even in the South, which attracted few immigrants, reform efforts were directed toward immigrants (Gordon 1994, 48, 85).

Maternalist reformers helped mobilize public assistance for impoverished families in the 1910s. Juvenile court judges in Chicago and in Kansas City, Missouri implemented widow's pension programs in 1907 and 1908, aiming to prevent sending mothers to the poor house and their children to foster homes. The 1909 White House Conference on Dependent Children helped boost "mothers aid" as a priority for female reformers. The General Federation of Women's Clubs, the NCL, and the National Congress of Mothers worked to secure these laws in their own states. Thirty-nine states enacted mothers' aid programs by 1920. Although most expanded eligibility and raised benefits in the following decade, both remained very low (Skocpol 1992, 424–479).

Progressives established the first federal grant-in-aid program to help mothers and children. Under the direction of Julia Lathrop, the U.S. Children's Bureau publicized research on infant and youth problems. The Bureau particularly emphasized efforts to improve birth records and information on child mortality. By 1917, the Bureau was advocating federal-state aid for the "public protection of maternity and infancy with federal aid" (Skocpol 1992, 482–506). This proposal evolved into the Sheppard-Towner Maternity and Infancy Protection bill. Medical associations opposed the bill because it threatened physicians' control of health care, but Congress passed the law in 1921 (Skocpol 1992, 480–524; Johnson 2006, 136–150). The Supreme Court upheld the law on the grounds that it did not "require the States to do or to yield anything. If Congress enacted it with the ulterior purpose of tempting them to yield, that purpose may be effectively frustrated by the simple expedient of not yielding." (*Commonwealth of Massachusetts* v. *Mellon*, 1923). Although Congress let the law lapse in 1929, it set a precedent for federal social-policy action that could survive a Constitutional challenge.

Maternalists also played a role in other Progressive Era reforms aimed at elevating family security and the nation's moral tone. Many maternalists joined in the battle to ban alcohol, seen as a family-destroying scourge that reached epidemic proportions among immigrants. Prohibition succeeded spectacularly, if temporarily, when the states ratified the Eighteenth Amendment to the Constitution, banning alcohol nationwide (Szymanski 2003). Several states enacted pension programs for the elderly and the blind, who could not be expected to work (Robertson and Judd 1989, 210–211). Congress responded to the needs of World War I servicemen with the War Risk Insurance Act of 1917, which established health, disability, vocational rehabilitation, and survivors' benefits for veterans and their families.

7 CONSEQUENCES

As the progressive tide retreated in the 1920s, it left an archipelago of new precedents, strategies, groups, networks and social policies. These legacies also provided a wealth of lessons and experience that shaped the ideas of the next generation of social policy innovators (Lubove 1968).

First, Progressive Era social policy expanded principally at the state and local levels. Most of the states enacted workmen's compensation, factory and work regulations, and mothers-aid laws. States with growing industrial hubs (such as Massachusetts, New York, Illinois, Ohio, Michigan, Wisconsin, and California) energized government with numerous tax, regulatory, and social policy reforms. In the early 1910s, a few optimistic reformers briefly believed that the United States was racing ahead of Europe in some aspects of social policy (Rubinow 1913, 184). By the 1920s, the state governments occupied many fields of social policy, abetted by a federal government that could build policy networks, disseminate information, and provide some funding. The Progressive Era laid the foundation for a system of federal grants-in-aid in which the federal government would lead in constructing national-policy action in partnership with the states.

Second, the Progressive Era produced stark geographical differences in social policy across the nation. Although some states were social-policy leaders, many others lagged far behind. For example, nearly all states limited women's working hours by the mid-1920s, and in New York, Ohio, and Massachusetts, these laws compared favorably to such regulations in Europe (Robertson 2000, 165). However, as late as 1933, Alabama, Florida, Georgia, Indiana, Iowa, and West Virginia did not limit women's weekly or daily hours at all, and more than a dozen other states permitted women to work more than 54 hours a week (Brandeis 1935, 458–459). The National Child Labor Committee set minimum standards for child labor laws in 1925, but only half the states met these standards in 1932, and the Southern textile states still fought them tenaciously (Johnson 1935, 450–456; Davidson 1939). A large majority of states enacted workers' compensation programs by 1920, but five ex-Confederate states did not create workers' compensation programs until much later. Only 13 of the state workers-compensation laws compelled employer participation at all (Robertson 2000, 236–237).

Third, American federalism restrained state experimentation and greatly limited the overall national effort to cope with poverty and unemployment. Interstate economic competition, coupled with limitations on state government capacity, reduced the scope and impact of Progressive Era state social policy. Those who opposed state labor laws and social-welfare policies routinely argued that any new policy would harm state industries and, therefore, state economic growth and prosperity (Robertson 2000, 17–18). Paul Douglas, an economist and reformer, wrote that interstate competition "restrained the more progressive states from pioneering as they would have liked and kept the country as a whole closer to the legal conditions in the less progressive states" (Robertson and Judd 1989, 211). Interstate competition generally made American workers-compensation benefits and coverage very low by the end of the 1920s (Robertson 2000, 237). Campaigns to establish health insurance and unemployment insurance were turned back by similar claims.

Fourth, racial and gender divisions permeated American social policy. Women's labor protections and mothers-aid programs established the legitimacy of segregating social policy by gender (McDonagh 2009). Mothers' aid programs stigmatized recipients and authorized the supervision of mothers' behavior (Gordon, 1994; Mink, 1996). Democrats in the Progressive Era enacted reforms and made administrative arrangements that underwrote racial segregation in the South. Their Republican successors left these arrangements in place (King 2007). Vocational-education grants to the states, for example, allowed Southern state boards of vocational education, channeled funds to white school districts, and "made it possible to train a racially segregated labor force" without federal-government interference (Werum 1997, 399–453).

8 CONCLUSION

By the 1920s, the unique nature of the U.S. social policy was clear to all American reformers. The disparities of state action would continue to haunt American social policy. According to historian Linda Gordon, "Not only did mothers' aid shape the welfare state, but the debate about it introduced the themes and questions that still dominate welfare policy discussions today" (Gordon 1994, 37).

The New Deal—constrained by the Supreme Court's narrow interpretation of federal regulatory power until the late 1930s—drew on the Progressive experience to make federal-state grants a more widely used and deeply embedded part of American social reform. At the same time, the New Deal ultimately surmounted many of the obstacles of federal jurisdiction, and its new regulatory authority, combined with a vast infusion of relief and grant in aid funds, marked a substantial shift away from progressivism.

Progressive Era social policy raises many questions for scholars. First, how did reformers understand the problems, opportunities, and constraints they confronted? How did reformers understand the institutional obstacles and constraints they faced? What did their strategies to overcome these obstacles have in common? In particular, how did outsiders use the system? Women profoundly shaped Progressive social policy, despite the fact that in most places they could not vote before World War I. A systematic comparison of the way the female reformers such as Florence Kelley and Jane Addams became so successful would shed light on some of the timeless features of the American social policy making. Second, we need a more systematic understanding of the way American government institutions shaped policy outcomes in this period. In the aggregate, did federalism advance or constrain social policy in the U.S. (Robertson 2011)? Third, we need a better understanding of the way policy and institutions change. Reform achievements gradually altered institutions, policies, and intergovernmental relationships in ways that continued to shape American social policy long after the Progressive impulse subsided.

REFERENCES

*Indicates recommended reading.

AALL (American Association for Labor Legislation). 1915. "The Prevention of Unemployment." *American Labor Legislation Review* 5: 176–192.

AALL. 1918. "Second National Conference of Health Insurance Commissioners." *American Labor Legislation Review* 8: 133–135.

AFL (American Federation of Labor). 1905. *Proceedings of the Annual Convention*. Washington, DC: Law Reporter Printing Co.

AFL. 1914. *Proceedings of the Annual Convention*. Washington, DC: Law Reporter Printing Co.

Alston, Lee J., and Joseph P. Ferrie. 1999. *Southern Paternalism and the American Welfare State: Economic, Politics and Institutions in the South, 1865–1965*. Cambridge and New York: Cambridge University Press.

Bailey v. Drexel Furniture Company. 1922. 259 U.S. 20.

Bensel, Richard Franklin. 2000. *The Political Economy of American Industrialization, 1877–1900*. Cambridge and New York: Cambridge University Press.

Brandeis, Elizabeth. 1935. "Labor Legislation." In John R. Commons, Don D. Lescohier, Elizabeth Brandeis, Selig Perlman, and Philip Taft., eds., *History of Labor in the United States*. New York: Macmillan, 3: 399–697.

Caporaso, James P., and David P. Levine. 1992. *Theories of Political Economy*. Cambridge and New York: Cambridge University Press.

Commonwealth of Massachusetts v. Mellon. 1923. 262 U.S. 447.

Congressional Record. Washington, DC: GPO.

Crenson, Matthew A. 1998. *Building the Invisible Orphanage: A Prehistory of the American Welfare System*. Cambridge, MA: Harvard University Press.

Davidson, Elizabeth. 1939. *Child Labor Legislation in the Southern Textile States*. Chapel Hill: University of North Carolina Press.

Duverger, Maurice. 1964. *Political Parties: Their Organization and Activity in the Modern State.* Rev. ed. London: Methuen, and New York: John Wiley and Sons.

Ernst, Daniel R. 1995. *Lawyers Against Labor: From Individual Rights to Corporate Liberalism.* Urbana: University of Illinois Press.

Fishback, Price V. 2007. "The Progressive Era." In Price Fishback et al., eds., *Government and the American Economy: A New History.* Chicago: University of Chicago Press, 288–322.

Fishback, Price V., and Shawn Everett Kantor. 2000. *A Prelude to the Welfare State: The Origins of Workers' Compensation.* Chicago: University of Chicago Press.

Flexner, Eleanor, and Ellen Fitzpatrick, 1996. *Century of Struggle: The Woman's Rights Movement in the United States,* enlarged ed. Cambridge, MA: Belknap.

Gompers, Samuel. 1916. "Voluntary Social Insurance vs. Compulsory." *American Federationist* 23 (May): 335–336, 350.

*Gordon, Linda. 1994. *Pitied But Not Entitled: Single Mothers and the History of Welfare, 1890–1935.* New York: Free Press.

Greenwald, Maurine W., and Margo Anderson. 1996. *Pittsburgh Surveyed: Social Science and Social Reform in the Early Twentieth Century.* Pittsburgh: University of Pittsburgh Press.

Haines, Michael R. 2000. "The Population of the United States, 1790–1920." In Stanley L. Engerman and Robert E. Gallman, eds., *The Cambridge Economic History of the United States, Vol. II, The Long Nineteenth Century.* Cambridge and New York: Cambridge University Press, 143–205.

Hamby, Alonzo. 1999. "Progressivism: A Century of Change and Rebirth." In Sidney M. Milkis and Jerome M. Mileur, eds., *Progressivism and the New Democracy.* Amherst, MA: University of Massachusetts Press, 40–80.

Hammer v. Dagenhart. 1918. 247 U.S. 251.

Hart, Vivien. 1994. *Bound by Our Constitution: Women, Workers, and the Minimum Wage.* Princeton, NJ: Princeton University Press.

Hofstadter, Richard. 1956. *The Age of Reform.* New York: Alfred A. Knopf.

Hunter, Robert. 1904. *Poverty.* New York: Macmillan.

Johnson, Elizabeth Sands. 1935. "Child Labor Legislation." In. John R. Commons et al., eds., *History of Labor Legislation in the United States,* 4 vols. New York: Macmillan, 403–457.

*Johnson, Kimberley S. 2006. *Governing the American State: Congress and the New Federalism.* Princeton, NJ: Princeton University Press.

Kangas, Olli. 2010. "Work Accident and Sickness Benefits." In Francis G. Castles, Stephan Leibfried, Jane Lewis, Herbert Obinger, and Christopher Pierson, eds., *The Oxford Handbook of the Welfare State.* Oxford and New York: Oxford University Press, 391–405.

Kaufman, Stuart B., Peter J. Albert, and Grace Palladino, eds., et al., eds. 1997. *The Samuel Gompers Papers,* vol. 6. Urbana: University of Illinois Press.

Kelley, Florence. 1906. "The Federal Government and the Working Children." *Annals* 27: 289–292.

King, Desmond. 2007. *Separate and Unequal: African Americans and the U.S. Federal Government.* Rev. ed. Oxford and New York: Oxford University Press.

Koven, Seth, and Sonya Michel, eds. 1993. "Introduction: 'Mother Worlds.'" In *Mothers of a New World: Maternalist Politics and the Origins of Welfare States.* London and New York: Routledge, 1–42.

Lindenmeyer, Kriste. 1997. *A Right to Childhood: The U.S. Children's Bureau and Child Welfare, 1912–46.* Urbana: University of Illinois Press.

Lochner v. New York. 1905. 198 U.S. 45.

*Lubove, Roy. 1968. *The Struggle for Social Security, 1900–1935*. Cambridge, MA: Harvard University Press.

McDonagh, Eileen. 2009. *The Motherless State: Women's Political Leadership and American Democracy*. Chicago: University of Chicago Press.

McGerr, Michael. 2003. *A Fierce Discontent: The Rise and Fall of the Progressive Movement in America, 1870–1920*. New York: Free Press.

Milkis, Sidney. 2009. *Theodore Roosevelt, the Progressive Party, and the Transformation of American Democracy*. Lawrence: University Press of Kansas.

Mink, Gwendolyn. 1996. *The Wages of Motherhood: Inequality in the Welfare State, 1917–1942*. Ithaca, NY: Cornell University Press.

Morone, James. 2003. *Hellfire Nation: The Politics of Sin in American History*. New Haven, CT: Yale University Press.

Moss, David A. 1996. *Socializing Security: Progressive-Era Economists and the Origins of American Social Policy*. Cambridge, MA: Harvard University Press.

Muller v. Oregon. 1908. 208 U.S. 412.

Muncy, Robyn. 1991. *Creating a Female Dominion in American Reform, 1890–1935*. Cambridge and New York: Cambridge University Press.

Nelson, Daniel. 1969. *Unemployment Insurance: The American Experience, 1915–1935*. Madison: University of Wisconsin Press.

New State Ice Co. v. Liebmann. 1932. 285 U.S. 262.

Nugent, John D. 2009. *Safeguarding Federalism: How States Protect Their Interests in National Policymaking*. Norman: University of Oklahoma Press.

*Numbers, Ronald. 1978. *Almost Persuaded: American Physicians and Compulsory Health Insurance, 1912–1920*. Baltimore, MD: Johns Hopkins University Press.

Ogburn, William F. 1912. *Progress and Uniformity in Child-Labor Legislation: A Study in Statistical Measurement*. New York: Columbia University Press.

Orren, Karen. 1992. *Belated Feudalism: Labor, the Law, and Liberal Development in the United States*. Cambridge and New York: Cambridge University Press.

*Robertson, David Brian. 2000. *Capital, Labor, and State: The Battle for American Labor Markets from the Civil War to the New Deal*. Lanham, MD: Rowman and Littlefield.

Robertson, David Brian. 2011. *Federalism and the Making of America*. Milton Park, Abingdon, Oxon, England, and New York: Routledge.

Robertson, David Brian, and Dennis R. Judd. 1989. *The Development of American Public Policy: The Structure of Policy Restraint*. Glenview, IL: Scott, Foresman/Little, Brown.

Rodgers, Daniel T. 1982. "In Search of Progressivism." *Reviews in American History* 10 (December): 113–132.

Rosen, George. 1972. "The Committee of One Hundred on National Health and the Campaign for a National Health Department, 1906–1912." *American Journal of Public Health* 62 (February): 261–263.

Rubinow, Issac M. 1913. *Social Insurance, with Special Reference to American Conditions*. New York: Henry Holt.

*Sanders, Elizabeth. 1999. *Roots of Reform: Farmers, Workers, and the American State, 1877–1917*. Chicago: University of Chicago Press.

Scheiber, Harry N. 1975. "Federalism and the American Economic Order, 1789–1910." *Law and Society Review* 10 (Fall): 57–118.

Sklar, Judith. 1995. *Florence Kelley and the Nation's Work*. New Haven, CT: Yale University Press.

Schwedtman, Ferdinand C., and James A. Emery. 1911. *Accident Prevention and Relief.* New York: National Association of Manufacturers.

*Skocpol, Theda. 1992. *Protecting Soldiers and Mothers: The Political Origins of Social Policy in the United States.* Cambridge, MA: Belknap.

Szymanski, Ann-Marie E. 2003. *Pathways to Prohibition: Radicals, Moderates, and Social Movement Outcomes.* Durham, NC: Duke University Press.

Teaford, Jon C. 2002. *The Rise of the States: Evolution of American State Government.* Baltimore, MD: Johns Hopkins University Press.

Tomlins, Christopher. 1985. *The State and the Unions: Labor Relations, Law, and the Organized Labor Movement in America, 1880–1960.* Cambridge and New York: Cambridge University Press.

Trattner, Walter. 1970. *Crusade for the Children: A History of the National Child Labor Committee and Child Labor Reform in America.* Chicago: Quadrangle Books.

U.S. Bureau of Labor Statistics. 1917. *Proceedings of the Conference on Social Insurance, Bulletin 212.* Washington, DC: GPO.

U.S. Commission on Industrial Relations. 1915. *Final Report of the Commission on Industrial Relations.* Washington, DC: GPO.

Werum, Regina. 1997. "Sectionalism and Racial Politics: Federal Vocational Policies and Programs in the Predesegregation South," *Social Science History* 21 (Fall): 399–453.

Wiebe, Robert H. 1962. *Businessmen and Reform: A Study of the Progressive Movement.* Cambridge, MA: Harvard University Press.

Wiebe, Robert H. 1967. *The Search for Order.* New York: Hill and Wang.

Weir, Margaret. 2005. "States, Race, and the Decline of New Deal Liberalism," *Studies in American Political Development* 19 (Fall): 157–172.

*Wood, Stephen B. 1968. *Constitutional Politics in the Progressive Era: Child Labor and the Law.* Chicago: University of Chicago Press.

CHAPTER 4

....

THE GREAT DEPRESSION AND WORLD WAR II

....

ANDREW MORRIS

1 INTRODUCTION: AMERICAN SOCIAL POLICY IN DEPRESSION AND WAR

A casual observer of American social welfare in 1929, particularly in industrial cities and states, might have been impressed by the results of the decade of New Era organization. Many cities had moved to rationalize the fundraising for their voluntary agencies through new "Community Chests," organized around the latest business principles; some leading employers were pioneering new "welfare capitalist" initiatives, including retirement pensions and unemployment plans, to provide for their workers; dozens of states were adding laws to the books to provide for the needs of widows with children, the elderly, and categories of the disabled, especially the blind. This patina of organization tarnished rapidly under the pressure of the mass unemployment of the Great Depression, though the administration of President Herbert Hoover desperately clung to a mode of provision that placed voluntary and local efforts at the forefront of relief.

Franklin Roosevelt, elected in 1932 and supported by Democratic majorities in Congress, proved far more willing to muster national resources to meet the emergency. Over time, using the political opening provided by the Depression, the New Deal inserted the federal government into social provision in ways that were sometimes unprecedented, such as in the creation of a national system of retirement insurance through the Social Security Act or the nationwide system of public employment embodied in the Work Progress Administration. Other New Deal programs, particularly in public assistance, essentially added federal funds to older programs, strengthening and spreading them but leaving tremendous discretion to the states. Even innovative programs such as unemployment insurance demonstrated strong continuities with earlier approaches to social welfare, particularly in the value placed on decentralized administration. Thus, by the late 1930s, the size and scope of public social welfare policy had dramatically changed but, with the exception of Old Age Insurance, it retained the crazy-quilt variations in benefits, eligibility, and administration that had characterized social policy the decade before.

World War II and the end of the employment emergency undermined the hopes of some advocates who anticipated gradually federalizing and expanding the core elements of the rudimentary public welfare state. Public employment programs were regarded as superfluous and were eliminated; welfare programs were expected to diminish except for the needs of an irreducible core of unemployables; and a labor movement empowered by the New Deal and the war worked with employers to expand the provision of pensions and health care through the workplace. At the war's end, the central elements of the mid-century "welfare regime" (Esping-Andersen 1990) had become clear: a core of public social provision through the programs of the Social Security Act; an expanding system of private social benefits organized around the workplace that built on these public programs; and a range of welfare programs that addressed the needs of nonworkers in a haphazard and often discriminatory manner.

2 MASS UNEMPLOYMENT, NEW ERA VOLUNTARISM, AND THE "ASSOCIATIONAL STATE"

The unemployment crisis of the Great Depression was not immediately dramatic; it unfolded inexorably in the years following the stock market crash of 1929. Industries that had struggled even during the boom times of the 1920s, such as coal mining or textiles, were among the first and hardest hit, but as consumer demand plummeted during 1930 and 1931, even industries at the cutting edge of the economy, such as autos and electrical goods, began to shed workers. Though unemployment statistics were not systematically gathered by the federal government until the 1930s, those that are available give some sense of the pace of unemployment's advance: unemployment rates outside of agriculture doubled from 1929 to 1930, rising from 3.2 percent to 8.7 percent, then almost doubling again the next year to 15.9 percent in 1931, and then rising to around 25 percent by the time that Franklin D. Roosevelt took office in early 1933. Although these numbers give a sense of the pace of the Depression's onset, they do not give an accurate picture of the true dimensions of unemployment. Not only were the statistics unreliable, but they also do not reflect the wage cuts and reduced hours that became common for those who managed to hold onto their jobs. If one included the reduction in work weeks, by some estimates, only half of all American workers were employed full-time by early 1933 (Badger 1989, 18–19; Kennedy 1999, 87).

Herbert Hoover, elected president in 1928, was by most contemporary standards the ideal person to marshal the nation's resources to address the unemployment crisis. The two-dimensional image of Hoover that emerged in the 1930s as a president who fiddled while Rome burned has given way to a more nuanced view. Hoover was clearly not a *laissez faire* conservative of the old order. He had built his career in public service on his background as a consummate organizer with a humanitarian bent, marshalling food relief to Europe during and after World War I, and then, as Secretary of Commerce under President Calvin Coolidge, coordinating relief after the Great Mississippi Flood of 1927. Hoover emerged with the reputation as an energetic, hypercompetent manager, and "Herbert Hoover: Master of Emergencies" (the title of a 1928 campaign film) entered the presidency with a toolbox full of ideas to address any potential disruption in the nation's economic well-being.

First and foremost among these was an innovative approach to using the power of the federal government. Hoover believed that the federal government could play an important new role in exhorting and coordinating the efforts of private industry, voluntary social welfare organizations, and local public officials to meet economic challenges that outstripped the capacity of purely local efforts to address. Hoover firmly believed that this combination of national energy and local provision was not only effective but represented the best possible synthesis of older American beliefs in localism and individualism and the demands of a twentieth-century industrial economy. The "American System," as Hoover called it, or the "associative state," as historian Ellis Hawley later labeled Hoover's approach, would meet the genuine needs of industrial dislocation but avoid the danger of dependency that a federally provided "dole" might present (Hoover 1928; Hawley 1974).

On paper, and particularly in the cities most visible to policy makers, the infrastructure existed to make Hoover's dreams come true. During the 1920s, several hundred cities had converted World War I fundraising organizations into Community Chests that streamlined and coordinated local charitable giving. The Red Cross, a national organization built on local chapters, also stood ready. And outside the more formal voluntary sector was a world of smaller charities and mutual aid associations (often in ethnic communities) to which the poor had often turned in times of need (Cohen 1990). When pressed by the sheer enormity of Depression era unemployment, though, this edifice of voluntarism faltered, cracked, and disintegrated. Hoover had hoped to use the bully pulpit of the presidency to provide publicity and information to local fundraising efforts, first through the President's Emergency Committee on Unemployment in 1930 (renamed the President's Organization on Unemployment Relief in 1931). However, unemployment increased far more quickly than voluntary resources could match. Local agencies, even in the cities with the best-organized and most prosperous voluntary sectors, such as New York or Chicago, were running in the red by 1932, and only a fraction of the unemployed or destitute might hope for assistance there. Smaller charities or ethnic organizations, often dependent on the contributions or membership of their working-class constituents, also ran dry. The handful of privately run corporate unemployment funds had similarly proved unable to keep up with the scale of need (Romansco 1965; Morris 2009).

The rhetorical celebration of voluntarism in the 1920s had also obscured the fact that public funds were already shouldering a large portion of the load of the safety net; historian Michael Katz estimates that public relief spending just prior to the Depression exceeded charitable spending by three to one (Katz 1996, 215–216). A welter of state programs initiated in the Progressive Era reforms had expanded the range of state-level responsibility, but largely to defined categories of recipients: 45 states had passed legislation for mother's-aid programs by 1931 and, by 1934, fully 28 states had established old-age pensions. Additionally, 27 states had created programs for aid to the blind. Here too, though, the appearance of a social safety net dissipated when tested by the Depression. Many state programs were unfunded; others offered only small amounts after recipients passed a humiliating "means test" to determine if they were truly needy. Local efforts remained the cornerstone of the early response to the Depression, but by 1932, localities were also at the end of their ropes. Property tax receipts, the basis of most municipal financing, had plummeted, and towns and cities went begging to states for assistance. By then, many states had reached the limits of constitutional restrictions on borrowing, and they had little or nothing that they could or would help cities with (Romansco 1965, 169–171). Thus, by 1932, the federal government appeared to be the court of last resort.

Hoover's steadfast opposition to federal relief may have seemed plausible at the onset of the Depression when it seemed to resemble earlier economic downturns. But as voluntary, local, and state social provision collapsed, activists in Congress pushed for a federal response. A coterie of urban and rural progressives from both parties, including New York Senator Robert Wagner (D), Wisconsin Senator Robert LaFollette Jr. (R), Colorado Senator Edward Costigan (D), and Representative David Lewis (D) of Maryland began to promote legislation expanding federal public works and directly funding unemployment relief. By the summer of 1932, the situation was so dire that both Congressional and White House resistance to federal intervention diminished. The passage of the Emergency Relief and Construction Act, which created the Reconstruction Finance Corporation (RFC), expanded federal funding for public works, and allotted $300 million in loans to states to provide direct unemployment relief. State and local administration of relief, plus the financing mechanism of a loan rather than grants, mollified Hoover somewhat, but in reality, most of the loans were never repaid and, in essence, became the first grants for unemployment relief provided by the federal government (Schwartz 1970, 172).

3 THE NEW DEAL: ROOSEVELT AND RELIEF

3.1 Emergency Relief

Hoover's opponent in the 1932 presidential race, though he shared some of the President's reservations about the "dole," had markedly different ideas about the role of government in providing a social safety net in a modern industrial economy. Franklin Roosevelt's thinking on social welfare, an amalgam of the *noblesse oblige* of the Hudson River aristocracy and a Progressive-era belief in the conservation of natural and human resources, lacked the finely honed philosophy of Hoover's. But those looking for evidence of what his vague promises of a "New Deal" meant for social policy could turn to the policies he supported during his tenure as governor of New York as the Great Depression deepened. Roosevelt, arguing for a program of emergency unemployment relief to the New York State Legislature, asked rhetorically, "What is the State? It is the duly constituted representative of an organized society of human beings, created by them for their mutual protection and well-being. One of the duties of the State is that of caring for those of its citizens who find themselves the victims of such adverse circumstances as make them unable to obtain even the necessities of mere existence without the aid of others" (Roosevelt 1932, 788). Roosevelt articulated a vision of *public* responsibility, and conceived of government as an instrument of mutual aid rather than as a threat to individualism. Governor Roosevelt authorized the creation in 1931 of the Temporary Emergency Relief Administration (TERA), under the leadership of social worker Harry Hopkins, the first state agency in the country to fund unemployment relief.

The TERA would be an important model for the national emergency when Roosevelt took office as President. In Congress, Lafollette, Costigan, and Murphy had, prior to Roosevelt's inauguration, advanced a new unemployment relief bill. Once Roosevelt took office, Congress moved quickly to pass the Federal Emergency Relief Act in May 1933. This legislation created the Federal Emergency Relief Administration (FERA) to grant, instead of loan, $500 million to states. Hopkins, appointed head of the agency in late May, on his first day of work found six urgent telegraphs from governors desperate for funds; he promptly approved them, and the image of Hopkins spending $5 million in his first two hours on the job has been an enduring symbol of the new spirit in Washington, D.C. (Leuchtenberg 1963, 121). FERA was one of the most significant avenues of federal expenditures in the "First" New Deal, ultimately distributing over three billion dollars by the time it was disbanded in 1936 (Brown 1940, 149).

FERA's direct relief program was one of the most immediate and tangible elements of the early New Deal. Federal relief spending backstopped the states, cities, and towns, and federal policies gradually encouraged higher standards of spending across the board. For example, the national average for family monthly grants almost doubled, from $15.15 in May 1933 to $29.33 in May 1935. Moreover, FERA's Washington administrators used federal monies as a lever to encourage or force states and localities to increase their appropriations for relief. Hopkins occasionally threatened to withhold federal funds entirely from states that sought to cut back their contributions. State spending on relief doubled from 1933 to 1935, and local spending increased 27 percent, often drawing on new forms of taxation. The federal contribution overall, though, was the most significant, averaging 70 percent of emergency relief spending in the same period. Despite the overall increase in spending, the average monthly grants varied wildly from state to state; in 1935, New York State had the highest, at $52.92, whereas South Carolina had the lowest of $11.32 (Brown 1940, 204–205, 248–249). The continued reliance on local and state administration of relief led advocates such as Edith Abbott, Dean of the School of Social Service Administration at the University of Chicago to complain that "the New Deal has been persuaded to try to keep alive a thoroughly antiquated pauper-relief system that belongs to the days of the ox cart and stage coach" (Abbott 1933, 402).

For the administration, federal direct relief was simply a stopgap on the way toward economic recovery and a broader social insurance approach to the safety net. Roosevelt himself had inveighed against the "dole," and had sent reporters into the field to assess the impact of relief policies on recipients' work ethic (Hickok, Lowitt, and Beasley 1983). Despite the aspirations of public welfare activists for a permanent nationwide structure for general relief, Roosevelt shrank from the idea. When he put forth the proposal for old-age insurance (now known as Social Security) and a restructured federal work relief program in 1935, he also announced that the federal government should "quit this business of relief," returning direct, general relief for those who could not work back to the states, localities, and charities (Roosevelt 1935).

3.2 Work Relief

The emphasis on work relief for the able-bodied unemployed on a mass, national level, was perhaps one of the most defining characteristics of New Deal social policy, and one that distinguishes it from subsequent policy regimes. Direct relief was the quickest, surest, and cheapest means to prevent starvation, which seemed the most pressing issue in the spring of 1933. But Roosevelt and Hopkins both preferred to integrate work into the relief program as soon as possible. In contrast to punitive "work tests" used in earlier eras of relief, Hopkins and Roosevelt saw work as a constructive relief strategy: a way to maintain the morale and the skills of workers, work relief would be more dignified and less corrosive to the work ethic, in their eyes, than direct cash grants that gave something for nothing (Amenta 1998). And while, according E. Wight Bakke's famous study of unemployed workers in the 1930s, relief was a last resort for most workers, they much preferred work relief to the "dole" (Bakke 1940, 29).

The first and most distinctive work relief program was one of the few New Deal relief programs directly shaped by the Roosevelt's own preferences—the Civilian Conservation Corps (CCC). The idea sprung from his interest in conservation projects and his belief in the salutary effects of outdoors work, as well as comparable projects in a handful of states and in Europe. Created in the spring of 1933, the CCC was open to young men ages 18 to 25 who were able and willing to work outdoors on a variety of conservation and recreation projects. A hybrid organization run jointly by the U.S. Army and federal civilian agencies such as the U.S. Forest Service, the CCC housed young unmarried men in military-style camps that were supervised by an Army officer and a civilian director. They were housed, fed, and paid $30 a month, $25 of which was sent back to their families, thus effectively broadening the impact of the wage. Enrollees worked on a wide range of projects on public lands: reforestation, erosion control, constructing roads and facilities in national and state parks and forestlands, and so on.

The CCC was immediately popular, and expanded to a maximum enrollment of over half a million young men in 2,900 camps in 1935 (Salmond 1967). But even at its height, the CCC only occupied a fraction of those in need, and the administration turned to other, broader measures to find productive work for the unemployed.

FERA provided the administrative structure for a general work-relief program. Many cities and towns, in previous depressions and in the early 1930s, had created local work-relief programs, but these tended to be haphazard and small scale. FERA aspired to create a more systematic program that would emphasize useful public works, but in the short run, during the summer of 1933, the Work Division mainly added federal funds to ongoing state and local projects. By the fall of 1933, though, the lack of economic recovery and the persistent high rate of unemployment led administrators to create a bigger, better funded, and better organized program within FERA: the Civil Works Administration (CWA). Roosevelt diverted $400 million from the Public Works Administration's (PWA) budget to the CWA with the aim of employing four million workers during the winter. The most important feature of the CWA, in the eyes of recipients, was that it was not simply an extension of existing relief—the CWA dispensed with the means test used by FERA and paid prevailing wages—making it popular with those it employed, but more expensive than the Administration would tolerate. Only a few months after it began, Roosevelt terminated the CWA, returning work relief back to the FERA's Work Division, the means test and "relief wages" (Schwartz 1984).

The stunning Democratic gains in the 1934 Congressional elections emboldened Hopkins and Roosevelt to reinvigorate the work relief program and to make it a permanent part of federal social welfare policy. Although Roosevelt proposed terminating federal direct relief in his 1935 State of the Union Address, he also laid out a plan for redoubling federal work relief efforts, in what would become known at the Works Progress Administration (WPA, renamed the Work Projects Administration in 1939). With a $4.5 billion initial appropriation, the WPA dwarfed the previous work-relief programs. It was a federal organization with federal staffs in the states, rather than operating through state agencies. By the time it was ended in 1943, the WPA had employed eight million workers, and at its height had over three million on the payroll at one time. WPA workers were drawn from relief rolls, but were paid a "security wage," lower than prevailing wages but higher than the relief wage paid to FERA workers. The WPA's emphasis on labor-intensive projects that would employ the maximum number of workers led it to fund many familiar types of public works projects, such as road building, sewers, and the construction of public facilities. However, the sheer range and variety of WPA projects also distinguished it from earlier efforts. WPA workers built golf courses, airports, and cleaned up after hurricanes. The WPA expanded the white-collar employment efforts of FERA; the educated unemployed were sent out to catalogue historical records; to survey local health and traffic conditions; to provide skilled nursing services; to bind library books, among other projects. Its most distinctive and controversial programs put unemployed artists and writers to work in the Federal Art Project, Federal Theater Project, and Federal Writers Project, leaving an impressive legacy of public imagery, performance, and literature (Howard 1943; Taylor 2008).

However, the limits of the WPA were as striking as its innovations. It shared some of the characteristic localism of other New Deal programs; despite federal oversight, projects required local sponsorship and some contribution of materials, and local and state politicians were often able to turn the WPA program into extensions of their own political operations. Congress never allocated the full amount of funds requested by Hopkins, and Roosevelt himself cut back WPA spending in early 1937 when it appeared that the economy was taking a turn for the better. The uncertainty of funding led to periodic cutbacks and layoffs that undermined the ability of the program to provide a sense of security for its employees, and forced the program to often use a means test to allocate work to the most needy. And, perhaps most damaging, was the critique of conservatives of waste and inefficiency in the program; WPA workers were derided as "shovel leaners," and periodic exposes of seemingly frivolous projects from the Federal Art Project overshadowed the relatively efficient operation of the WPA under the circumstances it was forced to deal with. Although work relief remained a vital part of the New Deal social safety net until World War II, and has achieved a nostalgic glow in retrospect, it was also the one strand of social policy innovation that would not persist into the postwar era (Amenta 1998; Taylor 2008).

3.3 Toward Social Security

Hopkins famously instructed his FERA staff after the Democratic victory in the 1934 midterm elections, "Boys, this is our hour. We've got to get everything we want—a works program, social security, wages and hours, everything—now or never. Get your minds to work on developing a complete ticket to provide security for all the folks in this country up and down across the board" (quoted in Sherwood 1950, 65). This policymaking window culminated in 1935 in the programs of the "Second New Deal," which instituted some of the widest ranging reform efforts of the Administration and Congress. The reinvention of social policy was at its core.

Up through 1935, federal support for direct and work relief had underwritten the emergency response to the unemployment crisis. However, reformers in the states, Congress, and the administration—as well as grassroots movements outside the political system—hoped to take advantage of the political opening provided by mass economic insecurity to do more. Social insurance advocates, who looked at the industrial economies of Europe and saw safety nets of unemployment insurance, pension plans for the elderly, even state-supported medical care, hoped to finally use the power of the national government to help cushion the impact on workers of the vicissitudes of economic life. Others aimed to use federal funds to reinvigorate or replace existing state programs that provided help for those deemed unable to provide for themselves: the elderly, the blind, and widows with children. The culmination of these various strands of activism into the Social Security Act of 1935 created some of the most durable elements of American public social policy, particularly in the programs of unemployment insurance and retirement security for workers.

Roosevelt had come into office sympathizing with the need for unemployment insurance in particular, thanks to the influence of Frances Perkins, who became his Secretary of Labor. The events of 1934 helped sharpen the Administration's attention toward moving forward on a broader program. Congressional liberals were advancing a variety of social welfare measures, attuned in part to external pressures from insurgent, often radical, movements. Most important of these was the "Townsend Movement," a grassroots organization of the elderly, which was flooding Congress with petitions to support the plan of Dr. Francis Townsend to provide all Americans over 60 with an astounding $200 per month pension, provided they stopped work and spent all the money each month (Amenta 2008).

Roosevelt convened a Committee on Economic Security, led by Edwin Witte of the University of Wisconsin, to make sense of the competing proposals for social insurance and to draft an administration plan. External pressure for generous pensions for the elderly undoubtedly moved old age to the forefront of the planning efforts of the CES. The Committee shied away from policies funded from the general revenues, such as the Townsend Plan. In their view, it would leave the program vulnerable to the vagaries of Congressional appropriations and the potential to use the program to curry political favor (the lesson that some took from the example of Civil War veterans' pensions). The CES instead proposed a contributory plan directly connected to employment: workers and employers would both be taxed to build up a fund that would, when workers turned 65, pay a pension based on the worker's lifetime earnings; the federal government would not contribute any additional funds from other sources. Roosevelt preferred this approach. He insisted that taxes be set high enough to ensure that the system remain completely self-supporting, and was convinced that a contributory system would create a constituency for protecting the program—if recipients perceived Old Age Insurance (OAI) as something earned rather than granted. As many noted, the payroll tax made the system far more regressive than one that could have been funded by a progressive income tax, but Roosevelt was convinced this was essential to the program's long term political viability (DeWitt, Béland, Berkowitz 2008). Over the long run, OAI proved to be quite popular and would become synonymous with the term *Social Security*, but in the short term, the welfare program for the elderly that was also included in the bill, Old Age Assistance (OAA) attracted far more attention and support (see Dewitt and Berkowitz's chapter, this volume).

As with OAI, the unemployment insurance program would have more long-term significance than short-term impact in the 1930s. Social insurance for the unemployed had been the focus of reformers dating back to the Progressive era, and an impressive body of work had been done researching various models in effect in Europe (Rogers 2000). Despite a heated debate within the CES about the structure of taxation, the most important element that emerged was the relatively decentralized system, funded by a federal payroll tax, but with states required to pass their own laws to manage the system. This left states with a reasonable amount of discretion over the structure of the system, and wide latitude on benefit levels. Political and legal considerations shaped the preference for a state-based, rather than nationalized system. In the event of a possible Supreme

Court rejection of the Social Security Act, CES planners hoped that state laws would persist (Berkowitz 1991, 32–33).

Finally, although Roosevelt had promised to have the federal government quit the relief business for employables, the Social Security Act did, in fact, support several means-tested welfare programs. OAA attracted the most attention at the time, but the Act also included federal support for female-headed households with young children, and for the blind. Those programs (Aid to Dependent Children [ADC] and Aid to the Blind) were relatively uncontroversial at the time, though ADC would loom much larger in the subsequent history of welfare policy. Originally designed for the CES proposal by the federal Children's Bureau, ADC sought, like OAA, to build on state programs, in this case state mothers' pensions laws, which had been widely adopted but meagerly funded. When the image of those families were those headed by widows, particularly white widows, the program sparked little opposition. Changes in federal policy, however, even in the 1930s would begin to affect the program's constituency. The first major amendments to the Social Security Act in 1939 extended benefits to the survivors of workers covered by OAI (and changed the program's name to Old Age and Survivors Insurance, or OASI), covering many widows, particularly of industrial workers, by a program whose benefits were perceived to have been earned (Mettler 1998). This left a growing group of female-headed households in ADC whose image (divorced, deserted, unmarried, and, increasingly, nonwhite) did not conform to the original ideal of a morally and economically deserving recipient.

3.4 Race and Gender in New Deal Social Policy

As this brief discussion of ADC suggests, racial politics and gendered assumptions about men's and women's proper roles deeply shaped the origins and trajectory of New Deal social policy. In both cases, New Deal policy ultimately did little to challenge prevailing racial and gender norms, in some cases because federal policy makers consciously or unconsciously adopted them, and in others because the structure of policies, particularly the largely decentralized nature of much of the social safety net, allowed for local mores and economic interests to dominate social policy.

The decentralization of relief administration, and eventually of the welfare programs of the Social Security Act, gave a sharp racial cast to relief. African Americans, the largest racial minority in the country, had far higher rates of unemployment and poverty than whites, and yet they consistently received less support through relief on an absolute and relative scale. In the early years of the Depression, African Americans in the South were often barred outright from white-run charities. Relief payments on the whole in the South (where the majority of African Americans lived) were lower than other regions, and here African Americans were excluded from relief at higher rates and were paid less than whites. White officials argued that blacks were used to surviving on less, and thus needed less relief; white employers, particularly in agriculture, also wanted to keep a cheap labor force available that would not have relief as an alternative. Blacks in the North faced less overt discrimination in relief, but employment discrimination led to disproportionate levels of unemployment and poverty (Sitkoff 2009).

The New Deal improved things somewhat for African Americans, but largely did not disrupt prevailing arrangements and attitudes. The single most noticeable fact was that relief spending increased, and impoverished African Americans received more than they had in the early 1930s. Particularly in the early emergency phase of FERA, the dependence on state and local administration ensured that whites would receive better treatment than blacks, particularly in the South. Hopkins and other FERA national officials were not ignorant of the racial inequities in relief distribution, but were handicapped by the local nature of relief distribution, the political powerlessness of blacks in the South to demand more equitable relief, and the powerful and watchful eye of Southern Democratic senators and congressmen who carefully scoured any relief legislation to ensure that it did not offer an entering wedge for federal interference that would undermine the social and economic dominance of Southern whites over blacks. Such disparities could be found in federal work relief and social insurance programs as well. The CCC, while offering equal pay to African American enlistees, enrolled far fewer young black men than white men, despite higher levels of black unemployment, and racially segregated its camps (Sitkoff 2009).

Later New Deal relief programs with a stronger federal role, particularly the WPA and the National Youth Administration (the NYA, a subsidiary program of the WPA that helped provide economic support and educational opportunities for high school and college age students) were able to lessen discrimination somewhat. African American political power and protest in the North also impacted the program. Following the Harlem Riot of 1935, a commission revealed systematic discrimination in relief administration in New York City, and more equitable treatment resulted (Greenberg 1991). The NYA, headed by Aubrey Williams, a liberal white Southerner, and with Mary McCloud Bethune as director of Negro Affairs (the highest placed African American official in Washington), established national standards of support, offered the same opportunities for training to both black and white students, and employed young African Americans in proportions roughly equivalent to their needs (Sitkoff 2009). Still, even in the most "national" element of all the New Deal's social welfare programs, OAI, African Americans were disadvantaged. The exclusion of agricultural and domestic workers (occupations that comprised a significant percentage of African American employment) from coverage under OAI and unemployment insurance left millions of African Americans ineligible for these core social insurance programs—an omission that would reverberate for decades (Lieberman 1998).

Relief policy also sharply differentiated between men and women. Young unmarried women without families, for instance, were largely invisible to relief administrators. Transient programs run by FERA were exclusively aimed at young men; no women were enrolled in the CCC, with only a tiny program run by FERA as an alternative. Work relief programs run by FERA and the CWA, oriented first and foremost to construction jobs, acknowledged the needs of women but struggled at first to find appropriate venues for women to work in (Ware 1981, 105–111).

The more profound and long-term impact of gendered assumptions about work and family came in the shaping of the Social Security Act. Here, scholars over the past two decades have revealed the explicit and implicit ways that men and women were given different support, and different women treated differently, by federal social policy (Abramovitz 1999; Gordon 1995; Kessler-Harris 2001; Mink 1995). The most noticeable were the social-insurance programs that were first and foremost designed around the assumption that men were the primary wage earners, and that cushioning the vagaries of an industrial economy, where white men were predominant in the work force, was the highest priority of federal policy. OASI was built around labor force participation, not a broader right of citizenship, and women tended to be included more as part of families than as individuals. For women who were in the labor force, OASI excluded a number of occupations, particularly domestic service, where women, just like racial minorities, were over-represented. This exclusion has formed the basis for a contentious debate among scholars, some of whom argue that this policy, as well as the exclusion of agricultural workers, reflected administrative obstacles: the wages of domestics and agricultural workers would be harder to keep track of than industrial workers (Davies and Derthick 1997). Some suggest it was part of a deliberate, incremental strategy in which policy makers recognized the opposition of white Southern lawmakers to the coverage of these groups, and hoped to fold these occupations in later (Lieberman 1998). Others argue that this policy reflected the gender and racial biases of the framers, in that domestics did not seem to be "workers" in the sense that factory or commercial workers did (Kessler-Harris 2001). Whatever the motive, it resulted in a generation of workers being left out of a program that would provide a vital economic safety net for old age. Those left out were often women and often African American; 3.5 million of 5.5 million African Americans working in the 1930s were employed in those two occupational sectors (Gordon 1995, 275).

Some women had access to the New Deal welfare regime through Aid to Dependent Children (ADC), if they headed a family with young children. Although ADC was virtually an afterthought in the drafting of the Social Security Act, the program's initial structure gives some indication of why it would become increasingly unpopular and stigmatized as "welfare" in the postwar era, because the fact that it was granted rather than "earned" would help undermine political support for the program in the long run. The dwindling number of widows in the program after 1939 meant ADC served families that often fell outside public norms of propriety, particularly unmarried mothers. As the percentage of mothers in the workforce grew after World War II, and as ADC recipients became increasingly nonwhite, it would become harder for the program's defenders to make the case for supporting this particular group of mothers. Decentralization also weakened ADC. Because of the opposition of Southerners in Congress, the Bureau of Public Assistance (the agency created to oversee ADC, OAA, and Aid to the Blind) was not able to set national standards for stipends, and left administration to the states under certain general federal guidelines. The result was the familiar wild variation of provision, higher in the industrial North and lowest in the South. Local interests in the South and Southwest would also often sharply restrict ADC eligibility to ensure that poor women would be forced to take jobs as domestics or at harvest time in agricultural areas, and African American women in the South were systematically under-represented in the early years of the program (Gordon 1995, 275–276).

Many similar constrictions could be seen in the creation of the nation's federal minimum wage in the Fair Labor Standards Act (FLSA) of 1938. "Wages and hours" (in the shorthand of reformers) was the last major piece of social welfare legislation passed during the New Deal. Although the Supreme Court had held as unconstitutional many earlier state-level attempts at a minimum wage (and had thrown out a set of federal minimum wages when it struck down the National Industrial Recovery Act in 1935), the Court's famous shift in response to Roosevelt's court-packing plan opened the door for another try. The FLSA set a federal minimum wage of 40 cents an hour, a 40-hour week, and banned child labor—but due to opposition from some unions (which opposed federal wage-setting) and many manufacturers, the categories of workers covered by the law was quite narrow. Women workers benefited from the inclusion of the garment and textile industries, but the now-familiar exclusion of agricultural and domestic workers from the minimum wage left vast swaths of the female workforce unprotected— though scholars disagree about the scale of the exclusions (Mettler 1998, 198–205; Kessler-Harris, 105–106). The agricultural exemption also disproportionately affected African Americans—as well as Hispanic and Asian workers in West Coast agriculture (Palmer 1995).

4 WORLD WAR II AND AMERICAN SOCIAL POLICY

By the late 1930s, the contours of what the New Deal had accomplished were relatively clear and at its core was a public insurance system to support workers separated from the work force due to unemployment or retirement. The Supreme Court's endorsement of broader federal authority rested those accomplishments on a firm legal base. Activists within the Social Security Administration hoped to expand these programs gradually over time, so that social insurance would gradually diminish the need for means-tested "welfare" programs such as OAA or ADC. For the long-term unemployed, public work relief would take up the slack when the economy could not generate enough jobs. For the most desperate, a mix of grudging "general" relief that bore the stamp of early welfare practices was available, or else they could turn to a voluntary sector that filled in some of the cracks between public programs.

World War II would change that landscape dramatically. Thanks to a level of federal spending inconceivable in the 1930s, the American economy achieved virtually full employment by 1943, and many of the most distinctive programs of relief were eliminated. Even prior to America's entry into the war, both the CCC and the WPA had begun to decrease enrollments and to shift over to defense-related work on military facilities.

By 1943, Congressional conservatives succeeded in eliminating both agencies. Relief expenditures also plummeted. The prospect of a full-employment economy and hopes for postwar prosperity altered the priorities of even the most ardent supporters of a robust public welfare state. A postwar planning effort convened by Roosevelt during the war, the National Resources Planning Board, envisioned an expanded program of social insurance, a revived public employment program, and a federal system of general relief that would even out regional variations, but rationalized first and foremost as a part of a Keynesian economic stimulus to guarantee prosperity, rather than a safety net in a hampered economy (Brinkley 1995).

One distinctive element of wartime social policy was that the workplace became further embedded at the center of a new mix of public and private social provision. This was an unanticipated consequence of collective bargaining and government regulation of wartime labor relations that had the end result of cementing support for the social-insurance aspects of the New Deal, reviving a system of private pensions that had been discredited by the Depression, and invigorating a system of private insurance for health care nurtured by favorable government tax treatment. In an effort to prevent inflation and stabilize employment in wartime industries, the federal government imposed wage and price controls, and, in return for a no-strike pledge from the AFL and the newly created Congress of Industrial Organizations (CIO), required workers in new wartime industries to be automatically enrolled in unions. Union membership surged and employers faced a more powerful bargaining partner. However, due to wage controls, wages could not be subject to negotiation; instead, union contracts began to expand to include retirement pensions and health-care provision. With the reality of private pensions for their working-class employees upon them, more and more employers came to see OASI as a boon; most pension plans deducted employees' Social Security payments from their final pension, with the employer only having to make up the difference. It also firmly committed the union movement to the Social Security program. Though it had played a relatively small role in the creation of Social Security, organized labor would emerge as one of the most important political forces supporting its expansion (Hacker 2002; Klein 2003).

The war also accelerated attention to health-care policy. The Committee on Economic Security had considered including health insurance as part of the Social Security Act, but Roosevelt feared a backlash from the American Medical Association, which could have jeopardized the entire effort. During the war, though, a variety of innovative programs offered alternative visions of health-care provision, most notably, the Emergency Maternal and Infant Care (EMIC) program, which provided health care to the wives and children of a majority of male military personnel. Social welfare advocates in the Children's Bureau hoped this might be an entering wedge for a broader public medical program, but they were unable to broaden the program beyond servicemen's families. Ultimately, the more significant trend was the inclusion of health care in contract negotiations between unionized employees and employers, and the favorable tax treatment of these fringe benefits by the federal government. Unions had experimented during the 1930s with a variety of methods of providing health care to their employees, but the peculiar conditions of wartime labor relations created an incentive for unions to bargain for employer-subsidized private health insurance. Though organized labor would remain a staunch supporter of an expanded and more generous Social Security program, the private provision of health insurance through employers to union members weakened the interest of unions in pursuing a broader public health insurance agenda (Hacker 2002; Klein 2003).

5 CONCLUSION

The economic trauma of the Great Depression convinced a generation of policy makers and their constituents that the federal government needed to play a central role in underwriting economic security. The emergency federal programs for relief and employment provided bare-bones but, nonetheless, vital sustenance to millions, and provided a dramatic counterpoint to the collapse of the state-local-voluntary apparatus of relief. By the end of World War II, a large swath of the American working class—particularly white men in unionized industries—began to benefit from a safety net anchored by federal policies and expanded by private benefits to a degree practically unimaginable in the 1920s. The limits of the New Deal/World War II welfare state, however, were as striking as the advances—a system in which the most generous and popular benefits were rooted in the workplace, rather than in broader notions of entitlement through citizenship, and in which decentralized administration of welfare programs led to wide variations in benefits that had profound racial and gender implications.

REFERENCES

*Indicates recommended reading.

Abbott, Edith. 1933. "The Crisis in Relief," *The Nation* 137, no. 3562 (October 11): 402.
Abramovitz, Mimi. 1999. *Regulating the Lives of Women: Social Welfare Policy from the Colonial Times to the Present.* Boston: South End Press.
*Amenta, Edwin. 1998. *Bold Relief: Institutional Politics and the Origins of Modern American Social Policy.* Princeton, NJ: Princeton University Press.
Amenta, Edwin. 2008. *When Movements Matter: The Townsend Plan and the Rise of Social Security.* Princeton, NJ: Princeton University Press.
*Badger, Anthony. 1989. *The New Deal: The Depression Years, 1933–1940.* Chicago: Ivan Dee.
Bakke, E. Wight. 1940. *The Unemployed Worker: A Study of the Task of Making a Living Without a Job.* New Haven, CT: Yale University Press.
*Berkowitz, Edward. 1991. *America's Welfare State: From Roosevelt to Reagan.* Baltimore, MD: Johns Hopkins University Press.
Brinkley, Alan. 1995. *The End of Reform: New Deal Liberalism in Recession and War.* New York: Knopf.

Brown, Josephine. 1940. *Public Relief, 1929–1939.* New York: Henry Holt.

Cohen, Lizabeth. 1990. *Making a New Deal: Industrial Workers in Chicago, 1919–1939.* Cambridge: Cambridge University Press.

Davies, Gareth, and Martha Derthick. 1997. "Race and Social Welfare Policy: The Social Security Act of 1935." *Political Science Quarterly* 112 (Summer): 217–235.

DeWitt, Larry W., Daniel Béland, and Edward Berkowitz. 2008. *Social Security: A Documentary History.* Washington, DC: CQ Press.

Esping-Andersen, Gosta. 1990. *The Three Worlds of Welfare Capitalism.* Princeton, NJ: Princeton University Press.

*Gordon, Linda. 1995. *Pitied but Not Entitled: Single Mothers and the History of Welfare, 1890–1935.* Cambridge: Harvard University Press.

Greenberg, Cheryl. 1997. *Or Does It Explode? Black Harlem in the Great Depression.* New York: Oxford University Press.

Hacker, Jacob. 2002. *The Divided Welfare State: The Battle over Public and Private Social Benefits in the United States.* New York: Cambridge University Press.

Hawley, Ellis. 1974. "Herbert Hoover, the Commerce Secretariat, and the Vision of an 'Associative State.'" *Journal of American History* 61 (June): 116–140.

Hickok, Lorena; Richard Lowitt, and Maurine Beasley, eds. 1983. *One Third of a Nation: Lorena Hickok Reports on the Great Depression.* Urbana: University of Illinois Press.

Hoover, Herbert. 1928. "New York City." In *The New Day: Campaign Speeches of Herbert Hoover.* Palo Alto: Stanford University Press, 149–176.

Howard, Donald S. 1943. *The WPA and Federal Relief Policy.* New York: Russell Sage Foundation.

Katz, Michael. 1996. *In the Shadow of the Poorhouse: A Social History of Welfare in America.* Rev. ed. New York: Basic Books.

Kennedy, David. 1999. *Freedom from Fear: The American People in Depression and War, 1929–1945.* New York: Oxford University Press.

Kessler-Harris, Alice. 2001. *In Pursuit of Equity: Men, Women, and the Quest for Economic Citizenship in 20th-Century America.* New York: Oxford University Press.

*Klein, Jennifer. 2003. *For All These Rights: Business, Labor, and the Shaping of America's Public-Private Welfare State.* Princeton, NJ: Princeton University Press.

Leuchtenberg, William. 1963. *Franklin D. Roosevelt and the New Deal, 1932–1940.* New York: Harper and Row.

Lieberman, Robert C. 1998. *Shifting the Color Line: Race and the American Welfare State.* Cambridge: Harvard University Press.

*Mettler, Suzanne. 1998. *Dividing Citizens: Gender and Federalism in New Deal Public Policy.* Ithaca: Cornell University Press.

Mink, Gwendolyn. 1995. *The Wages of Motherhood: Inequality in the Welfare State, 1917–1942.* Ithaca: Cornell University Press.

Morris, Andrew. 2009. *The Limits of Voluntarism: Charity and Welfare from the New Deal through the Great Society.* Cambridge: Cambridge University Press.

Palmer, Phyllis. 1995. "Outside the Law: Agricultural and Domestic Workers Under the Fair Labor Standards Act." *Journal of Policy History* 7 (October): 416–440.

Rogers, Daniel. 2000. *Atlantic Crossings: Social Politics in a Progressive Age.* Cambridge: Harvard University Press.

Romansco, Albert. 1965. *The Poverty of Abundance: Hoover, the Nation, the Depression.* New York: Oxford University Press.

Roosevelt, Franklin. 1932. (October 13) "Radio Address on Unemployment and Social Welfare." In *The Public Papers and Addresses of Franklin D. Roosevelt*. New York: Random House, 1938, 1: 786–795.

Roosevelt, Franklin. 1935. (January 4) "Annual Message to Congress." In *Public Papers and Addresses of Franklin D. Roosevelt*. New York, Random House, 1938, 4: 15–25.

Salmond, John. 1967. *The Civilian Conservation Corps: A New Deal Case Study*. Durham, NC: Duke University Press.

Schwartz, Bonnie Fox. 1984. *The Civil Works Administration, 1933–1934: The Business of Emergency Employment in the New Deal*. Princeton, NJ: Princeton University Press.

Schwartz, Jordan. 1970. *The Interregnum of Despair: Hoover, Congress and the Depression*. Urbana: University of Illinois Press.

Sherwood, Robert. 1950. *Roosevelt and Hopkins: An Intimate History*. Rev. ed. New York: Harper and Bros.

Sitkoff, Harvard. 2009. *A New Deal for Blacks. 30th Anniversary Edition*. New York: Oxford University Press.

*Taylor, Nick. 2008. *American Made: The Enduring Legacy of the WPA*. New York: Bantam Books.

Ware, Susan. 1981. *Beyond Suffrage: Women in the New Deal*. Cambridge: Harvard University Press.

CHAPTER 5

....

FROM THE FAIR DEAL TO THE GREAT SOCIETY

....

JENNIFER KLEIN

1 INTRODUCTION

....

WHEN President Franklin Roosevelt presented his fourth State of the Union Address, in January 1944, he linked the imperatives of winning the war against fascism and securing peace and democracy to the necessity of an Economic Bill of Rights at home. For him, the end of the war should not become the opportunity for dismantling the foundations for economic and social security built over more than a decade, but rather a new stage in turning these into expanded citizenship rights, in areas such as health care, jobs, housing, and income support (Roosevelt 1944; Sunstein 2004).

The Economic Bill of Rights, however, remained aspirational. At first, it appeared the continuation of the New Deal occupied center stage at the end of the war, but political and social struggles shifted its development in a slightly different direction. Moreover, social policy after World War II, as before, reflected the structural, regional, and legal particularities of the United States.

To grasp the trajectory of the American welfare state from the 1940s through the 1960s, this chapter will focus on four areas of social policy: social insurance (Social Security), health insurance, welfare, and housing. Each of these fields embodied the tensions of American federalism, race, and gender that had long shaped American political economy. Programs may have been enacted at the national level during and after the New Deal, but most had to be implemented through states or municipalities. In some cases, racial and gender exclusion were explicitly built into the national law. In others, local and state officials implemented programs through various discriminatory or coercive mechanisms—or occasionally, rejected the federal program altogether. The 1940s and 1950s represented a period of consolidation of New Deal programs, further bifurcation between public and private, and incremental extensions of social benefits that often still left African Americans out. The 1960s reopened the possibilities for broad-based reform and indeed included a sweep of new programs. By the 1970s, some of the most explicit racial barriers had been eliminated, and African Americans and women had gained greater access to core programs of the American welfare state. At the same time, the ideological and programmatic split between social insurance and public assistance—the assumptions about the deserving and undeserving—had only deepened.

2 THE FAIR DEAL

President Harry Truman (1945–1953), Roosevelt's successor, initially sought to extend the New Deal welfare state after the war was over, pushing forward a comprehensive agenda that included a higher minimum wage, federal commitment to public housing, increased unemployment insurance, and national health insurance. Although the Democrats lost heavily during the 1946 Congressional elections, Truman and a broad-based coalition of labor unions, workers, liberals, and small farmers held together the Roosevelt coalition during the 1948 elections. Interpreting his surprising re-election as a vindication of the New Deal project, Truman declared early in 1949, "Every segment of our population and every individual has a right to expect from our government a fair deal" (Truman 1949; Klein 2012).

The Fair Deal would succeed in modest ways—and certainly solidified the basic elements of the New Deal welfare state. But the Fair Deal neither achieved the ambitious social transformation of the New Deal nor realized the tenets of the Second Bill of Rights. While countries in Western Europe and Scandinavia built comprehensive social democracies, the American reliance on public and private, federal and state, policies often worked at cross purposes. Moreover, Southern Democrats, or "Dixiecrats," increasingly wary that Fair Deal labor policies and civil rights initiatives would threaten white supremacy in the states of the Old Confederacy, now formed a generation-long alliance with anti-New Deal Republicans. This Republican-Dixiecrat Congressional bloc ultimately turned back many Fair Deal proposals, especially one Truman most sought: public health insurance (Katznelson 2005).

The Servicemen's Readjustment Act, or G.I. Bill of Rights as it is popularly called, can also be understood as an extension of the New Deal for the postwar period. Enacted in 1944, it offered college scholarships and living expenses, low-interest, government-backed home mortgages with no down payment, vocational training, loans to start a small business, and extended unemployment compensation. A Veterans' Preference Act gave them preferential hiring in jobs receiving federal funds. And the Veterans Administration dramatically expanded medical and hospital services. By the mid-1950s, it had provided benefits to over eight million World War II veterans, although its local implementation often discriminated against African Americans

(Katznelson 2005). Yet the GI Bill did not provide an alternative open channel for the Fair Deal.

The struggle over the balance of power in the political economy significantly shaped the trajectory of the postwar U.S. welfare state. The American labor movement, like its European counterparts, emerged from the war with economic power that also was explicitly political. Basic employment decisions from wages to time shifts to compensation had been decided publicly, with the participation of state actors. Coming out of the war with an unprecedented 15 million members (35 percent of the American workforce), organized labor sought to use New Deal and war-time political structures to transform economic relationships and realize labor's broader economic security goals. Business leaders fought back to tip the balance of power in their favor, a project that was as much ideological as economic. Although American policy makers may have had to accept labor-management co-determination in war-torn Europe in order to proceed with reconstruction and sustain noncommunist governments, American business had no intention of accepting a dramatic restructuring of production and power at home. Whether a redistributive social policy would be realized through social insurance or the Wagner National Labor Relations Act or other corporatist means, it had to be stopped (Klein 2003, 2012).

3   UNIONS, THE PRIVATE WELFARE STATE, AND HEALTH CARE

To counter the growing pressure of the new labor movement and welfare state, corporations turned, as they had in previous eras, to "welfare capitalism"—a wide range of social welfare benefits, from insurance and pensions to paid vacations, athletic and leisure programs to mortgage assistance and even college scholarships, offered by the firm. American employers recognized the popular legitimacy attached to economic security as a political imperative. Pressured to accede to workers' demands for security, American business leaders sought to re-privatize the meaning of security. Ideologically, this meant resuscitating a more individualized understanding of risk and security. Tactically, it entailed separating security from any form of shared economic management and working-class political power.

The potential of a labor-government partnership that could tip the balance of power between workers and owners had begun to unfold in mining. Great strikes swept across the country throughout 1946. In the spring of that year, John L. Lewis, leader of the United Mine Workers (UMW), pursued a broad program of economic security through collective bargaining, especially seeking a union health and welfare program. Miners had long suffered debilitating health problems and notorious medical neglect in camps and towns run by authoritarian mine companies. When coal owners balked, Lewis led the miners out on strike. Facing a strike that could choke the economy, President Truman intervened through the War Labor Disputes Act. With the mines officially under federal jurisdiction, Truman was ready to make a deal, whereas the mine owners were not. Truman and the Secretary of the Interior pressured mine owners into signing a contract in which they would pay for a union Welfare and Retirement Fund—hospital, medical, and retirement plans—all financed by a royalty assessed on the amount of coal extracted by union workers (Klein 2003, 2012).

What we may think of as a "private" welfare plan, therefore, came into existence through active government intervention. The Social Security Administration provided technical assistance in designing the mineworkers' union-run welfare program and, along with the U.S. Public Health Service, helped recruit staff for the UMW program. Physicians, public health experts, and industrial health experts came from the Public Health Service and the Farm Security Administration, which had successfully run rural medical programs during the 1930s and World War II. As part of the settlement, the federal government investigated the health-care needs of miners and their families, entering the long insular realm of mining camps, surveying conditions, and testing coal operators' claims that they took care of their employees. Here was a direct and threatening intervention of the state into the once private relations of employment (Berkowitz 1980, 236–237; Krajcinovic 1997).

American labor leaders were impressed by what Lewis and the UMW had done. Leaders of the new industrial union movement, the Congress of Industrial Organizations (CIO), perceived it as a victory. The UMW had extracted resources from the coal operators that would be shifted into a comprehensive workers' security program. It took several years to implement, but through this fund, the UMW built a network of well-equipped, modern hospitals, bringing about a major improvement in living standards. The settlement was industry-wide, thus equalizing the sharing of risk and the benefits of "social" insurance. Guaranteed health security, through government partnership, went a long way toward giving workers much greater security, independence, and power in relation to their employers. The UMW story pointed toward one possible legacy of the National War Labor Board and the New Deal's legitimation of economic and social security.

Labor's health experts promoted a vision of health security linked to communities, not employers. According to this model, they envisioned a not-for-profit community plan in which a board of delegates, or a nonprofit foundation, contracted with providers for medical and health services. Public members and labor representatives would have representation on the Board, as well as health professionals. The United Automobile Workers (UAW) presented a similar version in 1946 (Klein 2003).

The initial set of postwar demands for health and pension plans, then, were envisioned as independent programs: union-run or union determined social-service programs. Such plans redistributed wealth and treated risk as social, not individual. They understood health and the debilitating effects of illness as a community, social responsibility. Nor was health provision seen as a private endeavor, walled off from public oversight and decision-making. This strategy did, in an important sense, attempt to shift power relations within the industry; it was intended to take security out of the realm of personnel policy, welfare capitalism.

Corporations and the National Association of Manufacturers (NAM) interpreted the demands of the UMW and UAW as a fundamental challenge to managerial prerogatives. As the NAM charged, "Not only do these plans represent a heavy payroll burden, but they go right to the heart of management's relations with employees by driving a wedge which tends to make the employee feel that his bargaining agent is more sympathetically concerned with his well-being than is his employer." Further, to business, this strategy smacked of European-style corporatism and "politicized bargaining" (quoted in Klein 2003, 220). The link between union power and the federal government would have to be severed.

Employers and commercial insurance companies became partners in creating and expanding private alternatives to public social insurance and community-controlled social-welfare institutions. To maintain full control over benefit plans, employers turned to public and private strategies to defuse government-backed collective bargaining. (National Association of Manufacturers 1947). On the legislative front, business interests had been circulating blueprints for revising the National Labor Relations Act throughout the first half of the 1940s. After the UMW won its union health and retirement program, revisions of the NLRA (what would become the Taft-Hartley Act) came to include restrictions on union trust funds and welfare funds. Corporate leaders even called for legislation excluding health insurance and pension benefits from collective bargaining. Given that collective bargaining was supposed to offer the sure road to industrial peace and boost productivity, Congress was not about to pass such outright bans. It did, however, pass the 1947 Taft-Hartley Act. Perhaps best known for its requirement of anticommunist loyalty oaths from labor officials, the social-welfare component of the act was critical, too. Congress also included a requirement that employers had to share equally in the administration of any welfare or retirement plans. Unions could not run them independently. Preventing union control of social security for American workers clearly became an essential component of curbing union power. With the Taft-Hartley Act, employers had improved their chances of restoring welfare capitalism (Millis and Brown 1950, 561–568; Jacoby 1997, 200; Klein 2003).

The National Labor Relations Board and the federal courts, though, subsequently made clear that health insurance, pensions, and welfare benefits were subjects for collective bargaining. In order to insulate the realm of bargaining from broader politics, managers created an alternative set of institutional arrangements, touted as "free collective bargaining," to tip the balance of power. First, negotiations would be at the level of the individual company, subsidiary, or, in many cases, a singular plant. American corporations organized to make sure they did not face the national level labor-management bargaining taking shape in Sweden or Norway, nor even the industry level bargaining of Germany or Great Britain.

Insurance companies enabled the second strategy. Insurance companies now saw a profitable market in the new expectations for security. To capitalize on it, they needed

steady, low-risk subscribers. Who could deliver these large groups? The largest corporate employers. Through a commercial group-insurance contract, a single policy would cover an entire group of employees but remain entirely in the hands of management. The employer was the only legal policyholder and, thus, for the most part, unions had little access to the exact terms of the insurance plan—especially premiums, costs per person, and dividends. Insurance companies sold policies that management could control—firm by firm, even plant by plant. The purchaser of a group plan could pick and choose exactly which services it did and did not want included and the amount of an employee's contribution (see for example, Metropolitan Life Insurance Company 1953; Klein 2003). By the late 1940s, unionized employers in the major sectors of the economy were primed and ready for the insurance pitch.

Insurance companies and corporate employers constructed a new ideology around risk and health security in the 1950s. Instead of community rating used by the health cooperatives and earlier models to share risk evenly, insurance companies used medical underwriting and experience rating. With medical underwriting, insurance plans divide people up and separate them according to their health profile. Insurers made the notion of risk an individualized one: "each insured will pay in accordance with the quality of his risk." Individuals or groups who are perceived to have higher risk for medical problems are charged more money and receive less coverage or insurers might just avoid them (Quadagno 2005, 3; Stone 1994, 33). Experience rating allowed firms with better conditions (or at least fewer workers seeking high-cost medical care) to pay less; industries deemed poor risks or firms with older or sicker workers paid more, fragmenting the social pooling of risk. Many occupations were left completely uncovered. Finally, because group insurance covered employees only during the term of their employment, in the long run, it generated cultural assumptions that health security was an achievement of individuals solely through their persistent hard work. It shrouded both the collective struggle that won these benefits and the role of politics and public power.

Instead of these broader political or social possibilities the New Deal and war had opened up, the "Treaty of Detroit," the landmark contract signed between General Motors and the UAW in 1950, became labor's model. The five-year Treaty of Detroit provided annual wage raises for productivity and cost-of-living increases, disability insurance, Blue Cross and Blue Shield benefits for hospital and medical care, and a pension of $125 a month (Lichtenstein 1995; Klein 2003) The UAW's comprehensive and independent Workers' Security Program was shelved—permanently. General Motors and the other large oligopolistic firms refused to hand over a percentage of payroll to union-run social-welfare programs. On the one hand, then, collective bargaining won employees' rights and benefits at work that changed their social expectations, social experience, and standard of living. As Jack Metzgar recalled about his father, a unionized steelworker at U.S. Steel Corporation, "no regular guy in the history of the world had seen the material conditions of his life improve more dramatically" (Metzgar 2000, 6). On the other hand, the new insurance-based contract represented quite a retreat from labor's vision of security just a few years earlier.

4 THE DEFEAT OF UNIVERSAL PUBLIC HEALTH INSURANCE

The spread of private hospital, surgical, and eventually medical insurance relieved some of the urgency to enact public, universal health insurance, especially as the medical profession's opposition became increasingly virulent, and anticommunist red-baiting again heated up. President Truman had ordered the Federal Security Agency to devote major resources toward planning and enacting a national health plan. Republicans, conservatives, and physicians attacked the national health plan relentlessly as an "insidious communist plot." The American Medical Association instructed state medical societies across the country to engage in an aggressive "educational" campaign to battle national health insurance and promote private health insurance instead. Likewise, the U.S. Chamber of Commerce ran coordinated propaganda campaigns, drumming up fear of "socialized medicine." They successfully allied with physicians in the 1950 elections to defeat liberal Democrats (Quadagno 2005, 31). By the end of 1950, the attempt to expand Social Security to include health insurance was dead. Private, employment-based insurance would become the primary way that Americans would gain access to hospital and medical care (Hacker 2002).

Those elements of the Fair Deal that stayed within the parameters of the welfare state already set—minimum-wage increase, means-tested public housing for the poor, improvements in Social Security pensions—passed into law. Proposals that would expand the welfare state in scope and curtail emerging private markets, like health insurance, were defeated. Although doctors and hospitals perceived national insurance as interfering with their "autonomy" and prerogative, they eagerly sought federal largesse for hospital and medical infrastructure. In addition to funding scientific and medical research, the Hill-Burton Hospital Survey and Construction Act of 1946 directed massive public investment into hospitals, medical and nursing schools, public-health centers, and skilled outpatient and nursing facilities. Like other major social policies, it delegated control to local officials and state and local medical authorities. Hill-Burton built an enormous number of hospitals in the postwar South, although these were mainly along segregated lines (Fox 1986).

5 CONSOLIDATING SOCIAL SECURITY IN THE POSTWAR PERIOD

When Americans mention Social Security, what they have in mind is the pension system, based on payroll tax contributions from workers and employers. The Act itself, however, actually established numerous support programs, including old-age assistance for indigent elderly, Aid to Dependent Children (ADC) for poor mothers with children, and public assistance for the blind and disabled. Unlike pensions, these programs—called welfare— were administered at the state level and carried the stigma of means-tested programs for the poor. The architects of Social Security intended old-age assistance and welfare for the disabled to fade away or scale down and be replaced by "earned" social insurance, as new generations of workers gained a foothold in the mainstream economy, built up a lifetime of contributions, and, therefore, qualified for benefits at retirement.

In the 1940s, this objective remained elusive. Twice as many people were still receiving old-age assistance in 1950 than receiving Social Security pensions. In some states, particularly rural ones, more than half of the elderly received such welfare payments. Moreover, the pension system covered jobs primarily in manufacturing—about half the jobs in the economy. Excluded were employees of nonprofit organizations (hospitals, for example), government employees, and agricultural and domestic workers (DeWitt, Béland, and Berkowitz, 2008, 8). The exclusion of farm and domestic workers—primarily African American and Mexican at the time—stemmed from Southern intransigence to any challenge to their control of black labor. Throughout the decade of the 1940s, pension coverage was not extended to excluded groups. Consequently, the public assistance titles of Social Security remained far more critical to millions of Americans, especially women, African Americans, and the aged.

After 1950, though, old-age social insurance (Social Security) became genuinely inclusive in scope, though modest in benefits. Amendments in 1950 added new groups of workers (including the self-employed and a proportion of full-time agricultural workers), raised benefits substantially, and raised both the tax rate and the taxable wage base. As a result, eight million new workers became participants in the program. In 1954, an additional two million agricultural and several hundred thousand domestic workers won inclusion in old-age social insurance. Owing to these amendments, old-age social insurance finally surpassed old-age assistance. Over the next decade, the number of excluded workers fell substantially and nonwhites gradually gained access to Social Security pensions. By 1960, the U.S. counted 68 million people in the workforce, with 4.6 million in occupations not covered by the pension program (Lieberman 2001, 85–87, 113). With each new group gaining inclusion, the support and popularity of Social Security also grew, as the notions of "earned" benefit and entitlement merged.

After the passage of the Social Security Act, many large companies had responded by instituting private pensions as "supplemental security." With the growing success of the labor movement, corporate employers sought to channel the postwar demands for security into private pensions in order to cultivate workers' loyalty to the company and check further growth of the welfare state. The ground rules of welfare capitalism remained in place: employers maintained control over benefit formulas, final eligibility rules, long-term service requirements for vesting, and how (or whether) a pension would be fully funded. Private pensions would never approach universality, yet, beginning in the 1950s, the U.S. tax code would encourage the development of a private pension system to "complete" Social Security (Klein 2003).

By the time Republican Dwight Eisenhower took office in January 1953, the New Deal welfare state, labor reforms, and state regulatory policies were firmly established. Although a Republican with strong ties to corporate elites, President Eisenhower shared the essential premises of liberal Keynesianism and the New Deal order. He raised the minimum wage, oversaw new amendments to Social Security that added disability pensions and expanded the range of old-age pensions coverage to more agricultural and to domestic workers, and created a new cabinet department of Health, Education, and Welfare (HEW).

6 Social Assistance as "Welfare"

The more Social Security gained legitimacy, the more it seemed to widen the ideological and political divide of the "two-channel" welfare state. When Aid to Dependent Children (ADC) was enacted, its drafters believed that single-mothers' duty was to stay home and take care of children, not work in the paid labor market. Although welfare administrators were concerned about children living with destitute mothers, there was tremendous anxiety and ambivalence over single women raising children without husbands. This ambivalence was built into ADC, which gradually took second-class status to the more generous social-insurance programs. It not only received less funding; the federal government would reimburse states a proportion of their spending and at a lower rate than for Old Age Assistance or Aid to the Blind (for those who were thought to be poor through no fault of their own). States had discretion over the ADC program, and consequently, benefits and eligibility criteria differed across the country. States could decide not to participate at all, as Nevada did, for example, up until 1955. Southern states set ADC payments particularly low in order to protect local southern interests' control over black labor. In the 1950s, states' ability to manipulate eligibility rules, cut benefits unilaterally, remove recipients from the welfare rolls, and enforce punitive rules increasingly stigmatized this program as "welfare"—in contrast to "Social Security," which was elevated to an entitlement (Abramovitz 1999; Gordon 1994; on Nevada see Orleck 2005).

Nonetheless, the program did expand, which had varying consequences. Far more women received benefits than had ever been the case under any previous public-assistance program. The number of families more than doubled between 1945 and 1950 and grew to three million clients by 1960. It became the largest federal public-assistance program. Yet this expansion created new tensions and anxieties, especially as the demographic profile of recipients began to shift. The *ideal* and predominant recipients of ADC initially had been white widows—women who were seen as honorably single and needy. White widows increasingly became eligible for survivors coverage under Social Security. This meant that more of the women applying for ADC were divorced, deserted, or never married. The number of nonwhite women among the clientele also rose. Although often referred to as the age of affluence, more than 20 percent of

Americans were poor in the late 1950s. African Americans were more likely to be poor and far less likely to be covered by Social Security. Hence, they began to rely dispro-portionately on ADC. The majority of recipients were still white but with the growing visibility of black migration from the South, the civil rights movement, and pressure by African American women for equal access to public support, whites came to see the program as welfare with a black face (Nadasen, Mittelstadt, and Chappell 2009, 23–25). Poor women began to demand greater rights at the same moment politicians stoked fears about welfare and immorality run amok. These conflicts drove welfare back onto the state and national political agenda in the 1960s.

7 Postwar Housing Policy

Housing policy in the United States replicated the dichotomies of American social policy—public and private, federal and local, white and black, the hidden and the vis-ible. The New Deal established two different primary programs for housing. The 1934 National Housing Act directed public policy toward private home ownership. A new Federal Housing Administration (FHA) would insure long-term mortgages made by private lenders, shielding them from risk. Under the FHA, home buyers could put down less than a 10 percent deposit, builders had to adhere to uniform construction standards, and mortgages could now be fully amortized for an unprecedented 30-year period. With government subsidization of risk, interest rates declined and average monthly payments came within the reach of millions of new families. The impact was dramatic, setting off a postwar home building boom, especially in the suburbs. Indeed, FHA loans privi-leged suburban homes; it became cheaper to own one of these homes than to be a renter. The FHA financed about a third of all new homes in the 1950s. With FHA-insured and VA-insured mortgages, by 1960, three out of five families owned their own home. Eleven million families became homeowners owing to FHA support (Jackson 1987). Since this homeownership surge occurred through the building, lending, and selling agents of the "private market," the actual public subsidy of private homeownership became, in a sense, invisible welfare. Further, the federal tax code provided an additional form of "invisible" subsidy, allowing owners to deduct their mortgage interest payments from their taxes. White Americans who became homeowners thus began to think of them-selves as "independent" of the welfare state—not reliant on or needing public social wel-fare (Radford 1997; Sugrue 1996).

Yet they were its primary beneficiaries. The FHA relied on a rating system for insur-ing mortgages that rated housing as higher or lower risk, depending on which social groups lived in the neighborhood. If a neighborhood was solidly white, FHA considered it a good risk and agreed to support mortgage lending there. If the neighborhood was socially "mixed"—having say, Jews, blacks, Latinos, or Asians living among whites—it was considered riskier and to be avoided. FHA did not support lending in black areas at all, marking them down as "D" or red. This discriminatory process became known as redlining and it profoundly shaped the geography of postwar cities in every region of the country. It buttressed other private, voluntary mechanisms such as restrictive covenants in deeds, prohibiting a sale of the house to nonwhites (Jackson 1987; Sugrue 1996; Brilliant 2010).

More visible was the other tier of America's divided welfare state: public housing. The 1937 United States Housing Act created the public-housing program. At first it seemed quite a success: 33 states immediately stepped forward to participate, and 130,000 new units had been built within a few years. Although it established a permanent role for the federal government in building public housing, it swept aside early New Deal progressive experiments in garden housing, community planning, and support for cooperatives. Instead, it tied the new construction of public housing to slum clearance and the principle of "equivalent elimination"—that is, new public housing units could only be built in a quantity equal to the amount of slum property condemned. Since it cost money to tear down buildings and clear land, this provision encouraged barracks-like high-rises to be built and, thereby, intensified the density of already poor neighborhoods. Housing Authorities made sure public housing did not get built on vacant land; that was for "development." Housing Authorities preserved suburban land for whites and private developers. The Act placed a means-test on public housing: one had to be poor to qualify. This restriction would eventually lead to segregation of the poor into these spaces, heightening the racial and class segregation of postwar urban America and creating what Arnold Hirsch has called "second ghettos" (Hirsch 1998). Finally, although it created a U.S. Housing Authority, public projects would be sited and developed through local housing agencies. Local officials, real-estate agents and developers, one observer noted, "greeted the idea of public housing... 'with the same enthusiasm as they might have greeted the introduction of bubonic plague'" (Radford 1997, 189–190).

President Truman had moved to address the needs of the "one-third of a nation.... ill-housed" soon after taking office, but new funding for public housing stalled in Congress until the end of the decade. Truman viewed public housing both as a stimulus to economic growth and a form of social welfare. For Truman, decent housing was essential to freedom, citizenship, and security. Southern Democrats, Republican conservatives, and real-estate interests combined to ideologically and fiscally attack the idea of public housing, not only charging that it was socialistic but also that it was unfair competition with the private building industry. And yet, public housing had become defined as housing for the low-income market that private builders wouldn't serve. Congress finally passed the Housing Act of 1949, which authorized the construction of 810,000 units of public housing, but cut from the Senate bill was an explicit prohibition of racial segregation (Hirsch 2006, 44).

The 1949 Housing Act delegated even greater power to local authority. Subsequently, each community had to make its own decision "as to whether or not a need existed." Application for federally subsidized public housing had to be voluntary. Broadened local prerogative hardened the lines of racial segregation in two ways. If a suburb didn't want public housing, it could refuse to create a housing agency; the federal government could do nothing to change that. And since hundreds of suburbs did not apply for federal funding, low-income housing became further concentrated in inner cities during the 1950s (Jackson 1987, 227).

The Housing Act of 1949 provided massive funds for "urban redevelopment," or what became known as "urban renewal." Local authorities, explains Jill Quadagno, could "assemble large parcels of land, bulldoze them to the ground, and then sell the land to private developers" at reduced cost (Quadagno 1994, 91). The Housing Act of 1954 added more funds to urban renewal. Throughout the 1950s and 1960s, local authorities used urban renewal to condemn and demolish homes of poor people. Instead of then building new public housing in their place, cities and private developers erected office buildings, hotels, shops, and convention centers. During the 1950s, more than 400,000 homes were destroyed but only 10,760 low-income units were built (Quadagno 1994, 91). As many of the homes condemned housed African Americans, urban renewal often became known among civil rights and community activists as "Negro removal." By the mid-1960s, the civil rights movement would help drive fair and accessible housing onto the agenda of Lyndon Johnson's Great Society.

8   THE GREAT SOCIETY AND A NEW ERA OF SOCIAL RIGHTS

Lyndon Johnson's Great Society offered the boldest comprehensive liberal agenda since the New Deal; still, the two-channel welfare state became further entrenched. In his State of the Union Address following Kennedy's death, Johnson, a Texas-born Southerner and ardent New Dealer, laid out an eloquent vision of hope and inclusion, recommending "the most Federal support in history for education, for health, for retraining the unemployed, and for helping the economically and the physically handicapped." These objectives could not be achieved, Johnson emphatically declared, without a simultaneous commitment to end racial discrimination (Johnson 1964). In contrast to the 1930s, this new round of liberal reform explicitly aimed to include—and enfranchise—African Americans, Latinos, the poor, seniors, immigrants, and farm workers. It included the legal revolution in civil rights, as well as the trumpeted War on Poverty, which expanded the slain President Kennedy's incipient job-training programs into a multifaceted attack on poverty. The War on Poverty also aimed to satisfy the rising expectations and demands of African Americans, especially in the cities that formed the national Democratic Party's base (Piven and Cloward 2005). Yet the War on Poverty was only one component of the Great Society. Between 1964 and 1968, the Great Society advanced a sweeping liberal agenda that included everything from immigration reform to education, civil rights and equal employment, medical care, housing, and legal assistance. Social Security minimum and maximum benefits rose, as did survivors benefits, representing yet another significant expansion of the pension program.

What truly marked this moment as a major period of reform, however, was the final passage of the long-fought for goal of some form of national social insurance for medical care. After the defeat of universal national health insurance in the Truman era, supporters regrouped around the idea of insurance for the elderly—the segment of the public that commercial insurance avoided as carrying too much risk. Since the late 1950s, then, leaders of the newly merged AFL-CIO and union retirees, along with grassroots and national organizations of seniors, committed themselves to the struggle for elder health insurance (Quadagno 2005, 58–59). They could make a case for them as worthy Americans and as those who would never be covered by the private market. The Golden Ring Clubs of Senior Citizens, the National League of Senior Citizens, Social Security Clubs of America, and the AFL-CIO's National Council of Senior Citizens sponsored rallies and picnics, organized petition drives, testified at hearings, and followed candidates to various campaign appearances during the 1960 elections. The laborite National Council of Senior Citizens and the Golden Rings Clubs kept up mass rallies, letter-writing campaigns, petitions, and appearances at hearings throughout the Kennedy years (Asbury 1960; Quadagno 2005, 64–69).

After Kennedy's death, a new Congress swept into power with decisive majorities for liberal Democrats in both the House and Senate. Johnson could now move forward, where Kennedy had been stymied (Marmor 2000; Berkowitz 1991; Oberlander 2003). Passed in 1965, Medicare included payment for hospital care (Part A), through the same type of payroll tax as Social Security. Medicare Part A would also cover skilled nursing care and home care for a limited period. To obtain physicians' care, recipients had to enroll in Part B, supplementary medical insurance based on individual payment of premiums and general revenues. Many services under Part B entailed a co-payment and deductible. Nonetheless, the majority of those eligible quickly signed up.

Medicare did not challenge America's divided welfare state—in two senses. First, it deferred to private insurance, which would implement Medicare as government contractors and remain the primary means of access for those under 65. It let the industry off the hook, since it would not be expected to pick up the costs for expensive hospitalization of the elderly. Insurers would still be players in an expanding market as providers of supplemental insurance, or "medigap" policies, to cover Part B medical expenses, as well as gaps in Part A (Oberlander 2003, 48–49; Hacker 2002). Second, the old split between social insurance and welfare, the deserving and the undeserving, was built into yet another social policy, because the Act also included another program, Medicaid, health coverage for the poor. Medicaid, known as Title XIX of the Social Security Act, continued the traditions of poor law and charity care, and for this reason labor and senior activists were initially quite opposed to it. It established a joint federal-state program for poor people's care and committed federal matching funds to states that chose to create a program. Again, state welfare departments supervised eligibility, and enrollment and benefits varied nationally. The law explicitly referred to potential enrollees as "recipients," while calling those in Medicare "beneficiaries" (Quadagno 2005, 74–75; Engel 2006, 48–49).

Since Medicare did not include sustained long-term care, Medicaid soon evolved into America's default long-term care program. Medicaid became the main funding source for institutional nursing home care. It also offered a vehicle through which states could finance in-home support for indigent elders and people with disabilities. Medicaid freed welfare administrators from having to piece together meager funding for homecare from child welfare, vocational education, and other small grants. Both Medicare and Medicaid certainly offered an opportunity for procuring a more robust right to care within the welfare state. Yet by having long-term care fall under Medicaid, it often meant the elderly had to "spend down" all their assets to poverty levels to access its benefits. This outcome thrust recipients, family members, and care workers into a persistent battle against the stigmatization and insecurity of welfare (Boris and Klein 2012, 86; Engel 2006, 34–39; Grogan 2006, 203–2012).

9 THE WAR ON POVERTY

Indeed, during the 1960s, welfare in general came under a magnifying glass. Critics of ADC became more vocal and demanding. Congressional conservatives targeted ADC as wasteful and bloated, especially as more African American women gained access, and immediately pressed President Kennedy's administration for changes. At the same time, defenders of welfare hoped that Kennedy's HEW appointments would showcase the latest research and thinking from social casework. The Public Welfare Amendments of 1962 tried to appease both sides (Mittelstadt 2005, 114–125).

Kennedy liberals embraced the notion that poverty and unemployment could be overcome through expanding individual opportunity without substantial income redistribution (O'Connor, 2001, 141–45). If public policies could modify individual behavior and skills, then poor people would be prepared to take advantage of labor-market opportunities. Manpower training programs were to supplant welfare by setting recipients on the road to self-sufficiency (Weir 1992, 64–69; O'Connor 2001, 232–234). Several months later, Congress passed major public welfare amendments that attempted to reconcile these critiques of poverty and welfare. ADC was renamed AFDC, Aid to Families with Dependent Children, with the added imperative of services to "restore families and individuals to self-support" (*Social Welfare in New York State in 1962*, 1963, 2–3; New Public Welfare System, 10; Gilbert 1966, 223).

To this end, the federal government allowed use of its matching funds for vocational training, which long had emphasized work-related independence. Now states had an additional incentive to emphasize ending "dependency" and moving public assistance recipients into work. AFDC would combine income support with work requirements, reclassifying poor mothers with young children as "employables." This designation as "employable" would take on heightened importance in coming years when Congress enacted more punitive workfare measures (Mittelstadt 2005, 118–9, 122).

Upon taking office, Lyndon Johnson was determined to make his mark fighting the poverty that persisted in America. The centerpiece of the War on Poverty, the Economic Opportunity Act of 1964, addressed the supply side of labor by offering education, training, and jobs. Directed by a new Office of Economic Opportunity (OEO), it initiated a group of programs based on manpower premises: Job Corps, Neighborhood Youth Corps, Adult Education Program, Volunteers in Service to America (VISTA), and Work Experience. The antipoverty warriors had faith that public policies could modify individual behavior and develop skills; poor people would be better prepared to take advantage of labor-market opportunities. There would be no public works programs per se, as in the New Deal. But the massive new infusion of public money (from multiple Great Society programs, including especially Medicare and Medicaid) into health, education, and social services created new jobs in the public sector and service industries of the economy. After all, Great Society programs doubled federal spending for social welfare. This growth posed opportunity for poor women, especially where new public-sector unions emerged. It also reflected the perpetual burden of racialized, gendered expectations about jobs and who should do them. The training that poor African American women received often directed them into the low-end ranks of service jobs, as if they hadn't been there before.

The War on Poverty both responded to and stimulated vocal and militant organizing (Piven and Cloward 2005, 253–269; Quadagno 1994). Community Action, a major piece of the Economic Opportunity Act, offered one way to challenge the links between political and economic marginalization and poverty. OEO would give grants to Community Action Agencies organized by neighborhood residents, who could then establish health centers, job training, literacy programs, legal assistance, food support, or home-care services. Community Action Agencies also became politicized organizations in some cities, linked with civil-rights groups, which began mobilizing poor people, long ignored by city hall, to fight back over tenant rights, welfare rights, exclusion from city services, and various forms of discrimination. Community Action enabled the poor to use federal money to fight city hall or go around it. In a number of places, they became so good at doing so that Democratic mayors went straight back to Washington demanding that Johnson or Congress pull the plug on the program (Quadagno 1994; Naples 1998). Although some scholars have criticized Community Action for being a poor substitute for a real employment policy (Katz 1989; Weir 1992), it had a dramatic impact where women organized welfare-rights movements; built coalitions with allies in churches, unions, nonprofit agencies, and social work; and secured funding to build their own institutions. In Las Vegas, for example, African American women did just that—and managed to construct the first public library and medical clinic in the all-black section of the West Side; they ran their own job training programs. They also won legal rights, greater welfare benefits, and genuine political inclusion (Orleck 2005).

10 HOUSING POLICY REVISITED

Just as African Americans and other poor Americans began to win inclusion within the rights of the New Deal welfare state, the era of FHA-subsidized housing drew to a close. Federal housing policy had encouraged private homeownership but then reinforced the racial boundaries of housing markets. The FHA and VA had financed $120 billion in new housing, but less than 2 percent went to nonwhite families. African Americans, Asians, and Jews had been organizing around fair and open housing in places such as Detroit, Los Angeles, Oakland, Chicago, New York, and New Haven, CT, for a decade, when Johnson took office. Reverend Martin Luther King, Jr. led marches in white neighborhoods against segregated housing. Some localities or states had passed fair-housing ordinances, but they remained difficult to enforce, especially when local white communities organized in hostile ways to scare off new families. Local and national real-estate interests aggressively opposed fair-housing legislation (Sugrue 1996; Brilliant 2010). President Johnson decided to take action applying to both public and private housing. The Civil Rights Act of 1964 banned discrimination in housing receiving federal assistance and mandated "open housing" (no segregation) for all new housing built in urban renewal areas. Legislation the following year created "rent supplements" but only for the very poor, reinforcing the view that federal housing support was only for the destitute and leaving the option to accept or reject it up to localities (Quadagno 1994, 93–94).

Still, Johnson and Great Society liberals could not get fair-housing legislation through Congress—until the assassination of Martin Luther King and two hot summers of urban riots. Title VIII of the Civil Rights Act of 1968 passed on April 10, a week after King's death. It banned discrimination in the sale, rental, and financing of most housing units. Even single-family homes of private individuals would now be covered by federal law. A federal Department of Housing and Urban Development (HUD) would oversee the civil rights agenda of new housing policy with responsibility for prohibiting discrimination in public housing and opening housing in the private market (Quadagno 1994, 100–101).

HUD also became responsible for a more ambitious plan, Model Cities, which offered grants and technical assistance to communities that sought to rebuild urban neighborhoods. Ideally, citizens would participate in the planning and decision-making process. In reality, local mayors and their associates did so, often excluding African Americans and using the funds to clear their areas. HUD, therefore, became a contested agency—over civil rights and social rights, black inclusion and white resistance (Quadagno 1994, 103–104). When Richard Nixon took office as president in January 1969, he accepted the existence of fair-housing legislation but undermined the potential for enforcement. The federal government, Nixon made clear, would not direct federal funds toward economic integration nor force "the economic pattern of a neighborhood" to change. In 1973, he declared a moratorium on construction of low-income subsidized housing. After 1974, the supply of affordable housing contracted significantly (Quadagno 1994, 110, 114).

11 CONCLUSION

By the end of the Great Society, more Americans had gained political and social rights. The Civil Rights Act of 1964 barred discrimination in employment and established an

Equal Employment Opportunity Commission. The landmark Voting Rights Act passed in 1965. Fair housing made a difference not only for African Americans but for Asians and Jews as well. The welfare rights movement, allied with antipoverty lawyers, had even won basic rights around welfare. In *King v. Smith* (1968), the Supreme Court held that searches for whether a "substitute father" was in the house violated the Social Security Act; *Shapiro v. Thompson* (1969) found that welfare residency rules violated recipients' right to mobility; and *Goldberg v. Kelley* (1970) found termination of AFDC benefits without a fair hearing violated due process. These seemed to make welfare an entitlement (Nadasen, Mittelstadt, and Chapell 2009, 51).

For white Americans, claims on social benefits deepened in legitimacy, even as these citizens perceived themselves relying less on the welfare state and benefiting more from the imagined private markets of housing and health care. The American welfare state expanded significantly through the 1950s and 1960s, but it never crowded out private insurers and providers of benefits. The provision of the most substantive and reliable public and private benefits remained tightly tethered to regular employment. The 1960s opened a new phase for the poor and marginally employed to fight their way into the rights and entitlements of the more valorized realms of the welfare state. A decade later, the War on Poverty was over but the War on Welfare politics was heating up. The New Deal and Fair Deal emphasis on security would give way to the new imperative of "ending dependency."

References

*Indicates recommended reading.

Abramovitz, Mimi. 1999. *Regulating the Lives of Women: Social Welfare Policy from Colonial Times to the Present*. 2nd ed. Cambridge, MA: South End Press.
Asbury, Edith Evans. 1960. "4,000 Aged Attend New York Democrats' Rally," *New York Times*, November 4.
Berkowitz, Edward D. 1980. "Growth of the U.S. Social Welfare System in the Post–World War II Era: The UMW, Rehabilitation, and the Federal Government." *Research in Economic History*. Vol. 5. Greenwich, CT: JAI Press, 236.
Berkowitz, Edward D. 1991. *America's Welfare State: from Roosevelt to Reagan*. Baltimore, MD: Johns Hopkins University Press.
*Boris, Eileen, and Jennifer Klein. 2012. *Caring for America: Home Health Workers in the Shadow of the Welfare State*. New York: Oxford University Press.
Brilliant, Mark. 2010. *The Color of America Has Changed: How Racial Diversity Shaped Civil Rights Reform in California*. New York: Oxford University Press.
DeWitt, Larry, Daniel Béland, and Edward D. Berkowitz. 2008. *Social Security: A Documentary History*. Washington DC: CQ Press.
*Engel, Jonathan. 2006. *Poor People's Medicine: Medicaid and American Charity Care Since 1965*. Durham, NC: Duke University Press.
Fox, Daniel M. 1986. *Health Policies, Health Politics: The British and American Experience, 1911–1965*. Princeton, NJ: Princeton University Press.
Gilbert, Charles E. June 1966. "Policy-Making in Public Welfare: The 1962 Amendments." *Political Science Quarterly* 81 (2): 196–224.

Gordon, Linda. 1994. *Pitied but Not Entitled: Single Mothers and the History of Welfare, 1890–1935*. Cambridge, MA: Harvard University Press.

Grogan, Colleen M. 2006. "A Marriage of Convenience: The Persistent and Changing Relationship Between Long-Term Care and Medicaid." In Rosemary Stevens, Charles E. Rosenberg, and Lawton R. Burns, eds., *History and Health Policy in the United States*. New Brunswick, NJ: Rutgers University Press.

*Hacker, Jacob S. 2002. *The Divided Welfare State: The Battle Over Public and Private Social Benefits in the United States*. New York: Cambridge University Press.

*Hirsch, Arnold R. 1998. *Making the Second Ghetto: Race and Housing in Chicago, 1940–1960*. 2nd ed. Chicago: University of Chicago Press.

Hirsch, Arnold R. 2006. "Less Than Plessy: The Inner City, Suburbs, and State-Sanctioned Residential Segregation in the Age of Brown." In Kevin M. Kruse and Thomas J. Sugrue, eds., *The New Suburban History*. Chicago: University of Chicago Press.

Jackson, Kenneth. 1987. *Crabgrass Frontier: The Suburbanization of the United States*. New York: Oxford University Press.

Jacoby, Sanford M. 1997. *Modern Manors: Welfare Capitalism Since the New Deal*. Princeton, NJ: Princeton University Press.

Johnson, Lyndon Baines. 1964. "Annual Message to the Congress on the State of the Union." January 8. Available at http://lbjlib.utexas.edu/johnson/archives.hom/speeches.hom/640.

Katz, Michael. 1989. *The Undeserving Poor: From the War on Poverty to the War on Welfare*. New York: Pantheon Books.

Katznelson, Ira. 2005. *When Affirmative Action Was White: An Untold History of Racial Inequality in Twentieth-Century America*. NY: W.W. Norton.

*Klein, Jennifer. 2003. *For All These Rights: Business, Labor, and the Shaping of America's Public-Private Welfare State*. Princeton, NJ: Princeton University Press.

Klein, Jennifer. 2012. "The Politics of Economic Security." In Katheleen G. Donohue, ed., *Liberty and Justice for All? Rethinking Politics in Cold War America*. Amherst, MA: University of Massachusetts Press.

Krajcinovic, Ivana. 1997. *From Company Doctors to Managed Care: The United Mine Workers Noble Experiment*. Ithaca: ILR Press, Cornell University.

*Lieberman, Robert C. 2001. *Shifting the Color Line: Race and the American Welfare State*. Cambridge, MA: Harvard University Press.

Lichtenstein, Nelson. 1995. *The Most Dangerous Man in Detroit: Walter Reuther and the Fate of American Labor*. New York: Basic Books.

Metropolitan Life Insurance Company. 1952. *Employee Security Founded On Group Insurance Safeguards Employee Morale and Loyalty*. New York: MLIC. Metropolitan Life Insurance Company Archives, NY, New York.

Metropolitan Life Insurance Company. 1953. *Tailored to Fit: A Group Insurance Plan Designed for the Employees of Your Company*. New York: MLIC. Metropolitan Life Insurance Company Records, Box 19 06 04, Group Insurance, Metropolitan Life Insurance Company Archives, New York, NY.

Metzgar, Jack. 2000. *Striking Steel: Solidarity Remembered*. Philadelphia: Temple University Press.

Marmor, Theodore. 2000. *The Politics of Medicare*. New York: Aldine.

Millis, Harry A., and Emily Clark Brown. 1950. *From the Wagner Act to Taft-Hartley: A Study of National Labor policy and Labor Relations*. Chicago: University of Chicago Press.

*Mittelstadt, Jennifer. 2005. *From Welfare to Workfare: The Unintended Consequences of Liberal Reform, 1945–1965*. Chapel Hill: University of North Carolina.

Nadasen, Premilla, Jennifer Mittelstadt, and Marisa Chappell. 2009. *Welfare in the United States: A History with Documents, 1935–1996*. New York: Routledge Press.

Naples, Nancy. 1998. *Grassroots Warriors: Activist Mothering, Community Work, and the War on Poverty*. New York: Routledge.

National Association of Manufacturers Labor-Management Relations Committee. 1947. Minutes, March 6, 1947. New York. NAM Records. Acc. 1412. Box 3, *Industrial Relations Division*. Hagley Museum and Library. Wilmington, DE.

"The New Public Welfare System: A Progress Report on the 1962 Amendments to The Social Security Act." In *Social Welfare in New York State in 1964*.

*Oberlander, Jonathan. 2003. *The Political Life of Medicare*. Chicago: University of Chicago Press.

O'Connor, Alice. 2001. *Poverty Knowledge: Social Science, Social Policy, and the Poor in 20th Century U.S. History*. Princeton, NJ: Princeton University Press.

Orleck, Annelise. 2005. *Storming Caesar's Palace: How Black Mothers Fought Their Own War on Poverty*. Boston: Beacon Press.

Piven, Frances Fox and Richard A. Cloward. 2005. "The Politics of the Great Society." In Sidney M. Milkis and Jerome M. Mileur, eds., *The Great Society and High Tide of American Liberalism*. Amherst: University of Massachusetts Press.

President's Commission on the Status of Women. 1963. *Report of the Committee on Home and Community*. October Washington, DC: GPO.

Quadagno, Jill. 1994. *The Color of Welfare: How Racism Undermined the War on Poverty*. New York: Oxford University Press.

*Quadagno, Jill. 2005. *One Nation Uninsured: Why the U.S. Has No National Health Insurance*. New York: Oxford University Press.

Radford, Gail. 1997. *Modern Housing for America: Policy Struggles in the New Deal Era*. Chicago: University of Chicago Press.

Roosevelt, Franklin. 1944. "State of the Union Address." January 11. Available at http://www.fdrli brary.marist.edu/archives/address_text.html.

Social Welfare in New York State in 1962. 1963. 96th Annual Report.

Stone, Deborah. 1994. "The Struggle for the Soul of Health Insurance." In James Morone and Gary S. Belkin, eds., *The Politics of Health Care Reform: Lessons From the Past, Prospects for the Future*. Durham, NC: Duke University Press, 26–56.

*Sugrue, Thomas. 1996. *The Origins of the Urban Crisis: Race and Inequality in Postwar Detroit*. Princeton, NJ: Princeton University Press.

Sunstein, Cass R. 2004. *The Second Bill of Rights: FDR's Unfinished Revolution and Why We Need It More Than Ever*. New York: Basic Books.

Truman, Harry S. 1949. "Annual Message to the Congress on the State of the Union." January 5. *The American Presidency Project*. http://www.presidency.ucsb.edu/ws/index.php?pid=13293&st =fair+deal&st1=.

Weir, Margaret. 1992. *Politics and Jobs: The Boundaries of Employment Policy in the United States*. Princeton, NJ: Princeton University Press.

CHAPTER 6

....

THE U.S. WELFARE STATE SINCE 1970

....

ALEX WADDAN

1 INTRODUCTION

....

IN the 1960s, President Lyndon Johnson's vision of the Great Society assumed that a resource rich country like the United States could afford an "unconditional war on poverty in America" (Johnson 1964). When analyzing the 1964 presidential election, the venerable political commentator Theodore White reflected on the apparent advantage that this brand of politics and policy gave the Democrats over their Republican opponents: "They [the Republicans] campaign, generally, *against* government; the Democrats, generally, *for* government. The Republicans are for virtue, the Democrats for Santa Claus. These are the rules of the game implacably stacked against Republicans" (White 1965, 2). Yet, 16 years later, the United States elected as president a Republican who explicitly called for a rollback of government's role in domestic life, especially with regard to its social-welfare functions. According to President Reagan, "In 1964 the famous War on Poverty was declared and a funny thing happened. Poverty, as measured by dependency, stopped shrinking and then actually began to grow worse. I guess you could say, poverty won the war" (Reagan 1986). Furthermore, the aftermath of the Reagan presidency, at least through 2008, saw a political and policy discourse that generally reflected on the dangers of excessive government involvement in social policy. However, just as the growth of the U.S. welfare state had been patchy and inconsistent through the New Deal and Great Society eras, the period of welfare-state retrenchment experienced many stops and starts and partial reversals.

In order to explore social policy development since the start of the 1970s, this essay begins with some brief observations about the American welfare state as the Great Society drew to an end. At that point, the welfare state had been expanding, albeit erratically, for 40 years. But then, in the mid-1970s, economic stagnation led to a political and policy rethink. The election of President Reagan produced a significant shift in the tone of social policy debate with conservative commentators, urging welfare state downsizing, coming to the fore. The chapter traces the political rhetoric of welfare-state rollback

embraced by Republicans through the 1980s and how this discourse subsequently influenced Democratic positioning on key social policy issues, before moving on to reflect on
whether this rhetoric was matched by substantive policy change. The chapter concludes
with a brief discussion of President Obama's health-care reform, especially in the light of
expectations at the time of his election that he might lead an administration committed
to renewing social-policy activism (Skocpol and Jacobs 2011).

2   The U.S. Welfare State at 40

If the modern American welfare state dates from the New Deal era, then its definitive
birth was the Social Security Act of 1935. Accordingly, this welfare state "celebrated" its
40th birthday in 1975, but this did not turn out to be a point at which "life begins." Yet
before concentrating on the era of austerity, it is worth briefly sketching out what welfare state structures had taken shape by this point, particularly as it was not immediately obvious in the mid-1970s that the politics of social policy was to shift direction.
Left-leaning Democrats may have vilified President Nixon, but his administration oversaw the continued expansion of social-welfare spending, and in November 1976 Jimmy
Carter was elected, ostensibly at least, as a New Deal Democrat. In addition, it is important to understand the welfare-state structures that had been put in place between the
1930s and 1970s in order to appreciate why some aspects proved resilient and other elements became vulnerable to retrenchment. The political and policy legacies of the New
Deal and Great Society "created the matrix for subsequent political struggles over public
social policies in America" (Skocpol 1995, 211).

The major pillars of the U.S. welfare state were established as part of the landmark
1935 Social Security Act and subsequent amendments, notably those in 1965 creating
the Medicare and Medicaid programs. Taken together, these programs refute the notion
that the U.S. neglected to build up social-welfare supports, but there were important
differences between programs according to whether they were deemed to constitute
social "insurance" or public "assistance." This distinction between insurance and assistance largely rested on whether a program had a contributory element and whether eligibility was determined by means testing, rather than reflecting an accurate assessment
of whether a program's rules properly matched the principles of insurance. Programs in
the former category tended to build up politically strong protective constituencies both
in terms of popular and interest-group politics (Campbell 2003), whereas those in the
latter group generally had less popular support and fewer powerful friends. One important exception to this generalization was the Medicaid program, which continued to
expand, if incrementally, through the 1980s and beyond (Jaenicke and Waddan 2006a).

The aspect of the original Social Security Act that proved to be the most politically
resilient and fiscally expansionary was old-age insurance, popularly known as Social
Security. Although this program had an uncertain beginning by the late 1960s and into
the early 1970s, political actors competed to gain praise for expanding Social Security

benefits (Béland 2007). Importantly, the program is funded by a dedicated tax on employees and employers, which contributes to the perception of it as an "earned" benefit. This impression is misleading but has worked to reinforce the notion that Social Security is a genuine insurance scheme and, as such, distinct from "welfare." In the early 1970s, in an effort to regulate the future growth of Social Security spending and also to prevent Democrats in Congress from introducing ad hoc benefit increases for their own political gain, President Nixon advocated that benefits be automatically indexed to rise in line with the cost of living. This was done, but only after a series of benefit increases were implemented (Béland 2007). These changes played a significant part in reducing the poverty rate of older Americans. In 1960, 35.2 percent of seniors had an income below the official poverty line. This had dropped to 24.5 percent by 1970 and fell further to 15.7 percent by 1980 (Palmer 1988, 10). Nevertheless, the rise in benefit levels also sowed the seeds of long-term fiscal instability for the program.

The Medicare program, although only created in 1965, also became seen as an "earned" benefit and quickly established its popular legitimacy (Marmor 2000). When it was created, Medicare had two main components: hospital insurance (Part A) and medical insurance (Part B). Part A, following the Social Security model, is a compulsory contributory scheme with payroll-tax financing. Part B is optional, with seniors having the choice to enroll in the program for a monthly fee, which most recipients choose to do. This fee covers about one-quarter of the cost, with general revenues funding the rest. In addition, the program has covered many nonelderly disabled Americans since 1972. Hence, much more rapidly than Social Security, Medicare became an embedded part of the American welfare state.

The social protections offered by Social Security and Medicare by the mid-1970s provided the bedrock of the American welfare state. The benefits are largely directed to the country's seniors, but, importantly, age, rather than means testing, is the primary eligibility criterion. In contrast, the major social welfare programs for the able-bodied, non-aged, population put means testing at the heart of eligibility. This reinforced the division between "social insurance" and "public assistance" programs, with the former perceived as serving legitimate needs and the latter being of more dubious merit.

The program perceived as particularly dubious was Aid to Families with Dependent Children (AFDC), which was established as part of the 1935 Social Security Act, with a cash benefit that distributed money to poor, largely single-parent families with children. It was originally designed to provide income support for poor single parents with children at a time when mothers were not expected to do full-time paid work but would concentrate on mothering. Importantly, AFDC split funding and regulation between federal and state governments, which meant considerable variation in how the rules were applied. Despite being enacted alongside Social Security, AFDC never enjoyed the status of that program, and by the early 1970s the demand for "welfare reform" had become increasingly strident (Weaver 2000).

A second, and much more expensive, program is Medicaid that provides health coverage to many public assistance beneficiaries, with costs shared between federal and state governments (Marmor 2000, 47–53). Medicaid is available only to the low income "medically indigent," but it does offer a comprehensive package of benefits to those who qualify as eligible. Since its creation, Medicaid has been the subject of many political fights over funding, and the program has never attained the same level of support as Medicare. However, it is also clear that predictions made in 1965 that Medicaid's status as a program for the poor would mean that it would remain a marginal program were wrong (Brown and Sparer 2003). Importantly, and in contrast to AFDC, Medicaid generates powerful supportive constituencies—older Americans who have exhausted their Medicare benefits leaving them "medically indigent," and health-care providers, for whom Medicaid offers an important income stream. The reimbursement rates paid by Medicaid frustrate some of those providers, but they remain powerful advocates who have a vested interest in opposing program retrenchment (Olson 2010).

In addition, the flurry of social policy activism in the Great Society era produced or expanded a number of other programs. For example, the Supplemental Security Income (SSI) program provides a minimum level of benefit for poor Americans who are blind, disabled, or aged. The Food Stamp Program, which helps low-income households, was expanded, and Head Start, which provides early-years education to disadvantaged children, was created. In addition, the Earned Income Tax Credit (EITC), which gives a federal-income-tax credit to low-income workers, was established in 1975 (Myles and Pierson 1997). Although the EITC differs from traditional welfare-state supports in which benefits or services are directly distributed by government, the government forfeits tax revenues through the program in the service of clear redistributive policy objectives. Hence the EITC involves "tax expenditures" that should be counted as part of the U.S. welfare state (Howard 2006). On the other hand, the EITC differs from antipoverty programs like SSI since the EITC only benefits people in work. In this way, the principles framing the EITC reinforced the notion that there were different levels of "deservingness" among the poor population—a theme that would grow in importance in the next stage of social-policy development.

3 CHANGING POLITICS

3.1 The End of the Golden Age

One simple measure of the changing political mood in the United States is the shift in electoral politics since 1968. Starting in 1968, Republican presidential candidates registered a series of triumphs that reversed the pattern of the previous 36 years. The turn against government activism, however, should not really be dated to Nixon's time in the White House. The hegemony in presidential politics enjoyed by New Deal Democrats ended in 1968, but, as president, Nixon did not lead an administration committed to welfare-state rollback. Such an administration only entered the White House in January 1981, led by President Reagan.

Reagan's triumph followed the Democratic presidency of Jimmy Carter that had been engulfed by a tide of economic woes. The mid-to-late 1970s saw a period of economic stagnation and rising inflation—so-called "stagflation." In 1980 the unemployment rate was 7.1 percent and inflation rate was 13.5 percent (U.S. Census Bureau 1998, Tables 644 and 772). With the two most visible economic indicators at such relatively high levels, it was unsurprising that there was an electoral backlash against the incumbent administration. It is difficult to identify an exact point at which the economic, political, and social bargain that had sustained the policy dynamics of the New Deal finally unraveled, but one clear indication of popular dissatisfaction came with the passage of Proposition 13 in California in 1978. This measure, which was a property-tax-cutting initiative, was not explicitly framed as an attack on the welfare state, but in Washington DC the so-called tax revolt was interpreted as a backlash against big government (Martin 2008). Furthermore, polling data showed that in the late 1970s an increasing number of people agreed with the statement that too much money was being spent on welfare rather than too little (Page and Shapiro 1992, 126). As these events unfolded, a revitalized conservative movement, rediscovering its long-time intellectual champions in figures such as Friedrich Hayek (1944) and Milton Friedman (1962), was boosted by interpretations of the economic crisis that placed the blame "not in the failure of markets but in the mistaken pursuit of those market usurping policies identified with the welfare state" (Pierson 1991, 41).

In hindsight, the economic slowdown of the 1970s decisively undermined the increasingly fragile New Deal political coalition. That electoral alliance had already been put under severe strain by divisions within the Democratic Party over civil rights and the Vietnam war. Now, economic stagnation seemed to turn decisions about social policy into a zero-sum game, pitting "taxpayers" against "tax recipients" and encouraging a "conservative coalition opposed to the liberal welfare state" (Edsall with Edsall 1992, 131). In this context, Reagan's emphasis on cutting taxes and reducing federal-government social spending resonated beyond traditional conservative constituencies. In his 1981 inaugural address, Reagan referred to a tax burden "which penalizes successful achievement," and, in a particularly memorable line, he declared: "In this present crisis, government is not the solution to our problem; government is the problem" (Reagan 1981).

For all the stridency of this language, the extent to which the Reagan and, subsequently, George H.W. Bush administrations cut welfare spending is disputed (Pierson 1994; details discussed later). What did diminish was the popular belief in the capacity of government to deal with social problems. The return of a Democrat to the White House did not see a return to the rhetoric of the Great Society. As a presidential candidate, Bill Clinton was keen to emphasize his credentials as a "New Democrat," and part of this political identity was to lessen the impression that Democrats were knee-jerk advocates of government programs. In fact, Clinton's campaign sent out contrary messages on key social-welfare issues. On health care he promised a comprehensive reform that would control costs and, in line with long-term Democratic aspirations, would also guarantee all Americans access to health insurance. Yet, simultaneously, he attempted to distance himself from the image of a Democrat who made no demands of those receiving public assistance.

As it was, health-care and welfare reform were major themes of Clinton's first term. The politics of health care dominated the first two years, whereas welfare policy came to the fore in 1996 as Clinton sought re-election. The institutional and partisan environment in which these two key social policy debates took place was very different. The 1992 elections had resulted in unified Democratic government in Washington, but the 1994 midterm congressional elections produced a seismic change in American politics as the Republicans gained majorities in both chambers of Congress. Moreover, Newt Gingrich (R-Ga.), who became the new Speaker of the House, was determined to follow a distinctly conservative path committed to reducing the size and role of government. More generally, congressional politics became increasingly polarized with both parties, but especially the Republicans, who had fewer moderates in their ranks (Sinclair 2006). In turn, this meant that the battles over social policy became ever starker.

In the end, both Clinton and Republican legislators in Congress were damaged by the battles over health care, whereas both sides claimed victory with respect to welfare. Another important development through the 1990s was the growing consensus that major entitlement programs needed reform, notably Medicare and Social Security, as well as Medicaid. That consensus did not extend to agreement on what exactly to do, and Clinton was skillful in presenting himself as a defender of these popular programs against Republican attacks. For example, he prevented the Republicans from enacting significant cuts to Medicare in 1995, and from converting Medicaid to a block grant. Nevertheless, discussion of how to impose fiscal constraints on these benefits was now more openly on the policy agenda than had previously been the case. Furthermore, in his 1996 State of the Union address, Clinton famously declared, "The era of big government is over." This phrase drew much attention, even though it was followed by the caveat, "we cannot go back to the time when our citizens were left to fend for themselves" (Clinton 1996).

The complex politics of "entitlement reform" was illustrated through the presidency of George W. Bush. President Bush espoused a philosophy of "compassionate conservatism" that implied that social welfare functions should be carried out, as far as possible, by organizations in the private sector, including faith-based groups, rather than by government (Bush 2002). With regard to the big-ticket items of Medicare and Social Security, Bush promoted his vision of the "ownership society"—the idea that personal ownership, rather than collective organization, is the best source of economic prosperity and security (for a discussion of Bush's conservatism, see Béland and Waddan 2008). Thus, the ownership society agenda was designed to encourage individuals to contribute toward and save for health care and pension provision through personal savings accounts, rather than through social insurance programs like Medicare and Social Security.

4 RETRENCHMENT AND EXPANSION IN THE ERA OF AUSTERITY

By the time Barack Obama was elected President in November 2008, the age of welfare-state "permanent austerity" (Pierson 2001) had lasted almost as long as the era of welfare-state expansion. Clearly the latter period had left in place many of the policy institutions established in the former. In this context, it is important to ask whether the changed political environment from the late 1970s onward had a real impact on the development of the American welfare state. Did the Reagan administration transform its rhetoric into reality and subsequently create a new template for social policy? Was there significant welfare-state retrenchment? The evidence appears contradictory. Paul Pierson argued that the U.S. welfare state had proven quite durable through the 1980s (Pierson, 1994). Yet, two years after that book was published, President Clinton signed into law the Personal Responsibility and Work Opportunity Reconciliation Act (PRWORA) that abolished the AFDC program and replaced it with a time-limited benefit with strict work requirements (Weaver 2000). On the other hand, Pierson's original argument, which highlighted the difficulties of "path departing" reforms, seemed vindicated when the Bush administration's effort to partially privatize the Social Security program floundered, despite unified Republican government in Washington DC (Béland and Waddan 2012). The narrative grew even more confusing when the Bush administration worked with congressional Republicans to enact the Medicare Modernization Act (MMA) in 2003. Apparently running against the grain of conservative ideas, this bill expanded Medicare significantly by adding a new prescription-drug benefit to the program. Yet, the bill also introduced a series of measures that advanced conservative preferences both in Medicare and the wider health-care system (Jaenicke and Waddan 2006b).

To make sense of the degree to which social policy decisively shifted in a more conservative direction after the mid-1970s, the best place to start is with the 1996 PRWORA—the most dramatic act of welfare state retrenchment. The law was the culmination of two decades of conservative attacks on the AFDC program (Weaver, 2000). Dramatic reform of welfare had been a long-term objective of conservative commentators who insisted that, rather than bringing economic security to the most vulnerable of American families, the program had encouraged dependency on government benefits and the formation of vulnerable, single-parent families (Mead 1992; Murray 1984). Although highly contested (Handler and Hasenfeld 2007), these views gained increasing currency outside the ranks of conservative thinkers and activists and, by the late 1980s, began to influence welfare policy experts with ties to the Democratic Party (Ellwood 1988). Even so, President Reagan had limited success in reining in the AFDC program. The income that families could earn and the asset amounts they could own while remaining eligible for AFDC were lowered as part of the Omnibus Budget Reconciliation Act of 1981. These changes reduced the AFDC rolls by about 400,000 recipients and cut benefits for nearly another 300,000 (Davies 2003, 211).[1] Although significant for the families affected, these measures did not constitute a repeal of AFDC, and the program largely survived intact through the rest of the 1980s. In Reagan's final year in office, the Family Support Act of 1988 (FSA) introduced a further series of reforms that were meant to act as carrots and sticks to move people off AFDC, but the measures made little impact on the ground.

One emerging political figure who had been involved in the development of the FSA was Arkansas Governor Bill Clinton. Later, when he became the Democratic Party's presidential nominee in 1992, he continued to promote welfare reform and, impor-tantly, made the issue a central part of his effort to brand himself as a "different kind of Democrat." Once in office, President Clinton introduced a reform proposal in 1994, but this made little legislative headway. Following the Republican capture of Congress in the 1994 midterm elections, it was the Republican leadership that took the initiative in formulating further reform plans. This led to a period of considerable legislative brink-manship before President Clinton, to the dismay of many Democrats, signed PRWORA in August 1996 (Weaver 2000). PRWORA finally ended the AFDC welfare-entitlement program for poor single-parent families and replaced it with a new conditional ben-efit named Temporary Assistance for Needy Families (TANF). TANF families are restricted to a five-year lifetime limit on receipt of federal-welfare benefits. The new law also imposed new work requirements on those receiving TANF that had a significantly tougher range of sanctions than had applied to AFDC. Overall, PRWORA was a much more radical transformation of welfare than Clinton had initially proposed, and some of his welfare policy advisors disputed the decision to sign rather than veto the legisla-tion (Ellwood 1996). In the aftermath of reform, conservatives claimed vindication as welfare rolls declined sharply, but critics worried that the drop in welfare receipt was not matched by a reduction in poverty. Whatever the merit of the 1996 reform, there has not been any serious political momentum to reverse the changes emphasizing work require-ments and time limits.

If, however, PRWORA presents a clear case of path-breaking social-policy reform, the remaining major pillars of that welfare state—Social Security, Medicare, and Medicaid—remain intact. Social Security, in particular, proved resilient to reform, gaining the reputation of being "the third rail" in American politics (that is, "touch it and die"). This is not to say that there were not attempts at restructuring the program. Both the Reagan and George W. Bush administrations launched reform initiatives, cit-ing worries about the long-term stability of the Social Security trust fund as providing objective grounds for concern about the program. In May 1981, the Reagan administra-tion caused a political storm when it announced plans to directly cut early retirement benefits. The hostility forced a quick re-evaluation by the administration, which backed away from its plans, and agreed to set up a bipartisan commission to find ways of provid-ing greater fiscal security for the program. The National Commission on Social Security Reform rejected radical options such as partial privatization of the system and largely reinforced the principles of the existing arrangements by turning to increased revenues rather than benefit cuts as the means to secure the long-term viability of the program. When enacting the Commission's recommendations, Congress also gradually increased the retirement age from 65 to 67, to be phased in by 2022. This last measure aroused the hostility of groups such as the AARP that lobby on behalf of America's seniors, but the overall package was not one of dramatic retrenchment.

The next major effort at reform came in 2005 when President Bush proposed restruc-turing Social Security in a manner compatible with his vision of the "ownership society." This followed a sustained debate between advocates of change who maintained that once again the program's finances needed re-balancing (Tanner 2004), and supporters of the existing system arguing that minor tweaking would suffice (Altman 2005). President Bush used concerns about fiscal stability to urge reform, and he claimed that his partial privatization plan would benefit those just embarking on their working lives. In his 2005 State of the Union address, he advocated a system of "voluntary personal retirement accounts" (Bush 2005), but this led to no legislative action. Congressional Republicans shied away from supporting their recently re-elected president and Democrats, demoralized by the 2004 elections, found a popular cause to fight for. By the summer of 2005, it was evident that Bush's effort to persuade the public had failed and the signature domestic policy commitment of his second term languished (Teles and Derthick 2009).

Prior to that legislative failure, the Bush administration had pushed through the controversial Medicare Modernization Act (MMA) of 2003, but that was not an unqualified rollback of social-welfare provision, either. In fact, the most immediate feature of the Act was a new prescription-drug benefit. Democrats had initially championed the new benefit, and one interpretation of the 2003 legislation is that it was driven by political expediency as President Bush and congressional Republicans sought to take an issue that was damaging to them off the political agenda and to win support from seniors. Moreover, the extra spending involved in paying for the benefit infuriated some conservatives (Bartlett 2006, 80). As described in the next section, other aspects of the MMA better fit a conservative narrative; but, before moving on, it is also worth noting that the Medicaid program, which, as a public-assistance program, might be seen as more vulnerable to retrenchment, in fact expanded during both the Reagan and George H.W. Bush presidencies. Due to a series of incremental changes to the rules governing Medicaid eligibility from 1984 to 1990, the program covered an increased number of pregnant women, children, seniors, and disabled Americans (Jaenicke and Waddan 2006a, 245–248).

5 A LESS EFFECTIVE WELFARE STATE?

The evidence already presented gives a mixed picture of welfare-state development in recent decades. It is certainly not an unambiguous story of retrenchment. Federal government spending on human resources increased as a percentage of GDP between 1980 and 2008 from 11.5 percent to 13.2 percent (U.S. Office of Management and Budget 2012, 51–54, Table 3.1).[2] Much of that rise was due to Social Security and Medicare spending, which, together, rose from less than 6 percent of GDP in 1980 to 8.4 percent in 2010 (Social Security and Medicare Boards of Trustees 2011). Yet, by 2005 some scholars were emphasizing how social policy in the United States *had moved* in a conservative direction (Hacker and Pierson 2005a, 2010). On occasion, as highlighted by PRWORA, this had come through explicit legislative action following intense political debate. However, some changes were more discrete, as conservative political actors adopted strategies to re-direct social policy through "subterranean" reform (Hacker 2004, 245).

For example, the headline aspect of the 2003 Medicare reform was an expansion of the Medicare program that seemed incompatible with a retrenchment agenda. At the same time, the MMA injected more market-oriented practices into the Medicare program. For instance, it gave private insurers an increased opportunity to compete in the Medicare market and expanded the availability of Health Savings Accounts (HSA)— tax-privileged savings accounts that are tied to insurance policies with high deductibles. Champions of HSAs maintain that the accounts give individuals the incentive to shop around more for their health insurance, allowing people to better determine their own health-care needs and keep costs down.

Beyond these specific changes, some scholars of the welfare state have looked beyond case studies of individual programs and focused on the bigger picture, asking what government does to protect the most economically vulnerable. In this context, Hacker and Pierson (2010) have brought attention to the phenomenon of "policy drift." They define government *inaction* as a form of policy making. The ongoing effectiveness of welfare-state programs can, over time, be undermined when these programs are not updated to deal with changing circumstances. Although programs' rules may look unchanged, "their ability to achieve the goals embodied in them has noticeably weakened" (Hacker 2004, 256). With this framework in mind, Hacker and Pierson compared how governments in industrialized nations had reacted to the processes of globalization, technological advance, and demographic change. Noting how these shifts in the broader economy and society had the potential to exacerbate economic disparities, the two writers argued that most rich nations had worked to mitigate rising inequality through policies designed to protect low-income families. In the United States, however, "the opposite is true. Government is doing substantially less to reduce inequality and poverty below the highest rungs of the income ladder than it did a generation ago" (Hacker and Pierson 2010, 52).

The data charting rising inequality are unambiguous. In 1980, the average after tax income of a household in the lowest income quintile was 13,900 dollars. In 2004 this figure was 14,700 dollars (all figures are in constant 2004 dollars). The average household in the middle quintile over that time period saw after-tax income rise from $39,900 to $48,400. In contrast to those modest gains, the highest quintile enjoyed an increase from an average after-tax household income of $92,100 in 1980 to $155,200 in 2004 (Aron-Dine and Sherman 2007). Conservative commentators might object that it is not government's job to reduce inequality and that social policy should concentrate on the narrower task of helping the least well-off. Even according to this criterion, the evidence suggests that policy has not always kept up with changing circumstances. Although poverty rates dropped significantly through the 1960s into the early 1970s, that pattern halted in the 1980s. In 1965 the official poverty rate was 17.3 percent, declining to a low of 11.1 percent in 1973. The figure then remained between 11 and 12 percent through the 1970s before rising in the 1980s. There was then a gradual decline through the late 1990s, but poverty increased through the 2000s even before the "Great Recession" that began in 2008. That downturn in the economy hurt many American households, with the poverty rate rising in 2011 to 15.1 percent (U.S. Census Bureau 2011, 14). Furthermore, many

Americans had found their living standards slipping even before the recession. The period from November 2001 through 2007 "marked the first time on record that poverty and the incomes of typical working-aged households worsened despite six years of economic growth" (Pavetti and Rosenbaum 2010, 4), with income gains through these years heavily skewed toward the top 1 percent of households (Feller and Stone 2009, 1).

One critical question is to what extent does social policy mitigate or exaggerate the uneven distributions rendered by the market. According to President George W. Bush's Treasury Secretary Hank Paulson, rising inequality "is simply an economic reality, and it is neither fair nor useful to blame any political party" (quoted in Krugman 2006). This suggests there is little that can be done in the short term to change the prevailing trends, and that inequality is not the consequence of choices made by political actors about the shape of social policy. President Clinton's Council of Economic Advisors (1994, 26) offered a slightly more activist perspective: "Although the underlying forces of the market are vastly more powerful than anything government can do, the right kinds of policy can make a difference." Illustrative of the Clinton administration's efforts to ameliorate the inequalities arising from market forces was the expansion of the EITC in 1993. This was part of the administration's agenda to "make work pay" but, whatever the merit of the EITC as a policy initiative, it did not do much to check the growth of inequality.

In 2004, a report sponsored by the American Political Science Association examining government policy and increasing income disparities in the United States maintained: "Policies pursued—or not pursued—help to explain sharper socioeconomic disparities in the U.S. compared to more muted inequalities in . . . other advanced industrialized countries" (Taskforce on Inequality and American Democracy 2004, 4). One clear example of a policy *choice* that exacerbated the rise in income inequality was the tax cut advocated by President George W. Bush and enacted in 2001: "36 percent of the cuts accrued to the richest 1 percent of Americans—a share almost identical to that received by the bottom 80 percent" (Hacker and Pierson 2005b, 33). Tax cuts are not framed as social policy, but when they have such an impact on real-world income distribution, then it is only logical to include them in an analysis of social- policy decision making.

6 PRESIDENT OBAMA: A NEW HEALTH-CARE STATE?

In January 2009, as Barack Obama entered the White House with Democratic majorities in Congress, it seemed as if this was another pivotal moment in U.S. politics. For American progressives, the hope (and, for conservatives, the fear) was that this moment signaled a reversal in the course of social policy of the previous 30 years, with a president and Congress committed to strengthening the safety net and reducing inequality.

President Obama's presidency quickly provoked much argument, with one critical area of controversy being the administration's efforts to push through comprehensive reform of the country's health-care "system."

Health-care reform had long been a contentious theme in American politics, dating back at least to President Harry Truman. Bill Clinton's presidency suffered huge political damage over its effort at health reform (Skocpol 1997), and President Obama's foray into the health policy arena was always likely to arouse formidable opposition. Yet, President Obama and Democratic leaders in Congress did steer the Patient Protection and Affordable Care Act (PPACA) through the legislative process. That process involved many compromises, and remarkably stiff opposition from Republicans, but the administration was determined to reduce significantly the number of Americans lacking health insurance and also to bring aggregate health-care spending under control. The former goal was a long-standing objective of Democrats, and the latter reflected that the United States, despite not having universal insurance coverage, spent a higher proportion of its GDP on health care than any other industrialized nation. In 2010, over 16 percent of Americans lacked insurance (U.S. Census Bureau 2011, 23). Yet, health-care spending consumed 17.4 percent of GDP in 2009 compared with 11.8 percent in France and 9.8 percent in the United Kingdom (OECD 2011). These numbers made the case for health care reform compelling, but produced little consensus on what reform should look like.

The legislative process that produced the PPACA featured an extraordinary endgame (Jacobs and Skocpol 2010), adding to the sense that the bill was nobody's first choice. Nevertheless, through a variety of means, including a major expansion of Medicaid, the new law promises to dramatically lessen the number of Americans without health insurance. Much of the revenue needed to finance this expansion will come from more affluent Americans. In addition, the bill prohibits private insurers from denying coverage to people on the basis of preexisting illness. In order to control the cost of care, the PPACA plans to slow down the growth of spending on Medicare and introduces changes to the incentive structure for health-care providers in order to encourage efficiency and greater health-system integration. After passage of the PPACA, supporters and opponents of the bill engaged in wildly conflicting arguments about the likely impact of the reforms, but, with full implementation spread out through to 2019, the final effects will not be known for some time. If implemented as planned, the PPACA would constitute an important re-distributive measure. Political scientists Lawrence Jacobs and Theda Skocpol (2011, 83) describe the bill as "a landmark in U.S. public social provision" that "draws resources from the privileged to spread access to affordable health insurance to most of the U.S. citizenry."

Importantly, however, this "landmark" was not universally welcomed. A series of legal challenges were quickly made to the law, which made their way to the Supreme Court. Beyond this, the Obama administration found it difficult to persuade the public of the virtues of the PPACA, even though particular aspects of it—such as restrictions on insurance companies—are widely popular. Even after it had been enacted, the law remained a contentious political issue. It became a central subject in the campaign for the 2010 midterm elections, with evidence suggesting that Democrats suffered as a consequence (Saldin 2010). It remains to be seen whether the PPACA will survive the political and legal challenges and, if it does, whether it will win over a skeptical public. Will those who benefit from the law form coherent, politically recognizable, supportive constituencies that protect the PPACA against retrenchment, allowing the major tenets of the law to become institutionally embedded? If so, could the Obama administration lay claim to achieving a major expansion of the U.S. welfare state? Given the complexity of the law and the hostility to it, this outcome is far from certain.

7 CONCLUSION

Social policy since the mid-1970s has taken a tortuous path. Clearly the policy environment changed as the political momentum switched to the Republican Party (Pierson and Skocpol 2007). Furthermore, that party re-oriented itself away from its Eisenhower and Nixon version of conservatism, which had accommodated the prevailing social policy activism, into a more ideologically coherent force committed to downsizing the welfare state. The wider public, however, has been more selective in its wish to retrench social programs. Although there was little support for "welfare" in the form of AFDC, Social Security maintained its status as a much-loved program, and politicians who embarked on reform efforts were defeated and punished. Hence conservatives have had only limited success in explicitly retrenching the biggest "Big Government" programs. Furthermore, a higher proportion of American households were receiving government aid in 2010 than had been the case a dozen years earlier. In 2010, 48.5 percent of American households received government benefits, compared with 37.7 percent in 1998. The former figure partially reflects the increased use of emergency safety-net programs such as unemployment insurance and food stamps during the economic downturn that started in 2008. Still, even by 2006, 44.5 percent of households received some government help (Applebaum and Gebeloff 2012). This type of data suggests that the U.S. welfare state in fact expanded rather than shrank even during the "era of austerity."

Ultimately, however, this picture is misleading if the aggregate impacts of social policy programs are examined. If one function of the welfare state is to reduce the inequality that arises from market outcomes, then U.S. social policy performed that task with diminishing effectiveness in the decades after 1970. The sharply rising levels of inequality in the United States (Bartels 2008) have not led to decisive government action to mitigate the growing disparities. The Obama administration did respond to the recession by expanding and extending access to food stamps and unemployment compensation, but the longer-term figures show that consistent movement in the direction of poverty reduction had ceased in the late 1970s.

This apparent discrepancy between the extended reach of government benefits into more households and the declining effectiveness of those benefits in terms of fulfilling the traditional functions of reducing inequality, or at least poverty, is explained by the nature of those benefits. First, the Social Security and Medicare programs serve the increasing number of senior households. These programs do significantly reduce poverty among seniors, but they can do little for the rest of the population. Second, partially reflecting the reliance on "tax expenditures" as a form of policy making (Howard 2006), the financial benefits of government activity have increasingly flowed to the middle class rather than the least well-off. Thus, whereas in 1979 the bottom quintile of U.S. households received 54 percent of government benefits, in 2007 that figure had dropped to 36 percent (Applebaum and Gebeloff 2012).

Overall, U.S. social-policy development in the four decades after 1970 has contradictory political implications. Conservative efforts to fundamentally reduce the size of government have run into the roadblocks of the still popular and expanding Social Security and Medicare programs. Liberals, on the other hand, have been unable to translate the support for those big- government programs into enthusiasm for a wider re-distributive agenda. In aggregate, the "era of austerity" has not lead to a shrinking of the federal welfare state. However, social-policy activism has been largely absent even as structural change to the American economy means that the rewards of economic growth have been divided ever more unevenly.

Notes

1. For an analysis of how the tax cuts and benefit cuts enacted in the early 1980s hurt Democratic voters and benefited Republican constituencies see Edsall with Edsall 1992, 158–162.
2. Human-resources spending comprises expenditures on: education; training; employment; social services; health, Medicare, income security; Social Security, and veterans benefits and services.

References

*Indicates recommended reading.

Altman, Nancy. 2005. *The Battle for Social Security: From FDR's Vision to Bush's Gamble.* Hoboken, NJ: Wiley.

Applebaum, Binyamin, and Robert Gebeloff. 2012. "Even Critics of the Safety Net Increasingly Depend on It." *New York Times*, February 11.

Aron-Dine, A. and A. Sherman. 2007. *New CBO Data Show Income Inequality Continues to Widen.* Washington, DC: Center on Budget and Policy Priorities. http://www.cbpp.org/cms/?fa=view&id=957.

Bartels, Larry M. 2008. *Unequal Democracy: The Political Economy of the New Gilded Age.* New York: Russell Sage Foundation.

Bartlett, Bruce. 2006. *Impostor: How George W. Bush Bankrupted America and Betrayed the Reagan Legacy.* New York: Doubleday.

*Béland, Daniel. 2007. *Social Security: History and Politics from the New Deal to the Privatization Debate (updated paperback edition)*. Lawrence: University Press of Kansas.

Béland, Daniel, and Alex Waddan. 2008. "Taking 'Big Government Conservatism Seriously? The Bush Presidency Reconsidered." *Political Quarterly* 79 (1): 109–118

*Béland, Daniel, and Alex Waddan. 2012. *The Politics of Policy Change: Welfare, Medicare and Social Security Reform in the United States*. Washington, DC: Georgetown University Press.

Brown, Lawrence D., and Michael S. Sparer. 2003. "Poor Program's Progress: The Unanticipated Politics of Medicaid Policy." *Health Affairs* 22 (1): 31–44.

Bush, George W. 2002. *President Promotes Compassionate Conservatism*. April 30. Washington, DC: The White House Office of the Press Secretary.

Bush, George W. 2005. *State of the Union Address*. February 2. Washington, DC: The White House, Office of the Press Secretary.

Campbell, Andrea L. 2003. *How Policies Make Citizens: Senior Political Activism and the American Welfare State*. Princeton, NJ: Princeton University Press.

Clinton, William J. 1996. "State of the Union Address." U.S. Capitol, January 23. http://clinton2.nara.gov/WH/New/other/sotu.html.

Council of Economic Advisors. 1994. *Annual Report of the Council of Economic Advisors*. Washington, DC: GPO.

Davies, Gareth. 2003. "The Welfare State." In W. Elliot Brownlee and Hugh Davis Graham, eds., *The Reagan Presidency: Pragmatic Conservatism and Its Legacies*. Lawrence: University of Kansas Press, 209–232.

*Edsall, Thomas B., with Mary D. Edsall. 1992. *Chain Reaction: The Impact of Race, Rights and Taxes on American Politics*. New York: W.W. Norton.

Ellwood, David. 1988. *Poor Support: Poverty in the American Family*. New York: Basic Books.

Ellwood, David. 1996. "Welfare Reform As I Knew It." *The American Prospect* 26: 22–29.

Feller, Avi, and Chad Stone. 2009. *Top 1 Per Cent of Americans Reaped Two-Thirds of Income Gains in Last Economic Expansion*. Washington, DC: Center on Budget and Policy Priorities.

Friedman, Milton. 1962. *Capitalism and Freedom*. Chicago: University of Chicago Press.

Hacker, Jacob. 2004. "Privatizing Risk without Privatizing the Welfare State: The Hidden Politics of Welfare State Retrenchment in the United States." *American Political Science Review* 98: 243–260.

Hacker, Jacob S., and Paul Pierson. 2005a. *Off Center: The Republican Revolution and the Erosion of American Democracy*. New Haven, CT: Yale University Press.

Hacker, Jacob S., and Paul Pierson. 2005b. "Abandoning the Middle: The Bush Tax Cuts and the Limits of Democratic Control." *Perspectives on Politics* 3 (1): 33–54.

*Hacker, Jacob S., and Paul Pierson. 2010. *Winner-Take-All Politics. How Washington Made the Rich Richer—And Turned Its Back on the Middle Class*. New York: Simon and Schuster.

Handler, Joel F., and Yeheskel Hasenfeld. 2007. *Blame Welfare: Ignore Poverty and Inequality*. New York: Cambridge University Press.

Hayek, Friedrich. 1944. *The Road to Serfdom*. London: Routledge and Kegan Paul.

Howard, Christopher. 2006. *The Welfare State Nobody Knows: Debunking Myths about U.S. Social Policy*. Princeton, NJ: Princeton University Press.

Jacobs, Lawrence, and Theda Skocpol. 2010. *Health Care Reform and American Politics: What Everyone Needs to Know*. New York: Oxford University Press.

Jacobs, Lawrence, and Theda Skocpol. 2011. "Hard Fought Legacy: Obama, Congressional Democrats, and the Struggle for Comprehensive Health Care Reform." In Theda Skocpol and Lawrence Jacobs, eds., *Reaching for a New Deal: Ambitious Governance, Economic*

Meltdown, and Polarized Politics in Obama's First Two Years. New York: Russell Sage Foundation, 53–104.

Jaenicke, Douglas, and Alex Waddan. 2006a. "Recent Incremental Health Care Reforms in the US: A Way Forward or False Promise?" *Policy and Politics* 34 (2): 241–264.

Jaenicke, Douglas, and Alex Waddan. 2006b. "President Bush and Social Policy: The Strange Case of the Medicare Prescription Drug Benefit." *Political Science Quarterly* 121 (2): 217–240.

Johnson, L. B. 1964. "State of the Union Address." U.S. Capitol, January 8. http://www.american rhetoric.com/speeches/lbj1964stateoftheunion.htm.

Krugman, Paul. 2006. "Wages, Wealth and Politics." *New York Times,* August 18.

Marmor, Theodore R. 2000. *The Politics of Medicare. 2nd ed.* New York: Aldine de Gruyter.

Martin, Isaac. 2008. *The Permanent Tax Revolt: How the Property Tax Transformed American Politics.* Palo Alto: Stanford University Press.

*Mead, Lawrence 1992. *The New Politics of Poverty: The Nonworking Poor in America.* New York: Basic Books.

Murray, Charles. 1984. *Losing Ground: American Social Policy, 1950–1980.* New York: Free Press.

Myles, John, and Paul Pierson. 1997. "Friedman's Revenge: The Reform of "Liberal" Welfare States in Canada and the United States." *Politics and Society* 25 (4): 443–472.

OECD. 2011. "Directorate for Employment, Labour and Social Affairs, OECD Health Data for 2011." http://www.oecd.org/document/16/0,3343,en_2649_34631_2085200_1_1_1_1,00.html.

Olson, Laura Katz. 2010. *The Politics of Medicaid.* New York: Columbia University Press.

Page, Benjamin, and Robert Shapiro. 1992. *The Rational Public: Fifty Years of Trends in Americans' Policy Preferences.* Chicago: University of Chicago Press.

Palmer, John. 1988. *Income Security in America: The Record and the Prospects.* Washington, DC: Urban Institute Press.

Pavetti, LaDonna, and Dorothy Rosenbaum. 2010. *Creating a Safety Net That Works When the Economy Doesn't: The Role of the Food Stamp and TANF Programs.* Washington, DC: Center on Budget and Policy Priorities.

Pierson, Christopher. 1991. *Beyond the Welfare State: The New Political Economy of the Welfare State.* Cambridge: Polity.

Pierson, Paul. 1994. *Dismantling the Welfare State? Reagan, Thatcher, and the Politics of Retrenchment.* New York: Cambridge University Press.

Pierson, Paul. 2001. "Coping with Permanent Austerity." In Paul Pierson, ed., *The New Politics of the Welfare State.* Oxford: Oxford University Press, 410–456.

*Pierson, Paul, and Theda Skocpol. 2007. *The Transformation of American Politics: Activist Government and the Rise of Conservatism.* Princeton: Princeton University Press.

Reagan, Ronald. 1981. "Inaugural Address." January 20. http://www.presidency.ucsb.edu/ws/index.php?pid=43130#axzz1oGALxBJX.

Reagan, Ronald. 1986. "Radio Address to the Nation on Welfare Reform." February 15. http://www.presidency.ucsb.edu/ws/index.php?pid=36875#ixzz1mdSViKgg.

Saldin, Robert. 2010. "Healthcare Reform: A Prescription for the 2010 Republican Landslide?" *The Forum* 8 (4): Article 10.

Skocpol, Theda. 1997. *Boomerang: Health Care Reform and the Turn Against Government.* New York: W.W. Norton.

Skocpol, Theda. 1995. *Social Policy in the United States: Future Possibilities in Historical Perspective.* Princeton, NJ: Princeton University Press.

Skocpol, Theda, and Jacobs, Lawrence. 2011 *Reaching for a New Deal: Ambitious Governance, Economic Meltdown, and Polarized Politics in Obama's First Two Years*. New York: Russell Sage Foundation.

Sinclair, Barbara. 2006. *Party Wars: Polarization and the Politics of National Policy Making*. Norman: University of Oklahoma Press.

Social Security and Medicare Boards of Trustees. 2011. "Status of the Social Security and Medicare Programs." http://www.ssa.gov/oact/TRSUM/index.html.

Tanner, Michael. 2004. *Social Security Time Bomb, and the Candidates Aren't Talking (Project on Social Security Choice)*. Washington, DC: CATO Institute.

Taskforce on Inequality and American Democracy. 2004. *American Democracy in an Age of Rising Inequality*. Washington, DC: American Political Science Association.

Teles, Steven, and Martha Derthick. 2009. "Social Security from 1980 to the Present: From Third Rail to Presidential Commitment-and Back?" In Brian J. Glenn and Steven M. Teles, eds., *Conservatism and American Political Development*. New York: Oxford University Press, 261–290.

U.S. Census Bureau. 1998. *Statistical Abstract of the United States: 1998*. Washington, DC: U.S. Department of Commerce.

U.S. Census Bureau. 2011. *Income, Poverty and Health Insurance Coverage in the United States 2010*. Washington, DC: U.S. Department of Commerce.

U.S. Office of Management and Budget. 2012. "Fiscal Year 2012 Historical Tables, Budget of the United States Government." Washington, DC: U.S. GPO. http://www.gpo.gov/fdsys/pkg/BUDGET-2012-TAB/pdf/BUDGET-2012-TAB.pdf.

*Weaver, Kent R. 2000. *Ending Welfare as We Know It*. Washington, DC: Brookings Institution Press.

White, Theodore. 1965. *The Making of the President, 1964*. London: Jonathan Cape.

CHAPTER 7

A CROSS-NATIONAL PERSPECTIVE ON THE AMERICAN WELFARE STATE

JULIA F. LYNCH

1 INTRODUCTION

COMPARATIVE studies frequently characterize the American welfare state as less precocious, less comprehensive, less decommodifying, and generally less successful than other welfare states in the advanced industrialized world. Classic comparative studies describe the United States as a welfare state "laggard"; a "residual" welfare state, in which "the state assumes responsibility only when the family or the market fails" (Titmuss 1958, 20); or, at best, a "liberal" welfare state whose heavy reliance on private, market-based social provision makes it hardly seem like a welfare *state* at all (Esping-Andersen 1990). These assessments are broadly accurate. Core social insurance policies at the federal level developed somewhat later than in Europe, and they provide less comprehensive protection against major social risks. The U.S. welfare state relies more on private provision than do others, and it generates worse outcomes in health, education, poverty, inequality, crime, homelessness, and the like.

At the same time, the U.S. welfare state is not *simply* "less than" other welfare states. T. H. Marshall (1950) suggested that democratic countries would ultimately, and necessarily, develop large, comprehensive welfare states as the culmination of democratic development. Esping-Andersen's (1990) tripartite typology of welfare state "worlds," however, made clear that even if one examined only the core social insurance programs, welfare states could have histories that gave them fundamentally different internal logics, as well as levels of generosity. These differences have been durable: Since the first oil crisis of 1973, when welfare states in the advanced industrialized world have faced common pressures from declining growth and demographic pressures, different *types* of welfare states have proved remarkably resistant to homogenization (Schmitt and Starke 2011). When it has changed in response to these potentially homogenizing pressures, the United States, like other states, has often changed in uniquely American ways.

This chapter explores similarities and differences in the patterns of welfare state development in the United States and other rich, mainly West European, democracies. All these welfare states consume a large share of Gross Domestic Product (GDP), and insure their citizens against a variety of risks. The U.S. welfare state is unusual, however, in its extensive reliance on private markets to produce public social goods; its geographic variability; its insistence on deservingness as an eligibility criterion; and its orientation toward benefits for the elderly, rather than children and working-age adults.

These differences are the result of political struggles among actors who were differently endowed with political power, and sometimes had different goals, than those who fought for social policies in other nations. American ideals and values have also contributed to American "exceptionalism," but the effects of these values are filtered through specific institutions and historical patterns, some of which have unintended consequences. To understand how, we need first to place the institutions and structures of the American welfare state in a comparative perspective.

2 The American Welfare State as a "Liberal" Regime

The single most influential piece of comparative welfare state research of the contemporary period, Esping-Andersen's *The Three Worlds of Welfare Capitalism* (1990), places the American welfare state in the Liberal category, along with the United Kingdom, Ireland, Canada, Australia, and New Zealand. Liberal welfare states rest on a political coalition that includes proponents of individualist and market-oriented philosophies (i.e., classical Liberalism, not liberalism in the American sense of progressive leftism.) The typical Liberal welfare state pushes individuals to secure their livelihood through participation in the market economy and to procure their own insurance against social risks, in part by ensuring that state benefits are means-tested, stigmatized, and generally "less eligible" (i.e., less desirable) than work.

The Liberal model is quite different from the Conservative Corporatist or Social Democratic welfare regimes that Esping-Andersen outlines. The former aims to protect the standard of living achieved by workers and their families during their working lives. It is essentially an occupational welfare state, providing insurance for workers against the risk of income loss due to unemployment, old age, or sickness, with a safety net for those excluded from the labor market. Reflecting the importance of Conservative parties in its historical development, the Conservative Corporatist welfare state model is designed to preserve social stratification while buffering the working classes from extreme risk. Germany resembles the ideal type, but most of the countries of continental Europe outside of Scandinavia conform loosely to this model.

Finally, the Social Democratic model, most closely approximated in Sweden, is a welfare state that emphasizes solidarity across classes and reduction of inequality. In the post-World War II period, Social Democratic welfare states have provided generous, citizenship-based rights to an extended array of social benefits, and have pursued full-employment policies that have created the broad tax base necessary for supporting such a system.

Esping-Andersen identifies the United States as a close approximation of the Liberal ideal type. The American welfare state's heavy reliance on private providers for everything from health insurance to old-age pensions; the stinginess and stigmatization of many of its poverty-alleviation measures; the stringent means-testing of many benefits; and the underdevelopment of public social services like early childhood education or elder care all mark the United States as a prototypical Liberal welfare state.

Nevertheless, there are important differences between the American welfare state and other Liberal regimes (Castles 2010). For example, even within the Liberal group, the U.S. welfare system is exceptionally private, requiring citizens to procure much of their protection in the realms of pensions, health care, vocational training, child care, education, and housing on private markets. The United States also relies on the tax system as a welfare delivery device to a much greater extent than do other rich countries, even other Liberal countries (Howard 1997; Adema, Fron, and Ladaique 2011). Such social "spending" includes tax exemptions on payments into employer-sponsored health insurance and pension programs; tax deductions for home mortgage interest, child care, and educational expenses; and the Earned Income Tax Credit (EITC).

Figure 7.1 shows the gap between gross public social spending (the most commonly used measure of welfare state "effort") and total (i.e., both private and public) *net* social spending. Among the rich democracies, only Australia has a similarly low level of gross public expenditure on welfare goods. But the United States climbs from 20th (last) place to 5th place in social spending if we measure net total spending rather than gross public expenditures (Figure 7.1). Significant private-sector spending, favorable tax treatment of such spending, and benefits delivered directly through the tax system augment the rather small visible, public side of the U.S. welfare state. (A reverse gap, as in the Nordic and some other countries, indicates a low level of private provision and significant taxation of social benefits.)

The visible, public and the private, "submerged" (Mettler 2011) parts of America's welfare system are not functional equivalents, however. Leaving aside whether public or private action is normatively preferable, public versus private and overt versus covert forms of social provision tend to have different distributive consequences, and differently affect public support for the welfare state (Hacker 2002; Mettler 2011).

No matter which kind of social spending we consider, however, it may be a flawed basis on which to compare welfare states. In Esping-Andersen's pithy formulation, "It is difficult to imagine that anyone struggled for spending *per se*" (1990, 21). In order to assess the strength of what welfare states do, rather than what they spend, Esping-Andersen devised a "decommodification score" summarizing the extent to which citizens in a welfare state could sustain themselves without relying on selling their labor power in the market in 18 rich democracies in 1980. In Esping-Andersen's original calculations, the United States and Australia had the lowest scores (Esping-Andersen 1990, 52). Subsequent attempts to replicate and update Esping-Andersen's work (e.g., Bambra 2006; Scruggs and Allan 2006) have found that the original decommodification

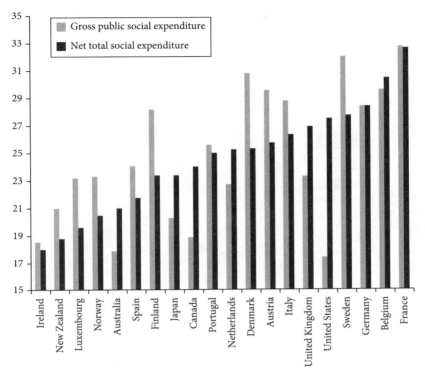

FIG. 7.1 Gross public versus net total (public+private) social expenditure as a percent of GDP, 2007.

Source: Adema, Fron, and Ladaique (2011), Table I.4

index wrongly categorized many countries. However, in every one of these studies, the United States remains at the bottom of the heap. Figure 7.2 compares the generosity of cash benefits (pensions, unemployment insurance, and social assistance for low income individuals and families) across nations. The United States ranks in the bottom quarter of countries for the generosity of its public benefits for the poor, the unemployed, and pensioners. Hence, it seems fair to portray the American welfare state, in general terms and on the basis of its core social insurance programs, as less generous and less comprehensive than almost any other welfare state in the community of democratic, industrialized nations. The United States, then, is not a typical welfare state—as is revealed when we examine its policies in more detail.

3 KEY DIFFERENCES IN SOCIAL PROGRAMS

Old-age and survivors pensions. The U.S. Social Security system is similar to Conservative Corporatist welfare states in linking earnings-related old-age benefits to

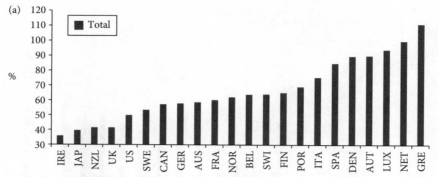

Net public pension benefit as a percent of prior earnings, for male earner with average wage and full contributory history (2008)

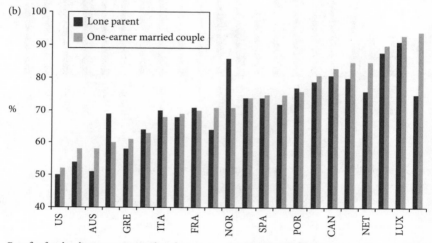

Benefits for the short-term unemployed as a percent of average wage (2010)

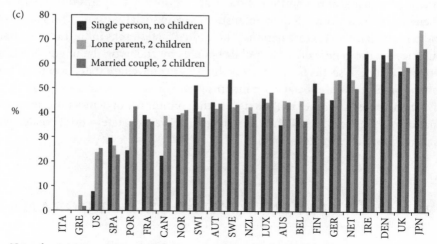

Net cash minimum assistance benefit as a percent of median household income (2010)

FIG. 7.2 Generosity of Social Programs.

Note: y axis = decommodification score

Source: OECD Stat ELS Pensions database http://stats.oecd.org/Index.aspx?DataSetCode=ELSPENSIONS

employment. The expansion of private old-age pension provision after WWII, however, means that public expenditure figures underestimate actual pension spending in the United States. Tax incentives for private pension provision would raise total pension spending considerably if they were included in accounts of social expenditure (Adema, Fron, and Ladaique 2011, 29–30). Like welfare states in other patronage-based political systems—for example, Southern Europe, Japan, Austria—the United States is a pension-heavy welfare state. Social Security benefits place a relatively effective safety net beneath senior citizens, something that cannot be said for all other program areas in the United States, but the private nature of much old-age provision in the United States entails significant stratification of risk within the elderly population.

Health care. The United States spends more than twice as much on health care per capita, from public and private sources, as the average rich OECD country (OECD 2012). Higher costs in the United States are largely a result of higher prices, not of major differences in the volume of services provided (Anderson et al. 2003). Until recently, the United States was unique in the advanced OECD countries for neither requiring enrollment in social or private health insurance plans, nor offering universally available primary health care services at minimal cost. Medicare, Medicaid, the Veterans Administration Health Service, and the Indian Health Service provided social insurance or national-health-service-type coverage for significant segments of the public. However, as of 2012, almost 50 million Americans remained without any health insurance coverage, and were entitled by federal law only to "stabilization" of life-threatening medical conditions. Upon implementation of the Patient Protection and Affordable Care Act (ACA) in 2014, the United States, like Switzerland and the Netherlands, relies on regulated private insurance markets and an individual obligation to purchase insurance to provide protection against the risk of ill health. Unlike these countries, however, neither U.S. states nor the federal government are required to provide insurance coverage for all citizens unable to afford insurance on private markets.

Unemployment benefits. A national system of unemployment insurance developed late in the United States (1935) compared to the United Kingdom (1911), France (1914), or Germany (1927). Each U.S. state operates distinct unemployment insurance schemes, but benefits are generally lower and of shorter duration in the United States than in most other developed OECD countries (see Figure 7.2). The United States joins Italy and Greece in offering no insurance against the risk of unemployment for first-time job seekers, which means that young adults unable to find employment must rely either on family support or social assistance benefits, for which childless adults may not be eligible.

Labor market policy. The United States maintains an unusually liberal labor market. Aside from rendering tax relief to attract businesses, neither the federal nor state-level governments frequently participate actively to promote employment. The United States' reluctance to spend substantial resources on job training or job creation, documented by Weir (1992), stands in contrast to many other OECD countries. Despite some local exceptions, the United States as a whole also has a weakly developed vocational education system compared to many European welfare states, in which publicly sponsored programs train and certify workers with specific skills that match the requirements of local businesses (Estevez-Abe et al. 2001). The United States also regulates employment and dismissal comparatively lightly: employers are required to make contributions for a limited range of social benefits, at-will employment contracts are the norm, and employers may essentially hire and fire workers at will. Even those European countries that have substantially liberalized their labor markets in the last decades have done so mainly by introducing short-term contracts, not by blanket reductions on the social duties of employers as a whole.

Social assistance and poverty relief. Whereas most advanced welfare states now have national-level, time-unlimited cash assistance programs designed to supply all citizens and households with an acceptable "minimum income," the federal Temporary Assistance for Needy Families (TANF) program allows for considerable state-level discretion in benefits and eligibility. Single childless men may be excluded from aid altogether, and aid for single female heads of households with children may be subject to time limits and contingent on work requirements. Cash transfers and services for the poor are often administered in a stigmatizing manner (Soss 2000; Schneider and Ingram 1993), and benefits are set low so as to encourage participation in a labor market in which the minimum wage still leaves many families with full-time earners in poverty. America's largest antipoverty program is, in fact, the Earned Income Tax Credit (EITC), which offers tax benefits to the working poor. Low wages lead to a relatively high prevalence of in-work poverty in the United States (12 percent as compared to an average of 6 percent in the rich OECD countries [data from OECD 2009, chapter 3]).

Child and family benefits. The United States is also a major outlier in the area of policies for families and children: paid parental leave, child allowances, public financing, and provision of care for young children (Gornick and Meyers 2005). The United States is unique in the OECD, and indeed is one of only four countries worldwide, in not offering paid leave with job protection for women following childbirth (Heymann et al. 2006). Fewer limitations on working hours and less paid leave and vacation give American parents less time to spend with children (Heymann et al. 2006). Unlike most West European countries, the United States does not offer per-child cash benefits for parents of dependent children. Tax credits for dependent children in the United States play a similar role, but even taking these into account, the United States spends less per child on allowances than most other rich countries; only Australia, New Zealand, and the United Kingdom paid less for single-earner, two-parent, two-child families in 1999 (Boeckmann, Budig, and Misra 2012).

The United States also offers relatively limited tax subsidies for child care and few public child-care spots. With the exception of 10 percent of spaces that may be set aside for families above the poverty line, eligibility for Head Start early childhood education programs is limited to children in families with incomes below the federal poverty level, in foster care, or receiving TANF benefits or SSI (Supplemental Security Income) (U.S. Dept. of Health and Human Services 2007, 1–2). No federal programs are aimed at providing broadly available care for 0–2- year-olds. Several states have universal pre-K programs for 3- and/or 4-year-olds, but the majority of state-level programs are not open to all children, and at less than 60 percent, the United States has the lowest rate of enrollment in preprimary (ages 3–5) education of any advanced industrial country save

Finland and New Zealand (Heymann et al. 2004). By way of contrast, France instituted public preschools in the late 19th century, and virtually all children ages 3–6 in France are enrolled in preprimary education.

Taken together, American child and family policies offer relatively little protection from child poverty, which is, by far, the highest in the OECD at 23 percent after taxes and transfers, and provide limited public support for the cognitive and emotional development of children, particularly poor children (Heymann et al. 2004, 2006). Siaroff (1994) has noted a strong negative correlation between public support for families with children and child poverty rates after accounting for taxes and social transfers. The United States scores at the bottom on both indicators (Pontusson 2005, 161).

Housing. Housing policy is often neglected as part of the welfare state, in part because of the many policy levers aside from direct public spending that affect the supply of housing (e.g., tax subsidies for developers, land-use restrictions, regulation of mortgage markets). Nevertheless, affordable, stable housing is an essential component of personal security that has implications for health and other social outcomes (Pollack and Lynch 2009, Pollack et al. 2010). True to the United States's generally liberal orientation, government has had very little direct involvement in constructing housing, with only 5–7 percent of all housing units either directly built by or subsidized by the federal government (Bardhan, Edelstein, and Kroll 2011, 7). Since the founding of Fannie Mae in 1938, government involvement in housing policy has included regulation of mortgage markets and guarantees of privately contracted mortgages. The tax code has been the other main tool for U.S. housing policy, including the significant tax exemption on mortgage interest (which, in 2012, will account for an estimated $105 billion [Center for American Progress 2012]) and the failure to tax imputed rent for owner-occupiers.

Both of these tax policies work to promote owner-occupation as the normative form of housing tenure. About two-thirds of housing units in the United States are owner-occupied—roughly similar to the other English-speaking countries, significantly higher than in Scandinavia, and significantly lower than in Southern Europe (Norris and Winston 2012). Government support of owner-occupied housing, if it comes at the expense of social (public) housing, is likely to limit income redistribution (Fahey and Norris 2011, 491). The U.S. housing policy profile, combined with a fragile safety net, has made lower- to middle-income households in the United States particularly vulnerable to housing market shocks. However, there is some evidence that government support for home ownership encourages redistribution across the life course, with housing assets substituting for other forms of income in old age (Castles 1998, DeWilde and Raeymaeckers 2008).

4 Structural Characteristics of The American Welfare State

Abstracting from the policy differences outlined earlier, four aspects of the organization and outputs of the U.S. welfare state stand out as unusual: the reliance on private provision; the degree of decentralized discretion; the persistent logic of deservingness; and the bias toward the elderly.

Private provision. The American welfare state relies to an exceptional extent on the market, rather than the state, to provide social goods. In many countries, both public and private entities provide health care, occupational pensions, child care, housing, and higher education. But only in the United States is the private sector the predominant provider of so many of them. Such an extensive system of private social provision has not emerged organically; it has been engendered by an ideology of the superiority of markets solutions, and by an extensive (and expensive) set of direct and indirect public subsidies to promote the provision and consumption of private benefits and services (Stevens 1988; Howard 1997; Hacker 2002).

Decentralized discretion. Even in nominally unitary states, subnational units may have important responsibilities for raising revenue, planning service delivery, and carrying out central mandates. Across welfare states, there is wide variety in the responsibilities delegated to subnational units, in the extent of redistribution of tax revenues across these units, and the extent of subnational variation in welfare outcomes. However, in most countries, standards for key welfare state attributes like population coverage, benefit packages, and eligibility criteria are agreed upon and enforceable by the national government.

U.S. states and localities, on the other hand, have significant discretion in establishing the *content* of even those welfare policies that the federal government mandates and finances. Furthermore, the fact that so much of the U.S. federal government's welfare activity comes in the form of low-visibility tax benefits and subsidies for private activity means that state- and local-level policies often appear to be where most of the welfare state "action" is in the United States The sheer size and diversity of the United States in cultural and economic terms also means that sub-national-level control and financing of welfare state institutions can lead to substantial geographic differentiation in programs and outcomes.

Logic of deservingness. If welfare state decentralization varies in degrees across the advanced democracies, the persistent and often explicit motivation of U.S. welfare policy by a logic of deservingness is really a difference in kind. Much of the expansion of the welfare state in Europe and elsewhere in the post-WWII period was justified politically by a rhetoric of social inclusion and solidarity that resonated nearly as strongly with the Christian social tradition as with the social democratic one (Kersbergen 1995; Berman 2006). Christian democratic and social democratic actors may have privileged different aspects of social inclusion, but welfare policies across Western Europe, Canada, and the Antipodes reflected the principle of inclusion with elements of universal entitlement based on need and adequacy. America, on the other hand, has maintained a welfare state logic that instead prioritizes personal responsibility, help for the deserving only, and the principle of "less eligibility."

This feature is particularly noticeable in the field of social assistance, as "welfare" beneficiaries are particularly strongly stigmatized (see e.g. Soss 2000; Schneider and Ingram 1993). Even in other program areas—for example, Social Security, Medicaid, primary and secondary education, public housing, programs for the long-term unemployed—the U.S. welfare state has maintained eligibility criteria and benefit levels that are quite explicit in their intent of excluding the undeserving (the idle and shiftless, noncitizens, those without lengthy contribution records, those who live in poor areas, drug users, convicted felons, etc.) from social solidarity, rather than reintegrating or rehabilitating them.

Elderly orientation. The population deemed by many to be most deserving of access to social support in the United States is consistently the elderly (Cook 1992). In addition to this cultural support, seniors have a powerful and effective lobby group, the AARP, and an activated electorate (Campbell 2003). The combination of the elderly's social and electoral desirability has merged with the particularistic political strategies of American politicians to make the United States one of the world's most elderly oriented welfare states (Lynch 2006, Ozawa and Lee 2013). Older Americans' access to social benefits has been consistently defended and expanded, whereas supports for working-aged adults and children are less emphasized, and less well funded. Aggregate spending data and analysis of individual income from social transfers show a distinct elderly orientation in the United States (Figure 7.3). Lynch (2006) further found a distinct skew toward the elderly in the United States in both tax expenditures for social purposes, and in health care spending.

Pontusson reports that only "[t]ransfer spending that is not targeted on the elderly has a strong positive effect on redistribution among working-age households [...]" (Pontusson 2005, 158). As a result of this elderly orientation of social spending in the United States, poverty, child poverty, and income inequality among the nonelderly population in the United States are all well above the OECD average (see chapters on poverty and inequality in this volume). Unfortunately, the same processes that drive elderly oriented social policy also tend to produce stratification of pension benefits, with the paradoxical result that elderly oriented welfare states like the United States also tend to have higher-than-average poverty among the elderly (Lynch 2006, 182).

5 COMPARATIVE WELFARE STATE DEVELOPMENT

Why does the U.S. welfare state not more closely resemble those of other rich countries? In ordinary public conversation, theories abound, including our Protestant heritage, our large and heterogeneous nation, the legacy of slavery, and the absence of a socialist party. Although each of these explanations contains a kernel of truth, none fully accounts for cross-national similarities *and* cross-national variation in welfare state institutions and outcomes. Comparative welfare state research has centered on the trinity of interests, ideas, and institutions to explain this variation.

Interests. Who was for and against the development of social policies in the United States? How do these coalitions compare to those in other countries? The configuration of

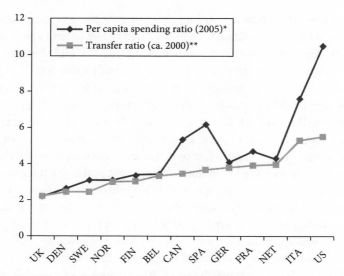

FIG. 7.3 Ratio of social spending on elderly/non-elderly populations.

Source: Ozawa and Lee (2012, Table 2)

interest groups in the United States did not augur well for the development of comprehensive, solidaristic welfare states. The strong sectoral split between the industrializing North and agricultural South, whose plantation economy relied on labor-repressive agriculture until well after emancipation, did nothing to encourage solidaristic social insurance programs, which more typically developed when smallholding land-owners formed coalitions with nascent urban working-class movements (Baldwin 1990; Esping-Andersen 1990). America did have a politically assertive smallholding class, centered in the country's Midwest and West, but despite their early joint success in establishing an income tax (Morgan and Prasad 2009), working-class partners for agrarian mobilization were notably weak. At the dawn of the American welfare state, unions were fragmented and lacking in the political "power resources" that have been hypothesized to drive welfare state expansion (Korpi 1983; Esping-Andersen 1985). Similarly, and in contrast to the strong social democratic parties in many parts of Europe, the United States has from the beginning lacked a labor-based party. As a result, "red-green" alliances of the type that drove welfare state expansion elsewhere were impossible in the United States.

Although there is much evidence for the argument that weak power resources on the left determined the relatively small size and private nature of the U.S. welfare state, it is not the whole story. Abundant comparative research has shown labor's power alone has not built welfare states—employers have played an important role as well (Mares 2006; Swank and Martin 2001; Swenson 1989). The United States' weak and fragmented organizations of employers, too, discouraged the formation of neocorporatist bargaining structures that elsewhere paved the way for comprehensive welfare states (Martin and Swank 2004). It would also be a mistake to view organized labor as a nonactor in the construction of the welfare state, at least after WWII. In fact, American labor (particularly the CIO), through its collective bargaining, aided the growth of substantial *private* welfare benefits like pensions and health care in the United States (Quadagno and Harrington Meyer 1989; Gottschalk 2000; Klein 2003), and played an important role in the development of public programs such as Medicare.

Ideas. Shared values surely explain some of the divergence between the United States and other welfare states. The Liberal welfare state embodies both an ideology—individual responsibility and laissez-faire liberalism—and a set of typical policies—means-testing, low benefits, reliance on markets. But the United States and the other Liberal welfare states like the United Kingdom are hardly carbon copies, as we have seen. A different hypothesized reason for the logic of deservingness that underlies American welfare policy is America's Puritan background, which is said to imbue our national discourse with a Protestant ethic that privileges work as the only road to salvation, and hence has resulted in welfare policies that are particularly meager and punitive toward those who are perceived as unwilling to work (Kahl 2009). But U.S. culture has many non-Protestant influences as well, and the predominantly Protestant countries of Northern Europe have welfare states marked by their universalism and generosity. So if we are to use ideas to explain the American welfare state's distinctive features, we must be more specific about the precise content of those ideas, and how they make their way into policies.

More than 20 years ago, sociologist Seymour Martin Lipset sought to outline the key features of the "American creed:" (negative) liberty, equality (of opportunity,) individualism, populism, and opposition to government intervention (Lipset 1989). To this list should be added the ideology of white supremacy, which has, as we shall see later, become embodied in the institutions of the welfare state. American values may indeed be causally related to the limited reach of direct state intervention to achieve redistribution (Brooks and Manza 2007; Page and Jacobs 2009), just as values of social solidarity, a strong state role, and equality of outcomes may have resulted in the construction of more comprehensive welfare states elsewhere (Brooks and Manza 2007; Svallfors 2007). However, existing social policies may themselves cause core values and beliefs about social solidarity among the public (Mau 2003; Rothstein and Uslaner 2005; Brooks and Manza 2007; Svallfors 2007). Powerful policy feedback effects make it hazardous to read welfare policies straightforwardly as results of public values.

Institutions. The translation of values and policy ideas into policies must occur by way of social and political institutions like political parties, legislatures, and labor and employer organizations. Comparative research has shed light on other institutions that may have even stronger effects on the contours of social policy. In numerous cross-national and case studies, multiple institutional veto points (such as those imposed by federal state structures, presidential systems, bicameral legislatures, and independent judiciaries) have been found to inhibit welfare-policy expansion (see, e.g., Immergut 1992; Huber, Ragin, Stephens 1993; Steinmo and Watts 1995). The United States' numerous institutional veto points have likely contributed to delays in the adoption of universal social programs, as well as to political compromises that have limited entitlements (see the chapter on institutions in this volume).

Veto points may have other important consequences, too. In a political context with large numbers of veto points, politicians will be tempted to turn to low-visibility tools— for example, tax expenditures as opposed to direct transfers or services, or policy drift as opposed to public debates over benefit levels (Hacker and Pierson 2010)—in order to secure their desired policy outcomes. In the American context, the use of low-visibility subsidies for private welfare activities has resulted in an ever-more private welfare "state," since the early adoption of private or particularistic solutions to collective welfare problems tends to make it more difficult to construct encompassing public programs later on (Hacker 2002; Lynch 2006).

Institutions of electoral competition, too, may explain the shape and redistributive capacity of welfare states. Iversen and Soskice (2006) find evidence that majoritarian electoral systems are associated with less redistribution because parties representing lower- and middle-class voters have less incentive to cooperate in pursuit of progressive tax and transfer regimes in majoritarian systems as compared to PR systems. Informal electoral institutions, too, may shape the welfare state in profound ways. The patronage-based party system of 19th- and early 20th-century America fueled growth of Civil War pensions and inhibited progress toward more universalistic measures (Skocpol 1992), and Lynch (2006) finds that, in a comparative context, particularistic electoral competition tends to produce more elderly oriented social spending.

Finally, the institution of white racial supremacy has had a profound effect on the American welfare state. The neo-Elizabethan emphasis in American welfare policy on deservingness noted earlier has persisted at least in part because of the association of African Americans with many of the characteristics deemed most undeserving. Some early welfare policies in the United States explicitly targeted African Americans for exclusion (Better 2008). New Deal policies did so indirectly, by excluding job classifications likely to be occupied by African Americans. Since the War on Poverty, social assistance and community development policies have become associated with African American beneficiaries and, as a result, have become less popular with the majority of the public (Quadagno 1994; Gilens 1999).

Most welfare states in the advanced democracies were built before there were significant nonwhite minorities in the population. Although religious and linguistic cleavages may have pushed some Continental European welfare states away from universalistic policies at the dawn of the welfare state, most of these welfare states took decisive steps toward broad, citizenship-based policies in the post-WWII period. In the United States, however, the racialization of welfare policy continued and in some cases intensified after WWII. Racial prejudice that was rooted in America's experience with African slavery filtered through a party system based on alliance between Northern industrialists and Southern landowners, and it affected welfare policy development in the United States. The result was a welfare state that allowed a very high level of subnational discretion over welfare policy, and a heightened emphasis on deservingness criteria.

6 ADAPTATIONS SINCE THE 1970S

Similar challenges have confronted welfare states in the OECD area since the mid-1970s: slower growth than in the post-World War II boom, deindustrialization, the disappearance of lifelong employment, the decline of the male-breadwinner-centered family model, population ageing, immigration, and the maturation of expensive social entitlement programs (Pontusson 2005; Esping-Andersen 1999; Pierson 2001). The United States has been somewhat buffered, however. Its large internal market, dollar-denominated currency reserves, and slower population ageing (due largely to high fertility among recent immigrants) have relieved pressure for austerity in the post-oil shock, and now post-financial crisis, periods.

Despite these advantages, however, the U.S. welfare state has also inherited unique challenges in accommodating to new social and economic realities. Many welfare states have reallocated their spending portfolios or invented new programs in order to better insure their populations against "new social risks" arising from economic and demographic shifts (Armingeon and Bonoli 2006; Häusermann 2010). However, several sources of rigidity have made it more difficult for the U.S. welfare state to adapt to the new environment. Nonportable employment-based pensions and health insurance prevent labor mobility and adjustment. The continuing importance of the race cleavage, as well as the newer wedge issue of immigration, has made it hard to introduce reforms that would strengthen the social safety net, rehabilitate segregated neighborhoods and schools, and improve the life chances of young Americans. Meanwhile, multiple institutional veto points and the severe elderly orientation of social spending in the United States have made it more difficult to adjust the welfare state to compensate for new social risks.

The American approach to welfare state reform since 1973 has been in some ways quite similar to other countries, particularly those in Esping-Andersen's Liberal world. Like other liberal welfare states, the United States has sought to avert fiscal catastrophe in a slow-growth world by promoting employment in private markets, spurring job growth with light labor market regulation, low wages, and low public social benefits (Iversen and Wren 1998); and compensating for the decreasing availability of public funds by shifting back onto individuals the burden of insuring themselves against risk (Hacker 2006). If the policy responses to new economic conditions are similar among liberal states, however, the liberal imprint has been more marked in the United States. The United States has relied on even lower wages and allowed much greater income inequality. Similarly, whereas many countries have adopted labor market activation policies, the United States has done it in a way that is both punitive and reminiscent of its traditional emphasis on deservingness (Levy 2004).

Despite the fiscal and institutional limits on welfare state expansion, welfare states have continued to grow, and the United States is no exception: Major new programs including the EITC, the Medicare prescription drug benefit, the State Children's Health Insurance Program (SCHIP), and the ACA have emerged since the 1970s. However, whereas welfare reforms in many other countries have focused on adapting the welfare state to new types of risk, expansions to the welfare state in the United States have, with the exception of SCHIP and the ACA, reinforced old patterns of elderly oriented spending and benefits for worthy (working) adults. In order for the U.S. welfare state to adjust successfully to insure against new social risks, it will need to focus more on key, underdeveloped program areas like health care, child care, early childhood education, and vocational training.

7 Conclusion

The American welfare state is distinctive from a cross-national comparative perspective. The protections against social risks that the U.S. welfare state affords to its citizens, particularly its younger and poorer citizens, are both narrower and shallower than in many other rich democracies. Nevertheless, the U.S. welfare state is not *sui generis*. The actors involved in the construction of the U.S. welfare state, the institutions created in response to social problems, and the contemporary pressures confronting the welfare state all have parallels in other countries. It may be tempting to view the welfare system as somehow more private, less statelike, in the United States than elsewhere, but the markets that provide so many social goods in the United States are the products of state action and state regulation, and hence should really be thought of as part of the welfare "state." Hence, in this case, comparisons are not odious but both justified and useful. If the U.S. welfare state comes off as odorous, as Shakespeare's Dogberry would have it, it should not invalidate the comparison, but rather spur the public and policy-makers to demand better.

References

* Indicates recommended reading.

*Adema, Willem, Pauline Fron, and Maxime Ladaique. 2011. *Is the European Welfare State Really More Expensive? Indicators on Social Spending, 1980–2012; and a Manual to the OECD Social Expenditure Database (SOCX)*. Paris: OECD.

Anderson, Gerard F., Uwe E. Reinhardt, Peter S. Hussey, and Varduhi Petrosyan. 2003. "It's the Prices, Stupid: Why The United States Is So Different From Other Countries." *Health Affairs* 22 (3): 89–105.

Armingeon, Klaus, and Giuliano Bonoli 2006. *The Politics of Post-Industrial Welfare States: Adapting Post-War Social Policies to New Social Risks*. London and New York: Routledge.

Baldwin, Peter 1990. *The Politics of Social Solidarity: Class Bases in the European Welfare State, 1875-1975*. Cambridge and New York: Cambridge University Press.

Bambra, Clare 2006. "Research Note: Decommodification and the Worlds of Welfare Revisited." *Journal of European Social Policy* 16 (1): 73–80.

Bardhan, Ashok, Robert Edelstein, and Cynthia A Kroll. 2011. *A Comparative Context for United States Housing Policy: Housing Markets and the Financial Crisis in Europe, Asia, and Beyond.* Washington, DC: Bipartisan Policy Center.

Berman, Sheri 2006. *The Primacy of Politics: Social Democracy and the Making of Europe's Twentieth Century.* New York: Cambridge University Press.

Better, S. J. 2008. *Institutional Racism: A Primer on Theory and Strategies for Social Change.* Lanham, MD: Rowman & Littlefield.

Boeckmann, I., M. Budig, and J. Misra. 2012. *The Work-Family Policy Indicators Dataset.* Department of Sociology, University of Massachusetts, Amherst.

Brooks, Clem and Jeff Manza. 2007. *Why Welfare States Persist: The Importance of Public Opinion in Democracies.* Chicago: University of Chicago Press.

Campbell, Andrea L. 2003. *How Policies Make Citizens: Senior Political Activism and the American Welfare State.* Princeton: Princeton University Press.

Castles, Francis G. 1998. "The Really Big Trade-Off: Home-Ownership and the Welfare State in the New World and the Old." *Acta Politica* 33 (1): 5–19.

*Castles, Francis G. 2010. "The English-Speaking Countries." In F. G. Castles, S. Leibfried, J. Lewis, H. Obinger and C. Pierson, eds., *The Oxford Handbook of the Welfare State.* Oxford: Oxford University Press, 630–642.

Center for American Progress. 2012. "Tax Expenditure of the Week: The Mortgage Interest Tax Deduction." www.americanprogress.org/issues/open-government/news/2011/01/26/8866/tax-expenditure-of-the-week-the-mortgage-interest-deduction/.

Cook, Fax Lomax, Barrett 1992. *Support for the American Welfare State: The Views of Congress and the Public.* New York: Columbia University Press.

DeWilde, Caroline, and Peter Raeymaeckers. 2008. "The Trade-Off between Home-Ownership and Pensions: Individual and Institutional Determinants of Old-Age Poverty." *Ageing & Society* 28 (6): 805–830.

Esping-Anderson, Gosta. 1985. *Politics against Markets: The Social Democratic Road to Power.* Princeton: Princeton University Press.

*Esping-Anderson, Gosta. 1990. *The Three Worlds of Welfare Capitalism.* Princeton, NJ: Princeton University Press.

Esping-Anderson, Gosta. 1999. *Social Foundations of Postindustrial Economies.* Oxford and New York: Oxford University Press.

Estevez-Abe, Margarita, Torben Iversen, and David Soskice. 2001. "Social Protection and the Formation of Skills: A Reinterpretation of the Welfare State." In D. Soskice and P. Hall, eds., *Varieties of Capitalism: The Institutional Foundations of Comparative Advantage.* Oxford: Oxford University Press, 145–183.

Fahey, Tony, and Michelle Norris. 2011. "Housing in the Welfare State: Rethinking the Conceptual Foundations of Comparative Housing Policy Analysis." *International Journal of Housing Policy* 11 (4): 439–452.

Gilens, Martin. 1999. *Why Americans Hate Welfare: Race, Media, and the Politics of Antipoverty Policy.* Chicago: University of Chicago Press.

*Gornick, Janet C. and Marcia K. Meyers. 2005. *Families That Work: Policies for Reconciling Parenthood and Employment.* New York: Sage.

Gottschalk, Marie. 2000. *The Shadow Welfare State: Labor, Business, and the Politics of Health Care in the United States.* Ithaca, NY: ILR Press.

Hacker, Jacob and Paul Pierson. 2010. "Drift and Democracy: The Neglected Politics of Policy Inaction." Annual Meeting of the American Political Science Association, Washington, DC.

Hacker, Jacob S. 2002. *The Divided Welfare State: The Battle over Public and Private Social Benefits in the United States*. Cambridge and New York: Cambridge University Press.

Hacker, Jacob S. 2006. *The Great Risk Shift: The Assault on American Jobs, Families, Health Care, and Retirement and How You Can Fight Back*. Oxford and New York: Oxford University Press.

Häusermann, Silja. 2010. *The Politics of Welfare State Reform in Continental Europe: Modernization in Hard Times*. Cambridge and New York: Cambridge University Press.

Heymann, Jody, Jeffrey Heyes, and Alison Earle. 2006. *The Work, Family and Equity Index: How Does the United States Measure Up?* Montreal: Project on Global Working Families.

Heymann, Jody, Alison Earle, Stephanie Simmons, Stephanie M. Breslow, and April Kuehnhof. 2004. *The Work, Family, and Equity Index: Where Does the United States Stand Globally?* Boston: Harvard School of Public Health.

Howard, Christopher. 1997. *The Hidden Welfare State: Tax Expenditures and Social Policy in the United States*. Princeton, NJ: Princeton University Press.

Huber, Evelyne, Charles Ragin, and John D. Stephens. 1993. "Social Democracy, Christian Democracy, Constitutional Structure, and the Welfare State." *American Journal of Sociology* 99 (3): 711–749.

Immergut, Ellen M. (1992). *Health Politics: Interests and Institutions in Western Europe*. Cambridge and New York: Cambridge University Press.

Iversen, Torben and David Soskice. 2006. "Electoral Institutions and the Politics of Coalitions: Why Some Democracies Redistribute More Than Others." *American Political Science Review* 100 (2): 165–181.

Iversen, Torben, and Anne Wren. 1998. "Equality, Employment, and Budgetary Restraint: The Trilemma of the Service Economy." *World Politics* 50 (4): 507–546.

Kahl, Sigrun. 2009. "Religious Doctrines and Poor Relief: A Different Causal Pathway." In Kees van Kersbergen and Philip Manow, eds., *Religion, Class Coalitions, and Welfare States*. Cambridge and New York: Cambridge University Press, 267–295.

Kersbergen, Kees van. 1995. *Social Capitalism: A Study of Christian Democracy and the Welfare State*. London and New York: Routledge.

Klein, Jennifer. 2003. *For All These Rights: Business, Labor, and the Shaping of America's Public-Private Welfare State*. Princeton, NJ: Princeton University Press.

Korpi, Walter. 1983. *The Democratic Class Struggle*. London and Boston: Routledge & Kegan Paul.

Levy, Jonah. 2004. "Activation Through Thick and Thin: Progressive Strategies for Increasing Labor Force Participation." In M. A. Levin and M. N. Shapiro, eds., *Transatlantic Policymaking in an Age of Austerity: Diversity and Drift*. Washington, DC: Georgetown University Press, 100–130.

Lipset, Symour Martin. 1989. *Continental Divide: The Values and Institutions of the United States and Canada*. Toronto: Canadian-American Committee.

Lynch, Julia. 2006. *Age in the Welfare State: The Origins of Social Spending on Pensioners, Workers, and Children*. Cambridge and New York: Cambridge University Press.

Mares, Isabela. 2006. *Taxation, Wage Bargaining and Unemployment*. Cambridge and New York: Cambridge University Press.

Marshall, Thomas H. 1950. "Citizenship and Social Class." In T. H. Marshall, ed., *Citizenship and Social Class and Other Essays*. Cambridge: Cambridge University Press.

Martin, Cathie Jo, and Duane Swank. 2004. "Does the Organization of Capital Matter? Employers and Active Labor Market Policy at the National and Firm Levels." *American Political Science Review* 98 (4): 593–611.

Mau, Steffen. 2003. *The Moral Economy of Welfare States: Britain and Germany Compared.* London and New York: Routledge.

Mettler, Suzanne. 2011. *The Submerged State: How Invisible Government Policies Undermine American Democracy.* Chicago: University of Chicago Press.

Morgan, Kimberly, and Monica Prasad 2009. "The Origins of Tax Systems: A French-American Comparison." *American Journal of Sociology* 114 (5): 1350–1394.

Norris, Michelle, and Nessa Winston. 2012. "Home-Ownership, Housing Regimes and Income Inequalities in Western Europe." *International Journal of Social Welfare* 21 (2): 127–138.

OECD. 2009. *Employment Outlook 2009.* Paris: OECD.

OECD. 2012. *OECD Health Data 2012.* Paris: OECD.

Ozawa, Martha, and Yung Soo Lee. 2013. "Generational Inequity in Social Spending: The United States in Comparative Perspective." *International Social Work* 56 (2): 162–169.

Page, Benjamin I., and Lawrence R. 2009. *Class War?: What Americans Really Think about Economic Inequality.* Chicago: University of Chicago Press.

Pierson, Paul. 2001. "Post-Industrial Pressures on the Mature Welfare States." In P. Pierson, ed., *The New Politics of the Welfare State.* Oxford and New York: Oxford University Press, 80–104.

Pollack, Craig Evan, Beth Ann Griffin, and Julia Lynch. et al. 2010. "Housing Affordability and Health Among Homeowners and Renters." *American Journal of Preventive Medicine* 39 (6): 515–521.

Pollack, Craig Evan, and Julia Lynch. 2009. "Health Status of People Undergoing Foreclosure in the Philadelphia Region." *American Journal of Public Health* 99 (10): 1833–1839.

*Pontusson, Jonas. 2005. *Inequality and Prosperity: Social Europe vs. Liberal America.* Ithaca, NY: Cornell University Press.

Quadagno, Jill 1994. *The Color of Welfare: How Racism Undermined the War on Poverty.* New York: Oxford University Press.

Quadagno, Jill, and Madonna Harrington Meyer. 1989. "Organized Labor, State Structures and Social Policy Development: A Case Study of Old Age Assistance in Ohio, 1916–1940." *Social Problems* 36 (2): 177–192.

Rothstein, Bo, and Eric M. Uslaner. 2005. "All for All: Equality, Corruption, and Social Trust." *World Politics* 58 (1): 41–72.

Schmitt, Carina, and Peter Starke. 2011. "Explaining Convergence of OECD Welfare States: A Conditional Approach." *Journal of European Social Policy* 21 (2): 120–135.

Schneider, Anne, and Helen Ingram. 1993. "Social Construction of Target Populations: Implications for Politics and Policy." *American Political Science Review* 87 (2): 334–347.

Scruggs, Lyle, and James Allan. 2006. "Welfare-State Decommodification in 18 OECD Countries: A Replication and Revision." *Journal of European Social Policy* 16 (1): 55–72.

Siaroff, Alan. 1994. "Work, Welfare and Gender Equality: A New Typology." In Diane Sainsbury, ed., *Gendering Welfare States.* London: Sage, 82–101.

Skocpol, Theda 1992. *Protecting Soldiers and Mothers: The Political Origins of Social Policy in the United States.* Cambridge, MA: Belknap Press of Harvard University Press.

Soss, Joe. 2000. *Unwanted Claims: The Politics of Participation in the United States Welfare System.* Ann Arbor: University of Michigan Press.

Steinmo, Sven, and Jon Watts. 1995. "It's the Institutions, Stupid! Why Comprehensive National Health Insurance Always Fails in America." *Journal of Health Politics, Policy and Law* 20 (2): 329–372.

Stevens, Beth. 1988. "Blurring the Boundaries: How the Federal Government Has Influenced Welfare Benefits in the Private Sector." In Margaret Weir, Ann S. Orloff, and Theda Skocpol, eds., *The Politics of Social Policy in the United States*. Princeton, NJ: Princeton University Press, 123–148.

Svallfors, Stefan., ed. 2007. *The Political Sociology of the Welfare State: Institutions, Social Cleavages, and Orientations*. Stanford, CA: Stanford University Press.

Swank, Duane, and Cathie Jo Martin. 2001. "Employers and the Welfare State." *Comparative Political Studies* 34 (8): 889–923.

Swenson, Peter. 1989. *Fair Shares: Unions, Pay, and Politics in Sweden and West Germany*. Ithaca, NY: Cornell University Press.

Titmuss, Richard M. 1958. *Essays on the Welfare State*. London: Allen and Unwin.

Weir, Margaret. 1992. *Politics and Jobs: The Boundaries of Employment Policy in the United States*. Princeton, NJ: Princeton University Press.

U.S. Department of Health and Human Services. 2007. "Enrollment Levels in Head Start, Department of Health and Human Services, Office of Inspector General." http://oig.hhs.gov/oei/reports/oei-05-06-00250.pdf.

PART III

THEORIES

CHAPTER 8

....

CULTURAL INFLUENCES ON SOCIAL POLICY DEVELOPMENT

....

J. TAYLOR DANIELSON AND ROBIN STRYKER

1 INTRODUCTORY OVERVIEW
....

IN their 2005 overview of comparative welfare state research, two influential scholars of social policy development noted that the power distributions of societal interests and state institutions have been treated as essential factors explaining how welfare states develop, expand, and contract over time (Huber and Stephens 2005, 567). However, these authors also noted that ideologies, or "self-conscious rationales and programs for political (and social) actions" (Goldstone 1991, 406), played an important role in driving cuts in state welfare provisions in the 1980s in the United States, New Zealand, and Great Britain. Drawing on literature emphasizing the causal force of cultural factors in social policy development, this chapter suggests that culture is far from a residual factor in understanding and explaining U.S. and comparative welfare state development. In the United States, culture—in the various meanings and roles that this chapter develops—has been an essential shaper of social policy.

Following Geertz (1973), we define culture broadly to include any "historically transmitted pattern of meaning embodied in symbols by means of which [people] communicate, perpetuate and develop their knowledge about and attitudes toward life" (Geertz 1973, 179). Our broad definition encompasses a number of social practices—and sociological concepts—as aspects of culture. These include ideas; ideologies; values; concepts and theories; categories; beliefs; attitudes; opinions; norms; cognitive schema and paradigms; frames; discourse; spoken, written, or signed language; and any material object to which meaning is attached. Each of these more specific concepts captures a unique aspect of culture; all shape social policies through meaning-making.

Indeed, meaning-making is the core of all cultural mechanisms influencing policy development. Like Froud and colleagues (2012, 80), we view conflicts over government agendas and policies as both interpretive and political-economic struggles, in which widely shared values and ideas both constrain the behaviors of political actors *and* provide them with political resources that can be used to recast policy debates, generate support for preferred policies, and undermine opponents' claims.

In this chapter we first explore how diverse aspects of culture play cognitive, normative-evaluative, and strategic roles in American social policy development (Campbell 1998, 2002; Steensland 2006; Béland 2009; Padamsee 2009; Schmidt 2008, Stryker and Wald 2009). Second, we review exemplary research exploring the relationship between different cultural forces and U.S. welfare state development. Third, we offer a series of methodological and theoretical suggestions about promising foci for future research. We conclude with some final thoughts about cultural influences on policy-making.

We argue that cultural factors alone are unlikely to provide a sufficient explanation for any aspect of U.S. social policy development. Yet understanding how cultural factors operate in the background and foreground of social policy debates is essential, because fully explaining the nature, timing, causes, and consequences of any particular American social policy development typically will require elucidating multiple aspects of—and roles played by—culture.

2 TYPES AND EXPLANATORY ROLES OF MEANING-MAKING IN U.S. SOCIAL POLICY DEVELOPMENT

The study of culture and its role in policy-making has experienced significant growth in the last 25 years. Discussions among political scientists tend to focus on "ideas" rather than "culture" (e.g. Bleich 2003; Schmidt 2008), but sociologists generally subsume ideas within a more generic concept of culture focusing on how "deep structures" of meaning, including fundamental values, and more surface frames of reference help guide action and make sense of material forces (see Alexander 2005; Eastwood 2005; Swidler 1986; Pedriana and Stryker 1997). When viewed from this perspective, ideas are aspects of culture that comprise "claims about descriptions of the world, causal relationships, or the normative legitimacy of certain actions" (Parsons 2002, 48). Ideas include assumptions as well as categories, discourse, and frames (Béland 2009; Schmidt 2008; Padamsee 2009).

Ideas enter policy-making in various ways. As Vivien Schmidt (2008, 306) noted, ideas operate "at three main levels of generality." The first signals specific policy solutions proposed by policy makers, the second refers to general programs providing the ideological foundation for these specific policy solutions, and the third encompasses what Campbell (1998, 2002) termed "public philosophies" or "public sentiments." Ideas at the programmatic level, including policy paradigms and programmatic beliefs, pro-vide assumptions, organizing principles, and frames of reference for policy develop-ment. Public philosophies or worldviews represent a "deep[er] core...of ideas, values and principles of knowledge and society" (Schmidt 2008, 306).

Because policy paradigms and programmatic beliefs typically are explicitly debated, they usually operate in the "foreground" of social policy-making (Schmidt 2008). Conversely, deeper worldviews—or what Somers and Block (2005) referred to as "ideational regimes"—tend to operate in the "background" of policy debates. Ideational regimes operate as taken-for-granted assumptions, constituting a broad but constraining cultural terrain for all phases of policy development, from agenda setting to policy enactment to policy administration. Ideational regimes are revealed in times of crisis when they become visible and open to contestation (Campbell 2002; Schmidt 2008).

Whether they operate in the foreground or background, policy paradigms, program-matic beliefs, and ideational regimes often are reinforced by or build upon other aspects of meaning-making, especially values. Values, or evaluative judgments or beliefs about whether something is good/bad or desirable/undesirable, may be foregrounded and debated explicitly. However, debates about specific extant meanings and implications of values typically are undergirded by more enduring "core" or "fundamental" values that are widespread and shared at an abstract and general level within societies or other discursive communities. Such fundamental values as democracy, freedom, liberalism, individualism, fairness, and equality of opportunity often are seen as defining features of American collective identity (Pedriana and Stryker 1997; Stryker and Wald 2009). These values typically convey different specific meanings across contexts and persons, and the widely noted "liberal value" tradition in the United States has coexisted with less noble value traditions such as white supremacy (Smith 1993; Quadagno 1994). In short, core values are similar to ideational regimes in that they provide an avail-able cultural repertoire that political actors can mobilize across time and space to (re) frame policy debates and influence policy development (Pedriana and Stryker 1997; Quadagno 2005).

Yet another aspect of culture—frames and framing—has garnered substantial attention among not only political scientists and sociologists, but also psychologists, economists, and communication scholars (Chong and Druckman 2007, 103). Some researchers define frames as overarching "cognitive and moral maps that orient an actor within a policy sphere" (Bleich 2003, 26; see also Guetzkow 2010, 175). Other researchers define frames more narrowly as "the central organizing idea[s] ... provid[ing] meaning to an unfolding strip of events" (Gamson and Modigliani 1987, 143; see also Benford and Snow 2000). Whereas frames as moral maps may operate in the background, frames as interpretive lenses for specific events typically operate in the foreground of policy debates, defining appropriate courses of action to address social problems (Schmidt 2008, 306) and evaluate the normative desirability/undesirability of each poten-tial policy (Gamson and Modigliani 1987, 143; Campbell 1998; see also Bleich 2003; Schmidt 2008, 306; Béland 2009; Stryker and Wald 2009). Elites and social movements alike engage in cognitive and normative aspects of framing purposefully or strategically to promote their preferred policies while undermining those of their opposition (Quadagno 2005; Pedriana and Stryker 1997).

The foregoing discussion is limited to those aspects of culture to which scholars of social policy have devoted the most attention. The following section provides empirical exemplars from U.S. social policy development to illustrate and develop further the explanatory power of this conceptual apparatus.

3 EMPIRICAL EXEMPLARS

3.1 Ideational Regimes and U.S. Policy Formation

Students of social science theory know that arguments about the causal role of ideas are not new; they date back at least to the classical writings of, among others, Karl Marx, Max Weber, and Antonio Gramsci (Zeitlin 2000; Gramsci 1995). Given these scholars' preoccupation with what we have called worldviews or ideational regimes—and notwithstanding their differences—none would be surprised at the profound role ideational regimes play in U.S. social policy development.

As illustrated by Clemens and Guthrie (2010), Somers and Bloch (2005), and Gieve and Provost (2012), conflict over the appropriate role of public and private relief and the impact of relief on aid recipients has been a durable feature of U.S. social policy. Clemens and Guthrie (2010) noted the widespread public perception, after the Civil War, that aiding the poor with public funds exemplified political corruption and encouraged sloth. This general belief set fostered private charitable aid and the development of public-private partnerships. But when voluntary organizations proved unable to aid the poor during the Great Depression of the 1930s, enduring economic crisis promoted political crisis. Charity became politicized and discredited, paving the way for public welfare programs (Clemens 2011; Clemens and Guthrie 2010).

The Red Cross proved pivotal in breaking down the old ideational and institutional antipoverty regimes in this period. President Herbert Hoover relied heavily on the voluntary actions of prominent businessmen and on the Red Cross to alleviate drought and unemployment. However, the Red Cross insisted that it could aid only victims of national disaster. It considered southern farmers to be architects of their own fate because they had opted for mono-crop agriculture (Clemens and Guthrie 2010, 85). The Red Cross's refusal to respond to southern drought and voluntary organizations' failure to alleviate unemployment spurred political actors to consider alternatives. Senator John Robinson (D-Ark.) proposed that the federal government provide $25 million to the Red Cross for food relief. When Hoover tried to defeat the proposal by emphasizing that the voluntary, charitable character of the Red Cross was fundamental to American collective identity, the Red Cross refused to accept federal aid, even though earlier it had accepted such aid to carry out its relief mission.

Interpreting the Red Cross's about-face as expressing its class-based alliance with the wealthy in opposing federal relief, defenders of the Robinson proposal reframed conflicts over federal relief in class-based terms, arguing that government funding of private aid organizations could not be considered the "dole." Rejecting assumptions about the superior moral virtues of private relief, opponents of voluntarism reconceptualized government relief as fully compatible with democratic citizenship. These new ideas paved the way for New Deal–instituted government antipoverty programs in the 1930s.

As illustrated by the New Deal, prior ideational regimes that no longer are embodied in government policies may experience periods of decline, yet they tend to be resistant to wholesale dismantlement. Regimes that have receded from dominance and are no longer institutionalized in government policies nonetheless persist, providing a repertoire of cultural resources that actors can mobilize with more or less policy success depending on diverse contextual factors. Such is the case with the worldview supporting private, voluntary poor relief in the United States.

Using a "most different cases" methodological strategy to compare enactments of the U.S. Personal Responsibility and Work Opportunity Act of 1996 (PRWORA) and Britain's 1834 New Poor Law, Somers and Block (2005) showed that in the post–World War II era in both the United States and United Kingdom, the dominant view was that labor markets were embedded in other social institutions, with poverty a structural condition for which the under- and unemployed were blameless. Still, even though political institutions and the dominant political culture had changed dramatically since the Depression, many people still believed that providing aid for the poor would create perverse incentives encouraging sloth. Both U.S. and UK actors mobilized this idea of perverse incentives strategically to act as a "wedge" for change from the "embedded markets" worldview to "market fundamentalism." The latter asserts that all social life, including social welfare programs, should be organized according to market principles. Once market fundamentalist ideas held sway, they became "causal mechanisms of revolutionary policy change" (Somers and Block 2005, 262).

Actors adopting perversity rhetoric argued that the welfare system established by the New Deal caused poverty by encouraging welfare dependency and other associated behavioral ills such as crime, illegitimacy, and idleness (Somers and Block 2005, 262). In turn, perversity rhetoric conjoined with the cultural strategy of value redefinition (discussed below) to promote enactment of the PRWORA. This legislation embodied free market values complemented by decentralization, voluntarism, and the reprivatization of relief in, for example, private faith-based social services (Stryker and Wald 2009).

When an ideational regime is fully entrenched in state policies, government elites may not perceive the need for substantial policy change until *after* a crisis has occurred to challenge the ideational regime. This can be seen dramatically in accounts of the 2007–2009 U.S. financial crisis, which followed many years of "light touch" regulatory policies embodying the idea that excessive government interference adversely affects markets, including financial markets (Gieve and Provost 2002; Froud et al. 2012).

Despite significant institutional innovations in the United States to strengthen public supervision, market "naturalization" (essentially equivalent to what Somers and Block termed "market fundamentalism") conjoined with failure to coordinate bank regulators, regulators' reliance on fee assessment as their major funding source, and scaled-back government oversight of housing markets to create a regulatory "race to the bottom," leading to the financial crisis (Gieve and Provost 2012; Froud et al. 2012). Just as the Great Depression's severity challenged taken-for-granted ideas and policies wedded to charitable and private poor relief, so the severity of the recent financial crisis challenged the market-naturalized ideational regime, spurring the fragmentation of post crisis regulatory narratives consistent with the diverse institutional positions and interests of various politicians, technocrats, and bankers (Froud et al. 2012).

3.2 Public Opinion, Public Sentiment, and the U.S. Welfare State

Research on the import of public opinion resonates best with the hypothesis that cultural factors can have independent causal effects on social policy development by constraining political courses of action or influencing politicians' perceptions of what policy interventions the public views as desirable (see Brooks and Manza 2007; Jacobs 1993).

Brooks and Manza (2007) used statistical regression techniques to examine how public support for the welfare state shaped total welfare state effort across advanced industrial democracies between 1980 and 2000. The authors measured public support with two International Social Survey Program items tapping individuals' attitudes toward government's role in job provision and inequality reduction. They measured welfare state effort with the ratio of total social spending to gross domestic product (GDP). Net of various control variables, policy preferences had a statistically significant impact, strongly influencing cross-country aggregate social welfare expenditures. Social democratic states had much higher rates of public support for welfare state expenditures than did liberal welfare states.

In his case-oriented comparative analyses of health policies in Britain and the United States, Jacobs (1993) found that adopted policies corresponded substantially with public opinion and public understanding as evidenced by public opinion polls and more qualitative evidence. However, neither Jacobs (1993) nor Brooks and Manza (2007) argued for a mono-causal, nonconjunctural explanatory role for public opinion. Brooks and Manza (2007) suggested that public opinion can have a direct effect on social policy development by shaping politicians' self-interested behavior, but that this effect is conditional on three additional factors: 1) whether the "signal" given by public opinion is strong and stable (see also Jacobs 1993); 2) whether the issue is salient for the public; and 3) whether public opinion is relevant to competing policy options. All three may hold in the medium term with respect to cross-national variation in aggregate welfare expenditures.

Institutional factors also may shape how public opinion influences policies. Reviewing data for the United States and various European countries, Jacobs (1993) suggested that public opinion's impact is conditional on policy networks, institutional context for policy formulation and political bargaining, and whether the policy situation is one of political stalemate. When policy bargaining takes place through pluralistic, decentralized, and fragmented political institutions, public opinion should have substantial impact, but when it takes place through centralized and corporatist political institutions, more diffuse public opinion should not have much impact. When policy-making is relatively closed and takes place through senior officials and policy experts, public opinion should have minimal impact. Public opinion should have substantial impact on policies when policy debates attract media attention, reverberating across the public sphere (Jacobs 1993).

Newman and Jacobs (2010) suggested conditions under which enacted policies were *not* likely to reflect public opinion. Based on public opinion data and letters sent to U.S. presidents, including Franklin Delano Roosevelt, Lyndon B. Johnson, Richard Nixon, Ronald Reagan, George Bush, and William Jefferson Clinton, Newman and Jacobs (2010) argued that major federal welfare policies in the United States were enacted despite popular resistance. New Deal (1930s) and Great Society (1960s) presidents went against substantial negative popular opinion toward helping the poor. Later presidents dismantled and retrenched despite the American public's lack of enthusiasm. In these instances presidents acted as leaders rather than followers. In addition, public opinion in *all* these eras exhibited substantial ambivalence, with Americans preferring to emphasize employment rather than cash relief (see also Stryker and Wald 2009). What is probably most important is not "the realities" of public opinion, but rather how public opinion *is perceived* by political and policy-making elites (Campbell 1998; Stryker and Wald 2009).

In sum, Newman and Jacobs's (2010) argument is consistent with that of Brooks and Manza (2007) and Jacobs (1993) in suggesting that when public opinion is not clear or points in multiple directions, political elites have more opportunity and incentive to promote particular programs and ideals. Elites will employ framing and coalition building that capitalizes on the ambiguities of public opinion. Indeed, New Deal bifurcation between Social Security and public assistance, the Social Security Administration's subsequent framing of its program as "insurance" for self-reliant working Americans (Cates 1983), and the later legislative and administrative push to increase work requirements as conditions for social assistance responded to ambivalences in public opinion. The next subsection discusses cultural framing and value reinterpretation. Political elites use these cultural strategies to build on and channel public opinion, sentiments, and beliefs.

3.3 Framing and Value Redefinition

While public sentiment may constrain political actors, the model adopted by Brooks and Manza (2007) assumes that governments are responsive to public preferences, providing a venue through which commonly shared values can influence the policy-making process. However, political actors do not "slavishly" follow public opinion when formulating social policies. Kenworthy's (2009) analysis of public opinion's impact on welfare state spending suggests, contrary to Brooks and Manza's findings, that welfare state spending may influence public opinion rather than vice versa. This is so even in the United States, where policy preferences closely map changes in welfare spending (Kenworthy 2009, 736). Given extant theory and research on policy feedbacks (Huber and Stephens 2001; Pierson 1996), there are likely reciprocal, reinforcing influences between public opinion and government social policies, except when ideational regimes break down or the redefinition of core or fundamental values occurs.

American politicians have become increasingly reliant on opinion polls and focus groups in recent years (Jacobs and Shapiro 2000). However, the politicians use polls mostly to identify symbols and cultural tropes that "resonate" with widely shared cultural values to affect public support for policies (Jacobs and Shapiro 2000; Stryker and Wald 2009).

Interviews and archival analyses of government documents conducted by Jacobs and Shapiro (2000) reveal that President Clinton *and* his Republican Party opponents used public opinion data to determine how best to frame their positions on Clinton's proposed health-care reform. These frames were used to "prime" the public by making its existing attitudes about the role of government more salient to the debate. Ultimately, Republicans were more successful in shaping public opinion about health-care reform; they did so by priming existing antigovernment sentiments within the electorate. When increased media coverage of political conflict stoked public uncertainty about the proposed bill, the Republicans' priming strategy resulted in lower public support for Clinton's proposed reforms.

Jacobs and Shapiro's (2000) analysis suggests that public opinion often shapes U.S. social policy development by serving as a political resource. Political actors also draw on public sentiment for strategic framing. Framing is used to identify social problems and how to solve them, to assign blame, to construct and evaluate appropriate policy solutions, to alter individuals' perceptions of their own self-interests, to recruit and motivate political allies, and to undercut the persuasive power of opponents (Alexander 2005; Béland 2009, 2010a, 2010c; Campbell 2002; Chong and Druckman 2007; Eastwood 2005; Jacobs and Shapiro 2000; Quadagno 2005; Pedriana and Stryker 1997; Schmidt 2008; Steensland 2006; Stryker and Wald 2009). Political actors use framing in all phases of policy development from agenda setting to enactment of social policy, and throughout problem, policy, and political "streams" subject to the rules of engagement of electoral politics, as well as legislative and executive branch policy-making at multiple levels of government (Kingdon 1995; Béland 2010a).

Quadagno (2005, 2010) showed how self-interested private insurers repeatedly used antisocialist and promarket choice rhetoric to persuade doctors and the American public that universal national health insurance was counterproductive. Given that private insurers existed, and given the specific political-institutional context for policy-making in which they operated, antisocialist and promarket choice rhetoric, in conjunction with other factors, was sufficient to forestall a single-payer national health system in the United States. Until the Obama administration managed to enact the Patient Protection and Affordable Care Act of 2010, anything close to universal insurance coverage, by any means, remained out of reach. In short, discursive frames building on more general cultural repertoires, including liberal values, have played a causal role in the development of American health care *in conjunction with—and through—*self-interested actors and a distinctive set of political institutions.

Stryker and Wald (2009) provided another example illustrative of the constitutive influence of core values coupled with a strategic framing contest for which these core values set the parameters. These authors found that in congressional debates in the 1990s over federal welfare reform, Democrats tried to forestall elimination of welfare entitlements by drawing on the then generally accepted, dominant meaning of compassion as requiring a government-provided safety net for the poor. Meanwhile, Republicans promoting elimination of entitlement *redefined* compassion to promote their preferred policies. Republicans conjoined this redefinition with negative attributions about welfare recipients, crafting a logically coherent symbolic package promoting entitlement-ending reform.

This rhetorical conjuncture occurred within a broader discursive field in which compassion was the taken-for-granted cognitive and normative backdrop for welfare reform supporters and opponents alike. In delineating a field of interrelated meanings and showing how, why, by which actors, in what contexts, and to what effects these meanings were elaborated, Stryker and Wald (2009) captured the essence of what Vivien Schmidt (2008) termed "discursive institutionalism" and provided evidence for her claim that "norms [and values] are dynamic, inter-subjective constructs rather than static structures" (Schmidt 2008, 303).

As shown by Stryker and Wald's (2009) analyses, value redefinition can promote radical policy change consistent with continuity in core values. Similarly, Pedriana and Stryker (1997) showed that supporters of affirmative action in the 1960s redefined fundamental equal opportunity values—previously understood as color-blindness—to promote race-conscious remedial action for past race discrimination (see also Skrentny 1996). Based on existing research, value redefinition seems to be a more general cultural strategy, used by promoters of progressive and conservative reforms alike when their preferred policies are inconsistent with dominant extant meanings of more enduring abstract, general values that have been institutionalized in government legislation (Pedriana and Stryker 1997; Stryker and Wald 2009).

Beyond value redefinition and normative reframing, political actors also may mobilize more cognitively oriented frames to recast social problems and the consequences of policies intended to address those problems. Examining debates surrounding the passage of the Economic Opportunity Act (EOA) of 1964, the Omnibus Budget Reconciliation Act (OBRA) of 1987, the Family Support Act of 1988, and the PRWORA of 1996, Joshua Guetzkow (2011) showed that from the 1960s through the 1980s there was dramatic reframing of the poor and of the causes of poverty. Consistent with Somers and Block's (2005) depiction of the post–World War II ideational regime of embedded markets, Guetzkow's (2010) analyses of congressional hearings found that 1960s policy makers traced poverty back to structural causes, against which the poor were helpless and were consequently blameless victims. Federal policies responded by empowering poor communities through community action programs and by mobilizing the Job Corps to provide the poor with skills and help them to escape broken communities.

By the time of OBRA, market fundamentalism was rising fast, and poverty was considered a disease requiring treatment. The poor "need[ed] to be coerced to work,...[B]ecause they lacked 'family' values, welfare recipients would not respond to positive incentives" (Guetzkow 2010, 189). To move people off of welfare, the OBRA reduced the Earned Income Disregard—the amount of money that could be earned to supplement welfare income—even though many experts feared that this would create perverse incentives on welfare recipients to reduce their work effort. This act and related 1980s legislation marked movement toward a new consensus on the causes and solutions of poverty among both Democrats and Republicans: "[T]he government would help [only those] individuals who took the personal responsibility to help themselves" (Guetzkow 2010, 190; see also Stryker and Wald 2009).

3.4 Moral Categorization: Class, Race, Gender, and the Distinction between the Deserving and Undeserving Poor

Somers and Block (1990), Stryker and Wald (2009), and Guetzkow (2010) also signaled another long-standing U.S. cultural tradition: distinguishing between the deserving and undeserving poor. Brian Steensland (2006, 2007) elaborated on this moral categorization, making it the centerpiece of his explanation for the failure of guaranteed annual income (GAI) policies in the United States. Outlining three mechanisms of influence for the deserving/undeserving poor moral categorization, Steensland captured the foregrounded strategic and backgrounded constitutive roles of culture, as well as how both descriptive (cognitive) and evaluative (normative) meaning-attribution had causal influence.

Steensland's (2006) discursive mechanism of cultural influence captured the strategic resource value of distinguishing between the deserving and undeserving poor in framing social problems and policy solutions in ways likely to be perceived as legitimate by politicians and the public. His schematic mechanism showed how this distinction constructed a mostly taken-for-granted backdrop that shaped "the range of cognitive perceptions and normative evaluations that people [found] comprehensible or plausible" (Steensland 2006, 1286). Because it was widely accepted that the GAI was about reforming "welfare," it was (mis)understood and evaluated against a backdrop in which presumed beneficiaries were "undeserving" former Aid to Families with Dependent Children (AFDC) recipients, even though the GAI would have benefited the working poor as well.

The third type of causal influence that Steensland found for categories of moral worth mirrored the institutional embodiment of culture emphasized by welfare regime scholars (Huber and Stephens 2005) and by Pedriana and Stryker (1997) and Stryker and Wald (2009). For Steensland (2006), the institutional embodiment of ideas reinforces their discursive and schematic influences, enhancing the overall explanatory power of cultural factors.

Whereas Steensland (2006, 2007) focused solely on categories of deservingness, feminist and critical race theorists have emphasized the long-standing interpretive associations among categories of race, gender, class, and deservingness. For example, the U.S. welfare state institutionalized separate programs and benefit delivery for those viewed as deserving and undeserving (Nelson 1990; Gordon 1990; Quadagno 1994). At the time of debates over the GAI, one U.S. welfare "track" included Social Security and other programs benefiting persons seen as deserving based on workforce participation. The other, including AFDC and Food Stamps, provided stigmatized relief to the nonworking poor. Work status was associated with race, class, and gender, and beneficiaries of means-tested programs were disproportionately female, nonwhite, and very poor, while those who got market participation–related assistance were disproportionately white, male, and less poor. Thus, gendered, classed, and racialized interpretations were integral to both U.S. welfare state institutions and debates over the GAI.

Feminist and critical race scholars have also shown how associations among class, race, gender, and welfare have been *reinterpreted* in tandem with racialized, classed, and gendered changes in family structures; patterns of labor market participation; and broader class, race, and gender ideologies, norms, and values (Gordon 1990; Orloff 2002; Hancock 2003). On the one hand, extant norms and values influenced policy debates and enacted policies. On the other hand, enacted policies influenced norms and values (Fraser and Gordon 1994; Quadagno 1994). This often, but not always, created a self-reinforcing cycle of ideas and institutions, consistent with our suggestion earlier in this chapter of typical reciprocal, mutually reinforcing influences between public opinion and public policies.

However, as Soss and Schram (2007) pointed out, welfare policies are valuable to mass publics in part because they affirm majority group identities, categories, and expectations. Although "progressive revisionists" in the Democratic Party strategized that 1990s welfare reform would "reduce race-coding of poverty politics and produce a public more willing to invest in anti-poverty efforts" (Soss and Schram 2007, 111), the reform had no such effects. Dramatic changes in the design of social assistance did *not* translate into decreased race-coding or increased public willingness to improve the standard of living of the poor. Soss and Schram (2007) suggested that this might be due to a combination of welfare's high visibility and its great distance from the lived experience of nonpoor Americans.

We suggest as well that—especially when a policy such as welfare reform is part of a broader transformation of ideational regime and when prefatory framing contests create new policy frames but retain fundamental values in their reinterpreted form—those who do *not* themselves experience the reform will continue to be influenced disproportionately by the new, and more general, winning ideational regime. In the case of the PWORA, this was market fundamentalism. The endurance of this ideational regime has contributed to the staying power of minimal poverty assistance and poor Americans' lack of entitlement to social assistance, notwithstanding substantial change in material conditions.

3.5 Future Directions

Incorporating culture into models of policy-making contributes substantially to our understanding of how social policies develop. Our review of exemplary research on the role of culture in U.S. policy-making has shown that we cannot account for the combination of continuity and change over time in key social policies, such as health care and social assistance, without considering the multiple causal roles played by cultural factors. At the same time, research has shown that it is not possible to understand how cultural factors work without understanding how they may interact with and through other analytical factors emphasized by this volume, including interests and institutions (Soss and Schram 2007; Steensland 2006; Schmidt 2008; Béland 2009; Padamsee 2009; Pedriana and Stryker 1997; Stryker and Wald 2009, Campbell 1998). We cannot explain U.S. social policy development by relying on cultural factors alone.

Even the explanatory role of public opinion is conditional on other factors, including both noncultural factors and other aspects of culture. Future research should develop further and test a variety of plausible conditions for the causal influence of public opinion. Included in conditions to be tested systematically based on extant analytical arguments should be centralized versus decentralized policy-making; corporatist versus pluralist bargaining institutions; closed versus open policy-making; the degree and type of media coverage; the level of issue salience to the public; the relevance of public opinion for policy options; the strength and stability of public opinion over time; whether public opinion points unequivocally in one direction or in multiple, potentially contradictory directions; and the clarity versus the ambiguity of public opinion (see e.g., Brooks and Manza 2007; Jacobs 1993; Newman and Jacobs 2010).

We have also suggested that, absent the breakdown of a dominant ideological regime or the redefinition of core or fundamental values, reciprocal, reinforcing influences between public opinion and state social policies are likely. This proposition invites substantial further empirical research, as do our empirically grounded suggestions that 1) economic crisis provides a key opportunity for ideational regime change; and 2) value redefinition is most likely to be attempted when political actors find that dominant extant interpretations of abstract, general values institutionalized in existing policies are inconsistent with their preferred policy reforms.

In addition, because of the reciprocal relationships that exist among culture, interests, power distributions, and institutions in the policy-making process, there is substantial consensus among scholars who take culture seriously that we must specify explanatory and interpretive connections between "cultural" and "political-economic" factors for many additional policy processes and outcomes (Béland 2009; Padamsee 2009; Pedriana and Stryker 1997; Stryker and Wald 2009). This can and should be done through multiple types of research, including qualitative and quantitative studies that examine the United States over time and in cross-national perspective. In all research going forward, researchers should attend carefully to the relationship between the specific analytical arguments being made and the evidence offered to support these claims.

This will ensure that quantitative models including cultural factors are appropriately specified. It also will ensure that the evidentiary details of qualitative-interpretive analyses match the analytical arguments, regardless of whether those details focus on specific episodes of strategic framing or provide broader analytical narratives and comparisons.

In addition to ensuring that the evidence provided matches the analytical arguments being made, our review of case-oriented research suggests that we need to distinguish between necessary and sufficient causation, investigate *multiple* potential cultural mechanisms of causal influence, and determine whether and how these mechanisms are mutually reinforcing (Jacobs 1993; Quadagno 2005; Pedriana and Stryker 1997; Stryker and Wald 2007). Given that some causal arguments suggest that cultural factors are necessary, while others suggest that cultural factors are sufficient conditions for particular policy processes or outcomes, and that many studies propose conjunctural causation among cultural and noncultural explanatory factors, research might make more use of case-oriented comparative methods. Formal methods of qualitative comparative analysis (QCA), including crisp set and fuzzy set analysis, allow us to examine such distinctions at the same time that they reveal conjunctural causation (Ragin 1987, 2000). Eliason and Stryker (2009) have made goodness-of-fit tests available for the "causal recipes" examined through fuzzy set QCA, so this method is now available for hypothesis testing as well as for more exploratory hypothesis generation.

In addition to their usefulness for identifying different causal pathways through which culture can influence policy-making, case-oriented methods also allow researchers to compare the effects of "cultural constants" such as abstract general values and ideational regimes on the policy-making process and to reveal the politically, problem-, and policy-related ways in which what is taken for granted in *one* country or timeframe may vary across countries or time frames so that actors in these contexts construct very different policy goals and policies for similarly labeled social problems such as race discrimination (Bleich 2003). Such an analysis could be used to help account for the weak path dependencies that exist *within* liberal, conservative-corporatist, and social democratic welfare state regimes versus the relatively stable patterns of variation *between* these countries.

By examining how cultural constants can be used to construct different policy goals, we also become attuned to the possibility of substantial policy and institutional change based on the *reinterpretation* of abstract general values embodied in the policy. Following Stryker and Wald (2009), we suggest that such reinterpretation of core values is a more general cultural mechanism promoting U.S. social policy change toward *both* more progressive policies and more conservative policies. Consistent with prior discussion, research should examine further the generality of this mechanism as well as whether the conditions we have suggested for its occurrence hold. By focusing on the constitutive role of ideas, especially when embodied in institutions, researchers may be better able to account for decades-long path dependencies within liberal, conservative-corporatist, and social democratic welfare state regimes versus the decades-long stable patterns of variation between them. This same approach promotes focus on the diverse ways that ideas and values embodied in institutions may operate as policy feedbacks, sometimes constraining action to particular paths but also providing opportunities to change paths (Béland 2010b). This approach also promotes a focus on the role of ideational regimes and on the conditions for change in ideational regimes.

Policy researchers should also look to additional theoretical literatures to identify more mechanisms linking cultural forces to the policy-making process. Research from social and political psychology improves our understanding of the micro-mechanisms through which culture affects policy development and what factors may make particular cultural tropes more or less effective in shaping public opinion. For example, Danielson (2013) used social identity theory (Tajfel 1982) to develop a theoretical model describing how differences in the ways that individuals define what it means to be "truly American" may interact with how policy interventions are framed to influence attitudes toward policies perceived to benefit racial minorities and immigrants. Consistent with his theoretical argument that individuals would be more supportive of policies that benefited in-group members, Danielson (2013) found that those adopting more inclusive forms of American national identity were more likely to support government expenditures on welfare, aid to African Americans, and assistance to immigrants, even net of individuals' demographic characteristics, perceived self-interest, and values.

Psychological models on persuasion and priming can be fruitfully applied to research on framing effects as well. Research on both the constitutive and strategic roles of framing has become more systematic in recent years. There is now substantial concern about the validity and reliability of frames identified as well as about the strength of the evidence offered for whatever causal influence on policy-making is claimed for framing (Chong and Druckman 2007; Stryker and Wald 2009). It is striking, however, that whereas U.S. social policy researchers often analyze the explanatory roles played by problem or issue or policy framing, they typically do not investigate what psychologists call "valence or equivalency" framing. As Chong and Druckman (2007) explained, this kind of framing effect occurs when people respond quite differently to logically equivalent phrases, such as 90 percent employment versus 10 percent unemployment.

Behavioral economists and experimental psychologists have shown that variation in valence or equivalency framing of an issue or policy implicates emotional responses in ways that can change individual preferences dramatically. Kahneman (2011, 363–370) provided examples of such valence framing effects relevant to social policy-making. Thus, research should examine the extent to which this type of framing strategy is used and whether it has met with any success in shaping which social policies are considered feasible or desirable by political elites or social movements.

3.6 Concluding Remarks

Drawing on exemplary research, this chapter has argued that cultural factors alone are unlikely to provide a sufficient explanation for any aspect of U.S. social policy development. However, understanding how cultural factors operate in the background and foreground of social policy debates is essential, because fully explaining the nature, tim-ing, causes, and consequences of any particular U.S. social policy development typically will require elucidating multiple aspects of—and roles played by—culture. Overall, research on the explanatory power of cultural factors, including ideas, values, frames, moral categorizations, and worldviews or ideational regimes, for U.S. social policy development has advanced considerably over the past 25 years. Advances have been commensurate with renewed attention given to cultural explanations after a period of relative drought.

Twelve years ago Campbell (2002, 21) suggested that future scholarship work to iden-tify "the actors who seek to influence policy making with their ideas, [to ascertain] the institutional conditions under which these actors have more or less influence, and [to understand] how political discourse affects the degree to which policy ideas are com-municated and translated into practice." Measured against these criteria, recent research has made significant strides. Similarly, there is substantial extant research responsive to Schmidt's (2008) pleas that scholars interested in the explanatory role of ideas examine how, why, by which actors, in what contexts, and to what effects interrelated fields of dis-cursive meaning relevant to policy-making are elaborated.

There is, of course, much more research to be done. But consistent with recent advances, and especially with the move to specify analytically the causal mechanisms through which the diverse aspects of culture work together with and through actors, interests, institutions, and power distributions, we expect that the next 10 to 15 years will bring a great deal more empirical research and many additional theoretical and empirical advances.

References

*Indicates recommended reading.

Alexander, Jeffrey C. 2005. "Why Cultural Sociology Is Not 'Idealist': A Reply to McLennan." *Theory, Culture, & Society* 22 (6): 19–29.
*Béland, Daniel. 2009. "Gender, Ideational Analysis and Social Policy." *Social Politics* 16 (4): 558–581.
Béland, Daniel. 2010a. "Policy Change and Health Care Research." *Journal of Health Politics, Policy and Law* 35 (4): 6125–6641.
Béland, Daniel. 2010b. "Reconsidering Policy Feedback: How Policies Affect Politics." *Administration and Society* 42 (5): 568–590.
Béland, Daniel. 2010c. "The Idea of Power and the Role of Ideas." *Political Studies Review* 8:145–154.
Benford, Robert D., and David A. Snow. 2000. "Framing Processes and Social Movements: An Overview and Assessment." *Annual Review of Sociology* 26:611–639.
Bleich, Eric. 2003. *Race Politics in Britain and France: Ideas and Policymaking Since the 1960s.* Cambridge: Cambridge University Press.
Brooks, Clem, and Jeff Manza. 2007. *Why Welfare States Persist: The Importance of Public Opinion in Democracies.* Chicago: University of Chicago Press.

Campbell, John L. 1998. "Institutional Analysis and the Role of Ideas in Political Economy." *Theory and Society* 27:377–409.

*Campbell, John L. 2002. "Ideas, Politics and Public Policy." *Annual Review of Sociology* 28:21–38.

Cates, Jerry. 1983. *Insuring Inequality: Administrative Leadership in Social Security 1935–1954.* Ann Arbor: University of Michigan Press.

Chong, Dennis, and James A. Druckman. 2007. "Framing Theory." *Annual Review of Political Science* 10:103–126.

Clemens, Elisabeth. 2011. "Nationalizing Reciprocity: Aligning Charity and Citizenship in the American Nation-State." Available at http://www.yale.edu/ccr/Clemens.pdf.

Clemens, Elisabeth S., and Doug Guthrie. 2010. "In the Shadow of the New Deal: Reconfiguring the Roles of Government and Charity, 1928–1940." *Politics and Partnerships: The Role of Voluntary Associations in America's Political Past and Present,* edited by E. S. Clemens and D. Guthrie, 79–115. Chicago: University of Chicago Press.

Danielson, J. Taylor. 2013. "The Boundaries of Being American: National Identity, In-Group Bias, and Attitudes toward Domestic Policy." Unpublished manuscript, Department of Sociology, University of Arizona.

Eastwood, Jonathan. 2005. "The Role of Ideas in Weber's Theory of Interests." *Critical Review* 17 (1/2): 89–100.

Eliason, Scott, and Robin Stryker. 2009. "Goodness-of-Fit Tests and Descriptive Measures in Fuzzy-Set Analysis." *Sociological Methods and Research* 38:102–146.

Fraser, Nancy, and Linda Gordon. 1994. "Dependency' Demystified: Inscriptions of Power in a Keyword of the Welfare State." *Social Politics* (Spring):4–31.

Froud, Julie, Adriana Nilsson, Michael Moran, and Karel Williams. 2012. "Stories and Interests in Finance: Agendas of Governance before and after the Financial Crisis." *Governance: An International Journal of Policy, Administration, and Institutions* 25(1):35–59.

Gamson, William, and André Modigliani. 1987. "The Changing Culture of Affirmative Action." *Research in Political Sociology* 3:137–177.

Geertz, Clifford. 1973. "Religion as a Cultural System." In *The Interpretation of Cultures*, 87–125. New York: Basic.

Gieve, John, and Colin Provost. 2012. "Ideas and Coordination in Policymaking: The Financial Crisis of 2007–2009." *Governance: An International Journal of Policy, Administration, and Institutions* 25 (1): 61–77.

Goldstone, Jack. 1991. "Ideology, Cultural Frameworks and the Process of Revolution." *Theory and Society* 20:405–453.

Gordon, Linda. 1990. "The New Feminist Scholarship on the Welfare State." In *Women, the State, and Welfare,* edited by Linda Gordon, 9–35. Madison: University of Wisconsin Press.

Gramsci, Antonio. 1995. *Selections from the Prison Notebooks of Antonio Gramsci.* New York: International.

Guetzkow, Joshua. 2010. "Beyond Deservingness: Congressional Discourse on Poverty, 1964–1996." *ANNALS of the American Academy of Political and Social Science* 629 (1): 173–197.

Hancock, Ange Marie. 2003. "Contemporary Welfare Reform and the Public Identity of the Welfare Queen." *Race, Gender, and Class* 10 (1): 31–59.

Huber, Evelyne, and John Stephens. 2001. *Development and Crisis of the Welfare State: Parties and Policies in Global Markets.* Chicago: University of Chicago Press.

Huber, Evelyne, and John Stephens. 2005. "Welfare States and the Economy." In *The Handbook of Economic Sociology,* 2nd ed., edited by N. J. Smelser and R. Swedberg, 552–574. Princeton, NJ: Princeton University.

*Jacobs, Larry R. 1993. *The Health of Nations: Public Opinion and the Making of American and British Health Policy.* Ithaca, NY: Cornell University Press.

Kahneman, Daniel. 2011. *Thinking Fast and Slow.* New York: Farrar, Straus and Giroux.

Kenworthy, Lane. 2009. "The Effect of Public Opinion on Social Policy Generosity." *Socio-Economic Review* 7:727–740.

Kingdon, John W. 1995. *Agendas, Alternatives and Public Policies.* 2nd ed. New York: HarperCollins.

Nelson, Barbara. 1990. "The Origins of the Two-Channel Welfare State: Workman's Compensation and Mothers' Aid." In *Women, the State, and Welfare,* edited by Linda Gordon, 123–151. Madison: University of Wisconsin Press.

Newman, Katherine S., and Elisabeth S. Jacobs. 2010. *Who Cares? Public Ambivalence and Government Activism from the New Deal to the Second Gilded Age.* Princeton, NJ: Princeton University Press.

Orloff, Ann Shola. 2002. "Explaining US Welfare Reform: Power, Gender, Race and the US Policy Legacy." *Critical Social Policy* 22 (1): 96–118.

*Padamsee, Tasleem. 2009. "Culture in Connection: Re-Contextualizing Ideational Processes in the Analysis of Policy Development." *Social Politics* 16 (4): 413–445.

Parsons, Craig. 2002. "Showing Ideas as Causes: The Origins of the European Union." *International Organization* 56 (1): 47–84.

*Pedriana, Nicholas, and Robin Stryker. 1997. "Political Culture Wars 1960s Style: Equal Employment Opportunity-Affirmative Action Law and the Philadelphia Plan." *American Journal of Sociology* 103:633–691.

Pierson, Paul. 1996. "The New Politics of the Welfare State." *World Politics* 48 (January): 143–179.

Quadagno, Jill. 1994. *The Color of Welfare: How Racism Undermined the War on Poverty.* New York and Oxford: Oxford University Press.

Quadagno, Jill. 2005. *One Nation Uninsured: Why the US Has No National Health Insurance.* Oxford: Oxford University Press.

Quadagno, Jill. 2010. "Institutions, Interest Groups, and Ideology: An Agenda for the Sociology of Health Care Reform." *Journal of Health and Social Behavior* 51:125–136.

Ragin, Charles. 1987. *The Comparative Method.* Berkeley: University of California Press.

Ragin, Charles. 2000. *Fuzzy Set Social Science.* Chicago: University of Chicago Press.

*Schmidt, Vivien. 2008. "Discursive Institutionalism: The Explanatory Power of Ideas and Discourse." *Annual Review of Political Science* 11:303–326.

Skrentny, John. 1996. *The Ironies of Affirmative Action: Politics, Culture and Justice in America.* Chicago: University of Chicago Press.

Smith, Rogers M. 1993. "Beyond Tocqueville, Myrdal and Hartz: The Multiple Traditions of America." *American Political Science Review* 87:549–566.

*Somers, Margaret, and Fred Block. 2005. "From Poverty to Perversity: Ideas, Markets, and Institutions over 200 Years of Welfare Debate." *American Sociological Review* 70:260–287.

*Soss, Joe, and Sanford F. Schram. 2007. "A Public Transformed? Welfare Reform as Policy Feedback." *American Political Science Review* 10 (1): 111–127.

*Steensland, Brian. 2006. "Cultural Categories and the American Welfare State: The Case of Guaranteed Income Policy." *American Journal of Sociology* 111:1273–1326.

Steensland, Brian. 2007. *The Failed Welfare State Revolution: America's Struggle over Guaranteed Income Policy.* Princeton, NJ: Princeton University Press.

*Stryker, Robin, and Pamela Wald. 2009. "Redefining Compassion to Reform Welfare: How Supporters of 1990s Federal Welfare Reform Aimed for the Moral High Ground." *Social Politics* 16 (4): 519–557.

Swidler, Ann. 1986. "Culture in Action." *American Sociological Review* 51:273–286.

Tajfel, Henri. 1982. Introduction to *Social Identity and Inter-Group Relations*, edited by H. Tajfel, 1–11. Cambridge: Cambridge University Press.

Zeitlin, Irving. 2000. *Ideology and the Development of Sociological Theory.* 7th ed. Upper Saddle River, NJ: Pearson.

CHAPTER 9

··

POLITICAL INSTITUTIONS AND U.S. SOCIAL POLICY

··

EDWIN AMENTA AND AMBER CELINA TIERNEY

1 INTRODUCTION

··

POLITICAL institutional explanations of social policy were rejuvenated over the last generation through the movement to bring the "state back in" to the analysis of politics (Skocpol 1985). They have often been invoked to explain the U.S. approach to public social policy (Weir, Orloff, and Skocpol 1988), with its comparatively late adoption of social programs, ungenerous coverage and benefits, and reliance on private social provision and indirect government efforts that are less effective in reducing poverty, insecurity, and inequality (see review in Amenta, Bonastia, and Caren 2001). Here we address the two main lines of political institutional explanation as they have been employed in scholarship on U.S social policy. The first includes large-scale formal political institutions—the organizations, rules, and procedures governing explicitly political activity, including electoral rules and practices, the division of authority within and across governments, and executive bureaucracies (Immergut 2010), as well as structural aspects of political party systems. These have been used singly or in combination to explain U.S. policy developments, especially the so-called "old" politics of social policy adoption and expansion. The second line of explanation views policies themselves as political institutions with important indirect influences on policy (see Pierson 2006). New policies create new politics, typically reinforcing programs by promoting political conditions that support the programs, through positive policy feedbacks (Pierson 2000; Béland 2005; cf. Weaver 2010). This line of argument has been at the center of the "new" politics of social policy, in which social policy has weathered both a period of austerity and retrenchment over the last three decades (Pierson 1996).

Political institutions are heavily implicated in historical developments and current features of U.S. social policy. Scholars have shown that the U.S. has exhibited extreme values on characteristics of formal political institutions unfavorable to social policy development, including long-standing restrictions in voting rights, national political institutions with many veto points, a majoritarian electoral system, fiscal federalism, weak domestic bureaucracies, patronage-oriented political parties, and a right-slanted and candidate-centered party system (reviews in Amenta 2003; Immergut 2010). United States social policy has Although scholarship has shown that established social programs have bolstered themselves and avoided severe retrenchment across capitalist democracies (Pierson 2011), indirect influences of policy have helped to keep U.S. public social policy marginal. remained tied to the least generous, liberal welfare state model (Esping-Andersen 1990; Scruggs and Allan 2008). Individual social programs, moreover, are sometimes claimed to lack positive policy feedbacks or have negative ones (Weaver 2010), including the means-tested programs standard to the liberal model (Weir et al. 1988) and patronage-oriented programs, which were adopted in early U.S. policy history (Skocpol 1992). Furthermore, the United States has extensive military (Hooks and McQueen 2010) and imprisonment policies (Manza and Uggen 2006; Uggen and Manza 2002), each of which competes with resources for social policy and diminishes political support for social policy. United States social policy also has been subject to policy "drift," in which programs are unable to keep up with inflation or new needs (Hacker 2004; Hacker and Pierson 2010).

We begin by addressing general issues surrounding political institutional theoretical claims and situate them among other perspectives that also employ the name "institutional." From there we move on to formal political institutional explanations of policy and the research supporting them. Next we address research on the influence of policies as political institutions. Political institutional explanations have flourished in "historical institutionalist" scholarship (Steinmo, Thelen, and Longstreth 1992; Pierson and Skocpol 2002), and in studies of American political development (Orren and Skowronek 2004), but they also have been confirmed in quantitative research (Amenta 2003). We conclude with some suggestions to advance the project, especially through historical research that might transcend the old and new politics distinction.

2 INSTITUTIONAL ARGUMENTS AND POLITICAL INSTITUTIONALISM

Institutionalists define institutions as emergent factors above the individual level that influence political processes and outcomes and tend to produce regular patterns. Institutions constrain or constitute the interests and political participation of actors "without requiring repeated collective mobilization or authoritative intervention to achieve these regularities" (Jepperson 1991: 145). Scholars who refer to themselves as institutionalists often differ about what constitutes an institution or an institutional causal argument. Rational choice institutionalists usually see institutions as rules resulting from strategic equilibria (Hall and Taylor 1996), whereas "sociological" institutionalists see institutions as centered on norms, practices, assumptions, and values, and typically make arguments that are ideational. Historical institutionalists are united by methodological approach, but theoretically most of them rely on political institutional arguments (see reviews in Hall and Taylor 1996; Campbell, 2004; Parsons 2007; Amenta and Ramsey 2010).

Political institutional arguments conceptualize institutions as procedures, routines, norms, and conventions in the organizational structure of politics (see Amenta 2005). Political institutionalists tend to view political actors as motivated by self-interest but not always, because actors are also constrained by the norms, ideas, cognitive models, and analytical capacities of organizations in which they are embedded. Political institutionalists, however, reject the ideas of rational choice institutionalists that institutions are simply the result of strategic equilibria or are created for functional reasons (Hall and Taylor 1996; Campbell 2004), and they are far more concerned with issues of power than are sociological institutionalists (see Amenta and Ramsey 2010). Political institutional arguments posit two forms of influence over political action. Institutions can be constraining, superimposing conditions of possibility for mobilization, access, and influence and limiting some forms of action while facilitating others. From this point of view, political institutions limit the conditions under which organized groups mobilize and attain collective goods, such as social spending. Institutions can also be seen as constitutive, establishing the available and viable models and heuristics for political action, and evoke an imagery of cultural frameworks or toolkits (Goodwin 2001).

The main analytical and explanatory focus of political institutionalism has been on the practices and activities surrounding the political organizations that constitute the "polity," and are directly connected to and engaged in formal political activity. Formal political institutions are those that determine political action directly and are centered in state organizations and rules and those political organizations seeking to govern states. These formal political institutions include the state organizations, rules, and practices surrounding who can participate in politics, how political officials are selected, and how laws are made, enforced, and administered (Immergut 2010). These institutions include the organizations, rules, and practices surrounding democratization, elections, the distribution of authority in national states, and the structure and size of state bureaucracies. Formal political institutions also include nonstate macrocharacteristics of the polity, notably the form and ideological makeup of political parties. Key characteristics of party systems, which remain fairly durable over time, include the number of parties; which parties are present, including whether there is a labor or socialist party and a unified right-wing party; overall ideological slant; and whether parties are oriented toward patronage or programmatic aims (Immergut 2010, Hicks 1999, Shefter 1977, Mayhew 1986; Schmidt 2010; Kitschelt 2012).

A second key political institutional influence is policy itself. Policies are lines of state action that provide a series of rules and executive organizations to enforce them; policies constitute the main connections between states and citizens, ranging from cash benefits to incarceration, and are posited to influence subsequent policy-making indirectly (Pierson 2006). Moreover, institutional arguments are associated with path dependence (Parsons 2007), in which key actions at critical junctures, typically the creation of new policy, bring about changes that are self-reinforcing (Mahoney 2000; Pierson 2000).

Among political institutionalists, some argue that path dependency and the "locking in" of policy does not often happen all at once (Mahoney and Schensul 2006), but occurs through a series of incremental changes (Thelen 2003; Streeck and Thelen 2005; Mahoney and Thelen 2010). These scholars agree that policies produce many indirect effects through "positive policy feedback" processes that buttress policies (see Pierson 2006; Béland 2010): new state bureaucracies may be created or existing ones strengthened to support the policies; preferences of key political actors may change in a favorable direction; organizations of beneficiaries may be buoyed or formed; categories of beneficiaries may become politically active in ways that bolster the policy; and policies may have self-reinforcing ideational or symbolic legacies. Politicians who seek to retrench spending policies impose harsh costs on their beneficiaries and thus fear negative electoral repercussions and must devise strategies to avoid blame (Pierson 1996; Weaver 1986). However, sometimes policies are deemed to have "negative feedbacks," that is, policy characteristics that undermine a specific program or related programs (Skocpol 1992; Weaver 2010).

Political institutionalists view political institutions at the individual country level as being distinctive and influential in shaping political outcomes (Amenta and Ramsey 2010). For that reason, unlike sociological institutionalists, political institutionalists rarely emphasize convergence in political processes and outcomes and often argue, instead, that country-level political institutions transmute global processes (see Campbell 2004). Political institutionalist explanations are prevalent in historical institutionalist scholarship and usually involve showing that some structural and systemic political conditions hindered a potential political change in one place and either aided or allowed the development in another; thus, for political institutionalists "comparison" usually means "contrast," such as between policy innovations and failures (Amenta 2012). Political institutionalists who focus on path dependency and policy feedbacks see the different policy choices made by countries as difficult to undo, despite similar changes in world economies (Steinmo 2010).

The first research about the influence of formal political institutional arrangements on U.S. social policy were historical studies that compared efforts to adopt social policy in the United States and other similarly situated countries (Orloff and Skocpol 1984; Weir and Skocpol 1983; see review in Amenta 2003). These historical studies were a reaction to larger-N quantitative studies of post-World War II spending efforts, and they focused, instead, on political institutions as shaping conflicts over social policy and on state actors in making policy during its formative period (see review in Skocpol and Amenta 1986). The historical studies argued that the timing of adoption and initial characteristics of social policy determined social spending and, therefore, effort would be better expended on explaining why and when policies were adopted and in the specific forms they took. More generally, historical scholars focused on identifying the "causes of effects" or complete explanations of important changes in social policy, rather than the "effects of causes" (Mahoney and Goertz 2006). The causes-of-effects strategy centers on isolating a few variables that explain the greatest variance in policy outcomes of interest in populations and is predominant in large-N quantitative research. Historical institutionalist scholars, by contrast, were driven by particular questions or puzzles, such as why Britain and the United States differed in the adoption of the core programs of their welfare states, why the United States never created a national health insurance system, or why the United States favored the development of extensive veterans' benefits. Given the complexity of these questions, historical institutionalists and American political development scholars often combine political institutional determinants with others in their explanations of policy developments (Amenta and Ramsey 2010).

3   FORMAL POLITICAL INSTITUTIONS IN EXPLANATIONS OF U.S. POLICY

The influence of formal political institutions was the focus of much early historical and comparative research on social policy, with studies finding that the U.S. polity obstructed the creation of national and direct social programs. This line of research began with small-N historical studies that compared the United States to other similarly situated countries and has been buttressed by findings in large-N quantitative research across rich democracies over time as well as across U.S. states.

Scholars generally see U.S. social policy as a negative, and often unusual, case (Amenta et al. 2001). The United States was relatively tardy in adopting the five major social insurance programs, enacting only workers' compensation before 1935, when most Western European countries largely completed adopting these programs. Old-age and unemployment insurance were added in 1935, health insurance was extended only to the aged and poor in 1965, and universal family allowances were never adopted (Weir et al. 1988). Moreover, U.S. social programs have been among the least generous and most restrictive of capitalist democracies (Pierson 2011). According to Esping-Andersen's (1990) three models of welfare state regimes, consolidated around the middle of the twentieth century, U.S. social policy is firmly in the "liberal" camp, with the least generous programs involving the greatest degree of means testing and private social policy, designed to aid markets. The United States also relies heavily on "tax expenditures" and other backdoor policy measures to achieve social aims, which are often less redistributive than direct spending would be (Howard 1997).

Partly as a result, in the post-World War II period, the United States expended relatively less "effort" on social policy (i.e. direct spending as a percentage of income). In 2007, U.S. spending efforts stood at 16.2 percent, ranking the country 19 among 20 long-standing Organization for Economic Cooperation and Development (OECD) countries, one place behind its position in 1980 (OECD 2012). United States social policy also lags in terms of reducing poverty, inequality, and insecurity. In the era of neoliberalism and social policy retrenchment efforts over the last three decades, U.S. social programs were subject to greater "systemic" retrenchment (Pierson 1996; Pierson 2011), in which future social spending is hamstrung by reductions in taxation (Steinmo 2010). Sometimes, however,

U.S. policy has stood out in terms of generosity with short-term, backdoor social programs, devoted to specific privileged groups, including the expansive Civil War veterans' pension benefits of the late 19th century (Skocpol 1992), the massive work programs of the Great Depression (Amenta 1998), and the wide-ranging veterans' benefits in the wake of World II in the so-called G.I. Bill (Mettler 2005).

The tardiness in adopting standard social insurance, the gaps in programs, the reliance on means-tested programs, indirect and backdoor public provision, and the significant role of the private sector in the U.S. welfare state have been frequently attributed to various aspects of U.S. political institutions (Amenta et al. 2001). Although the U.S. polity was democratized early for white males, in key ways it was also democratized very late—the late-nineteenth-century disfranchisement of southern African-Americans was not rectified until the 1960s—which greatly truncated policy possibilities during the period in which capitalist democracies were adopting social programs. In addition, political authority in the United States was born divided, with each branch of government granted legislative, executive, and judicial authority. Having a president that can veto legislation, a Supreme Court that can override legislation, and a bi-cameral legislature that frequently requires supermajorities to pass legislation hindered, and still hinders, legislative breakthroughs and opens up veto points for their opponents. Taken together, these institutional arrangements reduce possibilities for adopting direct social spending and provide incentives for indirect social provision. What is more, the U.S. executive bureaucracy was underdeveloped from the start, and remained so, given the polity's early democratization. Developing coherent bureaucratic authority in domestic policy areas has proved difficult, leaving programs without bureaucratic advocates, sources of expertise for policy advocates, and guardians of administrative efficiency (Orloff 1993). Legislative authority over social policy has always been shared with state and local governments (Finegold 2005). These fiscal competitors have generally acted as a drag on social policies. States have all the institutional obstacles prevalent in the national polity, but typically to a greater degree and some of them in extreme form, rendering non-national social programs typically less generous and more racially discriminatory (Lieberman 2001; Weir 2005).

Several aspects of the U.S. party system also have been identified as hindrances to direct social policy (see review in Amenta et al. 2001). The U.S. party system has two catchall parties, with no labor or socialist party, and historically it has been slanted to the right. The Democratic Party did not move toward the center-left until the 1930s and, until the late 1970s, its reform elements were weighed down by a southern contingency from under-democratized states devoted to upholding a racial/economic order that would be threatened by generous, nationally administered social policy (Hicks 1999; Amenta 1998). Both U.S. parties were historically oriented toward patronage, and patronage-oriented parties have been hostile to modern social policy reform (Mayhew 1986). The parties were weakened as organizations during the 20th century, as candidate-centered political campaigns became the norm (Clemens 1997), sapping the sort of party discipline needed to pass controversial social legislation. These party characteristics result, in part, from formal state political institutions, because a polity that is democratized before it is bureaucratized is likely to be dominated by patronage-oriented parties (Shefter 1977; Skocpol 1992). In addition, the majority electoral requirements discourage socialist parties and promote right-slanted party systems (Lipset and Marks 2000; Iverson and Soskice 2005). The strongest political institutional arguments claim that formal political institutions discourage social policy directly while also encouraging forms of political organization, such as patronage-based parties, that slow the development of social programs and discourage forms of political organization, such as left parties, that promote social policy (see Amenta 2005).

Claims about the influence of political institutions on social policy were developed mainly in research that treated the United States historically and comparatively, documenting divergent policy trajectories in similarly situated countries, and then analyzing the reasons behind the divergence (see review in Amenta 2003). Several early comparative historical accounts, often examining the U.S., British, and Swedish cases, noted the discouraging influences of lagging U.S. domestic bureaucratic capacities (Heclo 1974; Orloff and Skocpol 1984; Weir and Skocpol 1985). Comparative historical studies of the impact of a wider array of political institutions on social policy soon followed (Immergut 1992; Skocpol 1992; Steinmo 1993; Maoini 1998), showing that broad-based social policy was frustrated by fragmented political institutions and incapable states. Historical studies indicated the debilitating influence of the underdemocratized South (Amenta 1998; Katznelson, Geiger, and Kryder 1993), and the influence of patronage party systems (Amenta 1998; see review in Amenta et al. 2001).

Research has also shown that political institutions are responsible in part for some of the comparatively unusual aspects of the U.S. welfare state, including the reliance upon nonsocial insurance programs to address risks to income, programs for privileged groups, and private and indirect forms of social policy. The patronage-based party system helped drive the short-term Civil War veterans' benefit programs that served as de facto old-age and survivors' insurance for a select group (Skocpol 1992), as well as the Depression-era work programs (Amenta 1998). More important for the present, the institutional barriers to forming political coalitions for passing direct social insurance measures for all citizens has often led to unusual social policy features, as reformers have been forced to settle for second- or third-best alternatives to address insecurity and poverty. Opponents of generous national social policy in Congress often succeeded in providing decision-making authority to states, which could choose to provide lower benefits and discriminate among groups in their provision (Lieberman 2001). An insufficient political coalition in favor of extending New Deal social policy initiatives helped spur the G.I. Bill of Rights, for veterans only (Amenta 1998). Similarly, political forces for social policy reform were unable to provide direct antipoverty income supports and allied with conservatives to provide it indirectly through the Earned Income Tax Credit (Howard 1997). The country's peculiar federalism, in combination with the polity's uneven democratization, local dominance of patronage-oriented parties, and state-level deficits in domestic administrative capacities, has led to disparities in social policy treatment, including those between races, and has hampered antipoverty efforts, because states over-represented by poor people are often the least generous (Weir 2005).

In dialogue with these studies, quantitative studies more frequently employed political institutional measures in analyses of policy outcomes. Cross-national analyses have examined social spending, "decommodification," and redistribution, usually across approximately 20 rich capitalist democracies over a series of time points spanning the last 60 years (see review in Immergut 2010). Institutional "veto points," powerful subnational fiscal competitors, and a presidential and majoritarian electoral system dampen social spending and redistribution and thwart the legislative process, more generally (Krehbiel 1998 Huber and Stephens 2001; Iverson and Soskice 2005; Hicks and Swank 1992; Swank 2002; see review in Immergut 2010). Center-right-leaning party systems, like that of the United States, have also been associated with lower social spending and redistribution (Schmidt 2010; Iverson and Soskice 2005), whereas bureaucratic development has been associated with social policy growth (Hicks and Swank 1992; Pampel and Williamson 1992). Other quantitative studies show that formal political institutions help explain policy differences at the U.S. state level, because states bear much responsibility for the administration of many social programs, such as Medicaid and public assistance (Amenta et al. 2001). Underdemocratized U.S. states, typically southern, had far less generous versions of Old Age Assistance and Aid to Dependent Children, programs enabled by the Social Security Act (Amenta and Poulsen 1996; Lieberman 2001). Similarly, studies of key congressional votes show a significant negative influence of southern Democrats on old-age and labor legislation (Amenta, Caren, and Olasky 2005; Farhang and Katznelson 2005). The dampening impact of underdemocratized regimes on social policy is also seen by quantitative work comparing policies in Latin America (Huber, Mustillo, and Stephens 2008), where polities differ on this dimension far more so than across capitalist democracies. In addition, patronage party development significantly lowers taxation efforts in states (Mayhew 1986), as well as the generosity of means-tested assistance programs under the Social Security Act (Amenta and Poulsen 1996).

Given that most characteristics of formal political institutions are slow to change, they have been invoked less frequently in explanations of policy developments in the burgeoning historical research on American political development (Orren and Skowronek 2004), but, nonetheless, there are some examples. Howard (2002) shows how workers' compensation laws have been defined and shaped by U.S. federalism, leading to an unusual system. United States workers' compensation laws remain at the discretion of state-level authorities, with national policy creating disability insurance and national standards for workplace safety to offset the inadequacies of workmen's compensation. Formal political party institutions are implicated in the scaling back of direct social policy, with social policy initiatives launched by southern Democrats in the late 1960s and early 1970s (notably, the EITC) undermining the New Deal welfarist model and helping to give birth to the modern workfare model (Bertram 2007).

Having many veto points has hindered the adoption of social policy in the United States, but has been only mildly effective in preventing retrenchment. Disunity in the policy-making process offers political actors plausible deniability in the blame-avoidance game, thus promoting retrenchment (Swank 2002; Pal and Weaver

2003; Immergut 2010). For the most part, however, to make sense of patterns of retrenchment, political institutionalists invoke policy feedbacks.

4 POLICY FEEDBACKS AND U.S. SOCIAL POLICY

Among political institutional scholars, especially those examining the U.S. case historically, attention has shifted to whether, how, and the conditions under which policies will influence politics in ways that will influence future social policy-making. The "new politics of the welfare state" approach (Pierson 1996) holds that many social programs have indirect and recursive influences on policy that may make them resistant to major retrenchment. Cuts to programs are held to be dangerous for their political proponents because they impose high and visible costs on recipients while providing only diffuse benefits, and programs may have other indirect influences that will buttress them. The most compelling policy feedback arguments show that policies influence politics in ways that reliably bolster social policy. Although, like others, the U.S. welfare state has largely resisted attempts at retrenchment and although some U.S. old-age programs were aided by positive feedbacks, policy feedbacks have been negative for some social programs, and some positive feedbacks buoy policy that conflicts with social policy.

Key big-picture evidence indicates that social policies have strong self-reinforcing effects. Despite three decades of lagging economic growth and postindustrial transition, austerity, and neoliberal policies from right-leaning governments, and a rapid decline of unionization, social spending in capitalist democracies remains remarkably stable, with core programs intact (Pierson 2011). More specifically, the major U.S. social programs, Social Security and Medicare, have not been greatly undermined, despite attempts by conservative politicians in the past three decades (Pierson 1996; Béland 2005), whereas right-wing forces easily prevented or slowed the initial adoption of U.S. social programs (Amenta 1998; see discussion in Hall 2003). The Social Security old-age pension program has been shown to benefit from most of the main indirect feedback influences and processes (see Béland 2010). The program is nearly universal, giving the entire population a stake in it (Weir et al. 1988). Unlike most U.S. programs, Social Security has had an expert-led bureaucracy that has been able to maneuver politically, provide expert plans for expansion, and administer the program efficiently, thereby aiding its expansion and protecting it (Béland 2005). The program also has helped bolster a political interest organization (the AARP) (Skocpol 1992; Pierson 1996), and spurred the political activity of senior citizens, both of which make Social Security difficult to retrench (Campbell 2003). Private pension programs were integrated into it (Hacker 2004), reducing employer opposition. The program also has technical characteristics that prevent retrenchment, such as the "double payment problem"—in which obligations to insured beneficiaries have to be paid out while taxes for a less generous initiative would also need collecting (Myles and Pierson 2001; Weaver 2010). Furthermore, the program is wrapped in a symbolic legacy of security, preventing it from being associated with the "unworthy" poor (Béland 2010; Steensland 2008).

All the same, these reinforcing influences on Social Security and social policy generally have not changed the nature of the U.S. welfare state. Although there is disagreement about whether countries continue to conform completely to Esping-Andersen's (1990) liberal, conservative, or social democratic welfare state regimes, the United States remains close to the liberal model (Scruggs and Allan 2008; for review of typologies see Arts and Gelisson 2002). Liberal regimes have done poorly in adapting to unemployment and other economic crises over the last decade (Steinmo 2010). In addition, even when resisting overall retrenchment, the polity's many veto points make it difficult to upgrade social programs, leading instead to policy drift. Policy fails to keep pace with inflation or new needs, and public social provision has declined relative to the subsidization of private policy efforts and the privatization of risk (Hacker 2004).

Scholars have found that some programs have negative feedback effects—features that tend to undermine them (Skocpol 1992; Weaver 2010). Liberal welfare state regimes like that of the Unuited States rely on income-tested programs that have smaller and fewer politically influential constituencies (Weir et al. 1988), making them more vulnerable to retrenchment efforts. However, the influence of institutions goes far back. The sorts of patronage-oriented programs that the United States pioneered in the nineteenth century hampered the building of political coalitions for modern social spending programs, as the high costs of Civil War pensions, which were de facto old-age pensions for Northern veterans, convinced progressives that reforming political parties was necessary before they could support social insurance on the European model (Skocpol 1992). Similarly, Hacker (2002) argues that extensive private benefits in health care inhibited public interventions in that area, helping to explain why the United States never adopted national health insurance.

In addition, defense and imprisonment policies come at the expense of social programs, are far more extensive in the United States than in other capitalist democracies, and have secondary effects that harm social policy. In 2011, U.S. military expenditures accounted for about 41 percent of the world's total military spending and 4.7 percent of U.S. GDP (SIPRI 2012)—much higher than the levels of any long-standing capitalist democracy—and reduced funds available for social programs. Because of standard policy feedbacks, weapons systems are notoriously difficult to cut and military bases difficult to close. Defense policy also has had negative influences on the potential political coalitions in support of social policy and positive influences on opponents. Social policy has advanced furthest when a liberal Democrat is president and Democrats overwhelmingly dominate the Congress, because this is one way of overcoming the institutional veto points (Amenta 1998). However, the creation of the U.S. military-industrial complex undermined congressional support for consolidating social policy at a critical juncture after World War II. Changes in aircraft manufacture employment coincided with an increased growth of the nonwhite population, contributing to New Deal Democratic electoral defeats in the North and West and strengthening the conservative coalition of southern Democrats and Republicans in Congress (Hooks and McQueen 2010).

Similarly, money spent on imprisonment, generally a state-level obligation, cannot be spent on social programs or education, and prisons are likewise difficult to close. The United States currently incarcerates its population at the world's highest rate—730 per 100,000—which is several times higher than that of any other long-standing capitalist democracy (International Centre for Prison Studies 2012). Imprisonment policy also has had negative influences on the potential political coalitions in support of social policy and positive influences on opponents. More recently, U.S. incarceration policies, which are also unusual in preventing nonincarcerated felons from voting in many states (Manza and Uggen 2006), have had secondary political effects, swinging many elections away from Democrats and undercutting coalitions that would support social policy and oppose retrenchment. Incarceration-related electoral contractions likely altered the outcomes of as many as seven recent U.S. Senate elections and the 2000 presidential election (Uggen and Manza 2002). Moreover, the expansive incarceration policy is likely to persist given current laws regarding probation, parole, and indeterminate sentencing (Uggen and Manza 2002).

Although political feedback influences have much empirical support, it is often difficult to ascertain how much they matter. Because policy feedbacks affect policies indirectly, the feedback can be only as influential as the direct cause of policy it is influencing, and most direct causes are partial. For instance, military spending significantly reduces support for the election of New Deal Democrats, who, in turn, are partially influential in enacting, consolidating, or protecting social policy. Tracing the influence of policy through another cause of policy and back to policy also poses methodological difficulties, with scholars usually only able to demonstrate the first step in the causal chain. In addition, the questions that policy feedbacks tend to address are often counterfactual and broad—why did a program not disappear or change form?—and thus are difficult to substantiate, given the many possible reasons that programs will persist. Often the lack of a challenge to a program does not mean that it is invulnerable to attack. The only way to ascertain the true internal strength of an institution, policy, or program would be to subject it to constant and varied challenges, which, in practice, never happens. Moreover, policies can produce feedbacks through several processes, and a given case may be subject to many of them. For instance, in its formative years, Social Security only occasionally faced significant challenges (Amenta 2006; Béland 2007) and, as noted earlier, generated many positive policy feedbacks. Thus, its avoidance of retrenchment was somewhat overdetermined. In addition, the program was aided in its formative years by an old-age-pension movement led by the Townsend Plan, which was well mobilized, politically active, and demanded more extensive benefits (Amenta 2006).

5 FUTURE RESEARCH

United States formal political institutions generally discouraged the development of public social policy, hindering it at crucial moments when the rest of the world was adopting it, and helping to sabotage the efforts of U.S. reformers. Policy feedbacks, moreover, help to explain aspects of U.S. policy that are reasonably strong, such as Social Security, but institutional approaches also help to explain why U.S. social policy has remained meager and has drifted over the last few decades. All that said, U.S. formal political institutions do not often explain the rise, expansion, and augmentation of policy—key questions for policy scholarship—and most policy feedback arguments are also biased toward stasis rather than change (cf. Orren and Skowronek 2004 on institutional dissonance and Weaver 2010 on negative policy feedbacks). Thus to address more fine-grained, change-oriented questions, such as why particular reforms took the forms that they did, historical institutionalists typically deploy political institutions in conjunction with other determinants of policy, such as the impetus of crises, the activity of social movements, the rise of new governments, the innovations of bureaucrats, the policy ideas of political actors, and the like in multicausal explanations (Campbell 2004; Orren and Skowronek 2004; Amenta and Ramsey 2010). We suggest that these other determinants be theoretically connected to political institutional arguments and developed through the sorts of historical and comparative research that initiated the perspective—searching for the causes of effects rather than the effects of causes. In this work, scholars need to bridge the differences in "old" and "new" approaches to social policy.

The most promising political institutional arguments are those that posit direct influences, but also indicate the conditions under which specific actors are likely to influence policy. In Halfmann's (2011) historical analysis of abortion politics in the United States, Britain, and Canada, the nature of the party system shaped the development of policy in each country, but also influenced the prominence of actors seeking to retrench initially liberal abortion laws. Decentralized, candidate-centered, and weakly disciplined U.S. political parties made them vulnerable to pressure from newly organized movements. The anti-abortion movement was able to force abortion policy onto the political agenda, and abortions became less accessible as a result. In Britain and Canada, differences in these political contexts deflected the efforts of well-organized anti-abortion organizations, and abortions became more accessible as the result of increased public funding and reduced medical gatekeeping. This work aligns with the political mediation model of social movement consequences, in which movement strategies must fit political contexts in order to have policy influence (see Amenta 2006; Amenta and Ramsey 2010). Such analyses address but go beyond the impact of political institutions on policy by simultaneously considering the influence of institutions, politically organized groups, and their strategies of action on policy outcomes.

Additional arguments about the determinants of policy, such as those surrounding ideas, should similarly be harnessed to a political institutional perspective. Béland (2005) notably argues that the content of new policies is heavily dependent on the national policy domains of state bureaucracies, interest groups, think tanks, academic research institutions, and social movements that monitor an issue area (see also Weaver 2006), and he proposes tracing the causal influence of policy paradigms from policy-producing organizations to decision-making authorities. This situates norms and schemas within the bounds of available and feasible analyses and proposals generated by policy domain actors, which are partly the product of national political structures (Campbell 2002). This research addresses the use of policy ideas by elected officials and policy advocates in framing policy innovations so as to draw public support or avoid resistance (see also Steensland 2008; Martin 2010). This use of ideas diverges from standard accounts of sociological institutionalism, in which global actors with largely similar policy ideas are expected to bring isomorphism in policy outcomes. Future work could explore the institutional conditions under which policy learning takes place, typically having to do with the structures and capacities of domestic bureaucracies and their political context. Scholars from this perspective should pursue the role of framing (McCammon et al. 2008; Martin 2010, see review in Amenta and Ramsey 2010), and address the conditions under which policy advocates can frame innovative policy initiatives that garner public support while avoiding potential resistance (Amenta and Ramsey 2010).

Valuable thinking and research about policy feedbacks has gone beyond showing how individual social programs help to buttress themselves, in two important directions. Scholars have begun to systematically analyze negative feedbacks, or aspects of programs that are inherently unstable or are unstable under the pressure of retrenchment efforts, beyond the standard universal/selective divide. Weaver (2010) has shown this in the case of public pension regimes in western industrial countries. Scholars have also begun to examine the repercussions of other state policy on social policy. The impact of military and imprisonment policies have negative feedbacks that go beyond simple tradeoffs between guns, or bars, and butter (Manza and Uggen 2006; Hooks and McQueen 2010). These cross-policy influences are systemic and may be more consequential to social policy than the positive feedbacks of individual programs on themselves. Another important line of institutional research should center on tax policy. The U.S. tax system is also constructed in ways that hamper the fiscal stability of the central state or federal government. The consumption taxes that support high spending on social policy in much of the world and are relatively immune from retrenchment (Steinmo 1993) are monopolized by states and localities in the United States, whereas the federal government heavily relies on income taxes that have drawn negative public attention and have been cut multiple times over the last half century (Campbell 2009; Morgan and Prasad 2009).

More generally, political institutional scholars need to go beyond the supposed divisions between old and new politics of welfare states (see also Myles and Quadagno 2002). Retrenchment efforts have been an important theme historically, with key programs being cut back even during the formative years of U.S. social policy (Amenta 1998; Martin 2010). Addressing new risks by way of new policy still matters in an era in which the United States has attempted to extend health insurance coverage to all and has tried and failed in other areas of social policy, as well as passing tax cuts that have weakened the fiscal stability of the state. The probability of major changes in policy has greatly increased, given the polarization of the political parties in the last two decades (Sinclair 2006). Following these leads will keep institutional analyses relevant for research on the past and present.

We thank the editors for valuable criticism and comments and the UCI Center for the Study of the Democracy for support of this project.

REFERENCES

*Indicates recommended reading.

*Amenta, Edwin. 1998. *Bold Relief: Institutional Politics and the Origins of Modern American Social Policy*. Princeton, NJ: Princeton University Press.

Amenta, Edwin. 2003. "What We Know About the Development of Social Policy: Comparative and Historical Research in Comparative and Historical Perspective." In Dietrich Rueschemeyer and James Mahoney, eds., *Comparative Historical Analysis in the Social Sciences*, 91–130. New York: Cambridge University Press.

Amenta, Edwin. 2005. "State-Centered and Political Institutional Theories in Political Sociology: Retrospect and Prospect." In Robert R. Alford, Alexander M. Hicks, T. Janoski, and Mildred A. Schwartz, eds., *The Handbook of Political Sociology*, ch. 4. New York: Cambridge University Press.

Amenta, Edwin. 2006. *When Movements Matter: The Townsend Plan and the Rise of Social Security*. Princeton, NJ: Princeton University Press.

Amenta, Edwin. 2012. "Historical Institutionalism." In E. Amenta, K. Nash, and A. Scott, eds., *The Wiley-Blackwell Companion to Political Sociology*, 47–56. Malden, MA:Wiley-Blackwell.

Amenta, Edwin, Christopher Bonastia, and Neal Caren. 2001. "US Social Policy in Comparative and Historical Perspective: Concepts, Images, Arguments, and Research Strategies." *Annual Review of Sociology* 27: 213–234.

Amenta, Edwin, Neal Caren, and Sheera Joy Olasky. 2005. "Age for Leisure? Political Mediation and the Impact of the Pension Movement on U.S. Old-Age Policy." *American Sociological Review*, 70: 516–538.

Amenta, Edwin, and Jane D. Poulsen. 1996. "Social Politics in Context: The Institutional Politics Theory and Social Spending at the End of the New Deal." *Social Forces* 75 (1): 33–60.

Amenta, Edwin, and Kelly M. Ramsey. 2010. "Institutional Theory." Pp. 15–40 in *Handbook of Politics: State and Society in Global Perspective*, eds. Kevin T. Leicht, and J. Craig Jenkins. New York: Springer.

Arts, Wil and Gelissen John. 2002. "Three Worlds of Welfare Capitalism or More? A State-of-the-art report,"*Journal of European Social Policy*, 12 (2): 137–158.

Béland, Daniel. 2005. "Ideas and Social Policy: An Institutionalist Perspective." *Social Policy and Administration*, 39:1–18.

Béland, Daniel. 2007. "Ideas and Institutional Change in Social Security: Conversion, Layering, and Policy Drift." *Social Science Quarterly*, 88: 20–38.

*Béland, Daniel. 2010: "Reconsidering Policy Feedback: How Policies Affect Politics." *Administration & Society* 42: 568–90.

Bertram, Eva C. 2007. "The Institutional Origins of 'Workfarist' Social Policy." *Studies in American Political Development* 21: 203–229.

Campbell, Andrea Louise. 2003. *How Policies Make Citizens: Senior Political Activism and the American Welfare State*. Princeton, NJ: Princeton University Press.

Campbell, Andrea Louise. 2009. "What Americans Think of Taxes." In Isaac Martin, Ajay Mehrotra, and Monica Prasad, eds., *The New Fiscal Sociology*, ch. 3. New York: Cambridge University Press.

Campbell, John L. 2002. "Ideas, Politics, and Public Policy." *Annual Review of Sociology* 28: 21–38.

*Campbell, John L. 2004. *Institutional Change and Globalization*. Princeton, NJ: Princeton University Press.

Clemens, Elisabeth S. 1997. *The Peoples' Lobby: Organizational Innovation and the Rise of Interest Group Politics in the United States, 1890–1925*. Chicago: University of Chicago Press.

Esping-Andersen, Gøsta. 1990. *The Three Worlds of Welfare Capitalism*. Cambridge: Polity Press.

Farhang, Sean, and Ira Katznelson. 2005. "The Southern Imposition: Congress and Labor in the New Deal and Fair Deal." *Studies in American Political Development* 19 (1): 1–30.

Finegold, Kenneth. 2005. "The United States: Federalism and Its Counter-factuals." In Federalism and the Welfare State, edited by Herbert Obinger, Stephan Leibfried, and Francis G. Castles, 138–178. Cambridge: Cambridge University Press.

Gelissen, J. 2002. *Worlds of Welfare, Worlds of Consent? Public Opinion on the Welfare State*. Leiden; Boston: Brill.

Goodwin, Jeff. 2001. *No Other Way Out: States and Revolutionary Movements, 1945–1991*. New York: Cambridge University Press.

*Hacker, Jacob S. 2002. *The Divided Welfare State*. New York: Cambridge University Press.

Hacker, Jacob S. 2004. "Privatizing Risk Without Privatizing the Welfare State: The Hidden Politics of U.S. Social Policy Retrenchment." *American Political Science Review* 98 (2): 243–260.

Hacker, Jacob. S., and Paul Pierson. 2010. "Winner-Take-All Politics." *Politics and Society* 38 (2): 152–205.

Halfmann, Drew. 2011. *Doctors and Demonstrators: How Political Institutions Shape Abortion Laws in the United States, Britain, and Canada*. Chicago: University of Chicago Press.

Hall, Peter A. 2003. "Aligning Ontology and Methodology in Comparative Research." In James. Mahoney, and Dietrich Rueschemeyer, eds., *Comparative Historical Analysis in the Social Sciences*, ch. 11. Cambridge: Cambridge University Press.

Hall, Peter A., and Rosemary C. R. Taylor. 1996. "Political Science and the Three New Institutionalisms." *Political Studies* 44: 936–957.

Heclo, Hugh. 1974. *Modern Social Politics in Britain and Sweden: From Relief to Income Maintenance*. New Haven, CT: Yale University Press.

Hicks, Alexander M. 1999. *Social Democracy and Welfare Capitalism: A Century of Income Security Politics*. Ithaca, NY: Cornell University Press.

Hicks, Alexander M., and Duane H. Swank. 1992. "Politics, Institutions, and Welfare Spending in Industrialized Democracies, 1960–82." *American Political Science Review* 86 (3): 658–674.

Hooks, Gregory, and Brian McQueen. 2010. "American Exceptionalism Revisited: The Military-Industrial Complex, Racial Tension, and the Underdeveloped Welfare State." *American Sociological Review* 75 (2): 185–204.

Howard, Christopher. 1997. *The Hidden Welfare State: Tax Expenditures and Social Policy in the United States*. Princeton, NJ: Princeton University Press.

Howard, Christopher. 2002. "Workers' Compensation, Federalism, and the Heavy Hand of History." *Studies in American Political Development* 16 (1): 28–47.

Huber, Evelyn, and John D. Stephens. 2008. "Politics and Social Spending in Latin America." *Journal of Politics* 70 (2): 420–436.

Huber, Evelyn, Charles Ragin, and John D. Stephens. 1993. "Social Democracy, Christian Democracy, Constitutional Structure, and the Welfare State." *American Journal of Sociology* 99: 711–749.

Huber, Evelyn, and John D. Stephens. 2001. *Development and Crisis of the Welfare State: Parties and Policies in Global Markets*. Chicago: University of Chicago Press.

Immergut, Ellen M. 1992. *Health Politics: Interests and Institutions in Western Europe*. Cambridge: Cambridge University Press.

*Immergut, Ellen M. 2010. "Political Institutions." In Francis G. Castles, Stephan Leibfried, Jane Lewis, Herbert Obinger, and Christopher Pierson, eds., *The Oxford Handbook of the Welfare State*, ch.15. Oxford: Oxford University Press.

International Centre for Prison Studies. 2012. http://www.prisonstudies.org/.

Iversen, Torben, and David Soskice. 2005. "Electoral Institutions, Parties, and the Politics of Class: Why Some Democracies Redistribute More than Others." *American Political Science Review* 100 (2): 165–182.

Jepperson, Ronald L. 1991. "Institutions, Institutional Effects, and Institutionalism." In Walter W. Powell and Paul J. DiMaggio eds., *The New Institutionalism in Organizational Analysis*, 143–163. Chicago: University of Chicago Press.

*Katznelson, Ira, Kim Geiger, and Daniel Kryder. 1993. "Limiting Liberalism: The Southern Veto in Congress, 1933–1950." *Political Science Quarterly* 108 (2): 283–306.

Kitschelt, H. 2012. "Parties and Interest Intermediation." In E. Amenta, K. Nash, and A. Scott eds., *The Wiley Blackwell Companion to Political Sociology*, 144–157. Oxford: Blackwell.

Krehbiel, Keith. 1998. *Pivotal Politics: A Theory of U.S. Lawmaking*. Chicago: University of Chicago Press.

Lieberman, Robert C. 2001. *Shifting the Color Line: Race and the American Welfare State*. Cambridge, MA: Harvard University Press.

Lipset, Seymour Martin, and Gary Marks. 2000. *It Didn't Happen Here: Why Socialism Failed in the United States*. New York: W. W. Norton.

Mahoney, James. 2000. "Path Dependence in Historical Sociology." *Theory and Society* 29 (4): 507–548.

Mahoney, James, and Gary Goertz. 2006. "A Tale of Two Cultures: Contrasting Quantitative and Qualitative Research." *Political Analysis* 14 (3): 227–249.

Mahoney, James, and Daniel Schensul. 2006. "Historical Context and Path Dependence." In Robert E. Goodin and Charles Tilly, eds., *Oxford Handbook of Contextual Political Analysis*, 454–471. Oxford: Oxford University Press.

Mahoney, James, and Kathleen Thelen. 2010. "A Theory of Gradual Institutional Change." In Mahoney, James, and Kathleen Thelen, eds., *Explaining Institutional Change: Ambiguity, Agency, and Power*, ch. 1. Cambridge: Cambridge University Press.

Maioni, Antonia. 1998. *Parting at the Crossroads: The Emergence of Health Insurance in the United States and Canada*. Princeton, NJ: Princeton University Press.

Manza, Jeff, and Christopher Uggen. 2006. *Locked Out: Felon Disenfranchisement and American Democracy*. New York: Oxford University Press.

Martin, Isaac William. 2010. "Redistributing Toward the Rich: Strategic Policy Crafting in the Campaign to Repeal the Sixteenth Amendment, 1938–1958." *American Journal of Sociology* 116 (1): 1–52.

Mayhew, David R. 1986. *Placing Parties in American Politics*. Princeton, NJ: Princeton University Press.

McCammon, Holly J., Soma Chaudhuri, Lyndi Hewitt, Courtney Sanders Muse, Harmony D. Newman, Carrie Lee Smith, Teresa M. Terrell. 2008. "Becoming Full Citizens: The U.S. Women's Jury Rights Campaigns, the Pace of Reform and Strategic Adaptation." *American Journal of Sociology* 113: 1104–1147.

Mettler, Suzanne. 2005. *Soldiers to Citizens: The G.I. Bill and the Making of the Greatest Generation*. Oxford: Oxford University Press.

Morgan, Kimberly J., and Monica Prasad. 2009. "The Origin of Tax Systems: A French-American Comparison." *American Journal of Sociology* 114: 1350–1394.

Myles, John, and Paul Pierson. 2001. "The Comparative Political Economy of Pension Reform." In Paul Pierson. ed., *The New Politics of the Welfare State*, ch. 10. Oxford: Oxford University Press.

Myles, John, and Jill Quadagno. 2002. "Political Theories of the Welfare State." *Social Service Review* 76: 34–57.

Organization for Economic Development and Cooperation (OECD). 2012. "StatExtracts: Social Expenditure—Aggregated Data." http://stats.oecd.org/Index.aspx.

Orloff, Ann Shola, 1993. "Gender and the Social Rights of Citizenship." *American Sociological Review* 58 (3): 303–328.

Orloff, Ann Shola, and Theda Skocpol. 1984. "Why Not Equal Protection? Explaining the Politics of Public Social Spending in Britain, 1900–1911, and the United States, 1880s–1920." *American Sociological Review* 49 (6): 726–750.

Orren, Karen, and Stephen Skowronek. 2004. *The Search for American Political Development*. Cambridge: Cambridge University Press.

Pal, Leslie A. and R. Kent Weaver. 2003. "Conclusions." In Leslie A. Pal and R. Kent Weaver, eds., *The Government Taketh Away: The Politics of Pain in the United States and Canada*, 293–328. Washington DC: Georgetown University Press.

Pampel, Fred C., and John B. Williamson. 1992. *Age, Class, Politics, and the Welfare State*. New York: Cambridge University Press.

Parsons, Craig. 2007. *How to Map Arguments in Political Science*. Oxford: Oxford University Press.

*Pierson, Paul. 1996. "The New Politics of the Welfare State." *World Politics* 48 (2): 143–179.

Pierson, Paul. 2000. "Increasing Returns, Path Dependence, and the Study of Politics." *American Political Science Review* 94 (2): 251–267.

Pierson, Paul. 2006. "Public Policies as Institutions: Government Institutions, Policy Cartels, and Policy Change." In Ian Shapiro, Stephen Skowronek, and Daniel Galvin, eds., *Rethinking Political Institutions: The Art of the State*, ch. 5. New York: New York University Press.

Pierson, Paul. 2011. *The Welfare State over the Very Long Run*. No. 02/2011. ZeS-Arbeitspapier.

Pierson, Paul, and Theda Skocpol. 2002. "Historical Institutionalism in Contemporary Political Science." In Ira Katznelson, and Helen V. Milner, eds., *Political Science: The State of the Discipline* 693–721. New York: W. W. Norton.

*Schmidt, Manfred. 2010. "Parties." In Francis G. Castles, Stephan Leibfried, Jane Lewis, Herbert Obinger, and Christopher Pierson, eds., *The Oxford Handbook of the Welfare State*, ch 14. New York: Oxford University Press.

Scruggs, Lyle. A., and James P. Allan. 2008. "Social Stratification and Welfare Regimes for the Twenty-First Century: Revisiting the Three Worlds of Welfare Capitalism." *World Politics* 60: 642–664.

Shefter, Martin. 1977. "Party and Patronage: Germany, England, and Italy." *Politics and Society* 7: 403–451.

Sinclair, Barbara. 2006. *Party Wars: Polarization and the Politics of National Policy Making*. Norman: University of Oklahoma Press.

Skocpol, Theda. 1985. "Bringing the State Back In: Strategies of Analysis in Current Research." In Peter B. Evans, Dietrich Rueschmeyer, and Theda Skocpol, eds., *Bringing the State Back In*, 3–37. Cambridge: Cambridge University Press.

*Skocpol, Theda. 1992. *Protecting Soldiers and Mothers: The Political Origins of Social Policy in the United States*. Cambridge, MA: Harvard University Press.

Skocpol, Theda, and Edwin Amenta. 1986. "States and Social Policies." *Annual Review of Sociology* 12: 131–157.

Steensland, Brian. 2008. "Why Do Policy Frames Change? Actor-Idea Coevolution in Debates over Welfare Reform." *Social Forces* 86: 1027–1054.

Steinmo, Sven. 1993. *Taxation and Democracy: Swedish, British and American Approaches to Financing the Modern State*. New Haven, CT: Yale University Press.

Steinmo, Sven. 2010. *The Evolution of Modern States: Sweden, Japan, and the United States*. Cambridge: Cambridge University Press.

Steinmo, Sven, Katheleen Thelen, and Frank Longstreth. 1992. *Structuring Politics: Historical Institutionalism in Comparative Analysis*. Cambridge: Cambridge University Press.

Stockholm International Peace Research Institute (SIPRI). 2012. "Military Expenditure by Country as a Percentage of Gross National Product, 1988–2010." Available at http://milex data.sipri.org/files/?file=SIPRI+milex+data+1988-2011.xls.

Streeck, W., and K. Thelen. 2005. *Beyond Continuity: Institutional Change in Advanced Political Economies*. Oxford: Oxford University Press.

Swank, Duane S. 2002. *Global Capital, Political Institutions, and Policy Change in Developed Welfare States*. New York: Cambridge University Press.

Thelen, Kathleen. 2003. "How Institutionalism Evolves: Insights from Comparative Historical Analysis." In James Mahoney, and Dietrich Rueschemeyer, eds., *Comparative Historical Analysis in the Social Sciences*, 208–240. New York: Cambridge University Press.

Uggen, Christopher, and Jeff Manza. 2002. "Democratic Contraction? Political Consequences of Felon Disenfranchisement in the United States." *American Sociological Review* 67 (6): 777–803.

Weaver, R. Kent. 1986. "The Politics of Blame Avoidance." *Journal of Public Policy* 6 (4): 371–398.

Weaver, R. Kent. 2006. "Government Institutions, Policy Cartels, and Policy Change." In Ian Shapiro, Stephen Skowronek, and Daniel Galvin, eds., *Rethinking Political Institutions: The Art of the State*, ch. 9. New York: New York University Press.

*Weaver, R. Kent. 2010. "Paths and Forks or Chutes and Ladders?: Negative Feedbacks and Policy Regime Change." *Journal of Public Policy* 30 (2): 137–162.

Weir, Margaret M. 1992. *Politics and Jobs: The Boundaries of Employment Policy in the United States*. Princeton, NJ: Princeton University Press.

*Weir, Margaret M. 2005. "States, Race, and the Decline of New Deal liberalism." *Studies in American Political Development* 19: 157–172.

Weir, Margaret M., Ann Shola Orloff, and Theda Skocpol. 1988. "Understanding American Social Politics." In Margaret M. Weir, Ann Shola Orloff, and Theda Skocpol, eds., *The Politics of Social Policy in the United States*, 3–27. Princeton, NJ: Princeton University Press.

Weir, Margaret M., and Theda Skocpol. 1983. "State Structures and Social Keynesianism: Responses to the Great Depression in Sweden and the United States." *International Journal of Comparative Sociology* 24 (1–2): 4–29.

Weir, Margaret M., and Theda Skocpol. 1985. "State Structures and the Possibilities for Keynesianism: Responses to the Great Depression in Sweden, Britain, and the United States." In B. Evans, D. Rueschmeyer, and T. Skocpol, eds., *Bringing the State Back In*, 107–163. Cambridge: Cambridge University Press.

CHAPTER 10

....

POLITICAL PARTIES AND SOCIAL POLICY

....

JEFFREY M. STONECASH

1 INTRODUCTION

....

POLITICAL parties play a significant role in shaping public policy.[1] The politicians who enact policy legislation are almost always elected on party lines. They support and advocate for specific policies to send a signal to voters they wish to attract (Sulkin 2011). They seek a majority coalition so they can control the Presidency and Congress. When deliberation over policies occurs, they seek to frame how debate develops. They set the terms of social policies, determining eligibility and benefits. Moreover, the relatively high levels of party polarization in Congress (McCarty, Poole, and Rosenthal 2006; Baumer and Gold 2010) suggests that, more than in the past, parties try to define themselves by presenting distinct policy alternatives. Nonetheless, some scholars remain skeptical that parties are central to the formation of public policy, with some arguing that parties do not keep their promises (Hibbing and Theiss-Morse 1995), whereas others believe they are more concerned with posturing and criticizing the opposition than in enacting policy (Mann and Ornstein 2006; Fiorina 2009).

This chapter examines whether parties play the roles just reviewed and have a major impact on social policy. Current understandings of these matters are not as developed as might be presumed for three reasons. First, the impact of parties on public policy has not been of primary concern to students of parties, and thus we lack much research on the subject. Second, the composition of parties has been steadily changing over time. In the 1960s through the 1980s, parties were less distinct in their composition. Now parties differ more in terms of their composition. That gradual change means we are tracking the effect of entities with changing electoral bases and unity. Third, during recent decades, it was often difficult to assess the impact of parties because for much of the 1980s and 1990s control of government was divided between Democrats and Republicans, limiting our ability to assess the impact of unified party control (Fiorina 2002). Given that situation, the concern was primarily whether divided control meant protracted policy stalemates, or whether parties could compromise and respond to pressing social problems. There have been extended periods of unified party control since 2000, making assessments of the impact of party control at least feasible. Still, assessing the role and impact of American political parties on policy is complicated.

This chapter begins with the issue of whether parties differ in their electoral bases and policy concerns and how these have changed over time. Then, the impact of growing party differences on policy discussions will be reviewed. Finally, the effect of party control differences on social policies will be examined.

2 POLITICAL CHANGE AND CONDITIONAL PARTY GOVERNMENT

To analyze the role of parties in forming public policy, scholars must first determine whether the parties represent coherent entities seeking different policies. This involves issues of their composition and internal homogeneity. Parties are more likely to matter when their composition is homogeneous, party unity is high, and the parties differ (Rohde 1991; Rohde and Aldrich 2010). When parties are diverse internally and do not differ much from each other, variations in party control are less likely to mean as much, and compromise between parties is more likely. Which party has control of institutions should affect public policy less.

The internal homogeneity and difference between parties have varied over time. These variations have, in turn, affected interest in the party—policy connection. Following the national elections of the 1930s, the Democratic Party was a coalition of conservative southern whites, northern urban ethnics, union members, and some blacks. The Republican Party was largely based in the North and drew its support from rural areas, small towns, and suburbs (Sundquist 1983; Polsby 2004, Brewer and Stonecash 2009, 66–103). Although the parties did differ in their electoral bases and policy preferences, from the late 1930s through the 1980s, the dominant coalition in Congress was drawn from conservative members within each party (Patterson 1967). The parties compromised more often, and bipartisan voting helped pass significant legislation involving, including the Social Security Act in 1935 (Derthick 1970), civil-rights laws (1964), Medicare and Medicaid (1965), Clean Air Act (1970), and reform of the tax code (1986) (Mayhew 1991). These bills rarely satisfied both sides, but they were passed. On many other matters, parties stalemated (Binder 1999).

This lack of internal coherence within the parties from the 1930s through the 1980s created significant internal tensions and desires to change their electoral bases. Northern liberals wanted a Democratic Party that stood for liberal causes such as civil rights and social programs that would enhance equality of opportunity (Mackenzie and Weisbrot 2008). Conservatives wanted a Republican Party that stood for less government, lower taxes, and traditional moral values (Reiter and Stonecash 2011). Each party had a strong faction that pushed for change. Republicans pursued conservatives in the South (Black and Black 1987, 2002), whereas Democrats sought the support of liberals in northern areas (Ware 2006).

These efforts have been successful, and during the last several decades there has been a gradual and steady realignment. Republicans have attracted fiscal and social conservatives and Democrats have attracted fiscal and social liberals (Stonecash, Brewer, and Mariani 2003; Polsby 2004; Brewer and Stonecash 2009; Reiter and Stonecash 2011). Liberals are now more likely to be Democrats and conservatives to be Republicans (Abramowitz 2010). Those with a strong attachment to religion are now more likely to be Republican (Layman 2001). The less affluent are now more likely to vote Democratic, and those who are more affluent are more likely to vote Republican (Stonecash 2000, 2010). The parties differ more and they have engaged in a lengthy process of creating more coherent messages and party images. They have recruited candidates for Congress and gradually have achieved greater consistency in presidential and Congressional election outcomes in House districts (Brewer and Stonecash 2009, 23; Stonecash 2013).

This process of realignment is by no means complete, meaning predictable and stable election bases cannot be assumed. Over the decade of the 2000s, neither party had a secure majority (Stonecash 2011). Each party has had to consider how much their policy proposals can differ and what will help the party win swing districts. The parties do, however, clearly represent different constituencies and have greater unity compared to 20–30 years ago. In the 1960s and 1970s, many Democrats had voting records similar to Republicans, whereas there were many Republicans with voting records similar to Democrats. There is little overlap now (Stonecash 2006), and the degree of polarization is greater than in the past.

The party policy-making process is now more cohesive within parties and party members vote together more. Parties now have less internal diversity, and members in Congress grant their leaders more power to pressure party members to go along with party goals (Rohde 1991). Leaders, in turn, use these powers to appoint loyal party members to committee and leadership positions (Sinclair 2006; Pearson 2008). These changes have come about because parties set goals, and pursued and attracted voters (Hillygus and Shields 2008; Cohen et al. 2008; Karol 2009).

The combination of more within-party similarity of electoral bases and leadership pressures results in members within each party being more likely to vote together. Figure 10.1 shows the percentage of Democrats and Republicans voting with a majority of their party in the Senate since 1952: In the 1960s, about 75 percent of members voted with their party; now it is up to 90 percent. The pattern in the House is very similar. In 2009–2010, Republicans stood united against Democratic legislation to stimulate the economy, to reform health care, and to regulate financial institutions. Parties' opposition to each other is more organized (Sinclair 2008), intense, and nasty (Eilperin 2006; Brownstein 2007). Compromise is more difficult and less likely.

Nevertheless, the study of the party-policy connection is not as well developed as might be expected. First, for some time, many believed we were witnessing the decline of political parties (Crotty 1984). Parties had less control over who was

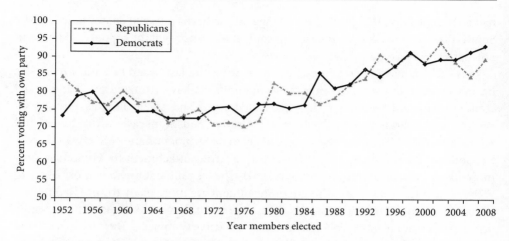

FIG. 10.1 Average Party Unity Score by Party, Senate, 1952—2010

nominated and candidates had more independent resources, so candidates were able to operate independently of formal party organizations (Aldrich 1995). The result was that campaigns were seen as increasingly candidate-centered (Wattenberg 1981, 1990, 1991). Some went so far as to argue that there really were not parties but just Members of Congress who arrived with differing views; they voted together when they shared views and not because they constituted a party (Krehbiel 1993). Further, there was evidence that the correlation between House and presidential results at the district level had declined significantly (Stonecash 2013). Not only were candidates seen as operating separately from party organizations but, also, their fate was not tied to that of their presidential candidates. It was unclear how much parties could be seen as unified entities pursuing coherent policy choices. Elites might be polarized, but this reflected a disconnection from the public (Fiorina 2009). This interpretation of party decline and autonomous politicians suggests that there is only a tenuous party-policy connection.

Further, some have claimed that the Democratic Party has been losing its working-class electoral base that might have encouraged it to advocate expanding social policies. Although the evidence was not persuasive, there was considerable writing that the white working class has abandoned the Democratic Party (Edsall and Edsall 1991) as Republicans have targeted cultural issues like abortion and gay rights (Frank 2004). Those with less education generally hold a more authoritarian orientation (Hetherington and Weiler 2009), and making cultural issues more salient was presumed to reduce working-class support for Democrats, reducing their ability to advocate for social programs. Although this argument lacks convincing evidence, it dominated for some time (Stonecash 2012) and for many years there was less focus on the policy pursuits and impacts of parties on policy.

The study of the party-policy connection has also been constrained because the range of issues subject to public debate is perhaps not as great as we might presume. As a number of scholars have noted in recent years, many of the things that government does are not very visible and subject to limited political debate. Many social benefits are seen as "givens" that support activities that society wishes to support, and are not highly visible and/or subject to regular political review (Howard 1997, 2007). Homeowners are allowed to deduct mortgage interest payments and property taxes because we wish to encourage homeownership. Businesses, small and large, are allowed to claim deductions to help them provide health insurance and retirement pensions to their workers. These tax benefits become "givens," their costs are generally not recognized, and they receive less attention than issues such as welfare, Medicaid, and Medicare. Most voters are largely unaware of the extent of these "programs" and who they benefit. When given more information about them, many voters are generally less supportive of their existence (Mettler 2011). Considering the sizable public ignorance about these benefits, however, most high-profile party debates about social policy do not fully incorporate these less visible programs.

3 STRUCTURING DEBATES: PARTY PRESENTATION OF POLICY ALTERNATIVES

As the legislative process unfolds in Washington, one of the primary concerns of parties is to structure the debate. Party leaders want voters to understand what are the central issues, how the party sees a given issue, the virtues of the party's approach, and the flaws of the opposing party's approach. Although many voters dislike these exchanges, regarding them as bickering, party leaders have high hopes for the positive effects of this process. Parties present differing sides of an issue to the public, thereby creating a meaningful dialogue about public policy. Parties are the vehicles for creating debates about desirable social policies (Key 1984 [1949]), and they are "mechanisms for comprising competing group demands" (Bibby and Schaffner 2008, 12). Ideally, strong parties enable better representation of differing concerns and groups, thus ameliorating the problems of citizen disengagement and excessive influence of special interests (Key 1984 [1949]). In this view, political parties are central to democracy because they are the vehicles by which the disparate interests of the public are represented in public policy.

Policy-making is often a contest over parties' different conceptions of realities in which the language they use "reflects, advances, and interprets" the alternative policy positions represented by parties (Rochefort and Cobb 1994, 9). As party differences have increased, parties have become more concerned about "framing" issues to their advantage. A frame is a "central organizing idea or storyline that provides meaning" (Gamson and Modigliani 1989, 1–37). Frames can embody broad, overarching principles, or they can involve narrower concepts. Parties use frames to present an issue to voters in a way that constructs a proposed policy's meaning and affects reactions among the public (Goffman 1974).

Framing an issue is valuable for parties because it provides the public with an interpretation, a way to think about an issue that connects with larger political battles (Callaghan and Schnell 2001). For example, Republicans in 2009 wanted voters to see the health care proposal in a way favorable to their agenda of less government and more individual freedom. To make that connection, they focused on the theme of restrictions in choice of doctors, framing the issue as involving an issue of fundamental importance, namely, personal freedom. Former vice-presidential candidate Sarah Palin depicted the Democratic Party's health-care reform plan as opening the door to "death panels." With this language, Palin portrayed the health-care plan as a policy that would deprive individuals of freedom over choices related to their health care.

Frames have such a powerful effect on citizens because many individuals do not have the time, energy, or resources to investigate policy implications. A large proportion of citizens lacks political knowledge and issue awareness (e.g., Converse 1966; Campbell et al. 1960; Delli Carpini and Keeter 1996; Gilens 1999), and thus often rely on cues provided by trusted members of one's political party. These messages work best when they are consistent, easily understood, and part of a broader narrative being presented by a party. For example, a person affiliated with the Democratic Party may support additional revenues for Social Security because prominent members of the Democratic Party have framed the issue in terms of "saving" the Social Security trust fund, rather than debate the general size and scope of government. The goal is to convince a voter to see the issue as a modest fix to a favorite program rather than a referendum about big government. These types of cues facilitate decision making because they serve as a substitute for the time-consuming process of obtaining full information.

4 POLARIZATION AND POLICY RHETORIC ON ISSUES

Although we lack long-term studies about how political actors frame issues, there is reason to suspect that the language on public policy issues has become more ideological as the parties have polarized in recent decades (McCarty et al. 2006; Stonecash et al. 2003; Stonecash 2006). In addition, there are more news outlets than in the past, and many of these sources—such as Fox News, MSNBC, right-leaning talk radio, and the left-leaning blogosphere—are more partisan than traditional news sources such as network television news (Hayes 2010). These more partisan venues allow for party advocacy (Jamieson and Cappella 2008) and enable parties to amplify and promote their messages, resulting in the recruitment and mobilization of their partisans. Indeed, some worry that the parties have gotten too good at the process of negatively portraying their opposition.

The rhetoric seems to have become more ideological, emotional, and intense, with some arguing the language has changed for the worse (Eilperin 2006).

Although we need more studies of how language has changed, it appears that political language is becoming more polarized. Three issues—economic policy, welfare, and health care—demonstrate how parties use language to discuss issues over time and indicate how policy discussions are enmeshed in party ideologies.

Economic Policy: Perhaps the most important effort by parties is to shape perceptions of what role government should play in the economy. The essential issue is what makes the economy work and whether or not government can increase economic growth through public spending. By the 1960s, it appeared that both parties had largely accepted Keynesian economics and the logic that government could affect the aggregate performance of the economy (Stein 1969). Economic policy was often discussed in terms of macroeconomic manipulations and the trade-off between inflation and unemployment. If the economy slumped and there were fewer jobs and a greater need for social programs such as welfare and Food Stamps, the widely shared view was that government should engage in countercyclical spending. This assigned a significant role to government action during times that unemployment and poverty increased.

Starting in the 1970s, that consensus began to break down. Since roughly the 1980s, the Republican Party has emphasized the positive role of individual entrepreneurs and the negative effects of government regulation and taxes. In the words of former President Reagan, "excessive taxation has robbed us of incentive" (cited in Smith 2007, 140). Over the last decade or so, Republicans have consistently highlighted the negative effects of government actions on economic growth. During debates in 2010 and 2011 about whether to raise taxes to reduce budget deficits, Republicans characterized them as "job-killing" taxes. With this narrative, the party has attempted to convince voters that government action does more harm than good (Smith 2007; Jones and Williams 2008). The result is two competing narratives championed by each party: one emphasizing how aggregate government spending has a positive effect and the other emphasizing its detrimental effects (Wapshot 2011).

Welfare: This debate over what makes the economy work is connected to discussions about various social programs such as public assistance and food stamps. The debate between the parties over public assistance has been contentious since AFDC (Aid to Families with Dependent Children) was adopted in the 1930s (Derthick 1970; Mettler 1998). Many Republicans were not supportive but struggled for some time to find a positive way to express their opposition. Beginning in the 1980s, they were able to frame their opposition in terms of how welfare created dependency, which sapped the resolve of recipients and ultimately harmed them (Murray 1984, 2012; Olasky 1992). This way of framing the debate has gradually grown in prominence (Mead 2011), creating a clear contrast between the parties in how they discuss programs that provide government support. Democrats argue that the economy is not generating sufficient jobs and that tax policies favor the more affluent, generating growing inequality (Congressional Budget Office 2011). Their argument is that the focus should be on the needs of individuals at a time when the economy is not providing widespread opportunity. This dispute has come to involve other social programs. Republicans also now argue that extended unemployment compensation and Food Stamps are detrimental because they discourage people from working.

Health Care: Another area in which party framing has been important is health care. In recent decades, more and more people have lost their health insurance. Whether this is seen as a problem and what role government should play in response has become a contentious partisan issue. President Bill Clinton tried to enact expanded health-care coverage through government in 1993 and 1994, and it prompted strong Republican resistance. During 2009-2010, President Barack Obama and Congressional Democrats pursued and enacted health-care reform legislation. The debate on health care reflected the polarized nature of parties' political communications, as well as the importance of constructing a clear and consistent narrative. Democrats focused on the need to manage the nation's health-care costs and stressed the role of government as a positive force to restrain costs through structured rules and incentives. They also emphasized issues of equality of access and told stories of people's lives ruined by lack of access or bills that bankrupted them. The emphasis was on government helping individuals denied help by the private sector. Fairness was central to their language.

Republican opposition to the reform proposals was organized around the values of freedom and personal responsibility. Republican members of Congress, activists, and citizens raised fears of "government takeover" or government-controlled health care. At town-hall meetings, throngs of people chanted "tyranny" and "just say no." As Sarah Palin stated it: "The America I know and love is not one in which my parents or my baby with Down Syndrome will have to stand in front of Obama's 'death panel' so his bureaucrats can decide…whether they are worthy of health care. Such a system is downright evil" (Seelye 2009). This language resonated strongly with Republicans who saw health care as a personal responsibility (Saad 2009).

These brief summaries indicate the consequences of the partisan framing contest. The language parties use to talk about issues of public policy has become more ideological and moral, and partisan debates appear to have become more emotional and intense. With this ideologically and emotionally charged rhetoric, party elites seek not only to win the support of public opinion but also to mobilize their bases to make a clamor about public policy issues. Increasingly polarized language over policy debates is not just an elite phenomenon. Today's voters—compared to voters in the 1970s—are more partisan (Bartels 2000; Stonecash 2006; Prior 2007). Many of these voters, especially those who are more politically aware, are attentive to the cues provided by party elites (Zaller 1992) and seek out information consistent with their political beliefs (Stroud 2008). When these voters encounter partisan messages—such as the Republican Party's communiqué that the Democrats' health-care plan would curtail Americans' freedom in the domain of health—they may hold stronger opinions and engage in action, including boisterous behavior at town-hall meetings, to oppose various policies and to help their party elites take control of the debate.

5 PARTIES, POLARIZATION AND POLICY DECISIONS

Although the parties have drifted farther apart and use language that presents different alternatives, have these trends produced differences in policies? We know that parties differ in the policies they propose (Hetherington and Keefe 2007, 143–157, Hershey 2011, 289–293). Republicans want lower taxes and fewer regulations and more limited social programs. Democrats want to maintain tax levels and a progressive tax system, and to use the revenues to provide more social programs such as job training, health care, and financial aid for college. Republicans generally want legislation that will support traditional moral values, and Democrats generally want government to stay out of such matters (Brewer and Stonecash 2007). But do these differences between parties affect policy? Has polarization prompted parties to be more intense in their opposition to change, such that gridlock occurs? Or, has polarization made each party more inclined to band together in unity and enact policies over the opposition of the other party?

We can test the effect of parties in two general ways. Parties battle for control of the presidency and Congress, and we can assess whether party control of institutions affects social policy in the short-term. Political parties are also engaged in the longer-term process of affecting public debate and getting their proposals established as credible social-policy alternatives. This route may shape policy without a party necessarily acquiring formal control of government. Each is an important means for parties to have influence.

Shifts in party control and short-term effects: Perhaps the most obvious way that a party can affect social policy is by acquiring control over institutions and enacting policy changes. Over the last 100 years, there have been times when a party had unified control, saw itself as having some sort of a mandate, and enacted significant policy changes. This occurred at the national level in the mid-1930s (Deckard 1976; Sundquist 1983; Brady 1988) and the mid-1960s (Mackenzie and Weisbrot 2008; Brewer and Stonecash 2009, 81–103). We also have case studies indicating that this has occurred in various states (Jennings 1977a, 1977b; Stonecash 2003).

Analyses of the effects of short-term changes in party control on social policy have been limited for two reasons. First, for a lengthy period of the last century, the condition of a coherent unified party was not met. From the late 1930s through some time in the 1980s, the Congressional parties were not highly unified. For most of that time Congress was dominated by the "Conservative Coalition," which consisted of conservative southern Democrats and northern Republicans (Patterson 1967; Shelley 1983). The parties differed, but each party had numerous moderates (Bond, Fleisher, and Stonecash 2008), and there was not a strong consensus within each party on what they wanted to achieve. For much of this time, the presidential and congressional wings of the party did not share the same electoral base. It was only in the mid-1990s that each wing of the party came from generally the same electoral base, and votes for president, House, and Senate candidates began to correlate at a fairly high level (Stonecash 2013).

The other important condition is that there be unified party control of institutions—the presidency and both houses of Congress. It has been difficult to assess whether parties really make a difference in enacting policy because there were few years of unified party control. Unified party control of government was not the norm from 1952 through 2000. That occurred only in 1961–1968, 1977–1980, and 1993–1994. Those years might be used as tests of the impact of parties, but most of those years were also ones in which the parties were still diverse internally. During the first two sets of years, each party contained some liberals and conservatives and many moderates. Within-party diversity was high, differences between the parties were at their lowest, and party unity in voting was low. Even in 1993–1994, the polarization in policy proposals that we now see was only beginning to be evident. The result was that many policy proposals drew support from both parties, and the goals of parties were not so clearly different. The exception involves the years 1965–1966. During those years, the large majorities that Democrats gained in the 1964 election resulted in the Great Society programs. That burst of legislation constitutes a clear case in which a party pursued an agenda, won an election, interpreted it as a mandate, and acted (Brewer and Stonecash 2009, 81–103).

From the 1970s through 2000, the more common situation was divided control, but with growing differences between the parties. There were few situations of clear party control, and no situations of Republican control such that we could see what an alternation in party control might mean. The persistence of divided control prompted many to focus on whether *anything* was achieved. The general conclusion was that government still continued to enact major legislation (Mayhew 1991), yet the rise of party polarization did slow down the rate of enactment and the rate of proposing major bills (Binder 1999, 2003). One exception was the major reform of welfare in 1996. In general, however, party polarization resulted in stalemate: the greater the difference between the parties, the less likely major bills would be enacted (Binder 1999; Jones 2001).

We know much less about how divided control affected policy negotiations. Did gridlock merely create initial policy positions that were further apart as a bargaining strategy, but which were then compromised to produce moderate policies? Or, was the greater cohesiveness of Republicans a vehicle to mount a sustained attack on taxes and social programs? Bartels presents data indicating that under situations of divided control, inequality in the distribution of income consistently increased when Republicans controlled the presidency, compared to when a Democrat was president (Bartels 2008, 29–63; but also see Campbell 2011). The evidence indicates that partisan control of at least the presidency matters.

Recent years provide a more interesting test of the joint impact of party control and party polarization. In 2000, for the first time in many decades, Republicans gained control of the presidency and both houses of Congress. In an era when the party had a more clearly conservative base, Republicans finally had power. Democrats won control of the House in 2006 and divided control prevailed for two years. Then, in 2008, Democrats won control of both houses; Barack Obama won the presidency and unified control prevailed. Did these alternations of party control affect policy?

The unified control under George W. Bush appears to have had a significant impact (Jacobson 2006; Hedge 2009). Bush quickly pursued a major tax cut, affirming Republicans' long-held view that existing tax levels served as a disincentive to entrepreneurs. The Republicans controlling Congress agreed, with a party-line vote supporting his proposal. The estate tax was significantly cut back, fulfilling a long-standing Republican goal (Graetz and Shapiro 2004). The rules for declaring bankruptcy were made more difficult, responding to the complaints of creditors. When Republicans enacted Medicare part D in 2003, they focused on making the program a subsidy to purchase benefits from private companies rather than government. The Bush administration was also able to cut back on many regulations affecting business and the environment (Hedge 2009). The goal of many of these actions was to reduce taxation and the accompanying resources available to government. The goal was to reduce the flow of revenues, which would lead to larger deficits and provide a basis for cutting social programs. Party control mattered because the condition of an ideologically cohesive party existed (Rohde and Aldrich 2010).

In the 2008 elections, after two years of divided control and stalemate, Democrats gained unified control. Early in 2009, Congress passed legislation that increased the ability of women to sue a company for wage discrimination, even if they do not discover the practice until years after it began, reversing a Supreme Court decision (Stolberg 2009). Republicans had declined to pass such legislation. The Democratic Congress then passed an economic stimulus bill in an effort to boost the sagging economy. Republicans wanted extensive tax cuts, but Democrats put more emphasis and spending on expanded unemployment benefits, Food Stamps, health-care subsidies for those laid off, aid to states, spending for construction of highways and bridges, and school renovations. The bill passed with almost no Republican support. In March 2010, after a lengthy battle, Democrats were able to pass health-care reform legislation (Jacobs and Skocpol 2010). Republicans uniformly opposed the bill. Democratic Party control meant the enactment of social policies and the pursuit of a policy agenda that Republicans would not have pursued, just as Republican control from 2001–2006 meant pursuit of an agenda that Democrats would not have pursued.

Long-term policy effects: Although assessments of short-term changes receive considerable attention, the long-term goals of parties are just as important. A crucial matter is the general degree of support for their positions (Katz 2010). Party leaders are very aware that, over time, public opinion can shift for or against them, and they must play a role in seeking to affect that. They also must be prepared to take advantage of any shifts that occur. Although we have only limited measures of general policy dispositions over time, scholars generally argue that there has been a gradual rise and fall of support for liberalism since the Second World War (Ellis and Stimson 2007; Coggins and Stimson 2012). From the 1950s through the 1960s, there was growing support for the liberal argument that government could be effective in managing society, and that policies promoting equality of opportunity should be enacted (Mackenzie and Weisbrot 2008). This liberal dominance of policy eventually prompted an effort by conservatives to present alternative interpretations of how society works and of the effect of liberal policies (Smith 2007; Hacker and Pierson 2010). They funded scholars to reinterpret the effects of programs like welfare (Murray 1984) and to recast policy debates within a conservative framework. They emphasized the argument that government was doing too much, taxes were too high, and programs should be restrained. Conservatives were able to create an alternative interpretation of how society works and what government should do. In 1994, after a lengthy process of trying to move the party in a more conservative direction, Republicans succeeded in winning control of the House and the Senate (Balz and Brownstein 1996; Drew 1997; Stonecash and Mariani 2000). Republicans were able to alter the climate of support for a liberal approach sufficiently that, in his 1996 State of the Union address, President Bill Clinton declared, "The era of big government is over." That was taken as evidence that the center of the policy debate had shifted in a more conservative direction.

The goal of conservatives was to reshape the presumed value of social programs, shifting the debate from whether to increase funding for social programs or maintain the status quo to whether these programs should be cut. There is some evidence they have succeeded. Over time, there have been reductions of benefits or restricted access (Hacker 2008; Hacker and Pierson 2005). Welfare was cut back; aid to attend college declined; income tax rates for the affluent were cut (Soss, Hacker, and Mettler 2007). The estate tax also was cut (Graetz and Shapiro 2004). We need more research on these long-term shifts, but it does appear that over the last several decades the efforts of conservatives to mobilize and shift the terms of debate have been effective. That has in turn reduced support for social programs.

Although those long-term efforts are important, parties have another way to influence social policy. In recent years, parties have been locked in a battle (Binder 2003; Brady and Volden 2006), each seeking to prevent the other from making major policy changes. Although engaged in that long-term battle, they also realize that when an opportunity comes along to change public policy, they must seize it as a means of changing the "givens" of social policy. Much policy making is incremental (Brady, Ferejohn, and Harbridge 2008). If the base situation can be altered, then it could affect the long-run availability of resources for social programs and the level of support for social programs. In the area of taxation, for example, Republicans have sought to preserve the tax expenditures that benefit their constituents (Mettler 2011) while reducing the flow of resources by lowering income tax rates and lowering the estate tax. That contributes to a situation of large deficits, which in turn prompts the question of whether America can continue to fund social programs such as unemployment compensation, Food Stamps, Medicaid, and Medicare at current levels.

Democrats have sought, when the opportunity arises, to ensconce programs in the federal budget and make them givens. This has happened with federal grants to attend college (Strach 2009), the establishment of the Food Stamp Program (Rosenfeld 2010), and the Earned Income Tax Credit (Ventry 2000). The result of establishing a program as an entitlement is that, when families experience income or job loss during a recession, the program automatically provides benefits to those who qualify. The result is that during a recession, such as that experienced in the late 2000s–early 2010s, the number of people supported increased significantly and the policy gridlock between the parties could not affect the provision of this benefit. If the economy is generating many jobs that provide only modest incomes, then the existence of the Earned Income Tax Credit makes many people automatically available. When the program began in 1975, it benefited 6.2 million families and cost $ 1.25 billion (Holt 2006). By 2011 there were 26.2 million families receiving benefits at a cost of $ 58.6 billion (IRS 2012).

6 CONCLUSION

The party-social policy link appears to be stronger now than several decades ago. Parties now present relatively coherent and strongly differing views about public policy. Increased polarization means that voters are presented with clearer portraits of the differences between Democrats and Republicans. They are presenting distinct arguments about which policies work well and which do not. If the goal is to have parties present and debate differing interpretations, we are getting that. The parties have influence over policy in several ways. When they do gain control over the presidency and Congress, they now seek and often do make significant policy changes. They also have long-run strategies. Each party devotes considerable energy and thought to how to frame the policy debates they present to voters. There are consistent efforts to shape and shift the debate in their favor. Some policies were established when a party held power, and they are somewhat less susceptible to short-term shifts in power.

There is still much to study about the impact of parties on public policy. Sorting this out has been difficult because the parties did not differ as much in prior decades and we had limited clear alternation of party power. Now we have parties that differ more and it appears that control means more. If polarization persists, we will have more and more cases for testing just how much party control matters for public policy.

NOTES

1. This presumption that parties are an important part of understanding policy developments is not shared by all scholars. In a recent review of the scholarship on the politics of inequality, only a few books that make parties central to the analysis are included. See Jacobs and Soss 2010.

REFERENCES

* Indicates recommended reading.

*Abramowitz, Alan I. 2010. *The Disappearing Center: Engaged Citizens, Polarization, and American Democracy*. New Haven, CT: Yale University Press.

Aldrich, John H. 1995. *Why Parties: The Origin and Transformation of Party Politics in America.* Chicago: University of Chicago Press.

Balz, Dan, and Ronald Brownstein. 1996. *Storming the Gates: Protest Politics and the Republican Revival.* Boston: Little Brown.

Bartels, Larry M. 2000. "Partisanship and Voting Behavior, 1952–1996." *American Journal of Political Science,* 44 (1) (January): 35–49.

Bartels, Larry M. 2008. *Unequal Democracy: The Political Economy of the Gilded Age.* Princeton, NJ: Princeton University Press.

Baumer, Donald C., and Howard J. Gold. 2010. *Parties, Polarization, and Democracy in the United States.* Boulder: Paradigm.

Bibby, John, and Brian Schaffner. 2008. *Politics, Parties, and Elections in America.* 6th ed. Boston: Thomson Wadsworth.

Binder, Sarah A. 1999. "The Dynamics of Legislative Gridlock, 1947–1996." *American Political Science Review* 93 (September): 519–533.

Binder, Sarah A. 2003. *Stalemate: Causes and Consequences of Legislative Gridlock.* Washington, DC: Brooking Institution.

Black, Merle, and Earl Black. 1987. *Politics and Society in the South.* Cambridge, MA: Harvard University Press.

Black, Merle, and Earl Black. 2002. *The Rise of Southern Republicans.* Cambridge, MA: Harvard University Press.

Bond, Jon R., Richard Fleisher, and Jeffrey M. Stonecash. 2008. "The Rise and Decline of Moderates in the House of Representatives." Presented at the Going to Extremes Conference, Dartmouth College, June.

Brady, David W. 1988. *Critical Elections and Congressional Policy Making.* Stanford: Stanford University Press.

Brady, David, and Craig Volden. 2006. *Revolving Gridlock,* 2nd ed. Boulder: Westview Press.

Brady, David W., John Ferejohn, and Laurel Harbridge. 2008. "Polarization and Public Policy: A General Assessment." In Pietro S. Nivola and David W. Brady, eds., *Red and Blue Nation?* Washington, DC: Brookings Institution, 107–133.

Brewer, Mark D., and Jeffrey M. Stonecash. 2007. *Split: Class and Cultural Divides in American Politics.* Washington, DC: CQ Press.

*Brewer, Mark D., and Jeffrey M. Stonecash. 2009. *Dynamics of American Political Parties.* New York: Cambridge University Press.

Brownstein, Ronald. 2007. *The Second Civil War: How Extreme Partisanship Has Paralyzed Washington and Polarized America.* New York: Penguin Press.

Callaghan, Karen, and Frauke Schnell. 2001. "Assessing the Democratic Debate: How the News Media Frame Elite Policy Discourse." *Political Communication* 18:183–212.

Campbell, Angus, Philip E. Converse, Warren E. Miller, and Donald E. Stokes. 1960. *The American Voter.* New York: John Wiley & Sons.

Campbell, James E. 2011. "The Economic Records of the Presidents: Party Differences and Inherited Economic Conditions." *The Forum* 9 (1). Available at http://www.bepress.com/forum/vol9/iss1/art7.

Coggins, K. Elizabeth, and James A. Stimson. 2012. "The Vanishing Liberal." Presented at the Southern Political Science Association Meetings, New Orleans. January 12–14, 2012.

Cohen, Marty, David Karol, Hans Noel, and John Zaller. 2008. *The Party Decides: Presidential Nominations Before and After Reform.* Chicago: University of Chicago Press.

Congressional Budget Office. 2011. *Trends in the Distribution of Household Income Between 1979 and 2007.* October: http:www.cbo.gov/doc.cfm?index=12485.

Converse, Philip E. 1966. "The Concept of a Normal Vote." In Angus Campbell, Philip E. Converse, Warren E. Miller, and Donald E. Stokes, eds., *Elections and the Political Order*. New York: John Wiley, 6–39.

Crotty, William. 1984. *American Parties in Decline*, 2nd ed. Boston: Little Brown.

Deckard, Barbara Sinclair. 1976. "Political Upheaval and Congressional Voting: The Effects of the 1960s on Voting Patterns in the House of Representatives." *Journal of Politics* 38 (2 (May): 326–345.

Delli Carpini, Michael, and Scott Keeter. 1996. *What Americans Know about Politics and Why It Matters*. New Haven, CT: Yale University Press.

Derthick, Martha. 1970. *The Influence of Federal Grants*. Cambridge, MA: Harvard University Press.

Drew, Elizabeth. 1997. *Showdown: The Struggle Between the Gingrich Congress and the Clinton White House*. New York: Touchstone Books.

*Edsall, Thomas B., and Mary D. Edsall. 1991. *Chain Reaction: The Impact of Race, Rights, and Taxes on American Politics*. New York: W.W. Norton.

Eilperin, Juliet. 2006. *Fight Club Politics: How Partisanship is Poisoning the House of Representatives*. Lanham, MD: Rowman and Littlefield.

Ellis, Christopher, and James A. Stimson. 2007. "On Symbolic Conservatism in America." Paper presented at the American Political Science Association Meetings, Chicago, Illinois, September.

Fiorina, Morris P. 2002. *Divided Government*. 2nd ed. New York: Longman.

*Fiorina, Morris P., with Samuel J. Abrams. 2009. *Disconnect: the Breakdown of Representation in American Politics*. Norman: University of Oklahoma Press.

Frank, Thomas. 2004. *What's the Matter with Kansas: How Conservatives Won the Heart of America*. New York: Metropolitan Books.

Gamson, William A., and Andre Modigliani. 1989. "Media Discourse and Public Opinion on Nuclear Power: A Constructionist Approach." *American Journal of Sociology* 95, (1): 1–37.

Gilens, Martin. 1999. *Why Americans Hate Welfare: Race, Media, and the Politics of Antipoverty Policy*. Chicago: University of Chicago Press, 1999.

Goffman, Erving. 1974. *Frame Analysis*. New York: Harper & Row.

Graetz, Michael J., and Ian Shapiro. 2004. *Death by a Thousand Cuts: The Fight Over Taxing Inherited Wealth*. Princeton, NJ: Princeton University Press.

Hacker, Jacob S. 2008. *The Great Risk Shift: The New Economic Insecurity and the Decline of the American Dream*. New York: Oxford University Press.

Hacker, Jacob S., and Paul Pierson. 2005. *Off Center: The Republican Revolution and the Evolution of Democracy*. New Haven, CT: Yale University Press.

*Hacker, Jacob S., and Paul Pierson. 2010. *Winner-Take-All Politics: How Washington Made the Rich Richer—and Turned Its Back on the Middle Class*. New York: Simon and Schuster.

Hayes, Danny. 2010. "Party Communication in a Transformed Media Age." In Jeffrey M. Stonecash, ed., *New Directions in Political Parties*. New York: Routledge, 44–62.

Hedge, David M. 2009. "The George W. Bush Presidency and Control of the Bureaucracy." Presented at the American Political Science Association Meetings, Toronto, September 3–6, 2009.

Hershey, Marjorie Randon. 2011. *Party Politics in America*. 14th ed. New York: Pearson/ Longman.

Hetherington, Marc J., and William J. Keefe. 2007. *Parties, Politics, and Public Policy*. Washington, DC: CQ Press.

Hetherington, Marc J., and Jonathan D. Weiler. 2009. *Authoritarianism and Polarization in American Politics*. Cambridge: Cambridge University Press.

Hibbing, John R., and Elizabeth Theiss-Morse. 1995. *Congress as Public Enemy: Public Attitudes Toward American Political Institutions*. New York: Cambridge University Press.

Hillygus, D. Sunshine, and Todd G. Shields. 2008. *The Persuadable Voter: Wedge Issues in Presidential Campaigns*. Princeton, NJ: Princeton University Press.

Holt, Steve. 2006. *The Earned Income Tax Credit at Age 30: What We Know*. Washington, DC: Brookings Insitution, February http://www.brookings.edu/~/media/research/files/reports/2006/2/childrenfamilies%20holt/20060209_holt.pdf.

Howard, Christopher. 1997. *The Hidden Welfare State: Tax Expenditures and Social Policy in the United States*. Princeton, NJ: Princeton University Press.

Howard, Christopher. 2007. *The Welfare State Nobody Knows: Debunking Myths about U.S. Social Policy*. Princeton, NJ: Princeton University Press.

IRS (Internal Revenue Service). 2012. *EITC Statistics*. http://www.eitc.irs.gov/central/eitcstats/.

Jacobs, Lawrence R., and Theda Skocpol. 2010. *Health Care Reform and American Politics*. New York: Oxford University Press.

Jacobs, Lawrence R., and Joe Soss. 2010. "The Politics of Inequality in America: A Political Economy Framework." *Annual Review of Political Science* 13:341–364.

Jacobson, Gary C. 2006. *A Divider, Not a Uniter*. New York: Longman.

Jamieson, Kathleen Hall, and Joseph N. Cappella. 2008. *Echo Chamber: Rush Limbaugh and the Conservative Media Establishment*. New York: Oxford University Press.

Jennings, Edward T. 1977a. "Some Policy Consequences of the Long Revolution and Bifactional Rivalry in Louisiana." *American Journal of Political Science* 21 (2): 225–246.

Jennings, Edward T. 1977b. "Competition, Constituencies, and Welfare Policies in the American States." *American Political Science Review* 73 (2): 414–429.

Jones, Bryan D., and Walter Williams. 2008. *The Politics of Good and Bad Ideas: The Great Tax Delusion and the Decline of Good Government in America*. Chicago: University of Chicago Press.

Jones, David R. 2001. "Party Polarization and Legislative Gridlock." *Political Research Quarterly* 54 (March): 125–141.

*Karol, David. 2009. *Party Position Change in American Politics: Coalition Management*. New York: Cambridge University Press.

Katz, Michael B. 2010. "The American Welfare State and Social Contract in Hard Times." *Journal of Policy History* 22 (4): 508–529.

Key, V.O. 1984 [1949]. *Southern Politics in State and Nation*. Knoxville: University of Tennessee Press.

Krehbiel, Keith. 1993. "Where's the Party?" *British Journal of Political Science* 23, no. 2 (April): 235–266.

Layman, Geoffrey. 2001. *The Great Divide: Religious and Cultural Conflict in American Party Politics*. New York: Columbia University Press.

Mackenzie, G. Calvin, and Robert Weisbrot. 2008. *The Liberal Hour: Washington and the Politics of Change in the 1960s*. New York: Penguin Press.

Mann, Thomas E., and Norman Ornstein. 2006. *The Broken Branch: How Congress Is Failing America and How to Get It Back on Track*. New York: Oxford University Press.

Mayhew, David R. 1991. *Divided We Govern: Party Control, Lawmaking, and Investigations 1946–1990*. New Haven, CT: Yale University Press.

*McCarty, Nolan, Keith T. Poole, and Howard Rosenthal. 2006. *Polarized America: The Dance of Ideology and Unequal Riches*. Cambridge, MA: MIT Press.

Mead, Lawrence M. 2011. "Welfare Politics in Congress." *PS: Political Science and Politics*, 44 no. 2 (April): 345–356.

Mettler, Suzanne. 1998. *Dividing Citizens: Gender and Federalism in New Deal Public Policy*. Ithaca, NY: Cornell University Press.

Mettler, Suzanne. 2011. *The Submerged State: How Invisible Government Policies Undermine American Democracy*. Chicago: University of Chicago Press.

Murray, Charles. 1984. *Losing Ground: America Social Policy, 1950—1980*. New York: Basic Books.

*Murray, Charles. 2012. *Coming Apart: The State of White America, 1960–2010*. New York: Crown Forum.

Olasky, Marvin. 1992. *The Tragedy of American Compassion*. Washington, DC: Regnery.

Patterson, James T. 1967. *Congressional Conservatism and the New Deal: The Growth of the Conservative Coalition in Congress, 1933–1939*. Lexington: University of Kentucky Press.

Pearson, Kathryn. 2008. "Party Loyalty and Discipline in the Individualistic Senate." In Nathan W. Monroe, Jason M. Roberts, and David W. Rohde, eds., *Why Not Parties? Party Effects in the United States Senate*. Chicago: University of Chicago Press, 100–120.

Polsby, Nelson W. 2004. *How Congress Evolves: Social Bases of Institutional Change*. New York: Oxford University Press.

Prior, Markus. 2007. *Post-Broadcast Democracy*. New York: Cambridge University Press.

Reiter, Howard L., and Jeffrey M. Stonecash. 2011. *Counter-Realignment: Political Change in the Northeast*. New York: Cambridge University Press.

Rochefort, David A., and Roger W Cobb. 1994. *The Politics of Problem Definition: Shaping the Policy Agenda*. Lawrence: University Press of Kansas.

Rohde, David W. 1991. *Parties and Leaders in the Postreform House*. Chicago: University of Chicago Press.

Rohde, David, and John Aldrich. 2010. "Consequences of Electoral and Institutional Change: The Evolution of Conditional Party Government in the U.S. House of Representatives." In Jeffrey M. Stonecash, ed., *New Directions in American Political Parties*. New York: Routledge, 234–250.

Rosenfeld, Sam. 2010. "Fed by Reform: Congressional Politics, Partisan Change, and the Food Stamp Program, 1961–1981." *Journal of Policy History* 22 (4): 474–507.

Saad, Lydia. 2009. "Many in U.S. See Health Insurance as Personal Responsibility," September 30: http://www.gallup.com/poll/123332/Many-U.S.-See-Health-Insurance-Personal-Responsibility.aspx.

Seelye, Katherine Q. 2009. "Sarah Palin Calls Health Care Overhaul 'Downright Evil.'" August 8. http://thecaucus.blogs.nytimes.com/2009/08/08/sarah-palin-has-weighed-in-on/.

Shelley, Mack C. II. 1983. *The Permanent Majority: The Conservative Coalition in the United States Congress*. Tuscaloosa: University of Alabama Press.

Sinclair, Barbara. 2006. *Party Wars*. Norman: University of Oklahoma Press.

Sinclair, Barbara. 2008. "Spoiling the Sausages: How a Polarized Congress Deliberates and Legislates." In Pietro S. Nivola and David W. Brady, eds., *Red and Blue Nation?* Vol. 2. Washington, DC: Brookings, 55–87.

Smith, Mark A. 2007. *The Right Talk: How Conservatives Transformed the Great Society into the Economic Society*. Princeton, NJ: Princeton University Press.

*Soss, Joe, Jacob S. Hacker, and Suzanne Mettler. 2007. *Remaking America: Democracy and Public Policy in an Age of Inequality*. New York: Sage.

Stein, Herbert. 1969. *The Fiscal Revolution in America*. Chicago: University of Chicago Press.

Stolberg, Sheryl Gay. 2009. "Obama Signs Equal-Pay Legislation," *New York Times*, January 20. http://www.nytimes.com/2009/01/30/us/politics/30ledbetter-web.html.

Stonecash, Jeffrey M. 2000. *Class and Party in American Politics*. Boulder: Westview Press.

Stonecash, Jeffrey M. 2003. *The Emergence of State Government: Parties and New Jersey Politics, 1950—2000*. Madison: Fairleigh-Dickinson University Press.

Stonecash, Jeffrey M. 2006. *Parties Matter: Realignment and the Return of Partisanship*. Boulder: Lynne Rienner.

Stonecash, Jeffrey M. 2010. "Class in American Politics." In Jeffrey M. Stonecash, ed., *New Directions in American Political Parties*. New York: Routledge, 110–125.

Stonecash, Jeffrey M. 2011. "Political Parties: The Tensions Between Unified Party Images and Localism." In Stephen Medvic, ed., *New Directions in Campaigns and Elections*. New York: Routledge, 115–128.

Stonecash, Jeffrey M. 2012. "Political Science and the Study of Parties: Sorting out Interpretations of Party Response." In Mark D. Brewer and L. Sandy Maisel, eds., *The Parties Respond*, 5th ed. Boulder: Westview Press, 1–14.

Stonecash, Jeffrey M. 2013. *Party Pursuits: the Presidential—House Election Connection, 1900—2008*. New York: Cambridge University Press.

Stonecash, Jeffrey R., Mark D. Brewer, and Mack D. Mariani. 2003. *Diverging Parties: Social Change, Realignment, and Party Polarization*. Boulder: Westview Press.

Stonecash, Jeffrey M., and Mack D. Mariani. 2000. "Republican Gains in the House in the 1994 Elections: Class Polarization in American Politics." *Political Science Quarterly* 115, no. 1 (Spring): 93–114.

Strach, Patricia. 2009. "Making Higher Education Affordable: Policy Design in Postwar America." *Journal of Policy History* 21 (1): 61–88.

Stroud, Natalie Jomini. 2008. "Media Use and Political Predispositions: Revisiting the Concept of Selective Exposure." *Political Behavior* 30 (3): 341–366.

Sulkin, Tracy. 2011. *The Legislative Legacy of Congressional Campaigns*. New York: Cambridge University Press.

Sundquist, James L. 1983. *Dynamics of the Party System: Alignment and Realignment of Political Parties in the United States*. Rev. ed. Washington, DC: Brookings Institution.

Ventry, Dennis J., Jr. 2000. "The Collision of Tax and Welfare Politics: The Political History of the Earned Income Tax Credit, 1969–99." *National Tax Journal* 53, no. 4, pt. 2 (December): 983–1026.

Wapshott, Nicholas. 2011. *Keynes Hayek: The Clash that Defined Modern Economics*. New York: W. W Norton.

Ware, Alan. 2006. *The Democratic Party Heads North*. New York: Cambridge University Press.

Wattenberg, Martin P. 1981. "The Decline of Political Partisanship in the United States: Negativity or Neutrality?" *American Political Science Review* 75, no. 4 (December): 941–950.

Wattenberg, Martin P. 1990. *The Decline of American Political Parties 1952—1988*. Cambridge, MA: Harvard University Press.

Wattenberg, Martin P. 1991. *The Rise of Candidate—Centered Politics: Presidential Elections of the 1980s*. Cambridge, MA: Harvard University Press.

Zaller, John. 1992. *The Nature and Origin of Mass Opinion*. New York: Cambridge University Press.

CHAPTER 11

··

INTEREST GROUPS

··

TRACY ROOF

1 INTRODUCTION

··

JAMES Madison (1787) famously argued that competition among numerous interests in a large, diverse democracy like the United States would control the "mischiefs of faction" by checking the power of any particular group, including one representing the majority. In contrast, many contemporary observers fear groups provide too much protection for organized minorities at the expense of the unorganized majority and the public interest (Hacker and Pierson 2010). The competition of interest groups, combined with a fragmented political system and historically weak but increasingly polarized political parties, encourages gridlock and limits the reach and redistribution of the American welfare state. But the social welfare policies that are adopted typically reflect both concessions to powerful, affluent interests and the influence of a diverse array of groups, including those that look out for the disadvantaged and the middle class. In exploring these themes, this chapter first examines the study of interest groups in American politics and comparative welfare state development, then reviews the role of various types of groups in shaping social welfare policy in the United States.

2 THE STUDY OF GROUPS IN AMERICAN POLITICS

··

Scholars have long debated the degree to which U.S. policy-making is shaped by a broad range of interests that reflect the needs and desires of the American people or by the interests of a privileged few who undermine American democracy. In the 1950s and 1960s several scholars developed the perspective of pluralism, which placed groups at the center of American democracy. Challenging the theory of elitism, which held that political power in the United States was concentrated in an exclusive group of decision makers, pluralists such as David Truman (1951) and Robert Dahl (1961) reasserted Madison's claim that the competition among groups prevented any one from dominating. The political system was democratic and responsive because all interests could organize, and politicians were inclined to consider the interests of unorganized groups that might coalesce if their concerns went unaddressed. This permeable pluralist system fostered stability and incremental policy change as the balance of power among group forces shifted to absorb new groups' demands.

In response, a range of scholars challenged many of the pluralists' assumptions by emphasizing sources of bias in the interest group system. E. E. Schattschneider famously observed, "The flaw in the pluralist heaven is that the heavenly chorus sings with a strong upper-class accent" (1960, 35). Economist Mancur Olson (1965) outlined a "logic of collective action" in which it was irrational for ordinary people to sacrifice their time and resources to join in pursuit of collective goods that would be widely shared. Business groups are more likely to organize because in small groups formed around narrow economic interests, each member gets a substantial share of the benefits of collective action. Since it is also irrational for citizens to dedicate considerable time to following and participating in policy debates, paid corporate lobbyists have substantial advantages in shaping outcomes. Moreover, as Peter Bachrach and Morton Baratz (1962) argued, corporate and affluent interests work to narrow the range of issues that are actively debated and to keep many issues—such as significant income distribution or the sanctity of private property—off the political agenda altogether.

Scholars investigating the claims of Olson and other critics of pluralism found sources of countervailing power against elites and business dominance. Collective action problems can be overcome by social movements; policy entrepreneurs; and patrons such as wealthy individuals, foundations, and even the federal government, which sponsor groups demanding collective goods or benefits for the disadvantaged (McAdam 1982; Salisbury 1969; Walker 1991). As a result, open, fluid policy networks of diverse contending interests, including many of the public interest groups born in the 1960s and 1970s, replaced closed policy-making systems in many areas where they once existed (Heclo 1978). Moreover, elites are often divided and may check each other.

In the last few decades the field of interest group research, once characterized as theory rich and data poor (Arnold 1982, 97), has generated a lot of data, but no overarching theory to replace pluralism (Baumgartner and Leech 1998). Efforts to catalog the groups active in national politics find significant diversity in the interest group universe, but affluent and corporate interests dominate (Schlozman and Tierney 1986; Schlozman, Verba, and Brady 2012). Dozens of studies on the impact of lobbying and political action committee (PAC) contributions to candidates have produced conflicting results, with some suggesting that groups have little influence in the policy process and others finding that groups, particularly those with significant resources, dictate policy outcomes (for reviews see Baumgartner and Leech 1998; Schlozman, Verba, and Brady 2012, 288–311). In the most comprehensive study of group influence on legislative outcomes to date, designed to address the methodological weaknesses of previous research, Baumgartner and colleagues (2009) find a strong status quo bias, with any group defending existing policy likely to prevail and a very weak relationship between group resources and success. Most issues pit diverse coalitions of the strong and the weak—such as pharmaceutical firms and patient advocacy groups—against each other, such that group efforts tend to cancel each other out. But when stalemate occasionally breaks, policy change is likely to be significant rather than incremental. Baumgartner and his colleagues caution that their study does not prove resources are unimportant, but rather that they are likely built into the status quo. They note that few issues dealing with the economic security of the poor or the working class even appeared on the agenda, although this finding may be skewed because their study was conducted over successive Republican-controlled Congresses. Some scholars argue that recent research, though not generating an elegant theory, reflects a new "neo-pluralist" perspective that stresses the uncertain and context-specific nature of interest group influence (Lowery and Gray 2004; McFarland 2004).

3   Comparative Theories of Welfare State Development

The role of organized interests has also figured prominently in another literature focused on explaining differences in the generosity and reach of welfare states in wealthy democracies. Business interests that control capital and the means of production are in a privileged position relative to laborers in any society, but in a capitalist democracy members of the working class can secure redistributive policies by leveraging the power of their greater numbers through mass organization. Building on this premise, power resource theorists argue that much of the variation in welfare state spending and entitlements across industrialized democracies can be explained by the relative strength of unions and leftist parties allied with labor that demand programs fostering greater economic security and equality (Korpi 1983; Esping-Andersen 1985). Power resource theorists thus argue that the low level of social welfare spending in the United States is a consequence of the comparative weakness of organized labor and the absence of an influential socialist, social democratic, or labor party, which has allowed corporate and affluent interests more sway over public policy.

Other comparative scholars have emphasized the importance of countries' political institutions in explaining the variation in the power of interest groups and the generosity of welfare states (for a detailed review, see the chapter on political institutions in this volume). Unlike both pluralists and power resource theorists, institutionalists stress that government policy is not a direct reflection of the balance of class forces or interests in society, because groups' influence is mediated by government structures and electoral rules (Immergut 1992). Organized interests face tremendous challenges in passing comprehensive welfare state programs because the American government, based on federalism and checks and balances, is very fragmented. Especially prior to the New Deal in the 1930s, social reformers' efforts were often targeted at the state and local levels, which inhibited the formation of strong national organizations and universal policies (Skocpol 1992). On the national level, there are multiple "veto points" in the House, the Senate, the executive branch, and the courts at which the passage or implementation of legislative proposals can be obstructed.

Interest groups are thought to be both numerous and powerful in the American policy-making process because the fragmented political system offers so many points of access. But groups such as labor that favor an activist government are at a disadvantage, because they must push legislation through every point in the policy gauntlet, whereas groups that favor limited government must only succeed at one veto point (Roof 2011). Fragmentation does not always work against the welfare state. Once programs like Social Security are established, beneficiaries and supportive groups are often able to fend off efforts to cut or eliminate them (Pierson 1995), and groups advocating for the disadvantaged have been able to expand programs for the poor and disabled through the courts and administrative rule-making processes when the elected branches were less receptive (Berry 1984; Melnick 1994; Erkulwater 2006). However, political scientists Jacob Hacker and Paul Pierson argue that over time legislative gridlock has produced "policy drift," as affluent interests in the United States have taken advantage of institutional veto points to stop legislation that would update social welfare policies to meet changing societal problems such as the rise in income inequality (Hacker and Pierson 2010).

The fragmented political system also makes it almost impossible to have corporatism, an institutionalized pattern of policy-making found in some European countries like Sweden, in which a highly centralized government negotiates policies with centralized "peak" organizations representing labor, business, or other major stakeholders. There is no centralized government capable of brokering and upholding compromises in the United States, and multiple groups typically claim to speak for major societal interests (Salisbury 1979). Rather than developing the type of coordinated economy typically associated with corporatism, the United States developed a liberal market economy (LME) that fosters business hostility to organized labor and welfare state programs (Iversen and Soskice 2009). Iversen and Soskice find that LMEs are also associated with majoritarian political systems, which discourage successful coalitions of interests supportive of redistributive policies.

3.1 The Relationship between Parties and Groups in the United States

Unlike the proportional representation systems common in many parliamentary governments, the plurality-based, majoritarian electoral system in the United States encourages the dominance of two parties (Duverger 1964), which shapes interest group behavior. Interests like labor and environmentalists, which have formed parties in other countries, instead mobilize as interest groups. The United States has also historically been characterized by the competition of a wide diversity of groups articulating concerns not well-represented by the two dominant parties.

Party discipline is also not as strong in Congress as in most parliamentary systems, which allows groups to lobby individual politicians away from the party line (Maioni 1998). Thus Democratic presidents and congressional leaders committed to party positions on health-care reform have faced the reluctance of many Democrats to challenge the interests of employers, insurers, and health-care providers (Starr 2011). Likewise, President George W. Bush's proposal to create private investment accounts in Social Security failed in part because many congressional Republicans were intimidated by the campaign of the AARP (formerly known as the American Association of Retired Persons) against it (Lynch 2011).

While interest groups often try to undermine party discipline, they have also contributed to growing ideological unity within parties, and polarization between them, in recent decades. Groups supporting an activist government have tried to pull the Democratic Party to the left, while antigovernment groups, such as those associated with the Tea Party movement, have pushed the Republican Party to the right. Wayward incumbents face the threat that a group such as the conservative Club for Growth or the liberal Moveon.org will fund primary challengers. While moderate Republicans once voted for programs like Medicare, only one Republican voted for the 2010 health-care law, in part because of the strident opposition of conservative groups. Deficit reduction and entitlement reform have been difficult to address because almost all congressional Republicans have signed a pledge not to raise taxes, under pressure from the influential leader of Americans for Tax Reform, Grover Norquist, while Democrats resist substantial cuts in social spending under pressure from liberal groups. Thus groups can constrain party leaders' ability to negotiate bipartisan compromises. But influence works both ways.

Given limited formal tools to enforce party discipline, leaders often utilize allied groups to secure votes in Congress. A striking example is the K-Street Project, an effort initiated by Republican congressional leaders to pressure business and trade associations to hire former Republican members of Congress and staffers. In addition to funneling business resources to Republican candidates, these close ties facilitated coordination on legislative strategy. The narrow passage of the Bush administration's Medicare prescription drug benefit in 2003 was made possible by the lobbying of business groups associated with the project—both with and without a direct interest in the legislation—of conservative Republicans reluctant to support a new entitlement (Morgan and Campbell 2011, 137). Groups make such useful allies for party leaders because of the range of tactics they can employ.

4 TACTICS

Jeffrey Berry (1977) identified four overarching categories of interest group tactics: 1) law, which includes involvement in litigation and administrative implementation; 2) confrontation, which includes protests and shareholders' actions; 3) information, such

as testimony before agency or congressional hearings, policy research, public relations campaigns, and direct lobbyist contacts; and 4) constituency influence, such as
letter-writing campaigns, issue advertising, and electoral efforts including campaign
contributions and voter mobilization. Groups choose tactics based on the issue; the
stage in the policy process, from agenda-setting to implementation; the larger political context, including the partisan balance in Congress; and their own resources and
strengths (for a review see Baumgartner and Leech 1998, 146–167). Some groups have
close relationships with congressional leaders and work quietly behind closed doors,
writing legislative language, while other groups with resources but few congressional
allies may run major media campaigns to influence voters. Groups with few resources or
allies, or those trying to call attention to a neglected issue, may resort to demonstrations.
All of these tactics have been used by groups to shape American social policy. The next
sections look at major categories of interest groups and their participation in the policy
process.

5 BUSINESS

Business interests have exerted significant influence over the development of the welfare state. Charles Lindblom (1977) famously argued that business has a privileged
position relative to other interests because the fortunes of politicians and government
officials are tied to economic strength, and officials are likely to accommodate business
concerns for fear that business will refuse to invest. Prior to the New Deal, when many
social welfare issues were handled by the states, states were leery of policies that might
increase business costs or reduce business autonomy and encourage businesses to move
to another state (Hacker and Pierson 2002). Many scholars argue that globalization and
capital mobility have shifted this threat to the national level in the last few decades, and
that this threat has had more influence on policy-making in liberal market economies
like that of the United States (Swank 2002). Lindblom and others emphasize that structural business power is heightened by extensive financial and organizational resources
deployed to influence politicians and public opinion. The American business community is considered one of the most antistatist among capitalist democracies, and it has
used its advantages to promote laissez faire ideology and oppose social welfare policies
that would strengthen workers' position in labor markets, interfere with management
prerogatives, or raise business costs.

But despite its advantages, business's political influence has fluctuated. Powerful
monopolies developed in the late 1800s and plowed money into politics. Protected by
the federal courts and Republicans, northeastern corporate interests largely weathered
challenges by the Populist and Progressive movements from the late 1890s through 1932.
But business was thrown on the defensive during the Great Depression, when sizeable
Democratic congressional majorities pushed through the New Deal, which included

policies that empowered organized labor, regulated business practices, and established the foundations of the modern welfare state. Although some scholars argue that the support of progressive business interests made passage of New Deal programs like Social Security possible (Swenson 2004), most business groups opposed public pensions, unemployment compensation, and numerous other New Deal programs (Hacker and Pierson 2002). Many scholars argue that big businesses, particularly in unionized sectors, accepted a social contract of collective bargaining and fair pay with benefits in exchange for workers' deference to managerial prerogatives in the postwar period, but conservative business interests continued to fight unions and the welfare state, helping to gut effective full employment planning legislation and pass anti-union provisions (Lichtenstein 2002).

Business was again thrown on the defensive in the late 1960s and early 1970s, when the environmental and consumer protection movements successfully pushed a wave of regulatory legislation over corporate opposition. But these defeats led to a reinvigoration of organized business (Vogel 1989; Hacker and Pierson 2010). Trade associations and business PACs proliferated. Business groups sought greater unity and coordination of their activities. Corporate and conservative interests also funded think tanks like the Heritage Foundation to popularize and give intellectual credibility to the merits of smaller government and market-based policies (Rich 2004). Business groups typically contribute to both Democratic and Republican incumbents to guarantee access, but these groups eventually became more strategic by shifting resources to more reflexively probusiness Republican challengers, which helped Republicans take control of both houses of Congress in the 1994 elections for the first time in 42 years. In the last three decades business interests have secured numerous favorable policies, including curtailment of union power under Republican presidents and tax cuts and deregulation under presidents of both parties. New welfare state programs also increasingly came to rely on private sector intermediaries (Mettler 2011; Morgan and Campbell 2011). For example, both Bush's Medicare prescription drug benefit and Obama's health-care reform law subsidize the purchase of private health insurance.

Despite efforts at coordination, one of the biggest constraints on business power remains fragmentation. Both in the past and today, the business community is divided by region, industry, size, labor force composition, and executives' ideological commitments. There are hundreds of organizations—including umbrella groups like the Business Roundtable, the Chamber of Commerce, and the National Federation of Independent Business, as well as industry-specific groups such as the American Beverage Association—that spent millions fighting the addition of a tax on high-calorie drinks to the 2010 health reform legislation. Most large businesses also hire lobbying firms and maintain their own offices in Washington to protect their particular interests. Businesses are often pitted against each other in policy struggles, and the umbrella organizations may fail to achieve enough consensus to actively lobby. Large businesses, which are less likely to oppose social welfare policies like universal health care or public investments in education and worker training, are typically less effective than the

organizations of small business that are ideologically unified in opposition to programs that might increase taxes or regulatory burdens. Political scientist Cathie Jo
Martin argues that while large companies often dominate regulatory politics, they do
not actively participate in some of the major social policy debates (Martin 1999, 6). In
contrast, the National Federation of Independent Business (NFIB), made up of small
businesses from every congressional district, has gained a reputation as one of the most
powerful players in Washington.

Business has also influenced social welfare policy by offering benefits that workers might otherwise receive from government. Prior to the New Deal, some employers endorsed "welfare capitalism," in which businesses either directly provided their
workers with services like education, housing, and health care or offered group insurance policies covering accidents and sickness. Welfare capitalists were always a small
minority of employers, and by the onset of the Great Depression most reformers had
abandoned the idea in favor of government insurance programs. However, in the 1940s
and 1950s more employers began to offer pensions and health insurance under pressure from unions and the need to attract workers, induced by favorable changes in
the tax code (Gottschalk 2000; Hacker 2002; Klein 2003). The spread of these benefits
produced powerful "feedback effects" shaping the context for future reform. Social
Security evolved as a complement to rather than a substitute for private pensions, and
employer-sponsored health insurance reduced the demand for government health
insurance (Hacker 2002). Health-care providers and insurers also gained a stake in the
private insurance system, making the adoption of national health insurance less likely
in the future. As a result, no president since Harry Truman has endorsed a program of
universal government-provided health insurance in office.

Recent struggles over health-care reform reflect the divisions among business groups
around social policy and the constraints of past policy choices. Most major business
organizations entered negotiations with the Clinton administration as it formulated its
universal health reform proposal built around the existing system of private insurance,
but over time they came to oppose the reform. Associations representing large insurers, which stood to gain business, offered lukewarm support. But the Health Insurance
Association of America (HIAA), a group representing small insurers that risked losing
business, came out against it and ran an influential series of ads featuring Harry and
Louise, a middle-class couple, discussing the dangers of Clinton's plan over their kitchen
table. Fearing a loss of revenue for their members, the American Hospital Association
and the Pharmaceutical Research and Manufacturers of America (PhRMA) also fought
the proposal. After securing an exemption for small businesses from a cost-sharing
mandate, the NFIB joined the opposition and became a leader in the fight. Although
many large employers burdened by high health-care costs that undermined their com-
petitiveness supported reform in general, the National Association of Manufacturers
and Business Roundtable eventually came out against Clinton's proposal. On the verge
of endorsing the bill, the Chamber of Commerce was "cross-lobbied" by the NFIB and
"reverse-lobbied" by conservative Republicans to withhold its support (Skocpol 1997,
158–160). After months of negotiations, the bill went down to defeat as the "losers"

under health-care reform fought the bill, but the groups representing businesses that would benefit did not actively support it (Starr 2011, 117).

Eager to avoid a repeat of Clinton's defeat, the Obama administration sought to secure prominent industry support early in negotiations over its proposal. In a deal with PhRMA, administration and Senate leaders agreed not to include Democratic proposals allowing Medicare to negotiate lower drug prices directly with manufacturers and permitting the importation of cheaper drugs from abroad in exchange for the industry's agreement to offer drug discounts in the Medicaid and Medicare programs and to bankroll a proreform advertising campaign (Starr 2011, 205). The hospital associations also backed the bill and agreed to accept reduced Medicare payments with the understanding that hospitals would gain more patients among the newly insured. Although insurers would also gain new customers, negotiators failed to reach a deal with America's Health Insurance Plans (AHIP, formed by a merger of the HIAA and other insurer groups) because of divisions within the industry (Starr 2011, 218–219). Some of the largest for-profit insurers ultimately funneled money through the AHIP to the Chamber of Commerce to help fund an antireform ad campaign. The AHIP did not come out against the bill, instead choosing to remain in the negotiations and fight proposals like the public option, which would have offered a government-run insurance plan to compete with private plans. The Chamber and the NFIB actively fought the bill, while other employer groups did not. The fracturing of the business community made it difficult for opponents to stop the bill while the Democrats briefly held the sixty Senate seats necessary to overcome a filibuster.

6 LABOR

Scholars have often pointed to the weakness of the labor movement in explaining the overall weakness of the Left and the limited welfare state in the United States. In trying to mobilize workers, unions have faced the hostility of employers; a strong strain of individualism in American culture; a belief in upward mobility; and divisions among workers based on skill level, race, and ethnicity (Greenstone 1977). In trying to mobilize politically, unions have confronted barriers to third parties; workers' attachments to one of the two parties based on local or ethnic ties; the historic hostility of the courts; and the fragmented, super-majoritarian features of the government. Organized labor is not nearly as influential in the United States as in other wealthy democracies with more centralized governments and more favorable rules governing organizing and collective bargaining, yet it has still played an important role in shaping the contemporary welfare state.

Prior to the 1930s labor was not very active in the policy-making process. The Knights of Labor, the first large, national labor organization, which rose to prominence in the 1880s, was largely unsuccessful in achieving policy goals such as the eight-hour day and prohibition of child labor. By the 1890s the American Federation of Labor (AFL) had replaced the Knights as the dominant national organization, a position it has maintained despite fleeting challenges from more radical movements like the Industrial Workers of the World. The AFL focused on collective bargaining for better wages and working conditions, rather than political mobilization as advocated by Socialist elements within the labor movement. Leaders like the AFL's long-serving president Samuel Gompers came to view political action as futile because of the courts' hostility to government regulation of working conditions (Forbath 1991; Hattam 1993). The courts even interpreted antitrust laws, originally written to restrain corporate monopolies, as restraints on workers' collective action, which threatened the very existence of unions. Although it occasionally supported state-level reforms, the AFL opposed many of the national welfare state programs advocated by social democratic labor movements in other countries at the time and focused on obtaining legal protections for unions' collective action. The AFL initially even opposed policies like a minimum wage, fearing it would become a ceiling rather than a floor. But the AFL's position slowly changed, and organized labor became the strongest advocate of welfare state programs such as unemployment compensation, public pensions, and national health insurance (Harrington 1972; Greenstone 1977).

Several factors encouraged the growth and politicization of the labor movement. First was the passage of the National Labor Relations Act (NLRA) in 1935, which recognized workers' rights to organize and bargain collectively. In accepting the NLRA's constitutionality two years later, the Supreme Court signaled a growing openness to regulation of social and working conditions, which opened up possibilities for labor's political action. After passage of the NLRA, dissidents within the AFL, who advocated large-scale organizing of unskilled industrial workers over the AFL's focus on skilled craftsmen, created a rival federation—the Congress of Industrial Organizations (CIO)—that was very politically active. The CIO became a key supporter of the New Deal and Fair Deal agendas of Democratic presidents Franklin Roosevelt and Harry Truman (Plotke 1996). Competition between the two federations, favorable government policies, and a tight labor market during World War II resulted in a surge in union membership to over a third of the nonagricultural workforce. Eager to rein in unions' growing economic and political power, conservative and corporate interests pushed the antilabor Taft-Hartley Act in 1947. This setback, as well as the failure to pass programs like national health insurance, encouraged the two federations to merge as the AFL-CIO in 1955 to strengthen labor's political muscle. Member unions, such as the United Auto Workers and the American Federation of Teachers, also engage in politics, but the AFL-CIO, despite periods of division, has historically taken the lead in coordinating labor's political activity, with very limited influence over organizing and collective bargaining.

Labor's new role in advocating expansion of the welfare state was limited by a number of factors (Roof 2011). While union membership in many states in the North, industrial Midwest, and Pacific Coast was on a par with that of more highly unionized Western countries after World War II, unionization rates were much lower in the South and western states with low levels of industrialization. Over half of all union members were located in just a handful of states. The political impact of this geographic imbalance was exaggerated by equal state representation in the Senate, the filibuster, and the role of seniority in Congress, with the latter awarding powerful committee chairmanships to conservative Southern Democrats, who often allied with Republicans to obstruct or water down legislation benefiting organized labor, the working class, and the poor. Given congressional resistance to policies like universal health care, unions sought these benefits through collective bargaining (Hacker 2002; Klein 2003).

Despite these limitations, labor remained active on public policy and helped secure the expansion of New Deal programs like the minimum wage and Social Security, as well as the creation of new programs—although these were often more incremental or targeted than the broad, universal programs labor favored. The AFL-CIO put the issue of Medicare on the congressional agenda and funded an influential new organization, the National Council of Senior Citizens, to build grassroots pressure (Marmor 1973). The AFL-CIO also worked closely with Democratic president Lyndon Johnson to pass other Great Society programs in the 1960s, including antipoverty measures, federal aid to education, and civil rights legislation.

Organized labor's membership and economic power declined considerably from the 1970s onward, but it remains an important player in national politics and policy-making (Dark 2001). Unionization has been reduced to a third of its 1950s peak, just 11.3 percent of the workforce and only 6.7 percent in the private sector in 2013 (BLS News Release 2014). But with 14.8 million members, labor still has more clout than many groups, although unlike business, labor's influence is largely limited to Democrats. Throughout the period of conservative dominance from Ronald Reagan to George W. Bush, labor worked with groups like the AARP to defend social welfare programs such as Medicare and Social Security from cuts, fundamental restructuring, and privatization. Labor also helped pass major new initiatives such as the 2010 health-care reform law, by both working behind the scenes and mobilizing grassroots support (Roof 2011).

Labor's ability to maintain its policy influence into the future faces many challenges. Largely because of the Senate filibuster, labor has been unable to secure laws making it easier to organize new workers in the face of intense employer opposition (Roof 2011). Tight government budgets amid the economic downturn starting in 2008 spurred conservative efforts in the states to weaken public sector unions, which have been one of the few growing sectors of the labor movement and now represent over half of union members. Membership is likely to continue to decline, which restricts the resources unions can commit to politics. Workers are also in a weakened position to demand better wages and the employer-provided benefits that are such an important part of the American social safety net. Thus, the decline of unions contributes to rising inequality in the United States (Hacker and Pierson 2010).

7 AGRICULTURAL GROUPS

Agricultural interests were also influential in the early development of many social welfare policies. The Populist movement attempted to build a coalition of small farmers and laborers favoring greater government regulation of the economy and working conditions, but it failed to gain control of the national government. However, the coalition's push for progressive taxation culminated in ratification of the Sixteenth Amendment in 1913, which permitted a federal income tax (Morgan and Prasad 2009). Farmers and labor again joined in the New Deal electoral coalition, but the representatives of southern farmers, who depended on a pliable, poor, and largely black labor force, demanded exemptions for agricultural labor from New Deal programs like Social Security and the minimum wage (Finegold 1988). By the late 1930s and throughout the postwar period, conservative Southern Democrats and Republican representatives of midwestern agricultural interests often found common cause in fighting expansion of the welfare state.

Agricultural groups also shaped nutritional assistance programs. The first school lunch and Food Stamps programs were originally created to dispose of agricultural surpluses during the New Deal. While the Food Stamps program was terminated because of declining farm support as surpluses all but disappeared during World War II, many farm groups joined children's advocates in supporting the National School Lunch Program in 1946 (Levine 2008, 74). The continued distribution of surplus commodities after the war proved inadequate in addressing the problem of hunger highlighted by politicians, the media, and civil rights and public interest groups. Yet farm interests feared that pilot food stamp programs created early in the Kennedy administration might threaten assistance to farmers and cloud the Department of Agriculture's mission (King 2000, 48). In a classic example of logroll politics, congressional representatives of agricultural interests agreed to support a national food stamp program in exchange for the support of urban representatives and nutritional advocates for legislation assisting tobacco, wheat, and cotton farmers. Farm groups were repeatedly party to similar logrolls as the program was expanded, and nutritional assistance and farm subsidies are often bundled together in legislation (King 2000; Finegold 1988). When Aid to Families with Dependent Children was converted to a block grant to the states in 1995, a similar effort on nutritional assistance was defeated in part because of the opposition of agricultural groups that feared reduced farm incomes (King 2000, 209).

Farmers are represented by two main umbrella organizations, the more progressive National Farmers' Union (NFU), dominated by small farmers, and the larger and more conservative American Farm Bureau Federation (AFBF). The NFU has typically allied with labor and other groups on the left in support of programs like Social Security and Medicare, whereas the AFBF has allied with conservative corporate interests to oppose the growth of the welfare state. There are also dozens of groups focused on particular crops.

8 PROFESSIONAL ASSOCIATIONS

While business, labor, and agriculture are the classic economic groups, a number of professional associations are also active in social welfare issues. The American Medical

Association (AMA), the largest group representing doctors, with influential members in every congressional district, has played a key role in health-care reform. Franklin Roosevelt's administration decided not to include health insurance in the Social Security Act for fear the AMA's opposition would kill the entire bill (Starr 2011, 38). The group also took the lead in defeating President Truman's national health insurance plan in the 1940s, launching a major public relations campaign warning about the dangers of socialized medicine (Poen 1979). It continued to fight any proposal it felt might involve government in the practice of medicine, including the addition of disability coverage to Social Security and Medicare. But after years of stalemate, both of these programs passed over the AMA's opposition, proving the group was not invincible (Quadagno 2005). However, to curb the vehemence of doctors' opposition, the Medicare legislation included no cost controls, which led to a windfall for doctors and soaring program costs.

Over time the AMA lost its reputation as the voice of doctors as groups representing specialists became more active, and rivals such as the much smaller Physicians for a National Health Program emerged. Although not as hostile to health-care reform as it once had been, the AMA did not join the American College of Physicians; groups representing specialists like pediatricians, neurologists, and family doctors; and other professional organizations such as the American Nursing Association in endorsing Clinton's health reform plan (Starr 2011, 114). The medical professions were more unified during Obama's health reform effort, and the AMA ultimately joined a broad range of provider groups in endorsing the legislation, which contributed to the momentum behind the bill.

Although they vary in influence, other professional organizations are active on a range of social policies. The National Education Association (NEA), the largest group representing teachers that operates as both a union and professional organization, lobbies on issues affecting children such as nutritional assistance. While not as powerful as the AMA or NEA, organizations of government and nonprofit professionals, such as the National Association of Social Workers, lobby on health, education, and antipoverty issues affecting their clients (Hays 2001). Even groups representing trial lawyers try to influence policies such as workers' compensation and disability insurance.

9 INTERGOVERNMENTAL ORGANIZATIONS

Intergovernmental groups representing states, cities, and counties engage in policy debates and provide critical information to Congress about how legislation and policy implementation affect other levels of government. These groups include generalist organizations based on the level of government, such as the League of Cities and the National Council of State Legislatures (NCSL); groups focused on a particular policy area, such as the American Public Welfare Association and the National Association of Housing and Redevelopment Officials; and individual units of government that maintain offices in

Washington or hire their own lobbyists (Cammisa 1995; Schlozman, Verba, and Brady 2012). Intergovernmental groups became active lobbyists in the 1930s with the growth of joint federal-state programs, such as unemployment insurance, and programs that relied on implementation by localities, such as public assistance. Their activities increased in the 1960s and 1970s as subnational governments sought greater control over growing federal streams of funding for programs such as Medicaid, elementary and secondary education, and workforce training (Cammisa 1995). In the last few decades intergovern-mental groups have been influential in debates over devolving responsibility from the federal government to states and localities. The National Governors Association (NGA) helped put welfare reform on the national agenda and played a prominent role in shap-ing the 1988 Family Support Act and the 1996 Temporary Assistance to Needy Families (TANF) legislation, which converted welfare to a block grant that gave states significant latitude in administering the program (Haskins 2008).

While intergovernmental groups almost always gain the ear of policy makers, the diversity of interests can compromise their effectiveness. Disputes between states and localities over control of federal funding limited their influence over affordable hous-ing legislation passed in 1990 (Cammisa 1995). Splits between governors over the block-granting of Medicaid have limited the NGA's ability to press the issue. Deep par-tisan divisions over health-care reform during the Obama administration also made it impossible for the NGA and NCSL to reach consensus (Dinan 2011). As a result, partisan organizations like the Republican Governors Association and individual states and gov-ernors played a prominent role in fighting the legislation, while the Obama administra-tion convinced the Democratic Governors Association not to raise concerns publicly. Although they did not get everything they wanted, states gained concessions on federal funding for the expansion of Medicaid coverage included in the law. Intergovernmental groups also convinced policy makers to retain a substantial state role in regulating insur-ers and setting up insurance exchanges, because they were more unified on these issues, and members of Congress recognized state expertise in these areas.

10 CITIZENS' GROUPS

Citizens' groups, with membership based on common interests and concerns rather than economic or occupational ties, have played an important role in social policy development throughout American history. They include public interest groups that pursue collective goods such as public health or a safe food supply; groups that repre-sent demographic categories such as the elderly or disabled; groups organized around an ideology or common policy goals, such as the American Conservative Union or civil rights groups; single-issue groups such as pro-life and pro-choice organizations; and groups that advocate for those without much political power, such as the poor and chil-dren. During the Progressive Era (1890s–1920s), reformers used citizens' groups to work around the two entrenched, patronage-oriented political parties that were hostile to their policy demands at both the state and national levels (Skocpol 1992). In her ground-breaking study, Theda Skocpol (1992) found that women's organizations helped create a "maternalist" welfare state in the early 1900s by securing policies such as mothers' pensions that provided for the welfare of mothers and children, while policies protecting male wage earners faced heavier political resistance.

The number of citizens' groups grew considerably in the last half of the twentieth century. Growth in government programs from the New Deal through the Great Society mobilized previously quiescent beneficiaries like the elderly into powerful political constituencies, represented by groups such as the AARP (Campbell 2005). Groups associated with the civil rights and women's rights movements in the mid-twentieth century demanded not only legal equality but—less successfully—programs to address economic inequality. These movements were followed by a surge in public interest groups in the 1960s and 1970s (Berry 1977). Most of these public interest groups focused on the "new liberal" interests shared by their upper-middle-class supporters, such as the environment and consumer protection (Berry 1999). But some focused on redistributive issues like expanding the Food Stamp Program (Berry 1984). Public Interest Research Groups (PIRGs), a network of state groups that formed on college campuses in the 1970s, lobby on a range of issues and recently joined with the United States Student Association to push an overhaul of government-subsidized college loans (Mettler 2011). Families USA has provided both research and grassroots mobilization in favor of universal health care for three decades.

Another influential category of citizens' groups has been Christian conservative organizations that first mobilized in the 1980s. While much of their agenda focuses on cultural issues like abortion, they typically support candidates with conservative social welfare positions, and their concerns bring them into the debate on policies such as welfare and health-care reform. They also supported the creation of the Child Tax Credit, which is one of the biggest government programs assisting families with children (Howard 2007, 87). While citizens' groups typically do not have the financial resources of business or even organized labor, some have substantial memberships, and others offer expertise and information valued by policy makers.

11 Conclusion

Competition among diverse interest groups adds even greater complexity and uncertainty to the fragmented and decentralized policy-making process. Although affluent groups often do get their wishes, they also often do not. However, interest group pressures make policy consensus more difficult and government action less likely, which on balance benefits the groups and interests opposed to an activist government. When new policies are adopted, both supporters and opponents typically shape them, and no side gets everything it wants. But accommodating various interests tends to make policies less coherent and efficient, and the deal-making itself often feeds public distrust in government—which in turn discourages government action.

Disentangling the effects of interest groups on public policy is difficult, and there is still a lot to be learned. Many factors contribute to outcomes, such as the partisan balance in government, the preferences of politicians and government officials, the legacies of previous policies, crises or other events, and public opinion. The body of interest group research suggests that this political context shapes which groups have the most influence in a policy battle and how much influence they have. The level of group participation and influence also varies with the stage of the policy process. While many groups become involved once an issue is actively debated in Congress, fewer groups work to put the issue on the agenda or shape its implementation. There is unlikely to be another grand theory like pluralism, but researchers should focus on developing more general principles based on the circumstances that determine groups' impact through both case studies and large-N studies, hopefully over an extended time horizon.

References

*Indicates recommended reading.

Arnold, Douglas. 1982. "Overfilled and Undertilled Fields in American Politics." *Political Science Quarterly* 97:91–103.

Peter Bachrach and Morton Baratz. 1962. "Two Faces of Political Power." *American Political Science Review* 56:947–952.

*Baumgartner, Frank R., and Beth L. Leech. 1998. *Basic Interests: The Importance of Groups in Politics and Political Science*. Princeton, NJ: Princeton University Press.

*Baumgartner, Frank R., Jeffrey M. Berry, Marie Hojnacki, David C. Kimball, and Beth L. Leech. 2009. *Lobbying and Policy Change: Who Wins, Who Loses, and Why*. Chicago: University of Chicago Press.

Berry, Jeffrey. 1977. *Lobbying for the People: The Political Behavior of Public Interest Groups*. Princeton, NJ: Princeton University Press.

Berry, Jeffrey. 1984. *Feeding Hungry People: Rulemaking in the Food Stamp Program*. New Brunswick, NJ: Rutgers University Press.

Berry, Jeffrey. 1999. *The New Liberalism: The Rising Power of Citizen Groups*. Washington, DC: Brookings Institution Press.

BLS News Release. 2014. January 24. http://www.bls.gov/news.release/pdf/union2.pdf.

Cammisa, Anne Marie. 1995. *Governments as Interest Groups: Intergovernmental Lobbying and the Federal System*. Westport, CT: Praeger.

Campbell, Andrea. 2005. *How Policies Make Citizens: Senior Political Activism and the American Welfare State*. Princeton, NJ: Princeton University Press.

Dahl, Robert. 1961. *Who Governs?* New Haven, CT: Yale University Press.

Dark, Taylor. 2001. *The Unions and the Democrats: An Enduring Alliance*. Ithaca, NY: ILR Press.

Dinan, John. 2011. "Shaping Health Care Reform: State Government Influence in the Patient Protection and Affordable Care Act." *Publius* 41 (3): 395–420.

Duverger, Maurice. 1964. *Political Parties: Their Organization and Activity in the Modern State.* 2nd ed. New York: Routledge, Kegan, and Paul.

Erkulwater, Jennifer. 2006. *Disability Rights and the American Social Safety Net.* Ithaca, NY: Cornell University Press.

Esping-Andersen, Gosta. 1985. *Politics Against Markets: The Social Democratic Road to Power.* Princeton, NJ: Princeton University Press.

Finegold, Kenneth. 1988. "Agriculture and the Politics of U.S. Social Provision: Social Insurance and Food Stamps." In *The Politics of Social Policy in the United States*, edited by Margaret Weir, Ann Shola Orloff, and Theda Skocpol, 199–234. Princeton, NJ: Princeton University Press.

Forbath, William. 1991. *Law and the Shaping of the American Labor Movement.* Boston: Harvard University Press.

Gottschalk, Marie. 2000. *The Shadow Welfare State: Labor, Business, and the Politics of Health Care in the United States.* Ithaca, NY: Cornell University Press.

Greenstone, J. David. 1977. *Labor in American Politics.* Chicago: University of Chicago Press.

Hacker, Jacob. 2002. *Divided Welfare State: The Battle over Public and Private Social Benefits in the United States.* New York: Cambridge University Press.

Hacker, Jacob S., and Paul Pierson. 2002. "Business Power and Social Policy: Employers and the Formation of the American Welfare State." *Politics & Society* 30 (2): 277–325.

*Hacker, Jacob S., and Paul Pierson. 2010. *Winner-Take-All Politics: How Washington Made the Rich Richer and Turned Its Back on the Middle Class.* New York: Simon and Schuster.

Harrington, Michael. 1972. *Socialism.* New York: Saturday Review Press.

Haskins, Ron. 2008. "Governors and the Development of American Social Policy." In *A Legacy of Innovation: Governors and Public Policy*, edited by Ethan G. Sribnick, 76–104. Philadelphia: University of Pennsylvania Press.

Hattam, Victoria. 1993. *Labor Visions and State Power: The Origins of Business Unionism in the United States.* Princeton, NJ: Princeton University Press.

*Hays, R. A. 2001. *Who Speaks for the Poor? National Interest Groups and Social Policy.* New York: Routledge.

Heclo, Hugh. 1978. "Issue Networks and the Executive Establishment." In *The New American Political System*, edited by Anthony King, 87–124. Washington, DC: American Enterprise Institute.

Howard, Christopher. 2007. *The Welfare State Nobody Knows.* Princeton, NJ: Princeton University Press.

Immergut, Ellen. 1992. *Health Politics: Interests and Institutions in Western Europe, 1930–1970.* New York: Cambridge University Press.

Iversen, Torben, and David Soskice. 2009. "Distribution and Redistribution: The Shadow of the Nineteenth Century." *World Politics* 61 (3): 438–486.

King, Ronald F. 2000. *Budgeting Entitlements: The Politics of Food Stamps.* Washington, DC: Georgetown University Press.

*Klein, Jennifer. 2003. *For All These Rights: Business, Labor, and the Shaping of America's Public-Private Welfare State.* Princeton, NJ: Princeton University Press.

Korpi, Walter. 1983. *The Democratic Class Struggle.* Boston: Routledge.

Levine, Susan. 2008. *School Lunch Politics: The Surprising History of America's Favorite Welfare Program.* Princeton, NJ: Princeton University Press.

Lichtenstein, Nelson. 2002. *State of the Union: A Century of American Labor.* Princeton, NJ: Princeton University Press.

Lindblom, Charles E. 1977. *Politics and Markets*. New York: Basic Books.

Lowery, David, and Virginia Gray. 2004. "A Neopluralist Perspective on Research on Organized Interests." *Political Research Quarterly* 57:163–175.

*Lynch, Frederick R. 2011. *One Nation Under AARP: The Fight over Medicare, Social Security, and America's Future*. Berkeley and Los Angeles: University of California Press.

Madison, James. 1787. *Federalist 10*.

Antonia Maioni, 1998. *Parting at the Crossroads: The Emergence of Health Insurance in the United States and Canada*. Princeton, NJ: Princeton University Press.

Marmor, Theodore. 1973. *The Politics of Medicare*. Chicago: Aldine.

*Martin, Cathie Jo. 1999. *Stuck in Neutral: Business and the Politics of Human Capital Investment Policy*. Princeton, NJ: Princeton University Press.

McAdam, Doug. 1982. *Political Process and the Development of Black Insurgency, 1930–1970*. Chicago: University of Chicago Press.

McFarland, Andrew S. 2004. *Neopluralism*. Lawrence: University Press of Kansas.

Melnick, R. Shep. 1994. *Between the Lines: Interpreting Welfare Rights*. Washington, DC: Brookings Institution.

Mettler, Suzanne. 2011. *The Submerged State: How Invisible Government Policies Undermine American Democracy*. Chicago: University of Chicago Press.

Morgan, Kimberly J., and Andrea Campbell. 2011. *The Delegated Welfare State*. New York: Oxford University Press.

Morgan, Kimberly J., and Monica Prasad. 2009. "The Origins of Tax Systems: A French-American Comparison." *American Journal of Sociology* 114 (5): 1350–1394.

Olson, Mancur. 1965. *The Logic of Collective Action*. Cambridge, MA: Harvard University Press.

Pierson, Paul. 1995. *Dismantling the Welfare State? Reagan, Thatcher and the Politics of Retrenchment*. New York: Cambridge University Press.

Plotke, David. 1996. *Building a Democratic Political Order: Reshaping American Liberalism in the 1930s and 1940s*. New York: Cambridge University Press.

*Poen, Monte. 1979. *Harry S. Truman versus the Medical Lobby: The Genesis of Medicare*. Columbia: University of Missouri Press.

Quadagno, Jill. 2005. *One Nation Uninsured, Why the U.S. Has No National Health Insurance*. New York: Oxford University Press.

Rich, Andrew. 2004. *Think Tanks, Public Policy, and the Politics of Expertise*. New York: Cambridge University Press.

*Roof, Tracy. 2011. *American Labor, Congress, and the Welfare State: 1935–2010*. Baltimore, MD: Johns Hopkins University Press.

Salisbury, Robert H. 1969. "An Exchange Theory of Interest Groups." *Midwest Journal of Political Science* 13:1–32.

Salisbury, Robert H. 1979. "Why No Corporatism in America?" In *Trends toward Corporatist Intermediation*, edited by Philippe C. Schmitter and Gerhard Lehmbruch, 213–230. Beverly Hills, CA: Sage.

Schattschneider, E. E. 1960. *The Semi-Sovereign People*. New York: Holt, Rinehart and Winston.

Schlozman, Kay Lehman, and John T. Tierney. 1986. *Organized Interests and American Democracy*. New York: Harper and Row.

*Schlozman, Kay Lehman, Sidney Verba, and Henry E. Brady. 2012. *The Unheavenly Chorus: Unequal Political Voice and the Broken Promise of American Democracy*. Princeton, NJ: Princeton University Press.

Skocpol, Theda. 1992. *Protecting Soldiers and Mothers: The Political Origins of Social Policy in the United States*. Cambridge, MA: Belknap Press of Harvard University Press.

Skocpol, Theda. 1997. *Boomerang: Health Reform and the Turn Against Government*. New York: W. W. Norton.

Starr, Paul. 2011. *Remedy and Reaction: The Peculiar American Struggle over Health Care Reform*. New Haven, CT: Yale University Press.

Swank, Duane. 2002. *Global Capital, Political Institutions, and Policy Change in Developed Welfare States*. New York; Cambridge University Press.

Swenson, Peter. 2004. "Varieties of Capitalist Interests: Power, Institutions, and the Regulatory Welfare State in the United States and Sweden." *Studies in American Political Development* 18 (1): 1–29.

Truman, David. 1951. *The Governmental Process: Political Interests and Public Opinion*. New York: Knopf.

*Vogel, David. 1989. *Fluctuating Fortunes*. New York: Basic Books.

Walker, Jack L. 1991. *Mobilizing Interest Groups in America*. Ann Arbor: University of Michigan Press.

CHAPTER 12

....

CONSTITUENCIES AND
PUBLIC OPINION

....

ANDREA LOUISE CAMPBELL AND MICHAEL W. SANCES

1 INTRODUCTION

....

THE American public is quite interested in social policy, recognizing that such policies touch the lives of virtually everyone in our society. Americans pay more attention to, are more knowledgeable about, and have a greater stake in social policy than in many other areas of government activity. Although public opinion is by no means the only factor influencing the shape of the American welfare state—interest groups, the institutional structure of American government, and the preferences of elected officials themselves all affect policy outcomes as well—the American welfare state's distinctive qualities arise in large part from the public's preferences. The modest level of redistribution, differential treatment of population subgroups, and frequent use of obscured means of social provision all reflect Americans' beliefs about the appropriate role of government and their feelings about who deserves what types of social protection. Thus, public opinion is a central element influencing social policy outcomes.

2 UNDERSTANDING PUBLIC OPINION
AND ITS LIMITS

....

Before discussing how public opinion matters, it is useful to consider some basic features of how the public thinks about politics. The first principle, long recognized by scholars of public opinion, is that the public simply does not pay as much attention to politics as do elites. When academics such as those from the University of Michigan's Survey Research Center began collecting systematic data on public opinion, they were shocked to learn just how little most citizens knew about politics and public policy (Campbell et al. 1960; Converse 1964). Nearly 40 percent of citizens could not identify the difference between "liberals" and "conservatives," terms that political elites consider the foundations of political debate. Rather than holding generally liberal or conservative policy positions, most citizens exhibited ideologically inconsistent bundles of opinions, taking a liberal stance on one policy issue and a conservative stance on another (Converse 1964). Opinions were also inconsistent across time: A liberal response on one issue was frequently followed by a conservative response on the *same* issue when respondents were reinterviewed two years later (Converse 1964).

These findings called into question the basis of centuries of democratic theory—which predicates government on the preferences of its citizens—and thus were much debated. Nevertheless, the fundamental finding of gross ideological inconsistency among the public has largely survived (Zaller 1992; Converse 2000; for a contrary view, see Ansolabehere, Rodden, and Snyder 2008). Furthermore, the public's ignorance of the basic facts of American politics—which party controls the lower house of Congress, the name of the vice president, the meaning of the words *liberal* and *conservative*—has persisted despite increases in education and media availability (Delli Carpini and Keeter 1996).

Given these shortcomings, how could it be that public opinion influences the shape of the American welfare state? In the wake of these original findings, some scholars have argued that instead of complex ideological schema, citizens use easy-to-recognize symbols such as race and party to organize their political thoughts (Sears et al. 1980), or utilize informational shortcuts, such as party identification and incumbency, in making political choices (Popkin 1991). Others have argued that individual inconsistencies in opinion cancel out in the aggregate, providing a coherent signal to policy makers about overall public preference (Page and Shapiro 1992; Erikson, MacKuen, and Stimson 2002).

More than symbols and shortcuts, however, perhaps the most important mechanism by which the public shapes welfare state policy is "latent opinion." Election returns and responses to surveys are but one form of public opinion; in order to keep their jobs, politicians must also worry about latent opinion, "the opinion that might exist at some point in the future in response to the decision-makers' actions and may therefore result in political damage or even the defeat at the polls" (Key 1961, quoted in Zaller 2003, 311). Elected officials constantly consider the attitudes of latent publics that might be activated if they were to vote one way or another on a given bill (Arnold 1990), discerning where the public stands from town hall meetings, media accounts, constituent contact, and so on (Peterson 1995). Thus, public opinion enters the policy-making process because elected officials are constantly thinking about what the public wants. The modern opinion poll merely augments the information-gathering processes that politicians have used for decades.

In the development of the American welfare state, latent opinion often spurred politicians to take action. For example, there were virtually no public opinion polls administered before the passage of the Social Security Act of 1935. Yet the plight of impoverished senior citizens was widely recognized, in part publicized by groups such as the Townsend Movement (Amenta 2006), but also made salient by the obvious failure of the private sector to provide adequate assistance (and by the desire of the business community to employ younger workers). Politicians did not need public opinion polls to tell them that addressing economic insecurity in old age was an important initiative that the public would support, although such support was overwhelming in the polls that appeared later in the decade (Schiltz 1970).

Even when the public is expressing its voice directly, however, it is typically more informative about the broad outlines of policy than specific provisions. As a result, the public can often be overruled by organized interest groups, which are much more capable of dealing in policy specifics. Thus, where organized groups have preferences that differ from those of the public, the organized interests often prevail. One example is the Medicare prescription drug benefit, enacted in 2003. The public was influential in forcing lawmakers to create a prescription drug plan after the 2000 election despite the fact that many in the GOP-controlled Congress would have preferred not to create a massive new entitlement, especially on the eve of baby boomer retirement. The public was able to shape the major parameters of the reform, in particular defeating the effort to limit the prescription drug benefit to private managed care plans.

Yet public opinion did not prevail on several other aspects of the program: Large majorities of the public told pollsters they wanted the government to have negotiating power over drug prices, wanted a Medicare option for getting prescription drugs rather than only private stand-alone plans, and desired the importation of cheaper drugs from abroad. None of these popular features was included in the final legislation. The pharmaceutical industry objected vehemently to government negotiating power and reimportation; the insurance industry fought against a Medicare option, which would surely have become the default for millions of seniors daunted by choosing among dozens of private plans. These stakeholder groups prevailed over the public (Morgan and Campbell 2011). Thus, policy reflected the public's general desire to add a prescription drug benefit to Medicare, but organized interests won out with regard to several important aspects of program design.

A final set of characteristics of public opinion with relevance for social policy concern political ignorance and susceptibility to framing effects. Possessing incorrect perceptions or misinformation can shape individuals' support for government policy. For example, individuals overestimate the proportion of government spending on welfare and the proportion of welfare recipients who are African American, and, in turn, feel negatively about social assistance programs (Gilens 1996; Gilens 2001). The impact of misinformation is revealed in experiments that supply respondents with the correct facts: for example, favorability toward the home mortgage interest deduction is quite high among the public, but drops when survey respondents are told that the majority of the benefits go to affluent households (Mettler 2011, 56–57). An even more problematic type of political ignorance is the belief in false information, such as myths and erroneous rumors (Berinsky 2011). For example, in summer 2010, a Kaiser opinion poll found that over 40 percent of Americans believed that the Obama health care reform included a provision for "death panels," which would make decisions about whether patients should live or die based on a subjective measure of societal productivity (Nyhan 2010). This belief persisted despite repeated demonstrations of its falsehood, and there is evidence that acceptance of the death panel rumor led to opposition to the reform (Berinsky 2011). Even more common than outright misinformation, seemingly subtle changes in the language used to frame problems, policies, and populations can have strong effects on public attitudes (Chong and Druckman 2007).

3 CHARACTERISTICS OF AMERICANS' ATTITUDES ABOUT SOCIAL PROGRAMS

Beyond these general characteristics, several aspects of public preferences shape the American welfare state. Most fundamentally, Americans are conflicted in their attitudes toward government in the social policy realm, wanting both small government, in the abstract, and substantial social protections, in their everyday lives. Americans' opinions about social programs are also deeply influenced by perceptions about beneficiary deservingness and attitudes toward race, inequality, and redistribution.

3.1 Americans Are Abstract Conservatives, but Operational Liberals

First and most fundamental is the conflicted, two-faced nature of American attitudes toward the role of government and social policy. As public opinion researchers Free and Cantril first reported in 1967, and as confirmed in the contemporary era (Page and Jacobs 2009; Morgan and Campbell 2011), most Americans say that they prefer small government and low taxes in the abstract. Further probing, however, reveals that the public also very much likes what government does, and supports increased spending for many specific programs. For example, even in 2008, a year when an apparent liberal surge catapulted Barack Obama into the White House, the small government proclivities of Americans were on full display: more Americans identified as conservative than as liberal in the 2008 National Election Study (32 percent versus 21 percent; 47 percent said they were "middle of the road" or hadn't thought much about it). Far larger proportions express skepticism about government in other ways. For instance, 70 percent of adult Americans say they trust the government to do the right thing only some of the time or not at all, 70 percent say the government in Washington is too strong, and 73 percent say the government wastes a lot of taxpayer dollars.

Yet when it comes to specific beneficiary groups and programs, Americans appear far more liberal. As shown in Table 12.1, when asked about programs for vulnerable populations, majorities of the same National Election Study respondents want greater spending. Fifty-eight percent want spending on the homeless increased, and 61 percent want spending on the poor increased. Programs benefiting the middle class are even more

Table 12.1 Preferences for Increased Government Spending among All Respondents and Government Skeptics, 2008

	All Respondents, %	Conservatives, %	Republicans, %	Trust Govt None/ Some of Time, %	Govt Wastes a Lot of Tax Dollars, %	Govt in Wash. Too Strong, %
Welfare	27	15	13	26	25	12[c]
The Poor	61	43	43	57	59	42[c]
The Homeless	58[b]	42[b]	43[b]	56[b]	53[b]	66[a]
College Financial Aid	53[b]	43[b]	43[b]	51[b]	50[b]	55[a]
Child Care	58	39	39	58	56	52[c]
Social Security	66	56	55	66	65	55[c]
Public Schools	75	61	62	73	73	66[c]

Note: Cells show percentage of respondents of each description who want program spending increased (rather than decreased or kept the same). Data from 2008 except [a]1992; [b]1996; [c]2000.
Source: American National Election Study cumulative file as calculated by Morgan and Campbell (2011, 39).

popular: The proportion of adult Americans wanting government spending increased is 53 percent for college financial aid, 58 percent for child care, 66 percent for Social Security, and 75 percent for public schools.

The magnitudes of these figures suggest substantial overlap between these two seemingly contradictory positions. And indeed, we see that a nontrivial portion of self-identifying small-government conservatives want spending in these social policy areas increased. Two-fifths of conservatives and Republicans want government spending on the poor, the homeless, college financial aid, and child care increased, and majorities of conservatives and Republicans want spending on Social Security and public schools increased. Solid majorities of those with low trust in government, who think government wastes a lot of tax money, and who believe the government in Washington is too strong, want spending in all of these areas increased as well. As we will see next, these conflicting tendencies are reflected in the shape of social policy and reform.

3.2 Views of Recipients Shape Program Support

A second characteristic of public opinion about social provision concerns the "deservingness" of various beneficiary groups and the distinctions that Americans make among them. Americans have long differentiated between earned (or universal) programs that benefit individuals of every income level, and unearned and targeted programs that benefit "only" the poor (Cook and Barrett 1992). "Deservingness" appears to be the chief characteristic that differentiates beneficiary groups and their programs in the public mind. Those who earned their benefits by paying into the system over time through payroll contributions or by serving the nation through military service are thought to be deserving. Others are regarded as deserving because they are not at fault for their neediness, including children and persons with disabilities. Those who are working but who simply cannot earn enough money to make ends meet are perceived as deserving as well. In comparison to these groups, the public views welfare recipients, those receiving AFDC/TANF, as the scourge of the American welfare state—able-bodied adults whose need to drink from the public trough is their own fault.

These differences in perceived deservingness spill over into other attitudes about beneficiary groups. In a comprehensive survey about perceptions of program recipients, Cook and Barrett (1992) found that 89 percent of respondents thought Social Security recipients "really need their benefits" compared to just 69 percent who thought that of Aid to Families with Dependent Children (AFDC) recipients. Similarly, respondents were far more likely to think that Social Security recipients would use their benefits wisely than would AFDC recipients, 89 percent to 42 percent (Cook and Barrett 1992, 98–100). Individuals also thought AFDC was much more likely than Social Security to foster dependence on government.

Although complementary explanations have been proposed for why different programs are favored and when—for example, Kam and Nam (2008) find a correlation between state economic conditions and welfare support, and Feldman and Steenbergen (2001) show that support correlates with a measure of "humanitarian values"—the deservingness hypothesis continues to receive both observational (Dyck and Hussey 2008) and experimental (Gollust and Lynch 2011) support. These perceptions about the deservingness and prudence of beneficiaries matter for policy making, with welfare the area in which there has been the most retrenchment—in part because of the public's skeptical stance.

Finally, as is common in the American context, race also shapes attitudes toward social programs and their recipients. Many white Americans overestimate the proportion of the poor who are African American and believe that African Americans disproportionately benefit from social welfare programs, particularly means-tested programs (Gilens 1999). At the same time, many whites view themselves as taxpayers who will never benefit from such programs but are forced to support minority recipients. These perceptions can make it difficult to enhance social welfare benefits overtly for fear of triggering race-based objections, and increase incentives for policy makers to resort to hidden or obscured means of providing social protections.

3.3 Americans Accept Inequality and Oppose Redistribution

Another aspect of public opinion that shapes the welfare state in profound ways is Americans' attitudes toward economic inequality and the desirability of

government-induced income redistribution. Even after the Occupy Wall Street movement of 2011 drew attention to economic inequality in the United States, the proportion
of Americans who say that income inequality is an "acceptable part of our economic
system" actually increased, from 45 percent in 1998 to 52 percent in December 2011
(Newport 2011). In the same December 2011 Gallup poll, more Americans said that
it is "extremely important" for the federal government to enact policies to "grow and
expand the economy" (32 percent) or to "increase the equality of opportunity for people to get ahead if they want to" (29 percent) than said the federal government should
enact policies to "reduce the income and wealth gap between the rich and the poor"
(17 percent) (Newport 2011). And in cross-national comparison, Americans are more
skeptical of government efforts to reduce economic outcomes through tax or transfer
programs than are citizens of other nations (Brooks and Manza 2007). In keeping with
these preferences, there is less redistribution than in other countries—in the United
States, post-tax and post-transfer poverty levels are not much different than pre-tax and
pre-transfer poverty levels (Smeeding 2005). And the redistribution that does happen
tends to occur through hidden means, such as within universal programs like Social
Security or through the tax code with the Earned Income Tax Credit (EITC) (Howard
1997).

In spite of their opposition to redistribution, Americans' attitudes toward the welfare state are partly structured by income. Even with regard to Social Security and
Medicare, universal programs that enjoy the strongest cross-class support, the affluent
are less supportive of increased spending than are their lower-income counterparts.
For means-tested programs, the income gradient in attitudes is even more pronounced,
because the affluent see themselves only as the unwilling funders of such programs, not
as potential beneficiaries. That the politically active affluent support universal programs
more than means-tested programs has made it easier for policy makers to trim the latter, given that public policy tends to be more responsive to the opinions of the wealthy
(Bartels 2008; Gilens 2005).

4 How Public Opinion Impacts the Welfare State

These characteristics of public opinion—feelings about the role of government in general, about deservingness and blame, about race, and about inequality and redistribution—shape the American welfare state in important ways. They help explain why some
programs have grown more than others, why attempts by conservative politicians to cut
or change the design of many welfare state programs have failed, why social spending
trends are unaffected by changes in party control of government, and why social programs in the United States so often have hidden or obscured policy designs.

4.1 Public Opinion Helps Explain Patterns of Program Growth

Over time, many welfare programs have grown, both universal ones such as Social Security and Medicare but even a number of means-tested programs as well, including Medicaid, CHIP (Children's Health Insurance Program), SNAP (Supplemental Nutritional Assistance Program; formerly food stamps), and the EITC (Earned Income Tax Credit). To the extent that public opinion factors into these patterns, the distinction is not between universal and means-tested program but rather between programs with deserving and sympathetic beneficiaries and those without. An analytical approach rooted in public opinion explains variation in program growth by asserting that the beneficiaries of these particular programs are viewed as relatively more sympathetic and less blameworthy than those in the reviled welfare program: disabled elderly patients dependent on Medicaid for their long-term care; children benefiting from CHIP and SNAP; the working poor benefiting from the EITC.

A related explanation for this growth is a combination of self-interest and economic forces: Greater inequality has forced more Americans into the recipient populations and thus made them more supportive of spending. This appears to be the case with the Food Stamp Program. Analyzing 1980s survey data, Cook and Barrett (1992) found that Food Stamps had the lowest public support, behind Medicare, SSI, Social Security, Medicaid, unemployment insurance, and AFDC. At that time, only 25 percent of the public wanted to increase food stamp benefits, compared to 33 percent who wanted to increase spending on AFDC (and 24 percent who wanted to decrease Food Stamps benefits). Since the 1980s, however, the public's stance toward Food Stamps has softened considerably. A March 2011 CNN poll found that 34 percent of respondents wanted to increase spending on Food Stamps, more than the 25 percent who said they wanted to decrease spending (CNN 2011). This change in support is likely due to increased usage among the public—in 2010, 13 percent of Americans used Food Stamps, up from 6 percent in 2000 (U.S. Department of Agriculture 2011)—and to a change in policy design. By June 2004, all states had switched to distributing benefits via debit cards rather than actual paper stamps (USDA 2011), and in 2008 Congress passed legislation changing the program's name to SNAP, or the Supplemental Nutritional Assistance Program, further reducing the stigma associated with the program.

4.2 Public Opinion Constrains Welfare State Retrenchment

The nature of public opinion has significant implications for welfare state reform as well. Conservative politicians and activists have long sought to cut back on social policy spending, or at least to change the designs of social programs to diminish the government's role. Although not the only factor shaping the outcomes of these efforts, public opinion is important in explaining what programs have been changed and how, as scholars of comparative welfare states are increasingly recognizing (Brooks and Manza 2007).

First, programs create constituencies that oppose retrenchment. Comparative scholars of the welfare state long hypothesized that recipients of social policies, particularly generous, universal ones, would act out of self-interest to defend their programs against threat (Baldwin 1990; Pierson 1993). Precisely this type of protective constituency developed around the Social Security program: As the program became more widespread and the benefits more generous, it helped transform senior citizens from the least to the most politically active age group in American politics. Social Security enhanced seniors' ability to participate in politics by giving them free time through retirement and a stable income, increasing their interest in politics by linking their well-being so visibly to a government program, and creating from this otherwise diverse group of citizens an identity as program recipients, which created the basis for mobilization by interest groups and political parties. Seniors subsequently used their political participation to beat back threats to their programs such as budget cuts and restructurings. Seniors' ability to assert their preferences—to defeat Reagan's Social Security cuts in 1981 and the unpopular Medicare Catastrophic Coverage law in 1987–1988—was due in part to how these programs had enhanced seniors' participatory capacity (Campbell 2003).

In contrast to Social Security, AFDC was vulnerable to fundamental reform in 1996 because it had not generated such feedback effects. Welfare benefits in most states fail to lift recipients above the poverty line, and are too low to have the kind of positive resource effect that Social Security does. Moreover, the program's administration through an arbitrary and capricious caseworker mechanism actually undermined political efficacy among recipients, resulting in political participation levels among welfare recipients even below what those individuals' low levels of education and income would predict (Soss 1999; 2000). Welfare recipients were virtually silent on the matter of program reform, and the 1996 reform remains one of the few examples of successful welfare state retrenchment.

Having failed to cut Social Security outright during the 1980s, conservatives later sought less politically explosive ways to achieve their goal of reducing the size and scope of government involvement in individuals' retirement. The idea was not to cut these programs directly but rather to introduce private elements into Social Security and Medicare that would indirectly achieve the same ends. In each instance, however, the public objected to the reforms and successfully combatted them.

In particular, Social Security privatization—which had been developed in conservative thinks tanks—got a boost when President George W. Bush made it the centerpiece of his second-term domestic agenda, barnstorming the country to build support. However, although many Americans felt the system should be reformed—a Time/SRBI poll in March 2005 found 72 percent of Americans felt it "extremely critical" or "very important" for Bush to address Social Security reform in his second term (Time/SRBI 2005)—privatization was deeply unpopular, as it threatened to replace a familiar system with one that was both new and might not provide the same benefits.

Anticipating latent opinion, Republican House Speaker Dennis Hastert warned as early as February 2005, "You can't jam change down the American people's throat"

(Toner 2005, A13). By fall 2005, Social Security privatization was dead, in part because of public pushback. Private accounts were never embraced by large majorities of the public, and support declined over time as opponents such as AARP and labor unions ran ads criticizing the proposal as undermining retirement security and exacerbating rather than improving problems in Social Security's long-term finances. Hearing almost entirely negative messages from constituents, members of Congress were deeply skeptical, and Bush's tactical mistake in making privatization a presidential rather than congressional initiative further undermined Member sentiment. No vote was ever taken in Congress (Campbell and King 2010).

Conservatives also tried to increase the role of private provision within seniors' retirement programs by linking a new Medicare prescription drug benefit to enrollment in a private managed care plan. Although President Bill Clinton first proposed adding a prescription-drug benefit in 1999, Republicans gained unified control of government in the 2000 election. Left with this popular proposal on their plate, they set about using prescription drug coverage as a carrot to change the design of Medicare.

However, senior citizens were deeply fearful of private managed care plans, which had abandoned millions of seniors by entering and then abruptly exiting the Medicare market during the 1990s. An ABC News/*Washington Post* poll from January 2003 found that only 21 percent of adult Americans supported the plan to cover prescription drug costs only for those who joined a managed care plan, whereas 64 percent preferred prescription drug coverage for all seniors regardless of their plan; among those aged 61 and older, support for the managed care version was only 15 percent (ABC News/*Washington Post* 2003). Seniors were joined in their objections by Republican Congressmen from rural areas who told their colleagues that the prescription drug benefit could not be limited to those in managed care, since there were few or no managed care organizations in their states (Morgan and Campbell 2011). In the end, conservatives were forced to back off from this proposal and instead make prescription drug coverage available to all Medicare beneficiaries, not just those in private managed care plans. Thus, whether faced with overt program cuts or more subtle changes in program design, program constituencies successfully fought off change to their programs.

A second aspect of public opinion that has thwarted retrenchment efforts is the failure of generational conflict to emerge. During the 1980s, some observers predicted that political backlash from younger citizens would arise (see Quadagno 1989 for an overview). The argument is that younger individuals would come to resent paying the payroll taxes that support generous pension and health benefits for retirees when they can barely afford to make ends meet themselves, particularly at a time when the long-term prognosis for these programs suggests that these workers might not benefit to the same degree when they reach retirement age. Such resentments would assist those interested in cutting back programs for senior citizens in particular.

Although the inevitability of such a backlash remains part of the conventional wisdom (e.g. Samuelson 2009), no such generational resentments have developed. Support for the major social insurance programs has been high for decades, and remains so, with those under 65 actually more likely than those 65 and over to support increased spending. A December 2008 Kaiser Family Foundation poll found that those under 65 are more likely to want spending on Medicare increased than those over 65: 54 percent to 36 percent (Kaiser Family Foundation 2008). Similarly, in a July/August 2009 National Academy of Social Insurance/Rockefeller Foundation poll, those under 65 are more likely than those over 65 to say that the government does not spend enough on Social Security: 48 percent compared to 37 percent (Reno, Lavery, and NASI 2009). Among those under 65, half told AARP in a 2004 survey that they think that "retired older Americans" have too little influence in "this country today," whereas two-fifths think they had the right amount; only a handful think older people have too much influence (AARP 2006).

Three aspects of non-seniors' attitudes explain why intergenerational conflict has failed to emerge: self-interest, financial emancipation, and altruistic societal considerations. Retirement programs enjoy public favorability because all workers pay in and hope to benefit themselves eventually. They represent financial emancipation for the adult children of retirees, who might otherwise have to support their elderly parents (in fact, in part because of Social Security and Medicare, seniors are three times more likely to give financial support to their adult children than to receive it [Pew Research Center 2005]). And these programs fulfill the societal aim of providing security for retirees, vastly reducing senior poverty over time. Public opinion data bear out each of these explanations: In the 2009 NASI/Rockefeller poll, large majorities of Americans say they don't "mind paying Social Security taxes," 72 percent because they know they will be getting retirement benefits themselves; 76 percent because otherwise they would have to support family members financially; and 87 percent because the program provides "security and stability" to millions of retirees, disabled persons, and survivors. The Great Recession has only strengthened these views (Campbell 2009), with 88 percent of 2009 NASI/Rockefeller respondents agreeing that "with the economy and the stock market as bad as it is right now, Social Security benefits are more important than ever to ensure that retirees have a dependable income when they retire" (Reno et al. 2009, 6).

4.3   Public Opinion Helps Explain the Non-Effects of Party Control

Another feature of the American welfare state that public opinion can help account for is the invariance of social spending to shifts in party control of government, a pattern that holds at both the federal (Faricy 2011) and state (Leigh 2008) levels. A public-opinion based explanation would argue that spending continues unabated because most of the American welfare state benefits middle- and upper-class voters through universal entitlements and tax expenditures. This creates strong political pressure from the most politically active subpopulations to maintain or increase spending. Small surprise, then, that conservatives' efforts to attack the welfare state have come to naught.

4.4 Public Opinion Helps Explain Obscured Program Designs

Finally, the nature of public opinion helps explain another distinguishing feature of the American welfare state, the enormous amount of social spending "hidden" in the form of tax expenditures (Howard 1997; 2007), or otherwise made invisible to the public via delegation to state and private authorities (Morgan and Campbell 2011; Mettler 2011). Obscuring the cost of social programs through tax expenditures is an ideal way to satisfy a Janus-faced public that wants both small government in the abstract and big spending on specific programs. In contrast to direct spending programs, tax expenditures can provide social protections without appearing to increase the size of government; in fact, by reducing tax collections, they actually shrink the formal size of government. Delegation of social programs to states takes the focus off the distrusted federal government, and delegation of program administration to nonprofit and for-profit firms appears to minimize the government role altogether, in keeping with Americans' small government preferences.

Another way in which social provision is obscured in the United States is the manner in which redistribution—whether through direct transfers or tax expenditures—is carried out. Not only does the American welfare state redistribute far less than those of other advanced industrialized nations, but also the most extensive redistribution occurs through veiled mechanisms. The most effective antipoverty program in the United States has not been AFDC/TANF (Temporary Assistance for Needy Families), Medicaid, Food Stamps, public housing, or any other means-tested program, but rather Social Security: Through its benefit formula, it redistributes payroll contributions from higher to lower income subgroups in a hidden way that does not trigger stigma and that is generous enough to dramatically reduce senior poverty (Skocpol 2000). Similarly, the amount of money refunded to the working poor through the EITC tax expenditure program far exceeds the value of any direct spending program for the poor; the program redistributes by sweeping the bottom 40 percent of earners out of the federal income tax system.

Moreover, when redistribution is not sufficiently obscured, public opinion objects. The framers of the Obama administration's landmark Patient Protection and Affordable Care Act of 2010 sought to win over public opinion with a policy design that neither introduced a universal, single-payer program—which most health economists argue is the most efficient system but which smacks of big government—nor fundamentally changed the existing system for purchasing private health insurance, as the 1993–1994 Clinton health reform effort would have done. Instead, the reform was designed to spread coverage to the uninsured by inducing them to obtain insurance through their employers or, failing that, through a private insurance plan purchased on a government-created "exchange," with subsidies for those below a certain income level (together with an expansion of Medicaid). The insurance arrangements of the vast majority of Americans covered by employers or Medicare would remain in place.

Despite these efforts to satisfy public preferences, the reform remained unpopular. Although individual pieces of the legislation were favored by large majorities, support for the reform as a whole never broke 50 percent for any extended time (Brodie et al. 2010). That the reform left intact the insurance arrangements of most Americans ironically did not win over their support, but rather reinforced their view that the reform was not universal and extended insurance coverage to the uninsured on their tax dollar. Exacerbating this perception was the fact that the redistribution was not hidden but quite overt: Tax dollars would pay for Medicaid expansion and help subsidize insurance purchases by lower income citizens; future increases in Medicare spending would be pared back to help fund the reform as well. The reform's designers may have dodged the "big government" bullet, but they failed to avoid the "redistribution" label.

5 PUBLIC OPINION VERSUS ALTERNATIVE EXPLANATIONS

Although public opinion is important in explaining patterns of social policy outcomes in the United States, it typically operates in conjunction with other factors, such as interest group influence or the institutional structure of the American system. For example, growth in Medicaid and CHIP has been encouraged by interest groups such as health care providers—mainly hospitals, but also doctors—who prefer insured patients to the uninsured, and by state governors who wish to maximize federal matching dollars and to secure reimbursement for services provided to the uninsured in public hospitals (Brown and Sparer 2003). The continued growth of social programs despite changes in party control of government is due not only to public opinion but also to a path-dependent lock-in effect: Neither universal programs nor tax expenditures are subject to appropriations, and so are simply on "auto-pilot," beyond the reach of politicians. Economic conditions also play a role. The economic and social needs that necessitate welfare spending are ever present, driving election-seeking politicians of both parties to respond (Erikson, Wright, and McIver 1993). And interest group politics might also explain why neither party can afford to abandon welfare state programs, perhaps because both parties are captured by special interests that will withdraw financial support if their programs are threatened. However, public opinion still matters, and, indeed, the latter two explanations are related to public opinion, as they ultimately involve electoral incentives and interest groups that, at least in part, serve to aggregate mass opinion.

6 CONCLUSION

Public opinion cannot explain the development and trajectory of American social policy by itself, but it remains a crucially important factor in explaining the nature of social provision in the United States and the outcomes of retrenchment efforts. Americans know just enough to give broad guidance to politicians, although ignorance, misperceptions, and susceptibility to framing influence the messages they send. And social policy outcomes reflect the preferences of American majorities in a variety of ways: In the differential generosity of programs for "deserving" and "undeserving" target populations, in the extensive use of hidden and obscured modes of social provision, and in the modest degree of redistribution the American welfare state achieves. Thus, the limited grasp of politics that most Americans possess may act as a buffer against massive change, whereas the more attentive and well-resourced members of the public are able to resist attempts at retrenchment and privatization as well. Any account of the development and future of the American welfare state that does not acknowledge the public's role is incomplete.

References

*Indicates recommended reading.

AARP. 2006. *Images of Aging in America 2004*. Washington, DC: AARP.

ABC News/*Washington Post*. 2003. January 30–February 1. Retrieved from the *iPOLL Databank, The Roper Center for Public Opinion Research, University of Connecticut.*

Amenta, Edwin. 2006. *When Movements Matter: The Townsend Plan and the Rise of Social Security*. Princeton, NJ: Princeton University Press.

Ansolabehere, Stephen., Jonathan Rodden, and James M. Snyder. 2008. "The Strength of Issues: Using Multiple Measures to Gauge Preference Stability, Ideological Constraint, and Issue Voting." *American Political Science Review* 102:215–232.

Arnold, R. Douglas 1990. *The Logic of Congressional Action*. New Haven, CT: Yale University Press.

Baldwin, Peter 1990. *The Politics of Social Solidarity: Class Bases of the European Welfare State, 1875–1975*. New York: Cambridge University Press.

Bartels, Larry M. 2008. *Unequal Democracy: The Political Economy of the New Gilded Age*. Princeton, NJ: Princeton University Press.

Berinsky, Adam J. 2011. *Rumors, Truths, and Reality: A Study of Political Misinformation*. Working paper, Department of Political Science, MIT.

Brodie, Mollyann, Drew Altman, Claudia Deane, Sasha Buscho, and Elizabeth Hamel. 2010. "Liking the Pieces, Not the Package: Contradictions in Public Opinion During Health Reform." *Health Affairs* 29 (6): 1125–1130.

Brooks, Clem, and Jeff Manza. 2007. *Why Welfare States Persist: The Importance of Public Opinion In Democracies*. Chicago: University of Chicago Press.

Brown, Lawrence C., and Michael S. Sparer. 2003. "Poor Program's Progress: The Unanticipated Politics of Medicaid Policy." *Health Affairs* 22 (1):31–44.

Campbell, Angus, Philip E. Converse, Warren E. Miller, and Donald E. Stokes. 1960. *The American Voter*. New York: Wiley.

*Campbell, Andrea L. 2003. *How Policies Make Citizens: Senior Political Activism and the American Welfare State*. Princeton, NJ: Princeton University Press.

Campbell, Andrea L. 2009. "Is the Economic Crisis Driving Wedges Between Young and Old?: Rich and Poor?" *Generations* 33 (3): 47–53.

Campbell, Andrea L., and Ryan King. 2010. "Social Security." In R. B. Hudson ed., *The New Politics of Old Age*. Baltimore, MD: Johns Hopkins University Press, 233–253.

Chong, Dennis, and James N. Druckman. 2007. "Framing Theory." *Annual Review of Political Science* 10:103–126.

CNN. 2011. Opinion research corporation poll. March 11–13. Retrieved from the *iPOLL Databank, The Roper Center for Public Opinion Research, University of Connecticut*.

Converse, Philip E. 1964. "The Nature of Belief Systems in Mass Publics." In D. Apter, ed., *Ideology and Discontent*. Glencoe, IL: Free Press, 206–261.

Converse, Philip E. 2000. "Assessing the Capacity of Mass Electorates." *Annual Review of Political Science* 3:331–353.

*Cook, Fay L., and Edith J. Barrett. 1992. *Support for the American Welfare State: The Views of Congress and the Public*. New York: Columbia University Press.

Delli Carpini, Michael, and Scott Keeter. 1996. *What Americans Know About Politics and Why It Matters*. New Haven, CT: Yale University Press.

Dyck, Joshua J., and Laura S. Hussey. 2008. "The End of Welfare as We Know It?: Durable Attitudes in a Changing Information Environment." *Public Opinion Quarterly* 72 (4): 589–618.

Erikson, Robert S., Gerald C. Wright, and John P. McIver. 1993. *Statehouse Democracy: Public Opinion and Policy in the American States*. New York: Cambridge University Press.

Erikson, Robert S., Michael MacKuen, and James A. Stimson. 2002. *The Macro Polity*. New York: Cambridge University Press.

Faricy, Christopher. 2011. "The Politics of Social Policy in America: The Causes and Effects of Indirect Versus Direct Social Spending." *Journal of Politics* 73 (1): 74–83.

Feldman, Stanley and Steenbergen, Marco R. 2001. "The Humanitarian Foundation of Public Support for Social Welfare." *American Journal of Political Science* 45 (3): 658–677.

Free, Lloyd A., and Hadley Cantril. 1967. *The Political Beliefs of Americans: A Study of Public Opinion*. New Brunswick, NJ: Rutgers University Press.

Gilens, Martin 1996. "Race and Poverty in America." *Public Opinion Quarterly* 60 (4): 515.

*Gilens, Martin 1999. *Why Americans Hate Welfare*. Chicago: University of Chicago Press.

Gilens, Martin 2001. "Political Ignorance and Collective Policy Preferences." *American Political Science Review* 95 (2): 379–396.

Gilens, Martin 2005. "Inequality and Democratic Responsiveness." *Public Opinion Quarterly* 69 (5): 778–796.

Gollust Sarah E., and Julia Lynch. 2011. "Who Deserves Health Care? Effects of Causal Attributions and Group Cues on Public Attitudes About Responsibility for Health Care Costs." *Journal of Health Politics, Policy, and Law* 36 (6): 1061–1095.

*Howard, Christopher 1997. *The Hidden Welfare State: Tax Expenditures and Social Policy in the United States*. Princeton, NJ: Princeton University Press.

*Howard, Christopher 2007. *The Welfare State Nobody Knows: Debunking Myths About US Social Policy*. Princeton, NJ: Princeton University Press.

Kaiser Family Foundation. 2008. "The Public's Health Care Agenda for the New President and Congress." Poll #2008-POL019.

Kam, Cindy, and Yunju Nam. 2008. "Reaching Out or Pulling Back: Macroeconomic Conditions and Public Support for Social Welfare Spending." *Political Behavior* 30 (2): 223–258.

Key, V. O. Jr. 1961. *Public Opinion and American Democracy*. New York: Alfred Knopf.

Leigh, Andrew 2008. "Estimating the Impact of Gubernatorial Partisanship on Policy Settings and Economic Outcomes: A Regression Discontinuity Approach." *European Journal of Political Economy* 24 (1): 256–268.

*Mettler, Suzanne 2011. *The Submerged State: How Invisible Government Policies Undermine American Democracy*. Chicago: University of Chicago Press.

*Morgan, Kimberly J., and Andrea L. Campbell. 2011. *The Delegated Welfare State: Medicare, Markets, and the Governance of Social Policy*. New York: Oxford University Press.

Newport, Frank 2011. "Americans Prioritize Economy Over Reducing Wealth Gap." Gallup report, December 16. http://www.gallup.com/poll/151568/Americans-Prioritize-Growing-Economy-Reducing-Wealth-Gap.aspx.

Nyhan, Brendan 2010. "The Persistence of the Death Panels Myth." *Pollster.com*, July 29.

Page, Benjamin I., and Lawrence R. Jacobs. 2009. *Class War?: What Americans Really Think About Economic Inequality*. Chicago: University of Chicago Press.

*Page, Benjamin I., and Robert Y. Shapiro. 1992. *The Rational Public: Fifty Years of Trends in Americans' Policy Preferences*. Chicago: University of Chicago Press.

Pew Research Center. 2005. Pew social trends poll, October 5–November 6. Retrieved from the iPOLL Databank, The Roper Center for Public Opinion Research, University of Connecticut.

Peterson, Mark A. 1995. *How Health Policy Information Is Used in Congress*. Washington, DC: American Enterprise Institute and Brookings Institution.

Pierson, Paul 1993. "When Effect Becomes Cause: Policy Feedback and Political Change." *World Politics* 45 (4): 595–628.

Popkin, Samuel L. 1991. *The Reasoning Voter: Communication and Persuasion in Presidential Campaigns*. Chicago: University of Chicago Press.

Quadagno, Jill 1989. "Generational Equity and the Politics of the Welfare State." *Politics and Society* 17 (3): 353–376.

Reno, Virginia P., Joni Lavery, and National Academy of Social Insurance. 2009. *Economic Crisis Fuels Support for Social Security: Americans' Views on Social Security*. Washington, DC: National Academy of Social Insurance.

Samuelson, Robert J. 2009. "Boomers versus the Rest." *Newsweek*, January 26, 77.

Schiltz, Michael E. 1970. *Public Attitudes Toward Social Security, 1935–1965*. Vol. 33. Washington, DC: GPO. Social Security Administration, Office of Research and Statistics.

Sears, David O., Richard R. Lau, Tom R. Tyler, and Harris M. Allen Jr. 1980. "Self-Interest vs. Symbolic Politics In Policy Attitudes And Presidential Voting." *American Political Science Review* 74 (3): 670–684.

Skocpol, Theda 2000. *The Missing Middle*. New York: Norton.

Smeeding, Timothy 2005. "*Government Programs and Social Outcomes: The United States in Comparative Perspective.*" Luxembourg Income Study, Working Paper No. 426.

Soss, Joe 1999. "Lessons of Welfare: Policy Design, Political Learning, and Political Action." *American Political Science Review* 93 (2): 363–380.

*Soss, Joe 2000. *Unwanted Claims: The Politics of Participation in the US Welfare System*. Ann Arbor: University of Michigan Press.

Time/SRBI Poll. 2005. March 15–17. Retrieved from *the iPOLL Databank, The Roper Center for Public Opinion Research, University of Connecticut*.

Toner, Robin 2005. "Hastert Warns Not to Hurry Overhaul of Social Security." *New York Times*, February 12, A13.

U.S. Department of Agriculture (USDA). 2011. "Supplemental Nutrition Assistance Program Participation and Costs." http://www.fns.usda.gov/pd/SNAPsummary.htm.

*Zaller, John 1992. *The Nature and Origins of Mass Opinion*. New York: Cambridge University Press.

Zaller, John 2003. "Coming to Grips with VO key's Concept of Latent Opinion." In M. MacKuen and G. Rabinowitz eds., *Electoral Democracy*. Ann Arbor: University of Michigan Press, 311–336

CHAPTER 13

....

RACE AND ETHNICITY IN
U.S. SOCIAL POLICY

....

ROBERT C. LIEBERMAN

1 INTRODUCTION

....

ISSUES of racial and ethnic diversity and inequality have long been central to the American welfare state. The welfare state is, among other things, an expression of social and political solidarity in a nation-state. Racially and ethnically divided societies, as many have noted, have posed barriers to the development of national welfare states that afford citizens broad protection against the risks of modern economies, from old age and unemployment to sickness and disability. In particular, racial conflict and inequality have substantially limited the reach and scope of the American welfare state and its capacity to reduce inequality, and have introduced sharp lines of conflict into debates about social policy in the United States.

Although early research on American social policy was largely silent about race and ethnicity, in the last few decades we have learned a great deal about the relationship between racial and ethnic divisions in American society and the American welfare state. This relationship runs in both directions. The racial character of American society has surely shaped policy-making and structured the welfare state itself. At the same time, the structure of American social policy has affected the welfare state's capacity to incorporate members of different racial and ethnic groups, shaping their access to social citizenship and their opportunities for full inclusion in (or isolation from) the American political economy. Much of the most fruitful research on race and American social policy has focused on describing and explaining these relationships.

But many open questions remain, and more recent research has begun to explore important new issues that reflect both the changing reality of race in American politics and society and trends in political science. Among the most important emerging issues is the definition of "race" in the context of American social policy. Much scholarship on race and American politics, especially where social policy has been concerned, has been about African-Americans. The subfield's conceptual apparatus has been based largely on a black-white paradigm. Although this may be a reasonable approach for much of American history, it is clearly no longer an adequate framework. Since the passage of the Immigration and Nationality Act of 1965, which eliminated racially biased national origins quotas, immigration has thoroughly reshaped the American population; in twenty-first-century American politics, "race" connotes a much more complex and multilayered set of identities and groups. It is not clear that the same models that scholars have developed to examine black-white race politics can apply to a multiracial, multiethnic, immigrant-heavy society.

Moreover, the role of race and ethnicity in American politics has changed. Although explicit racist attitudes have declined, racial inequality remains resilient in many domains of American life, and the mechanisms that maintain and reproduce racial inequality in the absence of clear racial motives remain poorly understood. Although the liberal rhetoric of equality is now nearly universal, many policy battles, especially over social welfare, are widely understood as proxies for fundamental conflicts over the racial order of society (King and Smith 2011). What is the relationship between race and social policy in a "postracist" society (Harris and Lieberman 2013)?

A second important frontier for the study of race and social policy is the impact of the changing American welfare state on racial inequality. Although much scholarship on American social policy focuses on the New Deal regime of the mid-twentieth century, the social-policy landscape has changed dramatically in recent decades. The Clinton administration's welfare reform of 1996 marked the first major change in the New Deal welfare alignment, invoking racially charged notions of dependency in significantly reshaping the contours of income support and other benefits for the poor. The Obama administration's Affordable Care Act of 2010 promised substantial reform of the motley and chaotic American health insurance system. Given the gathering fiscal crisis of the American state, expensive entitlement programs including Social Security, Medicare, and Medicaid, which together compose nearly half of federal spending, face unprecedented political challenges. And the increasing importance of private social benefits—health insurance, pensions, and the like—has eroded the capacity of public policies to protect citizens against the emerging risks of a globalized economy, as policies have remained in place while economic reality has changed (Hacker 2002). Scholarship on American social policy has kept pace remarkably well with these and other changes over recent decades, but it remains unclear what these changes portend for racial and ethnic minorities in the American political economy or how they might alter historic links between race and social policy.

Race also lay at the center of the urban crisis in the late twentieth century—shorthand for the intricately linked political and economic challenges of joblessness, criminality and violence, and physical and fiscal decay that plagued American cities and became a critical political and intellectual pivot for debates about race and social policy. More generally, race and social policy were central to fundamental changes in American politics over the last third of the twentieth century, including ideological shifts, partisan change, and political polarization. Understanding the race–social-policy nexus, then, is critical to comprehending broader transformations of American politics.

2 RACE AND WELFARE STATE DEVELOPMENT

Many scholars have studied the operation and outcomes of social policies themselves, focusing attention on the sources of racial inequality and the disparate treatment of racial and ethnic minorities in the welfare state. My primary focus here, however, is on a second category of studies, which focus on the *politics* of race, ethnicity, and the welfare state—the ways in which political processes, institutions, and struggles shape policy outcomes, and vice versa. The central questions that this body of literature has sought to address have been the following: How does race help to explain the particular characteristics of American social policy? By what causal mechanisms does the welfare state either reduce or reproduce racial inequality in American society? These questions have produced a very fertile literature, which has led to a host of newer questions about race, ethnicity, and social policy that are now at the forefront of the subfield.

Before the late 1980s and 1990s, race and ethnicity did not figure prominently in studies of American social policy or the welfare state (Lubove 1968; Berkowitz and McQuaid 1980; Flora and Heidenheimer 1981; Patterson 1981; Katz 1986). In hindsight, this seems perhaps a curious omission. Economic welfare and social rights have long been a core part of the agenda for racial equality, and the politics of American social policy in the 1960s and 1970s revolved largely around racial questions, emerging from the civil rights movement and the War on Poverty (Hamilton and Hamilton 1997; MacLean 2006). These events focused attention and extensive policy effort specifically on the challenges of urban poverty and on barriers to equal economic opportunity. Nevertheless, studies of the American welfare state in the 1960s and 1970s emerged largely out of the concerns of comparative political economy and sought to explain the United States' apparently "laggard" and limited welfare state compared with continental European models (Wilensky and Lebeaux 1965). These studies focused primarily on the absence of European patterns (such as strong labor movements, labor or social democratic political parties, and strong centralized bureaucracies) in American political development (Skocpol 1992b). Led by Theda Skocpol (1992a), later studies began to focus not on what was absent in the United States, but on what was present—the distinctive characteristics of American state formation, political institutions, and social relations that could account for the particular shape of the American welfare state without measuring it against a normalized European standard.

But race—arguably a key defining characteristic of American politics—remained a lacuna in this literature through the 1990s. Much of the earliest work concerning race and the development of the American welfare state focused on the New Deal era and its aftermath. These accounts argue that the structure of American politics in the middle of the twentieth century produced social policies that tended to systematically exclude African Americans and afforded them less protection from the risks of a changing industrial economy. Robert Lieberman (1998) argued that the structure and configuration of American policymaking institutions in the New Deal era—such as the party system and the organization of Congress, which allowed the South to dominate national policy-making, and federalism, produced a limited and race-laden national welfare state that integrated minorities unevenly into social provision. Michael Brown (1999), by contrast, focused on the interaction of fiscal conservatism and racial antagonism (a theme that others have also noted) in constraining the growth of American social policy. Later work, particularly by Deborah Ward (2005), showed that the race-welfare link was present in the Progressive Era as well. Other studies have shown how race and gender interact in welfare policy to create overlapping and reinforcing categories of marginalization and exclusion (Gordon 1991; Mink 1990).

Importantly, these arguments were not primarily about racial attitudes or explicit discrimination as a causal factor in limiting the reach of the American welfare state (although there is some evidence of racial discrimination in the local administration of New Deal welfare policies; see Lieberman and Lapinski 2001). Rather, they emphasized structural features of American politics that systematically disadvantaged racial minorities in policy-making and confer power along racial lines. This distinction has produced something of a debate about the causal role of race in key policy decisions. Critics of the racial-structure school of thought have argued that the lack of direct documentary evidence of racially motivated decision-making (for example, in the decision to exclude agricultural and domestic workers from coverage in the Social Security Act, a key choice that left African-Americans largely unprotected by old-age insurance for a generation) means that race did not have a large influence on policy-making (Davies and Derthick 1997; DeWitt 2010). However, Mary Poole (2006) has found ample evidence of racial bias behind these exclusions, particularly in the Roosevelt administration's dominant emphasis on protecting the overwhelmingly white (and male) industrial working class. Moreover, these arguments tend to sidestep the role of race in structuring political power in the United States (Lieberman 2008).

Work at the intersection of race and social policy has also contributed to the increasing depth and scope of explorations of the power in American politics and the American state. Linda Williams (2003) shows, for example, how the protection of white privilege has long been a central organizing structure of American politics and policy-making, especially in social policies that confer selective, categorical benefits that have consistently categorized African-Americans as "dependents" rather than honorable, deserving beneficiaries (like retired workers or veterans, for example). Ira Katznelson (2005) reveals how generations of American social policies, from New Deal social policies to labor law and the G.I Bill, have systematically advantaged whites and effectively widened the gap between whites and minorities as state-provided social benefits and protections have expanded over the past century. Accounts of race-laden limitations on social policies and the growth of the welfare state have recently fed into broader discussions of the American state's distinctive characteristics, especially in comparative perspective (Alesina and Glaeser 2004; King and Lieberman 2009). At the same time, certain domains of social policy have contributed to the continued oppressive potency of the American state and implicated the state in the reproduction and perpetuation of racial inequality. Examples are housing policy, where federal policies long contributed to residential segregation and urban decay, and criminal justice policy, where patterns of mass incarceration have led many scholars to define and describe a vastly powerful and deeply racialized "carceral state" (Dawson 2012; Jackson 1985; Weaver and Lerman 2010).

Integral to these new considerations of the racialized American state have been issues of political inclusion and representation. The welfare state has also been a central site of political struggle over citizenship and belonging in the United States; Chad Alan Goldberg (2007) has shown how African Americans have repeatedly been required to forego the full exercise of the rights of citizenship and belonging in return for the benefits of relief. The political capacity of African Americans—and, increasingly, other racially and ethnically defined minority groups—to participate in policy-making coalitions has also been an increasingly important theme in accounts of American social policy, and it connects the field to other important themes in the study of African American politics (Browning, Marshall, and Tabb 1984; Lieberman 2005; Preuhs 2006).

Finally, scholarship on race and social policy has been instrumental in illuminating the critical role of regionalism and the South in shaping American political development and structuring American politics. The South's distinctive political economy and its compromised democratic institutions were both built on racial exclusion and domination, and these institutions shaped not only the region's own particular path of political development but also national politics and policy (Key 1949; Mickey forthcoming). This was particularly true in the mid-twentieth century, when the Democratic Party dominated the region and segregationist Southern Democrats reigned in Congress due to the relatively stable seniority and committee systems and the emerging importance of the filibuster in the Senate (Shepsle 1989; Wawro and Schickler 2006). For a somewhat one-dimensional account of the Senate's role in blocking civil rights progress, see Caro 2002.) As Ira Katznelson and colleagues have shown, the influence of Southern Democrats in this period was especially strong in policy areas relating to civil rights and labor, but this broad area of Southern influence extended widely across the range of New Deal social policy enactments (Farhang and Katznelson 2005; Katznelson, Geiger, and Kryder 1993; Katznelson and Lapinski 2006; Lieberman 1998; Quadagno 1988).

The analytical importance of the South helps explain why studies about race and social policy have focused on a black-white paradigm in the United States. To some degree, this focus is defensible; the politics of race for most of the twentieth century revolved around the exclusion and oppression of African Americans and their particular place in the American political economy through a distinctive history of slavery, emancipation, Jim Crow, migration, and the civil-rights revolution. This history profoundly shaped not only the lives and fortunes of African Americans themselves but also the very structure of American politics and the possibilities of social policy. Nevertheless, this perspective has its limitations, as I will suggest below.

3 RACE, SOCIAL POLICY, AND THE URBAN CRISIS

Although race was an important and often defining dimension of social policy in the New Deal era, it has also been central to a critical episode in the recent history of American social policy: the urban crisis of the late twentieth century and debates about the "underclass" in American society and "dependency" in the welfare state. In the decades after World War II, the American political economy underwent a series of critical transformations that exacerbated racial conflict and inequality, particularly in the big industrial centers of the Northeast and Midwest: the mass migration of African-Americans from the rural South to the urban North; the gathering civil rights movements that led to the toppling of Jim Crow; federal policies that outlawed racial discrimination in a variety of settings, desegregated public schools, and secured voting rights; the beginnings of the deindustrialization of the American economy; and the rise of suburbs that allowed (mostly white) middle-class families to escape decaying inner cities. By the 1960s, American inner cities were in decline—increasingly racially segregated, economically deprived, and socially isolated. As Thomas Sugrue (1996) has shown, racial conflict in northern cities had been brewing for decades, the result of continual friction over jobs, homes, neighborhoods, policing, and other arenas of industrial urban life. When a series of race riots broke out in American cities in the mid-1960s—beginning in Harlem in 1964 and the Watts neighborhood of Los Angeles in 1965 and continuing in cities large and small around the country over the next few summers—the racial and economic crisis of American cities and the effects of urban inequality were on full view to the nation and began to capture the attention of citizens, policy-makers, and scholars alike. The fraying of the civil rights movement and the rising tide of racial conflict in urban American were among the factors that helped to doom Lyndon Johnson's War on Poverty (Quadagno 1994).

One of the earliest and most celebrated analyses was the Labor Department's report, "The Negro Family," colloquially known by the name of its principal author, Assistant Secretary of Labor Daniel Patrick Moynihan, as the "Moynihan Report" (U.S. Department of Labor 1965). This report described and diagnosed what Moynihan saw as the deteriorating structure of the African American family, especially in cities, leaving black communities mired in a "tangle of pathology"—patterns of crime, violence, low school achievement, and chronic joblessness—that accounted for much of the social and economic dislocation then occurring in American cities. Moynihan argued for federal policies to address the inadequacies of inner-city life and provide opportunities for education and employment that would break the self-reinforcing spiral of urban deprivation (Scott 1997). But Moynihan's many critics, on both the left and right, attacked the report for either effacing individual responsibility for bad behavior or "blaming the victim" (Rainwater and Yancey 1967). As a consequence, the scholarly community shied away from research that directly addressed the conditions of black urban life for many years (Wilson 1987, chap. 1).

By the time scholars began to revisit these themes, the political landscape had changed significantly. First, the urban unrest of the mid-late 1960s appeared to raise the stakes for debates about urban inequality. The Kerner Commission, appointed by President Lyndon Johnson to investigate the causes of urban violence, concluded that the United States was "moving toward two societies, one black, one white—separate and unequal" (National Advisory Commission on Civil Disorders 1968, 1). The more widespread public response was one of antagonism toward inner-city residents and especially toward people of color. Second, the ideological center of American politics began to drift rightward, as American conservatism increasingly found its voice (often through repurposing liberal ideas such as "color-blindness" or "equality of opportunity") and expanded its organizational base (Horton 2005; Phillips-Fein 2009; Skowronek 2006). Third, organized political conflict in the United States was increasingly aligned along racial lines as the parties diverged sharply on civil rights and other issues with racial valence, the result of a gradual shift in constituencies and electoral strategy that began with the Republicans' nomination of civil rights opponent Barry Goldwater for president in 1964 and the emergence of the "law and order" issue onto the national agenda in the midst of the urban unrest later in the decade. By the 1970s and 1980s, racial conflict and concerns about welfare dependency were increasingly built into American political alignments (Feinstein and Schickler 2008; Gilens 1999; Lowndes 2008; Weaver 2007).

Out of this political and intellectual context emerged a generation of debate about the urban "underclass," a term coined by Swedish economist Gunnar Myrdal (1963, 19) and popularized by journalist Ken Auletta (1982). An imprecise but evocative term, the "underclass" denoted the inner-city urban poor who were increasingly isolated—spatially, economically, and socially—from mainstream American society. The "underclass" was defined in a variety of ways: in terms of location (inner cities, particularly in the northern industrial core), economics (chronic joblessness and welfare dependency), education (low achievement), and behavior (criminality, violence, out-of-wedlock childbearing) (Jencks 1990). Even though these phenomena were not always linked and were trending in different directions during the 1970s and 1980s, they came to be lumped under the "underclass" rubric, which dominated debates about poverty and social policy during this period. [This was so, even though inner-city poverty constituted only a relatively small slice of the overall problem of poverty in the United States (Ellwood 1988)]. Above all, these characteristics were associated with inner-city African Americans, an association abetted, as Martin Gilens (1999) shows, by the media's relentless portrayal of poor African Americans as undeserving.

Into this breach stepped Charles Murray, whose 1984 book, *Losing Ground*, was a sustained attack on the American welfare state on the grounds that federal social policies perpetuated and sometimes even aggravated low educational achievement, joblessness, out-of-wedlock childbearing, crime, poverty, and long-term welfare dependency in the United States. Murray drew particular attention to racial disparities on each of these dimensions and his argument, which gained wide notoriety, helped to buttress claims about the racial underpinnings of the urban "underclass" and its apparent pathologies. Most of Murray's claims about the causal relationship between policy and social outcomes—such as the suggestion that higher welfare benefits provided "incentives" for out-of-wedlock childbearing because Aid to Families with Dependent Children, the primary federally funded assistance program for poor families, was generally not available to two-parent families—did not stand up to empirical scrutiny (Ellwood and Bane 1985). As the historian Michael Katz (1993, 16) observed, "critics have subjected the evidence and methods of few books to such withering and authoritative criticism as they meted out to *Losing Ground*." Nevertheless, Murray's book continued to shape policy debates about race and poverty.[1]

The most vigorous response to Murray came from the sociologist William Julius Wilson, particularly in his 1987 book, *The Truly Disadvantaged*. Wilson highlighted the impact of economic change, particularly the decline of manufacturing and other industries that had long been stable sources of urban jobs. As these industries began to leave the cities, so did the (predominantly white) middle class. At the same time, the civil rights revolution was helping to expand the black middle class, who joined their white counterparts in escaping the city, leaving behind increasingly poor and segregated urban ghettos whose residents were increasingly disconnected from the mainstream of the political economy. Wilson thus offered a structural account of the urban "underclass" that emphasized the importance of urban joblessness for understanding the challenges of inner-city poverty and the behavioral responses of the urban poor.[2]

The arguments of Murray and others who attacked the War on Poverty and the Great Society as misguided and counterproductive tapped into more general public anxieties not just about race but also about the proper size and scope of government and, in particular, the fiscal burden of the welfare state (Edsall and Edsall 1991; Quadagno 1994). Attempts to cut back or eliminate programs for the poor were common toward the end of the twentieth century, culminating in the historic welfare reforms of 1996 (Gilens 1999; Katz 1989; Schram, Soss, and Fording 2003; Weaver, this volume). Moreover, in what we might call a "postracist" era, when conventional open attitudes about racial inferiority were no longer the explicit driving force in politics and policymaking, racial antagonism was increasingly displaced into policy arenas where it could be framed in race-neutral terms such "law and order" and, more recently, voter suppression (Cobb, Greiner, and Quinn 2012; Harris and Lieberman 2013; Weaver 2007).

4 RACE AND WELFARE REFORM

The debates of the 1970s and 1980s about the urban crisis, dependency, race, poverty, and social policy culminated in the welfare reform act of 1996. The 1996 act bundled together a number of reforms that had been brewing in various forms for more than 30 years: welfare-to-work requirements for public assistance recipients, time limits on the receipt of cash assistance, further devolution of policy authority to the states, and eligibility limits on immigrants, among others. These provisions addressed perceived inadequacies in Aid to Families with Dependent Children, the New Deal public assistance program for poor families, that derived largely from the policy's race-laden character—its parochial decentralization, its association with family decay and the "undeserving poor" (Gilens 1999; Lieberman 1998; see also Weaver this volume). This context helped shape the direction and substance of reform (Fording 2003; Williams 1998).

More recent research has begun to suggest that the racial context that helped produce the welfare reform act has also shaped its implementation and effects. As Sanford Schram (2005) has shown, although the act was couched in scrupulously race-neutral terms, it arose out of a racially biased political context and actually deepened racial disparities. On average, African Americans and Latinos start down the welfare-to-work path with disadvantages in education, work readiness, family support, residential segregation, and other factors that affect the program's key outcomes. Limits on immigrants' eligibility for federally funded benefits have had far-reaching consequences for the health, welfare, and social inclusion of immigrants and their children, affecting an increasingly diverse swath of the American population (Fix 2011; Kretsedemas and Aparicio 2004). As Schram (2005, 260) writes, "'equal' treatment ends up producing more racial disadvantage" (see also Harris and Lieberman 2013).

The 1996 reform devolved considerably more policy-making authority to state governments than had been the case even under the relatively decentralized AFDC regime. Devolution led to substantial policy variation among states, and scholars have begun to parse the role of race in the implementation of welfare reform. This work has taken several important directions, focusing variously on the impact of racial diversity on state policy choices (Fording 2003; Hero 1998; Soss et al. 2001;) and on the role of bureaucratic discretion in the implementation of reform (Keiser, Mueser, and Choi 2004). More generally, Joe Soss, Richard Fording, and Sanford Schram (2011) have threaded together many of these strands into an important argument about social policy and poverty governance in the United States that identifies race as a central factor in a range of political, economic, and social mechanisms that effectively isolate poor people of color and constitute the welfare state as a means of social control, thereby updating and extending Frances Fox Piven and Richard Cloward's (1971) argument about the political economy of American poor relief and connecting to other arguments about race and social control in contemporary American politics, especially in the criminal justice system (Wacquant 2009; Weaver and Lerman 2010).

5 FUTURE DIRECTIONS

Broad arguments about race, class, and the "underclass" in late-twentieth-century social policy have left a deep imprint. In a recent book, *More Than Just Race*, William

Julius Wilson (2009) argues passionately and compellingly that the choice often posed between culture and structure as the foundations of poverty and social isolation is a false one, that these two causes of racial inequality have reinforced one another, and that neither the cultural nor material hypotheses of previous generations of scholarship are sufficient to account for contemporary patterns of racial inequality. But even Wilson's persuasive deconstruction and reconstruction of the roots of racial inequality leaves open questions of the mixture of structural and cultural causes that lie behind the persistent racial gap that remains in American society, the precise mechanisms that underlie these causal relationships, and the conditions under which these mechanisms do and do not operate to produce and perpetuate racial inequality.

More generally, many contemporary scholars of race and social policy seek an account of what the sociologist Eduardo Bonilla-Silva (2003) has called "racism without racists": the ways in which social relations, political institutions, and other features of American society often advance the interests of whites and thus reproduce existing patterns of inequality (see also Katznelson 2005; Williams 2003). Here is the central puzzle of the "postracist" society: how do institutions that are, on their face, scrupulously racially neutral have systematically racially imbalanced consequences, resulting over time in the replication of old lines of racial inequality or the construction of new ones, even as still others seem to dissolve? Earlier studies have documented the deeply "race-laden" character of much of American politics and policy, the tendency to divide the population along racial lines without saying so explicitly. But the notion of "race-laden" policy goes beyond the merely incidental unintended consequences of apparently race-neutral arrangements to suggest that more systematic sources of racial bias might be "built into" the structure of political, social, and economic structures and processes. These structures might reflect more hidden racially structured power arrangements—class conflicts, party coalitions, political institutions, markets, political and social attitudes, and the like—whose characters are shaped by racial distinctions. Moreover, such arrangements can be expected to affect whites and people of color differently in the course of their normal operations, whether or not the people who designed them or inhabit them intend that result (King and Smith 2005; Lieberman 1998). These questions, which grow largely out of these earlier debates, animate much contemporary work on race and inequality in American politics and policy (Harris and Lieberman 2013).

These recurring themes in the study of race and social policy, particularly the connection between policy and the production and reproduction of racial inequality, suggest a set of important new directions for this rich and still-underdeveloped research agenda.

First, we need a fuller analysis of the role of race in the emerging and still-changing welfare regime, going beyond the important analyses of the racial politics and impact of welfare reform of the last decade. This line of analysis could profitably take several directions. The 1996 welfare reform was passed during a period of strong economic growth and low unemployment, which made the act's welfare-to-work provisions relatively more plausible. But the financial crisis of the late 2000s, which has brought sustained unemployment rates at a level not seen in decades, has made these provisions of the new welfare regime considerably more difficult to achieve, leaving both states and the federal government searching for flexible and innovative means to continue to implement the work provisions of Temporary Assistance for Needy Families (TANF), the principal cash relief program for poor families (the subject of a flashpoint of controversy during the 2012 presidential campaign, when Mitt Romney falsely attacked the Obama administration's flexible approach as an attempt to gut the work requirements of welfare reform in a television advertisement that many observers saw as racially inflected). More generally, the Great Recession and its aftermath have been especially catastrophic for African-Americans and Latinos, for whom unemployment rates have risen to depression-like levels in many metropolitan areas (Austin 2011a, 2011b). And certain features of the economic crisis and the limited federal response—in particular the collapse of state and local government finance and the mortgage and foreclosure crisis—have fallen especially sharply on already precarious minority communities (Johnson 2011). But we know precious little about the impact of welfare reform over a long period of time and a wide range of economic conditions, and further research on the consequences of reform and its impact on minority communities remains necessary.

Similarly, research on current issues at the forefront of contemporary social politics needs to focus more directly on questions of racial inequality. Much research on race and American social policy has focused on means-tested programs. But this focus tends to neglect more inclusive welfare state programs, such as Social Security, Medicare, disability insurance, and tax expenditures, which, in fact, constitute a large share of the American welfare state and have significant but largely unexplored racial consequences (Buto et al. 2004; Lieberman 1998). To take two prominent examples, emerging discussions of both the Patient Protection and Affordable Care Act of 2010 and the prospects for reform of entitlement programs such as Medicare and Medicaid have been largely devoid of mention of the racial implications of these policy developments. African Americans and Latinos disproportionately lack health insurance, and the disparity was increasing in the years before the passage of health-care reform; they are more than twice as likely as whites to be covered by Medicaid (DeNavas-Walt, Proctor, and Smith 2011). The progress of health care and entitlement reform over the coming years and decades will clearly be of great moment for the future of racial equality in the United States and is a critically important direction for future research.

Finally, research on race and social policy (and on race in American politics more generally) needs to recognize that the American racial and ethnic palette has always been broader than black and white, and especially since the reopening of immigration into the United States in the 1960s. American society has grown more multiracial, multiethnic, and multicultural. More recent scholarship is beginning to address this development, considering particularly the increasingly important role of Latinos and other immigrant groups in the American welfare state. In the first decade of the twenty-first century, for example, the Latino share of TANF beneficiaries increased from 25 percent to 30 percent, whereas the African American share declined from 39 percent to 32 percent. The shift in Medicaid enrollment has been even more dramatic: Latino enrollment has increased from 20 percent to 29 percent, outstripping black enrollment, which fell from 25 percent to 20 percent over the same period. Rodney Hero and Robert Preuhs (2007), for example, find that benefit levels tend to degrade over time in states with liberal rules for including immigrants in welfare programs because multiculturally inclusive social policies tend to fragment the polity and erode public support for the welfare state. Cybelle Fox (2012) examines the historical importance of immigration and ethnic politics in the early evolution of the American welfare state, finding striking parallels between the experiences of Mexican-Americans and African-Americans in early twentieth-century poor relief. Fox finds that European immigrants in northern cities benefited extensively from social assistance whereas blacks and Mexicans were more often exposed to the intrusive and punitive hand of the state. These works are enormously suggestive, but the role of increasing racial and ethnic diversity and immigration in both the past and future of the American welfare state remains one of the field's most important open questions.

These and other emerging questions in the study of race and social policy touch on a wide range of topics in the broad mainstream of American politics scholarship—from public policy and American political development to electoral politics and political institutions. The politics of inequality, moreover, is moving to the forefront of American politics, as political conflict is increasingly waged as a contest between the haves and have-nots of American society. Even in the "postracist" era of the twenty-first century, race and ethnicity remain key lines of American inequality, and careful exploration of the racial causes and consequences of future directions in American social policy are essential if we wish both to understand and to remedy growing inequality in the United States. As both scholars and citizens, we ignore these connections at our peril.

NOTES

1. The racial undertones of Murray's argument became explicit in his subsequent book, *The Bell Curve* (Herrnstein and Murray 1994), which argued that racial differences in genetically heritable intelligence explain many of the same "underclass" phenomena. That book's methods and findings were widely disparaged by scholars from a range of disciplines (Fraser 1995; Gould 1996).
2. Wilson (1991, 1996) eventually disavowed the term *underclass* because of the racial and cultural connotations it had acquired over a decade of this argument.

REFERENCES

*Indicates recommending reading.

Alesina, Alberto, and Edward L. Glaeser. 2004. *Fighting Poverty in the US and Europe: A World of Difference*. Oxford: Oxford University Press.
Auletta, Ken. 1982. *The Underclass*. New York: Random House.

Austin, Algernon. 2011a. "High Black Unemployment Widespread Across Nation's Metropolitan Areas." Issue Brief 315. Washington, DC: Economic Policy Institute.

Austin, Algernon. 2011b. "Hispanic Unemployment Highest in Northeast Metropolitan Areas." Issue Brief 314. Washington, DC: Economic Policy Institute.

Berkowitz, Edward, and Kim McQuaid. 1980. *Creating the Welfare State: The Political Economy of the Twentieth Century.* New York: Praeger.

Bonilla-Silva, Eduardo. 2003. *Racism Without Racists: Color-Blind Racism and the Persistence of Racial Inequality in the United States.* Lanham, MD: Rowman and Littlefield.

Brown, Michael K. 1999. *Race, Money, and the American Welfare State.* Ithaca, NY: Cornell University Press.

Browning, Rufus P., Dale Rogers Marshall, and David H. Tabb. 1984. *Protest Is Not Enough: The Struggle of Blacks and Hispanics for Equality in Urban Politics.* Berkeley and Los Angeles: University of California Press.

Buto, Kathleen, Martha Priddy Patterson, William E. Spriggs, and Maya Rockeymoore, eds. 2004. *Strengthening Community: Social Insurance in a Diverse America.* Washington, DC: National Academy of Social Insurance.

Caro, Robert A. 2002. *Master of the Senate.* New York: Alfred A. Knopf.

Cobb, Rachael V., D. James Greiner, and Kevin Quinn. 2012. "Can Voter ID Laws be Administered in a Race-Neutral Manner? Evidence from the City of Boston in 2008." *Quarterly Journal of Political Science* 7:1–33.

Davies, Gareth, and Martha Derthick. 1997. "Race and Social Welfare Policy: The Social Security Act of 1935." *Political Science Quarterly* 112:217–235.

DeNavas-Walt, Carmen, Bernadette D. Proctor, and Jessica C. Smith. 2011. "Income, Poverty, and Health Insurance Coverage in the United States: 2012." U.S. Census Bureau, Current Population Reports, P60–239. Washington, DC: GPO.

Dawson, Michael C. 2012. "Blacks and the Racialized State." In Henry Louis Gates Jr., Claude Steele, Lawrence D. Bobo, Michael Dawson, Gerald Jaynes, Lisa Crooms-Robinson, and Linda Darling-Hammond, eds., *The Oxford Handbook of African American Citizenship, 1865–Present.* 400–424 Oxford: Oxford University Press.

DeWitt, Larry. 2010. "The Decision to Exclude Agricultural and Domestic Workers from the 1935 Social Security Act." *Social Security Bulletin* 70 (4): 49–68.

Edsall, Thomas Byrne, with Mary D. Edsall. 1991. *Chain Reaction: The Impact of Race, Rights, and Taxes on American Politics.* New York: W. W. Norton.

Ellwood, David T. 1988. *Poor Support: Poverty in the American Family.* New York: Basic Books.

Ellwood, David T., and Mary Jo Bane. 1985. "The Impact of AFDC on Family Structure and Living Arrangements." *Research in Labor Economics* 7:137–207.

Farhang, Sean, and Ira Katznelson. 2005. "The Southern Imposition: Congress and Labor in the New Deal and Fair Deal." *Studies in American Political Development* 19:1–30.

Feinstein, Brian, and Eric Schickler. 2008. "Platforms and Partners: The Civil Rights Realignment Reconsidered." *Studies in American Political Development* 22:1–31.

Fix, Michael E., ed. 2011. *Immigrants and Welfare: The Impact of Welfare Reform on America's Newcomers.* New York: Russell Sage.

Flora, Peter and Arnold. J. Heidenheimer. 1981. *The Development of Welfare States in Europe and America.* New Brunswick, New Jersey: Transaction Publishers.

Fording, Richard C. 2003. "'Laboratories of Democracy' or Symbolic Politics? The Racial Origins of Welfare Reform." In Sanford F. Schram, Joe Soss, and Richard C. Fording, eds., *Race and the Politics of Welfare Reform.* Ann Arbor: University of Michigan Press.

*Fox, Cybelle. 2012. *Three Worlds of Relief: Race, Immigration, and the American Welfare State*. Princeton, NJ: Princeton University Press.

Fraser, Steve, ed. 1995. *The Bell Curve Wars: Race, Intelligence, and the Future of America*. New York: Basic Books.

*Gilens, Martin. 1999. *Why Americans Hate Welfare: Race, Media, and the Politics of Antipoverty Policy*. Chicago: University of Chicago Press.

Goldberg, Chad Alan. 2007. *Citizens and Paupers: Relief, Rights, and Race, from the Freedmen's Bureau to Workfare*. Chicago: University of Chicago Press.

Gordon, Linda. 1991. "Black and White Visions of Welfare: Women's Welfare Activism, 1890-1945." *Journal of American History* 78:559–590.

Gould, Stephen Jay. 1996. *The Mismeasure of Man*. Rev. ed. New York: W. W. Norton.

Hacker, Jacob S. 2002. *The Divided Welfare State: The Battle Over Public and Private Social Benefits in the United States*. Cambridge: Cambridge University Press.

Hamilton, Dona Cooper, and Charles V. Hamilton. 1997. *The Dual Agenda: Race and Social Welfare Policies of Civil Rights Organizations*. New York: Columbia University Press.

Harris, Fredrick C., and Robert C. Lieberman. 2013. "Beyond Discrimination: Racial Inequality in the Age of Obama," In Fredrick C. Harris and Robert C. Lieberman, eds., *Beyond Discrimination: Racial Inequality in a Postracist Era*. New York: Russell Sage.

Hero, Rodney E. 1998. *Faces of Inequality: Social Diversity in American Politics*. Oxford: Oxford University Press.

Hero, Rodney E., and Robert R. Preuhs. 2007. "Immigration and the Evolving American Welfare State: Examining Policies in the U.S. States." *American Journal of Political Science* 51:498–517.

Herrnstein, Richard J., and Charles Murray. 1994. *The Bell Curve: Intelligence and Class Structure in American Life*. New York: Simon and Schuster.

Horton, Carol A. 2005. *Race and the Making of American Liberalism*. Oxford: Oxford University Press.

Jackson, Kenneth T. 1985. *Crabgrass Frontier: The Suburbanization of the United States*. New York: Oxford University Press.

Jencks, Christopher. 1990. "Is the American Underclass Growing?" In Christopher Jencks and Paul E. Peterson, eds., *The Urban Underclass*. Washington, DC: Brookings Institution.

Johnson, Olatunde C. A. 2011. "Stimulus and Civil Rights." *Columbia Law Review* 111:154–205.

Katz, Michael B. 1986. *In the Shadow of the Poorhouse: A Social History of Welfare in America*. New York: Basic Books.

Katz, Michael B. 1989. *The Undeserving Poor: From the War on Poverty to the War on Welfare*. New York: Pantheon.

Katz, Michael B. 1993. "The Urban 'Underclass' as a Metaphor of Social Transformation." In Michael B. Katz, ed., *The "Underclass" Debate: Views from History*. Princeton, NJ: Princeton University Press.

Katznelson, Ira. 2005. *When Affirmative Action Was White: An Untold Story of Racial Inequality in Twentieth-Century America*. New York: W. W. Norton.

Katznelson, Ira, Kim Geiger, and Daniel Kryder. 1993. "Limiting Liberalism: The Southern Veto in Congress, 1933–1950." *Political Science Quarterly* 108:283–306.

Katznelson, Ira, and John S. Lapinski. 2006. "The Substance of Representation: Studying Policy Content and Legislative Behavior." In E. Scott Adler and John S. Lapinski, eds., *The Macropolitics of Congress*. Princeton, NJ: Princeton University Press.

Keiser, Lael, Peter R. Mueser, and Seung-Whan Choi. 2004. "Race, Bureaucratic Discretion, and the Implementation of Welfare Reform." *American Journal of Political Science* 48:314–327.

Key, V. O., Jr. 1949. *Southern Politics in State and Nation*. New York: Alfred A. Knopf.

King, Desmond, and Robert C. Lieberman. 2009. "Ironies of State Building: A Comparative Perspective on the American State." *World Politics* 61:547–88.

King, Desmond S., and Rogers M. Smith. 2005. "Racial Orders in American Political Development." *American Political Science Review* 99:75–92.

King, Desmond S., and Rogers M. Smith. 2011. *Still a House Divided: Race and Politics in Obama's America*. Princeton, NJ: Princeton University Press.

Kretsedemas, Philip, and Ana Aparicio, eds. 2004. *Immigrants, Welfare Reform, and the Poverty of Policy*. Westport, CT: Praeger.

*Lieberman, Robert C. 1998. *Shifting the Color Line: Race and the American Welfare State*. Cambridge, MA: Harvard University Press.

Lieberman, Robert C. 2005. *Shaping Race Policy: The United States in Comparative Perspective*. Princeton, NJ: Princeton University Press.

Lieberman, Robert C. 2008. "Legacies of Slavery? Race and Historical Causation in American Political Development." In Joseph E. Lowndes, Julie Novkov, and Dorian T. Warren, eds., *Race and American Political Development*. New York: Routledge.

Lieberman, Robert C., and John S. Lapinski. 2001. "American Federalism, Race, and the Administration of Welfare." *British Journal of Political Science* 31:303–329.

Lowndes, Joseph E. 2008. *From the New Deal to the New Right: Race and the Southern Origins of Modern Conservatism*. New Haven, CT: Yale University Press.

Lubove, Roy. 1968. *The Struggle for Social Security, 1900–1935*. Cambridge, MA: Harvard University Press.

MacLean, Nancy. 2006. *Freedom Is Not Enough: The Opening of the American Workplace*. New York: Sage; Cambridge, MA: Harvard University Press.

Mickey, Robert. Forthcoming. *Paths Out of Dixie: The Democratization of Authoritarian Enclaves in America's Deep South 1944–1972*. Princeton, NJ: Princeton University Press.

Murray, Charles. 1984. *Losing Ground: American Social Policy, 1950–1980*. New York: Basic Books.

Mink, Gwendolyn. 1990. "The Lady and the Tramp: Gender, Race, and the Origins of the American Welfare State." In Linda Gordon, ed., *Women, the State, and Welfare*. Madison: University of Wisconsin Press.

Myrdal, Gunnar. 1963. *Challenge to Affluence*. New York: Pantheon.

National Advisory Commission on Civil Disorders. 1968. *Report of the National Advisory Commission on Civil Disorders*. Washington, DC: GPO.

Patterson, James T. 1981. *America's Struggle Against Poverty, 1900–1980*. Cambridge, MA: Harvard University Press.

Phillips-Fein, Kim. 2009. *Invisible Hands: The Making of the Conservative Movement from the New Deal to Reagan*. New York: W. W. Norton.

Piven, Frances Fox, and Richard A. Cloward. 1971. *Regulating the Poor: The Functions of Public Welfare*. New York: Pantheon.

Poole, Mary. 2006. *The Segregated Origins of Social Security: African Americans and the Welfare State*. Chapel Hill: University of North Carolina Press.

Preuhs, Robert R. 2006. "The Conditional Effects of Minority Descriptive Representation: Black Legislators and Policy Influence in the American States." *Journal of Politics* 68:585–599.

Quadagno, Jill. 1988. *The Transformation of Old Age Security: Class and Politics in the American Welfare State*. Chicago: University of Chicago Press.

*Quadagno, Jill. 1994. *The Color of Welfare: How Racism Undermined the War on Poverty*. Oxford: Oxford University Press.

Rainwater, Lee, and William Yancey. 1967. *The Moynihan Report and the Politics of Controversy*. Cambridge, MA: MIT Press.

Schram, Sanford F. 2005. "Contextualizing Racial Disparities in American Welfare Reform: Toward a New Poverty Research." *Perspectives on Politics* 3:253–268.

*Schram, Sanford F., Joe Soss, and Richard C. Fording, eds. 2003. *Race and the Politics of Welfare Reform*. Ann Arbor: University of Michigan Press.

Scott, Daryl Michael. 1997. *Contempt and Pity: Social Policy and the Image of the Damaged Black Psyche*. Chapel Hill: University of North Carolina Press.

Shepsle, Kenneth A. 1989. "The Changing Textbook Congress." In John E. Chubb and Paul E. Peterson, eds., *Can the Government Govern?* Washington, DC: Brookings Institution.

Skocpol, Theda. 1992a. *Protecting Soldiers and Mothers: The Political Origins of Social Policy in the United States*. Cambridge, MA: Harvard University Press.

Skocpol, Theda. 1992b. "State Formation and Social Policy in the United States." *American Behavioral Scientist* 35:559–584.

Skowronek, Stephen. 2006. "The Reassociation of Ideas and Purposes: Racism, Liberalism, and the American Political Tradition." *American Political Science Review* 100:385–401.

*Soss, Joe, Richard C. Fording, and Sanford F. Schram. 2011. *Disciplining the Poor: Neoliberal Paternalism and the Persistent Power of Race*. Chicago: University of Chicago Press.

Soss, Joe, Sanford F. Schram, Thomas P. Vartanian, and Erin O'Brien. 2001. "Setting the Terms of Relief: Explaining State Policy Choices in the Devolution Revolution." *American Journal of Political Science* 378–395. Volume 45, Number 2.

Sugrue, Thomas J. 1996. *The Origins of the Urban Crisis: Race and Inequality in Postwar Detroit*. Princeton, NJ: Princeton University Press.

U.S. Department of Labor, Office of Policy Planning and Research. 1965. *The Negro Family: The Case for National Action*. Washington, DC: GPO.

Wacquant, Loïc. 2009. *Punishing the Poor: The Neoliberal Government of Social Insecurity*. Durham, NC: Duke University Press.

Ward, Deborah E. 2005. *The White Welfare State: The Racialization of U.S. Welfare Policy*. Ann Arbor: University of Michigan Press.

Wawro, Gregory J., and Eric Schickler. 2006. *Filibuster: Obstruction and Lawmaking in the U.S. Senate*. Princeton, NJ: Princeton University Press.

Weaver, Vesla M. 2007. "Frontlash: Race and the Development of Punitive Crime Policy." *Studies in American Political Development* 21:230–265.

Weaver, Vesla M., and Amy E. Lerman. 2010. "Political Consequences of the Carceral State." *American Political Science Review* 104:817–833.

Williams, Linda Faye. 1998. "Race and the Politics of Social Policy." In Margaret Weir, ed., *The Social Divide: Political Parties and the Future of Activist Government*. Washington, DC: Brookings Institution; New York: Russell Sage.

Williams, Linda Faye. 2003. *The Constraint of Race: Legacies of White Skin Privilege in America*. University Park: Pennsylvania State University Press.

Wilensky, Harold L., and Charles N. Lebeaux. 1965. *Industrial Society and Social Welfare: The Impact of Industrialization on the Supply and Organization of Social Welfare Services in the United States*. New York: Free Press.

*Wilson, William Julius. 1987. *The Truly Disadvantaged: The Inner City, the Underclass, and Public Policy*. Chicago: University of Chicago Press.

Wilson, William Julius. 1991. "Studying Inner-City Social Dislocations: The Challenge of Public Agenda Research." *American Sociological Review* 56:1–14.

Wilson, William Julius. 1996. *When Work Disappears: The World of the New Urban Poor.* New York: Alfred A. Knopf.

Wilson, William Julius. 2009. *More Than Just Race: Being Black and Poor in the Inner City.* New York: W. W. Norton.

CHAPTER 14

....

GENDER

....

ELLEN REESE, STEPHANIE D'AURIA AND SANDRA LOUGHRIN

1 INTRODUCTION

....

WELFARE programs shape, and are shaped by, gender relations and ideologies. As feminist scholars emphasize, gender is not a product of biological sex differences; masculinity and femininity, and male dominance, are socially constructed and reproduced within particular contexts through social interaction as well as through culture and institutions. As Orloff (2010, 252–253) explains, "Gender is not an attribute of individuals but a social relationship, historically varying, and encompassing elements of labour, power, emotion, and language; it crosses individual subjectivities, institutions, culture, and language." Although varying historically and cross-nationally, gender relations tend to be characterized by inequalities in power, resources, and status as well as by conflicts and resistance rooted in such inequalities.

Feminist scholarship on the welfare state developed in reaction to the traditional literature on welfare state development. That literature focused almost exclusively on the impact of political parties, industrialization, and the political economy on the development of social policy. It also emphasized programs that mainly served male workers, such as pensions, unemployment insurance, and workers' compensation, without considering the gendered consequences of the welfare state. In contrast, feminist scholars drew attention to programs previously neglected by welfare scholars, such as mother's pensions, that were not linked to wage employment or industrialization but, instead, to reproductive labor in the home. More generally, they highlighted the ways in which welfare programs were deeply gendered in terms of their underlying philosophies, recipient populations, and distribution of benefits. Drawing insights from poststructuralist theories, feminist scholars emphasized how welfare policies reinforced, or challenged, dominant discourses or traditional "ideologies, about proper gender roles. In the U.S. context, they showed how the welfare state provided distinct forms of entitlement and support for particular types of male and female subjects—the citizen-soldier, the "male bread-winner," the female widow, the "retired worker," etc.—who upheld normative standards of masculine or feminine behavior, and withheld or minimized support for those who deviated from such standards—the "single mother," the "able-bodied unemployed," and so on (Gordon 1994; Haney 2000; Orloff 2003).

Feminist scholars have long been divided in their assessments of the U.S. welfare state and its capacity to serve women's interests (variously conceived) and to challenge (or reproduce) gender inequalities and traditional gender roles.[1] Some scholars note how aid for single mothers, originally designed by female reformers, serves women's interests by helping them to overcome material hardships, enabling some women to be economically independent of individual men, and publicly recognizing the social value of women's reproductive labor. In contrast, other scholars emphasize the patriarchal character of U.S. welfare policies, arguing that male policy makers adopted policies that upheld male privileges, women's greater responsibility for reproductive labor (or care work), and women's subordination. These scholars point out how welfare programs targeting women, such as mothers' pensions or later Aid to Dependent Children, were stingy, stigmatizing, and reinforced traditional gender roles for women and the devaluation of care work. In contrast, programs that historically serve mostly men, such as veterans' programs or Social Security, provide higher levels of benefits and are viewed as entitlements or rights for worthy citizens. Feminist scholars thus show how so-called "universal programs," like Social Security are not so egalitarian, and tend to treat men and women differently.

Although early feminist scholarship on the welfare state in the United States overlooked how race and ethnicity as well as class mediated women's relationships to welfare programs, more recent research, building on the analytical concept of intersectionality, has addressed these gaps (Misra and Akins 1998; Orloff 2009a). Critical race feminist, or intersectionality, theory emphasizes how male domination, or patriarchy, is embedded within a broader "matrix of domination" (Hill Collins 2000 [1990]) that includes racism, capitalism, heterosexism, and other types of "interlocking inequalities" (Baca Zinn and Dill 1996, 322). This perspective emphasizes the relational nature of dominance and subordination as well as the interplay of social structure and agency. It thus portrays male domination and resistance to it as occurring at multiple levels (the individual, the cultural, and the institutional). This perspective highlights the diverse nature of women's and men's lived experiences, and the inequalities that exist not only between men and women but among them. Following this perspective, feminist scholars documented how the welfare state reproduced gender inequalities in interaction with other kinds of social inequalities. In doing so, they showed how women's and men's relationships to the welfare state varies across race, ethnicity, immigration status, class, age, sexual-orientation, and so on.

This chapter provides an overview of feminist scholarship on the welfare state in the United States, beginning with cross-national perspectives. We then discuss the historical development of the "two-tiered" U.S. welfare state and how it has reinforced gender inequalities. After a brief review of the historical trajectory of welfare policies targeting low-income families, we examine more recent scholarship on welfare reform policies since 1996. Finally, we examine how gender shapes public attitudes toward welfare. We conclude by discussing fruitful avenues for future research on gender and the U.S. welfare state.

2 CROSS-NATIONAL FEMINIST PERSPECTIVES ON THE U.S. WELFARE STATE

Feminist research on cross-national differences in welfare systems has drawn insights from, but has also challenged, Esping-Andersen's (1990) typology of welfare state regimes, which focused on market-state relations and the extent to which welfare policies "decommodified" labor. Feminist scholars reconceptualized welfare state regimes in terms of the interactions between markets, states, and gender and family relations, distinguishing welfare regimes in terms of how (and the extent to which) welfare policies redistributed and recognized care work, encouraged female employment, and facilitated the formation of autonomous female households (Orloff 1996, 2010).

Cross-national scholarship reveals that the United States is relatively more "market-based" in its approach to both employment and care work than other wealthy democracies. Other affluent democracies better regulate the labor market and provide families, even middle-class families, with far more generous welfare benefits and support, including universal child allowances, national health insurance, subsidized child care, and paid family leave (Gornick and Meyers 2003). As a result, female poverty, especially of lone mothers, is far higher in the United States compared to other wealthy democracies (Christopher 2002).

Overall, compared to 12 other industrialized countries, Gornick and Meyers (2003) showed that the United States offered the lowest levels of income transfers and services and had the highest post-tax and post-transfer rate of poverty among families with children under six. Even after welfare benefits were distributed in the United States, families with children had higher poverty rates than those without. Countries with extensive child-care support and maternity leave, and generous income transfers, had the highest rates of maternal employment, greater equality between families with and without children, and the lowest post-tax and post-transfer poverty rates. Although the United States also has high maternal employment rates, the prevalence of low-wage work means that many working families cannot escape poverty (Meyers and Gornick 2001).

In most advanced industrialized states, countries provide workers with relatively lengthy and paid family leave after the birth of a child or to take care of sick relatives. Family leave policies are most generous in the Nordic countries of Denmark, Finland, and Sweden. There, workers are guaranteed one to three years of leave after the birth of a child and receive about two-thirds of their usual pay during most or all of this period. In contrast, the U.S. Family and Medical Leave Act of 1993 allows workers to take up to 12 weeks of unpaid leave following the birth or adoption of a child, or to care for "seriously ill" family members. Workers in small companies and new workers are exempt, and many eligible families cannot afford to take the time off from work without pay. As of 2012, paid family leave is only available in California, New Jersey, and the District of Columbia.

Subsidized child care is also far less generous and accessible in the United States compared to other wealthy democracies. In the United States, most working parents rely on private day care or make informal child-care arrangements. While nonpoor families can receive tax breaks for dependent-care expenses, directly subsidized child care is only available to very poor families. Moreover, only between 10 and 15 percent of eligible families actually receive support from the primary source of funding for subsidized child care, the Child Care and Development Fund (Giannerellis and Barsimantov 2000, 1). Meanwhile, most child-care workers (largely women) earn low wages and lack benefits; this encourages high employee turnover and reduces the quality of care. By contrast, in much of Western Europe, countries provide most working parents with access to subsidized child care and early education, which is delivered by better-educated and better-paid staff (Bolzendahl and Olafsdottir 2008; Gornick and Harrington Meyers 2003).

Although policies supporting maternal employment reduce women's dependence and vulnerability, in most countries, being a mother is still associated with a "long-term gender earnings gap" and a "motherhood wage penalty" (Mandel and Semyonov 2006). Affordable child care and paid family leave facilitate mothers' employment, but may channel women toward particular forms of work, particularly in countries with a large public sector. For instance, in countries that offer lengthy statutory leave for new mothers, private employers may hesitate to hire women because of the cost of replacing them during maternity leave. Thus, women are more likely to work in the public sector, resulting in higher levels of occupational segregation as compared with countries with less generous leave policies (Estevez-Abe, Iverson, and Soskice 2001; Estevez-Abe 2005a, 2005b). These patterns may also result from antidiscrimination and affirmative-action policies, which are more developed in the United States than in the European Union (Zippel 2009).

Although feminist scholars critique welfare policies in wealthy democracies for reproducing women's disproportionate responsibility for care work and its devaluation, they are divided on the relative merits of extended paid family leave, policies to reduce work hours, and the provision of subsidized child care as mechanisms for reconciling work and family obligations and for promoting gender equality. Some feminists critique the devaluation of care work in advanced welfare states and call for "supporting unpaid care work as a civic activity, and attempting to redistribute the responsibility for it" (Herd and Meyer 2002, 677). Others warn against a "one size fits all strategy," arguing that policies should ultimately aim to expand both men's and women's choices regarding employment and at-home care (Orloff 2009b).

3 GENDER AND THE ORIGINS OF A "TWO-TIERED" WELFARE STATE

Paying attention to the gendered and racialized consequences of social provision has led feminist scholars to reconceptualize the origins and development of the U.S. welfare state in terms of a "two-track" system. "First tier" programs provided relatively generous benefits and mainly served men; their beneficiaries were portrayed as "deserving" or "worthy citizens." These programs included veterans' pensions, first authorized at the end of the Civil War, and other benefits for war veterans, military personnel, and their families (Gifford 2006; Mettler 2005; Orloff 2003; Skocpol 1992). Other "first-tier" programs, created in the first half of the 20th century, included Unemployment Insurance, Workers' Compensation, and Social Security. Historically, these three programs were earnings-based, disproportionately served men and whites, and were portrayed as "income supplements" rather than "antipoverty" programs (Lovell 2002, 193; Mettler 1998; Nelson 1990).

In contrast, public assistance programs were "second tier" programs that provided relatively meager benefits. Whereas Aid to Dependent Children (ADC) primarily served women (initially mostly white widows), other public assistance programs, such as Old Age Assistance and state and local general relief, served both men and women and were often associated with racial minorities. Public assistance was highly stigmatized, with ADC benefits contingent on conformity to strict behavioral rules and regulations (Lovell 2002; Nelson 1990; Orloff 2003). Although ADC benefits were meager when compared to "first tier" programs, they provided single mothers with income support and services not available to men (and childless women) who did not qualify for first-tier welfare programs.

Various feminist scholars portray the early U.S. welfare state as reinforcing the family wage system and traditional gender division of family labor in which men were expected to be the main breadwinner and women the main caregivers and domestic workers, and to be dependent upon male wages (Collins and Mayer 2010; Gordon 1994; Mettler 1998; Mink 1995; Nelson 1990; Orloff 2003; Reese 2005; Skocpol 1992). Civil War pensions helped disabled and retired military veterans to continue in their male breadwinner role. Likewise, during the Progressive Era, "alliances of overwhelmingly male working-class movements and male intellectual, political, and reform elites advocated programs that would give public benefits to male breadwinners that they might continue to support their families financially even when they lost their jobs or wage-earning capacities" (Orloff 2003, 229). In response, nearly all states passed workmen's-compensation laws requiring employers to provide insurance for workers affected by industrial accidents, which disproportionately affected the male workforce. Some states also passed old-age pensions, but these were very limited (Orloff 2003). In 1939, Old Age Insurance benefits were extended to the survivors of covered workers and the spouses and children of retired workers. These changes increased women's access to the program and helped to ensure that male workers could fulfill their obligations as the "male breadwinner" even after their retirement or death (Gordon 1994; Kessler-Harris 1995; Mettler 1998).

Female reformers also played a role in policies that reinforced traditional gender roles and racial hierarchies. According to Skocpol (1992, 464), the "wildfire spread" of mothers' pension laws in the early 20th century was the outcome of "deliberate, organized, state-by-state efforts of associations of (mostly) married women, who worked in coalition with a few key reformers." These women's associations, largely composed of white upper- and middle-class women, included the General Federation of Women's Clubs, Mothers' Congresses, and Consumers' Leagues. Women's groups such as these were active prior to initial mothers' pension legislation in at least 80 percent of the 40 states that enacted Mothers' Pensions between 1911 and 1920 (Skocpol 1992, 424–478). Some reformers drew on nativist and racist discourse, arguing that mothers' pensions would help to improve "the race" and to assimilate immigrants. More commonly, they made the case for welfare in maternalist terms, emphasizing the value of motherhood. Many made the traditional claim that children received the best care from full-time mothers. They also argued that single mothers, frequently portrayed as "worthy" white widows, deserved compensation for the work of raising good citizens (Gordon 1994; Mink 1995). On the other hand, Civil War army nurses' pensions, teacher's pensions, and the implementation of mothers' pensions (discussed more fully below) show that women were often expected to work for wages (Leroux 2009).

4 GENDER AND THE DEVELOPMENT OF "FIRST-TIER" WELFARE PROGRAMS

Not only has feminist scholarship drawn attention to the "second-tier" programs described earlier, but it has led to a reconceptualization of first-tier social insurance programs. Federal welfare programs created by the 1935 Social Security Act reinforced both gender and racial inequalities in the labor market and continue to do so today. Along with agricultural workers, domestic workers (disproportionately women) were excluded from coverage from Social Security and Unemployment Insurance when these programs were first designed. Many of these workers remained ineligible for coverage until a series of amendments were adopted to the Social Security program in the 1950s, and to the Unemployment Insurance program in 1974 (Derthick 1979; Lovell 2002).

More generally, Social Security (now known as Old Age and Survivors Insurance, or OASDI) and Unemployment Insurance benefit levels were, and continue to be, tied to earning histories and wage levels, and hence reproduce gender and racial inequities in workers' incomes during periods of unemployment and retirement. As women's labor-force participation and earnings relative to men have been increasing, this has reduced the gender gaps in benefits and coverage for these programs and Workers' Compensation. Unemployment Insurance reforms under the Obama Administration also made that program more inclusive of low-wage workers and women (who might be unemployed for family-related reasons, sexual harassment, etc.) (Wentworth 2011). On the other hand, declining marital rates, along with rising divorce rates, have slowed the closing of the gender gap and contributed to the racial gap in OASDI coverage (Harrington Meyer et al. 2005).

As of December 2010, more women than men receive OASDI benefits, but this is because women are more likely than men to survive their spouses and to qualify for benefits as survivors or spouses of retired and disabled workers. Women still make up less than half of beneficiaries of retired workers' benefits, although the gender gap in receiving such benefits has been shrinking over time. On average, women's benefits remain less than men's among retired workers, although the reverse is true among survivors and spouses of retired and disabled workers due to the persistent gender gap in male and female earnings (Social Security Administration 2012). Consistent with previous research suggesting that "individuals who are socio-economically vulnerable and thus more likely to benefit from the welfare state . . . are more likely to support it," surveys reveal that women tend to be more opposed than men to efforts to privatize welfare programs, such as Social Security (Yang and Barrett 2006).

Herd (2005a) contends that Social Security is an outdated structure that disproportionately benefits individuals who either have consistent lifetime work histories or who get and stay married and are never employed. She argues that providing minimum benefits is the most effective method for increasing the percentage of noncontributory benefits to the poorest women, including black women and single poor parents (although it also diverts noncontributory benefits to wealthy women). Other countries provide flat pensions for retirees so that gender inequalities in the labor market are not reproduced in uneven benefit levels (see Berkowitz and DeWitt's chapter in this volume).

Another major first-tier welfare program, and one that mainly serves men, is military benefits for veterans and the families of active military personnel (see Kleykamp and Hipes, this volume). The expansion of military benefits since the Civil War era increased access to many vital resources among war veterans and active-duty military personnel (mostly men) and their dependents. Veterans' organizations successfully pushed for expansions in military pensions, and they gained access to various other benefits, including educational benefits, through the G.I. bill after World War II (Mettler 2005; Skocpol 1992). Gifford (2006) claims that military benefits were further expanded to active-duty personnel and their families in order to better recruit and retain them, especially during wartime and after the end of forced conscription. These benefits, including medical services, family housing, and family separation and subsistence allowance, "are direct transfers to breadwinners designed to support the maintenance of the family household, which are extended as a social right, regardless of income" (Gifford 2006, 381). These are similar to rights-based benefits for families found in other countries (such as family allowances or national health insurance), but they are selectively provided to active-duty military families. As such, these benefits constitute a "distinct welfare institution," divergent from both social assistance and social insurance models because benefits are contingent on military service and compliance with norms of "military propriety."

5 GENDER AND THE DEVELOPMENT OF WELFARE FOR LOW-INCOME FAMILIES

Much feminist scholarship on the early U.S. welfare state focuses on the history of mothers' pensions, and shows that support for maternalist policies was, from the start, weak and selective. State-level mothers' pensions were adopted through enabling legislation; counties were not required to provide pensions, and few rural areas did so (Skocpol 1992, 471–477). Mothers' pensions were almost exclusively given to "deserving" white widows. "Suitable home" and other rules were commonly used to deny aid to unwed, divorced, and separated mothers and women of color (Abramovitz 1989; Mink 1995). In fact, it was not uncommon for pension applicants to be pressured to work outside the home, and many recipients had to work because benefits were so low (Goodwin 1995, 257–258; Reese 2005).

Maternalist reformers, including Grace Abbott, Katherine Lenroot, and Martha Eliot, succeeded in expanding mothers' pensions through the development of a new federal program (Aid to Dependent Children, or ADC) during the Great Depression when President Roosevelt and other New Deal Congressional Democrats pushed for greater governmental relief for the poor in response to public agitation. Following maternalist reformers' recommendations, Congress gave states administrative authority over the implementation of ADC, required counties to establish a program, and broadly defined "needy children." Other bureau recommendations, such as national standards for benefits, were defeated within congressional committees that were dominated by southern politicians (Gordon 1994). Lack of funding, demands for cheap labor, restrictive eligibility criteria, and discrimination against unwed mothers and racial minorities combined to limit ADC coverage. Like mothers' pensions, ADC almost exclusively served white widows in the late 1930s. Welfare offices pressured poor mothers to work by steering them into employment offices, providing meager benefits, or refusing aid entirely (Abramovitz, 1989, 329; Reese 2005).

Support for maternalist welfare policies, never strong, was further weakened as maternal employment grew and as more women of color and unwed mothers gained access to welfare. Beginning in 1939, and especially after World War II, ADC served increasing numbers of unwed mothers and racial minorities. In part, this was because many poor widows became eligible for the more generous Old Age and Survivors' Insurance program in 1939 and left ADC (Curran 2005, 115). Rapid growth of ADC and its changing composition sparked a strong backlash against the program in the 1950s and 1960s led by business interests and racist politicians. Critics, often targeting women of color, charged that the program had become too lax and fostered dependency. Various U.S. states, especially in the South and West, adopted new eligibility restrictions—including "man in the house," "suitable home," and "employable mother" rules—that were disproportionately applied to unwed mothers and women of color (Mayer 2008; Reese 2005).

In 1962, Congressional amendments expanded the ADC program and provided more social services for recipients in an effort to encourage labor-force participation. The program was renamed Aid to Families with Dependent Children (AFDC) since greater access was provided for two-parent families (Orloff 2003, 233). Even after the 1962 amendments, however, the vast majority of adult AFDC recipients remained single mothers.

By the late 1960s, as the AFDC program grew in size, both the left and the right attacked it. To reduce "welfare dependency," Congress enacted the first federal-level work requirements for adult recipients of AFDC in 1967 and expanded these further in 1971. A national welfare-rights movement also emerged in this period, demanding greater access to welfare benefits for poor families. They and their allies pushed for the replacement of the restrictive and stigmatizing AFDC program with a more universal guaranteed annual income program. Some conservatives, including Nixon, also began to push for a guaranteed-income program (albeit a less generous one) as a way to make the distribution of welfare more efficient, calm social unrest, and discourage family dissolution, especially among blacks. These proposals were rejected by Congress, however, because conservatives claimed the program would undermine work incentives and liberals rejected the proposed income levels as insufficient (Quadagno 1990; Waddan 1998).

The failure to replace AFDC with a less stigmatizing alternative in the 1970s paved the road for the backlash against welfare and expansion of welfare-to-work (WTW) programs in the 1980s and 1990s (Reese 2005). Opposition to AFDC spending had both gender and racial dynamics, with the greatest opposition directed toward black single mothers (Moller 2002).

6 GENDER AND THE RISE OF SUBSIDIZED CHILD CARE

As more women entered the labor force, the U.S. system of publicly subsidized child care expanded but remained minimal compared to the more generous and universal day-care programs found in other wealthy democracies. Congress also adopted policies that reinforced class differences, offering "tax subsidies to support private day care for the middle class, federally funded day care for the very poor, and indifference to the plight of working low-income families...." (Morgan 2001, 243). Politicians justified these policies in terms of both maternalist rhetoric and market-based values.

Initial federal investments in day care were adopted as short-term solutions to national emergencies. The first federal investment in public day care occurred in the 1930s when Congress temporarily authorized funding to establish Emergency Nursery Schools, mainly to provide work for unemployed school staff in the midst of the Great Depression (Michel 1999). During World War II, the Lanham Act provided federal funding for day-care centers in order to meet the wartime demands for factory labor. When the war ended, Congress withdrew these funds, reflecting the widespread presumption that most working mothers would depend on male incomes or find private solutions to their child-care needs. Afterward, wartime child-care centers closed in most areas, although they persisted in some cities, such as New York City, and in California in response to public agitation by working mothers, child care providers, and their allies (Michel 1999; Reese 1996).

Nationally, discourses emphasizing the negative impacts of maternal deprivation on child development along with Cold War anticommunism strengthened opposition to public day care. Recognizing these obstacles, the Women's Bureau and the Children's Bureau helped to document the need for public day care for low-income mothers who had to work. In response to such concerns, and in favor of keeping day-care provision in the private sector, Congress authorized an income-tax deduction for child-care expenses in 1954. The income ceiling for eligibility for this tax deduction was very low, however, and other restrictions limited its reach (Michel 1999; Morgan 2001).

Support for public day care increased in the 1960s in response to "concerns about welfare dependency" and new research on the benefits of early-childhood education (Morgan 2001, 221). Women's labor force participation and demands for equality were also growing in the 1960s, giving fuel to feminist demands for governmental support for child care. In this context, federal funds for child care for low-income families expanded along with other social services in the 1960s in order to reduce welfare dependency. Federal funds for early childhood education were also authorized through the Head Start program, which began in 1965 as part of the federal War on Poverty (Morgan 2001, 222).

Child-care policies under the Nixon Administration set the tone for later developments, solidifying the class-divided approach to child-care policy in place today. In 1971, a broad coalition emerged in support of the Comprehensive Child Development Act (CDA), which sought to establish publicly supported day care that would serve for both low-income and middle-class parents with sliding-scale fees. Republican support for the bill waned, however, when administration of the program became tied to War on Poverty programs and civil rights. Conservatives also claimed that the bill would undermine the traditional family and was a communist policy. Republican President Richard Nixon vetoed the legislation (Morgan 2001, 215), but the next day signed a bill that expanded the income ceiling for claiming tax deductions for child care and allowed middle-class families to claim the deduction at a lower amount. The Nixon administration, like Congress, also supported expanding funds for child care for welfare recipients. Since the 1970s, publicly subsidized day-care services for very poor families have mainly been provided through Head Start and welfare programs, although at levels insufficient to meet the growing demand for them. Meanwhile, the income ceiling was raised for tax deductions for child-care expenses in 1975, and these deductions became a nonrefundable tax credit in 1976. Since then, middle and upper class families have gained the most from family policies implemented through the tax code (Morgan 2001; Orloff 2003; see also Michel's chapter, this volume).

7 THE WELFARE REFORM ACT OF 1996 AND ITS REAUTHORIZATION

The backlash against welfare mothers, on the rise since at least the 1980s, led to the Congressional passage in 1996 of the Personal Responsibility and Work Opportunity Reconciliation Act. PRWORA replaced AFDC with a more restrictive program called

Temporary Assistance for Needy Families (TANF). As Orloff (2002) suggests, the act, and its reauthorization in 2006, expressed a "farewell to maternalism," by expanding welfare-to-work (WTW) participation requirements for adult recipients, imposing new time limits on welfare receipt, and expanding publicly subsidized child care. Since 1996, many states adopted even more strict work requirements and time limits of TANF receipt (Mettler 2000). Observations of WTW trainings reveal that workshop leaders often encourage participants, mostly mothers, to adopt masculine work norms, such as working long hours and putting employers' needs above those of their children (Korteweg 2006).

Federal welfare reform policies also reflected traditional expectations regarding men's and women's proper roles within families. For example, PRWORA strengthened the child support requirements for welfare receipt, reinforcing the expectations that fathers fulfill their role as "male breadwinners" within families. In response to agitation by Christian right organizations, Congress allocated federal welfare funds to promote marriage and sexual abstinence and to reward states that reduce their rates of unwed motherhood. The act also authorized states to adopt "family cap" policies that refuse additional benefits for children conceived while a woman receives welfare, despite the lack of evidence that welfare generosity is linked to fertility patterns (Reese 2005). Ethnographic research suggests that caseworkers frequently neglect the "marriage promotion" aspects of welfare reform, however, when interacting with welfare recipients (Hays 2003; Ridzi 2009). "Marriage promotion" has mainly been carried out through special government-funded workshops, which have reinforced traditional gender roles and the marginalization of same-sex couples (Heath 2009).

The implementation of welfare reform policies reinforced racial inequalities among poor women. States were more likely to adopt more restrictive types of welfare-reform policies in the 1990s when blacks and Latinos made up a larger percentage of the overall population, the welfare caseload, or the low-income population (Reese 2005, 2011; Zylan and Soule 2000). Unequal implementation of welfare policies across racial groups has also persisted in the "welfare-reform" era (Gooden 2004; Schram et al. 2009).

Feminist scholars highlight the gender dimensions of discourses that justified welfare reform policies in the 1980s and 1990s. Politicians often portrayed poor single mothers as morally deficient and in need of strict rules imposed by a paternalistic state. They and other critics of AFDC appealed to racist and sexist stereotypes of black and Latina women, as welfare mothers were portrayed as lazy, sexually promiscuous, and irresponsible "welfare queens" (Mink 1998; Reese 2005). Fraser and Gordon (1994a, 1994b) critique the dominant policy discourses on "welfare dependency" that emerged in this period, arguing that they reflected the emphasis on individualism and self-reliance, the hegemony of wage labor and devaluation of unpaid domestic and caregiving work, and psychological discourses that associated dependency with pathology. These latter discourses attributed recipients' disadvantage to their "poor" choices and character flaws and justified efforts to discipline and regulate their behavior through punishments and rewards (Haney 2004). The term "dependency" thus obscured the social relations of subordination, power, and domination that shaped the need for welfare, and the view that welfare mothers were more dependent than other types of parents or workers (who depended on the support of family members or bosses). Antiwelfare rhetoric thus drew attention away from structural sources of poverty among female-headed households and women of color, such as the shortage of living wage jobs, employer discrimination, and lack of affordable child care (Reese 2005; Luther, Kennedy, and Combs-Orne 2005).

Political attacks on welfare mothers largely resonated with the public. Negative and racialized stereotypes of welfare mothers reduced public support for welfare spending and increased support for welfare-reform policies (Foster 2008; Gilens 1999; Harris 2002). Although most Americans surveyed did not oppose aid for poor people or poor children in the 1990s, most opposed spending on "welfare" or "AFDC" and most supported many of the tough new welfare- reform policies (Reese 2005; Weaver 2000).

Given women's greater vulnerability to poverty and greater need for welfare, as well as women's traditional role as caregivers, it is not surprising that men's and women's attitudes toward welfare differ in significant ways. Research generally indicates that U.S. women are much more likely to support welfare spending than men. Women are also more likely than men to perceive structural rather than individual causes as more important determinants of poverty than men and to support governmental provision of basic needs (Shirazi and Biel 2005). Research suggests that women are more likely than men to favor policies that will improve women's status in society or assist women with children, including welfare policies that provide resources for women, children, and other disadvantaged groups or that reduce the burden of carework (Eagly and Diekman 2006; Edlund et al. 2005; Iversen and Rosenbluth 2010).

Feminist scholarship has also brought to light how women's and feminist organizations sought to influence welfare debates and contested welfare reform policies in terms of women's rights. Although they otherwise had little influence over national welfare policies, feminist organizations, such as National Organization for Women and other advocacy groups for battered women, were nevertheless instrumental in Congress' decision to adopt a "domestic violence option" that allowed states to exempt battered women from new work requirements and time limits, although the reach of such policies has been uneven and limited. After PRWORA's passage, feminist organizations filed legal challenges to the "family cap" policy, claiming that this policy discriminated against children based on the conditions of their birth, and restricted women's reproductive choices. Various welfare-rights organizations also protested the devaluation of women's care-giving work implicit in WTW requirements and defended poor mothers' rights to care for their children at home. Feminists and welfare rights groups also protested the use of federal welfare money to promote marriage, pointing out how it discouraged women's independence and encouraged poor women to stay in abusive relationships (Abramovitz 2000; Reese 2011). Meanwhile, unionized home-based child-care providers (mostly women) and their clients, both of whom grew in number as WTW programs expanded, played critical roles in state-level campaigns to improve, protect, and further expand the subsidized child-care system in the decade following PRWORA's passage (Reese 2011).

In terms of policy outcomes, advocates of welfare reform have pointed to the sharp reduction of welfare caseloads that followed the implementation of welfare reform, from a monthly average of 4.8 million families in 1995 to 1.7 million in 2008, as signs of its success (Brown 2010). Yet, these trends were partly the product of the employment boom of the 1990s, not just the change in welfare policies; TANF caseloads subsequently rose as labor market conditions worsened in the next decade (Collins and Mayer 2010; Zedlewski and Loprest 2003; Legal Momentum 2010). In the context of racial inequality in the labor market, white women left the welfare rolls more quickly than black and Latino recipients because their income exceeded eligibility criteria (Brush 2003). Moreover, the vast majority of former welfare families, even those with employed parents, remained in poverty. WTW programs often tracked women into low-wage jobs (often in "pink collar" service and clerical occupations). Most earned just above the minimum wage and did not work full-time or year-round (Collins and Mayer 2010; Negrey et al. 2003; Legal Momentum 2011). Like current recipients with meager benefits, recipients who left welfare for work commonly faced material hardships (Edin and Lein 1997; Legal Momentum 2011, 7). Perhaps most alarming are indications that the loss of welfare has contributed to the rise of homelessness among women and children and to the loss of child custody (Burnham 2001; Reese 2011).

The failure of welfare reform to reduce poverty among single mothers is not surprising given that it did little to address common employment barriers such as mental or physical disabilities, the lack of stable, living wage jobs, and employer discrimination (Burnham 2001; Legal Momentum 2011). "Work-first" models prioritizing employment also significantly reduced access to secondary education and vocational training among adult welfare recipients (Collins and Mayer 2010; Jones-DeWeever and Gault 2006; Pearson 2007).

Research shows that the implementation of welfare reform has not really affected rates of marriage or out-of-wedlock childbearing. Some research has shown that the implementation of welfare reform policies, such as time limits on welfare receipt, has led some low-income women to be more dependent on male partners after they were denied welfare (Scott, London, and Myers 2002). Other research, however, found that current or former welfare recipients generally sought to have greater financial independence from men and relied more heavily on help from other women than from male partners (Rogers-Dillon and Haney 2005).

8 FUTURE DIRECTIONS

Feminist scholarship on the U.S. welfare state has demonstrated how assumptions about men and women, proper gender roles, and the relative value of men's and women's labor, have shaped the design of welfare programs, the relative distribution of benefits, and how these policies are justified. Much of the feminist scholarship on the U.S. welfare state has focused on particular welfare programs serving low-income mothers, namely A(F)DC/TANF and subsidized child care. Such research reveals how the influence of traditional maternalism, never very strong, has waned, whereas financial support and services for working parents increased, but remained class divided and minimalistic in comparison to benefits provided by other wealthy democracies. Feminist scholarship has also shown how the U.S. welfare state has historically reinforced the "male bread-winner" role within families through various programs, including benefits for active military personnel, workers' compensation, and unemployment insurance. Feminist scholars have also revealed how purportedly gender neutral programs, such as Social Security and Unemployment Insurance, reproduce gender inequalities in the labor market through the uneven distribution of benefits.

Although much feminist research has focused on the TANF program already, there are some notable gaps in it. It largely focuses on the experiences of single mothers, rendering invisible the experiences of two-parent families (especially adult males) receiving TANF and recipients of "child only" TANF grants, which make up growing shares of TANF cases. Building on the insights of Haney (2000), Critelli (2007), and Roberts (2002), greater feminist research is also needed on how welfare reform interacts with other kinds of social policies, such as criminal justice and child-welfare policies, in regulating the lives of low-income mothers. Finally, the gender dynamics within faith-based welfare reform initiatives would be especially fertile ground for feminist research.

Greater research is needed on the gender dynamics of other welfare programs such as general relief, Supplemental Security Income, Medicare, food stamps, and the Earned Income Tax Credit. Such research would also help to uncover how women without dependent children relate to the welfare state. Likewise, feminist analyses of recent policy shifts—including the implementation of the economic recovery programs adopted in 2008, the federal health-care reforms enacted in 2010, and social-service cutbacks since 2008—would broaden our understanding of gender and U.S. social policy.

NOTES

1. For a good review of this debate, see Haney (2000).

REFERENCES

*Indicates recommended reading.

*Abramovitz, Mimi. 1989. *Regulating the Lives of Women: Social Policy from Colonial Times to the Present.* Boston, MA: South End Press.
Baca Zinn, Maxine, and Bonnie Thornton Dill. 1996. "Theorizing Differences from Multiracial Feminism." *Feminist Studies* 22: 321–331.

Bolzendahl, Catherine, and Sigrin Olafsdottir. 2008. "Gender Group Interest or Gender Ideology? Understanding U.S. Support for Family Policy Within the Liberal Welfare Regime." *Sociological Perspectives* 51: 281–304.

Brown, Kay E. 2010. "Temporary Assistance for Needy Families: Implications of Caseload and Program Changes for Families and Program Monitoring." Statement of Kay E. Brown, Before the U.S. Senate, Committee on Finance, GAO-10-815T, September 21. Available http://www.gao.gov/products/GAO-10-815T.

Brush, Lisa D. 2003. "Impacts of Welfare Reform." *Race, Gender & Class* 10: 173–192.

Burnham, Linda. 2001. "Welfare Reform, Family Hardship, and Women of Color." *Annals of the American Academy of Political and Social Science* 577: 39–47.

Christopher, Karen. 2002. "Single Motherhood, Employment, or Social Assistance: Why Are U.S. Women Poorer Than Women in Other Affluent Nations?" *Journal of Poverty* 6: 61–80.

*Collins, Jane L., and Victoria Mayer. 2010. *Both Hands Tied: Welfare Reform and the Race to the Bottom in the Low-Wage Labor Market.* Chicago and London: University of Chicago Press.

Critelli, Filomena, M. 2007. "Caregiving and Welfare Reform: Voices of Low-Income Foster Mothers." *Journal of Human Behavior in the Social Environment* 15: 55–80.

Curran, Laura. 2005. "Social Work's Revised Maternalism: Mothers, Workers, and Welfare in Early Cold War America, 1946–1963." *Journal of Women's History* 17: 112–136.

Derthick, Martha. 1979. *Policymaking for Social Security.* Washington DC: Brookings Institution.

Eagly, Alice H., and Amanda B. Diekman. 2006. "Examining Gender Gaps in Sociopolitical Attitudes: It's Not Mars and Venus." *Feminism & Psychology* 16: 26–34.

Edin, Kathyrn, and Laura Lein. 1997. *Making Ends Meet.* New York: Russell Sage.

Edlund, Lena, Laila Haider, and Rohini Pande. 2005. "Unmarried Parenthood and Redistributive Politics." *Journal of the European Economic Association* 3: 95–119.

Esping-Andersen, Gøsta. 1990. *The Three Worlds of Welfare Capitalism.* Princeton, NJ: Princeton University Press.

Estevez-Abe, Margarita. 2005a. "Gender Bias in Skills and Social Policies: The Varieties of Capitalism Perspective on Sex Segregation." *Social Politics* 12: 180–215.

Estevez-Abe, Margarita. 2005b. "Feminism as Industrial Policy in Japan." Washington, DC: Woodrow Wilson. Rev. April 2012. Available at http://faculty.maxwell.syr.edu/mestevo2/Feminism%20as%20Industrial%20Policy%20in%20Japan%202005.pdf.

Estevez-Abe, M., T. Iversen, and D. Soskice. 2001. *Varieties of Capitalism: The Institutional Foundations of Comparative Advantage.* London: Oxford University Press.

Foster, Carly Hayden. 2008. "The Welfare Queen: Race, Gender, Class and Public Opinion." *Race, Gender & Class* 15: 162–179.

Fraser, Nancy, and Linda Gordon. 1994a. "A Genealogy of Dependency: Tracing a Keyword of the U.S. Welfare State." *Signs: Journal of Women in Culture and Society* 19: 309–336.

Fraser, Nancy, and Linda Gordon. 1994b. "'Dependency' Demystified: Inscriptions of Power in a Keyword of the Welfare State." *Social Politics* 1: 4–31.

Giannarelli, Linda, and James Barsimantov. 2000. *Child Care Expenses of America's Families.* Occasional Paper no. 40. Washington, DC: Urban Institute. Available at http://www.urban.org/UploadedPDF/310028_occa40.pdf.

Gifford, Brian. 2006. "The Camouflaged Safety Net: The U.S. Armed Forces as Welfare State Institution." *Social Politics* 13: 372–399.

Gilens, Martin. 1999. *Why Americans Hate Welfare: Race, Media, and the Politics of Antipoverty Policy.* Chicago: University of Chicago Press.

Gooden, Susan. 2004. "Examining the Implementation of Welfare Reform by Race: Do Blacks, Hispanics, and Whites Report Similar Experiences with Welfare Agencies?" *Review of Black Political Economy* 32 (2): 27–53.

Goodwin, Joanne L. 1995. "'Employable Mothers' and 'Suitable Work': A Re-Evaluation of Welfare and Wage-Earning for Women in Twentieth Century United States." *Journal of Social History* 29: 253–274.

*Gordon, Linda. 1994. *Pitied but Not Entitled: Single Mothers and the History of Welfare.* New York: Free Press.

*Gornick, Janet C., and Marcia K. Meyers 2003. *Families That Work: Policies for Reconciling Parenthood and Employment.* New York: Russell Sage.

Haney, Lynne. 2000. "Feminist State Theory: Applications to Jurisprudence, Criminology, and the Welfare State." *Annual Review of Sociology* 26: 641–666.

Haney, Lynne. 2004. "Introduction: Gender, Welfare, and States of Punishment." *Social Politics: International Studies in Gender, State, and Society*, 11 (3): 333–362.

Harrington Meyer, Madonna, Douglas A. Wolf, and Christine L. Himes 2005. "Linking Benefits to Marital Status: Race and Social Security in the US." *Feminist Economics* 11 (2): 145–162.

Harris, Cherise A. 2002. "Who Supports Welfare Reform and Why?" *Race, Gender, & Class* 9 (1): 96–121.

*Hays, Sharon. 2003. *Flat Broke with Children: Women in the Age of Welfare Reform.* New York: Oxford University Press.

Heath, Melanie. 2009. "State of Our Unions: Marriage Promotion and the Contested Power of Heterosexuality." *Gender & Society* 23: 27–48.

Herd, Pamela. 2005a. "Ensuring a Minimum: Social Security Reform and Women." *Gerontologist* 45 (1): 12–25.

Herd, Pamela. 2005b. "Reforming a Breadwinner Welfare State: Gender, Race, Class, and Social Security Reform." *Social Forces* 83 (4): 1365–1393.

Herd, Pamela, and Madonna Harrington Meyer. 2002. "Care Work: Invisible Civic Engagement." *Gender and Society* 16 (5): 665–688.

Hill Collins, Patricia. 2000 [1990]. *Black Feminist Thought.* Boston: Unwin Hyman.

Iversen, Torben, and Frances Rosenbluth. 2010. *Women, Work, and Politics: The Political Economy of Gender Inequality.* New Haven, CT: Yale University Press.

Jones-DeWeever, Avis A., and Barbara Gault. 2006. *Resilient and Reaching for More: Challenges and Benefits of Higher Education for Welfare Participants and Their Children.* Washington DC: Institute for Women's Policy Research.

Kessler-Harris, Alice. 1995. "Designing Women and Old Fools: The Construction of the Social Security Amendments of 1939." In Linda K. Kerber, Alice Kessler-Harris, and Kathryn Kish Sklar, eds., *U.S. History As Women's History: New Feminist Essays.* Chapel Hill: University of North Carolina Press, 87–106.

Korteweg, Anna C. 2006. "The Construction of Gendered Citizenship at the Welfare Office: An Ethnographic Comparison of Welfare-To-Work Workshops in the United States and the Netherlands." *Social Politics: International Studies in Gender, State, and Society* 13: 313–340.

Legal Momentum, The Women's Legal Defense and Education Fund. 2010. "TANF Caseloads Fall Again the Second Quarter of 2010." New York: Legal Momentum. Rev. April 2011. Available at http://www.legalmomentum.org/sites/default/files/reports/tanf-caseload-declined-again-in.pdf.

Legal Momentum, The Women's Legal Defense and Education Fund. 2011. "Welfare Reform at Age 15: A Vanishing Safety Net for Women and Children." New York: Legal Momentum. Rev. April 2011.

Available at http://www.ncdsv.org/images/LM_WelfareReformat15VanishingSafetyNet_4-2011. pdf.

Leroux, Karen. 2009. "Unpensioned Veterans: Women Teachers and the Politics of Public Service in the Late-Nineteenth Century United States." *Journal of Women's History* 21: 34–62.

Lovell, Vicky. 2002. "Constructing Social Citizenship: The Exclusion of African American Women from Unemployment Insurance in the U.S." *Feminist Economics* 8: 191–197.

Luther, Catherine A., Deseriee A Kennedy, and Terri Combs-Orme. 2005. "Intertwining of Poverty, Gender, and Race: A Critical Analysis of Welfare News Coverage from 1993–2000." *Race, Gender & Class* 12: 10–34.

Mandel, Hadas, and Moshe Semyonov. 2006. "A Welfare State Paradox: State Interventions and Women's Employment Opportunities in 22 Countries." *American Journal of Sociology* 111 (6): 1910–1949.

Mayer, Victoria. 2008. "Crafting a New Conservative Consensus on Welfare Reform: Redefining Citizenship, Social Provision, and the Public/Private Divide." *Social Politics: International Studies in Gender, State and Society* 15: 156–181.

Mettler, Suzanne. 1998. *Dividing Citizens: Gender and Federalism in New Deal Public Policy.* Ithaca, NY: Cornell University Press.

Mettler, Suzanne. 2000. "States' Rights, Women's Obligations: Contemporary Welfare Reform in Historical Perspective." *Women & Politics* 21: 1–34.

Mettler, Suzanne. 2005. *Soldiers to Citizens: The G.I. Bill and the Making of the Greatest Generation.* New York: Oxford University Press.

Meyers, Marcia, and Janet Gornick. 2001. "Gendering Welfare State Variation: Income Transfers, Employment Supports, and Family Poverty." In Nancy J. Hirschmann, and Ulrike Liebert, eds., *Women & Welfare: Theory and Practice in the United States and Europe.* New Brunswick, NJ: Rutgers University Press, 215–243.

Michel, Sonya. 1999. *Children's Interests/Mothers' Rights: The Shaping of America's Child Care Policy.* New Haven, CT: Yale University Press.

*Mink, Gwendolyn. 1995. *The Wages of Motherhood: Inequality in the Welfare State, 1917–1942.* Ithaca, NY: Cornell University Press.

Mink, Gwendolyn. 1998. *Welfare's End.* Ithaca, NY: Cornell University Press.

Misra, Joya, and Frances Akins. 1998. The Welfare State and Women: Structure, Agency, and Diversity. *Social Politics* 5 (3): 259–285.

Moller, Stephanie. 2002. "Supporting Poor Single Mothers: Gender and Race in the U.S. Welfare State." *Gender & Society* 16: 465–484.

Morgan, Kimberly. 2001. "A Child of the Sixties: The Great Society, the New Right, and the Politics of Federal Child Care." *Journal of Policy History* 13 (2): 215–250.

Negrey, Cynthia, Sunhwa Golin, and Barbara Gault. 2003. "Job Training for Women Leaving Welfare: Assessing Interest in Non-Traditional Employment." *Research in the Sociology of Work* 12: 231–257.

Nelson, Barbara J. 1990. "The Origins of the Two-Channel Welfare State: Workmen's Compensation and Mothers' Aid." In Gordon, Linda, ed., *Women, the State, and Welfare.* Madison: University of Wisconsin Press, 123–151.

*Orloff, Ann. 1996. "Gender in the Welfare State." *Annual Review of Sociology* 22: 51–78.

Orloff, Ann. 2002. "Explaining US Welfare Reform: Power, Gender, Race and the US Policy Legacy." *Critical Social Policy* 22: 96–118.

Orloff, Ann. 2003. "Markets Not States? The Weakness of State Social Provision For Breadwinning Men in the United States." In Lynne Haney, and Lisa Pollard, eds., *Families of a*

New World: Gender, Politics, and State Development in a Global Context. New York: Routledge, 217–243.

Orloff, Ann. 2009a. "Gendering the Comparative Analysis of Welfare States: An Unfinished Agenda." *Sociological Theory* 27: 317–343.

Orloff, Ann. 2009b. "Should Feminists Aim for Gender Symmetry? Why a Dual-Earner/Dual-Caregiver Society Is Not Every Feminist's Utopia." In Janet C. Gornick and Marcia K. Meyers, eds., *Gender Equality: Transforming Family Divisions of Labor*. London: Verso, 129–157.

Orloff, Ann. 2010. "Gender." In Francis G., Castles, Stephan Leibfried, Jane Lewis, Herbert Obinger, and Christopher Pierson, eds., *The Oxford Handbook of the Welfare State*. Oxford: Oxford University Press, 252–264.

Pearson, Fiona. 2007. "The New Welfare Trap: Case Managers, College Education, and TANF Policy." *Gender & Society* 21: 723–748.

Quadagno, Jill. 1990. "Race, Class, and Gender in the U.S. Welfare State: Nixon's Failed Family Assistance Plan." *American Sociological Review* 58: 11–28.

Reese, Ellen. 1996. "Maternalism and Political Mobilization: How California's Postwar Child Care Campaign Was Won." *Gender & Society* 10 (5): 566–589.

*Reese, Ellen. 2005. *Backlash Against Welfare Mothers: Past and Present*. Berkeley and Los Angeles: University of California Press.

Reese, Ellen. 2011. *They Say Cutback, We Say Fightback! Welfare Rights Activism in an Era of Retrenchment*. New York: American Sociological Association's Rose Series.

Ridzi, Frank. 2009. *Selling Welfare Reform: Work-First and the New Common Sense of Employment*. New York: New York University Press.

Roberts, Dorothy E. 2002. *Shattered Bonds: The Color of Child Welfare*. New York: Basic Books.

Rogers-Dillon, Robin and Lynne Haney. 2005. "Minimizing Vulnerability: Selective Interdependencies After Welfare Reform." *Qualitative Sociology* 28: 235–254.

Schram, Sanford F., Joe Soss, Richard C. Fording, and Linda Houser. 2009. "Deciding to Discipline: Race, Choice, and Punishment at the Frontlines of Welfare Reform." *American Sociological Review* 74 (3): 398–422.

Scott, Ellen K., Andrew S. London, and Nancy A. Myers. 2002. "Dangerous Dependencies: The Intersection of Welfare Reform and Domestic Violence." *Gender & Society* 16: 878–897.

Shirazi, Rez and Anders Biel. 2005. "Internal-External Causal Attributions and Perceived Government Responsibility for Need Provision: A 14-Culture Study." *Journal of Cross-Cultural Psychology* 36: 96–116.

*Skocpol, Theda. 1992. *Protecting Soldiers and Wives: The Political Origins of Social Policy in the United States*. Cambridge, MA: Belknap Press of Harvard University Press.

Social Security Administration 2012. "Fast Facts and Figures About Social Security." Available at http://www.ssa.gov/policy/docs/chartbooks/fast_facts/2012/fast_facts12.html.

Waddan, Alex. 1998. "A Liberal in Wolf's Clothing: Nixon's Family Assistance Plan in the Light of the 1990s Welfare Reform." *Journal of American Studies* 32: 203–218.

Weaver, Kent. 2000. *Ending Welfare As We Know It*. Washington, DC: Brookings Institution.

Wentworth, George. 2011. "How the Great Recession Changed the Politics of Unemployment Insurance." Presented at the Reconnecting to Work Conference, at the Institute for Research on Labor and Employment, UCLA, April 2.

Yang, Philip, and Nadine Barrett. 2006. "Understanding Public Attitudes Towards Social Security." *International Journal of Social Welfare* 15: 95–109.

Zedlewski, Sheila R., and Pamela Loprest. 2003. "Welfare Reform: One Size Doesn't Fit All." *Christian Science Monitor*. Rev. Aug, 25. Available at http://www.urban.org/publications/900648.html.

Zippel, Kathrin. 2009. "The Missing Link for Promoting Gender Equality: Work-Family and Anti-Discrimination Policies." In Janet C. Gornick and Marcia K. Meyers, eds., *Gender Equality: Transforming Family Divisions of Labor*. London: Verso, 209–229.

Zylan, Yvonne, and Sarah A. Soule. 2000. "Ending Welfare As We Know It (Again): Welfare State Retrenchment, 1989–1995." *Social Forces* 79(2): 623–652.

PART IV

....

PROGRAMS FOR THE ELDERLY

....

CHAPTER 15

....

SOCIAL SECURITY

....

EDWARD D. BERKOWITZ AND LARRY DEWITT

1 INTRODUCTION

....

MORE than 75 years after the creation of Social Security in 1935, it endures as America's largest social program. The sheer size of Social Security testifies to its importance. In December 2011, more than 55 million people of all ages received benefits from the program, including some 38 million retirees and their dependents and more than 6 million survivors of people insured by the Social Security system (SSA 2012a). Many of the remaining recipients claimed their benefits as part of the extensive Social Security Disability Insurance program, which is the subject of a separate chapter in this volume. In 2011, about 158 million people worked in jobs that were covered by Social Security, which meant that 94 percent of the nation's workers participated in the system (SSA 2011a). Of those already over 65, some 89 percent received benefits that averaged $1,181 a month and typically replaced about 40 percent of a worker's preretirement income (SSA 2011b). Given these numbers, the program inevitably involves large expenditures. For calendar year 2010, the Social Security Old Age and Survivors Insurance trust fund (exclusive of disability) received more than $677 billion in income and paid out nearly $585 billion in benefits (SSA 2012b). For most of the last 20 years, the Social Security program has been the single largest expenditure in the U.S. government's budget.

As these numbers illustrate, Social Security has become the nation's primary program that pays benefits to the elderly. It also serves as a life insurance program for families in which the principal breadwinner dies and leaves dependents behind. Because it reaches so many of the nation's elderly, it helps to pull many of them out of poverty. The National Academy of Social Insurance estimates that in 2010, Social Security lifted nearly 13.9 million adults 65 years or older out of poverty. The elderly adult poverty rate, which might have been 44 percent in the absence of Social Security, stood at just 9 percent (National Academy of Social Insurance 2011).

As suggested below, although popular, Social Security remains a controversial program. Some critics have questioned the program's fairness to any number of groups (e.g., younger workers, women, racial minorities). Others have debated how best to keep it on sound fiscal footing over the coming decades. Politically, Social Security may be difficult to change, but that does not stop many from trying.

2 A BASIC PROGRAM DESCRIPTION

From the beginning, Social Security has relied on payroll taxes as its principal means of revenue. Between 1937 and 1949, the tax rate amounted to 2 percent, shared equally by employers and employees, on the first $3,000 of an employee's income. Over time, that rate has risen substantially; currently it stands at 12.4 percent of the first $106,800 of a worker's income (leaving aside the transient matter of the Social Security payroll tax "holiday" that applied in 2011 and 2012). Some 85 percent of this goes into a trust fund for retirees and survivors and the remainder into a trust fund for disability payments (Tax Policy Center 2011).

The program relies on a fundamentally simple concept. Workers and their employers (or in the case of the self-employed, simply the worker) make contributions to a trust fund from the nation's payrolls. The Social Security Administration (SSA) keeps a record of these contributions, linked in each case to an employee's Social Security number. On a worker's retirement, the government uses a formula that takes wage inflation into account and converts a worker's average earnings into a basic benefit level. Once a worker begins to receive monthly benefits, those benefits are indexed to the rate of inflation on an annual basis, so that benefit levels keep up with prices.

Benefits vary not only by a worker's average earnings but also by his or her family status. Married workers receive more than single workers in many cases. Divorced people who have been married for at least 10 years, divorced for two years, and are 62 years of age and unmarried may receive a benefit based on the wage earnings of their former spouse. Widows of insured workers may collect benefits at age 60. Like the rest of the Social Security system, these family benefits have evolved over the years. Legislation passed in 1939, for example, allowed widows to receive a benefit that was only three-quarters of a basic benefit, but Congress has gradually raised the widow's benefit to the same level as the basic Social Security benefit (Berkowitz 2002).

At bottom, Social Security uses involuntary contributions from payroll taxes to pay a defined benefit to the great majority of the nation's retirees. The worker and his or her family receive these benefits as a matter of right. No one is too rich to qualify for Social Security, even though richer beneficiaries—as many as a third of all beneficiaries—must pay income taxes on their benefits. Because of increases in the size and nature of benefits and changing economic and demographic conditions, the percentage of nation's GDP dedicated to Social Security has risen from less than 3 percent in 1962 to 4.4 percent in 2008. Current actuarial estimates predict that percentage will increase in the future, reaching 6.2 percent of GDP in 2035 and then declining gradually to about 6 percent for the remainder of the 75-year period over which the estimates range. When one factors in the income that comes to the program through payroll taxes and other sources, it leaves a likely shortfall in the system over the course of the next 75 years of some 0.9 percent of GDP. Expressed in dollar terms, the system's current long-range unfunded liability amounts to $6.5 trillion over the next 75 years (Congressional Budget Office 2010).

3 THE HISTORICAL CONTEXT

Although Social Security is now one of the largest and most popular parts of government, the program had to overcome numerous challenges during its early years. In 1935, the system's founders—social insurance experts from academia and private pension consultants who worked on the staff of a cabinet-level committee headed by Franklin D. Roosevelt's secretary of labor, Frances Perkins—made what might be described as a social policy bet. They wagered that a social insurance system financed completely by payroll contributions could be successfully implemented and sustained into the future. At the same time, they hedged their bets by simultaneously creating a state-administered system of public assistance payments to elderly individuals who could demonstrate financial need to state and local authorities. The federal government and the states shared the costs for this system. In 1935, a state-administered system enjoyed far more congressional support than did "old-age insurance" or, as we know it today, Social Security (Béland 2005).

The reasons were many. The state system could begin benefit payments immediately; indeed, many states were already paying such benefits by virtue of programs created before the passage of the Social Security Act. Old-age insurance, by way of contrast, needed to build up a pile of contributions before it could start benefits (otherwise, benefits early on would have to be funded in part by general revenues, rather than contributions from participants). In the original plan, payroll deductions would begin in 1937, but the first regular benefits would not be paid until 1942. Congress modified this arrangement in 1939 so that benefits would begin in 1940, but that still left the gap between 1937 and 1940. Until 1940, any elderly person in need of financial assistance had to turn to the state programs for help. These state programs had a means test— only those deemed indigent could receive benefits—but old-age insurance had more fundamental restrictions. In particular, one had to work in a job that was covered by Social Security in order to qualify for benefits. Half of all workers, those people outside the industrial and commercial labor force, did not participate in the system and hence were ineligible for benefits. Average benefits in the state program were in fact higher than benefits under old-age insurance. Social Security looked to be superfluous, less essential to the nation's social provision than the state public assistance programs (Berkowitz 1991).

The Social Security program was also difficult to finance in the short run. In its first years, it collected taxes from workers already facing difficulties making ends meet in

bad economic times, and it only paid out small, lump-sum death benefits to contributors who died before they could begin receiving regular benefits. A program that existed
primarily as a tax rather than a benefit—one that had not elicited much congressional enthusiasm on the initial passage of the bill in 1935—faced the prospect of repeal.
Moreover, large surpluses developed in the Social Security accounts, especially during
the full-employment economic boom of the World War II economy. Because tax rates
were scheduled to increase over time, these surpluses were forecast to grow for many
years. People questioned a program that was in surplus when its potential beneficiaries were in need and that impounded money from a depressed economy (at least until
World War II, and even then people feared that a new depression would develop after
the war). And people wondered how one program could be in surplus when the federal
budget itself was in deficit.

The question whether employers who already ran pension programs would be exempt
from Social Security hung over the new program. The issue was volatile enough that the
Senate actually passed an amendment in 1935, later removed in conference, that would
have allowed some employers to opt out of the program. An employer who offered a
private pension program at least as generous as Social Security could have chosen not to
participate in it. Because Social Security was slated to pay relatively low benefits, most
private plans would have qualified. Furthermore, the notion of self-insurance already
existed in social insurance programs, such as workers' compensation, so the proposal
enjoyed the comfortable cover of political precedent. The issue of allowing private
employers offering pensions to opt out of Social Security arose again in 1936, only to be
put aside. If Social Security had become, in effect, voluntary depending on the actions
of private employers, it would have been much more difficult for it to grow into a fiscally
viable system or to attract a political following. The largest and richest companies might
well have opted out, leaving Social Security with the poorest workers who constituted
what insurers would have described as the worst risks (DeWitt et al. 2008).

The program also faced the challenge of judicial review at a time when the Supreme
Court was declaring many New Deal programs unconstitutional. The program passed
this test in 1937, the beneficiary of the Court's new-found deference to Congress in the
midst of Roosevelt's court-packing plan (Shesol 2010).

Even after meeting these initial challenges, the program still received substantial
congressional scrutiny in 1939 that resulted in significant revisions, even before the
program went into full effect. In an effort to reduce the size of the fund held in reserve
for future benefits, Congress expanded the range of benefits to include survivors and
family benefits. Significantly, in the period between 1935 and 1939, Republicans and
Democrats alike criticized the program that, some four decades later, would develop a
substantial political following and become one of the most durable parts of America's
welfare state.

The challenge of private pensions, the legal hurdles posed by judicial review, and the
difficulties of starting a program from scratch and funding it through dedicated payroll taxes all underscored the fact that Social Security was not an inevitable triumph. It
survived its initial period because the popular Roosevelt administration, buttressed by

large Democratic majorities, managed to put the program in place. Once the program existed, it became difficult for opponents to repeal it. In addition, program administrators took deliberate steps to remove some of the program's political liabilities and to present it as a more attractive social program than public assistance (Cates 1983).

Even with the changes made in 1939, Social Security still played a secondary role to state public assistance programs in America's social provisions for the elderly. Throughout the 1940s, Social Security lagged behind state public assistance programs in terms of the number of people it served and even in the average size of the benefits it paid. Congress routinely brushed aside suggestions to expand Social Security and, in fact, passed two separate laws that slightly reduced the number of jobs it covered. Congress also regularly postponed increases in the payroll tax rate that, by the terms of the 1935 law, were supposed to occur at three-year intervals beginning in 1937 (DeWitt et al. 2008).

4 THE TRIUMPH OF 1950

It took until 1950 to correct these problems. In a truly momentous step for the program, Congress broadened coverage to include the self-employed and other previously excluded workers and raised the benefit level. These changes made Social Security benefits more valuable when compared with state public assistance programs, and expanded coverage gave more congressional representatives, such as those from predominantly rural or agricultural districts, a stake in the program. As a result, Social Security's political base expanded.

Robust economic conditions made it possible for Congress to raise benefit levels without raising taxes. The actuaries who advised Congress on the program's financial condition utilized the simplifying assumption that wages would remain level into the future. When wages, in fact, rose, the program developed a temporary surplus. Congress "spent" this surplus by raising benefit levels. In this manner, a regular ritual developed after 1950 of raising benefits in election years. The wager policy-makers had made in 1935 had begun to pay off for the proponents of Social Security.

The new Social Security program, once safely implemented, offered many advantages over the state public assistance programs. These included the possibility of keeping future expenses under control or at least visible, since benefit increases would show up in cost projections made over a 75-year period. The public assistance programs, which varied greatly from state to state, did not have this feature. State politicians could expand benefit rates and pressure the state's congressional delegation to expand the federal contribution to the states without much consideration of long-term consequences. In hard times, the pressure to raise public assistance benefits was intense. Indeed, one of the original rationales for Social Security was that a public assistance system was not sustainable in the long run (Berkowitz 1991).

Because Social Security benefits were paid to retired workers as a matter of right, they carried less stigma than welfare benefits, particularly in the post-World War II period, when welfare came to be associated with the mothers of dependent children, a majority of whom were not married and a disproportionate number of whom were African American. Social Security's proponents touted the program as a uniquely American response to the problems of old age, one that reinforced the free market and a capitalist economy by providing portable benefits that allowed workers to move freely from job to job and that linked benefit levels to earnings (Berkowitz 1991).

Between 1950 and 1972, Congress expanded Social Security in four ways. It raised the basic benefit levels, for example in 1950, 1952, 1954, and 1958. It expanded the range of benefits, as in the creation of disability insurance in 1956. It brought more jobs and more occupations into the Social Security system, for example adding agricultural workers to the system in 1950 and again in 1954. Finally, it eased some of the restrictions, for example on widows' benefits and, after 1956, on disability benefits. Each Congress, it seemed, made the program more generous by easing the restrictions on the receipt of benefits. (Berkowitz and DeWitt 2009; Altman and Marmor 2009)

5 CREATING COST-OF-LIVING ADJUSTMENTS

Before the expansionary era of Social Security came to an end in the 1970s, Congress once again altered the program in a fundamental way. In 1972, program administrators, who enjoyed a close and collaborative relationship with the congressmen on the tax committees who essentially legislated on behalf of Congress, persuaded these members to change the actuarial assumptions that governed the program. Instead of assuming that wage rates would remain the same in the future, actuaries would now factor in future wage growth. As a result of this change in the accounting rules, a surplus showed up in the Social Security accounts, which Congress used to enact a 20 percent benefit increase in 1972.

Much of this debate took place in elite and technically oriented policy circles (Derthick 1979). The public, to the extent that it participated in Social Security policy-making at all, understood the matter as a simple one of raising benefits. In general, the issue enjoyed far less visibility, even within the responsible congressional committees, than did the more politically contentious matters of the moment, such as welfare reform.

At the same time Congress legislated the 20 percent increase, it resolved an internal debate among program experts and policy-makers that had been conducted since 1969. Some program proponents andprogram congressional proprietors of the program, notably Ways and Means chair Wilbur Mills, favored the system in which Congress made periodic, ad hoc adjustments in benefit levels in order to keep up with the inflation rate and, in general, to raise the level of Social Security benefits to make them more politically appealing. That way, Congress gained credit for each increase, boosting the political appeal of the Democrats, who controlled Congress for all but two years of the period 1949–1981 (Zelizer 1998). In addition, Congress often raised benefits by more than the inflation rate, actions that were welcomed by program proponents as making the program more adequate. Others, however, argued that the system was essentially capricious and could result in both irrational benefit increases and long delays between benefit increases. To remedy that problem, they suggested that benefit increases be automatically linked to the inflation rate, without need for any congressional action. President Richard Nixon and other Republicans, in particular, welcomed indexation because it allowed them to share in the credit for benefit increases, which, from the Republican point of view, seemed to take place with alarming frequency in the booming economy of the 1960s (Weaver 1988).

Hence, in 1972 Congress created what became known as automatic cost-of-living adjustments (or COLAs, as they were popularly known; Berkowitz 2003). This important provision went into effect in 1975, after a series of final ad hoc benefit increases in 1973 and 1974. The so-called automatic adjustments protected the program from the high inflation of the 1970s, when the real value of many other social benefits was falling. Beginning in 1974, the federal government also took over administration of the state public assistance programs for the elderly and disabled and instituted a minimum benefit that applied to every state, under a new federal program known as Supplemental Security Income (SSI) (Berkowitz and DeWitt, 2013).

6 The 1970s and 1980s

The switch to the "automatic" procedures collided with the rampant inflation and high levels of unemployment experienced in the 1970s and produced a crisis in Social Security financing. The Congress and the administrations of presidents Jimmy Carter and then Ronald Reagan responded with two sets of major amendments, one in 1977 and one in 1983. Both of these legislative interventions were driven by concerns over the program's finances, and they marked the beginning point of a period of policy retrenchment that continued to characterize the program for the remainder of the century and into the present (Béland 2005).

The 1983 amendments became a celebrated event in Social Security's history that in the future would be singled out as an example of how the program could handle crises in a pragmatic manner. Reagan officials proposed solving the program's financial problems through major changes in the disability and early retirement programs. Legislation that made cuts in the still popular Social Security program without providing beneficiaries with advance warning attracted little political support from either party. In frustration, Reagan appointed a bipartisan commission to tide his party through the 1982 congressional elections and to formulate new proposals that would have the support of Democrats and Republicans alike. Although the commission made little progress, a bargaining group of members broke off from the main group at the end of 1982 and facilitated direct bargaining sessions between President Reagan and House Speaker Thomas P. O'Neill (D-Mass.). The resulting agreement formed the basis of the 1983 amendments (Berkowitz 2003; Light 1994).

Although the 1977 legislation sought to restore financial balance to the system principally through moderate payroll tax increases and some corrections to the benefit formulas, the more wide-ranging 1983 amendments relied on a roughly equal combination of revenue increases and benefit reductions. Among the major changes introduced in 1983 were the partial income taxation of Social Security benefits, a long-term increase in the retirement age, the coverage of all federal government employees, and a six-month delay in the payment of the 1983 COLA. In a manner analogous to a bank skipping an interest payment, this delay amounted to a permanent benefit cut for Social Security recipients.

7 CONSERVATIVE ALTERNATIVES TO SOCIAL SECURITY

Liberals believed they had made real concessions in the 1983 amendments. Conservatives, by way of contrast, felt a sense of frustration that the essential elements of the program—such as its contributory nature financed through compulsory payroll deductions and defined benefits that were indexed to the rate of inflation—remained in place. Even though America had undergone a political shift to the right, as President Reagan's growing popularity demonstrated, its New Deal social programs seemed as invulnerable as ever.

The politics of retrenchment, to use the phrase popularized by political scientist Paul Pierson (1994), did not appear to apply to Social Security. Even as the influence of labor unions, which had traditionally served as major defenders of Social Security in Congress, declined, new groups and organizations arose to protect the program. Prominent among these new organizations was the American Association of Retired Persons (AARP), which would grow into a 40-million-member group of people over 50 years of age (Lynch 2011) dedicated to exploiting the purchasing power of the elderly and protecting their perceived political interests. Indeed, as Andrea Campbell (2003) has argued, the highly visible benefits provided by the Social Security and Medicare programs mobilized the elderly as "uber-citizens . . . an otherwise disparate group of people who were given a new political identity as program recipients." In Campbell's political arithmetic (2002, 2), "policy begets participation begets policy." In other words, Social Security recipients made up a strong vested interest that conservative politicians, even as they were winning in general elections, found difficult to dislodge.

The 1983 experience convinced Social Security's opponents that they needed a more politically attractive alternative to it (Teles 2007). Over time, conservative theorists such as University of Chicago economist Milton Friedman, an articulate proponent of relying on the free market to solve social problems, and analysts at the libertarian Cato Institute and other such Washington think tanks promoted the idea of private alternatives to public Social Security (Friedman 2002; Ferrara and Tanner, 1998). They argued that—due to a mix of economic and social factors—workers no longer enjoyed substantial job stability, in which they would remain with a single employer throughout their careers. Employers, they argued, no longer had the same interest they had once had in providing employees with defined benefit pensions that were linked to the Social Security system. With this linkage, the more Social Security paid, the less private employers would have to pay. The new trends in private pensions undermined this traditional arrangement, necessitating a movable private pension plan that they could manage themselves. To respond to these new economic/social conditions and the perceived change in the political climate, conservatives promoted using government regulation and favorable tax treatment to facilitate new financial instruments that workers could use to save for their retirements. These newer financial instruments, such as 401(k) plans, would allow workers more freedom to manage their own retirements. Conservatives hoped that as these new private plans grew in popularity, there would be a decline in popular support for Social Security.

As the financing problems of the Social Security system continued and the economy recovered from its 1970s doldrums, the number of private alternatives grew, and the returns on these private investments looked attractive. Conservatives promoted a narrative in which Social Security was about to go bankrupt and private plans offered potentially higher benefits. Individuals would be allowed to shift at least some portion of their payroll taxes to private equity investments that promised a potential of higher benefits, with, however, the risk of greater losses as well depending on the behavior of financial markets. Proponent of these plans emphasized potential rewards and downplayed potential losses. Under the conservative narrative, opportunity would replace government coercion, and nearly everyone would be better off. To be sure, the private plans would not pay defined benefits, but if the Social Security system ran out of money, then it would not be able to meet its obligations and pay promised benefits (Teles and Derthick 2009).

In the political fight over Social Security, conservative groups suffered from several disadvantages. For one thing, Social Security recipients were already mobilized as a strong political force, most notably through the AARP. The supporters of private alternatives still needed to be mobilized, and the tangible benefits they would receive lay in the future, if they materialized at all. Policy based on regulation and tax breaks represented a form of what Suzanne Mettler (2011) has called "submerged" government, whose benefits were often less apparent to people than the very tangible deposits the Social Security program made to the bank accounts of elderly citizens. For another thing, the Social Security Administration, dedicated to the preservation and extension of the Social Security program, continued to enjoy a substantial degree of influence within the still relatively closed world of Social Security policy-making.

Not surprisingly, then, conservative proposals took time to establish themselves as serious alternatives to the Social Security program. Nonetheless, they made measurable progress, aided not only by specific factors in Social Security but by more general developments that broadened the scope of political participation in the issue. Within the political sphere, these external developments included the creation of more subcommittees in key congressional committees, and the emergence of administrative difficulties in the disability and SSI programs undermined confidence in the Social Security Administration and its programs (Derthick 1990). The emergence of microcomputers as powerful computing tools meant that complex policy analyses that previously could only be conducted by agencies with access to expensive computers, such as the Social Security Administration, could now be performed by nearly anyone. That lessened the Social Security Administration's monopoly on policy expertise and opened the door for conservative organizations to make credible proposals.

If conservatives had lost the battle over the 1983 amendments, they succeeded in influencing subsequent Social Security politics. One indication of this new influence came in the report of the Social Security Advisory Council that met in the Clinton era, between 1994 and 1996. In the past, Social Security Advisory Councils had made recommendations that closely tracked the policy aims of program advocates, and these councils served as arenas for political pre-negotiations that often led to successful legislation. The Clinton-era council broke with these precedents. It put three competing alternatives forward, including a call for "personal security accounts" that would largely supersede Social Security (Berkowitz 2003). The privatization of Social Security had made it to the policy table. Less than a decade later, President George W. Bush decided to make Social Security privatization a centerpiece of his second administration. Privatization now not only had a seat at the policy table but appeared to be driving the president's policy agenda.

Despite these advances, the privatization of Social Security failed to take hold. One problem was technical in nature: the transition from Social Security to private accounts would be costly and difficult to manage in a pay-as-you-go system in which present benefits needed to be protected, even as workers began to save money for their own privately funded benefits. Another problem was both technical and political: the private sector did not appear capable of handling complex social risks, such as disability, that needed to be included in any Social Security package (Berkowitz 1987). Still another problem was that the private and voluntary nature of the conservative proposals undermined financial discipline. It was difficult to argue that a worker's private retirement fund should be reserved for retirement if that worker should face a calamity, such as extended unemployment or sickness, along the way to retirement. But if a worker spent his or her retirement fund before retirement, it left the worker at the mercy of the government's generosity—precisely the outcome the privatizers hoped to avoid. In a more basic sense, the private plans became as vulnerable to external shocks as the public Social Security program had been susceptible to adverse effects that stemmed from the economy's bad performance in the 1970s. In particular, the returns on stocks and other private investments turned sharply lower in the period after 2001, undercutting the appeal of privately managed retirement funds. A defined benefit plan began to look more attractive, and people began to consider ways to preserve that benefit (Teles and Derthick 2009).

8 A PROGRAM BALANCE SHEET

Today Social Security remains firmly in place, as important as ever. When it was created in 1935, proponents regarded it as a way of protecting workers against the insecurities of an industrial economy prone to periodic downturns in the business cycle, and against the economic hazards of old age. The solution was to force employees to save money over their working lifetimes and to pay them benefits when they reached old age.

The founders of Social Security wanted to create a well-run, impartially administered program that did not bequeath an unmanageable financial load to future generations. In those aims, they largely succeeded against considerable odds. Although some people complained that program administrators promoted their program over other viable alternatives, almost no one accused Social Security administrators of political favoritism, in the sense of withholding benefits from people who opposed the program (Derthick 1979). When President Nixon wanted to send a notice of a benefit increase wrapped in a message that gave him credit for the increase, Social Security officials insisted on a more neutral message that did not call attention to the president. Social Security officials took pride in the small percentage of program funds that went to the costs of administration (Derthick 1979). The overhead of the Social Security program was considerably less per capita than that of a private insurance company offering similar products, and Social Security did not have the luxury of adjusting its rates to reflect risks or of refusing coverage to a particular group.

Over time, however, new tests for the efficacy of social programs emerged. They came to be judged on how effectively they reduced poverty and on their racial and gendered effects. The very size of the Social Security program made it an effective antipoverty program, but this success came at the expense of what might be called "target efficiency." Many of the people who received Social Security did not need it. If money spent on those people could be redirected to the poor, then more of the nation's elderly, as well as other groups, such as children, could be brought out of poverty. Experience demonstrated, however, that means-tested programs, particularly those for people with little or no history of labor force participation, failed to generate large political followings that could advocate for benefit levels that met people's needs and protected against inflation. Hence, Social Security was the nation's most important antipoverty program, in part because it did not target its benefits exclusively to the poor (Hacker 2004).

9 SOME CURRENT ISSUES—RACE AND GENDER

The perception that Social Security, at some point in the future, will not have enough money on hand to pay 100 percent of the benefits that have been promised has defined much of the program's politics in recent years. The program's defenders (generally, political liberals) argue that any shortfall can and should be handled through incremental adjustments that leave the program basically intact. The program's critics (generally, political conservatives) charge that Social Security has the potential to bankrupt the nation's already shaky economy, and that the government will not be able to keep the promises it has made, and therefore requires fundamental change. Such critics want to reduce the program's income guarantee and require workers to make contributions to private pension plans. In other words, the critics, particularly conservatives and libertarian policy advocates, advocate the program's conversion from a defined benefit to a defined contribution program.

If one leaves aside the fundamental matter of privatizing the system, many issues, such as those related to race, remain to be considered. In the period after 1964, race became an important factor in the evaluation of federal social policy. The Social Security program conferred its benefits on blacks and whites alike. Still, because it was employment oriented and because its benefits were based on average wages, blacks tended to receive lower benefits on average than whites. The chronically unemployed also did not qualify for Social Security and, if they became old and impoverished, had to depend on SSI rather than Social Security. At the same time, features of the complex Social Security system cut in the opposite direction. Blacks benefited disproportionately from the disability insurance program, survivors' benefits, and the features in the benefit formula that gave lower income beneficiaries a greater return on their contributions than higher income ones (SSA 2011c). Although Social Security exemplified social policy not explicitly based on race, it also benefited the less advantaged, such as minority workers who were paid less.

Much of the criticism of Social Security on the issue of race holds that the program does not benefit African Americans sufficiently, in part because it contains historic biases built into its very structure. The original program, for example, did not cover agricultural or domestic workers, who were the majority of black labor force participants at the time (DeWitt 2010). Furthermore, the program's reliance on wage work in the economy might have worked to the disadvantage of African Americans over the long run. Nonetheless, studies by the Social Security Administration show that when all of the conflicting factors are figured into the calculations, the present Social Security system actually benefits racial minorities more than whites (Lieberman 1998; Hendley and Bilimora 1999).

Issues of gender have also produced many policy debates in Social Security circles. A single man and a single woman of the same age with identical employment records receive exactly the same Social Security benefits on retirement. The program has been explicitly gender neutral since at least 1983, and such gendered policies as did exist before then tended to benefit women and disadvantage men. Indeed, various features of the program, combined with demographic factors such as the longer life expectancy of women, have the effect of benefiting women more than men. But in a contributory, wage-based social insurance scheme, inequalities that exist in the workplace get reflected in Social Security benefits.

Women often receive less pay for doing the same job as men, and Social Security faithfully reflects that inequity in the labor market. Furthermore, women who bear children often drop out of the labor force for extended periods of time, which makes their ultimate Social Security benefits, based on their average wages, lower than those of men. As sociologist Ann Orloff (1993, 308) has noted, "men make claims as worker citizens to compensate for failure in the labor market: women make claims as workers but also as members of families, and they need programs especially to compensate for marriage failures and for the need to raise children." Social statistics underscore that need. In the final three decades of the twentieth century, the percentage of women who were married dropped, the percentage of women who were divorced more than doubled, and the percentage of families headed by single mothers rose from 10 percent to 27 percent (U.S. Census Bureau 2001).

The Social Security program has not been agile in responding to these changes for two reasons. The program's sheer complexity defeats efforts at what might be called "women-friendly" reforms. Because the program has paid spousal benefits since 1939, and because in earlier decades a nonworking spouse was more likely to be a woman than a man, a married woman who never joined the labor force can in some circumstances receive a higher benefit than a woman who worked for her entire life. It is also possible that a household containing two married workers can generate more income than a household with just one married worker and still receive lower benefits. Critics perceive these outcomes as expressions of gender bias against some women (Herd and Harrington Meyer 2007; Berkowitz 2002).

The second reason for the program's inability to respond to feminist critiques relates to conservative efforts to privatize and reform Social Security. Social and demographic changes tied to gender and the family have resulted in a "mismatch" between existing policy and present circumstances. In the past, program administrators responded to such changing circumstances by expanding and liberalizing the program to embrace new contingencies. In today's newly constrained policy environment such expansions and liberalizations have been hard to enact. Mere program preservation has become the goal of those who favor a defined benefit program, and program preservation can perpetuate and even accentuate problems and perceived inequities.

Policy-makers have, nevertheless, proposed many possible solutions to the problems raised by feminist critics. One widely discussed reform involves care credits. In one variant, individuals "may substitute up to half of the US median annual wage... for up to five years if they have one child and up to nine for those with more than one child, within the 35 years used to calculate her benefit" (Herd 2005, 1371). Still, this proposal adds costs, and requires that if funding problems are not to be aggravated, sacrifices—for example abolishing spousal benefits—be made elsewhere in the system. And such sacrifices would certainly meet with opposition from those who are mobilized to defend the Social Security program. Given the cost constraints under which the program has operated since the late 1970s, reforms that increase costs to the system or that disadvantage current program participants do not stand a good chance of political success.

10 THE LONG-TERM FINANCING PROBLEM

The reality that defines the system today and has, indeed, tended to crowd out other policy concerns is the long-term financing problem. In every annual report issued since 1989, the system's trustees have reported that the program is not financially solvent over the next 75 years. Reform proposals need to correct that problem to the satisfaction of the actuaries who act as financial gatekeepers for the system.

Ideas about what the nation should do to ease the program's finances abound. Some suggest raising the retirement age at which people qualify for basic benefits. In 1935, Congress set the retirement age at 65, although it later (1956 for women and 1961 for men) created an early retirement program, with reduced benefits, for people 62 or older. In 1983, in the midst of debates over the program's solvency, Congress, against the advice of many Social Security proponents, legislated a gradual increase in the retirement age. Someone born between 1943 and 1954, a group that includes a substantial number of baby boomers, now has a retirement age of 66, and those born 1960 or later may not retire with full benefits until age 67. Some people think that the retirement age should be set still higher. However, as the full retirement age rises, the gap between the early retirement age (still set at 62) and the full age increases, which results in a greater penalty for early retirement. Raising the retirement age—without compensating adjustments elsewhere in the system—acts as a de facto benefit cut for workers who retire before their full retirement age. In addition, some believe that raising the retirement age discriminates against those involved in manual labor and other occupations that take a physical toll on the body. Better-off workers in terms of health and longevity would have additional advantages over their less fortunate co-workers (Berkowitz 2003).

Another set of proposals to deal with the long-term funding problem involves making "technical adjustments" in the way initial benefits are computed and in how those benefits are subsequently increased to reflect increases in the inflation rate. By using different measures of wage growth and inflation, program costs could be reduced. All such proposals have the result of reducing benefits for both current and future program participants and in this manner, such "technical" adjustments decrease the funding shortfall (Berkowitz 2003).

As already noted, libertarian policy advocates, for example those at the Cato Institute who are in the vanguard of the privatization movement, hope to abandon the system altogether, preferring that the government not be in the business of providing social insurance to its citizens. For the scholars at Cato and similar policy advocates, the long-range solvency of Social Security functions less as a problem to be solved than as an opportunity to be seized to discredit the system entirely. Another frequently heard proposal calls for means-testing Social Security benefits. Suggestions to cut or eliminate benefits for wealthier participants have an intuitive appeal. Why should Bill Gates or David Rockefeller collect Social Security benefits when the system faces financing shortfalls? People on the other side of this question point to what might be called the political logic of Social Security: it is precisely because Social Security does not target its benefits to the poor that it has done so much to alleviate poverty and reduce economic insecurity for the nonwealthy (Skocpol 1995). To use standard insurance terms, means-testing benefits might produce an "adverse selection" situation in which higher income workers see the program as biased against them and lobby to be removed from the system—taking their payroll taxes with them.

Other reform proposals move in the opposite direction. The cap on the amount of annual earnings subject to Social Security payroll taxes stood at $106,800 in 2011. Some call for raising or even removing the cap in order to generate additional tax revenues, at least in the short term. The problem is that this action would also obligate the system to pay higher benefits for wealthier workers in the long term, thus offsetting some of the expected additional income. One solution to this problem involves "clawing back" some of the increase in benefits, not giving higher income workers the full benefit of their increased payroll taxes. This clawing back of benefits risks the creation of an "adverse selection" dilemma similar to the one that arises with direct means testing. In a complex policy system like Social Security, therefore, pushing in at one place invariably produces a bulge somewhere else.

In a fundamental sense, the immediate challenge for the Social Security system involves demographics. As the large post–World War II baby boom generation move into their retirement years, demands on the system will inevitably grow. As this demographic "bulge" works its way through the system, the ratio of current workers to beneficiaries will decline, making the system more costly and reducing relative income inflows. In the long run, this demographic "bulge" will dissipate, but it presents an acute challenge.

The Social Security system functions in a larger fiscal context that also will have a major influence on the program's future. The program operates as a transfer payment system: payroll taxes from current workers fund the benefits of current recipients. By law, payroll taxes collected beyond current needs must be invested in U.S. Treasury securities. To date, the Social Security Trust Funds have accumulated approximately $3 trillion in such securities, making the Social Security system the largest single holder of U.S. government debt. At the same time, the United States has been running increasingly larger annual deficits and has accumulated a massive public debt in excess of $15 trillion. The deficit/debt has become a major concern of policy-makers. Because the Social Security program is a major creditor, actions taken to address the government's fiscal condition might alter the balance of the Social Security Trust Fund and exacerbate the program's financing problems.

11 CONCLUSION

Many people recognize Social Security as a highly successful program, one that legitimized the receipt of government benefits among many Americans and changed the nature of old age in the United States by providing the elderly with a modicum of support. Although this success took many years to achieve, it has produced a large and costly program that has evolved into America's major antipoverty program. Some say that this program favors the elderly over other age groups and represents an inefficient and unfair form of government coercion. Others cite Social Security as one of the few successful examples of overcoming the antistatist bias in U.S. social policy and one of the best examples of the federal government's ability to undertake complex tasks. After more than 75 years, America clings to its Social Security program, but whether it will be sustained in the future or modified in a significant way remains a critical question for the future of U.S. social policy.

REFERENCES

* Indicates suggestion for further reading.

Altman, Nancy, and Marmor, Ted. 2009. "Social Security from the Great Society to 1980: Further Expansion and Rekindled Controversy." In Brian Glenn and Steven Teles eds., *Conservatism and American Political Development*. New York: Oxford University Press, 154–187.

*Béland, Daniel. 2005. *Social Security: History and Politics from the New Deal to the Privatization Debate*. Lawrence: University Press of Kansas.

Berkowitz, Edward D. 1987. *Disabled Policy: America's Programs for the Handicapped—A Twentieth Century Fund Report*. New York and London: Cambridge University Press.

Berkowitz, Edward D. 1991. *America's Welfare State: From Roosevelt to Reagan*. Baltimore, MD: Johns Hopkins University Press.

Berkowitz, Edward D. 2002. "Family Benefits in Social Security: A Historical Commentary." In Melissa M. Favreault et al., eds., *Social Security and the Family: Addressing Unmet Needs in an Underfunded System*. Washington, DC: Urban Institute Press, 19–46.

*Berkowitz, Edward D. 2003. *Robert Ball and the Politics of Social Security*. Madison: University of Wisconsin Press.

*Berkowitz, Edward D., and Larry DeWitt. 2009. "Social Security from the New Deal to the Great Society: Expanding the Public Domain." In Brian Glenn and Steven Teles eds., *Conservatism and American Political Development*. New York: Oxford University Press, 53–85.

Berkowitz, Edward D., and Larry DeWitt. 2009. "Social Security." In Paul Quirk and William Cunion, eds., *Governing America: Major Policies and Decisions of Federal, State, and Local Government*. New York: Facts on File, 809–819.

Berkowitz, Edward D., and Larry DeWitt. 2013. *The Other Welfare: Supplemental Security Income and the American Welfare State*. Cornell: Cornell University Press.

Campbell, Andrea. 2002. "Social Security, and the Distinctive Participation Patterns of Senior Citizens." *American Political Science Review* 96, no. 3 (September): 565–574.

*Campbell, Andrea. 2003. *How Policies Make Citizens*. Princeton, NJ: Princeton University Press.

Cates, Jerry R. 1983. *Insuring Inequality: Administrative Leadership in Social Security, 1935–1954*. Ann Arbor: University of Michigan Press.

Congressional Budget Office. 2010. "Social Security Policy Options." www.cbo.gov/doc.cfm?index=11580.

*Derthick, Martha. 1979. *Policymaking for Social Security*. Washington, DC: Brookings Institution.

*Derthick, Martha. 1990. *Agency under Stress: The Social Security Administration in American Government*. Washington, DC: Brookings Institution.

DeWitt, Larry. 2010. "The Decision to Exclude Agricultural and Domestic Workers from the 1935 Social Security Act." *Social Security Bulletin* 70 (4): 49–68.

*DeWitt, Larry, Daniel Béland, and Edward D. Berkowitz, eds. 2008. *Social Security: A Documentary History*. Washington, DC: Congressional Quarterly Press.

Ferrara, Peter, and Michael Tanner. 1998. *A New Deal for Social Security*. Washington, DC: Cato Institute.

Friedman, Milton. 2002. *Capitalism and Freedom: Fortieth Anniversary Edition*. Chicago: University of Chicago Press.

Hacker, Jacob. 2004. "Privatizing Risk without Privatizing the Welfare State: The Hidden Politics of Social Policy Retrenchment in the United States." *American Political Science Review* 98, no.2 (May): 243–260.

Harrington Meyer, Madonna. 2009. "Why All Women (and Most Men) Should Support Universal Rather Than Privatized Social Security." In Leah Rogne et al., eds., *Social Insurance and Social Justice*. New York: Springer, 149–164.

Herd, Pamela. 2005. "Reforming a Breadwinner Welfare State: Gender, Race, Class, and Social Security." *Social Forces* 83, no. 4 (June): 1365–1393.

Herd, Pamela, and Madonna Harrington Meyer. 2007. *Market Friendly or Family Friendly? The State and Gender in Old Age*. New York: Russell Sage Foundation.

Hendley, Alexa A., and Natasha F. Bilimora. 1999. "Minorities and Social Security: An Analysis of Racial and Ethnic Differences in the Current Program." *Social Security Bulletin* 62 (2): 59–64.

Lieberman, Robert. 1998. *Shifting the Color Line: Race and the American Welfare State*. Cambridge, MA: Harvard University Press.

Light, Paul Charles. 1994. *Still Artful Work: The Continuing Politics of Social Security Reform*. New York: McGraw Hill.

Lynch, Frederick R. 2011. *One Nation under AARP: The Fight over Medicare, Social Security, and America's Future*. Berkeley: University of California Press.

Mettler, Suzanne. 2011. *The Submerged State: How Invisible Government Policies Undermine American Politics*. Chicago: University of Chicago Press.

National Academy of Social Insurance. 2011. "Thankful for Three Key Social Security Insurance Programs That Kept Nearly 24.2 Million out of Poverty in 2010." www.nasi.org/discuss/2011/11/thankful-three-key-social-insurance-programs-kept-nearly-242.

Orloff, Ann Shola. 1993. "Gender and the Social Rights of Citizenship." *American Sociological Review* 58 (June): 303–328.

Pierson, Paul. 1994. *Dismantling the Welfare State: Reagan, Thatcher, and the Politics of Retrenchment*. Cambridge: Cambridge University Press.

Shesol, Jeff. 2010. *Supreme Power: Franklin Roosevelt vs. the Supreme Court*. New York: Norton.

Skocpol, Theda. 1995. *Social Policy in the United States: Future Possibilities in Historical Perspective*. Princeton, NJ: Princeton University Press.

SSA (Social Security Administration). 2011a. "Annual Statistical Supplement, 2011," table 4-B1. www.ssa.gov/policy/docs/statcomps/supplement/2011/4b.html#table4.b1.

SSA. 2011b. "Fact Sheet." www.ssa.gov/pressoffice/factsheets/basicfact-alt.pdf.

SSA. 2011c. "Social Security Is Important to Race." www.ssa.gov/pressoffice/factsheets/africanamer.htm.

SSA. 2012a. "Monthly Statistical Snapshot, December 2011." www.ssa.gov/policy/docs/quickfacts/stat_snapshot/.

SSA. 2012b. "Trust Fund Data, 2012." www.ssa.gov/cgi-bin/ops_period.cgi.

Tax Policy Center. 2011. "Historical Social Security Tax Rates." www.taxpolicycenter.org/tax facts/content/pdf/ssrate_historical.pdf.

Teles, Steven. 2007. "Conservative Mobilization against Entrenched Liberalism." In Paul Pierson and Theda Skocpol, eds., *Transformation of the American Polity*. Princeton, NJ: Princeton University Press, 160–188.

*Teles, Steven, and Martha Derthick. 2009. "Social Security from 1980 to the Present." In Brian Glenn and Steven Teles, eds., *Conservatism and American Political Development*. New York: Oxford University Press, 261–290.

U.S. Census Bureau. 2001. "America's Family and Living Arrangements: Population Characteristics." Report No. P20-537, June, pp. 6–7, 9–10.

Weaver, R. Kent. 1988. *Automatic Government: The Politics of Indexation*. Washington, DC: Brookings Institution.

Zelizer, Julian E. 1998. *Taxing America: Wilbur D. Mills, Congress, and the State, 1945–1975*. Cambridge: Cambridge University Press.

CHAPTER 16

···

PRIVATE PENSIONS

···

TERESA GHILARDUCCI

1 INTRODUCTION

···

LIKE health care, retirement pensions in the United States are a complicated mix of public and private elements. Although Social Security is the best-known and most important pension program, it was never intended to be the sole source of retirement income. Many individuals are also expected to have pensions from their employers. Employer-provided pensions did not spring forth from the brains of employers as Athena sprung forth from Zeus's head. Nor does the government mandate that all employers provide retirement plans in addition to Social Security. Instead, employer pensions in the United States are voluntary, expressed in collective and individual labor contracts, highly regulated, and highly subsidized through favorable federal and state tax treatment of contributions and earnings. Between 1950 and 1979, the share of all employees who have any kind of pension plan at work more than doubled from 25 percent to 60.5 percent, and then the share stagnated. In the most recent decade, private sector pension coverage declined precipitously. The share of workers whose employers' sponsor any type of retirement plan, a defined benefit or defined contribution plan, fell from a high of 60.5 percent in 2000 to a low of 50.9 percent in 2010 for workers ages 25–64 (SSA 2008; Gale 1998).[1]

Incomplete retirement plan coverage matters; it portends a retirement income crisis (Eisenbrey 2010). Declining sponsorship and subsequent low participation rates will mean higher rates of poverty and inequality among retirees. Even when people are covered by a plan, many do not have sufficient savings. The median 401(k) plan balance for a near retiree, for example, is currently less than $52,000. The Center for Retirement Research (Munnell, Webb, and Golub-Sass 2010) at Boston College calculates that a growing share of working-age households are at risk of being unable to maintain their preretirement standard of living in retirement. Roughly one-half of households who are near retirement now, ages 50–64, will likely not have enough income to maintain their living standards in retirement at age 65. When health care and long-term care costs are included, the share of households "at risk" increases to 65 percent.

The unprecedented decline in pension coverage in the United States presents a paradox because recent trends indicate that employer retirement plan coverage should have increased. First, workers are much older, and older workers value employer pensions and health insurance more than younger workers do. (The average age of workers was 38.3 years in 1980, rising to over 48 years of age in 2010.) Second, defined contribution (DC) plans, mostly 401(k) plans, have grown in use and popularity as the tax expenditures for these plans have grown (Office of Management and Budget 2010). And third, confidence in Social Security has weakened as political elites discuss its uncertain financial future and possible future benefit cuts (Ghilarducci 2008). Fears about Social Security, by itself, should have increased retirement savings incentives and actual retirement savings.

On balance, other factors outbalanced, or overwhelmed, the trends favoring expansion. Declining unionization is chief among the factors explaining the decline in employer pension coverage.

2 ORIGINS AND DEVELOPMENT OF EMPLOYER-PROVIDED PENSIONS

In the late nineteenth century, management employees and soldiers were the only groups routinely covered by a pension plan at work. Many private-sector family-owned firms also provided pensions, but they were more informal. Otherwise, some employers provided pensions to their rank-and-file workers when they unionized or threatened to unionize (Sass 1997; Ghilarducci 2008).

As described elsewhere in this volume, the first stable pension plans in America were for Union-side soldiers and their beneficiaries in the Civil War. (Revolutionary War officers were given lump-sum pensions for service, and many of the other postservice payments to members of the armed forces before the Civil War were for disability.) The first civil-service pensions for public employees were established in several states about the time of World War I. The real expansion of pensions to nonmilitary and nonpublic sector workers started when the American labor movement bargained for pensions after World War I (Clark, Lee, and Wilson 2003). More than three hundred pension plans, covering 15 percent of the workforce, had been established by 1919. Coverage, however, was quite uneven. By 1924, just four firms—two railroads plus AT&T and U.S. Steel—covered one-third of all pension-plan participants. Moreover, working for a firm that offered pensions did not mean one would ever receive a pension. In these early years most workers died or left the firms they worked for before the age of compulsory retirement— age sixty at many firms. Rank-and-file workers were less likely to ever receive a benefit than were management employees.

From the 1900s to the 1920s, the largest American corporations adopted welfare capitalism programs, which are employee benefits that supplement or serve as social insurance and thus replaces income for workers who lose wages because of sickness, superannuation, and other factors that prevent work. Firms adopted these programs as tactics in their strategies to maximize profits and minimize labor costs while attracting and retaining the best employees (Esping-Andersen 1990). They also created personnel management departments that were linked to wide-ranging efforts to rationalize the work process, pay, recruitment, and promotion. Then, as now in the second decade of the twenty-first century, employers used pensions as personnel devices designed to maximize profits by minimizing the costs of maintaining a productive workforce. Pensions were (and are) used to attract, retain, and ease the leave-taking of the right employees at the right time. The optimal pension plan from the employer's point of view balanced the potentially conflicting objectives of making some employees loyal while encouraging others to leave.

In the 1920s, the few single-company plans that had existed for 30 or so years became more mature and more expensive. Consequently, many employer-based pension plans disappeared during the 1930s Depression. Thirteen international union pension funds collapsed; only four survived after World War II. Public-sector worker plans, such as those for New York City employees, fared better. The creation of Social Security in 1935, despite the insurance companies' opposition based on their fears that the program would diminish the demand for their products, cemented the idea of a legitimate retirement and created a base from which unions and employers would later build employer pension plans.

Employer pensions rebounded in the 1940s. The growth of pensions was aided not only by the end of the Depression, but also by unintended effects of macroeconomic policy during World War II. Wage and price control policies adopted during the war had to solve two problems, inflation and profiteering. Defense and related firms, desperate for workers, were bidding up wages and putting pressure on prices. Some of these same firms were also making enormous and politically unsavory profits from the war. Congress passed four excess profits statutes between 1940 and 1943.[2] President Roosevelt created the War Labor Board in 1942 in order to develop a "comprehensive national economic policy" to control prices, wages, and profits. The Board controlled prices to ensure that profits were not "unreasonable or exorbitant." In a boost to pensions, the Board deemed that money spent on employee benefits (e.g., pensions, health insurance, vacation benefits) was exempt from wage and price controls. The Board reasoned that because this form of payment did not cause labor costs to rise immediately nor put money in people's pockets, inflation would not spike (Ghilarducci 2008; Sass 1997).

The U.S. government used other tools to encourage and shape private pensions during this time. Since the 1920s, the government had given favorable tax treatment to employer pensions, provided that companies did not offer pensions solely to top managers. These "nondiscrimination" rules were developed further during the war, and the expansion of the income tax to finance World War II made favorable tax treatment even more valuable. The courts also played a key role. Companies often wanted to offer pensions, but did not want to enter into contracts about how to pay pensions. In the late

1940s and 1950s, Supreme Court decisions sided with unions against employers and made pensions subject to collective bargaining, similar to wages, hours, and working conditions (Ghilarducci 2008; Sass 1997).

Unions were in a good position to bargain for pensions after the War. Membership was near its historic peak, and many employers did not have to worry about stiff international competition for their goods and services. It was no coincidence that company pensions spread at a time when the labor movement was relatively strong and could influence wages, hours, and working conditions throughout the economy.

The American labor movement shaped employer pension design and retirement policy, as well as retirement expectations. Union contracts throughout the years have strengthened traditional pension plans, called defined benefit plans, and in the last two decades unions have negotiated 401(k) supplements (defined contribution plans) to those defined benefit plans. (Almost all defined contribution plans are 401(k) plans; profit sharing plans; money purchase plans; individual retirement accounts; and 403(b) plans, which are 401(k) plans for employees in the public sector.)

The union' effect is strongest for workers most at risk of not having a pension. The decline in union influence over wages, benefits, and working conditions is imperfectly measured by the portion of the labor force (public and private) represented by unions, which fell from 35 percent to less than 11.3 percent from 1953 to 2011. A decline in unions means a decline in pensions and a decline in defined benefit plans in particular. Union membership has declined since the 1950s, but the decline in power and influence over key employment contracts accelerated in the 1980s and 1990s. Unions consolidated power in key industries—auto and steel—in the 1950s and 1960s and negotiated pensions and health insurance plans. That ability waned with weakened enforcement of labor law and import penetration (Western and Rosenfeld 2011).

Unions supported the expansion of the employer pension system and, for the most part—especially the United Auto Workers—ushered in the major regulatory framework to govern private-sector defined-benefit pension plans, Employee Retirement Income Security Act (ERISA) in 1974 (Wooten 2004). In 1978, section "k" was added to the 401 section of the income tax code that allowed a new legal, tax-advantaged means of saving for retirement, and employers readily adopted it starting in 1980. Commonly known as 401(k) plans, they allow workers to defer income taxes on the portion of their salary they save for retirement. These employer-based individual retirement plans, along with individual retirement accounts (IRAs), are often collectively referred to as "defined contribution" plans since their balances at retirement are determined by the volume and size of the contributions to the plans, rather than by a predetermined benefit formula.

2.1 ERISA

The Employee Retirement Income Security Act of 1974 aimed to promote and maintain the defined-benefit pension system. ERISA established minimum standards for retirement plans (and for other employee trust plans such as health and other welfare benefit plans). ERISA rules and regulations of the fiduciaries for pension plans require detailed reporting and accountability to the federal government. ERISA defines parameters about how much employers have to fund a pension promise and how employees are considered eligible to be covered in the plan. Nevertheless, ERISA did not mandate that employers have a retirement plan. Both the House and Senate approved ERISA by overwhelming majorities. A larger share of Congressional Republicans supported ERISA than voted in favor of Social Security in 1935 (Wooten 2004).

The Act established the Pension Benefit Guaranty Corporation (PBGC)—a quasi-governmental agency—that pays for its operations by charging premiums to companies that sponsor defined-benefit pension plans. In exchange, the agency will take over the payments to retirees of a bankrupt company's pension up to an annual limit that usually covers most regular pensions. However, early retirement benefits are not covered, and the big losers in a PBGC-administered plan are long-service workers who lose their jobs in a bankruptcy before the age of 65. The Pension Benefit Guaranty Corporation also has the ability to terminate a pension plan before it becomes indebted during a troubled time leading up to bankruptcy. In the early 2000s, the PBGC, in a departure from its previous stance, aggressively terminated many defined-benefit pension plans in the airline industry because their projected liabilities were growing and the PBGC determined it needed to stem its losses (Wooten 2004).

3 How the Employer Pension System Works

Private pensions come in two basic forms, defined benefit (DB) and defined contribution (DC). The simplest definition of a DB plan is that the benefits payable to participants are predetermined by the plan's formula and are based on years of service and earnings. The employer contribution to a DB plan is mandatory. Most economists maintain that the cost of the employer contribution is ultimately paid by workers because employers reduce the wages and other benefits they would have paid in order to provide pensions (Baicker and Chandra 2006). When workers are covered by a DB plan, the employer uses an actuary to define the liabilities and the annual required contribution to pay off those liabilities in a process defined by ERISA.

When workers participate in a DC plan, the employer or employee (or both) pay into a tax-qualified retirement account; the employer contribution is optional. In DC plans, the contributions into an individual account are predetermined but not the benefits. Types of DC plans include money purchase, thrift and profit sharing, 403(b), 457 (which are basically 401(k) plans for people who work for governments and not-for-profit employers), and the largest category, the 401(k) plan. Despite the convenience of payroll deduction and expensive campaigns to educate workers about these plans—marketing campaigns by Fidelity, Smith-Barney, Charles Schwab ("ask Chuck")—the participation rate (which is not the coverage rate, but, rather, it is the people who elect to participate after they are covered) for 401(k)-eligible workers is still too low. This means that more than 50 percent of workers are not eligible to be in a 401(k) plan, and the eligibility rate is much lower for workers under age 40 (Ghilarducci 2008; Munnell and Sundén 2004; author's calculations from the Current Population Survey [CPS] 2012).

The best way of differentiating between DB and DC pensions is by determining who bears the risks. In a DB plan, the employer underwrites the vast majority of risk, so that if investment returns are poor or costs increase because people are living longer or more people retire than expected, the employer must find the needed revenue or somehow re-negotiate their pension obligations. In a defined contribution plan, the risks of poor investment returns or longer lifespans will be felt directly by workers.

Not surprisingly, then, employers have been moving away from DB and toward DC plans. Firms that led the way to DC conversions included PepsiCo, Northwest Airlines, and Bank One. One study found that employers who switched their funding to a DC plan away from a DB plan saved money from 1980 to 2006. A 10 percent increase in the employers' use of DC plans is associated with between a 1.7 percent and a 3.5 percent reduction in employers' pension costs per worker. One source of savings is that fewer workers chose to participate in DC plans. Therefore, taking into account how much DC plans, including 401(k) plans, have expanded, the average firm lowered its pension costs by more than 10 percent by adopting DC plans, or by expanding the DC plans that were already provided (Ghilarducci 2008, chap. 3).

Initially, unions enthusiastically accepted employers adding 401(k) plans to supplement the traditional DB plans. However, as employers sought to replace their DB plans by resisting improvement in the DB portion and adding more contributions to the DC portion, labor opposed 401(k) substitutions and in some instances negotiated switches from DC plans to DB plans. Unions eventually realized that substituting DC plans for DB plans was not a dollar for dollar substitution (more below) (Ghilarducci and Sun 2006).

Strictly speaking, employer pensions are not "private" pensions. They receive considerable funding from the U.S. government in the form of favorable tax treatment. The government spends indirectly over $140 billion in income taxes forgone (OMB 2010). All contributions and earnings on those contributions in DB plans, DC plans (including 401(k) plans), individual retirement accounts, and other retirement savings vehicles are eligible for this tax favoritism. Contributions to these plans and investment earnings on the contributions are not taxed; only the pensions paid out at retirement are taxed, but commonly at a much lower tax rate than when the employee was working.

The tax-favored treatment for retirement plans has been, until 2006, the largest of all categories of federal government tax expenditures. In 2011, taxes not collected on pension funds and contributions will be the federal government's second-largest tax expenditure (OMB 2010). Moreover, this tax expenditure is over and above the expense for Social Security and Medicare, further tilting the welfare state to the aged and also to upper income workers.

The value of pension tax expenditures varies substantially by income. Say, for example, that all workers save 10 percent of their income. A worker earning $20,000 per year is at the 15 percent tax bracket and receives a federal tax break, that is, a pension subsidy, worth 15 percent of his or her $2,000 pension contribution, equal to $300. In contrast, a worker earning $200,000 per year is at the 36 percent tax bracket, and, therefore, receives 36 percent of her pension contribution of $20,000, worth $7,200. This pattern is particularly evident in 401(k) plans because many lower-income workers contribute little or no money to them. Overall, the top 20 percent of taxpayers receive approximately 79 percent of the tax expenditures for retirement plans (Toder, Harris, and Lim 2010 Burman, Toder, and Geissler 2008; Burman et al. 2004). Given the growth of 401(k) plans, this skew in favor of the affluent will likely become more pronounced.

Much like tax breaks for health insurance, tax expenditures for pensions have enjoyed bipartisan support (Faricy 2011; Howard 2006, 2007). Democrats support these tax breaks in large part because of their historic ties to organized labor. Republicans can portray them as tax cuts, as subsidies for more affluent (and often more conservative) voters, and, in the case of pensions, as support for the financial services industry. However, Republicans, employers, and money managers have been much less enthusiastic about government regulation of pension funds. For instance, they fought hard to keep at bay legislation requiring 401(k) fee regulations. In 2007, 12 organizations submitted voluntary guidelines, arguing that mandated disclosure was unnecessary. "Our organizations believe the Department of Labor has both the statutory authority and institutional expertise to improve disclosure of fee information to participants without new legislation" (ICI 2007). The House Labor committee voted along party lines in favor of mandating fee disclosure in 2008, the Bush Administration was opposed, and the bill never made it to the floor. The next year Senator Harkin (D-IA) introduced the same bill and it died (see legal blogs at a website devoted to 401(k) fee disclosure, 401(k) Help Center http://www.401khelpcenter.com/cw/cw_planfees.html.)

3.1 Who Gets What from Employer Pensions

Currently, substantial numbers of retirees receive income from employer pensions. Among households with members over age 65 in 2001, the *median* present value of the future pension income stream, which we refer to as pension wealth, was only $10,700, having decreased by 69.3 percent from 1983. Since the distribution of retirement wealth is very skewed toward the top, the *mean* (i.e., average) present value of pension wealth is $105,400, and the *mean* is also increasing by 69 percent, which eerily mirrors the rate of decline in the pension wealth for the lower-paid median worker (Butrica, Iams, and Smith, 2003). As described earlier, about half of the current workers in the private sector are participating in an employer-sponsored retirement plan and three-fourths of Americans who are age 50–64 have annual incomes below $52,000 per year, which explains why the median retirement account balance is zero. The average account balance for all people in that age range, the near-retirees, is $15,837. The bottom

Table 16.1 Average and Median Retirement Account Balances in the U.S., (November 2010 for all people ages 50–64)

Total Personal Income Quartiles		All Retirement Accounts
Bottom 25th percentile (–$10,800)	Mean	$16,034
	Median	$0
25–50th percentile ($10,801–$27,468)	Mean	$21,606
	Median	$0
50–75th percentile ($27,469–$52,200)	Mean	$41,544
	Median	$6,500
75–100th percentile (More than $52,201)	Mean	$105,012
	Median	$52,000

Source: SIPP and author's calculations

three-fourths of near-retirees have retirement account balances of less than $16,000, and the top one-quarter, with incomes above $52,000, have a median balance of just $52,000 and an average balance of $105,012 (Table 16.1).

Typically, the account balances are reported for those workers with account balances, leaving out those with no balances. Most Americans (51 percent) nearing retirement have no private retirement accounts at all. Those with more income, the top one-fourth, are much more likely to have private retirement accounts. Only 23 percent in the top income group have none, whereas 77 percent of those Americans with incomes in the bottom fourth lack any pension besides Social Security.

Even if we ignore those people with zero balances, the picture is still troubling. The median and mean account balances are much higher, but still leave an inadequate amount for most Americans nearing retirement to comfortably supplement Social Security. The average retirement-account balance for those with incomes in the top quartile is $135,000, which yields a monthly annuity at 65 of about $1000 per month. This amount with Social Security would be well above poverty—about $1000 per month—but far too little to come near to replace 80 percent of their preretirement standard of living (Table 16.2).

3.2 Pension Coverage

Recall that only about half of current workers have a pension at work, and that number has been falling. The highest rates of coverage—workers in jobs where employers sponsor pension plans—are among public sector employers, and they have not fallen as much; over two-thirds of the 15 million workers in the public sector are covered. Note that *coverage rates* and *participation rates* are different. People who work for an employer who provides a DB pension plan or a DC pension plan are considered *covered*. But the actual participation rate is smaller. Many workers are not included in the pension plan, that is, they are not *participating*, either because they may not have met the threshold

Table 16.2 Average and Median Retirement Account Balances in the U.S. for Person with Nonzero Balances, as of November 2010

Total Personal Income Quartiles		All Retirement Accounts
Bottom 25th percentile (–$10,800)	Mean	$71,971
	Median	$30,000
25–50th percentile ($10,801–$27,468)	Mean	$61,232
	Median	$22,000
50–75th percentile ($27,469–$52,200)	Mean	$69,309
	Median	$36,100
75–100th percentile (More than $52,201)	Mean	$135,914
	Median	$90,000

Source: SIPP and author's calculations

for eligibility—over 20 hours per week or tenure, which is usually one year—or because they choose not to contribute to the defined contribution plan, most likely a 401(k).

Another way we can view the steady erosion of retirement income is through the rising income inequality among the elderly. Among current retirees, the average income of the richest 20 percent of 67-year-olds is almost double the average income of the bottom 20 percent (we used age 67 as a snap shot of the income distribution among the elderly because income falls as people age so we wanted a pure income distribution measure). By the time the late boomers (born between 1956 and 1963) are 67, the ratio of income for the top 20 percent to that of the bottom 20 percent will be 3.35 to 1; the top 20 percent will have three-and-one-third times more income (Butrica, Iams, and Smith 2003).

In the first part of the twenty-first century, workers with the lowest rates of pension coverage are nonunion, low-wage earners employed by small firms. Unions are a good route for all workers to get retirement plan coverage. Unionization doubles pension coverage rates for workers (private and public) earning in the bottom third of the earnings distribution from 30 percent to 62 percent, and in the middle third from 58 percent coverage to 82 percent. The reason why the coverage rates are higher than reported in the first section is because I am including private and public sector workers. (See Table 16.3)

4 RETIREMENT INCOME

4.1 Effects on Future Retiree Income and Elderly Poverty

In the United States, retirement income, in order of magnitude, comes from Social Security[3]; employer-provided pensions; personal savings and assets; earnings; and, to a very small extent, family networks and welfare. Employer plans and programs are a

Table 16.3 Union Workers in Small Firms Have More Pensions: Full Time Private and Public Sector Workers Working for Employers Who Sponsor a Pension, by firm size and income in 2010

	Not unionized with a pension	Unionized with a pension	Unionized and in Small Employers: Firm with 99 Employees or less with a pension
Low income (wage income $1–$24,999)	32%	60%	47%
Middle income ($25,000–$49,999)	58	52	69
High income ($50,000+)	73	88	76
Total	55%	87%	67%

Source: Author's calculations from the Current Population Survey (CPS)

key element in securing enough income in retirement. Social Security benefits are the predominant income source for retirees. Urban Institute economists Barbara Butrica, Howard Iams, and Karen Smith used a forecasting model and data on assets and retirement plan coverage to calculate the adequacy of pension income and future adequacy as cohorts age. Though the data are nine years old, their modeling was the most comprehensive. Since coverage has gotten worse and assets fell during the financial crises, the projections could not have improved. The results were sobering. In 2003, retired married men, aged 67, replaced 90 percent of their preretirement earnings; those who are now in their 40s are expected to replace only 81 percent when they reach 67, which is still adequate, but the security is falling. The decreases in the replacement rate (i.e., the part of income before retirement that is replaced by income during retirement) are worse for retired married women and unmarried men: their replacement rates fall 13 percentage points to 79 percent and 83 percent, respectively. Retired nonmarried women aged 67 replaced almost all of their income in 2003, but their counterparts in the mid-2020s are expected to replace only 83 percent (Butrica, Iams, and Smith 2003).

Many retirees have income from paid work while they identify themselves as retired—allowing for a bit of illogical identity! But the earnings from work by retirees, which helps offset the fall in preretirement income replacement rates, is not enough to make up for losses from pension income and Social Security income. In 2003, earnings to retired elderly households constituted 13 percent of their retirement income; earnings are expected to make up 17 percent in 2023. Between those same years, the share of retirement income from defined benefit pensions is projected to fall from 21 percent to 9 percent. The average preretirement income—or, more specifically, the income during the year immediately preceding retirement for married men who will be age 67 in 2027 (calculated in 2003)—is predicted to rise by 69 percent.

Preretirement income is a good measure of an accustomed standard of living for most researchers (Aon 2008). However, the retirement income of those retiring in 2027 is expected to be only 52 percent higher than the retirement income of those who retired at age 67 in 2003. Late-boomer women (born 1956–1963), who are not married at age 67, will have the most difficulty keeping their standard of living in retirement. Their pre-retirement income is expected to rise by 60 percent, but their retirement income will increase by only 37 percent (Butrica, Iams, and Smith 2003). Women are making improvements in obtaining employer pensions of their own, although the improvements are small, and women over age 65 will still suffer higher rates of poverty than men.

The good news in the United States regarding the income of elderly people, over the age of 65, is that it improved considerably since 1974, from almost 58 percent of the median income to people over the age of 15 to a whopping 75 percent two decades later (U.S. Census Bureau 2012). This is good news in part because it has been commonly accepted that the income needed in retirement is between 60 percent and 85 percent of preretirement income, depending on how high or low that income is (people with lower incomes need a higher percentage). The bad news is that, despite these trends, nearly one out of five elderly women is poor, and every elderly woman's chances of falling into poverty increases by 470 percent if she does not have a husband. That translates to 22.8 percent of nonmarried women falling below poverty level compared to about 4 percent of married women. Poverty rates for married women are predicted to be a low 2 percent in the mid-2020s. The predictions for never-married and divorced women in the mid-2020s are 11 percent and 15 percent, respectively.

Compared to the bad news on replacement rates, the predictions are mixed for the poverty rate. Large increases in the benefits from Social Security in the 1960s and 1970s helped elevate elderly households (households containing 67-year-olds and older) out of poverty—from 19 percent below the poverty level in the 1960s to 8 percent in 2003 (Butrica, Iams, and Smith 2003).

Ghilarducci, Saad-Lessler, Schmitz (2011) used the 2008 panel of the Survey of Income and Program Participation (SIPP) to make projections of vulnerability to poverty at age 65. These projections differ from others because they do not assume that the elderly will continue to work after retirement age (65). These estimates show what percentage of the elderly will have to face deprivation or supplement their incomes through work or other means. For workers aged 50–64 in 2010, when they reached age 65, 12.9 percent will have incomes at or below 100 percent the federal poverty line, and 35.3 percent will have incomes at or below 200 percent the federal poverty line. These projections indicate growing rates of poor and near-poor at retirement age; coupled with a growing elderly population, this trend would lead to large increases in economically vulnerable elders in the United States.

5 Current Challenges

The U.S. retirement income security system may fail to provide adequate and guaranteed retirement income for most workers. If current trends continue, the early baby boomers (born between 1946 and 1955) will be the last generation with more retirement security than their parents. Much of this shortfall comes about because almost half of workers do not have an employer-based retirement plan. This problem is widely known among public officials and experts, and yet it persists—despite the growth in advertising for retirement plans, despite a large and growing tax subsidy for retirement plans, and despite the aging of the workforce, which creates a pressing and acute demand for retirement accounts.

Clearly, the links between tax policy and retirement policy need to be changed. Rather than increasing savings, research suggests that current tax breaks mostly induce high-income households to shift savings they already have in financial assets that are taxed over to tax-favored accounts. A simple change, though a politically challenging one, is that the tax deduction for retirement-account savings could be converted to a tax credit of $600. A conversion to a credit from a deduction will not cost the government a cent over the cost of the current system. By rearranging the tax break for retirement savings, this fix could cover the 50 percent of American workers in 2010 who do not participate in an employer retirement plan. Because retirement plans are tax favored through deductions and not tax credits, the subsidy perversely subsidizes high-income individuals who can contribute the maximum—up to $46,000 (not including their employer contribution) on a tax-free basis. For higher income workers, that tax favoritism is worth over $7,000.

States could convert their tax deductions even if Congress doesn't move. Many states, like California and New York, copy federal tax policy. Workers earning the minimum wage or a bit more obtain nothing from the federal tax break because their income is too low to file taxes. If a worker does not participate in a pension plan, of course, he or she gets nothing from the federal program subsidizing pensions. The California tax expenditures for 401(k) plans cost $2.3 billion in 2010. If every California worker received a pension credit, $145 per year could be deposited in each employee's retirement account. This would be important seed money for the workers who need it most. In New York the conversion is worth $114 for each worker (SCEPA 2010; Schmitz 2012). A conversion to a tax credit of $600 would provide a universal subsidy and help solve the problem of chronic under accumulation.

The politics of pensions is often couched as intergenerational conflict, but in most cases the dynamic is one of capital- and labor-making deals when capital has more economic power. Labor, whether represented by public officials or unions, must make deals with firms who often have more bargaining power, whether it is to lower taxes or reduce environmental standards. The challenge for unions is to manage the inevitable intergenerational debate when the union agrees to pension cuts in order to save jobs. Hawthorne (2008) describes the deal the Unite-HERE union made in managing Cone Mills' bankruptcies as a choice between active workers and pensioners. This is a common but faulty analysis, in this case and others. In 2003, Cone management filed for bankruptcy; all future pension accumulations would be lost as well as American union jobs. To save the jobs, the union aligned with financier Wilbur Ross to buy the failing company, who then kept the union and dumped the DB plan. The union did not conspire against pensioners in favor of active workers (Hawthorne 2008, chap. 3)

Bankruptcy has become one way that traditional pensions are transformed into less costly 401(k) plans. What I call "intensive-care" bankruptcy (i.e., filing for reorganization under Chapter 11 rather than "death" bankruptcy, Chapter 7) has become a common way companies discharge traditional pension obligations onto the quasi-governmental insurance agency, the PBGC. When unions are present and the PBGC has to take over a DB plan, the two parties have been able to negotiate better terms. Examples are the airlines bankruptcies and the General Motors and Chrysler reorganizations, which greatly diminished or eliminated the traditional DB pension plans, but replaced them with 401(k) and hybrid plans that were more generous than the average 401(k) plan.

At bottom, the challenges for public policy are to increase individuals' retirement-account accumulations, help individuals manage their accumulations well, and direct accumulations to be paid out in an annuity. A specific policy proposal known as 'State Guaranteed Retirement Accounts" (Ghilarducci 2007; Government Accountability Office 2009; Ghilarducci 2011; Schmitz 2012) would have state legislators and governors create Guaranteed Retirement Accounts for private sector workers to be managed by state or local pension fund, such as California's large-scale public sector plans CalPERS and CalSTERS. The already existing financial infrastructure that manages pension investments—the government-fund apparatus—would help private-sector workers deposit their retirement savings, earn a safe return, and withdraw a stream of income for life.

This proposal seeks to meet the underfunding and pension design challenges by providing private sector workers more choice in retirement investment vehicles over and above employer 401(k) plans and IRAs, and to mandate that all employees be enrolled in low-risk personal retirement accounts managed by state-level public retirement institutions. In addition, state and local pension plans for their employees are united into one system, which helps achieve economies of scale—that is, the cost per person falls as the size of the system grows. The costs are lower than for commercial 401(k) accounts because the government pension plans are managed on a not-for-profit basis. In sum, the retirement income security challenge facing the nation can be met with mandating more pension savings with an advanced–funded individual retirement account tier sitting atop Social Security.

6 CONCLUSION

A shocking number of older workers are underprepared for retirement. Over a third of Americans approaching retirement age have less than $10,000 in liquid assets, which means at least 37 percent approaching retirement are projected to be poor or near poor in retirement. That translates into an average budget of about $7 per day for food and $600 a month for housing. In addition, working longer is becoming an unattractive option for strapped older people or retirees facing limited income. For the first time, older unemployed Americans remain unemployed longer than younger job seekers, even teenagers.

The Aon Consulting Group (2008) has been analyzing the needs of retirees since its first report for the President's Commission on Pension Policy in 1980. The plain math is that, in order to replace working income for retirement, people should save about 17 to 20 percent of their income. Let's count Social Security for 12 percent of that goal; thus, people need to save an extra 8 percent every pay period. Hardly anyone does; the retirement asset deficit has been estimated at $6 trillion. (And if they do, they are likely to withdraw from their pension during times of economic stress.) Aon shows that people who are 50 to 64 years old and earning $30,000 to $90,000 per year save between 2.8 and 5.6 percent of their income. If they saved consistently for the past 30 years, they would be fine at that savings rate. Given the minimal assets that people in this age group have accumulated, they should be saving, in some retirement vehicle, 33 to 45 percent. People need to have set aside the equivalent of 10–20 times their annual salary at retirement to adequately supplement Social Security. People who have contributed to a DB plan over 15–20 years of work likely have enough, but people with DC plans have less than two year's salary on average.

As the use of individual-retirement-account plans (DC plans or 401(k)-type plans) increases, an opposite and perverse relationship has developed between death and work. People with the lowest levels of education and income are being forced to work longer, which minimizes their retirement time because they also tend to die sooner. Higher-income workers who live longer accumulate more retirement income and can retire earlier because the federal and state governments heavily subsidize their retirement accounts with a top-heavy tax subsidy. The gap in retirement time by class will grow, reversing a remarkable achievement of the U.S. retirement system that, despite the increasing gaps in income, wealth, housing, and health, retirement time was converging between people in different socioeconomic classes.

The move away from company pensions in favor of pensions that rely on a workers' taking a "do-it-yourself" approach has failed. Such an approach relies on individuals to save for retirement from each pay check—regardless of a child's need, financial urgency, or tempting vacation. No developed or developing nation depends on its inhabitants making long-term plans to secure their retirement income without a great deal of institutional support (Burtless 2009).

A good retirement-income security system is comprehensive, provides adequate retirement income, and is administrated efficiently. The American pension system falls short on all four counts. Only 50 percent of workers have a pension at work—the best and most practical way to save for retirement. American workers do not save enough, and when they do they are restricted access to the best quality investment managers, appropriate portfolio structures, low fees, economies of scale, and cost effective annuities because of the growing use of defined contribution (DC) plans, such as a 401(k) plans, rather than a traditional defined benefit (DB) plan. In 401(k) plans, workers are not required to save consistently and often make lump sum withdrawals before and at retirement. Many American elderly will be near poor or poor and many current middle class workers will face downward mobility in retirement because of the lack of coverage of the employer based system, it has failed and bold public policy is needed to protect retirement for working Americans.

NOTES

1. Author's calculations from the 2001 and 2011 Current Population Survey, March Supplement.
2. Excess profits were usually defined in comparison to prewar levels.
3. In 2009, Social Security benefits constituted 58 percent of total retiree income and more than 85 percent of income for retirees in the lowest 40 percent of the income distribution. Social Security benefits represented more than one-third of income to retirees in the top 20 percent of the income distribution. Over the past 37 years, the share of retiree income from Social Security has averaged 53 percent (SSA 2010).

REFERENCES

*Indicates recommended reading.

*401(k) Help Center. N.d. http://www.401khelpcenter.com/cw/cw_planfees.html.

Aon Consulting. 2008. "The 2008 Replacement Ratio Study." http://www.aon.com/aboutaon/intellectual-capital/attachments/human-capital-consulting/RRStudy070308.pdf.

Baicker, Katherine, and Amitabh Chandra. 2006. "The Labor Market Effects of Rising Health Insurance Premiums." *Journal of Labor Economics*, 24 (3): 609–634. http://www.jstor.org/stable/10.1086/505049.

Burman, Leonard, Eric Toder, and Christopher Geissler. 2008. "How Big Are Total Individual Income Tax Expenditures, and Who Benefits from Them?" Tax Policy Center Discussion Paper No. 31 (December). www.taxpolicycenter.org/UploadedPDF/1001234_tax_expenditures.pdf.

Burman, Leonard E., William G. Gale, Matthew Hall, and Peter R. Orszag. 2004. "Distributional Effects of Defined Contribution Plans and Individual Retirement Accounts." Tax Policy Center Discussion Paper No. 16 (August). www.taxpolicycenter.org/UploadedPDF/311029_TPC_DP16.pdf.

Burtless, Gary. 2009. "Financial Market Turbulence and Social Security Reform." In Mitchell Orenstein, ed., *Pensions, Social Security and the Privatization of Risk*. New York: Columbia University Press.

Butrica, Barbara A., Howard M. Iams, and Karen Smith. 2003. "It's All Relative: Understanding the Retirement Prospects of Baby Boomers." Center for Retirement Research at Boston College. Available at http://www.bc.edu/crr.

Butrica, Barbara A., Howard M. Iams, Karen E. Smith, and Eric J. Toder. 2009. "The Disappearing Defined Benefit Pension and Its Potential Impact on the Retirement Incomes of Boomers." Center for Retirement Research, WP#2009-2 (January). http://crr.bc.edu/working_papers/the_disappearing_defined_benefit_pension_and_its_potential_impact_on_the_retirement_incomes_of_boomers.html.

Butrica, Barbara A., Howard M. Iams, Karen E. Smith, and Eric J. Toder. 2009. "The Disappearing Defined Benefit Pension and Its Potential Impact on the Retirement Incomes of Baby Boomers." *Social Security Bulletin* (69): 3.

*Center for Retirement Research. 2010. "National Retirement Risk Index." http://crr.bc.edu/special-projects/national-retirement-risk-index/.

Clark, Robert Louis., Lee A. Craig, and Jack W. Wilson. 2003. *A History of Public Sector Pensions in the United States*. Philadelphia: University of Pennsylvania Press

Eisenbrey, Ross. 2010. "The Wobbly Stool: Retirement (In)security in America." Testimony before the U.S. Senate, Health, Education, Labor and Pensions Committee. http://help.sen ate.gov/imo/media/doc/Eisenbrey.pdf.

Esping-Andersen, G. 1990. *The Three Worlds of Welfare Capitalism*. Princeton, NJ: Princeton University Press.

Faricy, Christopher. 2011. "The Politics of Social Policy in America: The Causes and Effects of Indirect versus Direct Social Spending." *Journal of Politics* 73: 74–83.

Gale, William G. 1998. "The Effects of Pension on Household Wealth: A Reevaluation of Theory and Evidence." *The Journal of Political Economy* 106, no. 4. (August): 706–723.

GAO (Government Accountability Office). 2009. "Alternative Approaches Could Address Retirement Risks Faced by Workers but Pose Trade-Offs." http://www.gao.gov/new.items/d09642.pdf.

Ghilarducci, Teresa. 2007. "Guaranteed Retirement Accounts." Economic Policy Institute Briefing Paper No. 204. http://www.sharedprosperity.org/bp204.html.

*Ghilarducci, Teresa. 2008. *When I'm Sixty-four: the Plot Against Pensions and the Plan to Save Them*. Princeton, NJ: Princeton University Press.

Ghilarducci, Teresa. 2011. "High Performance Pensions for All Californians." In Nari Rhee, ed., *Meeting California's Retirement Security Challenge*. Berkeley: UC Berkeley Center for Labor Research and Education.

Ghilarducci, Teresa, Joelle Saad-Lessler, and Lauren Schmitz. 2012. "Are New Yorkers Ready for Retirement." Schwartz Center for Economic Policy Analysis. http://comptrollernyc.com/rsnyc/pdf/RetReadiness_Summary_v15.pdf.

Ghilarducci, Teresa, and Wei Sun. 2006. "How Defined Contribution Plans and 401(k)s Affect Employer Pension Costs." *Journal of Pension Economics and Finance* 5: 175–196.

Hawthorne, Fran. 2008. *Pension Dumping: The Reasons, the Wreckage, the Stakes for Wall Street*. New York: Bloomberg Press.

Howard, Christopher. 2006. *The Welfare State Nobody Knows: Debunking Myths about U.S. Social Policy*. Princeton, NJ: Princeton University Press.

Howard, Christopher. 2007. "The Haves and the Have Lots: The American Welfare State Is Bigger Than You Think, and More Unfair Than You'd Want." *Democracy: a Journal of Ideas* (Spring): 48–58.

ICI (Investment Company Institute). 2007. "Fee and Expense Disclosures to Participants in Individual Account Plans." Letter to the Department of Labor. July 24. http://www.ici.org/pressroom/speeches/ci.07_dol_401k_joint_com.print.

*Munnell, Alicia H., and Annika Sundén. 2004. *Coming Up Short: The Challenge of 401(k) Plans*. Washington, DC: Brookings Institution Press.

Munnell, Alicia, Anthony Webb, and Francesca Golub-Sass. 2009. "The National Retirement Risk Index: After the Crash." Center for Retirement Research at Boston College, October, Report No. 9-22. http://www.oecd.org/dataoecd/2/27/46263009.pdf.

OMB (Office of Management and Budget). 2010. *Analytical Perspectives on the Federal Budget.* http://www.whitehouse.gov/sites/default/files/omb/budget/fy2010/assets/spec.pdf.

Schmitz, Lauren. 2012. "How Policymakers and State Pension Funds Can Help Prevent the Coming Retirement Income Crisis." 64th Annual Meeting of the Labor and Employment Relations Association: Proceedings of a Meeting held January 6–8. Chicago, University of Illinois, Labor and Employment Relations Association.

*Sass, Steven A. 1997. *The Promise of Private Pensions: The First Hundred Years.* Cambridge, MA: Harvard University Press.

SSA (Social Security Administration). 2008. "Income of the Population 55 and Older." http://www.ssa.gov/policy/docs/statcomps/income_pop55/

SCEPA (Schwartz Center for Economic Policy Analysis). 2010. "Backgrounder for Tax Expenditures." http://www.economicpolicyresearch.org/images/docs/research/retirement_security/WP%202012-2%20Lauren%20Schmitz.pdf.

*Toder, Eric J. Benjamin, H. Harris, and Katherine Lim. 2010. "Distributional Effect of Tax Expenditures." Schwartz Center for Economic Policy Analysis. http://www.urban.org/UploadedPDF/411922_expenditures.pdf.

U.S. Census Bureau. 2012. "Historical Tables on Income." http://www.census.gov/hhes/www/income/data/historical/people/.

Western, Bruce, and Jake Rosenfeld. 2011. "Unions, Norms, and the Rise in U.S. Wage Inequality." *American Sociological Review* 76 (August): 513–537.

Wooten, James. 2004. *A Legislative and Political History of ERISA of 1984.* Berkeley: University of California Press.

CHAPTER 17

....

MEDICARE

....

JONATHAN OBERLANDER

1 INTRODUCTION

MEDICARE is America's federal health-insurance program for the elderly and younger adults with permanent disabilities. It provides a crucial measure of security, assuring access to medical care for nearly 50 million persons and contributing to their "improved health and quality of life" (Moon and Davis 1995, 31). Medicare helps pay for hospital stays, physician services, prescription drugs, home healthcare, and much more—vital assistance given the staggering costs of medical care and complex health needs of its beneficiaries. Medicare is a program that almost all American families come to rely on— it is a foundation of the welfare state and a secure retirement.

Medicare also has a major impact on the healthcare system and the federal budget. As the single largest purchaser of medical services in the United States, Medicare represents an important source of income for hospitals, physicians, and other medical providers. Medicare supports graduate medical education through funding for physician training programs and pays supplemental funds to hospitals serving a disproportionate share of low-income patients (NASI 1999). Changes made in Medicare policy reverberate throughout American medical care.

Medicare spending currently comprises about 20 percent of national healthcare expenditures and 14 percent of the federal budget (KFF 2010). In 2013, the federal government spent $590 billion on Medicare, and its costs are expected to climb much higher in the coming years. Medicare consequently stands at the center of debates over how to contain healthcare spending and reduce the federal deficit. It is a crucial front in broader partisan and ideological conflicts over health reform and the welfare state. Debates over the program are likely to intensify against the backdrop of population aging, budget pressures, partisan polarization, and healthcare reform.

This chapter provides an overview of how Medicare works, its political dynamics, and policy challenges. I begin by sketching Medicare's origins and its development over the past five decades. Next, I summarize Medicare's mechanics, including who it covers, what benefits it provides, and how it is financed. I then examine key themes in Medicare politics, including the influence of interest groups and erosion of bipartisanship. Finally, I discuss political and fiscal challenges to Medicare, and possible directions for program reform.

2 ORIGINS

Medicare's historical roots lie in 20th century fights over healthcare reform. From 1915 through the 1940s, American reformers tried unsuccessfully to follow the path of European nations that had established national health insurance systems. In 1945, Harry Truman became the first president to propose a government health-insurance plan for all Americans. Stymied by the conservative coalition of Republicans and Southern Democrats in Congress, the fierce resistance of the American Medical Association (AMA), which represented physicians, the Cold War stigma of "socialized medicine," and the president's reluctance to fight harder for reform, the Truman administration failed to secure passage of national health insurance (Blumenthal and Morone 2009; Harris 1966; Marmor 1973; Starr 1982).

By 1949, administration officials were searching for an alternative reform strategy. Medicare emerged as that alternative, conceived as a more pragmatic path to adopting federal health insurance. The original Medicare proposal in 1951 called for 60 days of hospital insurance for elderly retirees receiving Social Security benefits. The substantive case for the government to cover the elderly was compelling. Although seniors required more medical services than younger populations, their uninsurance rate was much higher and they had much lower incomes. In 1962, at a rate far above the national average, 47 percent of elderly families had incomes below the poverty line, (Moon 2006, 47). Once retirees left employer-sponsored health insurance, they had trouble obtaining coverage since insurers saw them as bad (expensive) risks. Before Medicare's enactment, only about half of seniors had any insurance coverage at all (Marmor 1973). Many of those policies had limited benefits: in 1963, only 25 percent of America's seniors had meaningful health coverage (Finkelstein 2005).

Still, the primary rationale for focusing on the elderly was political. By limiting federal health insurance to the aged, reformers hoped to improve health reform's legislative prospects (Marmor 1973). Reformers intended to draw on seniors' sympathetic image as a population deserving of government assistance to overcome American cultural ambivalence about social welfare programs and to dampen fears of socialized medicine (Jacobs 1993). By initially limiting benefits to 60 days of hospital coverage, Medicare's advocates hoped to moderate the opposition of their most formidable opponent, organized medicine. By tying the program to Social Security, they hoped to build on the program's familiarity and popularity, while emulating the social- insurance philosophy and arrangements considered key to its success.

Workers would establish their eligibility for Medicare through compulsory payroll tax contributions; the connection to work reinforced the perception that enrollees deserved their benefits. Medicare benefits were to be viewed as an earned right, not a handout. Medicare's supporters wanted to avoid the political and social stigmas that charity and welfare evoked, so Medicare would not impose a means test to restrict eligibility to the poor (Ball 1995; Marmor 1973). Medicare's universalism and mandatory financing ensured that it would have a broad pool of enrollees across which to spread risk, a critical requirement of a stable health insurance program. As with Social Security, Medicare payroll tax revenues would be dedicated to a federal trust fund that advocates believed would safeguard program finances from political intervention.

The Medicare strategy was one of incrementalism, shaped by the Truman plan's defeat and the constraints of American politics, including public ambivalence about government power and a fragmented political system that complicated efforts to pass major reform legislation through Congress. As Robert Ball, one of the program's key architects later explained, "insurance for the elderly [was] a fallback position, which we advocated solely because it seemed to have the best chance politically" (Ball 1995, 62–63). The strategy worked, but not immediately. The same sides that had earlier fought over national health insurance re-formed, with liberals and labor unions supporting Medicare (union-affiliated seniors groups joined the fray), and conservatives, business groups, and organized medicine opposing it (Marmor 1973). AMA president David Allman declared in 1957 that the Medicare proposal "is at least nine parts evil to one part sincerity" and "the beginning of the end of the private practice of medicine" (JAMA 1957, 2090). Ronald Reagan famously warned in a 1962 AMA recording that if Medicare passed, then a slippery slope of socialism would surely follow, as "behind it will come other federal programs that will invade every area of freedom as we have known it in this country" (quoted in Morone 1990, 262).

Although Medicare attracted considerable support in Congress, it could not overcome the opposition of the conservative coalition and Arkansas Democrat Wilbur Mills, chair of the powerful House Ways and Means committee. The 1964 elections, which produced a landslide victory for President Lyndon Johnson and brought overwhelming Democratic Party majorities to both the House of Representatives and Senate, transformed Medicare's political fortunes. Johnson pushed immediately for Medicare's enactment and Mills acquiesced. Indeed, Mills orchestrated, with Johnson's support, a major, unanticipated expansion of the program. Mills worried that Medicare's limited benefits package would disappoint seniors and, by adding coverage for physician services on his terms, he sought to preempt any future efforts to liberalize program benefits by raising Social Security payroll taxes. The 1965 law also created Medicaid, a program for low-income Americans that Mills hoped would forestall pressures to expand Medicare into a broader system of national health insurance (Marmor 1973; Blumenthal and Morone 2009).

Only one year after its enactment, Medicare was up and running, with 19 million beneficiaries enrolled and broad participation of hospitals and doctors secured. Medicare's impressive takeoff reflected the Social Security Administration's (SSA) administrative excellence, political skills, and flexibility. The Medicare statute authorized the SSA to contract with private insurers to handle Medicare claims processing and payment. The SSA had no experience with health insurance, so program officials believed that contracting with private organizations was essential to launching Medicare quickly. The arrangement had the additional benefit of reassuring medical providers that they would work with private sector intermediaries, rather than directly with the government.

Medicare had a dramatic impact on seniors' medical care burdens, reducing out-of-pocket costs substantially for elderly Americans who used the most services (Finkelstein and McKnight 2005). Medicare's contribution to beneficiaries' health remains powerful today; previously uninsured adults with serious health conditions increase their utilization of medical services after entering Medicare, and Medicare eligibility is associated with a lower death rate among very sick elderly patients admitted to the hospital (McWilliams et al. 2007; Card, Dobkin, and Maestas 2007).

Medicare's implementation also had important effects beyond seniors' medical care. As a condition of receiving federal payment, hospitals had to certify that they were not discriminating on the basis of race. Social Security administrators aggressively enforced this requirement, which compelled many hospitals to admit black patients. Medicare thus helped promote desegregation of hospitals in the South (Smith 1999; NASI 2001; Quadagno 2006).

3 MEDICARE'S EVOLUTION

In 1972 Medicare expanded to cover persons receiving Social Security Disability Insurance (SSDI) and patients with end-stage renal disease (ESRD). Medicare's administrators had anticipated, given the program's close links to Social Security, extending coverage to SSDI enrollees. The addition of ESRD patients to Medicare had a more peculiar genesis (Rettig 1991). Dialysis emerged in the 1960s as a life-saving technology. The question was how to guarantee access to this vital medical procedure in a country that lacked national health insurance. Medicare became the home for dialysis largely because it provided an available federal program into which dialysis could be folded—a development emblematic of the inchoate character of the American health-care system.

Although the additions of nonelderly Americans with permanent disabilities and kidney disease broadened Medicare's reach, program architects had grander ambitions. They envisioned Medicare as a first step, the cornerstone of national health insurance. The goal was to establish federal health insurance for the elderly and then eventually expand it to cover the rest of the population, with children next in line (Ball 1995). That plan never came close to fruition. The political prospects of national health insurance faded as American politics shifted rightward in the 1970s and 1980s. Vietnam, Watergate, and economic stagflation eroded public trust in government. Meanwhile, Medicare's rising costs—from its earliest days, critics labeled it a "runaway program"—meant that issues of cost control rather than expansion dominated the policy agenda (Oberlander 2003; Brown and Sparer 2003). Intermittent trust-fund crises and warnings about approaching insolvency plagued Medicare, further cementing policy makers' preoccupation with controlling spending and diminishing any chance to realize "Medicare for All."

Rising costs helped defuse pressures to expand Medicare benefits. Medicare's original benefit package changed little during the program's first two decades of operation (Schlesinger and Wetle 1988; Oberlander 2003). In 1988, Congress enacted the Medicare Catastrophic Coverage Act (MCCA), which liberalized the program's limited hospital benefits, capped the amount that beneficiaries had to pay out of their own pockets for other Medicare-covered services, and added coverage of outpatient prescription drugs. However, the MCCA's financing arrangements—including a surtax on higher-income beneficiaries—triggered fierce resistance from many seniors who already had supplemental insurance coverage (Himmelfarb 1995). Medicare beneficiaries' confusion about the scope of both the law's benefits and surtax, amplified by misleading attacks from interest groups, further fueled opposition to catastrophic health insurance.

Congress repealed the MCCA in 1989, and Medicare benefits remained largely static until the 2003 Medicare Prescription Drug, Improvement and Modernization Act (MMA). The MMA again added outpatient prescription drug coverage to Medicare, albeit through a bizarre benefit design—the government initially covered 75 percent of medication costs up to $2250 of expenditures, after which beneficiaries fell into a "doughnut hole" where coverage stopped completely, only to start up again after $5100 of expenses (Moon 2006; Oliver, Lee, and Lipton 2004). In addition, the MMA substantially increased payments to private insurance plans that contract with Medicare to serve program beneficiaries. The MMA's enhanced payments were designed to ramp up beneficiaries' enrollment in private insurance, an aim that 1997 legislation had tried and failed to accomplish.

The most important changes in Medicare since 1980 arguably have been reforms to slow program spending. Medicare initially paid providers for their costs and charges generously, retrospectively, and with little oversight. The 1965 Medicare statute declared that "Nothing in this title shall be construed to authorize any Federal officer or employer to exercise any supervision or control over the practice of medicine or the manner in which medical services are provided..." (quoted in Oberlander 2003, 109). Medicare's payment rules emulated lenient policies employed by private insurers at the time. Controlling healthcare spending was not a public or private policy issue in 1965, and Medicare officials saw the program's primary goal as ensuring that seniors had access to mainstream medicine (Marmor 1988). "There was," explained Robert Ball, "overwhelming political agreement that Medicare did not have a mission to reform delivery of, or payment for, medical care" (NASI 2001, 2).

Medicare's permissive reimbursement system and promise not to interfere with prevailing medical arrangements also represented a political accommodation to hospitals and doctors. Medicare's first administrators were determined to show that federal health insurance could work. Mindful of the AMA's intense opposition to the law and the threat of doctors' strikes, they sought to assure the cooperation of the medical care industry through, in part, generous payments for Medicare patients (Brown 1985; Derthick 1979; Feder 1977). Permissive payment policies were a political price paid to mollify medical providers and assure Medicare a smooth start.

Rising budget deficits eventually rendered Medicare's original inflationary bargain untenable. In 1983, Congress adopted the Prospective Payment System (PPS) for hospitals. Under PPS, the federal government established in advance what it would pay hospitals for inpatient care according to a Medicare patient's diagnosis, giving Congress a powerful new lever to produce budgetary savings. Then, in 1989, Congress adopted the Medicare Fee Schedule, which similarly set predetermined payment rates for physician services (Smith 1992). As part of the 1997 Balanced Budget Act, federal policy makers further extended prospective payment to home health, skilled nursing-facility, and hospital-outpatient services, completing Medicare's transformation away from retrospective reimbursement, and underscoring Medicare's "subordination to fiscal policy" (Mayes and Berenson 2006, 104).

Medicare's new cost containment policies proved effective in slowing the rate of growth in program spending. Excess cost growth per Medicare beneficiary (growth beyond general inflation and demographic changes) declined from an average annual rate of 5.6 percent during 1975–1983 to 2.1 percent during 1992–2003 and 0.5 percent during 1997–2005 (White 2008).

4 MEDICARE AND HEALTHCARE REFORM

The 2010 Patient Protection and Affordable Care Act (ACA) expanded Medicare benefits. It gradually fills in the infamous "doughnut hole" in prescription drug coverage over the next decade and enhances Medicare's coverage of preventive care, eliminating beneficiary cost-sharing for recommended screenings. The ACA additionally reduces projected Medicare spending, alters the program's financing system, establishes a new independent board to develop policies to further slow program expenditures, and uses Medicare as a platform to experiment with a variety of reforms in how medical care is delivered and paid for—changes discussed in detail later in the essay.

The ACA was significant as well for what it did not do, namely establish a Medicare-like government insurance program for Americans under age 65. The so-called "public option" emerged as a major reform goal for liberals during 2009–2010 (Hacker 2009) but it failed, even in limited form, to clear the Senate. So, too, did a compromise plan that would have expanded Medicare by enabling persons age 55–64 to buy into the program. These proposals' defeat underscores the fact that, for all its successes, Medicare has not realized the original expectations that it would evolve into a full-fledged system of national health insurance.

5 How Medicare Works

Medicare is open to all Americans age 65 and over who receive Social Security retirement benefits. Unlike means-tested programs such as Medicaid that are limited to lower-income persons, Medicare has a universalist philosophy for the elderly. There is no income or assets test for Medicare eligibility. American citizens and permanent residents who are not eligible through Social Security can buy into the program, and state Medicaid programs typically pay for some low-income seniors to join Medicare. In practice, Medicare covers about 98 percent of all persons age 65 and older. Seniors not covered by Medicare include American citizens who have not worked long enough to qualify for Social Security and unauthorized immigrants (Birnbaum and Patchias 2010; Moon 2006).

In addition to elderly Social Security beneficiaries, Medicare covers nonelderly persons with permanent disabilities who have received Social Security Disability Insurance for two years. Medicare's crucial role in covering this population "is often overlooked" (Cubanski and Neuman 2010: 1725). The two-year waiting period creates significant problems for persons with disabilities—about one-third of them go without any health insurance during this time (Moon 2006), though the 2010 health reform law will increase their access to coverage. The nonelderly disabled use more medical services than elderly Medicare enrollees, and they are much more likely to report problems paying for and delaying medical care (Cubanski and Neuman 2010). Medicare additionally covers persons with end-stage renal disease who require dialysis or transplantation and those diagnosed with Amyotrophic Lateral Sclerosis (ALS) or Lou Gehrig's disease (ESRD and ALS patients face no waiting period for Medicare coverage).

All told, Medicare had 49 million enrollees in 2011, encompassing 40 million beneficiaries over age 65, over 8 million persons under age 65 with disabilities, and about 437,000 persons with end-stage renal disease. Their need for help is clear. Half the Medicare population has per capita income below $22,000, 45 percent have three of more chronic conditions, 29 percent have cognitive or mental impairments, and 4 percent are residents of a long-term care facility (KFF 2010).

Americans who turn 65 and receive Social Security benefits are automatically enrolled in Medicare coverage for hospital and physician services. People can opt out of physician coverage. However, if they enroll at a later date, a premium penalty is assessed. Medicare also offers optional outpatient prescription drug coverage. Beneficiaries who do not sign up for coverage when first eligible and later enroll must pay a premium penalty. Once a person over 65 joins Medicare they are typically enrolled for life, ensuring continuity of coverage.

Medicare does not discriminate on the basis of health status. It does not reject persons with preexisting health conditions or charge them higher premiums, common practices in private insurance markets (though they will be greatly restricted by the 2010 health reform law). Medicare's commitment to equal treatment and solidarity is crucial given the costly medical needs of its covered populations, populations that would have extraordinary difficulty securing private insurance. These principles have helped keep Medicare's administrative costs low, since in addition to not requiring a profit, the program does not engage in medical underwriting.

6 Benefits

Medicare beneficiaries can choose to receive coverage through the traditional Medicare program operated by the federal government or from private insurance plans that contract with the government to arrange for beneficiaries' medical care. Those private plans comprise Medicare Advantage (Part C) and currently enroll about 30 percent of Medicare beneficiaries. Medicare covers a wide range of medical services, and as a defined-benefit program, that coverage is specified in law. Medicare is a legal entitlement—all persons who meet eligibility criterion are entitled to program coverage and the federal government must pay for covered services (Jost 2003).

Medicare is divided into four parts, a separation that reflects the program's political history, but fosters considerable confusion and runs counter to the contemporary emphasis in health policy on integration of medical services. Medicare Part A covers inpatient hospital care, post-hospital stays in skilled nursing facilities, and hospice care. Medicare Part B covers physician care and other outpatient services including chemotherapy, diagnostic tests and laboratory services, dialysis, durable medical equipment, home healthcare, and preventive screenings. Medicare Part D rounds out the benefit package by paying for outpatient prescription medications.

Although Medicare provides far-reaching benefits, it has serious limits. Medicare does not cover long-term stays in nursing homes, a substantial expense for many seniors (and one that Medicaid covers but only after seniors spend down their assets and income). Nor does Medicare pay for most dental and vision care, or for hearing aids. Medicare additionally requires substantial cost-sharing from beneficiaries. Medicare Part A (hospital insurance) charges no premiums for coverage because retired workers have established their eligibility previously through payroll taxes. However, in 2012, the Medicare hospital insurance deductible was $1156 per illness episode, and beneficiaries can incur more than one deductible in a given year. After the deductible, there is no copayment for the first 60 days of hospitalization. Then, during the next 30 days of a hospital stay, Medicare beneficiaries are responsible for a 25 percent daily copayment ($289 in 2012). After 90 days, Medicare beneficiaries can draw on 60 lifetime reserve days during which they are responsible for a 50 percent ($578 in 2012) copayment. When that reserve is exhausted, beneficiaries must pay all costs (CMS 2012).

The Medicare deductible for physician services was $140 in 2012 and Medicare enrollees pay 20 percent of doctors' bills thereafter. Notably, there is no total cap on the cost-sharing associated with hospital and physician services that Medicare beneficiaries can pay in a year, a protection against catastrophic medical expenses that many private insurance policies have. Other Medicare benefits have substantial holes in their coverage. Stays in skilled nursing facilities, for example, are insured only for 100 days and in 2012, required a daily $145 copayment for days 21–100. Home health services are restricted to "part time" and "intermittent" care (CMS 2012).

Medicare's benefit package and cost-sharing liabilities do not compare well with either Medicaid or insurance plans offered by large employers. Indeed, most Medicare beneficiaries carry additional coverage, with many receiving supplemental coverage from former employers. Others purchase Medigap policies, federally regulated private insurance plans with varying benefits that typically pay for beneficiaries' cost-sharing liabilities, including deductibles and copayments. Medicare enrollees also obtain extra benefits from the aforementioned Medicare Advantage plans, which often limit beneficiaries' total out-of-pocket spending for hospital and physician services and provide enhanced vision and dental coverage. Eight million low-income Medicare beneficiaries are simultaneously enrolled in Medicaid as "dual eligibles," with Medicaid covering gaps in Medicare coverage and paying for their premiums and cost-sharing. Only 11 percent of Medicare beneficiaries rely exclusively on traditional Medicare (KFF 2010), underscoring its limitations and the complexities of American health insurance arrangements.

7 Financing and Administration

Medicare is financed through multiple sources, with general revenues and payroll taxes together accounting for about 75 percent of its funds in 2010 (CBO 2011). Working Americans must contribute a payroll tax that finances Medicare hospital insurance (Part A). The Medicare payroll tax is levied against all earnings, unlike the Social Security tax, which in 2012 applied to a maximum of $110,100 in earnings. Historically, the Medicare payroll tax rate has been the same (1.45 percent in 2012) regardless of a worker's income. Beginning in 2013, Americans making over $200,000 must pay a higher payroll tax rate (2.35 percent). Federal income taxes assessed on retirees' Social Security benefits generate additional revenues for Part A.

Medicare Part B, coverage for physician and other outpatient services, is financed through general federal tax revenues (75 percent) and beneficiary premiums (25 percent). Traditionally, all Medicare beneficiaries were charged the same premium, though states subsidized lower-income enrollees. Since 2006, Medicare has formally varied premiums by income, with higher-income beneficiaries (currently, those with annual incomes over $85,000) paying larger premiums (KFF 2010). Medicare Part D draws on a similar combination of beneficiary premiums and general revenues, and it too charges higher-income enrollees larger premiums. Part D additionally receives funds from states for dual eligible enrollees who previously had their medication costs covered by Medicaid (KFF 2010). Revenues from all these sources are credited to two separate

Medicare trust funds, hospital insurance (Part A) and supplementary medical insurance (Parts B and D).

Medicare beneficiaries have government health insurance, yet they receive their medical care mostly from private doctors, hospitals, and other care providers. The revenues that Medicare collects are thus paid out to medical care providers. Medicare pays physicians according to a preset fee schedule based on the "relative value" of medical procedures, whereas hospitals are paid a set amount according to a patient's diagnosis. The government pays private insurance plans that are part of the Medicare Advantage program on the basis of plan bids and benchmarks tied to spending for beneficiaries in traditional Medicare. Prescription drug plans in Medicare Part D are paid on the basis of bids they submit to cover their enrollees' costs.

Medicare is a federal program, administered by the Centers for Medicare and Medicaid Services (CMS) within the Department of Health and Human Services. The federal government enacts laws and sets rules that govern program eligibility, benefits, financing, and payment policies for medical services. Medicare contracts with private organizations to process claims and pay bills.

Congress plays an important role in Medicare policy making. Several committees— including Ways and Means and Energy and Commerce in the House, and Finance in the Senate—actively engage with Medicare issues. An independent agency, the Medicare Payment Advisory Commission (MEDPAC) advises Congress on program policy. Congress additionally draws on the expertise of the Congressional Budget Office and Congressional Research Service.

8 THE POLITICS OF MEDICARE

Medicare operates in a political environment loaded with powerful interests. Lobbies for doctors, hospitals, insurers, drug companies, medical-device manufacturers, and numerous other medical care suppliers aggressively seek to shape Medicare policy. Healthcare spending represents income to the medical care industry; for most providers, Medicare is their single largest payer. Not surprisingly, the "Medicare-industrial complex" (Vladeck 1999) seeks to maximize Medicare payments and resist spending controls. Such groups have an enormous stake in Medicare politics, and they possess the expertise, political skills, and financial resources to promote their economic interests. Provider lobbies exert their influence on Medicare issues large and small, from major bills to obscure payment and coverage rules. As we have seen, Medicare's original payment rules favored physicians and hospitals, and medical care providers profited handsomely from those arrangements in the program's early years. Since then, legislative provisions have repeatedly advanced the interests of individual hospitals and classes of hospitals (Vladeck 1999). Moreover, the pharmaceutical industry shaped the 2003 Medicare Modernization Act to its favor, as did private insurers. Additionally, throughout the 2000s, physicians successfully pressed Congress to overturn scheduled payment cuts (Oberlander 2007).

This familiar picture of Medicare politics is somewhat deceptive, however, because it neglects far-reaching changes in Medicare policy. Medicare politics has not, in fact, been consistently dominated by the medical industry—their influence actually has declined over time (Jost 1999; Oberlander 2003). The erosion of providers' power in Medicare is largely attributable to the rise of budget-deficit politics. The large and rapidly growing federal bill for Medicare made it a prime target for budget cutters. As federal deficits became a preoccupation, policymakers increasingly took on the medical care industry in the name of fiscal discipline. The presence of another formidable political interest with both organized representation and far more voting power than providers can muster—seniors—made political life more difficult for the industry. As fiscal pressures mounted, policy makers generally preferred imposing pain on medical care providers than on retirees—a political calculus that elderly advocacy groups like the AARP supported.

The advent of prospective payment systems during the 1980s and 1990s signaled a transformation not only in Medicare reimbursement rules, but also in program politics. Medicare policy increasingly was driven by deficit politics, rather than by industry demands. To be sure, Medicare providers continue to fight relentlessly for more funds and often shape specific policies to preserve (or expand) their slice of the program. Nonetheless, since the 1980s federal policy makers have resisted industry pressures sufficiently to moderate the growth of the Medicare pie, as evidenced by the aforementioned slowdown in excess cost growth.

The George W. Bush administration (2001–2008) offered a major exception to the predominance of deficit politics in Medicare policy. It took office at a time of projected budget surplus and even after the surplus evaporated showed little interest in fiscal restraint. The Bush administration adopted no major Medicare cost-control measures and helped pass legislation expanding program coverage for prescription drugs—without paying for the new benefit. Yet with the Obama administration in office and deficits soaring following the Great Recession and subsequent federal stimulus efforts, Medicare policy returned to its more familiar pattern of recent decades. The 2010 Affordable Care Act is projected to generate major program savings largely by reducing the growth in payments to hospitals and private Medicare Advantage plans (Merlis 2010). Given rising concern over federal deficits, Medicare providers are likely to face additional payment cuts in coming years. Interest groups, then, greatly influence but ultimately do not run Medicare.

A second theme in Medicare politics is that the program has emerged as a front in broader partisan and ideological struggles over healthcare reform and the welfare state. As enacted in 1965, Medicare was in key respects a liberal program, defined by the principles of social insurance and universalism. It embodied government health insurance—single-payer in the parlance of contemporary health policy—a model favored by its liberal designers. They assumed that government-run insurance was more efficient, egalitarian, and reliable than private coverage.

The original vision of Medicare prevailed during the program's first three decades. Policy makers focused on rationalizing, rather than replacing, the existing Medicare model, and rationalizing politics often produced a surprising degree of bipartisanship. Both Democrats and Republicans, for example, supported prospective payment reforms during the 1980s (Oberlander 2003). Nonetheless, conservatives have always preferred a different model, with the government subsidizing beneficiaries to buy private insurance. They have emphasized the virtues of market competition, individual choice, and deregulation. The ascendance of Republican Congressional majorities—in 1994, the GOP won majority control of the House and Senate for the first time in 40 years—enabled the party to push Medicare policy closer to their programmatic vision. Since 1995, bipartisanship in Medicare politics has eroded and program policy has moved rightward.

The 2003 Medicare Modernization Act (MMA) represented the largest step to date in efforts to promote market-based policy in the program (Oliver et al. 2004; Jaenicke and Waddan 2006; Morgan and Campbell 2011; Oberlander 2007, 2012). The newly created prescription drug benefit was offered exclusively through private plans, the first time in Medicare's history that an entire area of the program had been privatized. The MMA dropped any pretense of cost savings by substantially boosting payments to private insurance (Medicare Advantage) plans above what it actually cost to deliver care to beneficiaries. Those subsidies represented an effort by the Bush administration and Congressional Republicans to induce Medicare beneficiaries to leave traditional Medicare for private coverage. The strategy worked, dramatically increasing Medicare beneficiaries' enrollment in private plans. Then, in 2010, President Obama Congress reversed that course, cutting extra payments to private plans (though subsequent policy adjustments reduced those cuts). The fight over the roles of private coverage and government insurance in Medicare rages on, intensified by mounting partisan and ideological polarization in Congress. That fight is part of a larger struggle concerning turning over responsibility for American social programs to the private sector (Morgan and Campbell 2011).

Finally, the structure of Medicare's financing arrangements has had a powerful impact on program politics. As previously noted, Medicare is financed by a combination of payroll taxes, general revenues, and beneficiary premiums that are credited to separate program trust funds. General revenue and premium funding for Medicare's supplementary medical insurance (Parts B and D) trust fund is adjusted annually to meet changing expenditures. Consequently, this trust fund has never had an insolvency issue—its funding sources automatically rise to meet program expenditures.

However, like Social Security, the Hospitalization Insurance (HI) trust fund is financed almost exclusively through dedicated payroll taxes. As a result, when payroll tax revenues decline or program expenditures rise rapidly, the trust fund appears to be in danger of insolvency, triggering a political crisis (Pierson 1994; Patashnik 2000; White 2001; Oberlander 2003). Indeed, Medicare politics has been driven by a cycle of crisis and reform, with policy makers leveraging warnings of funding trouble in the Medicare trust fund to adopt their preferred changes in the program (Oberlander 2003). Crisis politics allow politicians to argue that urgent action is required to save a program, in this case to stop Medicare from going bankrupt. If Medicare was funded exclusively from general revenues, like defense programs, then policy makers would surely still fret over rising costs, but impending "bankruptcy" would never be an issue.

The structure of Medicare financing thus explains both the character of debates over Medicare and the timing of reforms, underscoring the political importance of differing institutional arrangements. That influence is not simply historical: Medicare's HI trust fund is currently projected to have insufficient funds to pay all its costs in 2030. As the next section explains, demographic changes and budget pressures have set the stage for a major clash over remaking Medicare, and trust-fund dynamics will occupy a central role in that drama.

9 REFORMING MEDICARE

Medicare's enrollment will swell in coming years—from 40 million in 2010 to 80 million in 2030—as the baby boomers retire. Meanwhile, the cost of medical care continues to increase. Consequently, federal Medicare spending will rise significantly. The Congressional Budget Office (CBO) projects that Medicare expenditures will increase from $560 billion in 2011 to over $1 trillion by 2022, and Medicare spending as a share of Gross Domestic Product (GDP) will grow from 3.7 percent in 2010 to 6.7 percent in 2035 (CBO 2011).

Medicare's cost and predicted growth rate make it a prominent target for deficit reduction. Major plans to reduce the federal deficit—including those offered during 2010–2012 by the Bowles-Simpson commission, President Obama, and Republican Congressman Paul Ryan—regularly count on substantial Medicare savings. Budget hawks argue, in the words of Connecticut Senator Joseph Lieberman (2011), that Medicare is "hurtling to its demise" and that federal deficits require immediate, major changes in Medicare.

Nonetheless, the challenge to Medicare and calls for entitlement reform are not simply a product of fiscal concerns or a response to economic circumstances (White 2001). After all, rising Medicare spending does not explain the sizable increase in the federal deficit during 2008–2012 (an increase attributable to the recession, declining tax revenues, and stimulus spending). Much of the impetus for Medicare reform is ideological; against the backdrop of a rightward swing in the Republican party, conservatives increasingly embrace plans that would privatize Medicare or otherwise fundamentally alter program arrangements.

How might Medicare change in response to these fiscal and political pressures? Four major categories of Medicare reform are currently in vogue in Washington (Marmor, Oberlander, and White 2011; Jost 2007). The first, advanced by the 2010 Affordable Care Act, seeks to curtail Medicare spending through an array of healthcare delivery and payment reforms, including patient-centered medical homes, bundled payment, and accountable care organizations (ACOs). In ACOs, groups of medical care providers will accept responsibility for an assigned population of Medicare patients and face financial incentives to hold spending down and improve quality.

ACOs sound appealing because they promise to control Medicare spending while improving health outcomes. The problem with ACOs and similar ideas is that, for all their promise, there is not much evidence yet that they will reliably slow healthcare spending. Delivery- and payment-system reforms could conceivably be strengthened by the newly created Independent Payment Advisory Board (IPAB). The IPAB is empowered to make recommendations to slow Medicare expenditures, and if Congress does not act, those recommendations become law. IPAB, though, is currently embroiled in political controversy—as is the entire ACA—and even if it escapes repeal, CBO projects that the board will have no impact during the next decade because Medicare spending will generally stay below the threshold that triggers its authority.

A second reform option is to reduce Medicare benefits by raising the age of eligibility. Given gains in life expectancy, Social Security's rising eligibility age for full benefits, and the ACA's establishment of health insurance exchanges, such a change initially appears sensible. Moreover, increasing the age of eligibility from 65 to 67 would certainly reduce federal spending on Medicare. However, this idea exemplifies the problem with focusing on Medicare spending and the federal budget, rather than on system-wide healthcare spending. If the federal government moves Medicare's eligibility age up to 67, then seniors who would have received their healthcare from Medicare will obtain it elsewhere, from private plans in the new health insurance exchanges, from Medicaid, or from employer-sponsored private insurance (some seniors could also become uninsured). Moreover, Medicare is less expensive than private insurance, so although this reform would reduce federal spending, it actually would increase total national healthcare spending. Put simply, it is an example of cost shifting rather than cost saving. Nor would it save much in federal Medicare spending.

A third category of reforms would increasingly differentiate Medicare beneficiaries by income and raise costs for higher-income enrollees. Medicare beneficiaries with more income already pay higher Part B and D premiums. Reform proposals would raise those premiums and expand the share of Medicare beneficiaries paying them. There is a strong normative case that wealthier Medicare beneficiaries who can afford it should pay higher premiums. But Part B and D are now funded mostly by general revenues, so progressive income taxes assure that wealthier beneficiaries contribute more (Vladeck 2004). Further, much of the Medicare population has only modest income, so income-related premiums can only generate modest savings unless a much broader portion of the Medicare population is subject to such premiums. Raising income-related premiums too high could lead some Medicare beneficiaries to opt out of the program, eroding its broad base.

The final category of Medicare reforms seeks to expand the role of private insurers and competition in the program. A 2011 Congressional Republican plan, sponsored by House Budget Committee chair Paul Ryan, would have eliminated the traditional Medicare program and enrolled beneficiaries exclusively with private insurers. Under this plan, the federal government would give each beneficiary a fixed amount or voucher each year to buy health insurance (with adjustments for age and health status), effectively creating a capped budget for Medicare.

The Ryan plan would indeed dramatically slow federal spending on Medicare. It would do so, though, by shifting costs to Medicare beneficiaries. The voucher amount provided to Medicare beneficiaries would grow much more slowly than healthcare costs. Over time its value would erode and beneficiaries increasingly would have difficulty affording meaningful insurance (Aaron 2011). The CBO concluded that, in 2030, a typical 65-year old Medicare beneficiary would pay 68 percent of the costs of their medical care under the Ryan plan, compared to 25–30 percent under current law. Moreover, because private insurance is more expensive than Medicare, moving all beneficiaries into private plans would increase healthcare spending. Once again, this proposal represents cost shifting, not cost cutting.

The Ryan plan ignited substantial controversy and subsequently Republican leaders, including Ryan himself, backed away from the original concept. They instead moved to endorsing a "premium support" system that would maintain the traditional Medicare program as part of a competitive market with private plans. The current Medicare system, though, already includes both government insurance and private plans. In order to reduce program spending, premium support plans, which vary greatly in how much protection they provide against rising healthcare costs (Aaron and Lambrew 2008; Aaron 2011), would have to strengthen financial incentives for beneficiaries to choose lower-cost plans (shifting costs to persons remaining in more expensive plans). Or they would have to generate savings from health-plan competition, savings that have often proven elusive (Marmor, Oberlander, and White 2011).

In sum, the prevailing menu of Medicare reform options leaves much to be desired. What, then, can be done to secure Medicare's fiscal future and moderate program spending? One simple step would be to implement already adopted reforms. Ironically, the conviction in much of Washington that Medicare spending is uncontrollable and that, therefore, the program must be restructured comes immediately in the aftermath of Congress enacting a law that will substantially slow Medicare spending—the 2010 Affordable Care Act. The ACA will generate projected savings of $500 billion in Medicare over the next decade, largely from reducing payments to hospitals and private Medicare Advantage plans (Merlis 2010). Assuming the ACA is not repealed and those measures are implemented, per capita Medicare spending is projected to grow at a rate very close to growth in GDP (Berenson and Holahan 2011). The ACA's Medicare savings underscore the fact that Medicare spending is controllable and amenable to public policy (White 2008, Vladeck 2011); program spending growth can be moderated without privatization or radical restructuring. Nonetheless, even if the ACA's Medicare reforms are fully implemented, additional measures to slow Medicare spending will likely be necessary in coming years.

A second remedy would be to enact an all-payer system in which public and private insurers in a given region, including Medicare, would pay medical providers according to the same fee schedule. All-payer reform would substantially strengthen the United States' capacity to hold down prices and control national health spending. It would focus policy-makers' attention where it should be: on the system-wide challenge of containing healthcare spending, rather than simply on limiting federal Medicare expenditures (Marmor, Oberlander, and White 2011).

Finally, Medicare revenues will have to be raised. Although rising medical costs continue to drive up program expenditures, Medicare spending is rising now in large part because program enrollment is growing substantially as the Baby Boomers retire (Feder and Cafarella 2011). Affording a growing Medicare program is largely a question of values, not economics (Vladeck 2004). After all, some of those who believe Medicare is unaffordable simultaneously support extending large tax-cuts for wealthy Americans that would significantly worsen federal budget deficits. Medicare's fortunes depend, then, on broader fiscal policy choices. As a share of GDP, tax revenues in the United States are significantly below historical averages and the average of industrialized nations. Sustaining Medicare, as well as Social Security and other social programs, means that taxes must rise to ensure their adequate funding (Aaron 2010).

10 CONCLUSION: THE FUTURE OF MEDICARE

Medicare has been a foundation of the American welfare state and critical source of health and economic security for nearly half a century. Yet, as Medicare approaches its 50th anniversary, it is ensnared in an intense political debate and unstable economic and fiscal environment. Change is coming to Medicare, but what kind?

Medicare could go in very different directions depending on shifting electoral outcomes. A Republican president and Congress could pursue broad restructuring of the program, whereas Democrats are more likely to retain the current Medicare model and implement the Affordable Care Act's provisions. Bipartisan agreement on changes like income-related premiums could emerge, but the polarized partisan environment makes broad agreement on comprehensive Medicare reform difficult. Confronted by fiscal pressures, policy makers will likely adopt a combination of financing changes, benefit cuts, revisions in cost-sharing, and payment reforms in Medicare, though the exact composition and scope of such changes is uncertain. Major political and economic shifts could produce unanticipated, more radical changes. What is certain is that Medicare will remain at the center of debates over healthcare reform, the budget, and the welfare state for years to come.

REFERENCES

*Indicates recommended reading.

*Aaron, Henry J. 2010. "How to Think about the U.S. Budget Challenge." *Journal of Policy Analysis and Management*, 29: 883–891.

Aaron, Henry J. 2011. "How Not to Reform Medicare." *New England Journal of Medicine*, 364: 1588–1589.

Aaron, Henry J., and Jeanne M. Lambrew. 2008. *Reforming Medicare: Options, Tradeoffs, and Opportunities*. Washington, DC: Brookings Institution Press.

*Ball, Robert. 1995. "What Medicare's Architects Had in Mind." *Health Affairs* 14 (4): 62–72.

Berenson, Robert A., and John Holahan. 2011. "Preserving Medicare: A Practical Approach to Controlling Spending." Urban Institute. http://www.urban.org/UploadedPDF/412405-Preserving-Medicare-A-Practical-Approach-to-Controlling-Spending.pdf.

Birnbaum, Michael and Elizabeth Patchias. 2010. "Measuring Coverage for Seniors in Medicare Part A and Estimating the Cost of Making it Universal." *Journal of Health Politics, Policy and Law* 35 (1): 49–62.

Blumenthal, David and James A. Morone. 2009. *The Heart of Power: Health and Politics in the Oval Office*. Berkeley: University of California Press.

Brown, Lawrence D. 1985. "Technocratic Corporatism and Administrative Reform in American Medicine." *Journal of Health Politics, Policy and Law* 10 (3): 579–599.

Brown, Lawrence D., and Michael Sparer. 2003. "Poor Program's Progress: The Unanticipated Politics of Medicaid Policy." *Health Affairs* 22 (1): 31–44.

Card, David, Carlos Dobkin, and Nicole Maestras. 2007. "Does Medicare Save Lives?" NBER Working Paper Series, Working Paper 13668.

Centers for Medicare and Medicaid Services (CMS). 2012. "Medicare & You." http://www.medicare.gov/publications/pubs/pdf/10050.pdf.

Congressional Budget Office (CBO). 2011. *CBO's 2011 Long-Term Budget Outlook*. Washington, DC: CBO.

Cubanski, Juliette, and Patricia Neuman. 2010. "Medicare Doesn't Work as Well for Younger, Disabled Beneficiaries as it Does for Older Enrollees." *Health Affairs* 29, (9): 1725–1733.

Derthick, Martha. 1979. *Policymaking for Social Security*. Washington, DC: Brookings Institution Press.

Feder, Judith M. 1977. *Medicare: The Politics of Federal Hospital Insurance*. Lexington, MA: D.C. Heath.

Feder, Judy, and Nicole Cafarella. 2011. *What's Driving Up the Cost of Medicare?* Washington, DC: Center for American Progress.

Finkelstein, Amy. 2005. "*The Aggregate Effects of Health Insurance: Evidence from the Introduction of Medicare*." NBER Working Paper Series. Cambridge, MA: National Bureau of Economic Research.

Finkelstein, Amy and, Robin McKnight. "*What Did Medicare Do (and Was It Worth It)?*" NBER Working Paper Series. Cambridge, MA: National Bureau of Economic Research.

Hacker, Jacob S. 2009. "Health Competition—The Why and How of 'Public Plan Choice.'" *New England Journal of Medicine* 360 (22): 2269–2271.

Himmelfarb, Richard. 1995. *Catastrophic Politics: The Rise and Fall of the Medicare Catastrophic Coverage Act of 1988*. University Park: Pennsylvania State Press.

Harris, Richard. 1966. *A Sacred Trust*. New York: New American Library.

Jacobs, Lawrence R. 1993. *The Health of Nations: Public Opinion and the Making of American and British Health Policy*. Ithaca, NY: Cornell University Press.

Jaenicke, Douglas, and Alex Waddan. 2006. "President Bush and Social Policy: The Strange Case of the Medicare Prescription Drug Benefit." *Political Science Quarterly* 121 (2): 217–240.

Journal of the American Medical Association. 1957. "Organization Section: Highlights of A.M.A. Clinical Session." 165 (16): 2090–2092.

*Jost, Timothy S. 1999. "Governing Medicare." *Administrative Law Review* 51: 39–116.

Jost, Timothy S. 2003. *Disentitlement: The Threats Facing Our Health Care Programs and a Right-Based Response*. New York: Oxford University Press.

Jost, Timothy S. 2007. "Medicare: What Are the Real Problems? What Contribution Can Law Make to the Real Solutions?" *St. Louis University Journal of Health Law & Policy* 1: 45–65.

*(KFF) Henry J. Kaiser Family Foundation. 2010. "Medicare: A Primer." http://www.kff.org/medicare/7615.cfm.

Lieberman, Joe. 2011. "How Medicare Can Be Saved." *Washington Post*, June 9.

*Marmor, Theodore R. 1973. *The Politics of Medicare*. Chicago: Aldine.

Marmor, Theodore R. 1988. Coping with a Creeping Crisis: Medicare at Twenty. In T. R. Marmor, J. L. Mashaw, eds., *Social Security: Beyond the Rhetoric of Crisis*, 186–99. Princeton, NJ: Princeton University Press.

Marmor, Theodore, Jonathan Oberlander, and Joseph White. 2011. "Medicare and the Federal Budget: Misdiagnosed Problems, Inadequate Solutions." *Journal of Policy Analysis and Management* 30: 928–934.

*Mayes, Rick, and Robert A. Berenson. 2006. *Medicare Prospective Payment and the Shaping of U.S. Health Care*. Baltimore, MD: Johns Hopkins University Press.

McWilliams, J. Michael, Ellen Meara, Alan A. Zaslavsky, and John Z. Ayanian. 2007. "Use of Health Services by Previously Uninsured Medicare Beneficiaries." *New England Journal of Medicine* 357: 143–153.

Merlis, Mark. 2010. "Adding Up the Numbers: Understanding Medicare Savings in the Affordable Care Act." Center for American Progress. http://www.americanprogress.org/issues/2010/10/pdf/medicare_aca_report.pdf.

*Moon, Marilyn. 2006. *Medicare: A Policy Primer*. Washington, DC: Urban Institute Press.

Moon, Marilyn, and Karen Davis. 1995. "Preserving and Strengthening Medicare." *Health Affairs* 14 (4): 31–46.

*Morgan, Kimberly J. and Andrea L. Campbell. 2011. *The Delegated Welfare State: Medicare, Markets, and the Governance of Social Policy*. New York: Oxford University Press.

Morone, James A. 1990. *The Democratic Wish: Popular Participation and the Limits of Democratic Government*. New York: Basic Books.

National Academy of Social Insurance (NASI). 1999. "Medicare and the American Social Contract." http://www.nasi.org/sites/default/files/research/med_report_soc_contract.pdf.

NASI. 2001. "Reflections on Implementing Medicare." http://www.nasi.org/usr_doc/med_report_reflections.pdf.

*Oberlander, Jonathan. 2003. *The Political Life of Medicare*. Chicago: University of Chicago Press.

Oberlander, Jonathan. 2007. "Through the Looking Glass: The Politics of the Medicare Prescription Drug, Improvement, and Modernization Act." *Journal of Health Politics, Policy and Law* 32: 187–219.

Oberlander, Jonathan. 2012. "The Bush Administration and Politics of Medicare Reform." In M. A. Levin, D. DiSalvo, and M. M. Shapiro, eds., *Building Coalitions, Making Policy: The Politics of the Clinton, Bush, and Obama Presidencies*, 150–80. Baltimore. MD: Johns Hopkins University Press.

Oliver, Thomas R., Phillip R. Lee, and Helene L. Lipton. 2004. "A Political History of Medicare and Prescription Drug Coverage." *Milbank Quarterly* 82 (2): 283–354.

Patashnik, Eric. 2000. *Putting Trust in the U.S. Budget: Federal Trust Funds and the Politics of Commitment*. Cambridge: Cambridge University Press.

Pierson, Paul. 1994. *Dismantling the Welfare State.* Cambridge: Cambridge University Press.

Quadagno, Jill. 2006. *One Nation Uninsured: Why the U.S. Has No National Health Insurance.* New York: Oxford University Press.

Rettig, Richard. 1991. "Origins of the Medicare Kidney Disease Entitlement." In K. Hanna, ed., *Biomedical Politics.* Washington, DC: National Academy Press.

Schlesinger, Mark, and Terrie Wetle. 1988. "Medicare's Coverage of Health Services." In D. Blumenthal, M. Schlesinger, and P. Brown Drumheller, eds., *Renewing the Promise: Medicare and its Reform*, 58–59. New York: Oxford University Press.

Smith, David Barton. 1999. *Health Care Divided: Race and Healing a Nation.* Ann Arbor: University of Michigan Press.

Smith, David G. 1992. *Paying for Medicare: The Politics of Reform.* New York: Aldine de Gruyter.

Starr, Paul. 1982. *The Social Transformation of American Medicine.* New York: Basic Books.

*Vladeck, Bruce C. 1999. "The Political Economy of Medicare." *Health Affairs* 18 (1): 22–36.

Vladeck, Bruce C. 2004. "The Struggle for the Soul of Medicare." *Journal of Law, Medicine and Ethics* 32 (3): 410–415.

Vladeck, Bruce C. 2011. "Statement on Medicare Statement on Medicare 'Reform.'" Hearing on "Health Care Entitlements: The Road Forward" Before the Committee on Finance, U.S. Senate. June 23. http://finance.senate.gov/imo/media/doc/Bruce%20Vladeck%20Testimony.pdf.

White, Chapin. 2008. "Why Did Medicare Spending Growth Slow Down?" *Health Affairs* 27 (3): 793–802.

*White, Joseph. 2001. *False Alarm: Why the Greatest Threat to Social Security and Medicare Is the Campaign to "Save Them."* Baltimore, MD: Johns Hopkins University Press.

CHAPTER 18

....

LONG-TERM CARE
FOR THE ELDERLY

....

MADONNA HARRINGTON MEYER AND JESSICA HAUSAUER

1 INTRODUCTION

....

As people grow older, or become chronically ill or disabled, they often require assistance with routine activities of daily life such as eating, bathing, dressing, or paying bills. Most medical care focuses on acute illnesses intended to cure the person and restore them fairly quickly to independent living. By contrast, long-term care often focuses on chronic physical or mental illnesses with the goal of helping those who can no longer live independently. Long-term care is provided by paid medical providers in nursing homes, assisted living facilities, and in one's own home in the community. Long-term care is also provided by unpaid family members and friends in all of these settings as well. Despite the growing need for long-term care, the United States does not have a coherent set of long-term care policies. The existing patchwork of programs and services can be difficult for patients and their families to understand and fails to adequately support many of those in need of care.

This essay pieces together the puzzle of long-term care in the United States. We begin by briefly tracing the historical background of long-term care policy and then take a more in-depth look at the three formal channels through which individuals currently navigate long-term care—Medicare, private long-term care insurance, and Medicaid. Medicaid is the primary payer of long-term care, and as a result, it faces a number of challenges. We investigate these challenges in detail and then address the question of who actually provides the greatest share of long-term care. Families, particularly women in families, continue to provide the lion's share of care through informal care work. We conclude by pointing out that it is the most vulnerable older and disabled Americans, particularly those who are women, black and Hispanic, and single, and their families who face the greatest difficulties under the current system and who will be most affected by future policy changes.

2 OVERVIEW OF LONG-TERM CARE IN THE UNITED STATES

Historically, around the world, families were expected to care for their own older or dis-abled relatives. This reliance on *filial* responsibility was certainly the case in the United States, where nineteenth-century poor laws encouraged families to provide for their own aging parents. Charitable groups provided alms only to those they felt were the deserving poor, and state assistance was limited mainly to almshouses with fairly harsh conditions (Katz 1986). Over time, modern welfare states took increasing responsibility for the provision of at least some basic needs for older people because they were gener-ally regarded as the deserving poor. As in many countries, U.S. policy makers recognized that filial responsibility concentrated risk, privatized cost, and maximized inequality among families (Harrington Meyer and Herd 2007). Public provision for the aging in the United States began to flourish when Medicare and Medicaid were created in 1965. Although Medicare specifically excluded from coverage nearly all forms of long-term care, Medicaid quickly became the largest public payer. Nursing homes shifted from those run primarily by counties and nonprofit church and charitable groups to more for-profit conglomerates (Estes and Swan 1993). Nonetheless, social provision for long-term care remained somewhat meager in the United States, and to this day families continue to provide most of the long-term care for frail older and disabled relatives (AARP 2008; Brody 2004; National Alliance for Caregiving and AARP 2009).

In fact, despite common reference to a long-term care system, the United States has a fragmented set of programs and policies that are expensive, difficult to navigate, and incomplete. The United States spent nearly $178 billion on long-term care in 2006, and $125 billion, or 70 percent, of that went to nursing home care (KFF 2009b; KFF 2011). Paid long-term care services are expensive, and nursing home care is often the most expensive. Nursing home care averages $72,000 per year and assisted living facilities average $38,000 per year. Home health services, which are rarely used around the clock and which do not include room and board, average $21 per hour (KFF 2011). The need for long-term care is increasing as most Americans, including disabled persons, experience ever greater life expectancy. Long-term care policies in the United States are fragmented across three main channels of formal care: social insurance-based Medicare, market-based long-term care insurance, and poverty-based Medicaid. We explore each in turn, assessing what they do and do not cover, and we end with an analysis of informal care provided by families.

2.1 Medicare

Medicare is a nearly universal social insurance program that provides limited coverage of long-term care. Unlike targeted programs that emphasize selective acceptance, social insurance programs boast broader eligibility, more redistributive benefit formulas, and more widespread approval by voters (AARP 2005; Estes and Associates 2001; Public Agenda 2005; Quadagno 2005). Supporters suggest that universal programs tend to be more effective than targeted programs at reducing poverty and inequality. Indeed, the combined value of Social Security and Medicare is credited with reducing poverty among the older adults from over 50 percent during the Depression, to 11 percent (Engelhardt and Gruber 2004; Korpi and Palme 1998).

Policy makers spent little time debating long-term care when Medicare was first enacted (Oberlander 2003). From the outset, Medicare coverage of long-term care was sparse. The decision to cover acute but not chronic care fragmented the health-care system for older and disabled people and created a great deal of diagnostic inequality wherein those with acute conditions receive broad coverage and those with chronic conditions receive relatively little coverage. Medicare generally only provides medical services for acute conditions such as heart attacks or hip replacements from which recipients are expected to recover (KFF 2009a). Medicare provides partial coverage of the first 100 days of nursing home care, but nursing home residents must meet several eligibility criteria and pay sizable deductibles, co-payments, and uncovered costs during those 100 days, thereby making the benefit unmanageable for many older and disabled persons (SSA 2009). In 2006, Medicare covered 23 percent of total long-term care expenditures, and just 17 percent of nursing home expenditures (KFF 2011; KFF 2009b). Coverage of long-term care in the community, which was never widespread, has been cut since the mid-1990s (Harrington Meyer and Herd 2007; MedPac 2008; SSA 2009). For example, the proportion of the Medicare budget dedicated to home health care decreased from 8 percent in 1994 to 4 percent in 2010, and there are now fewer types of care covered, licensed providers, persons receiving home health care, and visits provided per person (Harrington Meyer and Herd 2007; KFF 2010; MedPac 2008).

Policy makers have also sought to reduce Medicare expenditures by shifting more and more of the costs onto older beneficiaries and their families. In addition to monthly premiums, Medicare recipients pay deductibles, co-insurance of 20 percent, any costs above the allowable rate, and uncovered goods and services such as preventive care, dental care, vision care, and eyeglasses (Harrington Meyer and Kesterske-Storbakken 2000; SSA 2009). All these out-of-pocket expenses have risen dramatically and are expected to continue rising at rates much higher than the cost of living. Some estimate that Medicare covers less than 50 percent of old age health care costs (SSA 2009). Four decades into the Medicare program, the costs of health care for older people are, in fact, a greater burden than before the program began both because of soaring health care costs and because Medicare coverage is spotty. Out-of-pocket expenses for older people rose from 15 percent of annual income in 1965 to 22 percent in 1998. By 2025, out-of-pocket health care expenses are expected to reach 30 percent (Moon and Herd 2002).

2.2 Long-Term Care Insurance

For decades there has been a tension between those who want to emphasize public long-term care insurance and those who want to emphasize private market-based policies. Neither side seems to be making much headway. Many aging activists have supported mandatory national long-term care insurance, funded and distributed similarly to Medicare (Estes and Associates 2001; Harrington Meyer and Herd 2007; Quadagno 2005). Weary of the price of public old age programs, however, opponents of big government have worked in recent years to downsize the federal government's provision of the social safety net. They aim to shift government spending on social provision to private market programs that would ostensibly meet the needs of older and disabled people and their families, lower costs to the government, and generate profits for private health care providers (Becker 2005; Estes and Associates 2001; Friedman 2002; Gilbert 2002; Hacker 2002; Quadagno 2005; Yergin and Stanislaw 1998).

People of all ages may purchase private long-term care insurance, and the Congressional Budget Office (CBO 2005) estimates that 40 percent could afford to do so, but only 10 percent actually hold a policy. Criticisms of private long-term care insurance policies include high premiums, coverage exclusions, and denial of those with common conditions (Brown and Finkelstein 2009). Most policies require that patients receive care for 30 to 100 days before benefits begin, a period longer than the average nursing home stay (Brown and Finkelstein 2009). Most policies have a maximum benefit period of 1 to 5 years with a cap on the maximum number of days that care can be covered. Additionally, most policies limit the dollar amount of coverage. In fact, the modal limit is $100 a day for nursing home care, well below the national average of $150 and rising. Such complaints about gaps in the coverage have discouraged many from purchasing a private long-term care insurance policy. Failure to purchase long-term care insurance, Brown and Finkelstein (2009) suggest, is also fueled by denial that individuals may need the services someday and the erroneous belief that Medicare or Medicaid will cover long-term care expenses (KFF 2009c; Harrington Meyer and Herd 2007). Despite the wishes of more conservative policy makers, the purchase of private long-term care insurance is merely holding steady.

2.3 Medicaid

Poverty-based Medicaid is the main public payer of long-term care generally and nursing home care in particular. As Figure 18.1 shows, Medicaid covers 40 percent of all long-term care. The next biggest payers are Medicare and older and disabled people themselves. As Figure 18.2 shows, Medicaid covers 43 percent of nursing home expenditures (KFF 2011; KFF 2009b). Although most Medicaid long-term care recipients are over age 65, a growing share, now 42 percent, are people with disabilities who are younger than 65 (KFF 2011). Proponents of targeted programs argue that they are less expensive because they target resources to the very poor and discourage dependency on the welfare state by encouraging individual responsibility, while critics argue that these benefits are politically divisive because they pit tax-paying contributors against highly stigmatized welfare recipients, emphasize gatekeeping, and have limited efficacy

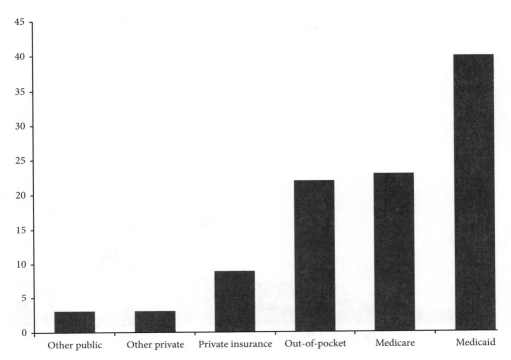

FIG. 18.1 Total long term care expenditures, 2006.

Source: Based on Kaiser Family Foundation 2009b. http://www.kff.org/medicaid/upload/2186_06.pdf.

(Harrington Meyer and Herd 2007; Korpi and Palme 1998; Korpi 2000; Quadagno 2005; Estes and Associates 2001; Katz 1986).

Because they live longer, and have fewer resources and greater long-term care needs, 69 percent of older Medicaid beneficiaries are women (KFF 2012, KFF 2009a; SSA 2009). For similar reasons, blacks and Hispanics are also much more likely than whites to rely on Medicaid. In one study of nursing home residents ages 65 and older, 46 percent of white men and 40 percent of white women, compared to only 20 percent of black men and 14 percent of black women, had never been on Medicaid (Harrington Meyer and Kesterke-Storbakken 2000). These socioeconomically disadvantaged groups have the most to gain or lose now and in the future, depending on how the United States addresses Medicaid coverage of long-term care.

3 MAJOR CHALLENGES FOR MEDICAID

As the major program covering long-term care, Medicaid provides much needed coverage for older and disabled persons in need of both institutional- and community-based

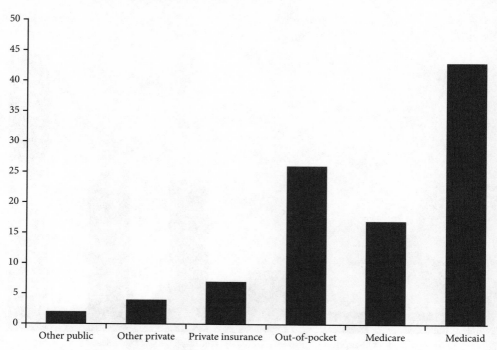

FIG. 18.2 Total nursing home expenditures, 2006.

Source: Based on Kaiser Family Foundation 2009b. http://www.kff.org/medicaid/upload/2186_06.pdf.

care. However, the program faces many challenges including institutional bias, frozen assets tests, admissions discrimination, frozen personal needs allowances, and estate recovery efforts. In this section we describe the issues and the competing suggestions for attending to these challenges.

3.1 Institutional Bias

One of the most vexing issues of Medicaid's long-term care policy is the ongoing institutional bias. Even though about 90 percent of older and disabled people prefer to receive long-term care services at home, and even though it is often, but not always, more cost effective to provide such services at home, Medicaid's long-term care policy still has a pronounced bias in favor of institutional care (AARP 2009). Such a bias derives mainly from differences in the income tests and in what services are covered. To put it simply, institutional bias means that it is easier to become eligible for Medicaid in a nursing home than in the community, and it is more difficult to garner Medicaid coverage of nonmedical personal care in the community than in the nursing home.

Medicaid income limits for the elderly and disabled are complex and often favor institutional care. First, states are required to provide Medicaid coverage to the *categorically needy*, or those who are eligible for Supplemental Security Income (SSI). Currently SSI regulations restrict eligibility to those whose incomes are below 75 percent of the federal poverty line. Eleven states, called the "209(b) states" have the option to set the income limits for categorical eligibility below the SSI standard. Conversely, some states set the income test for categorically needy applicants a bit higher than the SSI limit, but do so mainly at their own expense (Harrington Meyer 1994; Kassner and Shirey 2000). For nursing home residents, however, the federal government permits states to establish income limits up to three times the SSI standard. This optional coverage, known as the 300 percent rule, allows states to set income limits for nursing home residents equal to 300 percent of the SSI guideline, an amount equal to about 225 percent of the federal poverty line. Although Medicaid coverage in nursing homes covers beds, meals, and personal care, categorical Medicaid coverage in the community generally covers only skilled nursing care and does not cover the vast array of nonmedical personal care services, such as homemakers, personal care, and adult day care, that many older and disabled people need (Kassner and Shirey 2000).

Second, since 1965, states have been permitted to extend Medicaid coverage to the *medically needy*. The medically needy are those whose incomes exceed state guidelines, but who become eligible when their incomes minus their medical expenses fall below the state guidelines (Harrington Meyer 1994; Kassner and Shirey 2000). The 209(b) states are required to provide medically needy coverage or to create a spend down program, through which people can become eligible for Medicaid by spending resources on medical care. For other states, this coverage is optional (KFF 2009d; Estes and Associates 2001; Kassner and Shirey 2000). Becoming eligible for the medically needy option is more difficult in the community than in the nursing home. To prove medical need in the community, older and disabled people must document that their medical expenses completely or nearly outweigh their income on a monthly basis for a period of one to six months, depending on the state. This requirement prevents persons with an isolated costly event such as a hip replacement or heart attack from qualifying for medically needy coverage (Kassner and Shirey 2000). Such documentation is easier to execute in nursing homes where residents are charged a monthly fee for services, making medical costs more consistent from month to month. Moreover, because the nursing home ultimately receives the benefit, staff members typically help families apply for and document medical need (Kassner and Shirey 2000). Additionally, because states often require a lengthy period of documentation, nursing homes will often accept payments retroactively.

In the community, however, individuals and their families often must document medical expenses on their own. Following the guidelines can be confusing and frustrating. Moreover, monthly medical expenses tend to fluctuate (Kassner and Shirey 2000). Applicants are not required to pay their medical bills during the deeming period, but failure to do so may dissuade providers from continuing to provide care. If medical services are then discontinued, the applicant's bills may drop below the standard, making them ineligible (Harrington Meyer 1994). Some states offer presumptive eligibility, assuming the person will be eligible, offering Medicaid coverage at the beginning of the deeming period, and keeping people from having to enter the nursing home prematurely (KFF 2009d). Some policy advocates are requesting that the federal government require presumptive eligibility in all 50 states (Kassner and Shirey 2000).

Third, in an effort to reduce institutional bias, many states have implemented Home and Community Based Services (HCBS) waivers (Estes and Associates 2001; KFF 2009d), part of a larger trend promoting waivers and experimentation within the Medicaid program. However, these efforts remain uneven. The Omnibus Budget and Reconciliation Act (OBRA) of 1981 allows states to apply for waivers that permit Medicaid to pay for medical and nonmedical services, including homemakers, personal care, and adult day care for those who might be able to avoid institutionalization, as long as the net effect is budget neutral (Kassner and Shirey 2000; Harrington Meyer 1994). Waiver services may be offered to those who would be eligible for Medicaid if they lived in a nursing home and would otherwise need the level of care offered by a nursing home. Under these rules, states may then expand the income limit for Medicaid eligibility to the 300 percent rule.

In general, Medicaid's institutional bias is easing. As Figure 18.3 shows, the proportion of the Medicaid long-term care budget devoted to institutional care dropped from 87 to 57 percent between 1990 and 2009, whereas the proportion devoted to community care rose from just 13 percent to 43 percent (KFF 2011). Institutional bias remains, however. According to an AARP study, in 2000, 13 of the 50 states had more restrictive income eligibility criteria for HCBS than for nursing home applicants, and 11 states

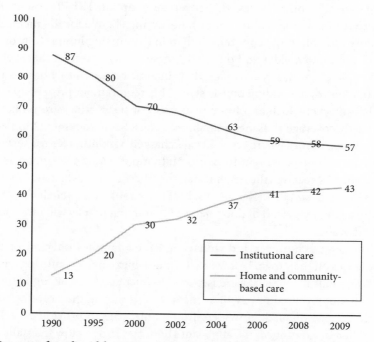

FIG. 18.3 Percent of medicaid long term care services bylocation of care, 1990–2009.

Source: Based on Kaiser Family Foundation. 2011. http://www.kff.org/medicaid/upload/2186-08.pdf.

applied medically needy or 209(b) spend down rules to nursing home participants but not to waiver participants (Kassner and Shirey 2000). Moreover, availability of the HCBS option varies dramatically by state. In New Mexico, Oregon, Washington, Alaska, and California, more than 50 percent of Medicaid long-term care spending for older and disabled people goes to HCBS (AARP 2009), but in 23 states, less than 20 percent of the budget goes to HCBS. Most troubling, however, is that the demand for HCBS far exceeds the availability. In fact, there are over 350,000 older and disabled Americans on waiting lists for HCBS (KFF 2011).

In the wake of the recent economic downturn, at least 25 states announced budget cuts between 2008 and 2010 that would effectively reduce community-based long-term care (Johnson, Oliff and Williams 2010). Oregon, which had developed a cost-cutting model program that provided assistance for bathing, preparing meals, cleaning house, and shopping to keep older people out of nursing homes responded to its $577 million deficit by eliminated the services of home aides to more than 4,500 low-income people. The *New York Times* (Leland 2010) spotlighted the case of Afton England, who lives in a trailer and has multiple chronic conditions that prevent her from walking for more than a few moments. She was told by state officials that her 45 hours per month of aide services would be eliminated. Her case manager said that this move was unlikely to reduce costs because it increased the likelihood that England, and many more like her, would end up in more expensive institutional care. As many state economies begin to rebound, the nursing home industry, mainly via the American Health Care Association, is requesting that states undo these budget cuts, requests that have thus far been declined (Baker 2012).

Whenever income tests are stricter and application procedures more oner-ous in the community, older and disabled persons and their families are pushed toward institutional solutions, fueling Medicaid's institutional bias and discouraging community-based long-term care solutions. Many policy experts favor making HCBS part of the mandatory Medicaid entitlement because that would expand the income test for many more community residents to 300 percent of SSI, make nonmedical personal care services available to community-based Medicaid recipients in all states, and pro-tect community-based services from budget cuts during recessions (Kassner and Shirey 2000). The risk, however, is that states would respond to such a mandate by tightening eligibility requirements for Medicaid.

3.2 Frozen Asset Tests

The proportion of older people relying on Medicaid decreased from 16 percent in 1970 to 13 percent in 2006. Reliance on Medicaid is down both because poverty among older people is now below 10 percent and because the Medicaid asset test has not kept pace with inflation (Harrington Meyer and Herd 2007). Under certain conditions, Medicaid applicants may exclude their homes, cars, and certain life insurance and burial space funds, but all other savings, bonds, stocks, mutual funds, and properties must total less than the asset test. The federal Medicaid asset maximum has been frozen since 1989 at $2,000 per individual and $3,000 per couple (KFF 2011; SSA 2009; Commonwealth Fund 2005). States can, and some do, set less restrictive assets tests.

A smaller subset of dual Medicare and Medicaid enrollees receive limited coverage under two relatively new federal programs that relax eligibility guidelines, increasing both the income and assets limits. Since 1998, Qualified Medicare Beneficiary (QMB) program and Specified Low Income Medicare Beneficiary (SLMB) reduce out-of-pocket costs to 13 percent of total annual incomes (KFF 2010). However, Congressional appropriations for SLMB are limited, and once the program funds are gone, no one is admitted to the program until new appropriations are granted.

Less than one-third of poor older people actually receive Medicaid (CBO 2005), and only one-half of those who are eligible receive the benefit (U.S. Congress 2000; Moon and Herd 2002; KFF 2003). Although some may choose not to receive their benefits out of lack of necessity, many are discouraged by the complicated and stigmatizing nature of the application process, as well as the restrictive eligibility rules.[1] QMB and SLMB provide relaxed eligibility guidelines, but also involve complex application procedures. Only 55 percent of those who qualify for QMB actually participate, and only 16 percent of those who qualify for SLMB actually participate (KFF 2010; Moon and Herd 2002; Quadagno 1999). Ultimately, the majority, fully 81 percent, of Medicaid beneficiaries are still subject to the standard asset test (KFF 2010). These low asset standards are problematic for community-based Medicaid recipients who are expected to pay for all of their nonmedical living expenses with virtually no savings or investments. They are also problematic for those receiving Medicaid in nursing homes. About one-third of current 65-year-olds will ever enter a nursing home, and, for most, that stay will last less than one year. Some who are medically able to leave the nursing home may be too impoverished by the low asset test to reestablish their lives in the community (Brown and Finkelstein 2009). Some policy makers want the asset tests indexed to inflation to better facilitate Medicaid coverage of long-term care for those with meager resources, whereas others argue that doing so would expand Medicaid eligibility and expenses dramatically (Brown and Finkelstein 2009; Estes and Associates 2001; Harrington Meyer and Herd 2007).

3.3 Admissions Discrimination

For those Americans who rely on Medicaid for their health care, access to that care can be problematic. Medicaid reimbursement rates to providers are often well below market and Medicare rates, leading many doctors, clinics, labs, hospitals, and nursing homes to refuse to treat, or to cap the number of, Medicaid patients (Commonwealth Fund 2005; Harrington Meyer and Kesterke-Storbakken 2000; MedPac 2008). Although the medical profession is often portrayed as a powerful influence on health policy (Quadagno 2005), its failure to boost Medicaid reimbursement rates is a notable exception. The American Health Care Association (2011) reported that for the nation, the average

Medicaid reimbursement for daily nursing home care was over $17 below cost and that the situation was growing worse each year. The impact of lower reimbursements is evident. Among primary care physicians in the United States in 2008, 84 percent were accepting new private payers, 61 percent were accepting new Medicare recipients, and only 42 percent were accepting new Medicaid patients (Cunningham 2011). Indeed, the lower reimbursement rates cause doctors to distinguish, and often discriminate, on the basis of payer source. Between 1980 and 1997, nursing homes and other health care providers could and did sue states on the grounds that Medicaid reimbursement rates were too low, using provisions in the Boren Amendment to the federal Medicaid statute in the Social Security Act. The courts became an important venue for policy making. However, that amendment was repealed by the 1997 Balanced Budget Act. As Medicaid rates stalled out, private pay rates continued to rise. In addition to causing hospitals, clinics, nursing homes, and other providers to eliminate or limit Medicaid admissions, lower reimbursements rates also cause private payers and Medicare recipients in all types of health care facilities to subsidize the costs of care for Medicaid patients in their same facility (Harrington Meyer and Herd 2007).

During the 1990s, Harrington Meyer interviewed nursing home administrators, Medicaid applicants and their families, and Medicaid officials in the state of Illinois. At that time, Medicaid was reimbursing nursing homes at just 70 percent of the private pay rate. For-profit and not-for-profit nursing home administrators alike reported that they were either not accepting Medicaid patients at all, capping the number they took in, or requiring a certain number of private pay months paid in advance of admission (Harrington Meyer and Kesterke-Storbakken 2000). Nursing home administrators reported that they were actively cross-subsidizing the care of Medicaid patients using fees paid by Medicare and private payers. One nursing home administrator said that the reimbursement rates for Medicaid were so low that he would rather leave the nursing home bed empty than fill it with a Medicaid patient (Harrington Meyer and Kesterke-Storbakken 2000). Another said that as soon as she realized that the patient would be on Medicaid, she would conclude the application interview and file the application in her circular file (her trash can). Several reported that they demanded proof of private payment, ranging from six months to two years, because they were unwilling to accept Medicaid recipients on admission. Medicaid reimbursement rates continue to fall behind Medicare and private insurance rates affecting both access to, and quality of, care (MedPac 2008; Intrator and Mor 2004)

Because they are more likely to be on Medicaid, older and disabled women, blacks, and Hispanics, and unmarried persons are more likely to face the consequences of lower reimbursement rates through denial of, or delays in, treatments or admissions (Harrington Meyer and Herd 2007). Some states, notably Minnesota, Florida, Ohio, and Connecticut have either prohibited or limited discrepancies between private and public pay rates and, as a result, admissions discrimination against Medicaid recipients is less frequent in those states (U.S. GAO 1990). In most states, however, the rate discrepancies persist and lead to widespread discrimination in admissions procedures. States have little incentive to make reimbursement rates competitive, given their emphasis on cost cutting. Health care providers, nursing homes included, have little incentive to admit nursing home residents given their emphasis on trying to maintain profit margins. Indeed, the nursing home industry has become increasingly for-profit and concentrated in the hands of a shrinking pool of owners, leading to ongoing concerns about the quality of care (Duhigg 2007). Some policy analysts favor setting Medicaid reimbursement rates equal to Medicare rates, arguing that rate equity would help reduce discrimination at the time of admission for nursing home applicants and may help improve quality of care, whereas opponents caution that the increased costs would be too much for state budgets to bare (Harrington Meyer and Herd 2007; American Health Care Association 2011).

3.4 Frozen Personal Needs Allowance

For those admitted to nursing homes, Medicaid policy reduces autonomy, sometimes in degrading ways. Unlike Medicaid recipients in the community, who keep their income and receive free health care through Medicaid, Medicaid recipients in nursing homes become wards of the state. Nursing homes are regarded as total institutions, meant to provide for all the basic needs of residents. Thus, all Medicaid recipients' Social Security and any private monies go toward paying their nursing home costs; Medicaid is payer of last resort. Since the personal needs allowance (PNA) was established in 1974, Medicaid recipients in nursing homes are permitted to keep a small monthly personal needs allowance to cover basic necessities not covered by Medicaid, including clothing, haircuts, transportation, phone calls, cable television, stamps, dentures, glasses, orthopedic shoes and devices, and dental work (Harrington Meyer and Kesterke-Storbakken 2000). The federal minimum personal needs allowance was set at $30 in 1988 and there it has remained. A few states have indexed the personal needs allowance to cost of living increases. In 2000, 21 states still used the federal minimum of $30 a month; 19 states allowed residents to keep an amount between $31 and $40 a month; 11 states allowed residents, including some veterans, to retain between $40, and $90 a month (Kassner and Shirey 2000).

3.5 Medicaid Estate Recovery

Since Medicaid was implemented in 1965, states have had the option to recover Medicaid costs from the estates of recipients, but only 12 states had employed any such recovery efforts. Then the 1993 Omnibus Budget Reconciliation Act required all states to do so (U.S. Department of Health and Human Services 2005a and b). Today, all states except Michigan are pursuing estate recovery, though they do so with various amounts of vigor and with rules that vary widely (Fox-Grage 2006). The logic is that many older people are cash poor but house rich. For example, when applying for Medicaid coverage of nursing home care, applicants are permitted to exempt their home and car. Prior to the Deficit Reduction Act of 2005, Medicaid disregarded the full value of primary residences, but now states may deem those with homes worth more than $500,000 ineligible unless a spouse or disabled child lives in the home or unless recovery presents undue hardship (U.S. Department of Health and Human Services 2005a). States may also permit eligibility up to $750,000 in home value and 11 states currently employ this more relaxed standard (KFF 2010). For all of those who are deemed eligible, however, states are required to attempt to recoup Medicaid expenditures posthumously as a means to reduce Medicaid expenditures.

The recovery is made from Medicaid patient estates after they die, before the remainder is distributed to those cited in the will (Wood and Sabatino 1996). Specifically, the Medicaid Estate Recovery Act requires states to recoup Medicaid expenses from the estates of anyone who has received Medicaid services after the age of 55 or has been determined by the state to be permanently institutionalized (U.S. Department of Health and Human Services 2005a). States must attempt to recover Medicaid expenses for nursing home care, home- and community-based services, hospital care, and prescription drug expenditures. States may elect to recover for additional care services, including physician services, hospice care, and technology assistance (Karp, Sabatino, and Wood 2005; U.S. Department of Health and Human Services 2005a). States may decide to exempt certain costs, such as Medicaid coverage of the Medicare Part B premium.

As described in the chapter by Grogan and Andrews on Medicaid (this volume), the national government pays for a larger share of Medicaid in some states than others. States with the highest proportion of federal matching for their Medicaid budget, typically the poorest states, appear to have the least incentive to recover because much of the recovered funds are then returned to the federal government. Nevertheless, recovery rates are in fact not linked to matching rates (Wood and Klem 2007; Kassner and Shirey 2000). States with higher property values have the greatest incentive to recover because home values are more likely to exceed recovery costs by a higher proportion. In total, only eight states recovered two or more percent of Medicaid nursing home expenditures in 2004, and seven states reported no or nearly no recoveries (Karp, Sabatino, and Wood 2005). Despite implementation of the federal requirement, Medicaid estate recovery has offset little of total Medicaid spending on nursing homes. In 1995, estate recovery in all states totaled $125 million, less than 0.5 percent of Medicaid nursing home expenditures for the aged (Wood and Sabatino 1996; Wiener and Stevenson 1998). By 2004, Medicaid estate recovery totaled over $360 million, an amount equal to less than 0.8 percent of Medicaid nursing home spending, and only about 0.13 percent of total Medicaid spending in that same year (U.S. Department of Health and Human Services 2005a and b). Clearly, Medicaid estate recovery helps a little to replenish the coffers for this financially strapped program. Though there have been some challenges from heirs, critics caution that the main concern is that estate recovery may discourage the aged from seeking needed medical care because they remain liable for their Medicaid benefits posthumously and because it converts a public benefit into a private loan (Karp, Sabatino, and Wood 2005; Katz Olson 2003; Schwartz and Sabatino 1994).

4 CLASS ACT

Before 2010, the main expansion to Medicare was the addition of a prescription drug benefit in 2003, and, to Medicaid, the addition of many more low-income mothers and children. In contrast, few expansions to the public provision of long-term care have even been
considered in the United States in recent decades. The one notable exception, the CLASS
Act (2010), would have provided workers a market-based, voluntary, long-term care
insurance plan. In exchange for a monthly premium, beneficiaries would have received a
basic lifetime benefit of a least $50 a day in the event of illness or disability. Benefits could
be used to cover medical and even nonmedical needs, such as making a house wheel-
chair accessible or hiring a home caregiver to assist with basic tasks. Championed by
the late Senator Edward Kennedy, and supported by the nursing home industry, CLASS
was meant to be a part of the national health care plan backed by President Obama
(American Health Care Association 2011; *Washington Post* 2011). Supporters saw it as a
way to increase long-term care insurance and help people cover chronic care services.
Conservative critics warned that the program would be too expensive and increase the
role of the federal government, and liberal critics warned that the benefits would be too
meager, and the premiums too steep, for most American consumers. In the end, the
Obama administration pulled the plug on the act, reporting that because the policy was
required to be financially self-sufficient, monthly premiums would likely soar to between
$400 and $1000, discouraging nearly all from participating (*Washington Post* 2011).

5 MAJOR CHALLENGES FOR FAMILIES

Given the dearth of public and private insurance, families provide about 80 percent of
all long-term care to their frail older relatives. Many family care providers are on call
seven days a week for several hours a day (National Alliance for Caregiving and AARP
2009; Navaie-Waliser, Spriggs, and Feldman 2002). In addition to helping with medical care, care work includes cleaning, helping with finances, running errands, cooking,
and assisting with eating, bathing, dressing, and mobility. The long-standing practice
of women providing most of the care work has diminished somewhat, but women continue to perform almost twice as much as men. Seventy percent of spousal care workers
are wives, and 60 percent to 80 percent of children who care for their older parents are
daughters (KFF 2009b; National Alliance for Caregiving and AARP 2004, 2009). Black
and Hispanic women report higher levels of care work than do whites. Given that black
and Hispanic women have lower incomes and worse health, these additional duties add
up to an even greater burden than for those with more resources (National Alliance for
Caregiving and AARP 2004).

Family care work has intensified in recent years (National Alliance for Caregiving and AARP 2009; AARP 2008; Estes and Associates 2001). Often families, mainly wives and daughters, are expected to perform highly technical work including tubal feedings, dressing changes, chemotherapy and phototherapy administration, apnea monitoring, and oxygen tent management. Such work is particularly stressful for family members who have had little medical training. Stone (2000) estimated that there are 40 unpaid informal care workers for every paid formal care worker. The total value of formal and informal care work, which is defined differently by various scholars, is estimated to be over $50 billion per year (Holtz-Eakin 2005; National Alliance for Caregiving and AARP 2004), with some sources estimating the total value to be as high as $375 billion per year (AARP 2008).

Most care workers report that the work is rewarding, but many also report that they experience substantial burden and stress. Some care workers report high rates of sleep-lessness, exhaustion, inadequate exercise, chronic conditions, anxiety, loneliness, family tension, and drug misuse (Brody 2004; National Alliance for Caregiving 2009; Pavalko and Woodbury 2000; Stone 2000). Care workers are at a significant risk for depression, with 50 percent of care workers reporting depressive symptoms (Clark and Diamond 2010). Some studies suggest that long-term provision of care tends to weaken the immune system, increase psychological distress, and accelerate aging (Epel et al. 2004; Pavalko and Woodbury 2000). Care workers take on emotional and physical labor in addition to their own daily responsibilities, placing them in stressful situations where they require increased social, physical, and economic supports that they often do not receive.

Efforts to relieve the social, emotional, and economic burdens on care workers have been few and modest in their effectiveness. Some workers, especially women, add unpaid care work to their paid responsibilities, whereas others tend to reduce or elimi-nate paid work. Pavalko and Henderson (2006) found that women whose jobs provide flexible hours, unpaid family leave, and paid sick leave are likely to remain employed, improving financial security for their own old age. For care workers who would like to take time off from work to provide assistance to frail older relatives, the Family and Medical Leave Act provides up to 12 weeks of unpaid leave. But the leave is only man-dated by law for large companies. The act only covers about 60 percent of private sector workers and just under 50 percent are both covered and eligible (Waldfogel 2001). Given that the leave is unpaid and covers only 12 weeks, taking it is not often a meaningful option for most long-term care workers.

6 CONCLUSION

The U.S. long-term care system is fragmented and inadequate, leaving many older peo-ple to turn to family members for care. Though the work is often meaningful, it tends to negatively affect care workers' health and financial status. Despite changes in families and in long-term care policies, families continue to grapple with rising out-of-pocket costs and barriers to adequate support from government programs. As the U.S. moves forward in developing and implementing national long-term care policy, it is important to remember that those older and disabled people who are affected by Medicaid are, by definition, poor, and disproportionately women, black and Hispanic, and single. These vulnerable older and disabled Americans, and their families, will be most affected by the policy changes to come.

Notes

1. See chapter on food stamps for comparative evidence.

References

*Indicates recommended reading.

AARP. 2005. *Public Attitudes toward Social Security and Private Accounts*. Washington, DC: AARP Knowledge Movement.

AARP. 2008. *Valuing the Invaluable: The Economic Value of Family Caregiving, 2008 Update*. Washington, DC: AARP Public Policy Institute.

AARP. 2009. *Across the States 2009: Profiles of Long Term Care and Independent Living*. Washington, DC: AARP Public Policy Institute.

American Health Care Association. 2011. "Issue Brief: Protect and Preserve Medicaid Funding for Long Term Care." http://www.ahcancal.org/advocacy/issue_briefs/Issue%20Briefs/IBProtectPreserveMedicaidFunding.pdf.

Baker, Sam. 2012. "Nursing Homes Say Its Time for States to Undo Medicaid Cuts." *Health Watch*. http://thehill.com/blogs/healthwatch/medicaid/221427-nursing-homes-say-its-time-for-states-to-undo-medicaid-cuts.

Becker, Gary S. 2005. "A Political Case for Social Security Reform." *Wall Street Journal*, February 15, A18.

*Brody, Elaine M. 2004. *Women in the Middle: Their Parent Care Years*. 2nd ed. New York: Springer.

Brown, Jeffrey R., and Amy Finkelstein. 2009. "The Private Market for Long-Term Care Insurance in the U.S.: A Review of the Evidence." *Journal of Risk Insurance* 76 (1): 5–29. http://www.ncbi.nlm.nih.gov/pmc/articles/PMC2799900/.

CBO (Congressional Budget Office). 2005. *The Long-Term Budget Outlook*. Washington, DC: CBO. http://www.cbo.gov/showdoc.cfm?index=6982&sequence=0.

Clark, Michele C., and Pamela M. Diamond. 2010. "Depression in Family Caregivers of Elders: A Theoretical Model of Caregiver Burden, Sociotropy, and Autonomy." *Research in Nursing and Health* 33: 20–34.

Commonwealth Fund. 2005. *The Long-Term Budget Outlook*. Washington, DC: CBO.

Cunningham, Peter J. 2011. *State Variation in Primary Care Physician Supply: Implications for Health Reform Medicaid Expansions.* Washington, DC: Center for Studying Health System Change. http://www.rwjf.org/files/research/72046.pdf.

Duhigg, Charles. 2007. "At Many Homes, More Profit, Less Nursing." *New York Times*, September 23. http://www.nytimes.com/2007/09/23/business/23nursing.html.

Engelhardt, Gary V., and Jonathan Gruber. 2004. *Social Security and the Evolution of Elderly Poverty.* NBER Working Paper No. 10466. Cambridge: National Bureau of Economic Research.

Epel, Elissa S., Elizabeth H. Blackburn, Jue Lin, Firdaus S. Dhabhar, Nancy E. Adler, Jason D. Morrow, and Richard M. Cawthon. 2004. "Accelerated Telomere Shortening in Response to Life Stress." *Proceedings of the National Academy of Sciences of the United States of America* 101: 17312–17315.

Estes, Carroll L., and James H. Swan. 1993. *The Long Term Care Crisis: Elders Trapped in the No-Care Zone.* Newbury Park, CA: Sage.

*Estes, Carroll L., and Associates. 2001. *Social Policy and Aging: A Critical Perspective.* Thousand Oaks: Sage.

Fox-Grage, Wendy. 2006. *Medicaid Estate Recovery.* Washington, DC: AARP Public Policy Institute. http://www.aarp.org/research/ppi/healthcare/medicaid/articles/fs127recovery.html.

Friedman, Milton. 2002. *Capitalism and Freedom.* 40th Anniversary ed. Chicago: Chicago University Press.

Gilbert, Neil. 2002. *Transformation of the Welfare State: The Silent Surrender of Public Responsibility.* New York: Oxford University Press.

Hacker, Jacob S. 2002. *The Divided Welfare State: The Battle over Public and Private Social Benefits in the United States.* New York: Cambridge University Press.

Harrington Meyer, Madonna. 1991a. "Organizing the Frail Elderly." In B. Hess and E. Markson, eds., *Growing Old in America*, 4th ed. New Brunswick, NJ: Transaction, 363–376.

Harrington Meyer, Madonna. 1991b. "Assuring Quality of Care: Nursing Home Resident Councils." *Journal of Applied Gerontology* 10 (1): 103–116.

Harrington Meyer, Madonna. 1994. "Institutional Bias and Medicaid Use in Nursing Homes." *Journal of Aging Studies* 8 (2): 179–193.

*Harrington Meyer, Madonna, and Pamela Herd. 2007. *Market Friendly or Family Friendly? The State and Gender Inequality in Old Age.* New York: Russell Sage.

Harrington Meyer, Madonna, and Michelle Kesterke-Storbakken. 2000. "Shifting the Burden Back to Families? How Medicaid Cost-Containment Reshapes Access to Long Term Care in the U.S." In Madonna Harrington Meyer, ed., *Care Work: Gender, Labor and the Welfare State.* New York: Routledge Press, 217–228.

Holtz-Eakin, Douglas. 2005. "*The Cost and Financing of Long-Term Care Services.*" Statement of Douglas Holtz-Eakin, Director, before the Subcommittee on Health Committee on Ways and Means U.S. House of Representatives. April 27. Washington,: CBO.

Intrator, Orna, and Vincent Mor. 2004. "Effect of State Medicaid Reimbursement Rates on Hospitalizations from Nursing Homes." *Journal of American Geriatric Society* 52: 393–398.

Johnson, Nicholas, Phil Oliff, and Erica Williams. 2010. *An Update on State Budget Cuts: At Least 45 States have Imposed Cuts that Hurt Vulnerable Residents and the Economy.* Washington, DC: Center on Budget and Policy Priorities. http://www.cbpp.org/cms/?fa=view&id=1214.

Karp, Naomi, Charles P. Sabatino, and Erica F. Wood. 2005. *Medicaid Estate Recovery: A 2004 Survey of State Programs and Practices.* #2005-06. Washington, DC: AARP Policy Institute. http://assets.aarp.org/rgcenter/il/2005_06_recovery.pdf.

Kassner, Enid, and Lee Shirey. 2000. *Medicaid Financial Eligibility for Older People: State Variations in Access to Home and Community-Based Waiver and Nursing Home Services.* Washington, DC: AARP.

*Katz, Michael B. 1986. *In the Shadow of the Poorhouse: A Social History of Welfare in America.* New York: Basic Books.

Katz Olson, Laura. 2003. *The Not-So-Golden Years: Caregiving, the Frail Elderly, and the Long-Term Care Establishment.* Lanham: Rowman and Littlefield.

KFF (Kaiser Family Foundation). 2003. "Dual Enrollees: Medicaid's Role for Low-Income Medicare Beneficiaries." *Kaiser Commission on Medicaid and the Uninsured.* Washington, DC: KFF.

KFF. 2009a. *Medicare's Role for Women Fact Sheet.* Washington, DC: KFF.

KFF. 2009b. *Medicaid and Long-Term Care Services and Supports. Fact Sheet.* http://www.kff.org/medicaid/upload/2186_06.pdf.

KFF. 2009c. "Closing the Long-Term Care Funding Gap: The Challenge of Private Long-Term Care Insurance." http://kff.org/health-costs/issue-brief/closing-the-long-term-care-funding-gap/

KFF. 2009d. *Advancing Access to Medicaid Home and Community-Based Services: Key Issues Based on a Working Group Discussion with Medicaid Experts.* Washington, DC: KFF. http://www.kff.org/medicaid/upload/7970.pdf.

KFF. 2010. *Medicaid Financial Eligibility: Primary Pathways for the Elderly and People with Disabilities.* Washington, DC: KFF. http://www.kff.org/medicaid/upload/8048.pdf.

KFF. 2011. *Medicaid and Long-Term Care Services and Supports. Fact Sheet.* http://www.kff.org/medicaid/upload/2186-08.pdf.

KFF. 2012. *Medicaid's Role for Women Across the Lifespan: Current Issues and the Impact of the Affordable Care Act.* Washington, DC: KFF. http://www.kff.org/womenshealth/upload/7213-03.pdf.

Korpi, Walter. 2000. *Faces of Inequality: Gender, Class and Patterns of Inequalities in Different Types of Welfare States.* Luxembourg Income Study Working Paper No. 224. Syracuse, NY: Syracuse University.

Korpi, Walter, and Joakim Palme. 1998. "The Paradox of Redistribution and Strategies of Equality: Welfare State Institutions, Inequality, and Poverty in the Western Countries." *American Sociological Review* 63: 661–687.

Leland, John. 2010. "Cuts in Home Care Put Elderly and Disabled at Risk." *New York Times,* July 21. http://www.nytimes.com/2010/07/21/us/21aging.html?_r=1&hpw.

MedPac. 2008. *A Data Book: Health Care Spending and the Medicare Program.* Washington, DC: Medicare Payment Advisory Commission.

Moon, Marilyn, and Pamela Herd. 2002. *A Place at the Table: Women's Needs and Medicare Reform.* New York: Century Foundation.

National Alliance for Caregiving and AARP. 2004. *Caregiving in the U.S.* Washington, DC: National Alliance for Caregiving and AARP.

*National Alliance for Caregiving and AARP. 2009. *Caregiving in the U.S. 2009.* Washington, DC: National Alliance for Caregiving and AARP.

Navaie-Waliser, Maryam, Aubrey Spriggs, and Penny H. Feldman. 2002. "Informal Caregiving— Differential Experiences by Gender." *Medical Care* 40: 1249–1259.

Oberlander, Jonathan. 2003. *The Political Life of Medicare.* Chicago: University of Chicago Press, 2003.

Pavalko, Eliza K., and Kathryn A. Henderson. 2006. "Combining Care Work and Paid Work: Do Workplace Policies Make a Difference?" *Research on Aging* 28: 359–374.

Pavalko, Eliza K., and Shari Woodbury. 2000. "Social Roles as Process: Caregiving Careers and Women's Health." *Journal of Health and Social Behavior* 41: 91–105.

Public Agenda. 2005. "*Medicare: Results of Survey Question re Federal Budget.*" PublicAgenda. org Issue Guides. April 18–22.

Quadagno, Jill. 1999. "Creating a Capital Investment Welfare State: The New American Exceptionalism." *American Sociological Review* 64 (1): 1–11.

*Quadagno, Jill. 2005. *One Nation, Uninsured: Why the U.S. Has No National Health Insurance*. New York: Oxford University Press.

Schwartz, Roger A., and Charles P. Sabatino. 1994. *Medicaid Estate Recovery under OBRA '93: Picking the Bones of the Poor?* Washington, DC: American Bar Association. Commission on Legal Problems of the Elderly.

SSA (Social Security Administration). 2009. "Annual Statistical Supplement 2008." *Social Security Bulletin*. Washington, DC: Department of Health and Human Services.

*Stone, Robyn I. 2000. *Long-Term Care for the Elderly with Disabilities: Current Policy, Emerging Trends, and Implications for the Twenty-first Century*. Washington, DC: Milbank Memorial Fund.

U.S. Congress. House Committee on Ways and Means. 2000. "*Green Book: Background Material and Data on Programs within the Jurisdiction of the Committee on Ways and Means.*" WMCP: 106–14. Washington, DC: GPO.

U.S. Department of Health and Human Services. 2005a. "Medicaid Estate Recovery." Policy Brief #1. http://aspe.hhs.gov/daltcp/reports/estaterec.htm.

U.S. Department of Health and Human Services. 2005b. "Medicaid Estate Recovery Collections." Policy Brief #6. http://aspe.hhs.gov/daltcp/reports/estreccol.htm.

U.S. General Accounting Office. 1990. *Nursing Homes: Admissions Problems for Medicaid Recipients and Attempts to Solve Them*. GAO/HRD-90-135. Washington, DC: GPO.

Waldfogel, Jane. 2001. "Family and Medical Leave: Evidence from the 2000 Surveys." *Monthly Labor Review* 124 (9): 17–23.

Washington Post. 2011. "White House Kills Long-Term Care Program." October 14. http://www.washingtonpost.com/national/health-science/white-house-kills-long-term-care-program/2011/10/14/gIQAVZLYkL_story.html.

Wiener, Joshua M., and David G. Stevenson. 1998. "*Long-Term Care for the Elderly: Profiles of Thirteen States.*" Assessing the New Federalism, Occasional Paper No. 12, August Washington, DC: Urban Institute Press.

Wood, Erica F., and Ellen M. Klem. 2007. *Protections in Medicaid Estate Recovery: Findings, Promising Practices, and Model Notices*. #2007-07. Washington DC: AARP Policy Institute. http://assets.aarp.org/rgcenter/il/2007_07_medicaid.pdf.

Wood, Erica F., and Charles P. Sabatino. 1996. "Medicaid Estate Recovery and the Poor: Restitution or Retribution?" *Generations* 20 (3): 84–87.

Yergin, Daniel, and Joseph Stanislaw. 1998. *The Commanding Heights: The Battle between Government and the Marketplace That Is Remaking the Modern World*. New York: Simon and Schuster.

PART V

PROGRAMS FOR THE POOR AND NEAR-POOR

CHAPTER 19

···

MEDICAID

···

COLLEEN M. GROGAN AND CHRISTINA M. ANDREWS

1 INTRODUCTION

MEDICAID is often described as America's health-care program for the poor. Yet, this description has never been entirely accurate. When Medicaid was enacted in 1965, it was only intended for select groups of poor people: low-income adults with dependent children, disabled persons, and older people. These groups became eligible for Medicaid primarily through receipt of cash assistance. Today, Medicaid remains a means-tested targeted program, but the link between Medicaid and cash assistance has largely been severed. Eligibility has expanded in many ways, largely because the federal government has mandated or, more often, provided optional coverage for certain groups, such as pregnant women and children in two-parent households, and provided financing to states that chose to expand coverage to certain additional groups, such as single childless adults. Even before the passage of the Affordable Care Act (ACA) in 2010, Medicaid had become the single largest health-insurance program in terms of number of people covered in the United States, surpassing even Medicare—the ever popular universal program for older people.

Under the ACA, Medicaid's role in financing health care in the United States will expand even further. For the first time since the Medicaid program was enacted over 45 years ago, all states will have the option to provide coverage to all low-income citizens, including many above existing poverty guidelines. In the single largest expansion in the program's history, roughly 16 million additional people could become eligible for Medicaid, accounting for nearly half of the total number of Americans who will obtain health insurance under the ACA (KFF 2013). Because the new law offers generous federal financing—covering 90 percent of the cost of new eligibles—for expanding coverage up to a federally defined eligibility level, health-care reform offers the potential to equalize Medicaid coverage across the states. Since many states have already declared their commitment toward expanding Medicaid under the ACA, it is clear that after 2014, many groups who were not covered in the past—single adult males, childless couples, and the homeless, for example—will receive access to public insurance.

Although this optional expansion will be substantial, it is a step back from what the Obama Administration and the majority in Congress wanted the ACA to achieve. In the original bill, the federal government required all states to expand Medicaid eligibility for all people with incomes below 133 percent of poverty. Twenty states submitted a lawsuit claiming the bill to be unconstitutional and, in particular, argued that the federal Medicaid mandate was too coercive. The Supreme Court ruled that the federal government could entice states with federal funds by allowing states the option to expand Medicaid coverage, but could not mandate expanded coverage. The lawsuit and the Supreme Court Decision reflect that larger political fight over Medicaid's role. As this chapter will demonstrate, many of these political struggles are rooted in Medicaid's institutional design, which fostered the gradual expansion of the program over time. In particular, an intergovernmental design with a generous federal matching rate and substantial state discretion has led to continual expansions. These expansions, in turn, have created a political constituency for Medicaid—both provider groups and enrollees— that fights against retrenchment. Yet, as program expenditures continue to increase, especially during fiscally distressed times, the partisan divide over the future direction of Medicaid became more stark.

2 Historical Background

Medicaid's roots can be traced to the nineteenth century with state and local government provision of health-care services for the poor. In this early period, responses to health-care needs were highly localized and varied. Growing concern about access to health care, particularly for poor seniors, led to the establishment of two federal programs by the 1960s. In 1950, the federal government created a grant-in-aid program that allowed funding for states to pay for the medical expenses of persons on cash assistance. The Kerr-Mills Act of 1960 expanded on this idea by allowing funding for states to cover poor seniors, who incurred high medical expenses relative to their income (Stevens and Stevens 1974).

Despite these advances in coverage, liberal policymakers continued their fight for a federal-level universal program. However, after the failure of national health insurance (NHI) under President Truman, they compromised their position to focus on national health insurance for older people. In the early 1960s, the Medicare proposal was publically discussed as an alternative to Kerr-Mills. Proponents of Kerr-Mills argued that the program would provide comprehensive services to those who truly needed it as opposed to limited services to seniors. Although the popular debate suggested a choice between Medicare's limited universalism or Kerr-Mills' comprehensive means-tested program, behind the scenes, the Chairman of the powerful Ways and Means Committee,

Representative Wilbur Mills, along with Wilbur Cohen, Under Secretary of Health, Education and Welfare (HEW), and President Johnson were working out a deal to make Kerr-Mills (which they called Medicaid) a supplement to Medicare. Medicare and Medicaid were both enacted in 1965 (Blumenthal and Morone 2009).

Although the 1964 Democratic landslide provided a large enough majority to pass Medicare and Medicaid, there was a divide at the start over what this dual adoption meant for the future trajectory of health-care reform. Representative Wilbur Mills viewed the Medicaid supplemental strategy as a way to reduce demand for universal coverage; by providing for "worthy" groups, Mills sought to stave off claims for broader health-care coverage (Patashnik and Zelizer 2001). In contrast, proponents of NHI continued to view Medicare as an important first step toward universal coverage and Medicaid as a mere residual program that could be swiftly eliminated when NHI was adopted (Stevens and Stevens 1974).

3 EARLY YEARS: RESIDUAL MEDICAID AMID EXPANSIVE CONTRADICTIONS

Although Medicaid was structured as a means-tested program, three crucial components of Kerr-Mills—the concept of the "medically indigency," comprehensive benefits, and intergovernmental financing with a generous federal matching rate—were carried over into Medicaid, and became the seeds of expansion over time (Grogan 2014). Almost immediately after the program was passed, some liberal states viewed Medicaid as an opportunity to expand coverage with federal funds. New York State was a pioneer in this regard. Using the medically needy provision, which included nonpoor people with medical needs, New York passed legislation in 1967 to set the Medicaid income eligibility requirements at a level high enough to encompass almost half its residents, thus including not only the poor, but also working- and middle-class families. New York's actions called into question the fundamental purpose of the newly created Medicaid program: Should it serve only as a safety net for the nation's neediest citizens, or as a stepping-stone toward universal health care coverage? Federal legislators responded to this question unequivocally by passing an amendment in 1968 that capped income eligibility for Medicaid at 133 percent of the state-mandated Aid to Families with Dependent Children (AFDC) eligibility line (Stevens and Stevens 1974; Grogan and Patashnik 2003a).

Meanwhile, liberal reformers at the federal level focused their efforts on expanding Medicare. Although logical, their strategy dashed the hopes of liberal states attempting to use Medicaid as a stepping-stone toward NHI. In so doing, Congress ensured that states would severely limit the expansion of coverage to citizens with incomes above state-defined cash assistance levels. Thus, early on its history, Medicaid was clearly defined as "welfare medicine" (Stevens and Stevens 1974).

Although the 1968 amendment tightened considerably the definition of medical indigency, it nonetheless maintained the concept, which meant the program had the potential to expand again in the future. The 1968 statute also expanded a series of well-child benefits for poor children, creating the Early and Periodic Screening, Diagnostic Treatment (EPSDT) program. The practical effect was to make the Medicaid benefit package even more comprehensive (Rosenbaum and Sonosky 1999).

The creation of the Supplemental Security Income (SSI) program in 1972 produced an enormous (though perhaps unintended) expansion of Medicaid. It consolidated five separate state-run cash assistance programs for the aged, blind, and disabled into a single, federal means-tested program (Stevens and Stevens 1974; Quadagno 1988). Because SSI, unlike most means-tested benefits, is run as a *nationally uniform* program, a clear bifurcation among Medicaid beneficiaries was established. Seniors, blind, and disabled—who tended to be viewed sympathetically—gained Medicaid eligibility based on a single *federal* eligibility standard. In contrast, poor mothers and their children gained eligibility according to (typically much lower) *state* eligibility standards, with few exceptions (Watson 1995).

4 THE MIDDLE YEARS: EXPANSION AND GROWTH

Even though Medicaid was a residual welfare program, expansionary seeds began to take hold during the 1980s and 1990s. Medicaid's structure of allowing state discretion over optional coverage combined with comprehensive benefits and intergovernmental financing prompted a series of incremental eligibility expansions for families, older people, and disabled, which, over time, led to major growth.

Because AFDC was primarily limited to single parents with children, most uninsured two-parent families—especially those in which an adult was working—were not eligible for Medicaid. These rules began to change in the 1980s, when it became more widely recognized that most uninsured children resided in working families. Led by Representative Henry Waxman (D-CA), the federal government passed a series of policies—first as options and later as requirements—to expand coverage for children regardless of parental status or attachment to the labor force, and ultimately led to coverage of many children in low-income families above the federal poverty line (FPL) (Grogan and Patashnik 2003a; Olson 2010).

The federal dynamics behind these expansions were important. The federal government was responding to state demand—in the 1980s the National Governor's Association lobbied for expanded coverage for children (Thompson and DiIulio 1998; Holahan, Weil, and Weiner 2003; Smith and Moore 2008; Olson 2010)—and the federal matching rate provided the incentive states needed to take up the offer. For example, when the federal government mandated expanded coverage for pregnant women and children in 1988 and again in 1990, the majority of states had already met the requirement (Grogan and Patashnik 2003a). By 1990, Medicaid guidelines mandated inclusion of all children and mothers living below 100 percent of the FPL, and provided numerous options through which states could provide coverage to families above the FPL and continue to receive federal matching contributions. Health insurance for children was expanded again in 1997 through the State Children's Health Insurance Program (SCHIP, now known as CHIP). The mechanism was similar to prior expansions: the federal government, through CHIP, gave states the *option* to cover uninsured children in families with incomes higher than Medicaid eligibility rates and with a matching rate even more generous than Medicaid (about 15 percentage points higher on average) (KFF 2011a). States can use CHIP funds to expand coverage under Medicaid, create a separate program, or a combination of the two. Because it is administratively easier, the majority of states use funds to expand Medicaid or do a combined approach. Not surprisingly, and similar to the pattern in the 1980s, many states quickly took advantage of this new opportunity to expand coverage (KFF 2012a). By 2006, the average CHIP eligibility level was 220 percent of the FPL, and 11 states set eligibility above 300 percent (Grogan and Rigby 2009). By 2002, 47 percent of all children were eligible for SCHIP (Seiden, Hudson, and Banthin 2004).

These institutional components of Medicaid—state discretion, comprehensive benefits, and federal matching rates—also work to expand the program on the long-term-care (LTC) side as well. Similar to pregnant women and children, Medicaid's role in financing services for older people and disabled individuals also began to grow in the late 1980s and 1990s. Although Medicaid acted as the "supplement" Wilbur Mills envisioned, demand for Medicaid's supplemental services grew way beyond what Mills or others predicted. The concepts of "medically needy" and "comprehensive benefits" embedded in Medicaid's enabling legislation were sufficiently elastic that Medicaid continually filled the gaping long-term-care hole, because no other state or federal program covers these costs. Medicare has never covered the costs of long-term custodial nursing-home care, and relatively few Americans have been able or willing to purchase private long-term care insurance during their working years (Konetzka and Luo, 2011). As early as 1970, Medicaid had already emerged as the primary public purchaser of nursing home care. Just 10 years later, Medicaid spending on nursing-home care reached $8.8 billion, equal to all other private and public sources for nursing home care combined (Olson, 2010). By the 1980s it was widely recognized that Medicaid had become America's "de facto LTC program" (Justice et al. 1988; Thompson and DiIulio, 1998).

Senior advocacy groups believed that Medicaid's means-test was stigmatizing and degrading to older people, and, therefore, fought to expand Medicare—not to new groups as advocates of national health insurance had hoped—but to expand the benefit package and reduce the out-of-pocket burdens on seniors. The old problem discussed at the time of Medicare's enactment—universal but limited benefits—came back to rear its ugly head. Congress responded to senior demands in 1988 by passing the Medicare Catastrophic Coverage Act (MCCA), which expanded Medicare's scope of services (to prescription drugs, hospice, and long-term hospital care), but also required all Medicare beneficiaries to pay special premiums pegged to income. Medicaid was mandated to pay the premiums for beneficiaries with incomes below the federal poverty level (Oberlander 2003). Although the MCCA was repealed just one year after its enactment, MCCA provisions requiring Medicaid to pay Medicare premiums for low-income seniors remained intact (Himelfarb 1995). Policymakers, advocates, and interest groups learned three crucial lessons from the failure of MCCA: first, despite Medicare's "favorable" politics, the program was extremely difficult to expand; second, Medicaid would remain America's *de facto* long-term-care insurance program for the foreseeable future (Oberlander 2003); third, and equally important, governors and state legislators learned that the federal government would continue to ask states to share in the burden of LTC coverage for older people and the disabled. Indeed, in the 1990s Medicaid expenditures for nursing-home care began to rise rapidly. By 1997, Medicaid nursing-home expenditures reached $39.4 billion, representing almost half of all nursing-home payments (Grogan and Patashnik 2003b).

This period also saw growth in Medicaid's disabled population. The definition of disability was expanded in 1999 by the Supreme Court case *Olmstead v. L.C.* The Court ruled that mental illness is a form of disability and must be granted protections under the Americans with Disabilities Act (ADA). This ruling made Medicaid coverage available to individuals with mental illness, leading to a significant increase in the number of individuals qualifying for Medicaid. The ruling also required state Medicaid programs to assume responsibility for financing community-based services for clients with mental illnesses. Traditionally, states assumed almost full financial and administrative responsibility for mental health services. Yet, these new rulings, combined with Medicaid's institutional structure, opened the floodgate for states to maximize Medicaid enrollment for all sorts of behavioral health-care services—previously paid for with state-only dollars—in order to leverage federal funds (Coughlin and Zuckerman 2002; Holahan, Weil, and Weiner, 2003; Mark et al. 2011).

Taken together, these expansions in Medicaid coverage increased the number of beneficiaries to 33 million in 2000, up from an average of 20–23 million during the 1970s and 1980s. Medicaid spending rose rapidly as well.

4.1 Program Description

Medicaid is a jointly financed intergovernmental program, largely administered by the states under a set of federal regulations. Since its inception, state participation in the Medicaid program has been optional, and, although all states opted to participate by 1972, each local program evolved somewhat differently. States are required to administer and contribute to their Medicaid programs, and each establishes its own eligibility standards, scope of services, reimbursement rates, and contract guidelines. Moreover, federal matching for state Medicaid programs is based on the average per capita income in each state. Consequently, matching rates vary from 50 percent to 75 percent; states with lower per capita incomes relative to the national average receive a higher federal matching rate. Federal spending levels for Medicaid are determined by the number of people participating in the program, the extent to which enrollees utilize services, and the scope of services covered. Thus, there are many different Medicaid programs—one for each state and territory in the United States (Smith and Moore 2008; Olsen 2010).

Medicaid's impact on the health-care system in the United States is enormous. In 2008, the program provided health-insurance coverage to approximately 60 million Americans (KFF 2012b). Under the ACA, states have the option to expand coverage to all individuals with incomes of up to 133 percent of poverty. For those states adopting this optional coverage, the traditional categorical restrictions on eligibility, which limit enrollment to parents, children, seniors, and disabled individuals who meet income requirements, will be abolished (KFF 2012c). If all states expand coverage, Medicaid would cover an additional 16 million people by 2019. Individuals who become eligible for Medicaid under health-care reform must be provided with a benchmark benefits package that meets minimum standards (Holahan and Headen 2010).

5 MAJOR THEMES

5.1 The New Politics of Middle-Class Medicaid

As the preceding history suggests, Medicaid's expansions for pregnant women and children, seniors, and disabled individuals have gradually extended its reach into the middle class over the 1980s and 1990s (Grogan and Patashnik 2003a; 2003b; Grogan 2008). For the last decade and still today, Medicaid has been America's largest health-insurance program. As a point of comparison, Medicare—our universal program for older people, which most observers thought would expand to national health insurance over time—covered 45 million people compared to Medicaid's 62 million in 2009 (KFF 2012d). That means one in five Americans is covered under Medicaid. The extent to which Medicaid finances the cost of delivering babies in the United States is extraordinary: in Arkansas and Oklahoma, 64 percent of all births were covered by Medicaid in 2009; even in relatively wealthy states such as Minnesota and Oregon, the rates were over 40 percent (KFF 2012e). As babies develop, many continue to be covered by Medicaid: 60 percent of America's children receive Medicaid services (KFF 2012f).

Moreover, Medicaid helps senior citizens (many of whom were considered middle-class all their lives and have children who fit squarely in the middle class) with high out-of-pocket expenses associated with care that is not covered by Medicare. In particular, Medicaid pays the premiums and copays for 20 percent of seniors on Medicare and covers the costs of 70 percent of those in nursing homes. After the federal government passed a number of asset-protection provisions in the 1990s, Medicaid incorporated many seniors into the program who were not low-income prior to entering a nursing home. Among nursing-home residents who do not have Medicaid as a payment at admission, only about one-third remain private payers throughout their stay. About two-thirds "spend down" their savings and eventually become Medicaid eligible (Grogan and Patashnik 2003b). Middle-class families rely on Medicaid for long-term care quite simply because nursing-home costs are astronomical: in 2005, the national average for a semi-private room was approximately $72,000 per year (U.S. Department of Health and Human Services 2010).

Medicaid thus plays a crucial role for a broad range of American families by providing health coverage to their children, older parents, and disabled family members. As a consequence, efforts to retrench the program are met with persistent and growing resistance from provider groups and the public. The nursing-home lobby has been remarkably effective across the 50 states in maintaining Medicaid payments to institutional care for older people and disabled (Sparer 1996; Olson 2010). Advocates for seniors have successfully lobbied states and the national government for more Medicaid coverage of home and community-based care (Grogan 1994; Olson 2010). Those who provide the bulk of primary-care services to Medicaid enrollees, the so-called safety-net providers—community health centers, public hospitals, and numerous nonprofit agencies—have gradually secured expanded Medicaid benefits and payments and expansions in infrastructure (Hall and Rosenbaum 2012; Mickey 2012).

Because Medicaid payments go directly to these provider groups (rather than reimbursing enrollees), these groups all have a vested interest in maintaining Medicaid payments and benefits. Although Medicaid provider payments are notoriously low, relative to rates paid by private insurance companies, Medicaid funds create financial sustainability for many nursing homes, home-care providers, and primary-care safety-net providers (Swan et al. 2000; *Modern Healthcare* 2002; Fornili and Alemi 2007). Indeed, when Texas and a dozen other states threatened to drop out of the Medicaid program when health care reform was passed in 2010, opponents feared the crippling effect such a move would have on the state's economy (as well as on enrollees). In Texas alone, a million people work in the health-care industry, and this was one of the few areas of job growth between 2005 and 2009. According to Tom Banning, chief executive of the Texas Academy of Family Physicians, "the downstream economic implications (of eliminating Medicaid) for Texas' health care infrastructure would be decimating" (Ramshaw and Serafini 2010, A21A).

Although public-opinion data regarding Medicaid are limited, it seems to have shifted over time as the program has expanded. The public's support for Medicaid has always been high. In 1972, when asked whether spending for Medicaid should be increased, decreased, or stay the same, 53 percent of Americans supported an increase in spending, 35 percent said stay the same, and less than 10 percent favored a decrease.[1] During the expansionary period in the 1980s, support for expanding Medicaid spending increased every year. By the late 1980s, more than 60 percent of Americans supported *increasing* Medicaid spending.[2]

Interestingly, questions regarding Medicaid support in national public opinion surveys changed after 1990, reflecting broader public discourse focused on federal budgetary politics. For the years 2008 and 2011, the Kaiser/Harvard Poll (2008) and the CNN/Opinion Research Corp Poll (2011) asked: "Thinking about the federal budget, do you want to see the next president and Congress increase spending on... Medicaid, the program that provides health insurance and long term care to low-income families and people with disabilities, decrease spending, or keep it about the same?" In response to this question in 2008, support for an increase dropped to 34 percent, whereas support for a decrease went up to 11 percent with the remaining 54 percent saying that spending should stay the same. As the fiscal climate continued to worsen across the American states, fewer Americans wanted spending to stay the same (41 percent) in 2011, and more supported a decrease in Medicaid (24 percent).[3] Nonetheless, it is important to realize that even in this extremely fiscally distressed period, the vast majority of American (75 percent) supported an increase or maintaining Medicaid funding. And, when asked pointedly whether Medicaid should be cut to reduce the federal deficit, a surprisingly high number (54 percent) are *strongly* opposed to this idea.[4]

A significant reason for this support may have more to do with middle-class self-interest than middle-class support for helping poor people. The Kaiser Monthly Health Tracking Poll focused specifically on public opinions regarding Medicaid in May 2011 and found that "about half of Americans (51 percent) report some level of personal connection to Medicaid." Consistent with health-coverage statistics, 20 percent report having received Medicaid coverage themselves, whereas the remaining 31 percent report having a friend or family member who received Medicaid at some point. Not surprisingly, this personal connection to Medicaid is strongly associated with beliefs about the program. Among those who have ever received Medicaid benefits, 82 percent say Medicaid is very or somewhat important to themselves and their family. Among those with family or friends who have relied on Medicaid, over half (55 percent) say the program is important. In contrast, among those who have no experience with Medicaid, only 32 percent say the program is important (KFF 2011c). Despite the repeated insistence of policymakers, pollsters, and policy experts on describing Medicaid as a health-care program for "the poor," these surveys suggest that at least half the American populace recognizes Medicaid's significant role for a broad range of American families.

5.2 Medicaid Partisanship and Cooperative Federalism?

The key partisan debate at the federal level has focused on changing Medicaid's financing structure from a matching rate to a federal block grant. Ever since the Reagan Administration first proposed block granting Medicaid in 1981, Republicans in Congress have advocated this reform, with Democrats adamantly fighting against it. When Republicans have control in Congress, a Medicaid block-grant proposal inevitably becomes a priority on the policy agenda. Examples include a block-grant proposal under the Gingrich Congress in 1994, under the Bush Administration's Deficit Reduction Act in 2005, and lately under Representative Ryan's plan to reduce the federal deficit (Thompson and DiIulio 1998; Holahan, Weil, and Wiener 2003; Grogan and Patashnik 2003a; Smith and Moore 2008; Grogan and Rigby 2009; Olson 2010). Part of the reason block-grant proposals have consistently failed, even under Republican control, is because they present tricky political dilemmas for the states. Typically, Republican governors are outwardly supportive of block-grant proposals, but, behind the scenes, there is reluctance due to the fixed budget that block grants represent and concerns that state Medicaid expenditures will not be significantly constrained (Smith and Moore 2008; Grogan and Rigby 2009).

Over the past decade, as states extended Medicaid coverage above the federal poverty level, they have increasingly advocated more flexibility to structure a Medicaid benefit that mimics employer-sponsored health insurance (Holahan, Weil, and Wiener 2003). Such flexibility, including greater ability to define eligibility, benefits, reimbursement, service delivery, rights of appeal, financing, and administration, has been a key objective of proposals supported by the National Governors' Association. Sometimes flexibility is discussed as desirable under block grants, but, more often, states prefer Medicaid's generous federal matching rate along with federal waivers, which provide more discretionary state-level decision-making (Thompson and Burke 2009).

Indeed, this tension over financing and flexibility was at the heart of the state lawsuits against the ACA. The attorneys general from 20 states jointly filed a lawsuit in the Florida U.S. District Court, and the Commonwealth of Virginia filed in a Virginia federal court, claiming that the ACA is unconstitutional. These lawsuits primarily focus on the individual mandate; however, one of the four main legal challenges concerns the federally mandated Medicaid expansion (Cauchi 2011). This challenge claimed that the ACA violated states' rights (and was "coercive") because the Medicaid expansions would have imposed massive financial burdens on the states—if states chose not to expand coverage they would have lost all their Medicaid funds. The federal government countered that Medicaid is an optional program, states are under no requirement to participate, and the federal government is picking up the vast majority of the costs associated with the expansion. In response, the plaintiffs argued that states have become so dependent on Medicaid that it is no longer practical to call state participation optional (Perkins 2011). As the foregoing analysis illustrates, Medicaid has reached substantially into the middle class, making it difficult for any state to cut the program without serious political and social ramifications.

The *price* of the ACA expansion is very low for the states. Indeed, the cost of Medicaid to a state, or the projected financial burden of the Medicaid expansion, has little to do with which states joined the lawsuit. Instead, partisanship drove whether states joined the lawsuit; all but two lawsuit states had Republican Governors.[5] Yet, despite this partisan divide, behind the scenes, states continue to seek federal assistance; all but four states have received infrastructure planning grants from the federal government since 2010. It defies Republican tea-party political rhetoric, but, for most mainstream Republicans, the funding is too difficult to turn down (Jones, Bradley, and Oberlander

2012). Front-stage fighting along with backstage cooperation has been a long-term trend in state Medicaid policy, because, at the end of the day, it has always made fiscal sense for states to leverage federal funds (Grogan 2007; Grogan and Patashnik 2003b, 821–858).

6 Current Challenges

6.1 Explosive Expenditures: Medicaid's Ever Expanding LTC Role

A persistent debate for Medicaid has been its role in financing long-term-care services in the United States. Harrington Meyer and Hausauer (this volume) describe in detail the main policy disputes. Here we wish to highlight some of the political dynamics. As mentioned earlier, the long-term-care services that seniors and the disabled need are extremely expensive. Although seniors and the disabled only account for about 25 percent of Medicaid enrollees, they consume over 65 percent of Medicaid expenditures. Most of the cost of these long-term-care expenses is *not* mandated by the federal government but reflects discretionary spending decisions by the states (60 percent of all Medicaid expenditures represent optional spending). Importantly, the bulk of discretionary spending is directed at the disabled and aged, whereas only about 30 and 15 percent of total spending (respectively) for these groups is mandated by the federal government (Courtot and Lawton 2012).

Thus, although states feel the extraordinary costs of long-term-care services on state budgets, they also feel political pressure to maintain Medicaid coverage for these services, and this creates numerous political challenges. On the one hand, the deep reliance of seniors on nursing-home coverage encourages politicians from both parties to offer families ever greater protections and economic security. All states except two (Indiana and Missouri) use federal options (300 percent SSI or Medicaid Needy program) to expand access to long-term care for older people. There is no correlation between state party control and adoption of the 300 percent rule, which substantially expands access to Medicaid for seniors. On the other hand, elected officials are deeply troubled by the use of Medicaid as a vehicle for protecting the assets of relatively well-off people, and policy makers will complain about the middle class "abusing" Medicaid (Grogan and Patashnik 2003b; Grogan 2014). The issue of home care and innovations has similar dilemmas. For example, many governors oppose providing payment vouchers to family caregivers because there is a strong belief that caregiving should be a familial obligation and not subsidized by the state. Yet, if subsidizing familial care would ultimately help keep older people and disabled in their homes, this seems like a reasonable investment. In sum, despite ever-rising LTC costs, there is a persistent tension over whether to expand or restrict various aspects of Medicaid's long-term care role (Thompson and DiIulio 1998; Olson 2010).

Consequently, state governments are constantly looking for creative ways to reduce long-term-care costs (Grogan and Smith 2008). State governors have been promoting alternatives to institutionalization since the early 1970s, mainly by relying on Medicaid waivers to increase use of home and community-based services (Abdellah 1978; Greene, Lovely, and Ondrich 1993; Thompson and Burke 2009). Home-health-care use has increased dramatically since the 1970s and, not surprisingly, expenditures followed suit (Grogan and Smith 2008). The share of Medicaid long-term-care spending in home and community-based settings more than doubled, from 19 percent in 1995 to 42 percent in 2008 (KFF 2011d). The vast majority of persons (82 percent) in need of long-term-care services and covered by Medicaid currently reside in the community. To the great disappointment of politicians and budget officials, however, this increase in home-care use has not resulted in significant Medicaid savings. Although there are indications of improved quality, most studies suggest that this hope for lower costs was not always realized (Abdellah 1978; Kemper, Applebaum, and Harrigan 1987; Kemper 1988; Greene, Lovely, and Ondrich 1993).

6.2 Explosive Benefits: Medicaid's Expanding Role in Financing Social Services

Over the past two decades, Medicaid has expanded its scope of services to include mental health, substance abuse treatment, child and foster care, school-based services, and supported employment. States' use of maximization strategies to expand Medicaid funding for social services have become ubiquitous; by 2012, all states use Medicaid to finance mental health services, and over 45 states provide at least some Medicaid coverage for services including substance abuse treatment and foster-care services (Buck 2011; Coughlin and Zuckerman 2002; Druss and Mauer 2011; Garfield et al. 2010). Although total Medicaid expenditures for social services is unknown, costs under the Rehabilitation Services Option increased 77 percent from 1999 to 2005, reaching over $6.4 billion (Congressional Research Service 2008). More politically liberal states, particularly those based in the Northeast, have been most aggressive in maximizing Medicaid to finance social services. Such states also tend to be wealthier, and thus better able to afford expanded services under Medicaid (Andrews 2012).

The quick rise in expenditures for social services has resulted in political controversy. For example, the Bush Administration tried to persuade Congress to restrict the scope of the Rehabilitation Services option as part of the Deficit Reduction Act in 2005. In response, a broad coalition of social-service advocacy groups successfully mobilized against the measure. At stake in this fight was whether social services should be considered health-related benefits. On behalf of the Bush Administration, Centers for Medicare and Medicaid Services official Dennis Smith argued that rehabilitation services in particular were "intrinsic elements of non-Medicaid programs," and that "the definition of rehabilitation services is so broad that there is a risk for federal dollars to be inappropriately claimed."[6] Following this logic, the Bush administration attempted to pass an administrative ruling that would prohibit the use of federal Medicaid funds for rehabilitative services. However, the Democratically controlled Congress passed a moratorium on the implementation of such administrative rules (Congressional Research Service 2008).

6.3 Persistent Problems: Access and Quality

Despite its remarkable growth in enrollment, Medicaid has experienced continuing problems with inadequate access to providers—both primary care and specialty services (Rosenbaum, 2011). Because rates of many chronic conditions (e.g., diabetes, asthma) are consistently higher among Medicaid beneficiaries than the general population, there is concern that enrollees are not receiving adequate care to manage these chronic conditions (Society of General Internal Medicine 2007; Winitzer et al. 2012). To address these issues, the federal government has long encouraged Medicaid managed care. The idea is that states pay a fixed rate to a health plan or a primary care provider to "manage" Medicaid recipients' care. In the 1980s, it funded managed care demonstration projects in the states (Hurley, Freund, and Paul 1993), and in 1993 President Bill Clinton ordered the federal government to make it easier for states to use Medicaid funds to introduce new health-care programs for low-income families (Friedman 1993). In the decade following, enrollment in managed care continued to increase so that, by 2006, 65 percent of the total Medicaid population in the United States was enrolled in some form of managed care, and by 2010 this had increased to 71 percent (KFF 2012g).

The federal government and the states are attracted to managed care because it promises to reduce costs, achieve budget predictability, improve access, and raise the quality of delivered services (Hurley and Somers 2003). Although some states realized reductions in inpatient use and improvements in quality of care (e.g., an increase in childhood immunizations), most states did not experience substantial cost savings (Davidson and Somers 1998). Nonetheless, states still favor managed care over the previous fee-for-service system and continue to look for ways to improve access under budget neutrality. For example, since 2006, more than 30 states have also advanced the "medical home" concept within Medicaid and CHIP, which designate a primary-care provider to Medicaid enrollees to provide comprehensive care management (National Academy for State Health Policy 2009).

7 Conclusion

Understanding how states' health-care policy for the poor evolved over time is crucial for grasping how a program that was intended to be charity care for the poor became an expensive comprehensive program for many nonpoor people. The three expansionary seeds imbedded in Medicaid's beginnings—medical indigency, comprehensive benefits, and intergovernmental financing—have pushed this program in ways no one quite envisioned. However, it is really the larger health-care system in the United States—a narrow Medicare program and an eroding employer-based health insurance system—that has always left a sizable group of uninsured, as well as older and disabled Americans knocking on states' doors. These demands, not only from the public but also from the providers who serve them, along with a federal matching rate that provides significant incentives for states to leverage Medicaid funds, have repeatedly pushed states toward Medicaid, even when states really do not want to go in that direction.

The ACA continues Medicaid's expansionary pattern by allowing states to eliminate categorical distinctions, increasing eligibility standards, and increasing the financing of social services. By almost any accounting, the ACA will further expand middle-class presence in Medicaid. The idea is that Medicaid will attempt to catch those "low to middle-income" persons before they get sick and lose their jobs, or before they enter a nursing home to keep them in the community. It is a preventive idea, which will likely save costs to the entire health-care system, but Medicaid expenditures will certainly increase. Thus, at the same time, the ACA invests heavily in new models of care—again building on past experience—to further incorporate Medicaid into managed care, medical homes, and community-based-care approaches. It remains to be seen the extent to which states will adopt the ACA Medicaid expansion, and if so, whether quality and access can be improved and costs controlled under these new models. To achieve such lofty goals, the ACA will need significant political support and cooperative governing. In the past, Medicaid has benefitted from remarkable bipartisan support, but as partisan rancor over the status of entitlements heats up at the federal level, Medicaid's future remains unclear.

Notes

1. "State of the Nation 1972" survey by Potomac Associates. Methodology: Interviewing conducted by Gallup Organization during May, 1972 and based on 669 personal interviews. Sample: National adult. Accessed online: http://webapps.ropercenter.uconn.edu.
2. For years: 1981, 1986, 1987, 1989, ABC News/ Washington Post polls. Question: please tell me whether you feel spending for that program should be increased, decreased or left about the same . . . Medicaid which provides free health care for the poor. Accessed online: http://webapps.ropercenter.uconn.edu.
3. In 2008 and 2011, one percent said they didn't know.
4. ABC News/ Washington Post poll, July 2011, based on 1,011 telephone interviews (included landline and cell-phone-only respondents.
5. Gubernatorial Party control and joining the lawsuit are correlated at.8, whereas projected increase in state spending due to ACA expansions is correlated at.15. Calculated by author.
6. Testimony by CMS Official Dennis G. Smith before the Senate Finance Committee in June 2005.

REFERENCES

*Indicates recommended reading.

Abdellah, Faye. 1978. "Long-Term Care Policy Issues: Alternatives to Institutional Care." *Annals of the American Academy of Political and Social Science* 438 (July): 28–39.

Christina Andrews. 2012. "State Medicaid Coverage and the Availability of Medicaid-Covered Outpatient Substance Abuse Treatment Services: Current Trends and Implications for Expansion under Health Reform." PhD diss., University of Chicago.

Blumenthal, David, and James A. Morone. 2009. *The Heart of Power: Health and Politics in the Oval Office.* Berkeley: University of California Press.

Buck, Jeffrey. 2011. "The Looming Expansion and Transformation of Public Substance Abuse Treatment under the Affordable Care Act." *Health Affairs* 30 (80): 1402–1410.

Cauchi, Richard. 2011. "State Legislation and Actions Challenging Certain Health Reforms." National Conference of State Legislatures. www.ncsl.org/default.aspx?tabid=18906.

CNN/Opinion Research Corporation Poll, Mar, 2011. Retrieved Aug-12-2014 from the iPOLL Databank, The Roper Center for Public Opinion Research, University of Connecticut. http://www.ropercenter.uconn.edu/data_access/ipoll/ipoll.html.

Congressional Research Service. 2008. "Medicaid Rehabilitation Services." U.S. Senate. Special Committee on Aging. http://aging.senate.gov/crs/medicaid13.pdf.

Coughlin, Teresa, and Stephen Zuckerman. 2002. "States' Use of Medicaid Maximization Strategies to Tap Federal Revenues: Program Implications and Consequences." Urban Institute. www.urban.org/uploadedPDF/310525_DP0209.pdf.

Courtot, Brigette, and Emily Lawton. 2012. "Medicaid Enrollment and Expenditures by Federal Core Requirements and State Options." Issue Paper: Kaiser Commission on Medicaid and the Uninsured. KFF (January update). http://www.kff.org/medicaid/upload/8239.pdf.

Davidson, Stephen M., and Stephen A. Somers, eds. 1998. *Remaking Medicaid: Managed Care for the Public Good.* San Francisco: Jossey-Bass.

Druss, Benjamin, and Barbara Mauer. 2011. "Health Care Reform and Care at the Behavioral Health-Primary Care Interface." *Psychiatric Services* 61: 1087–1092.

Federal Register. 2010. "Federal Matching Shares for Medicaid, the Children's Health Insurance Program, and Aid to Needy Aged, Blind, or Disabled Persons for October 1, 2011 through September 30, 2012." <frwebgate.access.gpo.gov/cgi-bin/getdoc.cgi?dbname=2010_register&docid=fr10no10-65.pdf>.

Fornili, Katherine, and Farrokh Alemi. 2007. "Medicaid Reimbursement for Screening and Brief Intervention: Amending the Medicaid State Plan and Approving State Appropriations for the Medicaid State Match." *Journal of Addictions Nursing* 18 (4): 225–232.

Friedman, Thomas. 1993. "President Allows States Flexibility on Medicaid Funds." *New York Times*, February 2, A1.

Garfield, R. L., J. R. Lave, and J. M. Donohue. 2010. "Health Reform and the Scope of Benefits for Mental Health and Substance Use Disorder Services." *Psychiatric Services* 61: 1081–1086.

Greene, V. L., M. E. Lovely, and J. I. Ondrich. 1993. "Do Community-Based, Long-Term Care Services Reduce Nursing Home Use? A Transition Probability Analysis." *Journal of Human Resources* 28 (2): 297–317.

Grogan, Colleen M. 1994. "The Political-Economic Factors Influencing State Medicaid Policy." *Political Research Quarterly* 47 (3): 589–622.

*Grogan, Colleen M. 2008. "Medicaid: Health Care for You and Me?" In James Morone, Theodor Litman, and Leonard Robins, eds., *Health Politics and Policy*. 4th ed. New York: Delmar Thompson, 329–354.

Grogan, Colleen M. 2014. "Medicaid: Designed to Grow." In James A Morone and Daniel Ehlke, eds., *Health Politics and Policy*. Stamford, CT: Cengage Learning, pp. 142–163.

Grogan, Colleen, and Erik Patashnik. 2003a. "Between Welfare Medicine and Mainstream Program: Medicaid at the Political Crossroads." *Journal of Health Politics, Policy and Law* 28 (5): 821–858.

Grogan, Colleen, and Erik Patashnik. 2003b. "Universalism Within Targeting: Nursing Home Care, the Middle Class, and the Politics of the Medicaid Program." *Social Service Review* 77 (1): 51–71.

Grogan, Colleen, and Elizabeth Rigby. 2009. "Federalism, Partisan Politics, and Shifting Support for State Flexibility: The Case of the U.S. State Children's Health Insurance Program." *Publius: The Journal of Federalism* 39: 47–69.

Grogan, Colleen M., and Vernon Smith. 2008. "Chapter 9. From Charity Care to Medicaid: Governors, States, and the Transformation of American Health Care." In Ethan Sribnick ed., *A More Perfect Union*. Philadelphia: University of Pennsylvania Press, 204–230.

Hall, Mark A., and Sara Rosenbaum. 2012. *The Health Care "Safety Net" in a Post-Reform World*. New Brunswick, NJ: Rutgers University Press.

Himelfarb, R. 1995. *Catastrophic Politics: The Rise and Fall of the Medicare Catastrophic Coverage Act of 1988*. University Park: Pennsylvania State University Press.

Holahan, John, and Irene Headen. 2010. *Medicaid Coverage and Spending in Health Reform*. Washington, DC: KFF: Kaiser Commission on Medicaid and the Uninsured. http://kaiserfamilyfoundation.files.wordpress.com/2013/01/medicaid-coverage-and-spending-in-health-reform-national-and-state-by-state-results-for-adults-at-or-below-133-fpl.pdf.

*Holahan, J., A. Weil, and J. M. Wiener, eds. 2003. *Federalism and Health Policy*. Washington, DC: Urban Institute Press.

Hurley, Robert, Deborah Freund, and John Paul. 1993. *Managed Care in Medicaid: Lessons for Policy and Program Design*. Ann Arbor, MI: Health Administration Press.

Hurley, Robert, and Stephen Somers. 2003. "Medicaid and Managed Care: A Lasting Relationship?" *Health Affairs* 22 (1): 77–88.

Jones, David K., Katharine W. V. Bradley, and Jonathan Oberlander. 2012. "Pascal's Wager: Health Insurance Exchanges and the Republican Dilemma." Presented at Midwest Political Science Association Conference. Chicago, IL, April 12.

Justice, Diane, Lynn Etheredge, John Luehrs, and Brian Burwell. 1988. "State Long Term Care Reform: Development of Community Care Systems in Six States, Final Report." U.S. Dept. of Health and Human Services and National Governors Association. http://aspe.hhs.gov/daltcp/reports/strfrm.htm#execsum.

KFF (Kaiser Family Foundation). 2013. *Medicaid: A Primer*. http://kaiserfamilyfoundation.files.wordpress.com/2010/06/7334-05.pdf.

KFF. 2010b. "Medicaid Financial Eligibility: Primary Pathways for the Elderly and People with Disabilities." Kaiser Commission on Medicaid and the Uninsured analysis of data collected by Medicare Rights Center, 2009. http://www.kff.org/medicaid/8048.cfm.

KFF. 2011a. "State Health Facts: Enhanced Federal Medical Assistance Percentage (FMAP) for the Children's Health Insurance Program (CHIP)." http://www.statehealthfacts.org/comparetable.jsp?cat=4&ind=239.

KFF. 2012a. "CHIP Enrollment: June 2011 Data Snapshot." http://kaiserfamilyfoundation.files.wordpress.com/2013/01/7642-06.pdf.

KFF. 2011c. "Kaiser Health Tracking Poll." Public Opinion on Health Care Issues. Pub. No. 8190-F. http://www.kff.org/kaiserpolls/8190.cfm.

KFF. 2011d. "Medicaid and Long-Term Care Services and Supports." www.kff.org/medicaid/upload/2186-08.pdf.

KFF. 2012b. "Medicaid Beneficiaries: Medicaid Enrollment by Gender, FY 2008." http://www.statehealthfacts.org/comparemaptable.jsp?ind=1007&cat=4.

KFF. 2012c. "A Guide to the Supreme Court's Affordable Care Act Decision." http://www.kff.org/healthreform/upload/8332.pdf.

KFF. 2012d. "Medicaid Beneficiaries: Total Medicaid Enrollment, FY 2009." http://www.statehealthfacts.org/comparemaptable.jsp?ind=198&cat=4. Medicare data under heading: "Medicare Enrollment: Total Medicare Beneficiaries, 2009." http://www.statehealthfacts.org/comparemaptable.jsp?yr=92&typ=1&ind=290&cat=6&sub=74.

KFF. 2012e. "Births Financed by Medicaid; As Percent of State Births." http://www.statehealthfacts.org/comparemaptable.jsp?ind=223&cat=4.

KFF. 2012f. "Health Coverage & Uninsured: Nonelderly with Medicaid: Distribution by Age, U.S. 2010." http://www.statehealthfacts.org/comparebar.jsp?ind=154&cat=3&sub=42.

KFF. 2012g. "Medicaid Managed Care: Key Data, Trends, and Issues." http://www.kff.org/medicaid/upload/8046-02.pdf.

KKF/Harvard School of Public Health. 2009. "The Public's Health Care Agenda for the New President and Congress." Chartpack, Chart 8, p.4. Accessed at http://www.kaiserfamilyfoundation.files.wordpress.com/2013/01/7854.pdf

Kemper, Peter. 1988. "The Evaluation of the National Long Term Care Demonstration." *Health Services Research* 23 (1): 161–74.

Kemper, Peter, R. Applebaum, and M. Harrigan. 1987. "Community Care Demonstrations: What Have We Learned?" *Health Care Financing Review* 8 (4): 87–100.

Konetzka, Tamara R., and Y. Luo. 2011. "Explaining Lapse in Long-Term Care Insurance Markets." *Health Economics* 20 (10): 1169–1183.

Mark, Tami, Katherine Levitt, Rita Vandivort-Warren, Jeffrey Buck, and Rosanna Coffey. 2011. "Changes in U. S. Spending on Mental Health and Substance Abuse Treatment, 1986–2005, and Implications for Policy." *Health Affairs* 30: 284–292.

Mechanic, David. 2012. "Seizing Opportunities Under the Affordable Care Act for Transforming the Mental and Behavioral Health System." *Health Affairs* 31: 376–382.

Mickey, Robert W. 2012. "Dr. StrangeLove; or, How Conservatives Learned to Stop Worrying and Love Community Health Centers." In Mark A. Hall, and Sara Rosenbaum, eds., *The Health Care "Safety Net" in a Post-Reform World*. New Brunswick, NJ: Rutgers University Press, pp. 21–66.

Modern Healthcare. 2002. "Late News—Layoffs at Duke—Three Hundred Workers at Duke University Health System Will Lose Their Jobs to Offset Planned Cuts in Medicaid Reimbursements." 32 (18): 4.

National Academy for State Health Policy. 2009. "Building Medical Homes in State Medicaid and CHIP Programs." www.nashp.org/sites/default/files/medicalhomesfinal_revised.pdf.

Oberlander, Jonathan. 2003. *The Political Life of Medicare*. Chicago: University of Chicago Press.

*Olson, Laura Katz. 2010. *The Politics of Medicaid*. New York: Columbia University Press.

Patashnik, Eric M., and Julian E. Zelizer. 2001. "Paying for Medicare: Benefits, Budgets, and Wilbur Mills's Policy Legacy." *Journal of Health Politics, Policy and Law* 26 (1): 7–36.

Perkins, Jane. 2011. "Florida Ruling on ACA Generates Some Surprise and a Lot of Confusion." National Health Law Project, Georgetown University Center for Children and Families.

http://ccf.georgetown.edu/ccf-resources/florida_ruling_on_aca_generates_some_surprise_and_a_lot_of_confusion/.

Pew Research Center for the People and the Press. 2011. "Public Wants Changes in Entitlements, Not Changes in Benefits." www.people-press.org/2011/07/07/public-wants-changes-in-entitlements-not-change-in-benefits/.

Quadagno, Jill S. 1988. *The Transformation of Old-Age Security: Class and Politics in the American Welfare State*. Chicago: University of Chicago Press.

Ramshaw, Emily, and Marilyn Serafini. 2010. "Battle Lines Drawn Over Medicaid in Texas." *New York Times*, November 12, A21. http://www.nytimes.com/2010/11/12/us/politics/12ttmedicaid.html?Pagewanted=all.

Rosenbaum, Sara. 2011. "Medicaid and Access to Health Care—A Proposal for Continued Inaction?" *New England Journal of Medicine* 365 (2): 102–104.

Rosenbaum, Sara, and Colleen A. Sonosky. 1999. "Child Health Advocacy in a Changing Policy Environment." Paper presented at conference on the Roles of Child Advocacy Organizations in Addressing Policy Issues, December 13–14. Washington, DC: Urban Institute.

Safety Net Medical Home Initiative. 2010. "Health Reform and the Patient-Centered Medical Home: Policy Provisions and Expectations of the Patient Protection and Affordable Care Act." www.qhmedicalhome.org/safety-net/upload/SNMHI_PolicyBrief_Issue2.pdf.

Seiden, T. M., J. L. Hudson, and J. S. Banthin. 2004. "Tracking Changes in Eligibility and Coverage among Children, 1996–2002." *Health Affairs* 23 (5): 39–50.

*Smith, D. G., and J. D. Moore. 2008. *Medicaid Politics and Policy: 1965–2007*. New Brunswick, NJ: Transaction.

Society of General Internal Medicine. 2007. "Redesigning the Practice Model for General Internal Medicine. A Proposal for Coordinated Care: A Policy Monograph of the Society of General Internal Medicine." *Journal of General Internal Medicine* 22 (3): 400–409.

Sparer, Michael S. 1996. *Medicaid and the Limits of State Health Reform*. Philadelphia: Temple University Press.

*Stevens, R., and R. Stevens. 1974 [2003]. *Welfare Medicine in America: A Case Study of Medicaid*. New York: Free Press.

Swan, James H., Charlene Harrington, Wendy Clemeña, Ruth B. Pickard, Liatris Studer, and Susan K. deWit. 2000. "Medicaid Nursing Facility Reimbursement Methods: 1979–1997." *Medical Care Research and Review* 57 (3): 361–378.

*Thompson, F. J., and J. J. DiIulio., eds. 1998. *Medicaid and Devolution: A View from the States*. Washington, DC: Brookings Institution Press.

Thompson, Frank J., and Courtney Burke. 2009. "Federalism by Waiver: Medicaid and the Transformation of Long-Term Care." *Publius: The Journal of Federalism* 39 (1): 22–46.

U.S. Department of Health and Human Services. 2010. "HHS Announces New Federal Support for States to Develop and Upgrade Medicaid IT Systems and Systems for Enrollment in State Exchanges." http://www.cms.gov/Newsroom/MediaReleaseDatabase/Press-releases/2010-Press-releases-items/2010-11-034.html.

Watson, Sidney D. 1995. "Medicaid Physician Participation: Patients, Poverty, and Physician Self-Interest." *American Journal of Law & Medicine* 21 (2–3): 191–220.

Winitzer R. F., J. Bisgaier, C. Grogan, and K. Rhodes. 2012. "'He Only Takes Those Type of Patients on Certain Days': Specialty Care Access for Children with Special Health Care Needs." *Disability and Health Journal* 5 (1): 26–33.

CHAPTER 20

....

TEMPORARY ASSISTANCE
FOR NEEDY FAMILIES

....

R. KENT WEAVER

1 INTRODUCTION

....

TEMPORARY Assistance for Needy Families (TANF) is a federal block-grant program that gives states funding to provide cash assistance and social services to low-income—primarily single-parent—families with children. TANF funding also goes to the District of Columbia, Indian tribes, and some U.S. territories. The TANF program was created in 1996 to replace Aid to Families with Dependent Children (AFDC), which focused on cash assistance to low-income families. This chapter reviews the problems of child poverty in the United States, discusses the policy controversies that led to the creation of TANF, and examines implementation of the TANF program and outcomes for low-income children and families in the first 15 years of the TANF program.

2 CHILD POVERTY IN THE
UNITED STATES

....

The perceived need for TANF and its predecessor AFDC is rooted in persistently high rates of child poverty in the United States. Although child poverty is sensitive to how poverty is measured (Blank 2008), there is substantial consistency across measures. Child poverty rates in the United States are among the highest in the Organisation for Economic Co-operation and Development (OECD) when conventional cross-national measures (viz., less than 50 percent of median income for households of a specified family size) are used (Gornick and Jäntti 2010; Rainwater and Smeeding 2003). In 2010, using the official U.S. poverty line (which uses an "absolute" dollar standard of income rather than one that is relative to median incomes), the poverty rate for persons aged 0–18 was 22 percent, more than twice the poverty rate for those aged 65 years and older (DeNavas-Walt et al. 2011).

Child poverty in the United States is also closely associated with race and ethnicity, family composition, educational level of the household head, and region (Danziger 2010). Although 12.4 percent of white non-Hispanic children were poor in 2010, 39.1 percent of black children and 35.0 percent of Hispanic children were poor. And whereas only 6.2 percent of married couple households were poor in 2010, 31.6 percent of female-headed households were poor. Children in the United States are also more likely than other groups to be *very* poor—that is, having a cash income below 50 percent of the poverty threshold.

Child poverty rates in the United States fell from 22.3 percent in 1992 to 16.2 percent in 2000. However, child poverty rates rose again after the turn of the century to 22 percent in 2010, erasing most of the gains in the previous decade (DeNavas-Walt et al. 2011, 68). Changing patterns of child poverty over time have been driven by the interaction of several factors. Deterioration of wages for the lowest-skilled workers and increases in the percentage of families headed by a single female have both increased child poverty rates, whereas rising female-labor-force participation generally worked in the opposite direction. Cyclical changes in unemployment and changes in government tax and transfer policies, which will be discussed further later, also affect child poverty rates (e.g., Hoynes, Page, and Stevens 2006). Reductions in child poverty in the 1990s are generally attributed to a growing economy and more generous governmental supports for low-income *working* families (notably a substantially expanded Earned Income Tax Credit (EITC) and improved access to health insurance for low-income families) that encouraged increased work among these families. Employment among single mothers with a high school education or less grew strongly in this period (Danziger 2010). Increases in child poverty in recent years, accompanied by a major increase in child homelessness, were caused in large part by the impact of the major recession on parental unemployment (Lovell and Isaacs 2010).

3 ORIGINS AND HISTORICAL DEVELOPMENT

Prior to 1935, assistance to low-income—almost always widowed—families was primarily a function of local governments, with states sometimes playing a supporting role (Gordon 1994; Skocpol 1995). The Social Security Act of 1935 created federal grant programs to the states to pay part of the cost of income-support programs for four categories of individuals or households who were not expected to work: the aged, blind, disabled, and families in which the (presumably male) breadwinner was absent. The first three categories were largely nationalized in the Supplemental Security Act of 1972 (Pierson 1995). The Aid to Families with Dependent Children program (originally Aid to Dependent Children) remained a shared federal-state program, and a program mired in controversy. The federal-state structure of AFDC gave substantial leeway over benefit levels, eligibility standards, and program administration to the states. Southern states tended to be more conservative on all these criteria than most states in other regions—and racially discriminatory in program administration during the early years of the program (Lieberman and Lapinski 2001).

Originally intended as a program to assist widows, AFDC increasingly came to serve families in which the mother was divorced from, deserted by, or had never been married to the father. It also grew to over-represent (relative to the overall population, if not the low-income population) African Americans. The politically weak and unpopular nature of AFDC's clientele meant that legislative expansions of the program were infrequent and modest.[1] AFDC rolls and expenditures grew dramatically between 1965 and 1973: The number of families receiving AFDC roughly tripled (Figure 20.1). These increases resulted primarily from court cases that struck down a number of state-imposed restrictions on eligibility rather than from more generous legislation, but decreased program stigma and a short-lived welfare rights movement also contributed to rising caseloads and costs (Melnick 1994).

President Nixon proposed in his first term to convert AFDC into a more nationally uniform negative income tax program labeled the Family Assistance Plan. However, this proposal foundered in Congress on both cost projections and conservatives' fear that these changes would lower work incentives and increase incentives for child-bearing

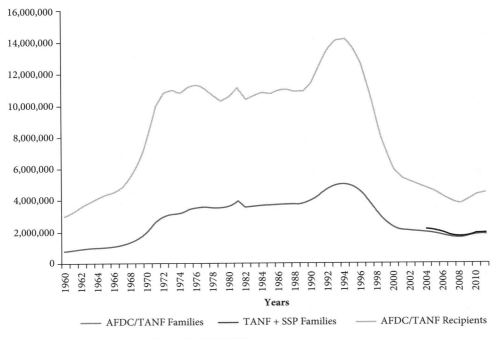

FIG. 20.1 AFDC-TANF CASELOAD TRENDS, 1960–2011.

by single mothers (Steensland 2008). A similar effort by President Carter in 1977 also failed to win congressional approval (Lynn and Whitman 1981). At the same time that national policymakers were considering (and ultimately rejecting) a negative income tax approach to supporting low-income families, they also sought to use AFDC policy to move recipients into the labor force. Efforts to increase paid work took many forms over the next 30 years. In 1967, Congress increased the amount of earnings disregarded in calculating benefit levels for AFDC recipients who entered employment (Melnick 1994); in 1981, however, those earnings disregards were reduced. The Family Support Act of 1988, a compromise between the Reagan administration and congressional Democrats, added (initially very weak) work requirements, and provided funding for training, child care, and other services to facilitate transitions into work.

4 Welfare Politics

Political conflict over the AFDC program grew substantially after enactment of the 1988 welfare reform legislation. A one-third jump in the AFDC caseload between 1989 and 1994, after it had remained largely stable for more than a decade (Figure 20.1), contributed to this conflict, but so did interrelated trends in elite opinion, public opinion, and state policy-making.

Concern over growing AFDC caseloads in the early 1990s was exacerbated by research indicating that half of all AFDC recipients at any given time were in the midst of very long (8 years or more) spells, that prolonged absence from work made labor-market re-entry more difficult, and that growing up in single-parent families could have negative long-term consequences for children. The result was a growing search for alternative policy approaches among policy-makers and policy intellectuals. Increasingly, "welfare dependency"—low rates of paid work among low-income families and high rates of nonmarital births, especially among children of welfare recipients—supplanted child poverty as policy-makers' main concern.

Several distinctive approaches vied as alternative solutions to addressing the problems of low-income families (Danziger 2010; Weaver 2000; Somers and Block 2005). Adherents of what can be called the "make-work-pay" approach (e.g., Ellwood 1988) focused on increasing work incentives through expansion of the Earned Income Tax Credit, as well as improved work supports (in particular expanded access to health care for low-wage workers) and provision of jobs for those who could not find them. Proponents of a "new-paternalist" approach emphasized stringent and strongly enforced work requirements (Mead 1992). Some conservative critics of the AFDC program—most notably Charles Murray in his 1984 book *Losing Ground*—focused on nonmarital births and the incentives offered by AFDC as the key problem, and suggested more radical cuts in programs for low-income families. Many state governments and some policy experts favored a devolution approach, arguing that giving states increased discretion to try alternative approaches would better reveal which approaches showed the most promise (Weaver 2000; Haskins 2006).

Public opinion in the United States has long emphasized that the able-bodied non-elderly should be expected to work. Moreover, Martin Gilens (1999) and others have shown that images of the poor, and especially welfare recipients, are heavily racialized. "Welfare" receipt is identified by Americans primarily with minorities, especially African Americans. Opposition to "welfare" is related to perceptions that minorities have a poor work ethic, and that too many recipients could get by without benefits if they really tried (Clawson and Trice 2000; Schram, Soss, and Fording 2003). The public consistently supports additional spending when questions ask them about "the poor" rather than "welfare," and they offer greater support for in-kind assistance (especially medical care) than cash assistance for the able-bodied poor (Heclo 1986; Heclo 1994).

The early 1990s saw a sharp spike upward in public discontent with welfare, and increased public support for measures such as work requirements and time limits. Research has linked this jump to "priming" by policy-makers and the media in this period that was highly critical of the AFDC program and the deservingness of program recipients (Schneider and Jacoby 2005; Weaver 2000).

State policy choices under the AFDC program reflected both differences in public opinion across states and a number of other factors. States with low per-capita incomes generally benefited from a higher federal "matching share" of AFDC program costs. States were allowed wide discretion over benefit levels, and variations were huge: In January 1994, for example, the maximum monthly AFDC benefit for a family of 3 was $120 in Mississippi and $680 in Connecticut. However, the real value of AFDC benefits fell precipitously across most states over time—from 1970 to 1994, the real value of the median state's maximum benefit for a family of three fell 47 percent (U.S. House of Representatives, 1994, 374–376).

Researchers have examined a number of possible explanations of variation in benefit generosity across states and over time. Higher benefits were generally found in states that had greater fiscal capacity, a lower African-American share of the AFDC caseload, and more liberal overall public opinion (e.g., Tweedie 1994; Rom, Peterson, and Scheve 1998; Howard 1999). Several studies also investigated whether the federal-state structure of the AFDC program led to a "race to the bottom" in benefit generosity: Because states have an interest in keeping their tax rates down, states might help the poor less than they would otherwise prefer out of a fear that they could encourage in-migration (and discourage out-migration) by the poor if they are more generous than neighboring states (Berry et al. 2003).[2] Most studies attempting to find a race to the bottom in AFDC benefits found that states allowed their benefits to erode over time with inflation, although actual cuts in the nominal level of AFDC benefits were infrequent (Schram, Nitz, and Krueger 1998; Volden 2002).

In the early 1990s, the federal government gave states increased flexibility to try new approaches to encourage or require work among welfare mothers, using waivers from federal AFDC program requirements. These innovations ranged from increased earnings disregards and extension of Medicaid coverage to those leaving the AFDC rolls to stronger work requirements and "family caps" (i.e., no additional benefit when an AFDC recipient had more children).

5 CREATING TANF: THE 1996 REFORM

Bill Clinton was well-aware of the unpopularity of AFDC, and in his 1992 presidential campaign he promised to "end welfare as we know it." He proposed to increase the Earned Income Tax Credit to "make work pay," increase access to health care and training, impose a work requirement after two years of AFDC benefits, and "revolutionize the culture of welfare offices" away from writing benefit checks and toward providing individually tailored services that would boost employment among recipients. A dramatic expansion of the Earned Income Tax Credit was enacted in 1993, but Clinton's health-care reform plan was not adopted by Congress, and legislation to reform AFDC was not passed by Congress in President Clinton's first two years in office, either. The president's AFDC proposals sparked opposition from both House Democrats, who found them too punitive, and from Congressional Republicans, who favored stronger work requirements and time limits as well as lower spending and stiffer provisions to discourage nonmarital births. Indeed, President Clinton's strong condemnation of AFDC and his reform initiative helped move congressional Republicans to the right on welfare reform to avoid "losing" the welfare issue by showing that they were tougher on welfare than the president and his congressional allies (Weaver 2000).

Welfare reform legislation was not enacted until after Republicans took control of Congress in the 1994 election. Legislation considered in the next Congress, drafted by Republicans, was considerably more conservative than Clinton's initial proposals. President Clinton twice vetoed welfare-reform legislation passed by Congress in 1995, largely over provisions unrelated to AFDC. Facing increased political pressure leading up to the 1996 presidential election, he signed the Personal Responsibility and Work Opportunity Reconciliation Act (PRWORA) passed by a Republican-controlled Congress in August 1996.

The PRWORA legislation replaced AFDC with a new Temporary Assistance for Needy Families program (TANF). TANF is intended to provide transitional rather than long-term assistance, while encouraging economic self-sufficiency and more responsible decisions concerning childbearing and family formation. States continued to have very broad flexibility in setting eligibility requirements and benefit levels, but PRWORA ended the individual entitlement to benefits that had existed under AFDC. TANF mothers were required to cooperate in establishing paternity of their children and in facilitating child-support payments by noncustodial parents (for details on PRWORA provisions, see U.S. House of Representatives, Ways and Means Committee 2004: chapter 7). The PRWORA legislation also substantially increased funding for child care for working low-income families, strengthened child-support-enforcement policies, and limited states' ability to use the TANF policy changes to restrict eligibility for Medicaid.

Federal funding levels under the TANF block grant were fixed in nominal terms after 1996 at $16.5 billion per year, rather than varying with caseload changes as had been the case with AFDC. As a result, the real value of funding from the basic TANF federal block grant fell by more than 25 percent in real terms over the program's first 15 years (Schott 2011). Federal funding no longer expanded automatically if an economic slowdown led to unemployment and caseload increases.[3] To lessen pressures for a race to the bottom, states were required to provide "maintenance of effort" of 75 percent of their prior expenditure levels (80 percent for states that do not meet work participation rate requirements) or lose federal TANF block-grant dollars.

States received more discretion in some important ways, notably freedom to spend their TANF block grant funds on a variety of services rather than just cash benefits. They were also allowed to institute family caps (i.e., no increase in benefits when a TANF recipient has another child) and given more freedom over a number of other policy measures such as how to disregard earnings in calculating benefits.

TANF also imposed new obligations and limitations on the states, however. States are required to assess the work readiness of TANF parents or other caretaker adults within 90 days after determination of eligibility, and to engage them in work activities within two years, with different minimum hours of work per week required for single-parent and two-parent families and for single parents with children less than 6 years old. The PRWORA legislation gave states some discretion in defining work activities for the purposes of this requirement from a federally approved list, but most activity had to be from "core" activities such as unsubsidized or subsidized employment. States are also required to sanction families that refuse to participate in required work activities—from a partial benefit reduction up to a "full-family" (i.e., entire-benefit) sanction. No more than 20 percent of the caseload receiving cash benefits financed with TANF dollars can get those benefits beyond a 60-month lifetime limit. States are also allowed to set shorter lifetime time limits.[4] Use of TANF funds to finance most noncash assistance for *working* families, such as child care and transportation, as well as state Earned Income Tax Credit programs, do not count toward the limit, however, and use of TANF funds to provide some forms of noncash assistance to these families beyond 60 months is permitted.[5] PRWORA also allowed states to create separate state programs funded entirely with their own funds (including maintenance-of-effort funds) that did not subject benefits to a 5-year time limit.

PRWORA required states to have a specified percentage of TANF recipients (50 percent of all such families and 90 percent of those with two parents) engaged in work-related activities for a specified number of hours per week, or face federal penalties. These requirements were phased in over 5 years. However, PRWORA allowed states to count caseload declines to meet the work participation standard, meaning that most states faced effective work participation requirements far below those specified in the statute in the initial years of the program. Some states with very high caseload declines initially had no effective work-participation rate requirement.

Federal TANF legislation has remained largely intact since its enactment. The Deficit Reduction Act of 2005 made a number of changes in TANF work-participation rate requirements for states. Responding to concerns that states were using "child-only" cases and State Separate Programs (SSPs) to avoid work requirements for hard-to-place household heads, parents in SSPs would henceforth be included in calculating work-participation rates. The set of activities that count toward meeting work participation requirements was also tightened, and the "caseload decline" credit was reset with 2005 rather than 1995 as the base year from which caseload changes were calculated—in most cases dramatically reducing the credit. All these changes make it much more difficult to meet work participation rate requirements and led states to develop a variety of new strategies to avoid penalties for failing to meet them (Allard 2007; GAO 2010).

6 IMPLEMENTATION OF TANF

The impact of greater discretion and new constraints depended on how states dealt with three questions during the implementation of the law. First, how would states choose to change rules and allocate resources under the new law? For example, how strict would their rules be for sanctioning noncompliance? Second, how would local welfare offices administer the new rules? Third, how would recipients and potential recipients respond to—and fare under—the new welfare regime?

States gained two important types of discretion under TANF: over how they spent federal funds, and over eligibility requirements. State spending priorities changed dramatically under TANF, away from cash assistance. In 1993, expenditures on AFDC cash benefits were approximately 20 times those on the AFDC jobs program (U.S. House of Representatives 1994, 389, 434). In Fiscal Year 2009, only 27.8 percent of federal and state maintenance of effort outlays under TANF were being spent on basic cash assistance.[6] Child-care expenditures were about one-sixth of total spending by 2009, with much of the rest spent on various other types of work supports plus program administration. Because the TANF block-grant allocation to individual states is based primarily on their federal funding levels under the old AFDC program, states that had spent little under AFDC (notably most southern states and states with low per capita incomes) now had far fewer federal dollars per child than those with higher spending histories to spend on the extended range of services such as child care that could be offered under TANF.

Substantial state variation in TANF policy exists on a number of dimensions. In 2007, for example, six states partially reduced benefits for noncompliance, whereas 23 states increased to full-family sanction policies for repeated noncompliance, and 21 states immediately imposed full-family sanctions—that is, withdrew all TANF benefits (Kauff et al. 2007). Some states impose intermittent time limits (e.g., no more than two years of cash assistance out of every four) in addition to federal time limits. Stricter provisions on "disciplinary" policy decisions such as time limits and sanctioning policy are, as in the AFDC waiver period, clearly associated with a higher African American share of the TANF caseload, whereas the ideology and partisanship of state government play a weaker role than it did in the earlier period (Soss, Fording, and Schram 2011). "Carrot" oriented policies offering positive incentives to work (e.g., state earned-income-tax credits), on the other hand, are most strongly affected by a state's resources, especially the resources per needy family member provided through the TANF block grants (Weaver and Gais 2002).

Outcomes for TANF applicants and recipients also depend heavily on how the program is administered at the "front-lines" in welfare offices. Even under the AFDC program, caseworkers in welfare offices had to exercise substantial discretion in making accurate eligibility determinations and calculating benefits— a difficult task given complex eligibility rules and the often very-complicated family structure and housing arrangements and fluctuating incomes of many low-income families. The TANF program institutionalized a "work-first" orientation toward job search and rapid movement into employment rather than provision of services to make them more employable. Many states have increased TANF application hurdles to "divert" them directly into employment rather than opening a TANF case (Brodkin and Majmundar 2010; Ridzi 2009). The TANF "work-first" focus increases the complexity and difficulty of tasks faced by front-line workers in welfare offices. Eligibility and benefit determinations have become more complicated as more recipients enter paid work, encountering the frequent earnings fluctuations that characterize the low-wage labor market. Caseworkers must also now assess the readiness of TANF recipients for work and link them with needed services (e.g., job search and job training, child care and transportation, and, in some cases, mental health, domestic abuse, and substance abuse) to prepare them for work. They must decide which cases merit exemption from work requirements. Moreover, they must exercise this discretion within the context of time limits that put enormous pressure on clients and caseworkers to move clients off cash assistance quickly, both to allow states to meet federal work rate performance standards and to allow clients to "bank" their limited number of months of eligibility for cash assistance for future spells of unemployment. At the same time, states must implement and document individual compliance with federal work-participation rate requirements, which takes time and resources away from efforts at getting recipients into work (GAO 2010; Falk 2011; Watkins-Hayes 2009).

Recent research suggests that states differ substantially in how rigorously they communicate the importance of time limits to TANF recipients and in how rigorously they enforce them (Farrell et al. 2008). There is also great variation across states in the frequency and severity of sanctioning of TANF recipients—and even variation across welfare offices within a single state (Pavetti et al. 2003). Not surprisingly, sanctioned individuals are more likely to face multiple barriers to gaining and sustaining employment, such as low education and poor access to transportation (Cherlin et al. 2002; GAO 2000). Even more disturbing, research suggests that minorities—especially African Americans—are more likely to be sanctioned than whites with similar observable background characteristics (e.g., education, work experience, and number of children) in the same communities. How strictly caseworkers apply sanctions for noncompliance with TANF work requirements and other program rules is affected not only by caseworkers' professional norms but by complex interactions between local political environments, racial stereotypes of client subgroups, and organizational pressures exerted on managers and front-line workers (Soss et al. 2011). Racial differences in sanctioning may occur for several reasons that do not involve overt and conscious racism, including racial stereotyping on the part of caseworkers that causes them to view minorities as undeserving and likely to be willfully avoiding program requirements when they engage in what appears to be noncompliant behavior. Greater social distance between caseworkers and clients and greater difficulties faced by minorities in meeting program requirements due to employment discrimination may also contribute to higher sanctioning rates for minorities (Keiser, Mueser, and Choi 2004; Monnat 2010).

7 Outcomes for TANF Recipients

The most obvious change in outcomes under TANF is a precipitous decline in caseloads that began after 1994, before enactment of PRWORA. As discussed in the chapter on poverty in this volume, the number of TANF recipients dropped more than 60 percent between 1994 and 2001 and continued to drop in later years before slowing down and reversing slightly after 2007. Caseload declines continued even as increases in the percentage of children in poverty and deep poverty rose after 2000. The composition of the TANF caseload also changed dramatically over its first decade: By 2008, 46 percent of TANF families were "child only" (without a parent in the TANF unit), compared to 12 percent in 1986 and 21.5 percent in 1996. In a few states, mostly in the South and Mountain West, more than two-thirds of TANF cases are "child only" (Farrell et al. 2000; Zedlewski and Golden 2010).[7]

There is also great variation across states in the percentage of poor families with children receiving TANF, with generally broader program coverage in richer and more politically liberal states (Zedlewski and Golden 2010). Low-income families in the United States are increasingly likely to draw on the Supplemental Nutrition Assistance Program (SNAP, formerly known as food stamps) without receiving cash assistance from TANF (Klerman and Danielson 2011). A particularly striking pattern is how little the caseload of TANF increased as a result of the very deep recession that hit the United States beginning in 2007, suggesting that TANF no longer serves as more than a marginal safety net during hard times. Moreover, there was substantial variation across states in TANF caseload trends after the onset of the recession that does not fully track changes in unemployment rates.

TANF's weak caseload responsiveness to the recession can be explained in part by its fixed block-grant structure. Federal TANF funding does not automatically increase during recessions as low-income families lose employment—and as states are simultaneously suffering reduced tax revenues and increased demands for scarce funds. The American Relief and Recovery Act of 2009 did provide a one-time injection of $5 billion in federal funds, but many states were reluctant to change their programs given the temporary nature of that funding. The structure of the TANF work-participation rate requirement and caseload-reduction credit also lower incentives for states to serve more families through TANF during recessions (Pavetti, Trisi, and Schott 2011).

The *social* impacts—notably effects on child well-being, parental employment, non-marital childbearing, maintenance and dissolution of marriages—of TANF and related policy changes are difficult to assess because of the complexity of causal relationships. TANF incorporated many policy changes, from time limits to increased funding for child care and more rigorous child-care enforcement—and these were implemented differently across states. Moreover, welfare reform occurred at the same time as a number of other policy changes, notably expansion of the EITC and greater access to publicly financed health-care programs (Medicaid as well as the Children's Health Insurance Program created in 1997) that also affected low-income families. Additionally, TANF policy changes occurred against a backdrop of—and interacted with—secular changes in family structure and income distribution and cyclical changes in the economy, as well as other social changes. Thus, even when overall patterns of outcomes are clear, establishing clear causal linkages between those patterns and specific policy causes often is not.

Efforts to analyze the aggregate impact of specific welfare reform initiatives suggest important trade-offs among objectives. For example, policy initiatives that provide increased earnings disregards, wage supplements, and other financial incentives to work generally produce higher incomes for program participants, but they also increase expenditures for government. Programs that focus on immediate job search for participants and require them to participate in unpaid work or other assignments if they do not find jobs, on the other hand, save government money but produce either no income gains or income losses for most participants (Greenberg, Deitch, and Hamilton 2009).

Studies of employment outcomes under TANF generally show a mixed picture. Overall, employment rates among single mothers increased significantly after welfare reform. Most studies done prior to the onset of the post-2007 recession showed that around 70 percent of single mothers who left TANF were employed when they left the program, generally at low wages. Increases in employment rates of single mothers are generally attributed to a combination of increased work requirements under welfare reform and greater work incentives, notably a substantially expanded EITC after 1993, and a relatively robust economy in the 1990s (Meyer and Rosenbaum 2001).

Longer-term employment outcomes for TANF leavers are heterogeneous, and far from universally rosy. Most welfare leavers endure substantial job instability and work for low wages. Because of the structure of the low-wage labor market, they frequently work less than full time and at irregular hours that make it more difficult to secure reliable child care. Many are unable to earn enough to pull their families above the poverty line based on their earnings. Many return to public assistance at least once after losing employment. Relatively few manage to get on a job trajectory that leads to better jobs—that is, significantly increased earnings and more stable employment— over time (e.g., Acs and Loprest 2004; Wu, Cancian, and Meyers 2010; Wood, Moore, and Rangarajan 2008; Morgen, Acker, and Weigt 2010; Livermore, Davis and Lim, 2011).

These mixed outcomes reflect not just problems in the low-wage labor market but also that many low-income single mothers face high barriers to successful labor-market transitions, notably limited education and prior work experience (Holzer, Stoll, and Wissoker 2004). Single mothers who have more children and younger children also tend to have less labor-market success (Pavetti and Acs 2001). Other constraints, such as health and mental health problems, difficulties in securing transportation and afford- able health care, residential instability (including homelessness), and substance abuse and domestic violence, add to the difficulties of some welfare recipients and welfare leav- ers in finding and keeping jobs. Women confronting multiple barriers to effective labor- market participation are most likely to have unsuccessful or intermittent labor market success (Danziger and Seefeldt 2003; Speiglman et al. 2011). A significant percentage of welfare leavers have become what are referred to as "disconnected mothers"—neither receiving cash public assistance nor working (Turner, Danziger, and Seefeldt 2006).[8]

The record of TANF (and other government initiatives) in achieving the other TANF statutory objectives—reduction of nonmarital births and promotion and maintenance of two-parent families—are also mixed. Rates of childbearing by unmarried adolescents declined between 1994 and 2005, largely leveling off thereafter (Federal Interagency Forum on Child and Family Statistics, 2011, 4). Overall, however, 41 percent of births in the United States were to unmarried mothers in 2009, an increase from 11 percent in 1970 and 28 percent in 1990.[9]

Failure to make progress in this area can be attributed to a large complex of societal factors, including high rates of premarital sex, a declining stigma attached to nonmari- tal births, and declining job prospects for low-skilled men that make them less attrac- tive marriage partners (Solomon-Fears 2008). Moreover, most programmatic models for reducing nonmarital births offer only modest results, and there is little agreement among policy experts on how to achieve family-formation objectives.

8 The Future of TANF

Over the past two decades, the AFDC/TANF program has been transformed from a program that primarily provided cash assistance for long periods of time to families with a nonemployed household head to a program that primarily provides services to help those household heads move into work. Cash assistance is now a secondary role for TANF, and it is provided on a temporary, time-limited basis. The TANF program plays a much smaller role in the social safety net for low-income families than its predecessor AFDC played in the past. Medicaid, the EITC, SNAP (the successor to food stamps), and school food programs all serve many more poor families than TANF.

At the federal level, the frequent legislative tinkering that characterized the later years of the AFDC program has been supplanted by a high degree of legislative resilience. Reauthorization of TANF proved contentious: it was scheduled for 2002, but not enacted until early 2006, as the Bush administration and Congressional Democrats squabbled over funding levels and forcing states to meet stricter work requirements. Work requirements were stiffened in those revisions, but a number of other changes proposed by the Bush administration were dropped (Allard 2007; GAO 2010). Temporary increased funding for TANF was provided to states as part of the Obama administration's American Relief and Recovery Act in 2009, but without making major changes in the program (Parrott 2009). Major changes in the program at the federal level are unlikely in the near future, reflecting a continued absence of elite consensus on how to address problems of low-income families in the United States.

At the state level, an AFDC program that already featured substantial heterogeneity across states in benefit levels has become dramatically more heterogeneous under TANF. All state programs are now much more work focused than in the past, but the percentage of poor families covered and the level of both cash assistance and the services offered vary dramatically across states.

Contrary to the hopes of some welfare reform proponents, the replacement of AFDC by TANF does not appear to have fundamentally shifted attitudes toward low-income Americans and programs that serve them. Images of the poor remain heavily racialized (Dyck and Hussey 2008). The fall in TANF caseloads along with time limits and increased emphasis on work appear to have led not, as advocates for the poor had hoped, to increased public support for antipoverty programs but rather to lower salience for the TANF program without fundamentally altering underlying attitudes toward welfare recipients (Soss and Schram 2007). As the politically most sensitive part of the safety net for poor families, there is little prospect that the diminished role of cash assistance under TANF will change in the near future.

Notes

1. Two exceptions were the extension of Aid to Dependent Children benefits to a caretaker parent in 1950 and creation of a state-option to cover two-parent families where both parents were unemployed in 1962.
2. Indeed the "welfare migration effect" need not be real for the effects of competitive federalism to cause policy to become more stingy or strict: it is enough that policymakers fear that it is real, or fear that they will be blamed for it by voters, even if they do not themselves believe in it (Schram and Soss 1998; Peterson and Rom 1990).
3. The PRWORA legislation did contain a small contingency fund that states could draw upon in periods of recession. It also included small supplemental grants for states seen as disadvantaged by the TANF funding formula and two funds for "high performance" in meeting TANF objectives. The performance funds were repealed by the Deficit Reduction Act of 2005. See Falk 2011, 6.
4. Months when working members of households received services such as child-care and transportation assistance but no cash assistance did not count toward the 60-month limit.

5. Technically, the critical distinction in Department of Health and Human Services regulations is between "assistance," defined as benefits designed to meet a "family's ongoing basic needs' (that is, for food, clothing, shelter, utilities, household goods, personal-care items, and general incidental expenses) plus supportive services such as transportation and child care for families who are not employed," and "'nonassistance' (including nonrecurrent, short-term benefits, work subsidies, and supportive services to employed families" (U.S. House of Representatives 2004, 7–5).

6. See U.S. Department of Health and Human Services, Administration for Children and Families, Tables A1 and A3, Fiscal Year 2010 TANF Financial Data, http://www.acf.hhs. gov/programs/ofa/data/2010fin/tanf_2010_index.html

7. Cases can end up as child-only for a variety of reasons, including parental absence and parental ineligibility—for example, because the parent in an ineligible immigrant of a citizen child or is receiving benefits from the Supplemental Security Income (SSI) program, or as a result of sanctioning, or (in a few states) because the parent has reached the 60-month time limit.

8. One recent study estimated disconnected mothers as about one-fifth of low-income mothers between 2004 and 2008. Almost 60 percent of this group "lived with adults connected to work or public assistance"; about one-third with a cohabiting partner (Loprest and Nichols 2011, 1). See also Blank 2007; Danziger, 2010.

9. Although about more than half (52 percent) of nonmarital births are to cohabiting couples, the figure is much higher for white (61 percent) and Hispanic (65 percent) than African American mothers (30 percent), according to 2001 data. Contrary to popular perceptions, only 21 percent of nonmarital births in the United States in 2009 were to teen mothers; 62 percent were to women in their 20s. (Wildsmith, Steward-Streng, and Manlove 2009). Nonmarital births are much more common among less well-educated women (DeParle and Tavernise, 2012).

References

*Indicates recommended reading.

Acs, Gregory, and Pamela Loprest. 2004. *Leaving Welfare: Employment and Well-being of Families That Left Welfare in the Postentitlement Era*. Kalamazoo, MI: Upjohn Institute for Employment Research.

Allard, Scott W. 2007. "The Changing Face of Welfare during the Bush Administration." *Publius: The Journal of Federalism* 37 (3): 304–332.

Berry, William D., Richard C. Fording, and Russell L. Hanson. 2003. "Reassessing the "Race to the Bottom" in State Welfare Policy." *Journal of Politics.* 65 (2): 327–349.

Blank, Rebecca M. 2007. "Improving the Safety Net for Single Mothers Who Face Serious Barriers to Work," *The Future of Children* 17, no. 2 (Fall): 183–197

Blank, Rebecca M. 2008. "Presidential Address: How to Improve Poverty Measurement in the United States." *Journal of Policy Analysis and Management* 27: 233–254

Brodkin, Evelyn Z. and Malay Majmundar 2010. "Administrative Exclusion: Organizations and the Hidden Costs of Welfare Claiming," *Journal of Public Administration Research and Theory* 20 (4): 827–848.

Cherlin, Andrew J., Karen Bogen, James M. Quane, and Linda Burton 2002. "Operating within the Rules: Welfare Recipients' Experiences with Sanctions and Case Closings." *Social Service Review* 76, no. 3 (September): 387–405.

Clawson, Rosalee A. and Rakuya Trice. 2000. "Poverty as We Know It: Media Portrayals of the Poor." *Public Opinion Quarterly* 64, no. 1. (Spring): 53–64.

* Danziger, Sandra K. 2010. "The Decline of Cash Welfare and Implications for Social Policy and Poverty." *Annual Review of Sociology* 36: 523–545.

Danziger, Sandra K. and Kristin S. Seefeldt. 2003. "Barriers to Employment and the 'Hard to Serve': Implications for Services, Sanctions and Time Limits." *Social Policy & Society* 2 (2): 151–160.

DeNavas-Walt, Carmen, Bernadette D. Proctor, and Jessica C. Smith. 2011. *Income, Poverty, and Health Insurance Coverage in the United States: 2010.* U.S. Census Bureau, Current Population Reports, P60-239. Washington, DC: GPO.

DeParle, Jason, and Sabrina Tavernise. 2012. "For Women Under 30, Most Births Occur Outside Marriage." *New York Times*, February 17.

Dyck, Joshua J., and Laura S. Hussey 2008. "The End of Welfare As We Know It? Durable Attitudes in a Changing Information Environment." *Public Opinion Quarterly* 72, no. 4 (Winter): 589–618.

Ellwood, David T. 1988. *Poor Support: Poverty in the American Family.* New York: Basic Books.

Falk, Eugene 2011. *The Temporary Assistance for Needy Families (TANF) Block Grant: A Primer on TANF Financing and Federal Requirements.* Report RL32748. August 2. Washington, DC: Congressional Research Service.

Farrell, Mary, Michael Fishman, Stephanie Laud, and Vincena Allen. 2000. *Understanding the AFDC/TANF Child-Only Caseload: Policies, Composition, and Characteristics in Three States.* U.S. Department of Health and Human Services. http://aspe.hhs.gov/hsp/child-only-caseloado0/.

Farrell M, Sarah Rich, Lesley Turner, David Seith, and Dan Bloom. 2008. *Welfare Time Limits: An Update on State Policies, Implementation, and Effects on Families.* New York: Manpower Demonstration Research.

Federal Interagency Forum on Child and Family Statistics. 2011. *America's Children: Key National Indicators of Well-Being, 2011.* Washington, DC: GPO.

GAO (General Accounting Office). 2000. *Welfare Reform: State Sanction Policies and Number of Families Affected.* Washington, DC: GAO.

GAO. 2010. *Temporary Assistance to Needy Families: Implications of Recent Legislative and Economic Changes for State Programs and Work Participation Rates.* Report GAO-10-525. Washington, DC: GAO.

* Gilens, Martin. 1999. *Why Americans Hate Welfare: Race, Media, and the Politics of Antipoverty Policy.* Chicago: University of Chicago Press.

Gordon, Linda. 1994. *Pitied but Not Entitled: Single Mothers and the History of Welfare.* New York: Free Press.

Gornick, Janet C., and Markus Jäntti. 2010. "Child Poverty in Upper-Income Countries: Lessons from the Luxembourg Income Study." In Sheila B. Kamerman, Shelley Phipps, and Asher Ben-Arieh, eds., *From Child Welfare to Child Well-Being.* Dordrecht: Springer, 339–368.

Greenberg, David, Victoria Deitch, and Gayle Hamilton. 2009. *Welfare-to-Work Program Benefits and Costs,* New York: Manpower Demonstration Research.

Haskins, Ron. 2006. *Work Over Welfare: The Inside Story of the 1996 Welfare Reform Law.* Washington, DC: Brookings Institution.

Heclo, Hugh. 1986. "The Political Foundations of Antipoverty Policy." In Sheldon H. Danziger and Daniel H. Weinberg, eds., *Fighting Poverty: What Works and What Doesn't*. Cambridge, MA: Harvard University Press, 312–340.

Heclo, Hugh. 1994. "Poverty Politics." In Sheldon H. Danziger, Gary D. Sandefur, and Daniel H. Weinberg, eds., *Confronting Poverty: Prescriptions for Change*. New York and Cambridge, MA: Russell Sage and Harvard University Press, 396–437.

Holzer, Harry J., Michael A. Stoll, and Douglas Wissoker. 2004. "Job Performance and Retention among Welfare Recipients." *Social Service Review* 78 (3): 343–369.

Howard, Christopher. 1999. "The American Welfare State, Or States?" *Political Research Quarterly* 52, no. 2 (June): 421–442.

Hoynes, Hilary W., Marianne E. Page, and Ann Huff Stevens (2006) "Poverty in America: Trends and Explanations." *Journal of Economic Perspectives* 20, no. 1 (Winter): 47–68.

Kauff, Jacqueline, Michelle K. Derr, LaDonna Pavetti, and Emily Sama Martin. 2007. *Using Work-Oriented. Sanctions to Increase. TANF Program. Participation. Final Report*. Washington, DC: Mathematica Policy Research.

Keiser, Lael R., Peter R. Mueser, Seung-Whan Choi. 2004. "Race, Bureaucratic Discretion, and the Implementation of Welfare Reform." *American Journal of Political Science* 48, no. 2 (April): 314–327.

Klerman, Jacob Alex, and Caroline Danielson. 2011. "The Transformation of the Supplemental Nutrition Assistance Program." *Journal of Policy Analysis & Management* 30, no. 4 (Fall): 863–888.

Lieberman, Robert C., and John S. Lapinski. 2001. "American Federalism, Race and the Administration of Welfare." *British Journal of Political Science* 31: 303–329.

Livermore, Michelle, Belinda Davis, and Younghee Lim. 2011. "Failing to Make Ends Meet: Dubious Financial Success Among Employed Former Welfare to Work Program Participants." *Journal of Family and Economic Issues* 32 (1): 73–83.

Loprest, Pamela, and Austin Nichols. 2011. "*Characteristics of Low-Income Single Mothers Disconnected from Work and Public Assistance*." Washington, DC: Urban Institute Low Income Families Fact Sheet. http://www.urban.org/UploadedPDF/412375-Low-Income-Single-Mothers-Disconnected-from-Work.pdf.

Lovell, Philip, and Julia B. Isaacs. 2010. "Families of the Recession: Unemployed Parents and Their Children." At Brookings Institution website: http://www.brookings.edu/papers/2010/0114_families_recession_isaacs.aspx.

Lynn, Lawrence, and David Whitman. 1981. *The President as Policymaker: Jimmy Carter and Welfare Reform*. Philadelphia: Temple University Press.

Mead, Lawrence M. 1992. *The New Politics of Poverty: The Nonworking Poor in America*. New York: Basic Books.

Melnick, R. Shep. 1994. *Between the Lines: Interpreting Welfare Rights*. Washington, DC: Brookings Institution.

Meyer, Bruce D., and Dan T. Rosenbaum. 2001. "Welfare, the Earned Income Tax Credit, and the Labor Supply of Single Mothers." *Quarterly Journal of Economics*, 116, no. 3 (August): 1063–1114.

Monnat, Shannon M. 2010. "The Color of Welfare Sanctioning: Exploring the Individual and Contextual Roles of Race on TANF Case Closures and Benefit Reductions." *Sociological Quarterly* 51: 678–707.

Morgen, Sandra, Joan Acker, and Jill Weigt. 2010. *Stretched Thin: Poor Families, Welfare Work, and Welfare Reform*. Ithaca, NY: Cornell University Press.

Murray, Charles. 1984. *Losing Ground: American Social Policy, 1955–1980*. New York: Basic Books.

Parrott, Sharon. 2009. *"Despite Critics Overheated Rhetoric, the Economic Recovery Bill Does Not Undermine Welfare Reform."* Washington, DC: Center on Budget and Policy Priorities (February 17). http://www.cbpp.org/files/2-17-09tanf.pdf.

Pavetti, LaDonna, and Gregory Acs. 2001. "Moving Up, Moving Out or Going Nowhere? A Study of the Employment Patterns of Young Women and the Implications for Welfare Mothers." *Journal of Policy Analysis and Management* 20: 721–736.

Pavetti, LaDonna, Michelle K. Derr, and Heather Hesketh. 2003. *Review of Sanction Policies and Research Studies: Final Literature Review*. Washington, DC: Mathematica Policy Research.

Pavetti, LaDonna, Danilo Trisi, and Liz Schott. 2011. *TANF Responded Unevenly to Increase in Need During Downturn*. Washington, DC: Center on Budget and Policy Priorities (January 25), http://www.cbpp.org/files/1-25-11tanf.pdf.

Peterson, Paul E., and Mark C. Rom. 1990. *Welfare Magnets: A New Case for a National Standard*. Washington, DC: Brookings Institution.

Pierson, Paul D. 1995. "The Creeping Nationalization of Income Transfers in the United States, 1935–94." In Stephan Leibfried and Paul Pierson, eds., *European Social Policy*. Washington, DC: Brookings Institution Press, 301–328.

*Rainwater, Lee, and Timothy M. Smeeding. 2003. *Poor Kids in a Rich Country: America's Children in Comparative Perspective*. New York: Sage.

Ridzi, Frank. 2009. *Selling Welfare Reform: Work-First and the New Common Sense of Employment*. New York: New York University Press.

Rom, Mark Carl, Paul E. Peterson, and Kenneth F. Scheve, Jr. 1998. "Interstate Competition and Welfare Policy." *Publius* 28 (3): 17–37.

Schneider, Saundra K, and William G. Jacoby. 2005. "Elite Discourse and American Public Opinion: The Case of Welfare Spending." *Political Research Quarterly* 58, no. 3 (September): 367–379.

Schott, Liz. 2011. *An Introduction to TANF*. (July 6.) Washington, DC: Center on Budget and Policy Priorities. http://www.cbpp.org/files/7-22-10tanf2.pdf.

Schram, Sanford, Lawrence Nitz, and Gary Krueger. 1998. "Without Cause or Effect: Reconsidering Welfare Migration as a Policy Problem." American Journal of Political Science 42: 210–230.

Schram, Sanford F., and Joe Soss. 1998. "Making Something Out of Nothing: Welfare Reform and a New Race to the Bottom." *Publius* 28: 67–88.

Schram, Sanford F., Joe Soss, and Richard Fording, eds. 2003. *Race and the Politics of Welfare Reform*. Ann Arbor: University of Michigan Press.

*Schram, Sanford F., Joe Soss, Richard C. Fording, and Linda Houser. 2009. "Deciding to Discipline: Race, Choice, and Punishment at the Frontlines of Welfare Reform." American Sociological Review 74, no. 2 (June): 398–422.

Skocpol, Theda. 1995. *Protecting Soldiers and Mothers: The Political Origins of Social Policy in United States*. Cambridge, MA: Harvard University Press.

Solomon-Fears, Carmen. 2008. *Nonmarital Childbearing: Trends, Reasons, and Public Policy Interventions*. Congressional Research Service Report for Congress RL34756, November 20.

Somers, Margaret R, and Fred Block. 2005. "From Poverty to Perversity: Ideas, Markets, and Institutions over 200 Years of Welfare Debate." *American Sociological Review 70*, no. 2 (April): 260–287.

Soss, Joe, Richard Fording, and Sanford F. Schram. 2011. *Disciplining the Poor: Neoliberal Paternalism and the Persistent Power of Race*. Chicago: University of Chicago Press.

Soss, Joe, and Sanford F. Schram. 2007. "A Public Transformed? Welfare Reform as Policy Feedback." *American Political Science Review* 101: 111–128.

Speiglman, Richard, Hana Brown, Johannes M. Bos, Youngmei Li, and Lorena Ortiz. 2011. "TANF Child-Only Cases in California: Barriers to Self-Sufficiency and Well-Being." *Journal of Children and Poverty* 17 (2): 139–163.

Steensland, Brian. 2008. *The Failed Welfare Revolution: America's Struggle over Guaranteed Income Policy*. Princeton, NJ: Princeton University Press.

*Turner, Lesley J., Sandra Danziger, and Kristin Seefeldt. 2006. "Failing the Transition from Welfare to Work: Women Chronically Disconnected from Employment and Cash Welfare." *Social Science Quarterly* 87 (2): 227–249.

Tweedie, Jack. 1994. "Resources Rather than Needs: A State-Centered Model of Welfare Policy-Making." *American Journal of Political Science* 38 (3): 651–672.

U.S. House of Representatives, Committee on Ways and Means. 1994. *1994 Green Book: Background Material and Data on Programs within the Jurisdiction of the House Committee on Ways and Means*. Committee Print 103-27. Washington, DC: GPO.

U.S. House of Representatives, Committee on Ways and Means. 2004. *2004 Green Book: Background Material and Data on Programs within the Jurisdiction of the House Committee on Ways and Means*. Committee Print WMCP 108-6. Washington, DC: GPO.

Volden, Craig. 2002. "The Politics of Competitive Federalism: A Race to the Bottom in Welfare Benefits?" *American Journal of Political Science* 46 no. 2 (April): 352–363.

Watkins-Hayes, Celeste. 2009. *The New Welfare Bureaucrats: Entanglements of Race, Class, and Policy Reform*. Chicago: University of Chicago Press.

*Weaver, R. Kent. 2000. *Ending Welfare As We Know It*. Washington, DC: Brookings Institution.

Weaver, R. Kent, and Thomas Gais. 2002. *State Policy Choices Under Welfare Reform*. Washington, DC: Brookings Institution Welfare Reform and Beyond Policy Brief No. 26 (April).

Wildsmith, Elizabeth, Nicole R. Steward-Streng, and Jennifer Manlove. 2011. *Childbearing Outside of Marriage: Estimates and Trends in the United States*. Child Trends Research Brief, Publication No. 2011-29 (November). http://www.childtrends.org/Files/Child_Trends-2011_11_01_RB_NonmaritalCB.pdf.

Wood, Robert G., Quinn Moore, and Anu Rangurajan. 2008. "Two Steps Forward, One Step Back: The Uneven Economic Progress of TANF Recipients." *Social Service Review* 82, no. 1 (June): 3–28.

Wu, Chi-Fang, Maria Cancian, and Daniel R. Meyer. 2008. "Standing Still or Moving Up? Evidence from Wisconsin on the Long-Term Employment and Earnings of TANF Participants." *Social Work Research* 32 (2): 89–103.

Zedlewski, Sheila, and Olivia Golden. 2010. *Next Steps for Temporary Assistance for Needy Families*. Urban Institute Working Families Brief 11 (February). http://www.urban.org/UploadedPDF/412047_next_steps_brief11.pdf?RSSFeed=UI_LowIncomeWorkingFamilies.

CHAPTER 21

THE POLITICS OF SUPPORTING LOW-WAGE WORKERS AND FAMILIES

DANIEL P. GITTERMAN

1 INTRODUCTION

THIS chapter highlights two major policies that supplement the earnings of low-wage workers: the federal minimum wage and the earned income tax credit (EITC). These policies reflect a core belief: all able-bodied workers must participate in the labor market full time; if they do so, they should earn enough to keep their families out of poverty. However, declining demand has pulled down the wages of the less skilled, both men and women, so employment alone often does not lead to economic self-sufficiency. Thus, despite decades of efforts to help low-wage workers, the challenge of making work pay for *every* American remains.

The need for earnings supplementation arises in part from the nature of the jobs held by less-skilled, low-wage workers. Such jobs are likely to be compensated on an hourly basis, not salaried, and are less likely to be full time. Moreover, the wages that these jobs pay have declined in relative terms. Over the past several decades the real hourly wage rate grew faster at the top of the wage distribution than at the middle and grew faster at the middle than at the bottom. For the foreseeable future, many less-skilled workers will continue to face low and even falling real wages. This trend provides a backdrop to policy efforts to use the minimum wage and refundable tax credits to supplement the earnings of low-income workers and their children. Such policies move many workers and families out of poverty, but by no means all of them.

A legally binding minimum wage is in place in twenty-one Organisation for Economic Co-operation and Development (OECD) countries (Immervoll and Pearson 2009). Nevertheless, minimum wages remain controversial. In part this is because they are redistributive; they "do not increase the pay of workers by magic" (Freeman 1996, 640), but rather entail gains for some and losses for others. In many OECD countries persistent labor market difficulties experienced by individuals with limited earnings potential have led to an interest in policies aimed at assisting them. A motivation to promote self-sufficiency has prompted ongoing discussions of rebalancing social safety nets. The result has been a growing interest in, and use of, "make work pay" policies such as the EITC (Immervoll and Pearson 2009).

A scholarly focus on the minimum wage and the EITC contributes to—and expands our understanding of—the US welfare state in two ways. First, it looks beyond social insurance and public assistance programs (such as welfare), which have been considered the main tools of social policy, to explore the importance of alternative policies. Second, it moves beyond income support to nonworkers (the elderly, the disabled, nonworking mothers with dependent children) to focus on efforts to support individuals who are *active* in the labor market. In so doing, it contributes to a scholarship that has reshaped thinking about the welfare state by introducing such concepts as the "hidden welfare state" and the "shadow" or "divided" welfare state (Howard 1997; Gottschalk 2000; Hacker 2002). As Chris Howard (2003, 414) observes, the "American welfare state is exceptional not so much for its small size—in terms of spending—as for its reliance on a broad range of policy tools to achieve social welfare objectives."

The policies highlighted in this chapter are not the only ways in which the government can boost the pretax earnings or after-tax incomes of low-income earners. The government can invest in human capital through education and training programs that help less-skilled workers prepare for higher-wage jobs. A range of means-tested benefits continues to help working poor families with basic expenses such as health care (Medicaid, CHIP), food security (SNAP), and child care. One consequence of our fragmented set of employer mandates, means-tested benefits, and tax credits is that working poor households in different circumstances receive different levels of support.

2 PROTECTING LOW-WAGE WORKERS IN THE UNITED STATES

The US Congress and President Franklin D. Roosevelt initially set the federal minimum wage at 25 cents per hour as part of the 1938 Fair Labor Standards Act (FLSA) (Grossman 1978). At the time most of the lowest-wage workers were employed in southern industries such as lumber textiles, and tobacco. Textiles and lumber were the two largest manufacturing employers; agriculture, the largest employer in the South, was originally exempted from coverage. Southern Democrats, responding to agricultural and other business groups, kept agricultural and domestic service occupations out of contributory social insurance and public assistance programs and out of federal labor standards (Linder 1987; Palmer 1995; Mettler 1998).

In recent decades the impact of the minimum wage has not been concentrated in one region. It largely affects teenagers and young adults; however, in recent decades an increasing number of adults have become its potential beneficiaries (Freeman 1996). Recent evidence suggests that the minimum wage reduces inequality in the lower end of the wage distribution (Autor, Manning, and Smith 2010). Congress has increased the minimum wage numerous times over the past seven decades, as shown in Figure 21.1. As of 2014 the minimum wage was $7.25 per hour. Nonetheless, because the minimum wage has not been indexed to inflation, it has not kept pace with the cost of living, and its real value has declined between each statutory increase. Currently all "covered nonexempt" workers are entitled to $7.25 per hour, and many states have minimum wages that exceed this amount. In cases where an employee is protected by both a state and federal minimum wage, the employee is entitled to the higher minimum wage. More than 130 million workers are protected by the minimum wage, which is enforced by the Wage and Hour Division of the Department of Labor (US DOL 2014).

Currently there are two ways in which an employee is covered: "enterprise coverage" and "individual coverage." Enterprise coverage applies to businesses that have at least two employees and an annual volume of sales or business of at least $500,000, or are hospitals, businesses providing medical or nursing care for residents, schools and pre-schools, or government agencies. When there is no enterprise coverage, employees are protected as individuals if they are "engaged in commerce or in the production of goods for commerce." Domestic service workers, such as housekeepers, full-time babysitters, and cooks, are examples of workers who are individually covered (US DOL 2014). Minimum wage exceptions apply to some workers such as full-time students and tipped employees.[1]

For service workers, tips and commissions can supplement their hourly wage. Many service-oriented employees regularly receive more than $30 per month in tips, and their employers may elect to use a tip credit provision and demonstrate that tipped employees receive at least the minimum wage when direct (or cash) wages and the tip credit amount are combined. For example, if an employee's tips combined with the employer's direct (or cash) wages of at least $2.13 per hour do not equal the minimum wage of $7.25 per hour, the employer must make up the difference. Thus, the maximum tip credit that an employer can claim is $5.12 per hour (the minimum wage of $7.25 minus the minimum required cash wage of $2.13). Employers can also pay a youth minimum wage of $4.25 an hour (to employees who are under twenty years of age during the first ninety days after initial employment). This includes protections for adult workers and prohibits employers from displacing any employee in order to hire someone at the youth minimum wage (US DOL 2014).

In 2012, 75.3 million workers in the United States age sixteen and over were paid at hourly rates, representing 59.0 percent of all wage and salary workers. Among those paid by the hour, 1.6 million earned exactly the prevailing federal minimum wage of $7.25 per hour. About 2.0 million had wages below the federal minimum. Together, these 3.6 million workers with wages at or below the federal minimum made up 4.7 percent of all hourly paid workers. the highest proportion of hourly paid workers earning at or

Mimimum Hourly Wage of Workers First Covered by

Effective Date	1938 Act[1]	1961 Amendments[2]	1966 & Subsequent Amendments[3]	
			Nonfarm	Farm
OCT. 24, 1938	$0.25			
OCT. 24, 1939	$0.30			
OCT. 24, 1945	$0.40			
JAN. 25, 1950	$0.75			
MAR. 1, 1956	$1.00			
SEPT. 3, 1961	$1.15	$1.00		
SEPT. 3, 1963	$1.25			
SEPT. 3, 1964		$1.15		
SEPT. 3, 1965		$1.25		
FEB. 1, 1967	$1.40	$1.40	$1.00	$1.00
FEB. 1, 1968	$1.60	$1.60	$1.15	$1.15
FEB. 1, 1969			$1.30	$1.30
FEB. 1, 1970			$1.45	
FEB. 1, 1971			$1.60	
MAY 1, 1974	$2.00	$2.00	$1.90	$1.60
JAN. 1, 1975	$2.10	$2.10	$2.00	$1.80
JAN. 1, 1976	$2.30	$2.30	$2.20	$2.00
JAN. 1, 1977			$2.30	$2.20
JAN. 1, 1978	$2.65 for all covered, nonexempt workers			
JAN. 1, 1979	$2.90 for all covered, nonexempt workers			
JAN. 1, 1980	$3.10 for all covered, nonexempt workers			
JAN. 1, 1981	$3.35 for all covered, nonexempt workers			
APR. 1, 1990[4]	$3.80 for all covered, nonexempt workers			
APR. 1, 1991	$4.25 for all covered, nonexempt workers			
OCT. 1, 1996[5]	$4.75 for all covered, nonexempt workers			
SEPT. 1, 1997	$5.15 for all covered, nonexempt workers			
JUL. 24, 2007	$5.85 for all covered, nonexempt workers			
JUL. 24, 2008	$6.55 for all covered, nonexempt workers			
JUL. 24, 2009	$7.25 for all covered, nonexempt workers			

[1] The 1938 act was applicable generally to employees engaged in interstate commerce or in the production of goods for interstate commerce.

[2] The 1961 amendments extended coverage primarily to employees in large retail and service enterprises as well as to local transit, construction, and gasoline service station employees.

[3] The 1966 amendments extended coverage to state and local government employees of hospitals, nursing homes, and schools, and to employees of laundries, dry cleaners, large hotels, motels, restaurants, and farms. Subsequent amendments extended coverage to the remaining federal, state, and local government employees who were not protected in 1966; to certain workers in retail and service trades previously exempted; and to certain domestic workers in private household employment.

[4] Grandfather Clause: Employees who do not meet the tests for individual coverage, and whose employers were covered by the FLSA on March 31, 1990, and fail to meet the increased annual dollar volume (ADV) test for enterprise coverage, must continue to receive at least $3.35 an hour.

[5] A subminimum wage—$4.25 an hour—is established for employees under twenty years of age during their first ninety consecutive calendar days of employment with an employer.

FIG. 21.1 Federal Minimum Wage Rates Under the Fair Labor Standards Act.

below the federal minimum wage was in service occupations, at about 12 percent. The industry with the highest proportion of workers with hourly wages at or below the federal minimum wage was leisure and hospitality (about 19 percent) (US DOL 2013).

(US DOL 2013). Thus the minimum wage affects primarily small businesses. The percentage of workers earning the minimum wage does not vary much by race or ethnicity (US DOL 2013).

Historically, proponents have viewed the minimum wage as an important antipoverty tool. Opponents have seen it as a burden on employers and an unwarranted interference with the labor market. The employment effects of the minimum wage have generated particular controversy. As early as the 1940s, George Stigler argued that "economists should be outspoken and singularly agreed" that the minimum wage does not reduce poverty (1946, 358). Opponents claim that the weight of the evidence supports the view that higher minimum wages reduce employment by forcing marginal businesses to lay off workers. However, empirical research suggests that the most recent increases have had little or no adverse effects on employment (Card and Krueger 1995; Freeman 1996). Moreover, some economists believe that the minimum wage offers benefits to firms, citing higher productivity, decreased turnover, lower recruiting and training costs, decreased absenteeism, and increased worker morale as gains that might offset some of the costs to employers of a wage increase (Fox 2006).

3 Taxing Low-Wage Working Families out of Poverty

Before examining the origins of the EITC, a useful way to think about the impact of the income tax on low-wage working families is to compare the income tax entry threshold and the federal poverty threshold. The tax entry threshold is the maximum income a family can earn before owing federal income tax (Maag 2004). The federal poverty threshold represents "the minimum dollar amount needed for individuals, couples, or families to purchase food and meet other basic needs" (US Dept. of Health and Human Services 2011). The poverty threshold increases with family size and is updated for inflation annually, using the consumer price index (CPI) (Maag 2004). If total family income is less than the threshold appropriate for that family, the family is in poverty. For example, if the tax entry threshold for a family of four falls at or below the poverty threshold, tax liabilities can push such families below the poverty line.

Because the personal exemption and the minimum standard deduction remained constant in nominal terms between 1948 and 1963, while the poverty threshold rose with inflation, the level at which low-income families started paying income taxes fell below the poverty line during this period. In 1964 Congress began to adjust the tax entry threshold—the amount a family could earn before having to pay federal income taxes—back up toward the poverty threshold (Atrostic and Nunns 1991). For the first time the income tax came to be seen as an antipoverty tool. But the tax entry threshold again fell below the poverty threshold during the late 1970s, and ad hoc increases were adopted in 1970, 1972, and 1979 to address the problem (Bakija and Steuerle 1991).

The 1980s brought tax relief for low-income families in two forms. First, the 1981 Economic Recovery Tax Act (ERTA) indexed the personal exemption, standard deduction, and tax brackets to inflation beginning in 1985. Second, the 1986 Tax Reform Act (TRA) expanded the EITC, which had been introduced in more modest form as the earned income credit in 1975, and indexed it to inflation as well. These changes, followed by increases in the EITC in the 1990s under the Bush and Clinton administrations, reduced the tax burden faced by low-income earners with children. Since the 1990s the tax entry threshold for a family of four has exceeded the poverty threshold, due largely to the EITC and more recently to the child tax credit (CTC) (Maag 2004).

Besides income taxes, most workers owe payroll taxes. When the federal payroll tax was first collected in 1937, it was only 2 percent of wages and salaries, evenly divided between employer and employee. By 1960 the rate had tripled to 6 percent, which approached the upper range of what President Franklin D. Roosevelt's Treasury Department had anticipated that low-income workers could bear without needing income tax relief. In 2011 the payroll tax rate was 15.3 percent of earnings (12.4 percent for Social Security and Disability Insurance and 2.9 percent for Medicare) (Burman and Leiserson 2007). Historically, Democrats and Republicans have disagreed over how to finance expansion of the Social Security program. Liberal Democrats preferred to increase the income ceiling on the payroll tax base, which would increase the tax burden on higher-income workers, while their more conservative colleagues favored increasing the payroll tax rate (Reese 1980). However, by the mid-1970s Democrats and Republicans expressed growing concern about the regressive effects of the payroll tax, which when combined with the income tax imposed a higher effective tax rate on low-income earners than high-income earners. In fact, many low-income taxpayers owed more in payroll taxes than in federal income taxes. To help such families, in 1975 Congress adopted the earned income credit—later known as the EITC—which reduced their tax liability.

The EITC reduces poverty by supplementing the earnings of workers with low earnings. Beginning with the first dollar, a worker's EITC grows with each additional dollar of earnings until the credit reaches the maximum value. This creates an incentive for people to leave welfare for work and for low-wage workers to increase their work hours. In 2011 working families, with children who had annual incomes below about $36,000 to $49,000 (depending on marital status and children) may have been eligible for the EITC. Working poor individuals without children who had incomes below about $13,600 ($18,700 for a married couple) could receive a small EITC (Center for Budget and Policy Priorities [CBPP] 2011). Twenty-five states, including the District of Columbia, have established EITCs to supplement the federal credit.

The amount of EITC depends on a recipient's income, marital status, and number of children (Figure 21.2). The amount rises with earned income until it reaches a maximum and then begins to phase out at higher income levels. In the 2009 tax year twenty-seven million working families and individuals received the EITC, which lifted about six million people out of poverty, including about three million children. The poverty rate among children would have been nearly one-third higher without the EITC. The EITC lifts more children out of poverty than any other social policy (CBPP 2011).

During the 2009 tax year the average EITC was $2,770 for a family with children and $259 for a household without children. Because of the credit, most low-wage working parents do not owe any federal taxes and often receive a tax rebate. There has been bipartisan agreement that a two-parent family with two children and at least one full-time, minimum-wage worker should not have to raise its children in poverty. At the minimum wage's current level, such a family can move above the poverty line only if it receives the EITC as well as SNAP (food stamp) benefits (CBPP 2011). The EITC for workers without children remains too small to fully offset federal taxes for workers at the poverty line. Currently, a childless adult or noncustodial parent who works full time at the minimum wage does not receive any EITC benefits. As a result, low-wage workers not raising children can still be taxed into poverty.

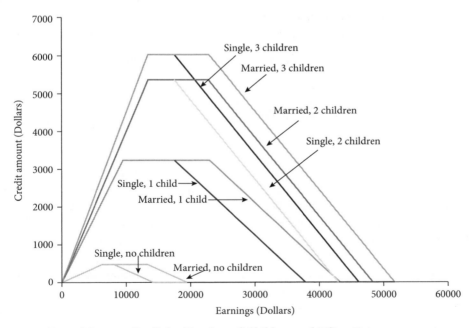

FIG. 21.2 Earned Income Credit by Number of Children and Filing Status, 2013

Source: Historical EITC Parameters, January 28, 2013, Tax Policy Center. http://www.taxpolicycenter.org/taxfacts/displayfact.cfm?Docid=36.

4 PARTISAN POLITICS

Agreement that full-time workers and their families should not live in poverty does not mean agreement over how best to achieve that goal. Political conflict over the minimum wage and EITC has mirrored major ideological and distributional divisions within American politics over the past several decades. There has been significant partisan conflict over increases in the minimum wage (and expansion of coverage), driven by the perceived trade-off between increases in workers' income and in labor costs for small business. Broader debates over the progressivity of the tax code have been partisan and divisive. Tax credits for low- to moderate-income earners with children, such as the EITC and CTC, have been a partial exception to this rule, drawing support across partisan, ideological, and economic lines. Nonetheless, partisan conflict has emerged over the EITC's "refundability," the costs of which have grown substantially over the past decades.

Democrats and Republicans have preferred different policies not solely for technical or ideological reasons, but also based on their distributive consequences for core constituents and interest groups. In forging the coalitions needed to enact policy change, both parties have sought to distribute tax relief or minimum wage increases (or exemptions) to the groups perceived as crucial to their electoral success. Moderates have played a pivotal role in brokering and shaping these final bargains. Both policies have been marked by repeated trade-offs between the demands of effectiveness and political support, and smaller, bipartisan groups of centrists have been critical at every stage of their evolution (Gitterman 2009).

5 THE FEDERAL MINIMUM WAGE, 1938–2013

The minimum wage emerged from the later New Deal as a mechanism to boost the pre-tax earnings of low-wage workers, regardless of their family size. The Great Depression had reached unprecedented depths by 1932–1933, with more than half of Americans living below a minimum subsistence level. The challenge was to lift wages and prices at the same time. Roosevelt's initial response was the 1933 National Industrial Recovery Act (NIRA), through which Congress empowered the president to set minimum prices, wages, and competitive conditions in all industries. The minimum wage was intended to increase workers' purchasing power. However, there was widespread evasion of the NIRA labor codes, and the US Supreme Court declared the program unconstitutional (Bernstein 1987).

Led by Roosevelt, Congress adopted the 1935 National Labor Relations Act (NLRA), which authorized most private-sector employees to join unions, to bargain collectively with their employers, and to strike. Congress established an independent entity, the National Labor Relations Board (NLRB), with the power to investigate and decide allegations of unfair labor practices and to conduct elections in which workers could choose whether to be represented by a union. Under the NLRA unionization rates doubled to more than one in four workers by 1940. However, collective bargaining was not a realistic option for many low-wage workers (Tomlins 1985).

To help unorganized workers, Roosevelt proposed a federal minimum wage at 80 cents per hour. Under his plan, Congress would delegate authority to a Fair Labor Standards Board, analogous to the NLRB, to set a minimum wage on an industry-by-industry basis and adjust the minimum wage to keep pace with inflation. However, to win passage of his proposal, the president had to secure the support of rural conservative southerners, who dominated the Democratic Party. In the early 1930s they favored an assertive role for the government in economic affairs and supported many of Roosevelt's labor-related initiatives, albeit with reservations and only after securing protection for their regional interests. As economic historian Gavin Wright (1986) has observed, all the distinguishing differences between the South and the rest of the United States had their roots in the "separateness" of the southern labor market. This "separateness" was evident in the low average wages paid, low investment in education, and low average value added in manufacturing per worker (Brand 1988).

In crafting a final bargain—a 25 cents per hour federal minimum wage, with many industries excluded—a conservative coalition of Republicans and southern Democrats chose to retain direct legislative control over the minimum wage rather than delegate authority to an independent body. This choice ensured that a new coalition had to be built *each and every time* policy makers sought to increase the minimum wage or expand its coverage. From 1938 to 1994 an enacting coalition had to include key members of the congressional labor committees, the House Rules Committee, the leadership of the majority party, and the president. By retaining political control, Congress could claim credit for a minimum wage increase, which had strong public support across all regions, as well as minimize blame from groups that feared its impact on labor costs by limiting coverage and the amount of the increase (Gitterman 2012).

In ensuing decades, policy makers made the most of this ability by fine-tuning increases (and limiting coverage) in response to the dictates of electoral politics. Congress adopted increases in a series of incremental steps rather than one large expansion, often directly before an election—a logic similar to Social Security benefit increases. Rather than work for repeal of the minimum wage, which was not in its members' electoral self-interest, the conservative coalition opposed any expansion of coverage from 1938 until 1961, as well as efforts to index it to inflation. However, the coalition did agree to modest and periodic increases in the minimum wage. Throughout this period liberal Democrats and their labor allies were forced to scale back their ambitions to win any support for wage increases from conservative legislators and their agricultural and small business allies. In the 1960s, however, moderates began to replace conservatives among southern Democrats in Congress, leading in 1961 and 1966 to the first major expansion of coverage since the New Deal. Each increase was made possible by intraparty bargaining between conservative southern and liberal Democrats (Gitterman 2012).

By the early 1980s the minimum wage emerged as "political enemy number one" for President Ronald Reagan and Senate Republicans. When Reagan took control of the White House, he was calling it an injustice, the cause of "more misery and unemployment than anything since the Great Depression." After regaining control of the Senate in 1986, Democrats aimed to increase the minimum wage to roughly half of the average wage (Cohodas 1987). Republicans blocked Democratic efforts to do so during the latter part of Reagan's second term. In late 1989 the moderate President George H. W. Bush agreed to a two-step increase to $4.25 (by 1991) in exchange for a temporary training wage for teenagers and a larger exemption for small businesses (Pytte 1989).

An unlikely agreement was struck between President Bill Clinton and the Republican Congress in 1996. As a candidate for president, Clinton had positioned himself as a moderate Democrat who promised to "end welfare as we know it" and make work pay. Although Clinton had promised to increase the minimum wage during his first year, he delayed proposing an increase because of concerns about antagonizing moderate-to-conservative Democrats. After Republicans took control of Congress in the historic 1994 midterm elections, Clinton proposed an increase from $4.25 to $5.15 over two years (Gitterman 2009).

Congressional Republicans in the 1990s were more conservative than their counterparts in the 1960s. Predictably, Republican leaders opposed any increase. Moderate Republicans, in contrast, supported a modest increase. Thus a new intraparty conflict emerged between conservative House leaders, primarily from the South, and a smaller group of moderate Republicans from the Northeast and Midwest, who feared that a vote against an increase would hurt them in the 1996 elections. The Republican leadership responded to concerns about an increase in labor costs by packaging a modest minimum wage increase with a tax relief package for small business. Ultimately, as part of the 1996 Small Business Job Protection Act, Clinton and a Republican Congress approved a two-step increase (from $4.25 to $4.75 and then to $5.15 by September 1997) (Gitterman 2009).

The 1996 agreement represented the first increase ever adopted when Republicans controlled at least one chamber of Congress. It reflected a new bargain: conservative southern House Republicans allowed a coalition of centrist northeastern Republicans and liberal Democrats to enact an increase, but only if it was coupled with tax relief for small businesses. Later in the decade Republicans were ready to make a similar deal. Although many remained opposed to the minimum wage on ideological grounds, they recognized it was important to moderate Republicans' electoral fortunes and thus to their control of Congress. Some supported a modest increase because they hoped to remove the issue from the Democrats' political arsenal, especially before the 1998 and 2000 elections (Gitterman 2009).

Between 2001 and 2006 President George W. Bush, backed by Republican leaders in Congress, refused to increase the minimum wage. After regaining control of Congress in 2006, the Democrats secured an increase as part of a supplemental defense

appropriations bill that provided emergency funds for the war in Iraq. The agreement—
the 2007 Small Business and Work Opportunity Tax Act—combined an increase to $7.25
an hour by 2009 with $4.84 billion in small business tax relief. During the 2008 cam-
paign Democratic presidential candidate Barack Obama pledged to increase the minimum wage to $9.50 and index it to inflation, but Congress was reluctant to support an
increase during the recent economic downturn (Gitterman 2009).

6 THE EARNED INCOME TAX CREDIT,
1975–2013

The EITC is a refundable tax credit, enacted with bipartisan support in 1975. It encourages low-income workers with children to enter and remain in the labor market by supplementing their earnings. Initially a temporary measure, it was made a permanent part
of the Internal Revenue Code (IRC) in 1978. Since then it has undergone expansions
with bipartisan support. The credit was expanded in 1986 under President Reagan, in
1990 under President Bush, and again in 1993 under President Clinton, when the size of
the credit was doubled and a small credit was added for workers without children (Holt
2006). The EITC's initial popularity was based on its ability to provide both work incentives and tax relief for low-income workers and their families. One bipartisan goal, often
espoused by President Reagan, was to eliminate income taxes on workers below the poverty line so they would not be taxed deeper into poverty.

The roots of the EITC can be traced back to the 1960s. President Lyndon B. Johnson
charged several antipoverty task forces with investigating the impact of nonindexation
of the personal exemption and standard deduction, as well as the effects of the payroll
tax. The rising payroll tax burden also helped fuel interest among some Democrats in
a proposal known as the negative income tax (NIT). The NIT would be a mirror image
of the income tax. Instead of tax liabilities varying positively with income according to
a tax rate schedule, benefits would vary inversely with income according to a negative
tax rate (or benefit reduction) schedule. This approach would allow policy makers to
increase the income of low-wage earners whose tax liability was already zero, but who
faced increasingly burdensome payroll taxes. More broadly, it would provide an additional policy tool for pushing low-income working families above the poverty threshold
and keeping them from turning to welfare or other cash assistance programs.

Although President Richard M. Nixon had not mentioned the NIT in the 1968 campaign, he included it as part of his Family Assistance Plan (FAP) in 1969. Under this proposal, a family of four with no income would receive $1,600—a guaranteed minimum
income. The idea was blocked by conservative Democrats, who argued that it would
undermine the incentive to work (Ventry 2000). Senator Russell Long (D-La.) proposed
a plan to distribute tax relief only to those "willing to work." This proposal called for
wage subsidies to low-income workers, known as a "work bonus," equal to 10 percent

of the wages subject to payroll taxes. Long argued that his proposal would offset payroll taxes, act as an earnings subsidy, and "prevent the taxing of people onto the welfare rolls" (Ventry 2000, 986). An attraction of the earnings subsidy, which became known as the earned income credit, was that its benefits rose positively with earnings up to a plateau, increasing incentives for very low income earners to work. However, more liberal House Democrats rejected the proposal three years in a row in the hope of passing an NIT instead.

In the mid-1970s President Gerald Ford proposed an $80 tax rebate for the poorest taxpayers. House Democrats went further by proposing a refundable credit, worth 5 percent of earned income, up to a maximum of $200 for lower-income earners with little or no tax liability (Ford 1975). This EIC, which closely matched the payroll tax on the first $4,000 of earned income, was expected to stimulate the economy because low-wage earners generally spend much of their increases in after-tax income (H.R. Rep. 94-19 1975). House Democrats viewed a one-time EIC as a way of offsetting the regressivity of the payroll tax, a subject of concern within both parties. More conservative Senate Democrats, in contrast, portrayed the EIC as welfare reform and sought to restrict the credit to low-income married couples with children. Because many low-wage workers were from nonpoor families, Senate Democrats concluded that extending earning subsidies to all workers would be "expensive and inefficient in reaching the poor" (S. Rep. 94-36 1975). The Senate reduced the number of eligible earners from 28 to 6.4 million. Ultimately, the 1975 measure created a one-year refundable credit of up to $400 for earners with dependents (and incomes below $8,000). Nonetheless, the EIC emerged as a tool to boost the paychecks of low-wage workers with children.

Initially policy makers were divided over the credit's purpose: whether to provide payroll tax relief to all low-wage workers or to increase the labor force participation of less-skilled workers who might otherwise rely on public assistance to support their families, or both. Ultimately Congress structured the credit to do both, but only for families with children, thus placing more emphasis on its role in welfare reform. In this way the EITC fulfilled its original purpose as set forth by Congress, "an added bonus or incentive for low-income people to work," and as a way to reduce welfare dependency by "inducing individuals with families receiving federal assistance to support themselves" (S. Rep. 94-36 1975).

Both parties in the 1980s supported the EITC as a mechanism to boost the paychecks of working poor families (Toder 1998; Steuerle 2008). This development was important given the stalemate over the minimum wage, which remained at the same level from 1981 to 1990. Not surprisingly, many of the same business groups that opposed increases in the minimum wage supported the EITC; they preferred that taxpayers boost wages for their workers (Howard 1997). In the early 1990s Clinton pledged that full-time work at the minimum wage plus the EITC (and any Food Stamps for which a family was eligible) would be enough to raise a family's after-tax income above the poverty threshold. The emphasis on helping low-income earners with jobs, rather than those on welfare, reflected a conviction often repeated by Clinton: the government should "make work pay" for those at the bottom. To achieve this distributional goal, the EITC would need to be increased, particularly for families with two or more children. These changes, followed by increases in the EITC under Clinton, reduced the tax burden faced by low-income earners with children. Although part of the EITC's growth was due to rising demand, the reason for expansion has been sizable real benefit increases legislated in 1986, 1990, and 1993 (Myles and Pierson 1997).

By the mid-1990s, however, the bipartisan consensus had started to unravel. Some Republicans now wanted to roll back the EITC. Many conservatives had come to view the refundable EITC as a form of welfare. Arguing that the EITC was supposed to off-set tax liability for low-income, full-time workers, Republicans claimed that the most recent Clinton expansion had transformed the EITC "into more of a welfare program than a tax refund" (Rubin 1995, 3057). In addition, many Republicans were concerned about fraud and abuse, as well as about the exponential growth of the refundable por-tion of the EITC. Republicans secured new rules to strengthen compliance and enforce-ment as part of the 1996 Personal Responsibility and Work Opportunities Act, the 1997 Taxpayer Relief Act, and the 1997 Balanced Budget Act (US Treasury 2003).

The opening decade of the twenty-first century brought modest gains to working poor families. The 2000 election gave the Republicans control of the White House and Congress for the first time since 1954. During the debates on President Bush's tax cuts in 2001, Senate centrists insisted on more tax relief for those at the lower end of the income distribution. For example, they won agreement on a *refundable* child tax credit for work-ing poor households earning at least $10,000 and set the income threshold for eligibility to satisfy Republicans, who opposed earnings subsidies for nonworking poor families. With a typical minimum wage worker earning a little more than $10,500 in 2001, the eligibility threshold allowed Republicans to claim that only families with the equivalent of a full-time, working parent would benefit from the refundable CTC (Nitschke and Swindell 2001). Single parents who worked less than full time and two-parent families with very limited earnings would not qualify for the credit.

During the 2008 campaign Obama proposed a making work pay (MWP) credit, worth $500 for single workers and $1,000 for families, which would eliminate the tax liability of ten million low-income earners (Tax Policy Center 2008). Obama pledged to expand—but did not succeed in expanding—the EITC and making the child and dependent care tax credit refundable for the first time in its history. Under the 2009 American Recovery and Reinvestment Act (ARRA), President Obama and congressio-nal Democrats approved the MWP credit and temporarily expanded the EITC in two ways. First, the act added a "third tier" of the EITC for families with three or more chil-dren, so that these families can receive up to $629 more than families with two children. Second, the ARRA expanded marriage penalty relief in the EITC, reducing the finan-cial penalty some couples experience when they marry by allowing married couples to receive larger tax benefits. These changes were scheduled to expire at the end of 2010, but Congress extended them through 2012 (CBPP 2011). By 2011, the recession and high unemployment, the Republican takeover of the House, and budget deficits loomed as stumbling blocks for Obama.

7 SUPPORTING LOW-WAGE WORKERS IN THE UNITED STATES

The minimum wage and EITC have followed distinct historical trajectories. As a result, they do not add up to a coherent policy regime. An enduring, fragile consensus rests on a simple idea: if able-bodied parents participate in the labor market, their take-home pay should be sufficient to lift their families out of poverty. The effectiveness of the minimum wage in alleviating poverty clearly depends on the workings of the tax system and vice versa. In the case of the minimum wage, this has meant slow and piecemeal growth. In the five decades after its passage, liberal Democrats had to accept limitations on coverage to gain support for modest increases from southern Democrats and Republicans. In the mid-1990s the price they paid for increases became tax relief for small businesses. Such bargains have allowed the minimum wage to endure through both liberal and conservative periods.

On the income tax side of the agenda, refundable credits have emerged as the centerpiece of efforts to help working poor families. This development has been fostered by growing reliance on the budget reconciliation process. Through reconciliation—a process first used in 1981—Congress decides which changes in mandatory spending and revenue programs are necessary to reach the overall goals set by the budget resolution for that fiscal year (Lindblom 2008). The process is governed by expedited procedures and restrictions, such as a ban on filibustering in the Senate, and produces huge omnibus packages. Together, these rules ensure that a bill moves quickly through the legislature, "beset by few of the procedural veto-gates that lie in wait for the typical piece of legislation" (Garrett 2000, 720). In this environment, tax credits have become a popular way for legislators to fine-tune the distributional impact of tax and spending packages and to deliver benefits to favored constituencies.

Thus, throughout its history the EITC has helped legislators deliver benefits to low-income families, alter the distributional balance of omnibus tax packages, and thereby secure bipartisan agreement. The 1986 EITC expansion resulted from a bipartisan effort to deal with some of the distributional unfairness of Reagan's tax relief in 1981. In 1990 both Republicans and Democrats saw expansion as a straightforward way to alter the distributional characteristics of the deficit reduction package and head off charges that it essentially benefited high-income earners. The 1993 EITC expansion made it easier for Democrats to support Clinton's first budget, which included more spending cuts and deficit reduction than they preferred.

Equally important, the period since the early 1980s has seen the consolidation of a consensus on the idea that working families should be the primary beneficiaries of tax-based assistance. It drove and was strengthened by the passage of welfare reform in 1996. This reform—which replaced Aid to Families with Dependent Children (AFDC) with Temporary Assistance to Needy Families (TANF)—shifted the focus of efforts to

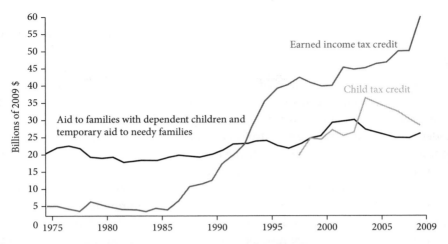

FIG. 21.3 Real Federal Spending on EITC, CTC, and Welfare, 1975–2009.

Source: Budget of the U.S. Government, Fiscal Year 2012, for AFDC/TANF; Internal Revenue Statistics of Income, various years for EITC and CTC; Bureau of Labor Statistics for CPI Deflator.

support poor families from cash assistance programs, such as welfare, to strategies to supplement labor market earnings, such as refundable tax credits (Haveman 2003). As Figure 21.3 shows, shifts in budgetary outlays on these programs and credits are indicative of the changing policy orientation.

In recent years the temporary refundable making work pay credit and recent (temporary) payroll tax reductions have offset Social Security and Medicare payroll taxes. Unlike the EITC, this tax relief is offered to moderate- and middle-income workers and families as well as lower-income families (up to their first $110,100 in wages). The payroll tax reduction was passed for one year when Obama and Republicans in Congress sought compromise on the Bush tax cuts. Moreover, unlike the CTC, it helps childless workers and married couples, as well as families with children, suggesting a turn toward universalism in policies to boost the after-tax income of working families. The MWP credit expired in 2010.

8 THE CHALLENGES AHEAD

Self-sufficiency and hard work lie at the heart of the idea of the "American Dream." Full-time participation in the labor market remains central to economic well-being, and the primary source of support for most working-age adults is their employment and earnings (Blank 2000; 2009). Americans expect their fellow citizens to work hard to support themselves and their households (Sawhill and Morton 2007). This emphasis on work as the route to self-sufficiency has driven many of the welfare reforms in recent decades. Yet minimum wage work alone is still not enough to keep some workers and their families out of poverty or to move others into the ranks of moderate-income families.

The original 1938 minimum wage agreement established a logic that helps explain its subsequent development. Instead of delegating authority to a wage-setting board, Congress chose to retain control over the amount and timing of any increase and the industries and occupations covered. Legislators guarded this power over the following decades. By retaining statutory control over its parameters, reluctant converts to the minimum wage were able to maximize the electoral benefits of a popular policy while minimizing the negative effects by limiting the costs imposed on business and agricultural groups. Since the late 1960s the principal casualties of these dynamics have been the real value of the minimum wage and the earnings of minimum wage workers. In 1977 Congress refused to index the minimum wage to inflation, and in 1990 it declined to establish a minimum wage advisory board even to "recommend" cost-of-living adjustments. Obama pledged to increase the minimum and to index it to inflation. But every prior effort to index the minimum wage has been defeated, and moreover, Obama could emerge as the first Democrat since the New Deal not to sign an increase.

The prevailing wisdom among political analysts is that narrowly targeted income transfers, such as direct cash assistance to poor families, have enjoyed only sporadic political support. They tend to be enacted or expanded in periods of partisan imbalance and to be vulnerable to retrenchment when elections shift the balance of power. However, many suggest that the EITC is a notable counterexample. It has been expanded under both Democratic and Republican administrations, often with bipartisan support. According to Robert Greenstein (1991, 450), the EITC's design—"a middle ground of maintaining a targeted program structure while incorporating near-poor and moderate-income working families that are struggling themselves"—has helped broaden its appeal.

However, the EITC is not immune to opposition, and the attacks on the program suggest the many challenges that credits may face in the future. Notably, some Republicans remain opposed to the concept of refundable credits, while many centrists are concerned about the cost in terms of budget outlays. Many critics of refundability would agree with George Yin (1996) that "programs should not be hidden in the tax system and therefore be subject to a lower level of scrutiny. If as a transfer program the EITC would not garner a sufficient level of political support to remain viable, there is no reason that it should continue to exist in the tax system and in the process be administered inefficiently" (1996, 316). In addition, some believe that everyone should pay at least some taxes, even if just one dollar, as a duty of citizenship and so that they feel they have some stake in governmental decisions (Batchelder, Goldberg, and Orszag 2006). This last argument, which opposes the rise of the "zero-filers" or those with no federal tax liability, is perhaps the most daunting for proponents of refundable credits.

Some research concludes that the EITC is more effective than the minimum wage in providing support for low-wage workers. Critics argue, for example, that the EITC is better targeted because many of the beneficiaries of minimum wage increases are not members of low-income families (Hotz and Scholz 2000). However, others conclude that the effectiveness of the EITC in raising the incomes of working poor families above the poverty threshold depends, in part, on regular increases in the minimum wage. Richard Freeman (1996) concludes that an appropriately set minimum wage can be a modestly effective redistributive tool—a risky but potentially profitable investment—particularly if it is linked with other social policies, such as the EITC, that support low-income earners and their families.

In forecasting the future of the minimum wage and the EITC, it is important to highlight the role of partisan political control of the White House and Congress on the one hand and coalition politics within Congress on the other. The differences between the parties over these policies have increased in recent decades as partisan polarization has soared. According to Nolan McCarty (2007), by almost all measures the divide between Democratic and Republican members of Congress has widened over the past twenty-five years, reaching levels of partisan conflict not witnessed since the 1920s. Polarization contributes to gridlock and stalemate, making it more difficult for Congress to respond to economic shocks and adopt measures such as minimum wage increases and expansions of the EITC.

Since the early 1980s both Republicans and Democrats have found their way around partisan gridlock to reach bargains on issues as contentious as tax policy and the minimum wage. With rare exceptions, neither party has had a sufficient majority or sufficient internal unity to legislate on its own in the past three decades. Relatively little attention has been paid to the effects of polarization on policy outcomes. Some political scientists conclude that polarization is not ideologically neutral; it has had a conservative effect on policy. Others argue that the main effect of polarization has been to produce less policy (McCarty 2007). However, most agree that polarization leaves centrists in both parties with the ever more important and demanding role of brokering policy bargains. Without a new bargain that balances partisan distributional and electoral goals, low-wage workers' families and the policies to support them remain at risk.

NOTE

1. For a complete list of minimum wage exemptions, see U.S. Dept. of Labor, "Fair Labor Standards Act Advisor: Exemptions," http://www.dol.gov/elaws/esa/flsa/screen75.asp.

REFERENCES

*Indicates recommended reading.

Atrostic, Barbara K., and James R. Nunns. 1991. "Measuring Tax Burden: A Historical Perspective." In *Fifty Years of Economic Measurement: The Jubilee of the Conference on Research in Income and Wealth* (1990), edited by Ernst R. Berndt and Jack E. Triplett, 343–420. Chicago: University of Chicago Press.

Autor, David H., Alan Manning, and Christopher L. Smith. 2010. *The Contribution of the Minimum Wage to U.S. Wage Inequality over Three Decades: A Reassessment*. Finance and Economics Discussion Series. Washington, DC: Divisions of Research & Statistics and Monetary Affairs Federal Reserve Board.

Bakija, Jon, and C. Eugene Steuerle. 1991. "Individual Income Taxation since 1948." *National Tax Journal* 44, (4): 451–475.

BarackObama.com. n.d. "Barack Obama: Tax Fairness for the Middle Class." http://obama.3cdn. net/b7be3b7cd08e587dca_v852mv8ja.pdf.

Batchelder, Lily L., Fred T. Goldberg Jr., and Peter R. Orszag. 2006. "Reforming Tax Incentives into Uniform Tax Refundable Credits." Policy Brief 156. Brookings Institution.

Bernstein, Michael. 1987. *The Great Depression: Delayed Recovery and Economic Change in America, 1929–1939*. Cambridge: Cambridge University Press.

*Blank, Rebecca M. 2000. "Fighting Poverty: Lessons from Recent U.S. History." *Journal of Economic Perspectives* 14 (2): 3–19.

Blank, Rebecca M. 2009. "Economic Change and the Structure of Opportunity for Less-Skilled Workers." *Focus* 26 (2): 14–20.

Brand, Horst. 1988. "Book Review of Old South, North South." *Monthly Labor Review* 111 (5): 58.

Burman, Len, and Greg Leiserson. 2007. "Two-Thirds of Tax Units Pay More Payroll Tax Than Income Tax." Tax Notes, April 9. http://www.urban.org/UploadedPDF/1001065_Tax_Units. pdf.

Card, David. and Alan B. Krueger, 1995. "Time-Series Minimum-Wage Studies: A Meta-analysis." *The American Economic Review* 85, no. 2. (1195): 238–243.

Center for Budget and Policy Priorities. 2011. "Policy Basics: The Earned Income Tax Credit." http://www.cbpp.org/cms/index.cfm?fa=view&id=2505.

Nadine, Cohodas, 1987. "Minimum Wage Getting Maximum Attention." *CQ Weekly*, March 7, 403–407.

*Ellwood, David T. 2001. "The Impact of the Earned Income Tax Credit and Social Policy Reforms on Work, Marriage, and Living Arrangements." In *Making Work Pay: The Earned Income Tax Credit and Its Impact on America's Families*, edited by B. Meyer and D. Holtz-Eakin. New York: Russell Sage.

Ford, Gerald R. 1975. "Address before a Joint Session of the Congress Reporting on the State of the Union.—" January 15. *American Presidency Project*. www.presidency.ucsb.edu/ ws/?pid=4938.

Fox, Lianna. 2006. "Minimum Wage Trends: Understanding Past and Contemporary Research." Washington, DC: Economic Policy Institute. http://www.epi.org/page/-/old/briefingpa pers/178/bp178.pdf.

Freeman, Richard. 1996. "The Minimum Wage as a Redistributive Tool." *Economic Journal* 106 (436): 639–649.

Garrett, Elizabeth. 2000. "The Congressional Budget Process: Strengthening the Party-in-Government." *Columbia Law Review* 100 (3): 702–730.

*Gitterman, Daniel P. 2009. *Boosting Paychecks: The Politics of Supporting America's Working Poor*. Washington, DC: Brookings Institution Press. http://www.brookings.edu/press/ Books/2009/boostingpaychecks.aspx.

Gitterman, Daniel P. 2012. "Making the New Deal Stick? The Minimum Wage and American Political History." *Journal of the Historical Society* 12 (1).

Gottschalk, Marie. 2000. *The Shadow Welfare State: Labor, Business, and the Politics of Health Care in the United States*. Ithaca, NY: Cornell University Press.

Greenstein, Robert. 1991. "Universal and Targeted Approaches to Relieving Poverty: An Alternative View." In *The Urban Underclass*, edited by Christopher Jencks and Paul E. Peterson, 437–459. Washington, DC: Brookings Institution Press.

Grossman, Jonathan. 1978. "Fair Labor Standards Act of 1938: Maximum Struggle for a Minimum Wage." *Monthly Labor Review* (June): 22–30.

Hacker, Jacob S. 2002. *The Divided Welfare State: The Battle over Public and Private Social Benefits in the United States*. Cambridge: Cambridge University Press.

Haveman, Robert. 2003. "When Work Alone Is Not Enough." In *One Percent for the Kids: New Policies, Brighter Futures for America's Children*, edited by Isabel Sawhill, 40–55. Washington, DC: Brookings Institution Press.

*Holt, Steve. 2006. "The Earned Income Tax Credit at Age 30: What We Know." Research Brief, Brookings Institution. http://www.brookings.edu/~/media/Files/rc/reports/2006/02childrenfamilies_holt/20060209_Holt.pdf.

*Hotz, V. Joseph, and John Karl Scholz. 2000. "Not Perfect, But Still Pretty Good: The EITC and Other Policies to Support the US Low Wage Labour Market." OECD. http://www.oecd.org/dataoecd/23/6/2697856.pdf.

Howard, Christopher. 1997. *The Hidden Welfare State: Tax Expenditures and Social Policy in the United States*. Princeton, NJ: Princeton University Press.

Howard, Christopher. 2003. "Is the American Welfare State Unusually Small." *Political Science and Politics* 36 (3): 411–416.

*Howard, Christopher. 2007. *The Welfare State Nobody Knows: Debunking Myths About U.S. Social Policy*. Princeton, NJ: Princeton University Press.

H.R. Rep. 94-19. 1975. Committee on Ways and Means. Report Accompanying H.R. 2166, the Tax Reduction Act of 1975.

Immervoll, Herwig, and Mark Pearson. 2009. "A Good Time for Making Work Pay? Taking Stock of In-Work Benefits and Related Measures across the OECD." IZA Policy Paper No. 3. http://www.politiquessociales.net/IMG/pdf/pp3.pdf.

Lindblom, Derek. 2008. "The Budget Reconciliation Process." Harvard Law School Federal Budget Policy Seminar. Briefing Paper No. 35 (May 11).

Linder, Marc. 1987. "Farm Workers and the Labor Standards Act: Racial Discrimination in the New Deal." *Texas Law Review* 65: 1335–1387.

Maag, Elaine. 2004. "Relationship between Tax Entry Thresholds and Poverty." Urban Institute–Brookings Tax Policy Center (March).

McCarty, Nolan. 2007. "The Policy Effects of Political Polarization." In *The Transformation of American Politics*, edited by Paul Pierson and Theda Skocpol, 223–255. Princeton, NJ: Princeton University Press.

*Mettler, Suzanne. 1998. *Dividing Citizens: Gender and Federalism in New Deal Public Policy*. Ithaca, NY: Cornell University Press.

Myles, John, and Paul Pierson. 1997. "Friedman's Revenge: The Reform of 'Liberal' Welfare States in Canada and the United States." *Politics & Society* 25: 443–472.

Nitschke, Lori, and Bill Swindell. 2001. "Grassley–Baucus Tax Blueprint Heads for Rough-and Tumble Markup." *CQ Weekly*, May 12, 1069–1070.

Palmer, Phyllis. 1995. "Outside the Law: Agricultural and Domestic Workers under the Fair Labor Standards Act." *Journal of Policy History* 7: 4.

Pytte, Alyson. 1989. "Labor: Minimum-Wage Bill Cleared, Ending 10-Year Stalemate." *CQ Weekly*, November 11, 3053.

Reese, Thomas J. 1980. *The Politics of Taxation*. Westport, CT: Quorum Books.

Rubin, Alissa J. 1995. "Low-Income Workers' Tax Credit among GOP Budget Targets." *CQ Weekly*, October 7, 3055–3057.

S. Rep. 94-36. 1975. *Report Accompanying H.R. 2166, the Tax Reform Reduction Act of 1975.*

Sawhill, Isabel, and John Morton. 2007 "Economic Mobility: Is the American Dream Alive and Well?" Pew Charitable Trusts. http://www.economicmobility.org/assets/pdfs/EMP%20 American%20Dream%20Report.pdf.

Steuerle, Eugene. 2008. *Contemporary U.S. Tax Policy.* Washington DC: Urban Institute Press.

Stigler, George J. 1946. "The Economics of Minimum Wage Legislation." *American Economic Review* 36 (3): 358–365.

Toder, Eric. 1998. "The Changing Role of Tax Expenditures: 1980–99." In *Proceedings of the Ninety-First Annual Conference of the National Tax Association.* Washington, DC.

Tomlins, Christopher. 1985. *The State and the Unions.* Cambridge: Cambridge University Press.

Urban Institute and Brookings Tax Policy Center. 2008. "An Updated Analysis of the 2008 Presidential Candidates' Tax Plans: Updated September 12, 2008." http://www.taxpolicycenter. org/taxtopics/presidential_candidates.cfm.

U.S. Department of Health and Human Services. 2011. The 2011 HHS Poverty Guidelines. http:// aspe.hhs.gov/poverty/11poverty.shtml.

US Department of Labor. Bureau of Labor Statistics. 2013. Characteristics of Minimum Wage Workers: 2012. http://www.bls.gov/cps/min wage2012.htm.

US Department of Labor. Wage and Hour Division. 2014. Minimum Wage: An Overview. http://www.dol.gov/whd/minimumwage.htm.

US Department of the Treasury. 2003. "Internal Revenue Service, Earned Income Tax Credit (EITC) Program Effectiveness and Program Management FY 1998–FY 2002." Doc 2002-5236, 2002 TNT 41-12, at 5 (February 28, 2002).

Ventry, Dennis J., Jr. 2000. "The Collision of Tax and Welfare Politics: The Political History of the Earned Income Tax Credit, 1969–99." *National Tax Journal* 53 (4) (pt. 2): 983–1026.

Wright, Gavin. 1986. *Old South, New South: Revolutions in the Southern Economy since the Civil War.* New York: Basic Books.

Yin, George K. 1996. "The Uncertain Fate of the EITC Program." In *Taxing America*, edited by Karen B. Brown and Mary Louise Fellows, 297–321. New York: New York University Press.

CHAPTER 22

....

FOOD ASSISTANCE PROGRAMS AND FOOD SECURITY

....

CRAIG GUNDERSEN

1 INTRODUCTION
....

MILLIONS of households in the United States are unable to acquire enough food for all their members. In 2010, for example, 14.5 percent of Americans were food insecure, meaning that they were uncertain of having or unable to acquire enough food because they had insufficient money or other resources (Coleman-Jensen et al. 2011). These proportions were substantially higher among certain subgroups of the population, including households with children, low-income households, and single-parent households. The high proportions of Americans who are food insecure, combined with the demonstrated serious health consequences associated with food insecurity, make it the leading nutrition-related public-health issue in the United States today.

Although research on the determinants and consequences of food insecurity in the United States is relatively recent, with a marked increase in the number of papers written on the topic in the past decade, the U.S. government has long recognized that millions of Americans face serious nutritional challenges. In response, policy makers have created a food-assistance safety net composed of several distinct programs, the two largest of which are the Supplemental Nutrition Assistance Program (SNAP; formerly known as the Food Stamp Program) and the National School Lunch Program (NSLP). This chapter begins with a discussion of food insecurity, focusing in particular on how it is measured and the extent and determinants of food insecurity. Next is a review of the origin and evolution of SNAP and NSLP and their consequences, concentrating on the impact of these programs on food insecurity. The chapter concludes with a discussion of how food insecurity research can influence best practices pursued by policy makers and program administrators.

2 Food Insecurity

2.1 Measurement

Many Americans were poor long before the government had a formal poverty line. Likewise, many people were hungry before the government had an official measure of "food insecurity."

Interest in food insecurity came to the forefront of policy discussions in the U.S. Department of Agriculture (USDA) and other government agencies during the early 1990s. In response, a task force was set up to establish methods that could be used to measure food insecurity (for more on the development of the CFSM, see Hamilton et al. 1997). These efforts culminated in a series of questions designed to measure food insecurity in the United States, which were introduced in the 1996 Current Population Survey (CPS). After some modifications, an official set of 18 questions used to measure food insecurity was established as the Core Food Security Module (CFSM). Ten of these questions are asked of all households and eight are asked only of households with children. The questions range from "I worried whether our food would run out before we got money to buy more," (the least severe item) to "Did a child in the household ever not eat for a full day because you couldn't afford enough food?" (the most severe item for households with children). Each question on the CFSM is qualified by the proviso that the conditions are due to financial constraints. As a consequence, persons who have reduced food intakes due to, say, fasting for religious purposes or dieting, should not respond affirmatively to these questions.

Based on the replies, the USDA delineates households into food-security categories. Households responding affirmatively to 2 or fewer questions are classified as food secure (defined as cases in which all household members had access at all times to enough food for an active, healthy life). Those responding affirmatively to 3–7 questions (3–5 questions for households without children) are classified as low food secure, meaning that at least some household members were uncertain of having, or unable to acquire, enough food because they had insufficient money and other resources for food. Those responding affirmatively to 8 or more questions (6 or more for households without children) are classified as very low food secure, which means that one or more household members were hungry, at least some time during the year, because they could not afford enough food. These latter two categories are often combined; a household responding affirmatively to 3 or more questions is thus identified as "food insecure."[1]

Researchers have established two other sets of food-security categories. The first is "marginal food insecure," which includes all households that respond affirmatively to one or more of the questions. One justification for this measure is that marginally food-insecure households often appear more similar to food-insecure households with respect to health outcomes and other characteristics, such as income, than to food-secure households. A second category is based on the 8 child-specific questions from the survey. A household is said to be "child food insecure" if 2 or more questions are answered affirmatively and "very low child food secure" if 5 or more questions are answered affirmatively (for a discussion of the child food-insecurity measures see, for example, Nord and Hopwood 2007).

Most research to date has used binary indicators of food insecurity such as food insecure versus food secure. These comparisons are clear and straightforward. Still, considerable information is being suppressed in such cases. In particular, information is not being utilized when broad categories are created from the 18 questions on the CFSM. Consider, for example, two households, with one responding affirmatively to 10 questions and the other responding affirmatively to 16 questions. Both households would be classified as very low food secure yet, arguably, the latter household has a higher level of food insecurity. In response, a more refined series of food insecurity measures was developed (Dutta and Gundersen 2007) and applied empirically (for example, Gundersen 2008). The close attention paid to the results based on the CFSM and the wide variety of ways the CFSM is used to measure food insecurity is a testament to how well established the CFSM has become within the set of measures of deprivation in the United States.

2.2 Extent of Food Insecurity

Figure 22.1 displays the proportion of all households that are food insecure and very low food secure, with those who are very low food secure being a subset of the food insecure group. From 2001 to 2007, the food-insecurity rate remained relatively steady at about 11 percent, with very low food-security rates ranging from 3–4 percent. These rates increased dramatically in 2008. The food-insecurity category increased more than 30 percent (from 11.1 percent to 14.6 percent), whereas for the very low food-security category, rates rose by almost 40 percent (from 4.1 percent to 5.7 percent). Rates of food insecurity remained high in 2009 and 2010. This increase, which is unprecedented since food insecurity was first measured, and continued high rates presumably reflect the economic recession and its lingering effects.[2] Even during better economic conditions, there are still a high percentage of Americans who are food insecure. As seen in Figure 22.1, food insecurity rates never fall below 10 percent, despite strong economic conditions throughout most of the 2001–2010 period.

Figure 22.2 shows similar trends in the proportions of children living in food-insecure households, food-insecure children, and very low food-secure children. (Note that Figure 22.1 is based on households rather than individuals, whereas Figure 22.2 is based on children.) As in Figure 22.1, the rates remained relatively static from 2001 to 2007. The proportion of children in food-insecure households ranged from 16.9 percent to 19.0 percent, the proportion of food-insecure children from 9.1 percent to 10.7 percent, and the proportion of very low food-secure children was always under 1 percent. Consistent with what occurred for the full population, in 2008 there were sizable increases in children living in food-insecure households and food-insecure children, and an over 60 percent increase in the number of very low food-secure children. These levels remained high in 2009 with slight declines in 2010.

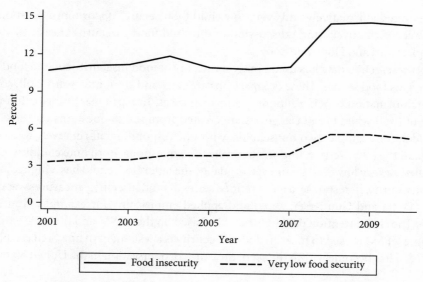

FIG. 22.1 Household food insecurity rates in the United States, 2001–2010.

Note: Figure is based on data from Coleman-Jensen et.al. 2011, Table 1A

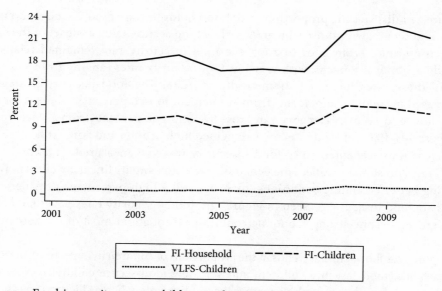

FIG. 22.2 Food insecurity among children in the United States, 2001–2010.

Note: Figure is based on data from Coleman-Jensen et.al. 2011, Table 1B

2.3 The determinants and consequences of food insecurity

Considerable research reveals the socioeconomic and demographic factors associated with food insecurity in the United States. For example, households headed by an African American, Hispanic, a never married person, a divorced or separated person, a renter, younger persons, and less educated persons are all more likely to be food insecure than their respective counterparts (Coleman-Jensen et al. 2011). In addition, households with children are more likely to be food insecure than households without children. This general set of findings holds whether the sample is all households, households with children, or households without children.[3]

Perhaps the most important factors are the resources available to a household, especially income. Figure22. 3 shows the relationship between food insecurity and income, normalized by the poverty line. This is a nonparametric representation with a bandwidth of 0.6 [see Fox (2000) for details on the estimation methods]. Vertical lines are placed at the eligibility cutoffs for SNAP (130 percent of the poverty line) and for free or reduced price lunches for NSLP (185 percent of the poverty line).

The figure supports three main points. First, the probability of food insecurity declines with income and the decline is more marked for food insecurity than for very low food security. Second, that poverty and food insecurity are not equivalent

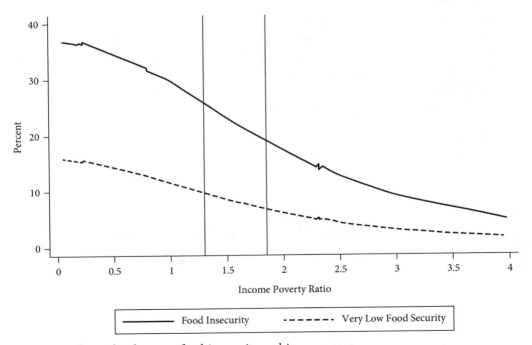

FIG. 22.3 Relationship between food insecurity and income, 2010.

Note: Author's calculation based on data from the December supplement of the 2010.

is reflected in the high proportions of households that are food secure *and* poor. For example, about two in three households close to the poverty line are food secure. Third, conversely, a nontrivial portion of households with incomes above the poverty line are food insecure: as the income-to-poverty ratio approaches 2, food insecurity rates are almost 20 percent, and, even as the ratio approaches 3, food insecurity rates are around 5 percent.

The inverse relationship between income and food insecurity is not surprising. What is surprising, perhaps, is the large number of poor households that are food secure and the large number of nonpoor households that are food insecure. This should be kept in mind in what follows insofar as the food assistance programs covered in this chapter are not available to those with incomes above 185 percent of the poverty line.

That millions of persons in the United States do not have enough food is a serious policy concern in and of itself. Making matters worse is that food insecurity has a well-established set of consequences. For children, research has shown that food insecure children are more likely to have fair or poor general health (Chilton et al. 2009), psychosocial problems (Alaimo, Olsen, and Frongillo 2001, 2002), frequent stomachaches and headaches (Alaimo et al. 2001), increased odds of being hospitalized (Cook et al. 2004), greater propensities to have seen a psychologist (Alaimo et al. 2001), behavior problems (Slack and Yoo 2005), lower intakes of important nutrients (Kaiser et al. 2002), worse developmental outcomes (Hernandez and Jacknowitz 2009), impaired mental proficiency (Zaslow et al. 2009), and higher levels of iron deficiency with anemia (Eicher-Miller et al. 2009) than are children in food-secure households. In comparison to food-secure adults, food-insecure adults have lower intakes of a variety of nutrients (Bhattacharya, Currie, and Haider 2004), a broad set of physical health problems (Pheley et al. 2002), mental health challenges (Huddleston-Casas, Charnigo, and Simmon 2009), and chronic diseases (Biros, Hoffman, and Resch 2005), including type 2 diabetes (ibid.). Among senior adults in particular, the negative health consequences of food insecurity include lower intakes of a variety of nutrients (Lee and Frongillo 2001), lower skinfold thickness (ibid.), greater likelihood of reporting fair or poor health (Ziliak, Gunderson, and Haist 2008), higher levels of depression (Holben, Barnett, and Holcomb 2006), poorer quality of life (Klesges et al. 2001), and lower levels of physical performance (ibid.).[4]

3 SUPPLEMENTAL NUTRITION ASSISTANCE PROGRAM

3.1 Overview

SNAP is by far the largest U.S. food-assistance program, serving approximately 40.3 million people in 2010, with total benefits of $68.3 billion.[5] These benefits can be used for the purchase of food in authorized retail food outlets. Benefits are distributed via an Electronic Benefit Transfer (EBT) card, which is operationally similar to an ATM card. The level of benefits received by a household is determined by income level and family size. In 2010, the average monthly benefit was $288/month for a family of four, with a maximum benefit level of $668. All SNAP benefits are funded by the federal government. The central goal of SNAP is to be a core component of the safety net against hunger (USDA 1999). Food stamps were first introduced as an experimental program between 1939 and early 1943. In 1959, Congress passed legislation that permitted the USDA to set up a limited food-stamp program along New Deal lines through 1961. Eisenhower did not implement this provision, and right before its expiration, Kennedy started the pilot program as a form of recession relief. After requests from the Kennedy and Johnson administration, Congress adopted the Food Stamp Act of 1964. A major contribution to the passage of this bill was the logrolling between rural Democrats who needed support for their commodity bill and the urban Democrats who needed support for the food-stamp bill (DeVault and Pitts, 1984; Ferejohn, 1986; Finegold, 1988). The Food Stamp Act of 1964 had a dual justification, to "help achieve a fuller and more effective use of food abundances" and to "raise the levels of nutrition among low-income households." A similar logroll has underpinned the continued relationship between these two objectives, even after the focus of the food stamp legislation moved away from absorbing some of the U.S. crop surpluses. And that relationship sometimes included Republican legislators from farm states, such as Senator Robert Dole of Kansas. From the beginning, food stamps enjoyed broader support in Washington than many other social programs targeted at low-income populations.

The 1964 Act authorized the Secretary of Agriculture "to formulate and administer" a program under which "eligible households with the State shall be provided with an opportunity more nearly to obtain a nutritionally adequate diet through the issuance to them of coupon allotment which shall have a greater monetary value that their normal expenditure for food." The Food Stamp Program thus intended to increase the food purchasing power of low-income households so they could afford the "Thrifty Food Plan"—the cheapest of the food purchasing plans developed by the USDA that aimed to help people obtain the recommended daily allowances of key nutrients as defined the National Academy of Sciences. To build support, the 1964 Act permitted, but did not require, food-stamp programs to be established in all counties. States could determine the eligibility requirements, but the federal government would fund the programs. During the 1970s, however, the national government took on a greater role, making Food Stamps much more uniform in its operation across the country (Finegold 1988). From here on, key policy decisions would be made in Washington, not the states. Medicaid and Aid to Families with Dependent Children, by contrast, continued to vary from state to state.

In the deep recession of the early 1980s, the need for food assistance grew, but so did the size of the federal budget deficit. During his first term, President Reagan pledged to tighten eligibility requirements and decrease benefit levels in the welfare system, which would have reduced access to Food Stamps. The President and the Senate at the time tried to separate the farm subsidy legislation and food stamp legislation in order to make it easier to make changes to the Food Stamp Program, but legislators continued to deal with both questions within omnibus bills that combined both issues. In 1983, President Reagan created a special Task Force on Food Assistance to report on the extent of America's hunger problem and to make recommendations on how to improve the Food Stamp Program. They concluded that people were going hungry in the United States, but that the Food Stamp Program was enough to help them. In 1985, some advocates believed that even greater budget cuts were possible and thus sought to publicize the degree of persistent hunger despite the economic recovery. They used the study by the task force to show that hunger was still present in the United States and that it had harmful effects on physical and psychological well-being. They also showed that the percentage of poor individuals receiving food stamp benefits had declined and that the safety net had proven insufficient.

In the past two decades, the program has been expanded and retrenched. The 1993 Mickey Leland Childhood Hunger Relief Act allowed households with children to gain access to Food Stamps more easily by raising the cap on the dependent-care deduction and simplifying the definition of a household. The Personal Responsibility and Work Opportunities Reconciliation Act of 1996 (PRWORA; discussed extensively in other chapters of this book) enacted other major changes, including restrictions on eligibility for most legal immigrants; time limits on food-stamp receipt for healthy adults with no dependent children; and requirements for states to implement the EBT system. In comparison to the cuts made to other assistance programs, the changes made to the Food Stamp Program were relatively mild.

A decade later, the Food Security and Rural Investment Act of 2002 made further changes, including re-establishing eligibility to qualified legal immigrants; modifying the standard deduction to vary by household size and inflation; and providing incentives for states to maintain high standards within the administration of the program. The recent American Recovery and Reinvestment Act Plan of 2009 lead to some temporary changes in SNAP in response to the sharp increase in hunger noted earlier along with the decline in economic conditions across a wide variety of other measures. In response, the ARRA provided an increase in the monthly benefits of SNAP participants, expanded eligibility for jobless adults, and added federal dollars to support the administration of the program.

3.2 Eligibility

Eligibility for SNAP is based on the household, which is defined as a unit containing people who live together and purchase and prepare meals together. To be eligible for SNAP, households first have to meet a monthly gross income test. Under this criterion, a household's income (before any deductions) must be less than 130 percent of the poverty line. As an example, in 2010, a SNAP household with three persons and a monthly income less than $1,984 would be gross-income eligible. There are exceptions;

for instance, households with at least one elderly member or one disabled member do not have to meet this test. Although the federal-gross income cutoff is 130 percent of the poverty line, some states have set higher gross-income thresholds.

Households with an elderly or disabled member and most other households have to pass the net income criteria, defined as gross income minus certain deductions. The allowable deductions include: a standard deduction for all households; a 20 percent earned-income deduction; a dependent-care deduction when care is necessary for work, training, or education; child-support-payments deduction; a medical-costs deduction for elderly and disabled people; and an excess-shelter-cost deduction. To be eligible for SNAP, this net income must be less than the poverty line. As an example, in 2010, a SNAP household with net income below $1,526/month would be net-income eligible. Households in which all members receive Supplemental Security Income (SSI) or Temporary Assistance for Needy Families (TANF) are automatically eligible for SNAP and do not have to pass the gross- or net-income tests. Although the vast majority of households that have incomes below 130 percent of the poverty line are also net-income eligible, many households that are gross-income eligible under higher state-specific thresholds are not net-income eligible.

The final test for SNAP eligibility is the asset test. As defined at the federal level, the total assets of a household must be under $2,000. Some resources are not counted, such as one's home and up to $4,650 of the fair market value of one car per adult household member. Similarly, one car per teenaged household member may be deducted if the teenager is using it for work, and a vehicle's value is not counted if it is needed to transport a disabled household member. There are three exceptions to these rules. First, households with an elderly or disabled person have a higher asset limit, namely $3000. Second, households in which everyone receives SSI or TANF benefits are not subject to the asset test. Third, states have the discretion to waive the asset test. Currently, about 80 percent of states do waive the asset test for all individuals.

Finally, able-bodied adults between the ages of 18 and 50 years without dependents (ABAWDs) must be employed to receive SNAP. If they are not employed, they can lose their SNAP benefits. In areas with particularly high unemployment rates or limited employment opportunities, this so-called "ABAWD requirement" is waived. This waiver is not automatic—states must make this request of the USDA.[6]

3.3 Impacts on food insecurity

Before turning to a discussion of the impact of SNAP on food insecurity, it is worth considering why many persons choose not to participate in SNAP. This choice is made despite, as discussed earlier, the potentially high monetary benefits of receiving SNAP—benefits that are high enough to have a nontrivial influence on the extent and depth of poverty in the United States (see, e.g., Jolliffe et al. 2005). In ways similar to other programs covered in this handbook, nonparticipation reflects three main factors. First, there may be stigma associated with receiving SNAP, due to a person's own distaste for receiving SNAP, the fear of disapproval from others when redeeming SNAP, and/or the possible negative reaction of caseworkers (Moffitt 1983; Rainwater 1982; Ranney and Kushman 1987; Stuber and Kronebusch 2004).[7] Second, transaction costs can diminish the attractiveness of participation, including travel time to, and time spent in, a SNAP office; the burden of transporting children to the office or paying for child-care services; and the direct costs of paying for transportation. A household faces these costs on a repeated basis because it must recertify its eligibility (see Ponza et al. 1999).[8] Third, the benefit level can be quite small—for some families as low as $10 per month. Given the inverse relationship between income and SNAP benefit levels, this explains why many households with incomes closer to the SNAP eligibility threshold are less likely to participate.[9] Interestingly, the latest recession prompted some state and local officials to publicize SNAP more heavily and to help people apply for benefits. Insofar as the national government pays for SNAP benefits, this is one further way that states and localities can bring more federal money into their jurisdictions (DeParle and Gebeloff 2010).

As noted earlier, the central goal of SNAP is the reduction in food insecurity. Of concern, then, is that rates of food insecurity among recipients are about double the rates among eligible nonrecipients (Coleman-Jensen et al. 2011), and these higher rates remain even after controlling for observed factors (see Gundersen, Joliffe, and Tiehen 2009). This is a counterintuitive result theoretically (it is difficult to see how shifting out the budget constraint can lead to an increase in food insecurity) and empirically (see Figure 22.3).

This puzzling result is presumably due to the fact that participation in SNAP is likely to be endogenous, and that SNAP recipients are likely to differ from nonrecipients across unobserved factors that contribute to their higher probability of food insecurity. Scholars have identified this selection effect. For instance, researchers found that SNAP participants were no more likely to be food insecure than nonparticipants once they control for selection into SNAP and selection into food insecurity (Gundersen and Oliveira 2001). Other recent scholarship has generally found that immigrants not facing restrictions on SNAP participation were less likely to be food insecure than immigrants facing restrictions. Researchers have concluded that SNAP leads to reductions in food insecurity for the general population as well (Van Hook and Ballistreri, 2006).[10]

Misreporting of SNAP participation status can also prevent researchers from accurately ascertaining the effect of SNAP on food insecurity. SNAP participation is systematically under-reported in major surveys, with errors of omission (that is, responding that one does not receive SNAP when one really does) being substantially more likely than errors of commission (Bollinger and David, 1997, 2001). As a result, a positive correlation between SNAP and food insecurity should be viewed as valid only if the researcher is willing to place a great deal of confidence in the reporting of SNAP participation within the dataset being used. Even when one imposes strong assumptions restricting the patterns of classification errors, SNAP-participation error rates are much smaller than 12 percent (a lower bound on the extent of SNAP misreporting derived from the literature) are sufficient to prevent one from concluding that there is a strong positive relationship between SNAP participation and food insecurity (Gundersen and Kreider 2008).

Although SNAP does help reduce food insecurity among those who are eligible, it is worth noting that millions of food-insecure Americans are ineligible for SNAP. (See the discussion of Figure 22.3 earlier.) In addition, those with incomes above 185 percent of the poverty line are ineligible for other food assistance programs. Thus, alongside the issue of nonparticipation of eligible families, many of whom are food insecure, there is the issue of ineligible, food-insecure families who would presumably benefit from participation in SNAP and similar programs.

4 National School Lunch Program

4.1 Overview

The National School Lunch Program (NSLP) is a federally assisted meal program that operates in over 100,000 public and nonprofit private schools. It provides nutritionally balanced lunches to children each school day. In 2010, more than 31 million students participated in NSLP. Of these, nearly 17 million received free lunches, slightly over 3 million received reduced-price lunches, and the rest of the children paid full price. Along with free commodities received by schools from the government, the cash payments to schools for the NSLP in 2010 were over $10 billion.[11] Most USDA support for this program comes from cash reimbursement for each meal served. Schools who provided more than 60 percent of their students with free or reduced-priced lunches the preceding year as well as schools in Alaska and Hawaii have higher reimbursement rates. Schools participating in this program also earn a small subsidy for those lunches that are bought at full price. Current reimbursement rates from the federal government for the contiguous states and those serving less that 60 percent free or reduced price lunches are: $2.77 for free lunches, $2.37 for reduced-price lunches, and $0.26 for paid lunches.[12]

The modern school-lunch programs began with sporadic food services by private associations as early as the 1850s.[13] Throughout the early twentieth century, lunch programs were created in major cities. Once these programs expanded, federal aid was distributed to most states. These programs proved very important during the Great Depression when children were especially in need of food. During World War II, due to shortages in food and workers, the number of lunch programs decreased, but in 1946 the National School Lunch Program bill was signed into law to assure continuation of the program. Like Food Stamps, the NSLP was designed to help needy citizens at the same time that it boosted demand for the nation's agricultural sector (Levine 2008).

Since the creation of the NSLP, some relatively minor changes have been made to the program over the years. For example, in 1962 there were amendments to the act to redefine the apportionment of funds between states because similar states were receiving the same funding without taking into consideration the program participation rate. Changes to the NSLP in the 1970s included increasing the types of schools that could participate and being able to certify students for two years of participation instead of just one in those schools with high percentages of low-income students.

The program was curtailed slightly during the Reagan administration. Namely, the Omnibus Budget Reconciliation Acts of 1980–1981 decreased the reimbursements for paid meals and increased the income range for free-meal eligibility. School food authorities were forced to raise prices for paid lunches, and school participation fell by 14 percent. Although key antipoverty programs were scaled back in 1996 under the Clinton administration, school lunches was not. Some scholars (e.g., Levine 2008) attribute the durability of the NSLP to the network of agricultural and commercial food interests who benefit indirectly from the program. In the 1990s and early 2000s, the focus shifted toward nutrition. In 1994, the USDA launched the School Meals Initiative for Healthy Children, which required nutritional improvements of school lunches based on the dietary guidelines. In 2004, part of the Child Nutrition and WIC Reauthorization Act required schools to create wellness policies that specify nutritional standards for all foods in school. Schools that participate in the NSLP must serve lunches that meet federal requirements. The meals must provide no more than 30 percent of an individual's calories from fat, less than 10 percent from saturated fat, and one-third of the Recommended Dietary Allowances of protein, vitamin A, vitamin C, iron, calcium, and calories. School districts must also offer free or reduced price lunches to eligible children.[14]

4.2 Eligibility

Eligibility for the NSLP begins at the individual level. Any child at a participating school may purchase a meal through the NSLP. (Children who are home-schooled or no longer attend school are not eligible.) Among children in these schools, families with incomes at or below 130 percent of the poverty level are eligible for free meals. Children with household income between 130 percent and 185 percent of the poverty level are eligible for reduced-price meals, which cannot cost more than 40 cents. Although children from families with incomes over 185 percent of poverty pay full price, their meals are still subsidized to some extent. These rules regarding eligibility are set at the national level.

4.3 Impacts on Food Insecurity

In comparison to studies of SNAP, relatively few studies examine the impact of the NSLP on food insecurity. One study provides indirect evidence of the importance of NSLP in alleviating food insecurity (Nord and Ronig 2006). This study exploits the fact that, during the summer, children do not participate in school-meal programs. Using this variation over the year and the timing of the CFSM in the CPS prior to 2001, they established that food-insecurity rates are higher for school-aged children during the summer months.

As with SNAP, food-insecurity rates are substantially higher among participants than among nonparticipants—39.9 percent versus 26.3 percent (Gundersen, Kreider, and Pepper 2012). Also like SNAP, it seems implausible that providing children an extra meal each day would lead to higher probabilities of food insecurity. Assessing the true effect of NSLP is made difficult, however, due to two fundamental identification problems akin to those found in SNAP. First, children receiving free or reduced-price meals are likely to differ from eligible nonparticipants in ways that are not observed in the data. Second, the association between participation in the NSLP and food insecurity may be, at least partly, an artifact of household misreporting of program participation.[15]

After addressing the selection and classification error issues, the authors find that the NSLP alleviates food insecurity.[16] If the data are treated as perfectly accurate, the program is estimated to decrease the prevalence of food insecurity between 2.3 and 9.0 percentage points. In the presence of participation classification errors, the estimated impacts range from 3.2 to 15.8 percentage point declines. Thus, after controlling for selection and measurement-error problems, one finds persuasive evidence that the NSLP leads to substantial reductions in food insecurity (Gundersen, Kreider, and Pepper 2012).

5 Major Challenges

The literature on the connection between food assistance participation and food insecurity in the United States has given policy makers and program administrators numerous insights. In addition, the extensive research that has been done on the determinants and consequences of food insecurity has enabled new approaches to alleviating food insecurity. I now turn to four major challenges that currently exist regarding food-assistance programs and food insecurity in the United States.

First, there is a substantial body of evidence that SNAP reduces the prevalence of food insecurity. This should be kept in mind as reconstructions of SNAP are being proposed. In particular, some have proposed changes to the structure of SNAP with respect to what types of food should be available for purchase. As an example, the New York City Department of Health recently proposed a ban on using SNAP benefits to purchase Gatorade and other sweetened beverages. (The USDA disallowed this ban, however.) Although the proposals have the goal of enhancing nutrition among SNAP participants, the effectiveness of the program on the whole could be compromised if more restricted food options discourage participation and lead to subsequent increases in food insecurity. Because SNAP has an explicit goal of alleviating food insecurity and is considered the leading program in the fight against hunger, proposals to modify the program must recognize that these proposals will likely lead to increased food insecurity.

Second, as was discussed earlier, the available evidence suggests that the National School Lunch Program also reduces food insecurity. Although the program focuses on specific nutritional objectives, policy makers have contemplated proposals to modify the program, such as imposing more nutritional requirements. In considering these modifications, policy makers may wish to keep in mind its alleviation of food insecurity. As with SNAP, proposals to modify the NSLP should consider the possibility that these changes could lead to increases in hunger by discouraging participation in the program. Namely, as seen in other assistance programs, limitations on benefits lead to reductions in participation.

Third, the negative health outcomes associated with food insecurity have been well established. Alongside the direct benefits associated with reducing food insecurity—for example, as a society, we may wish to avoid having children go to bed hungry due to economic constraints —potential reductions in medical expenditures should be incorporated into relevant benefit-cost considerations of programs like SNAP and NSLP.

Fourth, millions of food-insecure households in the United States have sufficiently high incomes to render them ineligible for food-assistance programs. Research findings regarding the role of assets and income shocks can provide some guidance for what types of policies might most effectively reduce food insecurity among middle-income households.

6 ACKNOWLEDGMENTS

The author acknowledges the excellent research assistance of Elizabeth Ignowski and financial support from the U.S. Department of Agriculture (USDA), Cooperative State Research, Education and Extension Service (CSREES), Hatch project no. ILLU-470-331.

NOTES

1. In some surveys, a six-item scale is used in lieu of the 18-item scale. When this scale is used, a household is said to be food secure if 0–1 questions are affirmed, low food secure if 2– 4 questions are affirmed, and very low food secure if 5–6 questions are affirmed.
2. For a discussion of the macroeconomic determinants of food insecurity see Gundersen, Kreider, and Pepper 2011.
3. These findings have used data from large scale data sets, which include the CFSM (or the full or portions of the six-item scale), namely the CPS, Panel Study of Income Dynamics (PSID), the Early Childhood Longitudinal Study—Birth Cohort (ECLS-B), the Early Childhood Longitudinal Study—Kindergarten Cohort (ECLS-K), the Survey of Income and Program Participation (SIPP), the Three City Study (TCS), and the National Health

and Nutrition Examination Survey (NHANES). Along with these datasets, a series of other smaller-scale datasets that are based on limited geographic areas have been used in these studies. For a more in-depth review of the determinants of food insecurity, see Gundersen, Brown, et al. 2011.

4. Other work showing that food insecurity leads to worse outcomes includes, for example, Cook et al. 2004; Cook et al. 2006; Dunifon and Kowaleski-Jones 2003; Gundersen and Kreider 2009; Kirkpatrick, McIntyre, and Potestio 2010; Yoo, Slack, and Hall 2009; Whitaker, Phillips, and Orzol 2006; Matheson et al. 2002; Jyoti, Frongillo, and Jones 2005; Rose-Jacobs et al. 2008; Skalicky et al. 2006; Dixon, Winkelby, and Radimer 2001; McIntyre et al. 2003; Stuff et al. 2004; Vozoris and Tarasuk 2003; and Sullivan et al. 2010.

5. The discussion here is based on Gundersen, 2012; King, 2000;

6. See Ziliak, Gundersen, and Figlio 2003 for a discussion of this requirement and subsequent implications for SNAP caseloads.

7. The introduction of EBT cards, discussed above, was one of the efforts of the USDA to reduce the stigma associated with the use of SNAP.

8. How often and the information needed to recertify differ by state and by category. With respect to the latter, for example, employed persons generally have to recertify more often than retired persons.

9. Along with households with lower incomes being more likely to participate, all else equal, the following household types tend to have higher SNAP participation rates: single mother-headed households, households with children, and households headed by an African-American.

10. Other work has also exploited variation in SNAP policy. A recent example is Nord and Prell (2011), who showed that the temporary increase in SNAP benefits due to the passage of the American Recovery and Reinvestment Act (ARRA) of 2009 led to reductions in food insecurity among those in the SNAP-eligible population. Other work examining selection issues in the context of SNAP include, for example, DePolt. Moffitt, and Ribar 2009; Kreider et al. 2012; Mykerzi and Mills, 2010; Nord and Golla, 2009; Ratcliffe, McKernan, and Zhang 2011.

11. The free commodities and other services received from the USDA reduce the price of meals for all children, even those who are not receiving free or reduced price meals.

12. USDA, NSLP Fact Sheet 2011 - http://www.fns.usda.gov/cnd/lunch/aboutlunch/NSLPFactSheet.pdf

13. The following discussion borrows heavily from Gunderson (2003) and Ralston et al. (2008).

14. Many schools also offer breakfasts through the School Breakfast Program, a program with eligibility criteria similar to the NSLP. This program is another important component of the social safety net against food insecurity.

15. Meyer, Mok, and Sullivan (2009), for example, find evidence of aggregate underreporting rates of 45 percent in the CPS and 27 percent in the PSID.

16. The authors impose three assumptions to address the selection problem: Monotone Treatment Selection (MTS), Monotone Treatment Response (MTR), and Monotone Instrumental Variable (MIV). The MTS formalizes the notion that the unobserved factors positively associated with participation in the NSLP are also positively associated with food insecurity, whereas MTR posits that receiving NSLP cannot increase the probability of food insecurity. An Income MIV assumption posits that children residing in higher-income households have no higher probabilities of food insecurity than children

residing in lower-income households. An Ineligible Comparison Group MIV assumption posits that: (1) income-ineligible children have no higher probabilities of food insecurity than income-eligible children; (2) children attending schools without a school-lunch program (which tend to be private, well-off schools) have no higher probabilities of food insecurity than children attending schools with a school-lunch program; and (3) children who have dropped out of school (and, hence, cannot participate in the NSLP) have at least as high probabilities of food insecurity.

To address the problem of misreporting NSLP participation, the authors impose restrictions on the extent of reporting error, using information on the difference between the self-reported participation rate and estimated true participation rate. This method, which was developed in Kreider et al. (2011), uses auxiliary administrative data on the size of the NSLP caseload to restrict the magnitudes and patterns of NSLP reporting errors.

REFERENCES

*Indicates recommended reading.

Alaimo Katherine, Christine Olson, and Edward Frongillo. 2001. "Food Insufficiency and American School-Aged Children's Cognitive, Academic, and Psychosocial Development." *Pediatrics* 108 (1): 44–53.

Alaimo, Katherine, Christine Olson, and Edward Frongillo. 2002. "Family Food Insufficiency, but Not Low Family Income, Is Positively Associated with Dysthymia and Suicide Symptoms in Adolescents." *Journal of Nutrition* 132: 719–725.

Bhattacharya, Jay, Janet Currie, and Steven Haider. 2004. "Poverty, Food Insecurity, and Nutritional Outcomes in Children and Adults. *Journal of Health Economics* 23: 839–862.

Biros Michelle, Pamela Hoffman, and Karen Resch. 2005. "The Prevalence and Perceived Health Consequences of Hunger in Emergency Department Patient Populations." *Academic Emergency Medicine* 12: 310–317.

Bollinger, Christopher, and Martin David. 1997. "Modeling Discrete Choice with Response Error: Food Stamp Participation." *Journal of the American Statistical Association* 92 (439): 827–835.

Bollinger, Christopher, and Martin David. 2001. "Estimation with Response Error and Non-Response: Food Stamp Participation in the SIPP." *Journal of Business and Economic Statistics* 19: 129–141.

Chilton, Mariana, Maureen Black, Carol Berkowitz, Patrick Casey, John Cook, Diana Cutts, Ruth Rose-Jacobs, Timothy Heeren, Stephanie Ettinger de Cuba, Sharon Coleman, Alan Meyers, and Deborah Frank. 2009. "Food Insecurity and Risk of Poor Health among US-Born Children of Immigrants." *American Journal of Public Health* 99 (3): 556–562.

Coleman-Jensen, Alisha, Mark Nord, Margaret Andrews, and Steven Carlson. 2011. *Household Food Security in the United States in 2010*. ERR-141. Washington, DC: USDA, Economic Research Service.

Cook, John, Deborah Frank, Carol Berkowitz, Maureen Black, Patrick Casey, Diana Cutts, Alan Meyers, Nieves Zaldivar, Anne Skalicky, Suzette Lenenson, Timothy Heeren, and Mark Nord. 2004. "Food Insecurity Is Associated With Adverse Health Outcomes Among Human Infants And Toddlers." *Journal of Nutrition* 134: 1348–1432.

Cook John, Deborah Frank, Suzette Levenson, Nicole Neault, Timothy Heeren, Maureen Black, Carol Berkowitz, Patrick Casey, Alan Meyers, Diana Cutts, and Mariana Chilton. 2006. "Child Food Insecurity Increases Risks Posed by Household Food Insecurity to Young Children's Health." *Journal of Nutrition* 136: 1073–1076.

DeParle, Jason, and Robert Gebeloff. 2010. "Once Stigmatized, Food Stamps Find Acceptance." *New York Times*, February 10.

DePolt, Richard, Robert Moffitt, and David Ribar. 2009. "Food Stamps, Temporary Assistance for Needy Families and Food Hardships in Three American Cities." *Pacific Economic Review* 14: 445–473.

DeVault, Marjorie, and James Pitts. 1984. "Surplus and Scarcity: Hunger and the Origins of the Food Stamp Program." *Social Problems* 31 (5): 545–557.

Dixon Lori Beth, Marilyn Winkelby, and Kathy Radimer. 2001. "Dietary Intakes and Serum Nutrients Differ between Adults from Food-Insufficient and Food-Sufficient Families: Third National Health and Nutrition Examination Survey, 1988–1994." *Journal of Nutrition* 131: 1232–1246.

Dunifon Rachel, and Lori Kowaleski-Jones. 2003. "The Influences of Participation in the National School Lunch Program and Food Insecurity on Child Well-Being." *Social Service Review* 77: 72–92.

Dutta, Indranil, and Craig Gundersen. 2007. "Measures of Food Insecurity at the Household Level." In Basudeb Guha-Khasnobis, Shabd S. Acharya, and Benjamin Davis, eds., *Food Security Indicators, Measurement, and the Impact of Trade Openness: Series: WIDER Studies in Development Economics*. Oxford: Oxford University Press, 42–61.

Eicher-Miller, Heather, April Mason, Connie Weaver, George McCabe, and Carol Boushey. 2009. "Food Insecurity Is Associated with Iron Deficiency Anemia in U.S. Adolescents." *American Journal of Clinical Nutrition* 90: 1358–1371.

Ferejohn, John. 1986. "Logrolling in an Institutional Context: A Case Study of Food Stamp Legislation." In Gerald Wright. Jr., Leroy Rieselbach, and Lawrence Dodd, eds., *Congress and Policy Change*. New York: Agathon Press, pp. 223–253.

*Fiese, Barbara, Craig Gundersen, Brenda Koester, and Latesha Washington, "Household Food Insecurity: Serious Concerns for Child Development." *Social Policy Report* 25 (3): 1–19. Society for Research on Childhood Development. (Also see associated commentaries, 20–27.)

Finegold, Kenneth. 1988. "Agriculture and the Politics of U.S. Social Provision: Social Insurance and Food Stamps." In Margaret Weir, Ann Orloff, and Theda Skocpol, eds., *The Politics of Social Policy in the United States*. Princeton, NJ: Princeton University Press, 199–234.

Fox, John. 2000. "*Nonparametric Simple Regression: Smoothing Scatterplots.*" Sage University Papers Series on Quantitative Applications in the Social Sciences. Thousand Oaks, CA: Sage, 7–130.

Gundersen, Craig. 2008. "Measuring the Extent, Depth, and Severity of Food Insecurity: An Application to American Indians in the United States." *Journal of Population Economics* 21: 191–215.

Gundersen, Craig. 2012. "Food Assistance Programs." In A. Catharine Ross, Benjamin Caballero, Robert Cousins, Katherine Tucker, and Thomas Ziegler, eds., *Modern Nutrition in Health and Disease*. Philadelphia: Lippincott Williams and Wilkins.

Gundersen, Craig, Julia Brown, Emily Engelhard, and Elaine Waxman. 2011. "*Map the Meal Gap: Technical Brief.*" Chicago, IL: Feeding America.

Gundersen, Craig, and Joseph Gruber. 2001. "The Dynamic Determinants of Food Insufficiency." In Margaret Andrews and Mark Prell, eds., *Second Food Security Measurement and Research Conference, Volume II: Papers.* 92–110. Washington, DC: USDA, ERS Food Assistance and Nutrition Research Report, 11–2.

Gundersen, Craig, Dean Jolliffe, and Laura Tiehen. 2009. "The Challenge of Program Evaluation: When Increasing Program Participation Decreases the Relative Well-Being of Participants." *Food Policy* 34: 367–376.

Gundersen, Craig, and Brent Kreider. 2008. "Food Stamps and Food Insecurity: What Can Be Learned in the Presence of Non-Classical Measurement Error?" *Journal of Human Resources* 43: 352–382.

Gundersen, Craig, and Brent Kreider. 2009. "Bounding the Effects of Food Insecurity on Children's Health Outcomes." *Journal of Health Economics* 28: 971–983.

*Gundersen, Craig, Brent Kreider, and John Pepper. 2011. "The Economics of Food Insecurity in the United States." *Applied Economic Perspectives and Policy* 33 (3): 281–303.

Gundersen, Craig, Brent Kreider, and John Pepper. 2012. "The Impact of the National School Lunch Program on Child Health: A Nonparametric Bounds Analysis." *Journal of Econometrics* 166: 79–91.

Gundersen, Craig, and Victor Oliveira. 2001. "The Food Stamp Program and Food Insufficiency. *American Journal of Agricultural Economics* 84 (3): 875–887.

Gunderson, Gordon. 2003. *The National School Lunch Program: Background and Development.* Hauppauge, NY: Nova Science.

Hamilton, William, et al. 1997. *Household Food Security in the United States in 1995: Technical Report of the Food Security Measurement Project.* Alexandria, VA: USDA, Food and Consumer Service, Office of Analysis and Evaluation.

Hernandez, Daphne, and Alison Jacknowitz. 2009. "Transient, but Not Persistent, Adult Food Insecurity Influences Toddler Development." *Journal of Nutrition* 139: 1517–1524.

Holben, David, Melissa Barnett, and John Holcomb. 2006. "Food Insecurity Is Associated with Health Status of Older Adults Participating in the Commodity Supplemental Food Program." *Journal of Hunger and Environmental Nutrition* 1 (2): 89–99.

Huddleston-Casas Catherine, Richard Charnigo, and Leigh Ann Simmon. 2009. "Food Insecurity and Maternal Depression in Rural, Low-Income Families: A Longitudinal Investigation." *Public Health Nutrition* 12: 1133–1140.

Jolliffe, Dean, Craig Gundersen, Laura Tiehen, and Josh Winicki. 2005. "Food Stamp Benefits and Child Poverty." *American Journal of Agricultural Economics* 87 (3): 569–581.

*Jolliffe, Dean, and James Ziliak, eds. 2008. *Income Volatility and Food Assistance in the United States.* Kalamazoo, MI: W. E. Upjohn Institute for Employment Research.

Jyoti, Diana, Edward Frongillo, and Sonya Jones. 2005. "Food Insecurity Affects School Children's Academic Performance, Weight Gain, and Social Skills." *Journal of Nutrition* 135: 2831–2839.

Kaiser, Lucia, Hugo Melgar-Quinonez, Cathi Lamp, Margaret Johns, Jeanette Sutherlan, and Janice Harwood. 2002. "Food Security and Nutritional Outcomes of Preschool-Age Mexican-American Children." *Journal of the American Dietetic Association* 102: 924–929.

*King, Ronald. 2000. *Budgeting Entitlements: The Politics of Food Stamps.* Washington, DC: Georgetown University Press.

Kirkpatrick, Sharon, Lynn McIntyre, and Melissa Potestio. 2010. "Child Hunger and Long-Term Adverse Consequences for Health." *Archives of Pediatrics and Adolescent Medicine* 164 (8): 754–762.

Klesges Lisa, Marco Pahor, Ronald Shorr, Jim Wan, Jeff Williamson, Jack Guralnik. 2001. "Financial Difficulty in Acquiring Food among Elderly Disabled Women: Results from the Women's Health and Aging Study." *American Journal of Public Health* 91: 68–75.

Kreider, Brent, John Pepper, Craig Gundersen, and Dean Jolliffe. 2012. "Identifying the Effects of SNAP (Food Stamps) on Child Health Outcomes When Participation is Endogenous and Misreported." *Journal of the American Statistical Association* 107 (499): 958–975.

Lee, Jung Sun, and Edward Frongillo. 2001. "Nutritional and Health Consequences Are Associated with Food Insecurity among Elderly Persons." *Journal of Nutrition* 131: 1503–1509.

Levine, Susan. 2008, *School Lunch Politics: The Surprising History of America's Favorite Welfare Program*. Princeton, NJ: Princeton University Press.

Matheson Donna, John Varady, Ann Varady, and Joel Killen. 2002. "Household Food Security and Nutritional Status of Hispanic Children in the Fifth Grade." *American Journal of Clinical Nutrition* 76: 210–217.

McIntyre, Lynn, Theresa Glanville, Kim Raine, Jutta Dayle, Bonnie Anderson, and Noreen Battaglia. 2003. "Do Low-Income Lone Mothers Compromise Their Nutrition to Feed Their Children?" *Canadian Medical Association Journal* 198: 686–691.

Meyer, Bruce, Wallace Mok, and James Sullivan. 2009. "The Under-Reporting of Transfers in Household Surveys: Its Nature and Consequences". Working Paper, University of Chicago.

Moffitt, Robert. 1983. "An Economic Model of Welfare Stigma." *American Economic Review* 73: 1023–1035.

Mykerezi, Elton, and Bradford Mills. 2010. "The Impact of Food Stamp Program Participation on Household Food Insecurity." *American Journal of Agricultural Economics* 92 (5): 1379–1391.

Nord, Mark, and Anna Golla. 2009. *Does SNAP Decrease Food Insecurity? Untangling the Self-Selection Effect*. Economic Research Report No. 85. Washington, DC: USDA, Economic Research Service.

Nord, Mark, and Heather Hopwood. 2007. "Recent Advances Provide Improved Tools for Measuring Children's Food Security." *Journal of Nutrition* 137: 533–536.

Nord, Mark, and Katherine Ronig. 2006. "Hunger in the Summer: Seasonal Food Insecurity and the National School Lunch and Summer food Service Programs." *Journal of Children and Poverty* 12: 141–158

Nord, Mark, and Mark Prell. 2011. *Food Security Improved Following the 2009 ARRA Increase in SNAP Benefits*. Economic Research Report No. 116. Washington, DC: USDA, Economic Research Service.

*Oliveira, Victor. 2007. *Informing Food and Nutrition Assistance Policy: 10 Years of Research at ERS*. Misc. Publication 1598. Washington, DC: USDA, Economic Research Service.

Pheley, Alfred, David Holben, Annette Graham, and Chris Simpson. 2002. "Food Security and Perceptions of Health Status: A Preliminary Study in Rural Appalachia." *Journal of Rural Health* 18: 447–454.

Ponza, Michael, James Ohls, Lorenzo Moreno, Amy Zambrowski, and Rhoda Cohen. 1999. *Customer Service in the Food Stamp Program*. Washington, DC: Mathematica Policy Research.

Rainwater, Lee. 1982. "Stigma in Income-Tested Programs." In Irwin Garfinkel, ed., *Income Tested Programs: For and Against*. New York: Academic Press, 19–46.

*Ralston, Katherine, Constance Newman, Annette Clauson, Joanne Guthrie, and Jean Buzby. 2008. *The National School Lunch Program: Background, Trends, and Issues*. Economic Research Report No. 61. Washington, DC: USDA, Economic Research Service.

Ranney, Christine, and John Kushman. 1987. "Cash Equivalence, Welfare Stigma, and Food Stamps." *Southern Economic Journal* 53: 1011–1027.

Ratcliffe, Caroline, Signe-Mary McKernan, and Sisi Zhang. 2011. "How Much Does the Supplemental Nutrition Assistance Program Reduce Food Insecurity?" *American Journal of Agricultural Economics* 93: 1082–1098.

Rose-Jacobs, Ruth, Maureen Black, Patrick Casey, John Cook, Diana Cutts, Mariana Chilton, Timothy Heeren, Suzette Levenson, Alan Meyers, Deborah Frank. 2008. "Household Food Insecurity: Associations with At-Risk Infant and Toddler Development. *Pediatrics* 121 (1): 65–72.

Skalicky, Anne, Alan Meyers, William Adams, Zhaoyan Yang, John Cook, and Deborah Frank. 2006. "Child Food Insecurity and Iron Deficiency Anemia in Low-Income Infants and Toddlers in the United States." *Maternal and Child Health Journal* 10 (2): 177–185.

Slack, Kristen, and Joan Yoo. 2005. "Food Hardship and Child Behavior Problems among Low-Income Children." *Social Service Review* 79 (3): 511–536.

Stuber, Jennifer, and Karl Kronebusch. 2004. "Stigma and Other Determinants of Participation in TANF and Medicaid." *Journal of Policy Analysis and Management* 23: 509–30.

Stuff, Janice, Patrick Casey, Kitty Szeto, Jeffrey Gossett, James Robbins, Pippa Simpson, Carol Connell, and Margaret Bogle. 2004. "Household Food Insecurity Is Associated with Adult Health Status." *Journal of Nutrition* 134: 2330–2335.

Sullivan, Ashley, Sunday Clark, Daniel Palline, and Carlos Camargo. 2010. "Food Security, Health, and Medication Expenditures of Emergency Department Patients." *Public Health in Emergency Medicine* 38: 524–528.

U.S. Department of Agriculture. 1999. *Annual Historical Review: Fiscal Year 1997*. Washington, DC.

Van Hook, Jennifer, and Kelly Stamper Balistreri. 2006. "Ineligible Parents, Eligible Children: Food Stamps Receipt, Allotments and Food Insecurity among Children of Immigrants." *Social Science Research* 35 (1): 228–251.

Vozoris, Nicholas, and Valerie Tarasuk. 2003. "Household Food Insufficiency Is Associated with Poorer Health." *Journal of Nutrition* 133: 1200–1206.

Whitaker, Robert, Shannon Phillips, and Sean Orzol. 2006. "Food Insecurity and the Risks of Depression and Anxiety in Mothers and Behavior Problems in Their Preschool-Aged Children." *Pediatrics* 118: e859-e868.

Yoo, Joan, Kristen Slack, and Jane Hall. 2009. "Material Hardship and the Physical Health of School-Aged Children in Low-Income Households." *American Journal of Public Health* 99 (5): 829–836.

Zaslow, Martha, Jacinta Bronte-Tinkew, Randolph Capps, Allison Horowitz, Kristin Moore, and Debra Weinstein. 2009. "Food Security During Infancy: Implications for Attachment and Mental Proficiency in Toddlerhood." *Maternal and Child Health Journal* 13 (1): 66–80.

Ziliak, James, Craig Gundersen, and David Figlio. 2003. "Food Stamp Caseloads over the Business Cycle." *Southern Economic Journal* 69 (4): 903–919.

*Ziliak, James, Craig Gundersen, and Margaret Haist. 2008. *The Causes, Consequences, and Future of Senior Hunger in America*. Special Report by the University of Kentucky Center for Poverty Research for the Meals on Wheels Association of America Foundation.

CHAPTER 23

....

PUBLIC HOUSING AND VOUCHERS

....

ALEX SCHWARTZ

1 INTRODUCTION

HOUSING policy in the United States follows two separate tracks. One track serves tens of millions of homeowners, most of them middle class or affluent, through several tax breaks. That track is described elsewhere in this publication. The second track helps a much smaller number of low-income households afford rental housing through public housing, vouchers, and other subsidy programs. As of 2012, about 7 million low-income households in the United States benefited from these programs, about one-quarter of all eligible low-income renters. About 5 million of these households benefit from "deep" subsidies that ensure that rents do not exceed 30 percent of their adjusted incomes; about 2 million additional renters receive smaller housing subsidies. In other western nations, governments help a far larger proportion of low-income families and individuals afford decent housing. This essay will focus on public housing and vouchers, which provide subsidized housing to about 3.5 million households.[1]

Public housing and vouchers represent two distinctive forms of housing assistance. Public housing epitomizes a supply-side, project-based subsidy, whereby the subsidy is attached to a specific housing unit. Vouchers reflect a demand-side, tenant-based approach, whereby the subsidy is provided to an individual or family to help cover the rent for any eligible housing unit in the United States. Public housing is the nation's oldest and most famous low-income housing subsidy program, having started in 1937. The voucher program began in 1974. But whereas the public housing program has contracted since the mid-1990s, the voucher program has continued to grow and is now the nation's single largest low-income housing subsidy program. Both programs are administered by public housing authorities (PHAs)—local governmental entities that report to and are funded by the federal government—and both serve extremely low-income populations.

This essay provides an overview and assessment of the two programs. It starts with a description of the two programs, focusing on their key elements, and then discusses their comparative strengths, weaknesses, and challenges.

2 PUBLIC HOUSING

The public housing program originated in 1937 in one of the last major pieces of legislation passed during the New Deal. Its enactment owed nearly as much to public housing's potential for employment generation and slum clearance than it did to its ability to meet the nation's need for low-cost housing (Bratt 1989; von Hoffman 2012). Public housing is the oldest and still best known housing subsidy program in the United States.

Until the 1980s, each successive decade saw increases in the production of public housing. In the past quarter century, however, far more resources have gone to the preservation and redevelopment of public housing than to its expansion. The stock of public housing reached its peak of 1.4 million units in 1994; by 2012, it had declined by 17 percent for a loss of more than 250,000 units. Only 5 percent of the public housing stock as of 2003 was built after 1985, and most of that replaced older public housing buildings that had been torn down. On the other hand, over half of all public housing units were more than 30 years old in 2003, and over one-third were 15 to 30 years old.

As of 2008, 3,148 public housing authorities (PHAs) owned and operated public housing in the United States and its territories (Sard and Fischer 2008). These PHAs operated a total of 1.12 million units. The smallest housing authorities, with 100 or fewer units, comprise nearly half of all authorities but account for only 5 percent of total units. On the other hand, just 12 housing authorities each manage 7,500 or more units, but they account for 23 percent of the total stock. The New York City Housing Authority alone accounts for 13 percent of the nation's public housing. The size of the average public housing development also varies, ranging from 48 units in the smallest housing authorities to 612 units in New York City.

Although many people associate public housing with high-rise buildings, most public housing consists of other building types. High-rise elevator buildings accounted for 30 percent of the total public housing stock in 2003—more in the largest cities and less elsewhere (the current percentage is lower as a result of subsequent demolition and redevelopment of public housing). Low-rise townhouses and row houses comprise an additional 25 percent. Other building types include midrise walk-up apartment buildings, semidetached houses, and even single-family homes. However, as will be discussed later, the design of public housing seldom blends in with the surrounding community, regardless of building type.

Public housing is no longer the nation's largest housing subsidy program for low-income renters, having been eclipsed by the Housing Choice Voucher program and the Low-Income Housing Tax Credit, but it is still, by far, the nation's most famous, if not infamous, housing program. It evokes many negative images in the popular imagination: extreme poverty, grim architecture, dilapidated buildings, neglected grounds, crime, and social pathology. These negative connotations are not true of all or even most public housing. They have applied mostly to some of the larger PHAs, mostly in big cities (except for New York City). Smaller public housing developments in suburbs, rural America, and small cities tend to be less troubled and stigmatized than their big-city counterparts (Bratt 2012; Schwartz 2010).

Many of the problems and challenges that have beset public housing for most of its history can be traced to the design of the program. The political compromises made in the 1930s in order to enact public housing severely constrained the financial resources available to public housing and made racial segregation virtually inevitable. However, other problems, especially those related to architectural design and property management stem from other factors, including the salience of modernism in mid-20th century architecture, and a tendency in many places to treat public housing as a backwater for political patronage. Moreover, the program has operated in relative isolation from other government agencies and with minimal coordination with other social programs aimed at the low-income population it serves (Hays 1995).

2.1 Tenants

Public housing is home to some of the nation's poorest, most vulnerable households. To overcome opposition from the real estate industry, advocates originally agreed that public housing would not compete with private housing. Families eligible for public housing would have incomes far below the level necessary to secure decent housing in the private market. The concentration of very low-income families in public housing is widely considered a source of many of public housing's most dire problems, including its difficulty meeting operating costs and the myriad issues associated with concentrated poverty (Vale 2000).

The program has always targeted low-income families. However, over time, the public housing population became increasingly impoverished. At first the program favored working people and their families who, because of circumstances outside their control, lacked the income necessary to afford housing in the private market. After World War II, many of these families moved into private housing because their growing incomes made them ineligible for public housing or because the rapid growth of low-cost homeownership, made possible by FHA mortgage insurance, enabled millions of working-class families to purchase modest homes, often in new suburban developments. As a result, the median income of public-housing residents fell from 57 percent of the national median in 1950 to 41 percent in 1960, 29 percent in 1970, and less than 20 percent by the mid-1990s (Nenno 1996). As of 2012, public housing residents earned on average just $13,500 annually, and only 12 percent earned more than $25,000 (HUD 2012a).

2.2 Project Location

From the beginning, public housing tended to be located in low-income, often minority neighborhoods. Given that the courts had ruled in 1935 that the federal government lacked authority to acquire property through eminent domain (Hays 1995), the original law gave local governments the right to establish public housing authorities (PHAs). As a unit of local government, PHAs had authority to exercise eminent domain to assemble sites for public housing. Thus, federalism became central to the program's development.

By relying on PHAs, the federal government gave local governments the right to decide whether to build any public housing at all. Localities that did not wish to create such housing within their jurisdictions were under no obligation to do so. Indeed, affluent suburbs and other municipalities had no obligation even to establish a PHA. As a result, public housing could be located only in jurisdictions that chose to participate in the program, virtually guaranteeing that public housing would be concentrated in central cities and working-class suburbs and absent from most affluent suburbs. Indeed, 65 percent of all public housing units in 2000 were located in central cities, compared to 43 percent of all rental housing. Conversely, suburbs accounted for only 17 percent of all public housing, less than half the suburban share of all rental housing.

Moreover, localities that decided to participate in the program had almost complete control over where public housing would be situated within their jurisdictions. This virtually guaranteed that public housing throughout the nation would be subject to racial segregation. White neighborhoods typically opposed the development of any public housing in their midst, and if such housing had to be built, it would be reserved for low-income whites (Hirsch 1998; Turner, Popkin, and Rawlings, 2009). African Americans and other minorities were the predominant population in many public-housing developments, especially in major cities.

2.3 Design and Construction Quality

Public housing is usually easily recognizable, especially developments completed before the mid-1990s. Whether high rise or low rise, the physical appearance of many public-housing projects differs sharply from the neighboring housing stock. Public housing is usually built more densely, often isolated from the surrounding streetscape, and almost always devoid of decoration and amenity. The physical quality of the housing is frequently markedly inferior to that of other rental housing.

The poor design and physical condition of public housing is partly, but not completely, due to severe financial limitations imposed by the program on funding for construction. The 1937 legislation set a maximum development cost of $5,000 per unit, or $1,250 per room, in cities with populations of at least 500,000 people, and $4,000 per unit, or $1,000 per room, elsewhere. Comparing these cost standards with the more generous ones set by the Housing Division of the Public Works Administration, Radford (1996, 191) writes that the "permanent [public housing] legislation mandated a markedly diminished physical standard for what Americans would come to know as 'public housing' as compared with the developments built by the PWA."

The 1937 legislation further constrained the funds that could go into the construction of public housing units by linking public housing with urban renewal. It required, at least initially, that a unit of slum housing be demolished for every unit of public housing built, thus imposing additional costs for public housing. The costs of site development were higher than if the public housing were located in less built-up areas farther from the city center.

Mary Nenno (1996, 104–105), a veteran observer of public housing, writes that the lack of financial support and the imperative to avoid the slightest appearance of competition with the private real estate market "left an indelibly dull architectural imprint on the [public housing] program. [These pressures] also managed to attach a stigma to it and propagandize public housing into a position apart from the mainstream." Many public-housing developments were designed to be as Spartan as possible. Closets were shallow and without doors; plaster walls were eschewed for cinderblocks. In many high-rise projects, elevators skipped every other floor; buildings lacked enclosed lobbies. Common spaces were kept to a bare minimum. Moreover, the building materials used were second rate and construction was often shoddy. Such measures could be, and were, rationalized as a means of complying with the program's strict restrictions on construction costs (Schwartz 2010).

The drive to save money in constructing public housing proved to be extremely short sighted. Inferior construction more often than not resulted in abnormally high maintenance and repair costs. Building systems broke down and needed replacement far more often than if the buildings had been constructed more soundly in the first place. Moreover, it could be argued that if public housing were more pleasant to start with, it would have seen much less vandalism and inspired more care from the residents.

The extremely tight budgetary conditions Congress imposed on the development of public housing certainly created challenges for the design and construction of public housing. However, the physical inadequacies of public housing cannot be blamed only on financial limitations. At least in hindsight, it is clear that the aesthetic preferences of public housing authorities and their architects for modernist high-rise structures were inappropriate for the population served by public housing. For instance, high-rise buildings made it difficult if not impossible for mothers to watch their children as they played outside (Schwartz 2010).

Decisions to separate public housing from the surrounding street grid made public housing stand apart from the rest of the community. The physical design of the grounds, as architect Oscar Newman famously showed, led to vandalism and crime. Long hallway corridors, interior courtyards, and other "anonymous public spaces made it impossible for residents to develop an accord on what was acceptable behavior in these areas, impossible for them to feel or assert proprietary feelings, impossible to tell resident from intruder" (Newman 1995, 130).

2.4 Management

If the financial difficulties and locational patterns of public housing stem at least in part from the design of the original legislation, other major problems of public housing derive from the choices, practices, and attitudes of public housing administrators and government officials. This is especially true of how public housing has been managed. Although many public housing authorities have professional, highly competent managers, others have long histories of ineptitude if not corruption.

Public housing in some cities has been treated as a source of patronage, with hiring decisions based on personal and political connections, rather than on experience, education, and competence. Poor management is evident in oversight of entire PHAs and in the administration of individual developments. It is reflected in lax tenant-selection procedures, failure to respond to tenant complaints, failure to repair and maintain appliances and building systems, and failure to develop and implement long-term plans to replace building systems as they approach the end of their useful life. In some cities, such as Washington, DC, Newark, New Jersey, and New Orleans, the federal government has intervened and put entire housing authorities in receivership, appointing independent administrators to bring order to the public housing stock. In the 1990s, the federal government took direct control of the Chicago Housing Authority (Schwartz 2010; Solomon 2005).

The problematic management of public housing also reflects systemic features of the program that render management much less effective than need be. Until recently, public housing tended to be cut off from the rest of the real estate industry. It was slow to adapt the technologies and management practices that have proven themselves among owners and managers of other rental housing, including subsidized rental housing. Moreover, public housing authorities adopted a much more complex and centralized organizational structure than is typical of the rest of the real estate industry (Byrne, Day, and Stockard, 2003: Harvard University Graduate School of Design 2003). Until the mid-2000s, PHAs maintained a much more centralized approach to property management, reporting expenditures and revenue on a system-wide basis and assigning limited authority and responsibility to on-site management personnel. In 2005, HUD issued regulations that required public housing authorities to drop their long-standing management system to an "asset management" approach in which each project is handled individually. The regulations require housing authorities to adopt project-based management, budgeting, and accounting (HUD 2009a).

2.5 Operating Subsidies

Public housing was originally structured so that the federal government paid the costs of building the projects and tenants paid the costs of operating them. Maintenance and other operating costs were covered by rental income. Local housing authorities issued bonds to finance the costs of project development; Washington paid principal and interest. The system worked reasonably well into the 1960s.

Eventually, however, operating costs increased faster than tenant incomes. At first, rents were increased regardless of the tenants' ability to pay, so it was not uncommon for residents to pay upward of 40 percent of their incomes on rent. To keep rents from rising too far out of line with tenant incomes, many housing authorities deferred basic repairs and maintenance. It was clear that the original way of funding public-housing operations was not working (von Hoffman 2012).

In the late 1960s and early 1970s, Congress responded to the problem with a series of amendments to the Public Housing Act that capped tenant rental payments at 25 percent of income (later raised to 30 percent). To compensate for the decreased rental income, these amendments, named after Senator Edward Brooke, instituted a new operating cost subsidy to supplement tenant rents. Although the federal government has several times changed the way it calculates and distributes operating cost subsidies, the subsidies quickly become integral to the public-housing program. As of 2003, operating subsidies amounted to about half of a typical PHA's operating budget (Byrne et al. 2003, 4). Although the system for allocating operating subsidies has evolved over time, the amount distributed to PHAs is subject to annual Congressional appropriation and often falls short of the amount needed. As a result of decreased support for public-housing operations, many PHAs have faced mounting budget deficits and have had to cut back on maintenance and repairs. Some have sought to lease units to higher income households so as to reduce their need for operating subsidies. A handful of authorities (e.g., San Diego) have sold off entire buildings and use the proceeds to support the remaining stock (Sard and Fisher 2008).

2.6 Capital Needs

Public housing has long struggled with the need to replace major building systems. For decades, public housing has had a backlog of billions of dollars worth of unmet capital needs, in part because of deferred maintenance due to insufficient operating revenue. Congress has allocated about $2.5 billion annually toward capital improvements since 2004; however, this does not adequately cover the costs of replacing equipment and other building elements that have just reached the end of their useful life, much less those that have been worn out for years.

Although the original legislation required housing authorities to set up capital reserve funds, Congress decided in the 1950s that PHAs should use them, instead, to offset federal debt service contributions on bonds issued to finance the construction of public housing (Nenno 1996, 112). As a result, no ready source of funds was available to meet the inevitable costs of keeping public housing in decent shape. Not until 1968, more than 30 years after the start of public housing, did the federal government create its first program to help meet the mounting need for capital improvement. Initially, public housing modernization priorities were determined in Washington and did not necessarily correspond to the most pressing needs of individual housing authorities. In some years, priority would be given to roofs and, in other years, to heating or other building systems. Because housing authorities had no other source of funding for capital improvements, it behooved them to take advantage of whatever modernization funds were available, regardless of the condition of the particular building system to be replaced.

Since 1980, Washington has given local housing authorities more leeway to determine their capital-improvement priorities, although the amount of financial assistance provided has almost always been insufficient. Adjusted for inflation (in 2007 dollars), annual federal expenditures for public housing modernization averaged $3.3 billion from fiscal 1990 through 2008. In recent years, funding levels trended downward, averaging $2.8 billion annually from fiscal 2001 to 2008—as against $3.6 billion from 1990 to 2000. As of 2010, public housing required $25.6 billion, or $23,375 per unit, to address the backlog of accumulated modernization needs. An additional $3.1 billion, or an average of $3,135 per unit, was estimated to be needed to meet accrual needs—that is, the cost of expected repairs and replacement beyond ordinary maintenance (Finkel et al. 2010). As substantial as the backlog of modernization needs is, after taking inflation into account, it has actually decreased by more than $10 billion since 1989 (29 percent)—although the cost of meeting accrual needs increased by 28 percent. Many of the public-housing developments in the worst condition in 1990—and thus with the greatest amount of backlogged modernization need—had been demolished or slated for demolition by 2008 under the HOPE VI redevelopment program (Finkel et al. 2010). Even so, public housing modernization needs still greatly exceed the funding made available through HUD's capital grants.

2.7 HOPE VI and the Transformation of Public Housing

The public housing stock decreased by more than 250,000 units (17 percent) from 1994 to 2010. In cities such as Atlanta, Chicago, Kansas City, Detroit, and Pittsburgh the supply of public housing decreased by 40 percent or more (Schwartz 2010; Goetz 2011). About half this decrease stems from the HOPE VI program for the redevelopment of distressed public housing. Under this program, PHA demolished many public-housing developments that were in the worst physical and financial condition and that suffered from high rates of crime and other social problems, and replaced them with smaller-scale, lower-density developments that usually accommodated a mix of income groups. Although about half the loss of public housing was associated with HOPE VI and other redevelopment programs, the other half resulted from demolition alone. Before 1995 PHA could not demolish public housing without replacing it with an equal number of new public housing units. Afterward, the federal government not only lifted the one-for-one replacement rule, it required them to demolish the most "unlivable," expensive projects and provide tenants with rental vouchers to secure housing elsewhere. If the costs of renovating and operating a public-housing project exceeded the cost of tenant-based vouchers, the government advised PHA to demolish the buildings and provide tenants with vouchers instead (Solomon 2005: Goetz 2011).

Congress launched the HOPE VI program in 1993 to demolish and redevelop distressed public housing. Funded initially with annual appropriations of $300 to $500 million, (though annual funding diminished by the mid-2000s to $100 million or less) the HOPE VI program has been central to the transformation of public housing since the early 1990s. From 1993 through 2007, HOPE VI funded the demolition of more than 150,000 units of distressed public housing and invested $6.1 billion in the redevelopment of 247 public housing projects in 34 states, plus the District of Columbia and Puerto Rico (Kingsley 2009; Schwartz 2010). In so doing, it changed the face of public housing. The Obama administration has phased out the Hope VI program in favor of a new, more broadly focused neighborhood revitalization program, Choice Communities (HUD 2012b).

Originally, HOPE VI focused on the physical reconstruction of public housing and resident empowerment. It sought to replace distressed public-housing projects with lower-density developments and to include a broader income mix by attracting working families whose low incomes made them eligible for public housing (Popkin et al. 2004, 14). The program's goals soon became broader and more ambitious, encompassing "economic integration and poverty deconcentration, 'new urbanism'; and inner-city revitalization" (Popkin et al. 2004, 14; see also Cisneros and Engdahl 2009).

By the mid-1990s, the program sought proposals from PHAs that combined public housing with housing financed through other subsidy programs and even market-rate homeowner and rental housing, thus expanding the income range of residents. Its design objectives promoted the principles of new urbanism and defensible space. The institutional look of traditional public housing was replaced by low-rise structures adorned with such features as front porches, bay windows, and gabled roofs. To help overcome the physical isolation of many public housing developments, HOPE VI projects are designed to blend in with the physical fabric of the surrounding community. In addition to innovations in development finance and design, the HOPE VI program also engendered changes in the management of public housing, in which each site has its own operating budget, and operating costs and performance are tracked on a project-by-project basis (Popkin et al. 2004, 26).

HOPE VI developments are built with a much higher level of amenity than the public housing they replaced. Apartments commonly include dishwashers, central air-conditioning, washers, and dryers (Popkin et al. 2004; Cisneros and Engdahl 2009). Such features, commonplace in market-rate housing, make it more feasible for HOPE VI developments to attract higher income households who, unlike typical public housing residents, have more options in the housing market.

Few would disagree that HOPE VI developments represent a dramatic improvement over the distressed public housing they replaced. However, the program does not necessarily improve the lives of all the residents of the original public housing. First, by replacing large public housing developments with smaller-scale, mixed-income projects, HOPE VI developments typically have fewer public-housing units than the projects they supplant (Cisneros and Engdahl 2009; Goetz 2011). For example, the 234 HOPE VI redevelopment grants awarded from 1993 through 2007 involved the demolition of 96,226 public housing units and the rehabilitation of 11,961 other units. These will be replaced by 111,059 units. However, only 59,674 of these new units, 54 percent, can be considered equivalent to public housing in that they receive permanent operating subsidies of the magnitude necessary to support households with very low incomes. The other replacement units will receive shallower subsidies and serve families who are not necessarily eligible for public housing or they will receive no subsidies and serve market-rate renters or homebuyers (Popkin et al. 2004, 21; Kingsley 2009).

A second and related criticism of HOPE VI concerns the fate of public-housing residents who do not get to live in the new housing developed under the program. Not all residents of public-housing projects redeveloped under HOPE VI are eligible to reside in the new housing that replaced the old. Local housing authorities and site managers have the latitude to devise and enforce stricter tenant eligibility criteria than is typical for public housing as a whole. HOPE VI developments may exclude families with poor credit histories, with criminal records, or that do not demonstrate acceptable housekeeping skills (Popkin, Cunningham, and Bart 2005).

If a former resident chooses not to return to the site after redevelopment or is not allowed to do so, he or she may be relocated to an apartment in another public-housing development or he or she may be given a Housing Choice Voucher to seek an apartment in the private market. If the resident is not in compliance with her public housing lease, or is not on the lease at all, however, he or she is not entitled to any subsidy.

2.8 Public Housing Summary

Despite its many problems, public housing has proven to be the most durable of the nation's low income housing programs. Notwithstanding substandard construction, inappropriate designs, often-weak management, inadequate funding for capital improvements and operating support, and concentrations of extreme poverty, most public-housing developments somehow manage to provide adequate housing. Most of the worst public housing has now been taken down and replaced with mixed-income developments built at lower densities and to superior design standards. Moreover, far fewer units are now located in the most distressed neighborhoods.

The secret to the program's longevity is public ownership. Unlike virtually all other types of subsidized housing, public-housing guarantees perpetual low-income occupancy. There are no subsidy contracts to renew and, unlike other project-based subsidy programs, owners do not have the option of eventually converting public housing to market-rate occupancy. Threats to the long-term viability of public housing include poor management and security and inadequate funding to replace worn out building systems and provide adequate maintenance. As long as the resources are in place to keep the housing in good condition and to cover operating costs not financed from rental income, public housing can continue to provide decent housing for very low-income families. However, operating subsidies have seldom been fully funded, and federal funds for capital improvements fall far short of what is needed to keep the stock of public housing in good physical condition.

In addition to the need for sufficient capital and operating support, another major challenge for public housing concerns the fate of residents displaced from projects slated for redevelopment. A large percentage of these households will fail to qualify for the new public housing built as part of mixed-income developments, and they also face severe challenges in finding new housing with rental vouchers. In particular, residents with felony convictions, substance-abuse problems, and erratic work histories are unlikely to meet the screening standards set for redeveloped public housing or to be welcomed by private landlords. Moreover, many residents in distressed public housing are not compliant with their leases, and some are not on the lease, which makes them ineligible for any relocation assistance at all.

Finally, it is important to note that the supply of public housing has been shrinking since the 1990s as a result of demolition and redevelopment into smaller, mixed-income projects. Although this new public housing often offers higher-quality accommodations than what stood before, there are fewer units than before, and access to this housing is more restricted. If this trend continues, public housing will become decreasingly available to the lowest-income families with the greatest need for affordable housing.

3 VOUCHERS

Housing vouchers help low-income households rent housing in the private market. Unlike public housing and other supply-side subsidies, vouchers are portable and recipients can use them for any eligible housing. Vouchers have been part of U.S. housing policy since the 1970s, and now constitute the single largest rental subsidy program for low-income households.

Although vouchers had been advocated in policy circles since the 1930s, they did not become part of federal policy until 1974 when the Nixon Administration created the Section 8 program (Hays 1995). This program included both supply- and demand-side housing subsidies. The supply-side program provided for-profit and nonprofit developers with a rental subsidy contract that would assure the payment of "Fair Market Rents" for units occupied by eligible households. The subsidy provided sufficient cash flow to cover debt-service and operating costs for new and rehabilitated rental housing. The supply-side component of Section 8 produced about 850,000 rental units before the federal government ceased funding new housing developments in the 1980s (Hays 1995; Schwartz 2010).

The Section 8 Existing Housing Program enabled eligible low-income households to rent apartments in existing buildings. Programmatic details have changed over time, as has the program's name (in 1998 the program was renamed Housing Choice Vouchers), but the concept has remained the same. Eligible households pay 30 percent of their adjusted gross income on existing housing (originally 25 percent), and the federal government pays the rest up to a limit that is determined by the local area's fair market rent (FMR). Fair market rent currently represents the 40th percentile in a metropolitan area (or other designated housing market) of rental housing that has experienced a recent turnover in occupancy. In some high-cost markets, FMR is set at the 50th percentile. Fair market rents are based on the cost of a recently rented two-bedroom apartment; FMRs for smaller or larger units are decreased or increased proportionately. In actuality, local housing authorities set the maximum eligible rent that can be covered by vouchers through a "payment standard," which is function of the FMR. Payment standards may range from 90 percent to 110 percent of the FMR. In addition, authorities may request permission from HUD to establish "exception rents" that exceed the maximum permissible payment standard (Schwartz 2010).

If a renter wishes to live in an apartment or house that costs more than the payment standard, he or she may pay the difference between the actual rent and the payment standard, provided that total rent payments do not exceed 40 percent of his or her gross income (i.e., any additional rental payments must not exceed 10 percent of gross income).

In addition to rent eligibility standards, households may use federal vouchers only if (a) the property owner agrees to accept the vouchers and (b) if the property meets the federal government's physical quality standards. Recipients may use their vouchers anywhere in the United States, although the great majority do not move across municipal boundaries and reside within the jurisdiction of the housing authority that issued the voucher.

Housing vouchers were once very controversial, and debate for and against vouchers divided along ideological lines, with conservatives favoring vouchers and liberals advocating for supply-side approaches (von Hoffman 2012; Hays 1995). Advocates claimed that vouchers are more cost-effective than supply-side subsidies, and, by providing the opportunity to exercise choice in the housing market, they enabled people to live in a wider array of neighborhoods. Opponents argued that vouchers could have an inflationary effect on local housing market, causing rents to increase across the board, and would not necessarily improve residential choice. Nearly 40 years of experience have illuminated strengths and flaws in both sides of the debate. Politically, the question of supply vs. demand side approaches is far less divisive than before. Although liberals now see merits in both types of assistance, conservatives are now mostly opposed to all forms of low-income housing subsidy—whether demand or supply side—just as they are against most other social-welfare expenditures (von Hoffman 2012).

3.1 Cost-Effectiveness

Vouchers are less expensive than supply-side subsidies. Public housing and other federal supply-side subsidies are more costly because they help pay for the cost of developing (constructing or rehabilitating) housing, and often also help cover operating costs as well. In contrast, demand-side subsidies cover the difference between 30 percent of tenant income and a market-based payment standard. Controlling for differences in unit size and location, the U.S. General Accounting Office, for example, found that public housing redeveloped under the Hope VI program costs 27 percent more than vouchers over their 20-year life cycle, and housing produced through the Low-Income Housing Tax Credit (LIHTC), costs 15 percent more (U.S. General Accounting Office 2002).

3.2 Residential Choice

Although vouchers are often championed for their potential to give households access to a wide range of neighborhoods, and to avoid neighborhoods with concentrations of poverty and high levels of racial segregation, this potential has not been fully realized. Voucher recipients do reside less often than public-housing residents in neighborhoods with the highest rates of poverty, but they tend to reside in areas with disproportionately large minority populations. For the most part, households have not used vouchers to move to neighborhoods with excellent schools and other services; few city residents have used vouchers to secure housing in more affluent suburban communities. Indeed, the voucher program's failure to help many low-income and minority households relocate to neighborhoods with greater opportunities for educational and economic achievement prompted the government to augment vouchers with counseling and other services to help people move to these neighborhoods (Briggs, Popkin, and Goering 2010; McClure 2008; Schwartz 2010).

As of 2008, voucher recipients could be found in 90 percent of the nation's 69,421 census tracts. However, in many of these tracts, voucher holders are underrepresented in relation to the tracts' share of total affordable (renting for less than FMR) housing in the region.

Table 23.1 compares the geographic distribution of voucher holders with that of housing subsidized under the public housing, LIHTC, and project-based Section 8 programs, as well as the total rental housing stock. The table shows that compared to public housing, voucher holders are far less concentrated in census tracts with the highest poverty rates and substantially less concentrated in tracts where minorities account for 80 percent or more of the total population. Vouchers are more successful than public housing, but they are less successful than other project-based subsidy programs in placing households in tracts with poverty rates below 10 percent. The voucher program underperforms public housing and the other project-based programs in placing households in tracts where minorities account for less than 10 percent of the total population.

Voucher holders, minorities especially, may reside in low-income and/or predominantly minority neighborhoods, and be underrepresented in more affluent, suburban neighborhoods, for several reasons:

- They may be reluctant to move away from the neighborhoods they know best, where they have family and friends and have access to various types of public services (Briggs et al. 2010; Schwartz 2010).

Table 23.1 Neighborhood Characteristics of Subsidized Housing in 2008

	Housing Choice Vouchers	Public Housing	Low-Income Housing Tax Credit	Project-Based Section 8[b]	All Rental Housing, 2005–2009
Tract Poverty Rate[a]					
<10%	24.5	14.6	33.1	26.6	33.1
10–19%	34.7	20.7	28.1	29.9	33.8
20–29%	21.4	20.1	16.9	19.2	18.0
30–39%	11.9	15.9	12.4	13.5	8.6
40%+	7.6	28.7	9.5	10.8	6.4
Percentage of Minority Population in Tract[a]					
<10%	15.4	18.9	21.7	25.5	17.0
10–29%	22.2	15.0	22.7	23.1	29.1
30–49%	15.6	11.5	14.7	14.0	18.8
50–79%	20.1	15.9	18.4	16.4	18.6
80%+	26.7	38.8	22.5	21.0	16.7

Notes:
[a] Poverty and population data are based on the 2000 census;
[b] Section 8 New Construction and Substantial Rehabilitation
Source: U.S. Department of Housing and Urban Development, A Picture of Subsidized Housing in 2008; Data on all rental housing is from the American Community Survey and covers the period of 2005–2009.

- They may be wary about moving to unfamiliar communities where they may encounter discrimination from landlords. If voucher holders do not own their automobiles, they may also be reluctant to move to places that lack sufficient public transportation (Schwartz 2010).
- The residential location of voucher holders is also influenced by the spatial distribution of affordable rental housing (i.e., renting for no more than the designated payment standard), and perhaps that of the overall rental housing stock (McClure 2010). As of 2009, only 17% of all rental housing (and only 15% of all housing renting for no more than the FMR), was located in tracts where the minority population was less than 10% of the total population, compared to 34% in 1990. Similarly, the percentage of rental housing units located in census tracts with poverty rates of 10% or less decreased from 41% in 1990 to 35% in 2009 (Schwartz and McClure 2012).

Another challenge is that not every household that is given a voucher succeeds in using it. Many households who are given vouchers fail to find housing that (a) rents for less than the payment standard; or (b) has an owner is willing to rent to a voucher holder; or (c) passes HUD's physical quality inspections. In 2000, the most recent year in which HUD analyzed voucher success rates, 69 percent of all participating households succeeded in leasing a home with a voucher, and the figure reaches 71 percent when

New York City and Los Angeles were excluded. In these two cities, the success rates were 57 percent and 47 percent, respectively. Whereas the voucher success rate exceeded 80 percent in 30 percent of the cities studied, it was less than 60 percent in 27 percent of them (Finkel and Buron 2001). The likelihood of securing a home with a voucher, controlling for a range of socioeconomic and demographic factors, was reduced in metropolitan areas with low rental vacancy rates among households headed by persons 62 years and older, among households with five or more members, and among formerly homeless single men (Finkel and Buron 2001; Schwartz 2010).

3.3 Voucher Summary

Vouchers offer several advantages over supply-side subsidy programs. They are less expensive per unit, potentially allowing the government to assist more households with the same amount of funding. They also provide a greater degree of residential choice than supply-side subsidy programs do, enabling recipients to live in a wider array of neighborhoods. Compared to public housing especially, but also to other project-based programs, a smaller percentage of voucher holders live in economically distressed neighborhoods. However, the voucher program is no guarantee against racial segregation. Minority voucher holders usually reside in minority neighborhoods. Moreover, the geographic distribution of affordable rental units (i.e., renting for no more than a housing authority's voucher payment standard) constrains the potential for voucher holders to access middle-class neighborhoods of any racial composition. When affordable rental units are in short supply, vouchers are of limited value in promoting opportunity.

More than 35 years of experience with vouchers also underscore fundamental limitations with this approach. Some types of households fare better than others under the program, and it is decidedly less effective in tight housing markets. Large families, the elderly, and families and individuals with special needs tend to be less successful in finding housing with vouchers than other types of households, and they stand to benefit from project-based subsidies. Supply-side subsidies can also enable low-income people to reside in affluent neighborhoods with few affordable units. They can also promote racial integration. In areas with very tight rental markets, project-based programs increase the supply of low-cost housing.

4 CONCLUSION

About 5 million low-income households receive "deep" housing subsidies in the United States, 25 percent of the eligible population. These subsidies are provided through three programs: public housing, "project-based Section 8," which supports privately owned rental housing, and vouchers. Of these three programs, only vouchers have seen any growth since the mid 1990s. The public housing stock has declined by more than 250,000 units, and the only new public housing built during this time has been to replace some of the public housing slated for demolition. The inventory of housing with project-based Section 8 has also declined with the expiration of subsidy contracts. Although vouchers are the largest program, subsidizing about 2 million households as of 2012, public housing is what most people associate with subsidized housing.

The public housing program, for all its problems, has proven to be the longest lived and in some ways most durable program. It is able to provide decent, affordable housing to families and individuals with a wide range of needs (including large families, people with disabilities) and in some cases provide access to desirable neighborhoods. Moreover, the overall quality of public-housing has improved, in large part because most of the worst public housing has been demolished under Hope VI and other programs (Sard and Fischer 2008). The management of many public housing developments has also improved in recent years. For decades many PHAs were isolated from the rest of local government and from the rest of the rental-housing industry—subsidized and market rate. Public housing was governed by rules and practices that were unheard of in the rest of the industry. In some PHAs, hiring and promotion decisions were based in large part on political patronage, not on professional qualifications (Bratt 2012). Since the late 1990s, housing authorities have been required to adopt the norms and practices of the rest of the industry, and to manage their housing on a decentralized, property-specific basis. In many cases, especially in Hope VI sites, management has been transferred to private firms.

If public housing was adequately funded and well managed, it could be a perpetual resource for low-income households. However, notwithstanding the construction of about 60,000 new public housing units under the HOPE VI program, and the demolition of the worst public- housing projects, the bulk of the remaining public-housing stock is aging and in immediate need of substantial capital improvement, improvements the government is unlikely to fund to any significant degree. Public housing has never been a major priority to the federal government, and it is less of one today in an era of fiscal austerity and partisan gridlock. As a result, public housing faces a very difficult future.[2]

Unlike public housing, the voucher program has continued to grow, if only in fits and starts. Much of its growth, however, had derived from the provision of vouchers to residents of public housing slated for demolition and to residents in privately owned housing whose project-based Section 8 contracts were expiring. The voucher program has shown itself to be less costly per unit than public housing and other project-based subsidy programs. It also provides recipients with more residential choices, as recipients may use vouchers to rent eligible units anywhere in the United States. However, recipients have not used vouchers as often as expected to access the most desirable neighborhoods. In addition, whereas public housing is accessible to any household that qualifies for the program—and finds itself at the head of the waiting list—when low-income households receive vouchers, many do not succeed in securing housing with them. Large families and the elderly face the greatest difficulty, and all households fare relatively poorly in areas where the rental vacancy rate is low.

Notes

1. Other low-income subsidy programs include project-based Section 8, the Low-Income Tax Credit, and the HOME Investment Partnership program. See Schwartz (2010) for details.
2. The Obama Administration launched in early 2013 a demonstration program that enables housing authorities to access private financing to help pay for essential capital improvements. The Rental Housing Demonstration program (RAD) allows a limited number of public housing developments(involving no more than 60,000 units) to be converted to the project-based Section 8 program. This will make the properties eligible for bank loans and for Low-Income Housing Tax credits to finance capital improvements.

References

*Indicates recommended reading.

Bratt, R. G. 1989. *Rebuilding a Low-Income Housing Policy*. Philadelphia: Temple University Press.

Bratt, R. G. 2012. "Public Housing." In A. T. Carswell, ed., *The Encyclopedia of Housing*. 2nd ed., 569–574. Thousand Oaks, CA: Sage.

*Briggs, X. de S., S. J. Popkin, and J. Goering. 2010. *Moving to Opportunity: The Story of an American Experiment to Fight Ghetto Poverty*. New York: Oxford University Press.

Byrne, G. A., K. Day, and J. Stockard. 2003. "Taking Stock of Public Housing." Paper presented to the Public Housing Authority Directors Association (PRADA) (September 16). http://www.haws.org/documents/Taking_Stock_of_Public_Housing.pdf.

*Cisneros, H. G., and L. Engdahl, eds. 2009. *From Despair to Hope: Hope VI and the New Promise of Public Housing in America's Cities*. Washington: DC: Brookings Institution Press.

Finkel, M., and L. Buron. 2001. *Study on Section 8 Voucher Success Rates: Vol. 1 Quantitative Study of Success Rates in Metropolitan Areas. Final Report*. Washington: DC: Report prepared by Abt Associates, Inc. for the U.S. Department of Housing and Urban Development, Office of Policy Development and Research (November). http://www.huduser.org/Publications/pdf/sec8success.pdf.

Finkel, M., K. Lam, C. Blaine, R. J. de la Cruz, D. DeMarco, M. Vandawalker, and M. Woodford. 2010. *Capital Needs in the Public Housing Program*. Report prepared by Abt Associates, Inc. for the U.S. Department of Housing and Urban Development. http://portal.hud.gov/hudportal/documents/huddoc?id=PH_Capital_Needs.pdf.

*Goetz, E. 2011. "Where Have All the Towers Gone?" *Journal of Urban Studies* 33 (3): 267–287.

Harvard University Graduate School of Design. 2003. *Public Housing Operating Cost Study: Final Report*. Washington: DC: U.S. Department of Housing Preservation and Development.

Hays, R. A. 1995. *The Federal Government and Urban Housing*. 2nd ed. Albany: State University of New York Press.

Hirsch, A. R. 1998. *Making the Second Ghetto: Race and Housing in Chicago, 1940–1960*. Chicago: University of Chicago Press.

*Hoffman, A. von. 2012. "History Lessons for Today's Housing Policy: The Politics of Low-Income Housing." *Housing Policy Debate* 22 (3): 321–376.

HUD (U.S. Department of Housing and Urban Development). 2009a. "Asset Management Overview." http://portal.hud.gov/hudportal/HUD?src=/program_offices/public_indian_housing/programs/ph/am/overview.

HUD. 2009b. FY2010 "Budget: Road Map for Transformation." http://www.hud.gov/budget summary2010/fy10budget.pdf.

HUD. 2012a. "Residents Characteristics Report." https://hudapps.hud.gov/public/picj2ee/Mtcsrcr?category=rcr_incomeanddownload=falseandcount=0andsorttable=table1.

HUD. 2012b. "Choice Neighborhoods." http://portal.hud.gov/hudportal/HUD?src=/program_offices/public_indian_housing/programs/ph/cn.

Kingsley, G. T. 2009. Appendix. In H. G. Cisneros and L. Engdahl, eds., *From Despair to Hope: Hope VI and the New Promise of Public Housing in America's Cities*, 299–306. Washington: DC: Brookings Institution.

McClure, Kirk. 2008. "Deconcentration of the Poor through Housing Programs." *Journal of the American Planning Association* 74 (1): 90–99.

McClure, Kirk. 2010. "The Prospects for Guiding Housing Choice Voucher Households to High-Opportunity Neighborhoods." *Cityscape* 12 (3): 101–122.

National Housing Law Project. 2002. "False HOPE: A Critical Assessment of the Hope VI Public Housing Redevelopment Program." http://nhlp.org/files/FalseHOPE.pdf.

Nenno, M. K. 1996. *Ending the Stalemate: Moving Housing and Urban Development into the Mainstream of America's Future.* Lanham, MD: University Press of America.

Newman, O. 1995. "Defensible Space: A New Physical Planning Tool for Urban Revitalization." *Journal of the American Planning Association* 61 (2): 149–156.

Popkin, S. J., B. Katz, M. K. Cunningham, K. D. Brown, J. Gustafson, and M. A. Turner. 2004. *A Decade of Hope VI: Research Findings and Policy Challenges.* Washington, DC: Urban Institute and Brookings Institution. http://urban.org/uploadedPDF/411002HOPEVLpdf.

Popkin, S. J., M. K. Cunningham, and M. Burt. 2005. "Public Housing Transformation and the Hard to House." *Housing Policy Debate* 16 (1): 1–24.

Radford, G. 1996. *Modern Housing for America: Policy Struggles in the New Deal Era.* Chicago: University of Chicago Press.

Sard, B. and W. Fischer. 2008. *Preserving Safe, High Quality Public Housing Should Be a Priority of Federal Housing Policy.* Washington, DC: Center for Budget and Policy Priorities. http://www.cbpp.org/files/9-18-08hous.pdf.

*Schwartz, Alex. 2010. *Housing Policy in the United States.* 2nd ed. New York: Routledge.

Schwartz, Alex, and Kirk McClure. 2012. "*The Changing Geography of Rental Housing in the US: Shrinking Limits to Opportunity?*" Unpublished manuscript, available from authors.

*Solomon, R. 2005. *Public Housing Reform and Voucher Success: Progress and Challenges.* Washington, DC: Brookings Institution, Metropolitan Policy Program (January). http://www.brookings.edu/metro/pubs/20050124solomon.pdf.

*Turner, M. A., S. J. Popkin, and L. Rawlings. 2009. *Public Housing and the Legacy of Segregation.* Washington, DC: Urban Institute Press.

U.S. General Accounting Office. 2002. "*Federal Housing Assistance: Comparing the Characteristics and Costs of Housing Programs.*" Washington, DC: GAO-02-76. http://www.gao.gov/new.items/d0276.pdf.

Vale, L. J. 2000. *From the Puritans to the Projects: Public Housing and Public Neighbors.* Cambridge, MA: Harvard University Press.

PART VI

PROGRAMS FOR THE DISABLED

CHAPTER 24

....

SOCIAL SECURITY DISABILITY INSURANCE AND SUPPLEMENTAL SECURITY INCOME

....

JENNIFER L. ERKULWATER

1 INTRODUCTION

....

SOCIAL Security Disability Insurance (DI) and Supplemental Security Income (SSI) are the foundation of the social safety net for Americans with disabilities. Both provide cash benefits, and because neither program is limited to specific impairments or to workers in particular occupations, as is the case with many public and private disability plans, they are broadly accessible to the American people and the most expensive of the nation's disability benefit programs. Excluding expenditures for health care, DI and SSI combined account for almost three-quarters of annual federal spending on the disabled (U.S. GAO 1999).

Disability benefits policy, though, has long been fraught with controversy. Conservatives have resisted broad income support for disabled workers, preferring, instead, workplace accommodations and limited public assistance. On the other hand, bureaucrats, the federal courts, and interest groups have been instrumental in expanding both social insurance coverage and public assistance to the disabled. As a result of their concerted efforts, DI and SSI have grown irrespective of which party controlled the White House or Congress. Today no other disability benefits program comes close to rivaling them, regardless of whether the measure is persons enrolled or dollars spent. Expansion, however, is not the same as largess, because, despite dramatic growth in DI and SSI since their enactment, poverty and unemployment still remain prevalent among Americans with disabilities.

2 ORIGINS AND DEVELOPMENT

The evolution of Social Security disability benefits policy can be divided into two eras, both of which featured growth in enrollment and program spending. During the first era, between 1935 and 1972, conservatives in Congress sought to limit federal power over the Southern political economy, which was premised on racial segregation and a steady supply of cheap African-American labor. This meant constraining liberal efforts to enact broad income-support guarantees for the nation's poor and disabled, programs that would lift the living standards of African Americans. By the late 1960s, the civil rights movement had brought down formal racial hierarchy in the South and weakened the power of conservative Democrats in Congress, and once disability benefits were created, lawmakers broadly supported expansion. During the second era, new ways of thinking about disability and social-welfare obligations raised challenges for the nation's disability policy. Rather than seeking an expanded social safety net, recently mobilized disability rights activists lobbied for civil rights protections that would open access to mainstream social institutions, including the workplace. The emphasis on work rather than welfare complemented conservative attempts to rein in social spending. Since 1972, lawmakers have sought to tighten eligibility for disability benefits while expanding job accommodations and work incentives, efforts that have largely failed to enhance employment among the disabled (this section relies heavily on Stone 1984; Berkowitz 1987; Quadagno 1988; Derthick 1990; Quadagno 2005; and Erkulwater 2006).

In the 1930s, lawmakers recognized the severe hardships endured by workers with impairments, but they were deeply divided over whether the federal government or the states should take primary responsibility for the disabled and whether aid should take the form of cash benefits. Lest these programs develop into income support programs for people with a vast array of disadvantages, lawmakers were willing to compensate only medical reasons for unemployment, not social ones. Yet they knew that drawing the line between medical and social handicaps would be exceedingly difficult. Thus, the Social Security Act of 1935 did not provide pensions for disabled workers. Instead, it provided matching grants to the states for programs that would offer cash assistance to senior citizens, persons with blindness, and single-parent families living in poverty. These programs—Old Age Assistance (OAA), Aid to the Blind (AB), and Aid to Families with Dependent Children (AFDC)—left states in charge of aid to the poor and ameliorated the concerns of Southern Democrats seeking to safeguard local control over black labor.

Nevertheless, shortly after World War II, with the basic Old Age and Survivors Insurance (OASI) program in place, officials at the Social Security Administration (SSA) made extending coverage to disabled workers and their families a top priority. However, experience with private insurance and veterans' pensions had taught policy-makers that disability was an inherently expansive administrative category, particularly during economic downturns. When jobs were scarce, even for the fittest of workers, administrators and judges took pity on down-and-out workers and stretched narrow definitions of disability, thus converting benefits reserved for the severely disabled into general compensation programs for the unemployed. To assuage wary members of Congress, SSA officials decided to start small. In its recommendations for the 1950 amendments, the Social Security Advisory Council dropped plans for covering temporary impairments and instead proposed a definition of disability that would encompass only permanent and severe physical or mental conditions that could be verified by medical examination. The program, however, immediately became entangled in the battle over national health insurance. The American Medical Association (AMA), Republicans, and conservative Democrats opposed disability benefits, fearing that they represented the entering wedge for greater federal intrusion into health care. In the face of steep opposition, Congress voted instead to create Aid to the Permanently and Totally Disabled (APTD). Like OAA, AB, and AFDC, APTD matched state spending on public assistance programs for the disabled, but it left each state free to set its own benefit levels and write its own legal definitions of disability.

Although conservatives regarded APTD as sufficient, liberals viewed the program as only the beginning. For the next 6 years, SSA officials worked tirelessly to bring disability benefits to fruition through piecemeal initiatives. In 1952, they proposed allowing a worker to "freeze" wages at the onset of a disability and then, upon reaching retirement age, receive benefits based on predisability earnings rather than the reduced earnings brought about because of the disability. Two years later, liberals succeeded in getting the disability freeze enacted into law. To appease the AMA and its congressional allies, lawmakers hammered out a compromise, which stipulated that, although SSA field offices would take initial applications for the freeze, the actual examinations of disability status would be made by designated state agencies operating under guidance from the SSA. Private physicians, not government doctors, would provide the medical documentation that state disability examiners needed. Although he objected to cash benefits for disabled workers, President Dwight Eisenhower did not oppose the freeze, which was similar to provisions in many private disability insurance plans. Moreover, Secretary of Health, Education, and Welfare Oveta Culp Hobby and assistant secretary Roswell Perkins believed that the freeze could serve as a conduit for channeling workers into the growing number of state vocational rehabilitation programs (Derthick 1979; Berkowitz 1987).

As soon as they had secured the freeze, SSA officials girded for a showdown over cash benefits. The AMA, the Chamber of Commerce, the private insurance industry, and congressional conservatives in both parties remained staunch opponents. SSA officials, however, pitched cash benefits as an early retirement pension for older workers with impairments. They argued that, because of their advanced age, these workers would have a difficult time learning new skills or adapting to a new occupation, making permanent withdrawal from the workplace appropriate. Officials succeeded in mollifying private insurers, who were not interested in covering older workers and simply wanted to safeguard their market among younger workers. Labor unions threw their organizational might behind disability benefits, and in 1956, Disability Insurance eked through the Senate by only a single vote (Quadagno 2005). The final version of the program adopted the state-run process for determining disability that had been established in 1954, and limited eligibility to workers aged 50 and over with severe and permanent impairments. Yet the program's restrictiveness, so crucial to its passage, undercut the goal of linking Social Security to rehabilitation. Because older workers made poor candidates for rehabilitation, the SSA failed to develop a close working relationship with rehabilitative services, even after younger workers became eligible for benefits in 1960.

Once DI was established, it ceased to be controversial and soon underwent a period of rapid growth. Throughout the late 1950s and the 1960s, Congress repeatedly made the program more generous: extending benefits to the disabled children and survivors of qualified workers, dropping the requirement that a worker had to be 50 years old to qualify for benefits, reducing the waiting period for benefits from 6 months to 5, and allowing benefits for impairments that, although not permanent, were expected to last at least a year. In addition, disability benefits became a form of constituency politics, as lawmakers frequently questioned SSA officials about why it took so long for the agency to process claims and why seemingly disabled claimants were denied benefits.

In the 1960s, changes in federal–state relations upended prevailing assumptions about welfare policy and opened the door to further expansion of disability benefits. The civil rights movement weakened the power of Southern Democrats in Congress, and the migration of the African Americans to the North and Midwest, where public assistance programs were administered more liberally than in the South, contributed to steeply rising welfare costs. Long defenders of local control of public assistance, conservatives lost faith in the ability of the states to properly manage the matching grant programs (Quadagno 1988). In 1969, President Richard Nixon proposed transferring responsibility for the state programs to the federal government and creating nationally uniform benefit levels and eligibility criteria. The adult programs for the aged, blind, and disabled would be rolled into one federal cash benefit program called Supplemental Security Income, and AFDC would become the Family Assistance Plan, open to all poor families.

AFDC quickly became embroiled in a bitter debate over whether Congress should provide the able-bodied poor, many of whom were African American, a minimum level of income support, but since neither the aged nor disabled were expected to work, SSI was less controversial. In 1972, lawmakers added it to a landmark bill that substantially raised Social Security benefits, indexed them to inflation, and made disabled workers eligible for Medicare. SSI represented an historic expansion of federal aid to the poor, especially the mentally ill, who, up until this point had been cared for at state expense in public hospitals and asylums, and disabled children, who had previously qualified for state assistance programs only if they were blind or crippled. Nevertheless, SSI sailed through Congress precisely because lawmakers expected the program to serve primarily the aged poor rather than the disabled poor. They had hoped that creating a means-tested supplement to Social Security would provide an adequate pension for low-income retirees, and they simply extended that guarantee to low-income people with disabilities with little thought given to the fact that the disabled clientele that SSI would aid would be far different from the older workers the SSA was accustomed to serving. Many had worked little, if at all, prior to enrolling in SSI, and their barriers to gainful employment were as much social as they were medical in origin (Erkulwater 2006).

The 1972 amendments marked the beginning of turmoil for DI and SSI as conflicting pressures to expand eligibility but also promote employment buffeted the programs. Throughout the early 1970s, DI and SSI experienced rapid and unexpected growth. Congressional and SSA studies indicated several reasons for this, including high levels of unemployment; declining stigma associated with disability and dependence on public assistance; high benefit levels relative to wages; and a growing backlog in claims, which created pressure for examiners to adjudicate claims quickly and led to rushed and sloppy evaluations. In 1980, President Jimmy Carter and a Democratic Congress enacted a set of amendments to slow program growth. In addition to reducing and capping DI benefits for younger workers, the bill expanded work incentives—for example, by increasing the length of time during which a beneficiary could work but then return to the disability rolls should employment prove impossible to maintain. The most significant provision of the 1980 amendments, however, was its mandate for continuing disability reviews. To strengthen program integrity, the amendments called for the SSA to conduct a review of every disabled beneficiary's status at least once every three years, unless the beneficiary suffered from a permanent impairment. Prior to this, the SSA reviewed a beneficiary's medical status only if the agency expected his or her medical condition to improve or if the individual had returned to work.

When President Ronald Reagan entered office in 1981, his administration greatly accelerated the reviews, using them as a pretext for removing hundreds of thousands of beneficiaries from DI and SSI. Rushed and poorly implemented, the disability reviews created a political firestorm that emboldened antipoverty and disability advocates. They filed hundreds of lawsuits challenging the legality of the rules the SSA used to deny benefits, and SSA hearing officers and federal judges overturned thousands of denials. Members of Congress excoriated the reviews in more than two dozen hearings between 1982 and 1984. Critics charged that the SSA had secretly tightened the standards of disability, that it was terminating benefits despite little evidence that beneficiaries' medical conditions had improved, and that the criteria for assessing mental impairments were far too restrictive and out of touch with current medical practice. Above all, critics objected to the heartlessness of the enterprise, noting that many individuals who had lost benefits had been on the rolls for years before being cut from their primary form of income support with little warning and after only perfunctory reviews of their medical status.

What also made the disability reviews difficult for the Reagan administration to maintain was the fact that medicine was moving in the opposite direction, toward an expansive understanding of impairment. In 1980, the American Psychiatric Association (APA) amended its diagnostic manual to recognize more mental disorders and to include fuller descriptions of the behaviors and functional limitations associated with these disorders. Psychiatrists also adopted an expansive understanding of mental illness that treated behavior that departed from statistical or social norms as possible indicators of a disorder. Similarly, by the 1970s, pediatricians began treating learning and behavioral problems in children as medical impairments rather than "bad behavior." Medical professionals, put simply, came to accept something that SSA officials had long known—that the boundary between medical and social reasons for one's inability to work or otherwise function was blurry at best. Assessing an impairment could not be done in isolation from assessing the environment in which a person functioned and societal expectations about what constituted "normal" behavior and abilities (Erkulwater 2006).

The diagnostic revolutions in psychiatric and pediatric medicine coupled with widespread outrage over the reviews led to sweeping changes in the administrative rules determining disability, in turn greatly altering the face of the Social Security disability rolls. With the SSA's disability process in disarray, Congress passed and Reagan signed the 1984 Disability Benefits Reform Act. The law significantly liberalized the standards of disability by, among other things, requiring that the SSA prove an individual's medical condition had improved (which is difficult to do) before determining that he or she was no longer disabled, requiring that the SSA evaluate the combined effect of multiple impairments rather than automatically denying benefits when no single impairment was severe enough to meet the legal standard of disability, and compelling the agency to rewrite its rules governing the evaluation of mental disorders with input from mental health professionals and advocates (Berkowitz 1987; Derthick 1990; Erkulwater 2006).

In 1985, the SSA released revised rules for evaluating mental impairments in adults, and 6 years later, a revamped series of rules for childhood disabilities. Whereas in the past, disability examiners had placed a great deal of emphasis on tangible or objectively verifiable signs of an impairment—a missing limb or diseased heart, for instance—the new rules required examiners to conduct a thorough assessment of whether a claimant could actually find and keep a job. Examiners had to consider a person's history of employment, assessments of his or her functioning, and even the presence of symptoms, like pain or depression, that could prevent work even if they were not objectively verifiable. In sum, the SSA adopted disability criteria that recognized a broader number of medical conditions, included more exacting descriptions of these conditions, and took into account the functional impact of impairments, resulting in a more thorough but, also, more expansive interpretation of disability (Erkulwater 2006).

The reforms brought an end to the upheaval caused by the disability reviews, but they did not end the contentiousness between the SSA and antipoverty advocates. If anything, resolution of the reviews brought new challenges to the SSA. During the 1980s, advocates came to appreciate the fact that, as one of the few national programs providing cash support to the disadvantaged, DI and SSI were central to the economic well-being of low-income groups. Groups as diverse as Legal Services, the APA, the American Academy of Pediatrics, the Arc, the Children's Defense Fund, the Bazelon Center for Mental Health Law, the National Law Center on Homelessness and Poverty, and the National Senior Citizens Law Center supported expansion of disability benefits. Over the next decade, advocates challenged virtually every SSA rule in an effort to pry DI and SSI open to more of the disabled, and they found ready allies among federal judges, who came away from the disability reviews with little regard for the SSA.

No single case illustrates the power of litigation in making disability benefits more accessible than *Sullivan v. Zebley* (1990). Prior to *Zebley*, the SSA determined whether a child was disabled by looking only at the severity of the child's medical condition with little attention to the way in which the child's condition affected his or her functioning. The agency argued that this approach was necessitated by the fact that the standard of disability used for adults was inappropriate for children. That standard assessed whether an adult had the functional capacity to remain employed, yet it could not be applied to children because children did not engage in paid work. Advocates, however, asserted that the SSA's childhood disability standard did not comport with the way in which medical professionals assessed children, and the Supreme Court in *Zebley* agreed. In a 7-2 decision, it ordered the SSA to devise an evaluation that considered whether a child functioned in an "age-appropriate" manner across a range of activities, such as school, daily self-care, play, and social relationships—activities that the Court deemed the "work" of children. These revisions made SSI accessible to children with a range of developmental delays and learning, mood, and behavioral disorders and led to an explosion in the number of children in the program (Erkulwater 2006).

Yet at the same time that disability rolls were growing, the rise of the disability rights movement called into question the assumption that people with disabilities were incapable of work and, therefore, automatically entitled to publicly provided income support. In the late 1960s, activists influenced by the civil rights movement objected to the exclusion of the disabled from workplaces, schools, and public spaces, and they rejected as prejudicial the compassion and pity that able-bodied members of society felt toward the disabled. The reason people with disabilities did not work, activists argued, was not because they were inherently incapable of doing so, but because the able-bodied discriminated against them and erected barriers, architectural and social, to their participation in paid work. Unlike previous groups representing the disabled, these new activists were not interested in more money or more services for the disabled; instead, they demanded that people with disabilities be fully integrated into mainstream society as a matter of right (Scotch 2001).

The early 1990s featured conflicting pressures in disability policy. The disability rights movement culminated in the enactment of the Americans with Disabilities Act (ADA) in 1990. The law sought to increase the employment of the disabled by banning discrimination and mandating that employers make reasonable accommodations for their disabled employees. The ethos of disability rights spilled over into Social Security as well. Since 1980, Congress has enacted a number of initiatives to encourage beneficiaries to return to work, including trial work periods, extended eligibility for Medicare or Medicaid, and a disregard of earnings and disability-related work expenses. However, no matter how much Congress tinkered with disability benefits, lawmakers could neither appease disability rights activists nor convince large numbers of the disabled to trade welfare for work. To many activists, social-welfare programs like DI and SSI were inherently flawed because they were premised on the belief that people with disabilities could not be productive citizens. For many people with disabilities, however, the ADA and work incentives were not sufficient to maintain employment, and DI and SSI continued to expand despite the passage of the ADA.

By 1993, rapid growth engulfed both programs in bitter controversy. SSI in particular became an easy target for budget-cutters in both political parties following escalating costs and media claims that the program was rife with fraud and abuse. In 1996, Democratic President Bill Clinton and a Republican Congress agreed to a major welfare reform bill that curtailed eligibility for AFDC, renamed Temporary Assistance for Needy Families (TANF), but realized most of its cost savings through cuts in SSI and Medicaid. The bill overturned *Zebley* by tightening SSI's disability standard for children, removed alcohol or substance abuse as a qualifying disability for DI or SSI, and made legal immigrants ineligible for a range of safety-net programs.

Welfare reform, however, did not put an end to Congress' efforts to tighten Social Security disability benefits and encourage the disabled to work. In 1999, lawmakers authorized Ticket to Work (TTW), yet another effort to assist working-aged DI and SSI beneficiaries trying to re-enter the workplace. Under TTW, beneficiaries can choose from a network of service providers that offer vocational rehabilitation and on-going employment support. While making the transition to work, they can keep Medicare or Medicaid coverage for an extended period of time, and for the first 9 months, can keep all earnings in addition to disability benefits. Meanwhile, the SSA will suspend its periodic review of beneficiaries' medical status and resume payment of disability benefits should earnings ever fall below $1,000 a month over the next three years.

Nonetheless, these measures did little to boost employment among people with disabilities or arrest growth in the number of applications filed for DI and SSI benefits. Instead, the job accommodations and protections of the ADA benefited the most advantaged of the disabled. Compared to their counterparts who were not employed, individuals who worked despite their disabilities were more likely to hold a college degree and to work in positions offering private health-care coverage (Russell 2002; Findley and Sambamorthi 2004). Yet for the vast majority of people with disabilities, the employment rate and earnings fell in the 1990s, and poverty rates climbed, even during the latter half of the decade when the economy expanded and poverty rates among able-bodied working-aged people plummeted (Stapleton, Burkhauser, and Houtenville 2004).

The 2000s were marked by several years of slow job growth followed by the Great Recession of 2007–2009, which hurt all workers, especially those with low levels of education. Workers with disabilities, however, were devastated. Although highly educated workers with disabilities were more likely to be employed compared to their disabled counterparts with less education, educational attainment did not afford the same protection against job loss that it did for able-bodied workers. At every level of educational attainment, disabled workers were more likely than their counterparts without disabilities to suffer unemployment and long spells of joblessness. Once the recession ended, the disabled remained less likely to work or to look for work than the able-bodied, and when they did work, they earned less and were more likely to be underemployed—that is, working at low wages or part-time jobs, even when they desired full-time employment (Fogg, Harrington, and McMahon 2010; U.S. Census Bureau 2011). Between 2009 and 2010, compared to households without a working-aged adult with a disability, households of the disabled experienced steeper declines in real median income and sharper increases in poverty (U.S. Census Bureau 2011).

The weak job market exacerbated fiscal pressures on DI. Between 2000–2012, the number of applications filed for DI and SSI doubled from 2.7 million to over 5.5 million (SSA Office of the Chief Actuary, 2013; Table 69, SSA 2013a). Although the share of DI applications approved for benefits has dropped from 47 percent in 2000 to 35 percent today, because claimants file so many applications, the ratio of awards to workers has skyrocketed from 4.6 benefit awards per 1,000 workers in 2000 to 6.8 today (Table 6. C7, SSA 2013b). As a result, between 2005–2013, the SSA paid out more in benefits to disabled workers than it was taking in payroll-tax contributions, resulting in a predicted shortfall in the DI trust fund by 2016 (Board of Trustees 2013).

3 A Primer

DI and SSI are administratively complex programs that defy easy generalizations. Although the programs use nationally uniform rules, claimants are by no means treated uniformly. Furthermore, although SSI was intended to supplement DI, it has evolved into both a safety net for the most disadvantaged of the poor and transitional assistance for impaired workers trading paychecks for disability checks. Yet, because paid employment is the primary form of income support for disabled and nondisabled alike, neither program fully compensates for the economic adversities brought about by disablement.

3.1 Eligibility and Enrollment

DI's program for workers and SSI's program for adults use the same definition of disability and the same process for determining disability. According to the Social Security Act, in order to qualify for benefits, a person must be unable "to engage in any substantial gainful activity by reason of any medically determinable physical or mental impairment which can be expected to result in death or which has lasted or can be expected to last for a continuous period of not less than 12 months." Not only must the disability examiner decide that the claimant cannot return to his previous job, but he must also agree that the claimant cannot perform any other job given his age, education, and work experience. Because children do not engage in paid employment, the SSA uses a different standard for children applying to SSI. They must demonstrate "marked and severe functional limitations" that last at least a year. The widows, widowers, and adult children of covered workers can also qualify for DI if disabled, although the disability standards for widows and widowers are stricter than those for workers or SSI recipients.

In addition to meeting the disability standard, applicants for DI must also satisfy an earnings test, whereas applicants for SSI must meet an income or means test. The earnings test for DI examines both how recently and how long the applicant worked before filing for benefits. In general, individuals filing for DI must have worked at least half of their adult life before filing for benefits. During this time, claimants are required to make contributions, paid as payroll taxes, to the DI trust fund.

Because SSI is a program of last resort, claimants must show that they have inadequate income and assets and that they have applied for other assistance programs for which they might be eligible. To qualify, a claimant's monthly income must not exceed SSI's income limit, which is equal to twice the maximum monthly benefit. This income limit is adjusted with inflation over time, so that, in 2012, individuals wishing to enroll in SSI had to show an income of no more than $1,396 per month. The limit for couples was $2,096. Because SSI excludes some of a claimant's earnings when calculating income, a claimant can receive SSI even though his or her family income exceeds the federal poverty line.

The Social Security Act's definition of disability is a strict one. Using a different definition of disability, the Census Bureau estimates that 54.4 million individuals in the United States are disabled, and two-thirds of these suffer from an impairment severe enough to limit daily activities (Brault 2010). However, because the programs are restricted to people with severe disabilities and because they include the earnings test or means test, taken together, DI and SSI pay benefits to only 13.7 million people with disabilities. Of the nearly 9.4 million individuals DI covers, almost 9 in 10 are disabled workers, and the rest are the disabled widows, widowers, or adult children of covered workers. SSI, on the other hand, is a smaller program, enrolling 5.4 million adults and 1.4 million children with disabilities (Table 7.A1, SSA 2013b; Chart 12, Table 65, SSA 2012; Tables 3 and 17, SSA 2013a).

Even though the two programs share the same definition of disability, SSI recipients are not simply DI beneficiaries, only poorer; rather, they tend to suffer from different types of disabilities. The most common impairments among SSI recipients are intellectual disabilities (formerly called "mental retardation") and mental disorders, which afflict nearly three out of five recipients. By contrast, only one-third of DI workers qualify based on a mental impairment. Instead, the most common impairments are musculoskeletal disorders, including chronic pain and repetitive stress injuries (Table 35, SSA 2013a; Table 68, SSA 2012).

At any given point in time, the overlap between DI and SSI is small, but over time, the overlap is substantial because SSI is both a bridge between employment and public support and a major source of income support in its own right. Originally, lawmakers expected SSI to supplement low Social Security payments, but only 1.4 million individuals receive concurrent benefits. By contrast, roughly 4.5 million recipients rely on SSI as their sole source of income support (Table 3.C6.1, SSA 2013b). Nevertheless, SSI serves as a key resource as claimants move from the workplace to the disability rolls. Although few remain dual beneficiaries for an extended period of time, over any given 5-year period, up to one-quarter of disabled claimants receive both DI and SSI, often relying on

SSI and then transitioning entirely to DI once the 5-month waiting period for workers' benefits elapses (Rupp and Riley 2011).

3.2 Benefit Levels, Expenditures, and Financing

Both DI and SSI are budgetary entitlements, meaning that individuals who meet the programs' means-test or contribution requirements and disability standard are entitled to full benefits absent congressional changes to the rules of eligibility or the formula used to calculate payments. To finance DI, covered workers and their employers each pay a tax of 0.9 percent on a wage base. Adjusted for inflation each year, this wage base stood at $113,700 in 2013. The amount of benefits a worker receives corresponds to his or her past earnings. In 2012, monthly benefits for DI workers averaged $1,130, and the program paid out a total of $136.9 billion in benefits to workers and their disabled spouses and children (Tables 4.A4 and 5.A1.2, SSA 2013b).

Funded through general revenues, SSI is a smaller program. In 2012, disabled adults enrolled in SSI received an average of $536 per month, whereas children received a mean benefit of $621. Together, SSI's annual costs for disability benefits in 2012 were $44.1 billion (Tables 7.A1 and 7.A4, SSA 2013b). Because DI is self-financing, the need to keep predicted benefit payments in line with payroll-tax revenues limits the program's capacity for expansion. SSI, on the other hand, faces no such limit to its expansion, though rapid program growth invites congressional scrutiny.

3.3 The Administrative Structure

Early supporters of Social Security distinguished it from public assistance by pointing to its uniformity throughout the nation. Under public assistance, eligibility and benefit levels could and often did vary widely from one region to the next. Social Security, on the other hand, sought to treat beneficiaries the same, regardless of place of residence. Yet uniformity is more descriptive of Social Security's retirement pension than its disability programs, where there has always been a great deal of variation between states and levels of review.

A major source of disparity is the decentralization of the disability determination process. Although SSA field officers take the application for disability benefits, examiners for state agencies conduct the initial determination of disability. They also perform the continuing disability reviews, in which once every three years, the SSA re-examines the medical condition of beneficiaries to ensure that they are still disabled. Although the SSA pulls cases for review, state examiners decide whether the beneficiary's medical condition has improved enough for him or her to work. When making both their initial and review determinations, examiners rely heavily on the records provided by third-party treating physicians or, in some cases, consulting physicians hired to conduct independent assessments of a claimant's medical condition.

The SSA provides examiners with guidance, but wide differences between states remain. At first glance, these differences appear regional. State examiners in the Mississippi Delta and Appalachia regions consistently turn away a larger share of applicants than elsewhere. Yet these states also have high application rates, high incidences of functional limitations in the working-age population, and chronic underemployment and poverty. After controlling for the demographic, health, and economic characteristics of states, the Southern and Appalachian states are no longer distinctive, though state variations in disability outcomes persist (McCoy, Davis, and Hudson 1994; Strand 2002; Social Security Advisory Board 2006; Brault 2010).

The multilayer appeals process introduces additional fragmentation and variability. Two-thirds of beneficiaries enter the disability rolls at the state level. Unfavorable state decisions can be appealed to an administrative law judge (ALJ) in the SSA's Office of Disability Adjudication and Review. The ALJ's review is not bound by the findings of the state examiners, and by this stage, claimants generally secure legal representation. If the claimant is unhappy with the ALJ's decision, he or she can appeal the case to the SSA's Appeals Council, the final step in the administrative review process. Claimants who have exhausted administrative review can then appeal to the federal courts. At the initial state level, disability examiners award benefits to one-third of applicants, but on appeal, three-quarters of cases are awarded benefits. This provides denied claimants strong incentives to appeal initial denials, if they can afford to hire a lawyer and weather the protracted process. Yet fewer than half of all denied claimants appeal their decision beyond the state level. Thus, how successful claimants are often depends on how doggedly they pursue their cases (Coile 2003/2004; Social Security Advisory Board 2006; Tables 60 and 62, SSA 2011).

3.4 The Impact on Economic Well-Being

Disability is a pervasive contributor to poverty and insecurity. In 2010, 28 percent of working-aged individuals who were disabled lived below the poverty line, a rate that was more than twice that of the nondisabled. Half of all working-aged adults who live below the poverty line for at least a year suffer from a disability, whereas 2 out of every 5 families that are poor have a member with a disability. In 2010, the median income for households in which at least one working-aged member reported a health problem that limited functioning was only $25,550, compared to $58,736 for households in which no one suffered such restrictions (Fremstad 2009; U.S. Census 2011).

Because African Americans are vulnerable to disability and poverty, Social Security disability benefits are important forms of income support for them. Relative to whites, blacks are more likely to live below the poverty line, to be unemployed, to earn lower wages over their lifetime, and to suffer from poor health. Because DI benefits are based on past earnings, DI does not rectify disparities in income across racial groups. However, because their incidences of disability are higher and lifetime earnings are lower, blacks receive higher benefits relative to taxes than do whites, and they are overrepresented on the disability rolls. Although 13 percent of the working-aged population in 2010 was African American, blacks comprised 18 percent of DI enrollment. Similarly, although most SSI recipients are white, African Americans represent 28 percent of the adults and 46 percent of children enrolled in SSI (U.S. GAO 2003; Rupp et al. 2005/2006; Table 3. C7b, SSA 2013b).

DI and SSI do much to ameliorate the hardships associated with disability and poverty, but they do not meet the full measure of need. Without them, almost one-fifth of DI workers and half of adults and children enrolled in SSI would live below the poverty line. For half of all disabled workers, disability benefits comprise 75 percent or more of total personal income (Koenig and Rupp 2003/2004; Social Security Advisory Board 2006; Strand and Rupp 2007). However, maximum federal SSI payments equal only 75 percent of the poverty threshold for individuals and 90 percent for couples.

To makes ends meet, households with a disabled member must supplement disability payments with other sources of income, the most important of which is earnings from employment, and, consequently, poverty rates vary dramatically depending on family or household situation (Strand and Rupp 2007). Among households with a disabled member, earnings account for one-third to one-half of total income, but because families with two parents are better able to take advantage of employment opportunities than families with a single parent, only one-quarter of families receiving SSI that are headed by a couple live below the poverty line. Likewise, couple-headed families receiving SSI are over 3.5 times more likely to live 200 percent above the poverty line than single-parent families. By contrast, single-parent households are more likely to live in deep poverty (below 50 percent of the poverty line) and to remain poor even after taking into account disability payments because they are poorly positioned to take advantage of paid employment (Koenig and Rupp 2003/2004; Kearney, Grundmann, and Gallicchio 1994, 1995; Rupp et al. 2005/2006; DeCesaro and Hemmeter 2008).

Disability, therefore, is a disadvantage that DI and SSI mitigate but do not eliminate. Because earnings constitute the primary source of income for Americans regardless of their disability status, individuals who are disadvantaged in the labor market—because of their medical condition, their family situation, or some other reason—will face lower incomes than those who are not. Even after taking disability benefits into account, poverty rates for the disabled in the U.S. are higher than in Western Europe, Australia, and Canada, where income support guarantees are broader (Fremstad 2009).

4 CHANGE AND CHALLENGES

When lawmakers enacted DI in the 1950s, they expected the program to aid mostly workers with age-related infirmities, like heart disease and arthritis, or severe impairments in mobility. Yet today's beneficiary is a far cry from that which lawmakers envisioned; not only is he younger than disabled beneficiaries of the past, but he is also more likely to suffer from mental, behavioral, or musculoskeletal impairments that can be difficult to measure and verify. Although policy-makers have sought ways of integrating employment with income support, as the plights of disabled children and the able-bodied poor illustrate, meeting the contemporary challenges of disability policy requires thinking beyond disability benefits and disability rights.

4.1 Transitions to Adulthood for Disabled Children

Many childhood disorders are neither totally nor permanently disabling, and this is particularly the case with deficits in cognition, emotional control, or behavior—the most common childhood impairments. Indeed, with proper care, some impaired children will eventually "catch up" with their age peers or learn to adapt to their disorders. The least functionally impaired of disabled children might even go on to lead economically productive lives as adults (U.S. Surgeon General 1999; Erkulwater 2006). Adequately preparing disabled children for adulthood, however, requires that SSA administrators track children as they mature and offer support services to those who are capable of eventually moving from SSI to employment. Yet because the SSA has its hands full simply conducting initial determinations of disability in a timely manner, re-evaluation and referral to support services rarely occur once a child enrolls in SSI (Wen 2010).

Without follow-up and support, teenagers enrolled in SSI as young children face a rocky transition to adulthood. Many are reluctant to accept part-time work even though they are able because SSI benefits provide a crucial and reliable source of income for their families. But because the adult and children's standards of disability are not the same, growing up on SSI does not guarantee growing old on SSI. Out of every 5 children who qualify for SSI as minors, 2 do not qualify as adults at age 18. For children with emotional, learning, or behavioral disorders, the odds are even worse; 2 out of every 3 are rejected, even though little provision has been made to ensure that they are prepared for a life on their own. Although the SSA has tried to create programs that encourage teenagers on SSI to transition to work, few families know about the programs or make use of them. Consequently, many children who leave SSI as young adults have difficulty adjusting to life on their own. Although the majority find work, their incomes remain low, often lower than their SSI payments, and half never complete high school (Loprest and Wittenberg 2005; Davies, Rupp, and Wittenburg 2009; Hemmeter, Kauff, and Wittenburg 2009; Wen 2010).

4.2 Neither Jobs Nor Support

Since 1980, policy-makers have sought to increase employment among the disabled through financial incentives, trial work periods, and the legal right to workplace accommodations. They have also added a patchwork of transitional services, such as health care, rehabilitation, and case management. Still, in any given year, fewer than one percent of disabled beneficiaries ever return to work, much less earn enough to leave the Social Security disability rolls (Rich 2011). Nevertheless, snapshots of the disability rolls present a distorted picture of beneficaries' work efforts. Workers beset by a medical condition that interferes with employment wait, on average, 7 to 8 years before filing for disability benefits (Burkhauser, Butler, and Weathers 2001/2002). Once on the rolls, many remain committed to work. Among DI beneficiaries tracked for a decade after entering the rolls, one-third found employment at some point during the 10-year period. One in 5 worked while receiving benefits, and 7 percent earned enough to spend some time off the rolls (Lui and Stapleton 2010). Persuading Social Security disability beneficiaries to return to work, however, is not nearly as daunting as helping them maintain employment. Although a significant number of beneficiaries can and do return to work, their employment rarely affords them a level of job security and economic well-being that allows them to forego disability benefits over the long run. In fact, among people with disabilities who already work, one-third are underemployed (Fogg, Harrington, and McMahon 2010).

At the same time that disability rights and work incentives have failed to provide remunerative employment to the disabled, recent reforms have scaled back the safety net and made citizens more vulnerable to economic dislocation with profound implications for disability benefits policy. In 1996, Congress greatly restricted benefits to low-income families with children by mandating that parents, even those with preschool children, work and by limiting families to TANF for only 2 years at any one spell and 5 years over an entire lifetime. By contrast, other than the possibility of a periodic medical re-evaluation, SSI has no behavioral requirements or time limits. Moreover, SSI benefits are generous when compared to cash payments under TANF. In half the states, the maximum TANF grant for a family of three does not come close to matching the average SSI grant to a single disabled child (Stapleton et al. 2001/2002; U.S. House of Representatives, Committee on Ways and Means 2009). As a result, efforts to tighten TANF have driven up applications for SSI given the similarity in the populations the two programs serve. Many low-income parents suffer from mental health problems or learning disorders or they have a child who does, and this is particularly true of TANF recipients who fail to transition successfully to work (Acs and Loprest 1999). Therefore, because of the porous boundaries between disability and ability, absent eliminating disability benefits outright, policymakers cannot dramatically reduce welfare spending overall without confronting head-on shortcomings in the labor market for disadvantaged workers (Nadel, Wamhoff, and Wiseman 2003/2004; Wamhoff and Wiseman 2005/2006).

Ultimately, the challenges that DI and SSI face grow out of policy-makers' inability to reconcile our conflicting attitudes toward need and work, social and personal responsibility. In an environment of uncertain job prospects and tenuous income support programs, DI and SSI have evolved into a shadow safety net for many Americans and their families. Although lawmakers have tried to facilitate the movement of the disabled into the workplace, disability rights and government services remain poorly coordinated with a steady supply of remunerative jobs. Addressing these policy challenges while remaining compassionate toward the disabled requires more than a mere tinkering with Social Security; it requires a wholesale rethinking of our obligations toward people with disabilities.

REFERENCES

*Indicates recommending reading

Acs, Gregory, and Pamela Loprest. 1999. "The Effects of Disabilities on Exits from AFDC." *Journal of Policy Analysis and Management* 18 (1): 28–49.
*Berkowitz, Edward D. 1987. *Disabled Policy: America's Programs for the Handicapped.* Cambridge: Cambridge University Press.
Board of Trustees for the Federal Old-Age and Survivors Insurance and Federal Disability Insurance Trust Funds. 2013. *2013 Annual Report.* Washington, DC: GPO.
Brault, Matthew W. 2010. "Disability Among the Working Age Population: 2008 and 2009." In *American Community Survey Briefs.* Washington, DC: U.S. Census Bureau.
Burkhauser, Richard V., J. S. Butler, and Robert R. Weathers II. 2001/2002. "How Policy Variables Influence the Timing of Applications for Social Security Disability Insurance." *Social Security Bulletin* 64 (1): 52–83.
Coile, Courtney. 2003/2004. "Errors in the Social Security Disability Awards Process." *NBER Bulletin on Aging and Health* Winter, Issue 6. http://www.nber.org/aginghealth/winter04/winter04.pdf.
Davies, Paul S., Kalman Rupp, and David Wittenburg. 2009. "A Life-Cycle Perspective on the Transition to Adulthood among Children Receiving Supplemental Security Income Payments." *Journal of Vocational Rehabilitation* 30 (3): 133–151.
DeCesaro, Anne, and Jeffrey Hemmeter. 2008. "Characteristics of Noninstitutionalized DI and SSI Program Participants." *Research and Statistics Note*, 2008-02. Baltimore, MD: Social Security Administration, Office of Policy, Office of Research, Evaluation, and Statistics.
Derthick, Martha. 1979. *Policymaking for Social Security.* Washington, DC: Brookings Institution Press.
*Derthick, Martha. 1990. *Agency under Stress: The Social Security Administration in American Government.* Washington, DC: Brookings Institution Press.
*Erkulwater, Jennifer L. 2006. *Disability Rights and the American Social Safety Net.* Ithaca, NY: Cornell University Press.
Findley, Patricia A., and Usha Sambamorthi. 2004. "Employment and Disability: Evidence from the 1996 Medical Expenditures Panel Survey." *Journal of Occupational Rehabilitation.* 14 (1): 1–11.
Fogg, Neeta P., Paul E. Harrington, and Brian T. McMahon. 2010. "The Impact of the Great Recession upon the Unemployment of Americans with Disabilities." *Journal of Vocational Rehabilitation* 33 (3): 193–202.
Fremstad, Shawn. 2009. *Half in Ten: Why Taking Disability into Account Is Essential to Reducing Income Poverty and Expanding Economic Inclusion.* Washington, DC: Center for Economic and Policy Research.
Hemmeter, Jeffrey, Jacqueline Kauff, and David Wittenburg. 2009. "Changing Circumstances: Experiences of Child SSI Recipients Before and After Their Age-18 Redetermination for Adult Benefits." *Journal of Vocational Rehabilitation* 30 (3): 201–221.

Kearney, John R., Herman F. Grundmann, and Salvatore J. Gallicchio. 1994. "The Influence of Social Security Benefits and SSI Payments on the Poverty Status of Children." *Social Security Bulletin* 57 (2): 27–43.

Kearney, John R., Herman F. Grundmann, and Salvatore J. Gallicchio. 1995. "The Influence of OASDI and SSI Payments on the Poverty Status of Families with Children." *Social Security Bulletin* 58 (3): 3–14.

Koenig, Melissa, and Kalman Rupp. 2003/2004. "SSI Recipients in Households and Families with Multiple Recipients: Prevalence and Poverty Outcomes." *Social Security Bulletin* 65 (2): 14–27.

Loprest, Pamela, and David Wittenburg. 2005. "Choices, Challenges, and Options: Child SSI Recipients Preparing for the Transition to Adult Life." Washington, DC: Urban Institute.

Lui, Su, and David Stapleton. 2010. "How Many SSDI Beneficiaries Leave the Rolls for Work? More Than You Might Think." Disability Policy Research Brief, No. 10-01. Princeton, NJ: Center for Studying Disability Policy, Mathematica Policy Research.

McCoy, John L., Miles Davis, and Russell E. Hudson. 1994. "Geographic Patterns of Disability in the United States. *Social Security Bulletin* 57 (1): 25–30.

Nadel, Mark, Steve Wamhoff, and Michael Wiseman. 2003/2004. "Disability, Welfare Reform, and Supplemental Security Income." *Social Security Bulletin* 65 (3): 14–30.

Quadagno, Jill. 1988. "From Old-Age Assistance to Supplemental Security Income: The Political Economy of Relief in the South, 1935–1972." In Margaret Weir, Ann Shola Orloff, and Theda Skocpol, eds., *The Politics of Social Policy in the United States*. Princeton, NJ: Princeton University Press, 235–264.

Quadagno, Jill. 2005. *One Nation Uninsured: Why the U.S. Has No National Health Insurance*. New York: Oxford University Press.

Rich, Motoko. 2011. "Disabled, but Looking for Work." *New York Times*, April 6, B1, http://www.nytimes.com/2011/04/07/business/economy/07disabled.html?pagewanted=all.

Rupp, Kalman, Paul S. Davies, Chad Newcomb, Howard Iams, Carrie Becker, Shanti Mulpuru, Stephen Ressler, Kathleen Romig, and Baylor Miller. 2005/2006. "A Profile of Children with Disabilities Receiving SSI: Highlights from the National Survey of SSI Children and Families." *Social Security Bulletin* 66 (2): 21–48.

Rupp, Kalman, and Gerald F. Riley. 2011. "Longitudinal Patterns of Participation in the Social Security Disability Insurance and Supplemental Security Income Programs for People with Disabilities." *Social Security Bulletin* 71 (2): 25–51.

Russell, Marta. 2002. "What Disability Civil Rights Cannot Do: Employment and Political Economy." *Disability and Society* 17 (2): 117–135.

Scotch, Richard K. 2001. *From Good Will to Civil Rights: Transforming Federal Disability Policy*. 2nd ed. Philadelphia: Temple University Press.

Social Security Advisory Board. 2006. *Disability Decision Making: Data and Materials*. Washington, DC: Social Security Advisory Board.

SSA (Social Security Administration). 2012. *Annual Statistical Report on the Social Security Disability Insurance Program, 2011*. Baltimore, MD: Social Security Administration.

SSA. 2013a. *SSI Annual Statistical Report, 2012*. Baltimore, MD: Social Security Administration.

SSA. 2013b. *Annual Statistical Supplement, 2012*. Baltimore, MD: Social Security Administration.

SSA, Office of the Chief Actuary. 2013. "Selected Data From Social Security's Disability Program." http://www.ssa.gov/oact/STATS/dib-g1.html.

Strand, Alexander. 2002. "Social Security Disability Programs: Assessing the Variation in Allowance Rates." ORES Working Paper Series, No. 98. Washington, DC: Social Security Administration, Office of Policy.

Strand, Alexander, and Kalman Rupp. 2007. "Disabled Workers and the Indexing of Social Security Benefits." *Social Security Bulletin* 67 (4): 21–50.

Stapleton, David C., Richard V. Burkhauser, and Andrew J. Houtenville. 2004. *Has the Employment Rate of People with Disabilities Declined?* Ithaca, NY: Rehabilitation Research and Training Center for Economic Research on Employment. Policy for Persons with Disabilities, Cornell University.

Stapleton, David C., David C. Wittenburg, Michael E. Fishman, and Gina A. Livermore. 2001/2002. "Transitions from AFDC to SSI Before Welfare Reform." *Social Security Bulletin* 64 (1): 84–114.

*Stone, Deborah A. 1984. *Disabled State*. Philadelphia: Temple University Press.

U.S. Census Bureau. 2011. *Income, Poverty, and Health Insurance Coverage in the United States: 2010*. Washington, DC.

U.S. Surgeon General. 1999. *Mental Health: A Report of the Surgeon General*. Washington, DC: Department of Health and Human Services.

U.S. General Accounting Office. 1999. *Adults with Severe Disabilities: Federal and State Approaches for Personal Care and Other Services*, HEHS-99-101.

U.S. General Accounting Office. 2003. *Social Security and Minorities: Earnings, Disability Incidence, and Mortality Are Key Factors That Influence Taxes Paid and Benefits Received*, GAO-03-387.

U.S. House of Representatives, Committee on Ways and Means. 2009. *Background Material and Data on Programs within the Jurisdiction of the Committee on Ways and Means*. Washington, DC: GPO.

Wamhoff, Steve, and Michael Wiseman. 2005/2006. "The TANF/SSI Connection." *Social Security Bulletin* 66 (4): 21–36.

Wen, Patricia. 2010. "The Other Welfare," 3-part series. *Boston Globe*, December 12, 13, 14. http://www.boston.com/news/health/specials/New_Welfare/.

CHAPTER 25

....

WORKERS' COMPENSATION

....

LESLIE I. BODEN AND EMILY A. SPIELER

1 INTRODUCTION

....

WORK involves risk. No matter how strong the commitment to safety, no matter how aggressive the regulatory system, workers get injured or sick at work in every work environment and in every country. This chapter describes the U.S. system of workers' compensation, which provides medical coverage for work-related injuries and illnesses, and cash benefits to workers who are injured or made ill by their work.

The chapter is organized as follows. In the initial sections, we provide a basic description of the workers' compensation system in the United States. This includes a brief history of the U.S. system, the legal framework and some of the key elements of this framework. This overview is intended to provide readers with an accurate but elementary understanding of the system. Because workers' compensation is largely state based and is not governed by any federal guidelines, this is more challenging than one might anticipate. The description here attempts to summarize the consistent elements among the state systems and to identify the main elements that differ from one state to another.

Next, we address some themes that have emerged in the provision of benefits to injured or ill workers. We focus on issues that are primarily of concern to injured workers. These include exclusions of many workers with work-related injuries and illnesses from the systems, both as a result of failure to file and denial of claims; the inadequacy of benefits; the labyrinthine nature of the systems, resulting in their inability to provide efficient, fair, consistent, and transparent justice to applicants for benefits; the impact of public campaigns against worker fraud; and the legal and institutional context of workers' compensation in the United States.

Finally, we turn to the key challenges and barriers to addressing the problems in the U.S. workers' compensation system, including political and economic issues.

2 The Basics of U.S. Workers' Compensation

2.1 History

Industrialization in the late 19th and early 20th centuries brought high rates of injury and death in the manufacturing, railroad, and mining sectors. With few exceptions, workers and their families bore the costs of work-related injuries and deaths. For most injured workers, there was no meaningful remedy in common law. In legal cases, injured workers had the burden to prove that their employers were negligent, that their injuries were work-related, and that the employers' negligence caused these injuries. Employers were able to defend themselves through use of powerful legal defenses: that the injured worker had assumed the risks of the workplace; that the injury was due to a fellow worker's negligence; or that the worker's own negligence was a contributory cause. As a result, most disabled workers and their families depended largely on their own resources and assistance from relatives, friends, and charities.

By 1910, some efforts had been made to provide better means of compensation to injured workers and their families. Larger corporations established private compensation schemes, and several states and the federal government enacted employers' liability acts that limited employers' common-law defenses.

These trends led to increased costs and greater uncertainty for employers, while retaining high levels of uncertainty and low likelihood of compensation for injured workers. At times, however, injured workers received substantial compensation from law suits in the courts. During the Progressive Era, a broad coalition of social reformers, unions, major corporations, and associations of manufacturers threw support behind social legislation that would provide greater certainty for both workers and employers (Fishback and Kantor 1998). Contemporaneous interpretations of the U.S. Constitution meant that social legislation had to be passed at the state, rather than federal, level. Political pressure gave rise to the passage of the first workers' compensation (originally called workmen's compensation) law in New York State. Although this initial law was held to be unconstitutional, soon the legal interpretations—and the tide—turned. By 1920, 43 states had passed compensation statutes. Mississippi was the last state to establish a workers' compensation system in 1948.

All of these laws met the goal of providing increased levels of certainty to both employers and workers. The laws shielded employers from law suits and, therefore, protected them from liability costs that had been rising for years (Weinstein 1968; Moss 1996; Fishback and Kantor 1998). Employers purchased coverage, most commonly from private insurers, although several states created exclusively state-run insurance programs.

At the same time, all the laws gave covered workers access to benefits if their injuries were caused by accidents and arose "out of and in the course of employment." Over time, states adopted administrative procedures for adjudicating disputes, with less formal procedural and evidentiary requirements than were required in courts of law. In general, a liberal standard was used to interpret evidence, giving the worker the benefit of the doubt when evidence of work-relatedness was contested or unclear. The employer was expected to "take the worker as he found him [or her]." If a work-related injury or illness contributed to a worker's disability, a worker's non-work-related health condition would not bar receipt of workers' compensation benefits.

Nevertheless, the early workers' compensation acts covered only a small proportion of workers. In 1913, six of the 22 states with workers' compensation laws limited coverage to hazardous industries (U.S. Bureau of Labor Statistics 1913). Due to initial state constitutional interpretations, many of the early laws created voluntary systems in which employers could choose whether to participate. A decision to opt out meant, however, that the employer would be liable for negligently caused injuries without the protection of the common-law defenses. Elective coverage persisted for decades: in 1972, there were 19 states that still retained optional coverage (National Commission 1972).

Before 1972, benefits were generally quite low. Maximum weekly benefits were set by statute and, therefore, difficult to change. As a consequence, maximum benefits as a proportion of average wages tended to fall over time. In 1972, only 13 states had maximum benefits that automatically increased with the state average weekly wage (National Commission 1973).

Occupational diseases were largely uncompensated as a result of outright exclusions or various technical aspects of the laws. For example, statutes of limitations did not allow for compensation for latent diseases like lung cancer, which could manifest themselves decades after exposure. "Ordinary diseases of life" like hearing loss were often explicitly excluded from coverage, even if caused by workplace exposures.

Faced with rising criticism regarding the adequacy of the existing state-based workers' compensation programs, Congress created the National Commission on State Workmen's Compensation Laws as part of the broader Occupational Safety and Health Act of 1970. The 1972 report of the Commission recommended minimum standards for all programs and identified major objectives, including broad coverage of employees and of work-related conditions as well as substantial protection against interruption of income. States were encouraged to meet these recommendations by the implicit threat that Congress would legislate federal standards or fully federalize workers' compensation if states failed to comply.

Although many states fell short of the Commission's recommendations, widespread changes in the state systems followed, expanding mandatory coverage, increasing benefits, and providing for automatic increases in weekly benefits. Beginning in the late 1980s, rapidly rising employer costs—in part attributed to the expansions of coverage that had followed the National Commission's report—led to a political backlash in many states. By 1997, most state legislatures had adopted statutory amendments that limited eligibility for compensation, resulting in a reduction of the number of claims filed and approved, the amount that would be paid to individual workers, and the aggregate costs of the system. Since 1997, this trend has continued, and legislation restricting the availability of benefits has passed in Florida, West Virginia, California, Missouri, Oklahoma, and South Carolina, among others. In California, Missouri, Oklahoma, and West Virginia, the changes were particularly sweeping in scope. For example, in California, lost-time claim frequency fell by 36 percent from 2004 to 2006 (WCIRB 2008). In addition, since 1990, well over half of state systems have strengthened provisions addressing fraud, often focusing on alleged worker fraud (Helvacian and Corro 1999).

These changes have generally resulted in reductions in overall costs to employers and insurers, reflecting a decrease in both the number of compensable claims and the cost per claim. Costs for employers declined from a peak of $2.18 per $100 of payroll in 1990 to $1.30 per $100 of payroll in 2009; benefit costs peaked in 1991 and 1992 at $1.65 per $100 of payroll and declined to $1.00 in 2009 and 2010 (Sengupta, Baldwin, and Reno 2013). In this report, employer costs and benefit payments are measured differently, so they are not directly comparable (see Sengupta, Baldwin, and Reno 2013, 32–36). Nevertheless, in privately insured workers' compensation systems, employer costs are typically substantially higher than benefit payments.

2.2 Workers' Compensation Today

Workers' compensation continues to be primarily a state-based program, despite federal involvement in almost every other U.S. social program (Howard 2002). All states now require employers to provide workers' compensation coverage, with two exceptions. Texas has never had a mandatory program for workers' compensation. In 2013, Oklahoma adopted legislation that allows employers to "opt out" of the pre-existing mandatory system.

Despite the continuing lack of federal guidelines or requirements, state programs share some basic similarities. Every program provides coverage for conditions "arising out of" and "in the course of" employment that are the result of traumatic events, generally referred to as "accidents." Every program provides temporary wage replacement benefits when an injured worker is unable to work and additional cash benefits to compensate for the permanent effects of the injury or illness. These benefits rarely provide full replacement for lost wages; the benefits are not subject to income taxation. Every program provides coverage for medical services related to a compensable work-related condition. Benefits are also paid to dependent survivors of fatally injured workers.

Coverage

Coverage must be viewed from three vantage points:

First, which employers participate in the system? Although all states except Texas and Oklahoma now require employers to obtain workers' compensation insurance to cover their employees, gaps in coverage still remain. For example, in many states, employers only enter the mandatory system if they have at least 3 to 5 employees.

Second, which workers are covered? Even when an employer has obtained insurance coverage, certain categories of workers may not be covered. Most importantly, independent contractors are excluded, as are many household employees and agricultural workers. Workers in the underground economy are, by definition, outside the system.

Third, what disabilities or conditions are covered? Although every state provides benefits for traumatic injuries that occur at work, coverage is much more variable for conditions that involve latency periods, such as occupationally caused cancers; conditions that evolve over time, such as carpal tunnel syndrome; or conditions that are caused by both work and nonwork factors. Even when such conditions are not explicitly excluded from coverage, difficulties in demonstrating work-relatedness often are substantial barriers to compensation.

Benefit Structure

Workers' compensation systems provide medical care, cash ("indemnity") benefits for temporary and permanent disability, and rehabilitation benefits.

Medical benefits: If a worker suffers from a compensable condition, then workers' compensation provides full coverage of medical costs associated with the injury or illness. This has been particularly important in the United States, where many workers still did not have health insurance in 2012. In fact, 77 percent of all workers' compensation cases involve only medical payments, often for minor injuries that involve little or no time away from work. These medical-only claims represent only a small fraction (8 percent) of the total costs of the program (Sengupta, Baldwin, and Reno 2013).

On the other hand, the medical costs for the entire program are quite high, and the overall level of these costs has risen dramatically in recent years, to $28.9 billion in 2009, the cost of medical care exceeded that of cash benefits paid to workers for the first time (Sengupta, Baldwin, and Reno 2013). In response, states have initiated a variety of programs that attempt to hold back medical cost increases, including fee schedules and restrictions on the doctors who may treat compensable injuries.

Temporary disability benefits: Cash benefits are provided to workers for temporary periods of disability, generally after a waiting period of three to seven days. After a period of 7 to 21 days off work, benefits for the waiting period are paid retroactively. The benefits are paid until the worker has reached "maximum medical improvement," has returned to full-time work, or has reached the statutory duration maximum. The majority of workers' compensation cases that involve cash benefits fit in this category and are resolved reasonably easily (Sengupta, Baldwin, and Reno 2013).

All states provide for temporary total disability benefits (TTD). These benefits are typically set at two-thirds of the pre-injury wage, with a maximum benefit level and a maximum duration, both of which vary by state. The maximum level is, most frequently, tied to the state's average weekly wage, resulting in lower levels of wage replacement for higher-income workers. As of 2014, the maximum weekly benefit varied from a low of $449 in Mississippi to a high of $1,543 in Iowa (Tanabe 2014).

During the recovery period, the worker may return to modified work or work fewer hours. If this results in reduced earnings, temporary partial disability (TPD) benefits are provided in many states. These benefits are generally set at two-thirds of the difference between the postinjury and pre-injury wage.

Permanent partial disability benefits (PPD): When an injured worker has recovered maximally from injury but still has a permanent impairment, the worker may be entitled to permanent disability benefits. PPD benefits are paid to workers with impairments that do not completely limit the ability to work. This is the most costly (66 percent of total costs) and contentious benefit type in workers' compensation (Sengupta, Baldwin, and Reno 2013). State systems vary tremendously in the availability of these benefits, the methodology for assessment, and the amount that is paid to workers.

States use several basic approaches in determining eligibility and amount of PPD benefits. Scheduled payments are specified in statutes, so that a worker will receive a predetermined benefit amount for loss of use of a particular body part (such as hands or feet) or function (such as vision or hearing). In addition, unscheduled PPD payments are based on one of the following approaches: 19 states determine PPD payments using a medically determined impairment rating; 12 states use a loss of earning capacity approach, which involves a forecast of the impact of the impairment on future earnings; 10 states calculate actual "wage loss," based on the difference between current and pre-injury earnings; and 9 states use a bifurcated approach, in which PPD benefits depend on the worker's employment status at the time of assessment (Sengupta, Baldwin, and Reno 2013). Most states place a limit on the length of time that unscheduled PPD benefits can be paid, typically between 300 and 500 weeks (Tanabe 2014).

Permanent total disability benefits (PTD): If an injury or illness leaves a worker permanently unable to be gainfully employed, the worker may then be eligible for permanent total disability benefits. In fact, these benefits are rarely awarded, as the level of proof required to show inability to work is very high. The resistance to awarding PTD benefits is also rooted in their costs: lifetime benefits (or benefits that run until eligibility for social security retirement benefits) can be very expensive. The insurer must reserve sufficient funds to pay the life of the claim at the time the award is made. These claims, therefore, meet strong resistance from both insurers and employers, resulting in tightening of eligibility standards and duration limits so that benefits may expire before the worker reaches full retirement age. Many workers in this category end up in the federal Social Security Disability Insurance (SSDI) system.

Fatalities: If a worker dies as a result of a work-related injury or illness, an amount is set aside for burial costs, and income benefits are typically paid to the worker's dependent spouse (until remarriage) and children during the age of dependency. If the worker dies without dependents, only burial expenses are paid.

Both PTD and fatality claims often involve many years of benefit payments. The costs of these claims can be very high compared to other cash benefits. Although these claims collectively represent only 0.7 percent of claims involving cash benefits, they are 10.4 percent of benefit payments (Sengupta, Reno, and Burton 2011).

Vocational rehabilitation benefits: Virtually all state systems provide for vocational rehabilitation benefits. Determination of eligibility for these benefits varies, but typically treating physicians and the workers' compensation agency can refer injured workers for a range of services that are designed to assist in reentry into the workforce. In addition to the continuation of cash benefits, sometimes beyond the general maximum duration, vocational rehabilitation provides funding for retraining and associated costs.

Financing and experience rating

Workers' compensation programs in the United States are financed directly by employers and indirectly by employees, as a result of reduced wages (Gruber and Krueger 1994). In general, employers must demonstrate that they have obtained the required coverage. Depending on the state, this can be done by purchasing private insurance; purchasing insurance from funds that are administered by the state; or maintaining self-insurance, assuming the employer can obtain the necessary approval from the state regulatory authority by demonstrating financial ability to cover the risk. In recent years, there has also been the growth of 'high deductible' policies, so that employers pay the initial costs and insurers pick up the remainder. Only four states currently offer insurance exclusively through a state fund; there is no private insurance market within those states.

In general, rates are established based upon the experience—the claims costs and the associated administrative expenses—for a risk class, which could be an industry group or an occupation group. An individual employer's rates within a class may vary, depending on the size of the employer and the loss experience in the preceding period. This variation is referred to as experience rating (Thomason, Schmidle, and Burton 2001).

Private insurance carriers compete for market share among employers by offering rate discounts, premium rebates, and additional services, including loss management advice regarding safety or disability management programs. Rates are highly regulated in some states and more market driven in others.

The overall cost of workers' compensation insurance varies based on several factors including how many claims are paid; the cost per claim of cash benefits; the cost of medical care associated with compensable injuries and illnesses; the administrative costs of the insurer; administration costs that are charged by the responsible state agency; marketing costs, legal expenses, and profit for the insurance carrier; and the effects of investment of premiums. As noted earlier, the cost of medical care accounted for 50 percent of the total benefit costs in 2009. Thus, the amount that is paid in cash benefits to workers is well under half the total cost of insurance to employers.

Federal Programs

Several federal programs cover specific categories of workers or diseases. Federal employees are covered by the Federal Employees' Compensation Act, which provides similar benefits to the state systems. Reacting to gaps in state systems, Congress has passed several laws to address particular occupational diseases, most notably the Black Lung Benefits Act for coal workers' pneumoconiosis (originally passed in 1969 as part of comprehensive coal mine health and safety legislation), and the Energy Employees Occupational Illness Compensation Program Act of 2000 for diseases resulting from work by civilians in the nuclear weapons industry. Separate federal programs cover longshore and harbor workers, employees of overseas contractors with the U.S. government, and railroad workers. In general, however, most workers have been covered—or not covered—by state workers' compensation statutes.

3 Emerging Themes

Workers' compensation programs in the United States are a continual source of political dispute and are under constant pressure in state legislatures. Many recent legislative changes have restricted the availability of benefits to injured workers. In this section, we focus on several themes related to this trend: (1) many injured workers never receive workers' compensation benefits; (2) when workers do receive benefits, they are frequently inadequate; (3) the system can be both opaque and demeaning to injured workers; and (4) allegations of fraud and malingering are used to argue for reduced access and benefits.

3.1 (Mis)match between injuries and awards of benefits

It is critical to understand that many workers with work-related injuries and illnesses never collect any benefits under these programs. Many studies have found that the number of people receiving workers' compensation benefits is substantially lower than the number of actual injuries and illnesses (Spieler and Burton 2012 and their references). Why is this true?

First, as noted earlier, some workers may not be eligible for compensation. One category—independent contractors—is on the rise. Many workers who are excluded from coverage, including agricultural workers, are employed in marginal but dangerous sectors of the economy. Being ineligible for benefits certainly does not mean that their work is free from hazards.

Second, many workers do not apply for benefits, although they might qualify. The reasons are multiple and complex. They may be unfamiliar with the filing procedures and eligibility requirements, or they may think that their injuries are not sufficiently severe to justify filing. For diseases, particularly latent diseases or conditions that worsen over time, workers may be unaware that the condition is work related—and their physicians may not know it, or, if they do, they may not provide them with essential information (Azaroff et al. 2002).

In other instances, workers know about the availability of compensation but choose not to file for benefits. They may fear retaliation by the employer. In some cases, workers have heard about negative experiences with the compensation system or retaliation within the workplace from co-workers or others. Unionized workers, who have far stronger job protections against retaliation, are more likely to file claims (Hirsch, MacPherson, and Dumond 1997). Management "behavioral safety" programs often focus on changing the behavior of individual workers rather than on environmental conditions. These include safety-incentive programs that discourage the filing of claims or reports of injuries to both employers and government agencies. Because employers pay for the program and insurance rates may reflect claims activity, there is a strong incentive to keep claim filing down (see Azaroff, Levenstein, and Wegman 2002 for more specifics).

This cluster of issues is also related to the stigmatization of disabled workers who file for benefits. The news media, as well as the insurance and economics literature, regularly disparage injured workers, suggesting that they file claims inappropriately or malinger in order to prolong cash benefits (Baker 1996; Dembe and Boden 2000). Consequently, injured workers may avoid workers' compensation entirely in order to avoid being portrayed in this manner.

Even if a worker files for benefits, many barriers remain. In recent years, well over half of state legislatures have restricted the availability of benefits, responding to agitation by employers and insurers to reduce their costs. These include states with large populations, such as California and New York, and states with dangerous industries such as West Virginia. Some states have changed the basic interpretation of the foundational statute from a liberal to a strict standard (e.g., Missouri, West Virginia), or required a claimant to prove the case by "clear and convincing" evidence (e.g., Alabama). In 1994, the U.S. Supreme Court held that federal claimants must prove compensation cases by a "preponderance of the evidence" (Dir., Office of Workers' Comp. Programs, Dep't of Labor v. Greenwich Collieries 1994). These changes move away from the historical assumption that gave injured workers the benefit of the doubt. As a result, injured workers' evidence must be much stronger if they are to prevail and receive benefits (Boden and Spieler 2010; Spieler and Burton 2012).

Other changes similarly restrict the availability of benefits. Some state courts and legislatures have moved to limit compensation for injuries involving aggravation of pre-existing conditions by creating a new requirement that work be the "major" or "predominant" cause or the "major contributing factor" of any disability. This changes the traditional rule that an injury was compensable even if the workplace only contributed to the condition. Conditions related to aging are now more often excluded from compensation systems as well.

All workers' compensation claims require proof of disability and work-related causation, but this proof can be difficult to obtain in complex cases. This is particularly true for occupational diseases and musculoskeletal conditions. Increasingly, state systems do not consider lay witnesses or the testimony of a worker's own treating physician to be sufficient. Few experts may be willing to support workers' claims; physicians also report significant pressure from employers and insurers to avoid linking diagnosis to work causation (GAO 2009).

Finally, workers with chronic occupational diseases face particular burdens in demonstrating that their illnesses arose "out of and in the course of employment." Medical and epidemiologic knowledge may be insufficient to distinguish clearly a disease of occupational origin from one of non-occupational origin. Estimates of failure to compensate occupational diseases range as high as 97 percent (Leigh and Robbins 2004).

3.2 (In)adequacy of income based benefits in awarded claims

The National Commission saw benefit adequacy as a primary objective for workers' compensation programs. In its landmark 1972 Report, the Commission set specific benchmarks for temporary total and permanent total disability benefits: programs should replace two-thirds of pretax lost earnings or 80 percent of after-tax lost earnings. Later, the Council of State Governments (1974) developed a consensus Model Act that suggested that benefits should replace 55 to 65 percent of pretax earnings losses for permanent partial disabilities.

By these measures, studies of benefit adequacy suggest that workers' compensation benefits often fall short of the mark (a description of these studies can be found in Hunt [2004]). In five states (California, Oregon, New Mexico, Washington, and Wisconsin), researchers found that a sharp drop in earnings occurred at the time of injury, followed by a long-term loss of about 30 percent that persists for many years—perhaps until retirement. For permanent partial disabilities, cash benefits replaced from 29 percent to 46 percent of before-tax earnings during the 10 years after injury (Reville et al. 2001). Because virtually all cash benefit payments cease during that 10-year period, lifetime average replacement rates are certain to be much lower.

A number of factors contribute to inadequate benefits. Statutory limits on weekly amounts and duration certainly affect adequacy. Permanent partial disability benefits are tied in many states to levels of impairment, rather than to loss of earnings; increasingly, the impairment is measured using the AMA *Guides to the Evaluation of Permanent Impairment*, which do not measure work limitations and may even understate functional impairment (Spieler et al. 2000). Even if they fully recover, workers whose injuries lead to substantial time off from work often suffer long-term earnings losses (Boden and Galizzi 1999). Promotion opportunities may be missed, the pre-injury job may be lost, and potential future employers may be less willing to hire them.

Because only a handful of recent studies address benefit adequacy, a number of questions remain: Have replacement rates been low for a long time, or have they been rising or falling in recent decades? Do states that have not been studied have similar replacement rates, or are they higher or lower? It seems very likely that workers' compensation benefits in the United States do not meet the standards of adequacy cited earlier, particularly for workers with long-term disabilities. The result is that other public and private benefit programs, and the workers' families and communities, are likely picking up the costs of occupational injury and disease.

3.3 (In)efficient and labyrinthine process

The workers' compensation system performs reasonably well for workers with uncomplicated traumatic injuries that are unquestionably work-related and that heal quickly. These workers typically receive appropriate health care and cash benefits once the waiting period has passed, and they return to their employers with workplace benefits—and long-term seniority and wages—intact. In most states, these cases are resolved quickly and without significant controversy.

However, for many injured workers, the system presents a quite different picture. For those with injuries that have complex causation, involve substantial medical treatment, permanent disability, or long periods of temporary disability, the system can be difficult to navigate. The issues of proof, as noted earlier, create enormous barriers to compensation. In addition, the claims process itself can be confusing at best and humiliating at worst. Multiple hearings and delays in obtaining medical evidence can force workers into a state of uncertainty and doubt.

Delays can leave injured workers without income and without money to pay for needed medical care. This creates pressure to settle claims, providing workers with a reduced lump sum payment instead of a guarantee of ongoing medical care and weekly benefits. These settlements have not been studied adequately. Anecdotally, it appears that workers in many states are pressured to accept a discounted amount on the claim, including the cost of medical care, and then may be cut off from further access to the system.

Studies have found that as few as 10 percent of injured workers feel that their overall experience with the system was positive (Imershein 1994). Workers complain that they are treated with disrespect by insurers and that they are given insufficient information in order to file and pursue claims (Imershein 1994; Sum and Stock 1996; Strunin and Boden 2004; Wall, Morrissey, and Ogloff 2009). Complicated processes often require representation by attorneys who may be inadequately responsive to their own clients, in part because they handle large numbers of claims.

Many injured workers report feeling stigmatized, humiliated, and doubted by their employers and the insurance carrier (Sum 1994). Workers also believe that they are mistrusted by medical providers (Strunin and Boden 2004). At the same time, medical providers report that they are pressured by employers and insurers to find that injuries are not work-related (GAO 2009).

3.4 Fraud

Many states have mounted legislative efforts to "reduce fraud" in response to concerns raised by employers and insurers. These concerns focus on unproven assertions that workers file intentionally fraudulent claims and that, when they receive benefits, they deliberately remain off work long after they should have returned (Burton and Thomason 1992; Michaels 1998). Newspaper articles have cited claims that many workers' compensation claims involve such fraud (see Kerr 1991), and television programs have regularly portrayed individual cases of worker fraud. Yet no evidence suggests that worker fraud exists in more than 1–2 percent of cases (see, for example, Wisconsin Division of Workers' Compensation 2000).

Fraud is also an issue on the employer side. The costs of employer premium avoidance (Fiscal Policy Institute 2007) and underpayment of claims by insurers (Fricker 2000) likely dwarf the costs associated with excessive filing by injured workers. In recent years, as evidence has mounted, more attention has been paid to these nonworker categories of fraud. Some states have launched efforts to identify employers who are not paying premiums in order to increase the revenue available to pay for benefits and reduce the costs to honest employers.

3.5 Workers' compensation in context

Workers' compensation is a critical component of American social insurance for disabled workers. It exists within a web of programs and policies that protect individuals at work as well as provide benefits for those with disabilities. From the standpoint of an individual who is unable to work as a result of disability, the complexity of these systems may be daunting.

The primary alternative source of public benefits for permanently disabled workers is the Social Security Disability Insurance (SSDI) system. As in most other countries, the U.S. Social Security Disability Insurance system only covers long-term total disabilities. Although workers' compensation requires proof that a disability was caused by work, SSDI requires only that the disabled worker has had a minimum amount of work in covered employment. After two years, SSDI beneficiaries become eligible for health insurance under the federal Medicare program. In size, SSDI and Medicare paid $187 billion in cash and medical benefits to the disabled in 2009, in contrast to $58 billion in workers' compensation (Sengupta, Reno, and Burton 2011). Interestingly, aggregate annual costs of workers' compensation have had an inverse relationship to claims and costs in SSDI for a number of years, and a significant portion of disability in SSDI claims has been shown to have at least some work etiology (Reville and Schoeni 2004). As SSDI costs and claims have risen in recent years while workers' compensation costs have fallen, the concern has been raised that cutbacks in workers' compensation programs may be externalizing costs from employers to the national social security system (Sengupta, Reno, and Burton 2011).

The patchwork nature of the U.S. medical insurance system also has an impact on workers' compensation claims. Employers may—or may not—provide private health insurance and short- and long-term disability coverage. Workers who lack general health coverage may seek benefits through workers' compensation in order to receive reimbursement for medical treatment, although this may have changed with the implementation of the Affordable Care Act, which expanded health insurance coverage in the U.S. beginning January 1, 2014. Alternatively, workers may choose to avoid the stress of filing for workers' compensation benefits if they have health insurance and do not need weekly cash benefits.

Unlike other social benefit programs, workers' compensation also exists *within* the employment relationship itself. Workers' general fears regarding retaliation are rooted in the nature of this underlying relationship. Under basic U.S. employment law, most employees are "at will" and are, therefore, legally subject to discharge without cause. In addition, employers have unilateral control over the offering of appropriate transitional or light-duty work options to returning injured workers. These decisions are influenced by concerns about productivity and cost, but also by the relationship between an employer and an individual worker. Although return to work is often critical to the economic and physical well-being of the worker, inappropriate work assignments can also damage the long-term health of the injured worker. Many workers report that their employers did not help them return to work or were disrespectful after injury (Strunin and Boden 2000, 2004). Others report that workers are forced to return to work prematurely or to jobs that they cannot perform due to their disabilities (Strunin and Boden 2000).

The employment relationship is also governed by laws that are relevant but not directly related to workers' compensation. These include, at the federal level, the Family and Medical Leave Act (forbidding discharge for up to 12 weeks of absence from work due to serious health conditions) and the Americans with Disabilities Act. Injured workers may have claims that grow out of their work injuries against their employers under these laws. The need to invoke these laws, and the willingness of a worker to pursue claims under them, is affected by the underlying relationship as well as by the outcome of the workers' compensation claim.

From the outset, workers' compensation programs have been linked to workplace safety. Do the costs of workers' compensation create incentives for employers to focus on safety improvements in the workplace? Some researchers have concluded that experience rating creates an important incentive for safety, particularly for large and self-insured employers (Thomason 2003; Tompa, Trevithick, and McLeod 2007). Others dispute this claim, either because they conclude that experience rating provides very limited safety incentives or that it creates incentives for employers to discourage the filing or approval of claims (Boden 1995; Hyatt and Kralj 1995; Mansfield et al. 2012). For employers that are not self-insured, insurance tends to soften incentive effects, despite rate adjustments based on actual claims cost and frequency experience. Further, claims may not be filed when real injuries occur. As a result, we are not confident that safety is significantly affected by workers' compensation programs.

Workers' compensation also intersects with the health and safety regulatory regimes established under the Occupational Safety and Health Act of 1970 and the Mine Safety and Health Act of 1977. Compensation claims can be an indicator of injuries and may highlight high-risk areas, providing guidance to strategic enforcement efforts. However, data from workers' compensation claims are generally not used effectively to investigate the cause of workplace morbidity and mortality, and the ability to use workers' compensation data to advance risk prevention strategies is still in its infancy (Utterback et al. 2012).

4 WHITHER WORKERS' COMPENSATION IN THE UNITED STATES?

The workers' compensation system in the United States is designed to accomplish two critical goals: first, to provide, in a fair and efficient manner, health care and adequate wage replacement benefits to workers injured on the job, irrespective of fault or negligence; and second, as a *quid pro quo*, to protect employers from common law liability for workers' injuries and illnesses that arise out of workplace conditions.

Because workers' compensation is state-based, discussions of the future of the program usually occur below the federal level. Unfortunately, the program is a political football in almost every state. The main parties to these disputes are employers and insurers (favoring cost reductions, typically through reducing cash benefits, medical costs, or payments to claimants' attorneys); unions, favoring improved benefits and access; medical providers and hospitals, hoping to maintain medical payment levels; and claimants' attorneys, favoring higher benefits and contingent-fee percentages.

Employers and their associations often raise the issue of costs in the context of interstate competition for business location, pointing to neighboring states in which some aspect of the system costs less. Lower workers' compensation costs, it is argued, will attract businesses to move from other states, whereas higher costs will drive them away. When successful, this argument produces a "race to the bottom," with declining workers' compensation costs and reduced benefits for injured workers in a downward spiral as state after state adopts the most restrictive aspects of another state's system. Although there have been no studies on this race to the bottom in workers' compensation programs, there is a substantial literature on this phenomenon in other contexts showing both international competition to offer subsidies for industrial location and municipal competition to reduce welfare benefits (Haaland and Wooton 1999; Figlio, Kolpin, and Reid 1999; Saavedra 2000).

The political problems are rooted in two fundamental aspects of workers' compensation. First, the lack of any federal framework leaves state governments with full discretion over their programs, regulated only by the political and economic forces within the state that are brought to bear on elected officials. Tremendous pressure from organized business interests is difficult to withstand at a time when the organized voice for workers is very weak. The average density of unionization in the private sector in the United States has been falling for years: from 1973 when the rate of unionization was 24.2 percent, to 2014 when the rate had declined to 6.7 percent (Hirsch and Macpherson 2014). Legislation amending state workers' compensation laws in the recent past reflects the increasing political imbalance between business and labor over time.

Second, if an injury or condition is compensable under the workers' compensation system, then the employer is protected from liability, irrespective of the level of benefits that are actually paid to the injured worker. Reduced costs for employers, achieved through reduced benefits, therefore, do not adversely affect the scope of liability protection. To the extent that employers are purchasing liability protection for themselves—as opposed to benefits for their employees—they lack any incentive to maintain benefits at an adequate level.

As workers' compensation benefits become more difficult to obtain for workers with complex disabilities, they turn to other means to support themselves and their families, raising the specter that the SSDI program may be subsidizing costs that "should" be paid through the workers' compensation programs. And as state systems have become more restrictive, workers are beginning to bring common law cases against employers, claiming that the failure to compensate a workplace health condition means that the employer has relinquished the liability protection that underlies the basic workers' compensation system.

The current status of workers' compensation in the United States is, therefore, troubling. There is little political consensus regarding basic aspects of the program, and the annual fights in state legislatures over benefits and costs are strident and polarized. Workers with occupational diseases and complex work-induced disabilities are unlikely to receive benefits in the state systems. Costs are declining for employers, whereas many workers coping with serious, long-term disabilities face substantially reduced income—even if they receive workers' compensation benefits.

This leaves us with important unanswered questions. First, is the historical design of workers' compensation appropriate as we go forward? This design assumes that employers must pay for the benefits and that benefit receipt must require a causal link between work and disability. Proof of work-relatedness has become both a focal point for legislated changes and a justification for increasingly higher barriers to and inordinate delays in the resolution of claims.

Second, as the United States moves toward universal health coverage, does it make sense to separate the treatment of work-caused injuries, illnesses, and impairments from the rest of the health-care system? This separation means that causation must be assumed or proven before medical care is reimbursed by the workers' compensation system, as opposed to general health insurance.

Third, the difficulties that workers face in these systems suggest that workers' compensation systems undermine basic human rights of injured workers, including both the right to income security and the right to be treated with dignity and respect (Hilgert 2012). Is the current system capable of improving the treatment of workers and satisfying the economic and political demands of employers? If not, an argument can certainly be made that, despite the loss of putative safety incentives, disability benefits for workers injured at work should be de-linked from the direct economic interests of employers. How such a system might be designed so that it could meet all the concerns regarding safety, worker health, and disability management is beyond the scope of this chapter.

REFERENCES

Asterisk (*) denotes recommended reading

*Azaroff, Lenore S., Charles Levenstein, and David H. Wegman. 2002. "Occupational Injury and Illness Surveillance: Conceptual Filters Explain Underreporting." *American Journal of Public Health* 92: 1421–1429.

Baker, Tom. 1996. "On the Geneology of Moral Hazard." *Texas Law Review* 75: 237–292.

Boden, Leslie I. 1995. "Workers' Compensation in the United States: High Costs, Low Benefits." *Annual Review of Public Health* 16: 189–218.

Boden, Leslie I. and Monica Galizzi. 1999. "Economic Consequences of Workplace Injuries and Illnesses: Lost Earnings and Benefit Adequacy." *American Journal of Industrial Medicine 36*, no. 5: 487–503.

Boden, Leslie I., and Emily A. Spieler. 2010. "The Relationship between Workplace Injuries and Workers' Compensation Claims: The Importance of System Design. In *Workers' Compensation: Where Have We Come From? Where Are We Going?* Cambridge, MA: Workers Compensation Research Institute.

*Burton, John F., Jr. 2007. An overview of workers' compensation. *Workers' Compensation Policy Review*, 7(3): 3–27. Available at http://www.workerscompresources.com/WCPR_Public/WCPR%20PDFs/MJ07.pdf. Accessed January 20, 2012. (This website is generally very informative.)

Burton, John F. Jr. and Terry Thomason. 1992. "Workers' Compensation Fraud: Let the Reader Beware." *John Burton's Workers Compensation Monitor* May/June: 21–23.

Dembe, Allard E. and Leslie I. Boden. 2000. "Moral Hazard: A Question of Morality?" *New Solutions. 10*, no. 3: 257–279.

Dir., Office of Workers' Comp. Programs, Dep't of Labor v. Greenwich Collieries, 512 U.S. 267 (1994).

Figlio, David N., Van W. Kolpin, and William E. Reid. 1999. "Do States Play Welfare Games? *Journal of Urban Economics 46*, no. 3: 437–454.

Fiscal Policy Institute. 2007. "New York State Workers' Compensation: How Big Is the Coverage Shortfall?" http://nycosh.org/uploads/injured_on_job/on_workers_comp/FPI_WorkersCompShortfall_Jan2007.pdf. Accessed July 27, 2014.

*Fishback, Price V. and Sean E. Kantor. 1998. "The Adoption of Workers' Compensation in the United States, 1900-1930." *Journal of Law and Economics 41*, no. 2: 305–342.

Fricker, Mary. 2000. "Workers' Comp Errors Worst in Decade: 28.5 Percent of Workers Paid Late, 22 Percent Shortchanged. *Santa Rosa Press-Democrat*. September 29, 2000.

GAO (Government Accountability Office). 2009. "Workplace Safety and Health: Enhancing OSHA's Records Audit Process Could Improve the Accuracy of Worker Injury and Illness Data. *GAO* 10–10.

Gruber, Jonathan and Alan B. Krueger. 1994. "The Incidence of Mandated Employer-Provided Insurance: Lessons from Workers' Compensation Insurance." *American Economic Review 84*, no. 3: 622–630.

Haaland, Jan I. and Ian Wooton. 1999. "International Competition for Multinational Investment." *Scandinavian Journal of Economics 101*: 631–650.

Helvacian, Nurhan M. and Dan Corro. 1999. "Effects of Antifraud Laws: Analysis Using the New NCCI Econometric Model." *Workers Compensation Fall Issues Report*. Boca Raton, FL: National Council on Compensation Insurance.

Hilgert, Jeffrey. 2012. "Building a Human Rights Framework for Workers' Compensation in the United States: Ideas and Policy Implications." *American Journal of Industrial Medicine. 55*, no. 6: 506–518.

Hirsch, Barry T. and David A. MacPherson. 2014. Unionstats.com. www.unionstats.com Accessed July 29, 2014.

Hirsch, Barry T., David A. MacPherson, and J. Michael Dumond. 1997. "Workers' Compensation Recipiency in Union and Nonunion Workplaces." *Industrial and Labor Relations Review 50*: 213–236.

Howard, Christopher. 2002. "Workers' Compensation, Federalism, and the Heavy Hand of History." *Studies in American Political Development 16*, no. 1: 28–47.

Hunt, H. Allan (ed). 2004. *Adequacy of Earnings Replacement in Workers' Compensation Programs: A Report of the Study Panel on Benefit Adequacy of the Workers' Compensation Steering Committee, National Academy of Social Insurance*. Kalamazoo, MI: W.E. Upjohn Institute.

Hyatt, Douglas E., and Boris Kralj. 1995. "The Impact of Workers' Compensation Experience Rating on Employer Appeals Activity. *Industrial Relations 34*, no. 1: 95–106.

Imershein, AllenW., Stephen Hill, and Andi M. Reynolds. 1994. "The Workers' Compensation System as a Quality of Life Problem for Workers' Compensation Claimants." *Advances in Medical Sociology* 5: 181–200.

Kerr, Peter. 1991. "The Price of Health: Employee Fraud—A Special Report.; Vast Amount of Fraud Discovered in Workers' Compensation System." *The New York Times*. December 30, 1991. Section D, Page 1, Column 1. Also http://www.nytimes.com/1991/12/29/us/price-health-employee-fraud-special-report-vast-amount-fraud-discovered-workers.html?scp=1&sq=employee%20fraud:%20a%20special%20report&st=cse Accessed January 19, 2012.

Leigh, J. Paul and John A. Robbins. 2004. "Occupational Disease and Workers' Compensation: Coverage, Costs, and Consequences." *The Milbank Quarterly 82*, no. 4: 689–721.

Mansfield, Liz, Ellen MacEachen, Emile Tompa, Christina C. Kalcevich, Marion Endicott and Natalie Yeung. 2012. A critical review of literature on experience rating in workers' compensation systems. *Policy and Practice in Health and Safety*, 10(1):3–25.

Michaels, David. 1998. "Fraud in the Workers' Compensation System: Origin and Magnitude." *Occupational medicine*. 13, No. 2, 439.

Moss, David A. 1996. *Socializing Security: Progressive-Era Economists and the Origins of American Social Policy*. Cambridge, MA: Harvard University Press.

*National Commission on State Workmen's Compensation Laws. 1972. *Report*. Washington, DC: *U.S. Government Printing Office*. http://www.workerscompresources.com/National_Commission_Report/national_commission_report.htm Accessed January 3, 2012.

——. *Compendium on Workmen's Compensation*. 1973.Washington, DC: U.S. Government Printing Office.

Reville, Robert T., Leslie I. Boden, Jeff Biddle, and Christopher Mardesich. 2001. *New Mexico Workers' Compensation Permanent Partial Disability and Return-to-Work: An Evaluation*. Santa Monica: RAND.

Reville, Robert T. and Robert F. Schoeni. 2004. "The Fraction of Disability Caused at Work." *Social Security Bulletin 65*, no. 4: 31–37.

Saavedra, Luz A. 2000, "A Model of Welfare Competition with Evidence from AFDC." *Journal of Urban Economics 47*: 248–279.

*Sengupta, Ishita, Marjorie Baldwin, and Virginia Reno. 2013. *Workers' Compensation: Benefits, Coverage, and Costs, 2001*. Washington, DC: National Academy of Social Insurance.

Spieler, Emily A., Peter S. Barth, John F. Burton Jr., Jay Himmelstein, and Linda Rudolph. 2000. "Recommendations to Guide Revision of the Guides to the Evaluation of Permanent Impairment." *Journal of the American Medical Association 283*, no. 4: 519–523.

*Spieler, Emily A. and John F. Burton Jr. 2012. "The Lack of Correspondence between Work-Related Disability and Receipt of Workers' Compensation Benefits. *American Journal of Industrial Medicine 55*, no. 6: 487–505.

Strunin, Lee and Leslie I. Boden. 2000. "Paths of Reentry: Employment Experiences of Injured Workers." *American Journal of Industrial Medicine 38*: 373–384.

*Strunin, Lee and Leslie I. Boden. 2004. The Workers' Compensation System: Worker Friend or Foe?" *American Journal of Industrial Medicine 45*, no. 4: 338–345.

Sum, Julie and Laura Stock. 1996. *Navigating the California Workers' Compensation System: The Injured Workers's Experience: an Evaluation of Services to Inform and assist Injured Workers in California.* Labor and Occupational Health Program, University of California at Berkeley.

Tanabe, Ramona P. 2014. *Workers' Compensation Laws as of January 1, 2014.* Cambridge, MA: Workers Compensation Research Institute.

Thomason. Terry. 2003. "Economic Incentives and Workplace Safety." In Sullivan F, ed. *Preventing and Managing Disabling Injury at Work.* London, UK: Taylor and Francis. 183–202.

Thomason, Terry, Timothy P. Schmidle, and John F. Burton, Jr. 2001. *Workers' Compensation: Benefits, Costs, and Safety under Alternative Insurance Arrangements.* WE Upjohn Institute, 2001.

Tompa, Emile, Scott Trevithick, and Chris McLeod. 2007. Systematic Review of the Prevention Incentives of Insurance and Regulatory Mechanisms for Occupational Health and Safety. *Scandinavian Journal of Work Environment and Health 33*, no. 2: 85–95.

United States Bureau of Labor Statistics (BLS). "Workmen's Compensation Laws of the United States and Foreign Countries." *U.S. Bureau of Labor Statistics Bulletin*, No. 126 (1913).

Utterback, David F., Teresa M. Schnorr, Barbara A. Silverstein, Emily A. Spieler, Tom B. Leamon, Benjamin C. Amick III. 2012. Occupational Health and Safety Surveillance and Research using Workers' Compensation Data. *Journal of Occupational and Environmental Medicine.* 54 (2) 171–176.

Weinstein, James. 1968. *The Corporate Ideal in the Liberal State, 1900-1918.* Boston: Beacon Press.

Wisconsin Division of Workers' Compensation. 2000. "Annual Report for Calendar Year 1999 on Allegations of Workers' Compensation Fraud." http://dwd.wisconsin.gov/wc/insurance/fraud/1999_Fraud_Report.htm. Accessed December 27, 2011.

Wall, Cindy L, Shirley A. Morrissey, and James R. P. Ogloff. 2009. The Workers' Compensation Experience: a Qualitative Exploration of Workers' Beliefs Regarding the Impact of the Compensation System on Their Recovery and Rehabilitation. *International Journal of Disability Management Research 4*, no. 2: 19–26.

Workers' Compensation Insurance Rating Bureau of California (WCIRB). *2008 Legislative Cost Monitoring Report.* 2008. Accessed December 18, 2008 at https://wcirbonline.org/wcirb/resources/data_reports/pdf/2008_cost_monitoring_report.pdf

PART VII

PROGRAMS FOR WORKERS AND FAMILIES

CHAPTER 26

··

UNEMPLOYMENT INSURANCE

··

STEPHEN A. WOODBURY

1 INTRODUCTION

··

UNEMPLOYMENT insurance (UI) is a social insurance program intended to provide temporary income support to workers who have lost their jobs through no fault of their own and are seeking reemployment. Its clearest purposes are to reduce the hardship of unemployment and to help stabilize the economy during downturns by maintaining demand for goods and services. UI is not means-tested, so it is not intrinsically an antipoverty program, although it does help households stay above the poverty threshold.

The next section recounts the origins of UI in the United States and outlines the principles and goals of the system. The following section describes how UI works, discussing eligibility, the structure of benefits, and how the system is financed. The chapter then turns to the political economy of UI, including discussions of the system's stakeholders and federal-state relations. This is followed by a review of current and recurring controversies over the system's effectiveness as an antipoverty program, trust-fund solvency, eligibility, and benefit adequacy. The chapter concludes with a brief review of the problems facing UI and speculation about its future.

2 HISTORICAL BACKGROUND AND GOALS

··

UI is unique among American social programs: each of the 50 states (plus the District of Columbia, Puerto Rico, and the Virgin Islands) finances and administers its own program, but under federal guidelines and oversight. Accordingly, UI differs from other social insurance programs like Social Security, which is national, and Workers'

Compensation, which has individual state programs with no federal involvement (Blaustein 1993).

Several considerations influenced this unusual federal-state arrangement (Rubin 1983; West and Hildebrand 1997). Although progressive reformers had pushed states to enact UI for decades, by 1935 only Wisconsin had done so, and it appeared that federal involvement was needed to overcome states' reluctance to adopt UI. On the other hand, when the Social Security Act (SSA) was drafted in 1935, no federal social program existed, and Congress was reluctant to enact a large, complex, and untested national program. Moreover, the novelty of such a program led many in Congress to believe that a national UI program would not survive a constitutional challenge. For these reasons, President Roosevelt stated a preference for "a maximum of cooperation between States and the Federal government" (Blaustein 1993, 133).

The solution, which has been attributed to Supreme Court Justice Louis D. Brandeis, was to create financial incentives under the SSA for each state to conduct its own UI system; specifically, to levy a federal payroll tax under the Federal Unemployment Tax Act (FUTA) on virtually all employers, then forgive most of that tax for employers in states operating a UI program that met federal requirements (Blaustein 1993). The most important requirements were and are quite general: administer a UI program using "methods of administration... reasonably calculated to insure full payment of unemployment compensation when due" [42 U.S.C. § 503(a)(1)] and raise revenues for that program through an experience-rated payroll tax levied on (at least) the federal tax base, and whose maximum tax rate is no lower than 5.4 percent. Payroll tax revenues must be deposited in a Trust Fund held by the U.S. Treasury and may be used only to pay UI benefits, but otherwise the states have much freedom in setting benefits and specific tax provisions (Rubin 1983; Hildebrand 1995–1996).[1] This freedom has led to marked differences among the states in program eligibility, benefit generosity, and program solvency.

Under the SSA, the federal government provides the funds to administer each state's UI program, conditional on the "methods of administration" requirement to meet basic quality standards such as timely payment and procedures to adjudicate appeals. Control over administrative funding gives the federal government added leverage over state UI programs, and as Rubin (1990, 213) notes, "has guaranteed continual conflict between the two parties." Both federal-state relations and debate over the merits of the federal-state system (versus a nationalized one) have been recurring themes.

Although UI is rife with controversy over specific provisions (discussed later), the principles and goals of the system are uncontested. Blaustein's (1993, chap. 2) review of existing statements of UI principles is comprehensive through 1993, and subsequent discussions (ACUC 1995; Blaustein, O'Leary, and Wandner 1997) mainly reiterate and elaborate on the earlier ones. A 1955 statement of "Major Objectives of Federal Policy with Respect to the Federal-State Employment Security Program" by the U.S. Department of Labor (USDOL) is close to definitive (quoted in Blaustein 1993, 47):

> Unemployment insurance is a program—established under Federal and State law—
> for income maintenance during periods of involuntary unemployment due to lack

of work, which provides partial compensation for wage loss as a matter of right, with dignity and dispatch, to eligible individuals. It helps to maintain purchasing power and to stabilize the economy. It helps to prevent the dispersal of the employers' trained work force, the sacrifice of skills, and the breakdown of labor standards during temporary unemployment.

Two purposes of UI are clear in this statement, which is "the last official federal expression of the program's overall objectives": first, to partially compensate for lost earnings and smooth consumption during periods of involuntary unemployment; second, to help stabilize aggregate economic output. Blaustein and others have interpreted the last sentence as encompassing two additional goals: to prevent unemployment (through an experience-rated payroll tax, which creates a disincentive to lay off workers); and to facilitate reemployment (through the work-search test and public employment services). The absence in the postwar years of any recorded debate over these principles suggests they are widely accepted.

3 How Unemployment Insurance Works

UI is a three-tiered system (Woodbury and Rubin 1997). Tier 1 is the "regular" system conducted by each state. It is always in effect, financed by payroll taxes collected from employers in the state, and in most states provides up to 26 weeks of benefits. Tier 2 is the "standby" Extended Benefits (EB) program, a federal-state program that is intended to activate automatically in a recession and lengthen the duration of benefits by 13 weeks (or 20 weeks by state option). Tier 3 is the succession of federal "emergency" benefit extensions that Congress has passed in every recession since 1958.

To be eligible for UI under any of these three tiers, an unemployed worker must file a claim and meet two broad sets of criteria: monetary eligibility criteria, which pertain to the worker's earnings history (ACUC 1995, chap. 7; Nicholson 1997); and nonmonetary eligibility criteria, which pertain to the conditions that led the claimant to become unemployed and whether the claimant is looking for work (ACUC 1995, chap. 8; Anderson 1997).

3.1 Monetary Eligibility

States differ markedly in their specific requirements, but all examine earnings or hours worked in a *base period*, usually defined as the first four of the five quarters completed before a claim is filed. Most states require that earnings exceed two thresholds: one for the base-period quarter in which earnings were highest (the "high quarter") and another for the entire base period (USDOL 2012, chap. 3). In most states, the thresholds are not high (for example, in 2012 the base-period threshold exceeded $4,000 in only six states), but they ensure that UI recipients have more than a casual attachment to the labor force.

For workers who meet the monetary criteria, the state determines the *weekly benefit amount* and *maximum payable benefits* (effectively, the potential duration of benefits) for the year following the UI claim—the *benefit year*. Most states calculate the weekly benefit amount as some fraction of high-quarter earnings, up to a maximum.[2] For example, in New York (a state near the median) the weekly benefit amount is 1/26 of high-quarter earnings up to a maximum of $405. In general, the weekly benefit amount replaces about one-half of average weekly earnings in the high quarter.

The weekly benefit formula has two implications for benefit adequacy (ACUC 1995, chap. 9). For seasonal workers, the weekly UI replacement rate—*relative to average base period earnings*—exceeds 50 percent because their high-quarter earnings are atypically high. But for most workers receiving the maximum weekly benefit amount, the weekly UI replacement rate is *less* than 50 percent. For example, all New York recipients with high-quarter earnings greater than $10,530 receive the same maximum weekly benefit—$405. Accordingly, the benefit formula aims to compensate low earners more than high earners.

In 2012, the maximum weekly benefit was below $300 in six states (Alabama, Arizona, Florida, Louisiana, Mississippi, and Tennessee) and above $500 in six others (Connecticut, Hawaii, Massachusetts, New Jersey, North Carolina, and Rhode Island). All but 17 states automatically adjust the maximum to be a percentage—usually between 50 and 67 percent—of the state's average weekly earnings in UI-covered employment. Five of the ten largest states (California, Florida, Georgia, Michigan, and New York) do *not* tie the maximum to state average earnings, and in all of these except California, the maximum is near or below the national median of $400.

In eleven "uniform duration" states (Illinois and New York alone among the 10 largest), all eligible claimants may receive up to 26 weeks of benefits. In all other states, potential benefit duration varies with base-period earnings. Most of these "variable-duration" states set maximum payable benefits so workers whose earnings are more stable have longer potential duration (Woodbury and Rubin 1997).

3.2 Nonmonetary Eligibility

A claimant must also meet two sets of *nonmonetary eligibility* criteria (USDOL 2012, chap. 5). The *separation criteria* require a worker to have lost a job due to lack of work and through no fault of his or her own. In principle, this implies that workers who are discharged for misconduct or voluntarily quit will be ineligible for UI. In practice, the separation criteria are somewhat less harsh. For example, employers often find it difficult to substantiate charges of misconduct when claimants appeal. Also, every state provides for workers who quit for "good cause" not to be disqualified, although states vary greatly in how they define "good cause." Most consider work-related issues—unsafe or unhealthy working conditions, a change in hours or pay, or being required to perform tasks different from those the worker was hired to perform—to be good causes.

In addition, most states have provisions that prevent a worker who quits for specified personal reasons from being disqualified. In the 10 largest states—California, Texas, New York, Florida, Illinois, Pennsylvania, Ohio, Michigan, Georgia, and North Carolina—workers are not disqualified if they move with a spouse whose employment has moved or quit due to an illness that is not work-related. In seven of these states, the same is true if a worker quits to care for an immediate family member who is ill or disabled (Florida, Michigan, and Georgia are the exceptions). When discharge for misconduct or a voluntary quit disqualifies a claimant, most states (including the 10 largest) postpone benefits for between four weeks (Illinois) and 17 weeks (Florida and Michigan).

The second set of nonmonetary eligibility criteria require a worker to be able, available, and seeking work—the *nonseparation* criteria (ACUC 1995, chap. 8). A worker who is ill or disabled, traveling or away on vacation, or lacking means to get to and from work is generally considered unable or unavailable to work. Also, most states disqualify workers who are available only for part-time work or enrolled in school or a training program (unless approved by the public employment agency). These latter two restrictions have been controversial and are discussed in the sections on recipiency, antipoverty goals, and "UI Modernization."

By law, the requirement that workers actively seek work—the *work-search test*—is administered by the Employment Service; however, the requirement is handled differently in each state, and little data exist on the procedures used or the stringency with which the requirement is enforced (O'Leary 2006). In general, the work-search test is applied through requirements that claimants register with the Employment Service and not refuse *suitable work* when referred to a job (Anderson 1997). Each state defines suitable work based on considerations like a worker's prior training, experience, and earnings, as well as the claimant's unemployment duration and distance between the claimant's residence and the job. If a claimant does refuse suitable work, 15 states (including California, Florida, and Michigan) postpone benefits for a specified number of weeks (between 2 and 21), and all others require the claimant to earn 5 to 10 times the weekly benefit amount to re-qualify. In addition, 10 states reduce benefits payable, usually by the number of weeks of the postponement.

3.3 Additional Eligibility and Benefit Provisions

Six additional issues relating to eligibility and benefits are important (USDOL 2012). First, under the SSA, every state must have an appeals process whereby a claimant who is denied benefits can obtain "a fair hearing before an impartial tribunal" (USDOL 2012, 7-1). In most states a single administrative law judge convenes the tribunal, and most states provide for a second appeal to a state review board.

Second, most states impose a one-week *waiting period* before UI benefits start. This serves as an insurance deductible and reduces the relative compensation paid during short unemployment spells.

Third, most states provide for workers who are *partially unemployed* to receive partial benefits. A week of partial unemployment is usually defined as a week of less than full-time work in which earnings are less than the weekly benefit amount for which the claimant would be eligible. The partially unemployed worker receives a benefit equal to the weekly benefit amount less earnings in excess of a disregard; all states set a disregard to create an incentive for workers to take short-term work.

Fourth, most states reduce benefits in weeks when a claimant receives *disqualifying income* such as severance pay, wages in lieu of notice, back pay, or vacation pay. Fifth, 15 states have special provisions for *seasonal employment*, typically limiting UI based on seasonal earnings to be paid during the time the industry is "in season." Finally, in 14 states (mainly in the Northeast and Midwest) UI recipients who have dependents receive an additional weekly *dependents' allowance*, which usually varies with the number of dependents.

3.4 Extended Benefits

In addition to the regular state UI programs described earlier (Tier 1), two extended benefit programs are important: standby EB and emergency extensions (Woodbury and Rubin 1997). Standby EB (Tier 2), enacted in 1970, automatically increases the duration of benefits when unemployment is high and rising. It is usually financed half from payroll taxes collected by the states and half from revenues raised under the FUTA. Accordingly, it shifts responsibility from the states to the federal government as economic conditions worsen.

Starting with the 1958 recession, Congress has enacted eight "emergency" extended benefit programs (Tier 3), one in each recession. These programs have become increasingly complicated, difficult to administer, and confusing to claimants (Woodbury and Rubin 1997; USDOL 2013). For example, Congress enacted the most recent emergency extension—Emergency Unemployment Compensation 08 (EUC08)—on June 30, 2008. It was effective the following week and provided up to 13 additional weeks of benefits. The measure included a "reach back" provision, so claimants who had exhausted regular benefits from a benefit year ending after May 1, 2007 could receive emergency benefits. States could pay EUC08 benefits *before* workers received EB, which appealed to states because EUC08 was fully federally financed. Initially, claimants in states with unemployment above 8 percent could receive up to 59 weeks of benefits.

In November 2008, Congress expanded EUC08 so claimants in high-unemployment states could receive up to 79 weeks of benefits. Congress further expanded EUC08 in November 2009 so that claimants in high-unemployment states could receive up to 99 weeks of UI benefits—substantially more than in previous recessions.[3] Between December 2009 and December 2011, Congress extended EUC08 six times, although twice the program lapsed, and states had to stop payments before Congress reinstated the program. Early in 2012, Congress again extended EUC08, but added provisions that started to wind down the program, reducing both the duration of EUC08 benefits and the number of states in which EUC08 would be paid (USDOL 2013). On January 2, 2013 (the day it was to have expired), Congress again extended EUC08 for another year.

The ad hoc and chaotic development of EUC08 typifies emergency extensions. Not surprisingly, state UI administrators consider emergency extensions difficult to administer, error-prone, and susceptible to fraud and abuse (Woodbury and Simms 2011). An effective standby program with established rules, activating automatically, and for which the states were prepared, would be a far more sensible approach to extending benefits in a slack labor market.

3.5 Recipiency

Most unemployed individuals do not receive benefits. New labor-force entrants and re-entrants typically have insufficient earnings to qualify, the conditions under which many workers leave employment disqualify them, and others are not able, available, and seeking reemployment (ACUC 1996, chap. 4; Wandner and Stengle 1997). As table 26.1 (column 4) shows, the percentage of unemployed individuals who received UI benefits— the *UI recipiency rate*—averaged about 35 percent during 2009–2011. Recipiency rates varied substantially by state and region, being above the national average in the northeast and east north central states, and well below average in the west south central states (Arkansas, Louisiana, Oklahoma, and Texas). This pattern reflects regional differences in labor markets as well as in eligibility rules and benefit levels (which are higher in the northeast).

Table 26.1 also reveals substantial differences in UI recipiency among demographic groups. UI recipiency tends to be higher for older workers, men, and white (non-Hispanic) workers. It tends to be lower for Hispanics, high-school dropouts, and part-time workers. In general, groups with lower recipiency rates tend to have lower earnings (for example, younger workers, nonwhite and Hispanic workers, and those with less education) and more transitions in and out of the labor force (younger workers and women). Also, the ineligibility (in many states) of those looking for part-time work contributes to the low recipiency of part-time workers. But research suggests that these factors alone do not explain low UI recipiency: analyses of four supplements to the Current Population Survey show that many workers do not claim UI because they are optimistic about becoming re-employed quickly or believe (perhaps incorrectly) that they are ineligible (Wandner and Stettner 2000; Vroman 2009; Gould-Werth and Shaefer 2012).

3.6 Financing Unemployment Insurance

UI is financed by a payroll tax that has federal and state components and is collected from most employers (USDOL 2012, chaps. 1 and 2; ACUC 1994, chap. 7; ACUC 1995,

Table 26.1 Labor force, unemployment, and UI recipiency rates, by region and population subgroup, 2009–2011 (weighted percentages)

Group	Percentage of labour force(1)	Percentage of unemployed(2)	Percentage unemployed at some time last year(3)	UI recipiency rate: percentage of unemployed receiving UI
All	100.0	100.0	11.9	35.3
Region				
New England	5.1	4.4	10.4	41.4
Middle Atlantic	13.2	12.0	10.8	41.2
East North Central	15.1	15.8	12.4	39.9
West North Central	7.2	6.6	10.8	34.1
South Atlantic	19.0	18.0	11.2	31.8
East South Central	5.7	6.0	12.6	32.5
West South Central	11.5	10.6	11.0	26.7
Mountain	7.2	7.5	12.4	33.0
Pacific	15.8	19.0	14.3	36.4
Age				
<25	13.3	22.6	20.1	12.4
25–34	21.6	25.7	14.1	34.0
35–44	21.2	19.4	10.9	41.5
45–54	22.8	18.9	9.8	48.4
>54	21.2	13.4	7.5	47.8
Male	52.8	59.7	13.4	36.8
Female	47.2	40.3	10.1	33.0
Race/ethnicity				
White(non-Hispanic)	68.2	61.1	10.6	38.9
Black(non-Hispanic)	10.6	13.6	15.3	33.0
Asian(non-Hispanic)	5.1	3.8	9.0	34.6
Other(non-Hispanic)	1.7	2.4	16.4	31.8
Hispanic	14.4	19.1	15.7	25.9
Educational attainment				
Less than high school	9.9	16.5	19.8	23.3
High school only	28.0	33.7	14.3	37.2
Some college	29.7	29.7	11.9	37.4
College graduate	32.4	20.0	7.3	38.8
Full-time	78.5	66.0	10.0	43.7
Part-time	21.5	34.0	18.7	18.9

Note: Recipiency rates show the percentage of individuals unemployed for at least one week in the preceding year who also received UI in that year.
Source: Author's tabulations of samples of the civilian labor force in the 2010, 2011, and 2012 Current Population Survey Annual Social and Economic Supplements (March CPS), extracted from IPUMS-CPS (King et al. 2010). The annual data in the March CPS pertain to the preceding year. Weighted percentages are based on samples of individuals who worked at least one week in the year preceding the survey (104,721 in the 2010 survey; 101,162 in the 2011 survey; 99,133 in the 2012 survey).

chap. 11).[4] Under the federal component (FUTA), a 6 percent tax is levied on the first $7,000 of each covered worker's annual earnings; however, employers in states with a UI program meeting federal standards receive a 5.4 percent credit. The 0.6 percent not credited is deposited in federal trust accounts that, in turn, finance UI's federal and state administrative costs, fund public employment services throughout the country, pay the federal share of the EB program, and make loans to states that have exhausted their UI trust funds.

Each state sets its own UI payroll tax base (or *taxable wage base*) and tax rates for financing regular state benefits. Both vary greatly from state to state (USDOL 2012): all but two states (Arizona and California) set their UI tax base higher than the $7,000 required under FUTA, but state UI tax bases are much smaller than the Social Security base ($110,100 in 2012). The UI tax base exceeded $25,000 in just 12 states in 2012, and in these 12, the base is adjusted automatically each year by indexation to the state's average annual wage. Of the 16 states that index, all but six are in the West, and of the 12 largest states, only New Jersey and North Carolina had 2012 tax bases greater than $12,000 *and* indexed their base. The tax base was $12,000 or less in 22 states, and in none of these was the tax base indexed. Vroman (2011) has shown that states with relatively low UI tax bases were more likely to exhaust their UI trust funds (and needed to borrow to pay UI benefits) following the 2007–2008 financial crisis (see the section on trust-fund solvency).

The tax rates levied on the base are *experience rated*, so that each employer's tax rate depends on the extent to which that employer has laid off workers who have received UI benefits (USDOL 2012, chap. 2). Experience rating was a hallmark of the UI law in 1935, and it remains a unique feature of the U.S. system. It was originally touted as a way to distribute the cost of UI equitably among employers and to discourage employers from laying off workers (Blaustein 1993). To implement experience rating, the same administrative records used to determine a claimant's monetary eligibility are used to identify the claimant's base period employer and to "charge" the benefits paid to each former employee back to the "responsible" employer.

Details and analysis of the formulas mapping benefit charges into tax rates can be found elsewhere (Topel 1984, 1990). More important is that not all benefits can (or should) be charged: those paid to workers who have quit with good cause, the federal share (50 percent) of EB, emergency extended benefits, and dependents' allowances are all *noncharged* benefits (traceable to an employer but not counted against the employer's layoff experience); and those traceable to employers that have gone out of business are *inactively charged*. Moreover, tax rates are capped at some maximum, leading to *ineffectively charged* benefits (charged to an employer but not affecting that employer's tax rate). These so-called socialized costs of UI have long been a source of complaints from stable employers whose workers rarely claim benefits (Blaustein, O'Leary, and Wandner 1997, 35).

The incentive effects of the tax-rate cap have been examined in detail and shown to be perverse. The cap leads to subsidization of unstable industries by stable industries, a reallocation of resources to unstable industries, and substitution of temporary layoffs for hours reductions when demand is slack (Topel 1984; Deere 1991; Card and Levine

1994). Topel (1990) has suggested that experience rating could be increased, and efficiency improved, by uncapping payroll tax schedules, charging interest on negative balances in employers' reserve accounts, and reducing the number of noncharging provisions in states' regulations.

Many strictly mechanical complications vex experience rating (ACUC 1994, chap. 7): Rules need to be worked out for charging benefits to employers of workers who have several base-period employers; for handling new employers (who have no experience on which to calculate a rate), and for the transfer of layoff experience when an employer merges, is acquired, or reorganizes. The details of all these provisions are inevitably arcane and often cryptic (USDOL 2012, chap. 2).

4 THE POLITICAL ECONOMY OF UNEMPLOYMENT INSURANCE

4.1 Interested Parties

The UI system has been shaped by diverse parties at both the federal and state levels. Employers, worker advocates, state UI administrators, researchers, and the Office of UI of the USDOL have all played key roles in shaping the system (West and Hildebrand 1997).

Employers have a financial stake in the system because benefits are financed from an experience-rated payroll tax. Their most prominent advocate has been UWC—Strategic Services on Unemployment and Workers' Compensation, a Washington-based membership organization whose mission is "to serve the business community by promoting unemployment insurance (UI)...programs that provide fair benefits to workers at an affordable cost to employers and the community" (UWC 2012). Among other activities, UWC advocates before state and national legislatures, holds annual meetings where members exchange information, and assists its members in resolving disputes with state UI authorities.

In recent years, the most prominent advocate for workers' rights to UI benefits and an expanded program—less restrictive eligibility requirements, higher benefit amounts, and longer benefit durations—has been the National Employment Law Project (NELP), a group funded primarily by foundations (NELP 2011). NELP's agenda for UI reform is extensive (Stettner, Smith, and McHugh 2004, with online updates), and it issues frequent briefing papers and reports on current UI issues and legislation. Organized labor also favors expanded UI benefits, and at the state and local level, legal-aid groups frequently assist denied UI claimants in litigating appeals (see Gray and Stevens 1995–1996). Despite support from these quarters, West and Hildebrand (1997, 588) have noted that "there is no specific 'UI lobby' for all individuals who might become unemployed," and as a result, UI does not "receive the political or moral support that it once did."

State UI and employment service agencies are at the center of the UI program. In 1937, they organized the National Association of State Workforce Agencies (NASWA, previously called the Interstate Conference of Employment Security Agencies) and have supported it strongly since. Although explicitly not a lobbying group, NASWA represents the states before Congress and the USDOL and provides a way for the states to network and exchange information through periodic conferences. NASWA refers to itself as "the collective voice of state agencies on workforce policies and issues" (NASWA 2012a), and West and Hildebrand (1997, 588–589) call NASWA "a positive force…that has performed an essential role in preserving the federal-state partnership."

The so-called federal partner in UI includes the U.S. Congress, the White House, and, most directly the Office of UI, the Chief Economist, and regional offices of the USDOL (West and Hildebrand 1997, 548). These groups have often held different views about the UI program, complicating matters for the states.

Researchers in academe and think tanks have performed numerous studies and field experiments on aspects of UI. Many of these studies have been sponsored by the USDOL and are readily available (http://wdr.doleta.gov/research/). The USDOL encourages researchers to make recommendations based on their work, and they occasionally testify before Congress. Researchers also meet frequently with UI administrators and the other interested parties at conferences organized by NASWA, NELP, UWC, and the USDOL, among others.

Because each state conducts its own UI program, most debates over UI occur at the state level and rarely reach the national stage. States have their own UI advisory councils, legislatures, and courts, all of which have different views (West and Hildebrand 1997, 549). Only during recessions, when Congress debates emergency extensions, does UI receive more than passing attention in the national press.

4.2 Federal-State Relations

Relations between the federal and state partners are most visible in the enforcement of federal requirements and funding for UI administration (Rubin 1983; Hildebrand 1995–1996–1996).[5] Although each state administers its own UI program, the federal government must both enforce conformity of state UI laws with federal requirements and ensure compliance of state administrative practices with federal requirements and state laws. Conformity cases have often pertained to states' interpretations of federal UI requirements, such as the prohibition on paying benefits to claimants like teachers, or the mandate to cover nonprofit organizations and state and local governments. (Hildebrand 1995–1996; Fanning 1995–1996).

Administrative compliance issues center on the SSA's "methods of administration" requirement ("to insure full payment of unemployment compensation when due"), which Rubin (1983, 42) has noted is broad enough "to permit virtually any federal control over administration [that] DOL sees fit to impose." In two pivotal federal court cases, the "methods of administration" requirement has been used successfully to challenge delaying payment of benefits during an employer appeal, and not using an alternative to the standard base period when doing so would benefit a claimant (Hildebrand 1995–1996; Fanning 1995–1996).

Although, as Rubin (1990, 219) has pointed out, "conflict is inevitable when responsibilities for a single program are shared by two levels of government with different perspectives," the USDOL has long preferred to negotiate informally with states to reach conformity and compliance. Indeed, the states often rely on USDOL's Office of UI for technical assistance in these and other matters. As a result, formal legal challenges to states and court cases like those mentioned earlier have been rare (Rubin 1983; Hildebrand 1995–1996).

A second important aspect of federal-state relations pertains to financing UI administration, which has long been a source of conflict (West and Hildebrand 1997, 574–583). The SSA [42 U.S.C. § 303(a)(8)] requires the federal government to provide grants to the states "in the amounts found necessary by the Secretary of Labor for the proper and efficient administration" of each state's UI program. In principle, FUTA payroll taxes are collected from employers nationwide and distributed to states based on program requirements. But UI administrative funding is discretionary, and less than half of FUTA revenues are returned to the states for UI administration (Hight 1982; NASWA 2012b). The result has been ongoing complaints from the states about inadequate funding for UI administration (Woodbury and Simms 2011). NASWA has proposed that at least 50 percent of FUTA revenue be guaranteed for UI administration (NASWA 2012b), but Congress has not acted on this proposal.

Equally important are the less tangible aspects of the federal-state partnership, especially the shifting balance of power between the two in deciding where responsibility for an adequate UI system will ultimately fall (Rubin 1990; O'Leary 2013). Although Congress has resisted calls for rigid federal standards on eligibility and benefits, the accretion of federal requirements, already discussed, suggests the increasing will of the federal government to assert its authority over UI. This continuing shift toward federal control was evident in the EUC08 benefit extensions and in the "UI Modernization" package passed by Congress in 2009, with its incentives to broaden eligibility (see the next section).

5 POLICY ISSUES

Despite general agreement over the principles of UI, many aspects of the program remain controversial. The issues stem from disagreement over the appropriate institutions for implementing the principles (e.g., effectiveness of the federal-state system), disagreement over interpreting the principles (e.g., the meaning of partial compensation for lost wages), and difficulties resolving tradeoffs inherent in the program (e.g., more adequate benefits and better countercyclical effectiveness may blunt job-search incentives and, through higher UI payroll taxes, inhibit job creation). This section focuses on a limited number of recurring policy issues.

5.1 Social Insurance and Antipoverty Goals

An overarching debate pertains to the effectiveness of UI as an antipoverty program. Since the mid-1990s, U.S. social policy has increasingly assumed that earnings will be the main source of income for nonelderly adults and their dependents, even when their earnings capacity is limited. Congress made this expectation clear by greatly expanding the Earned Income Tax Credit effective 1994 and replacing Aid to Families with Dependent Children with Temporary Assistance for Needy Families effective 1997 (Decker, Gustafson, and Levine 2001).

The added emphasis on employment as a source of income for the poor has inevitably placed added pressure on UI: insurance against loss of earnings is more important when society emphasizes employment and earnings as the primary means of support. The question then is whether UI should change in response to changes in income maintenance policy, or if some other accommodation is needed.

Some researchers (Shaefer 2010; Vroman 2010) and worker advocates (Stettner et al. 2004) do not question UI's underlying principles, but do favor UI reform. They have criticized UI provisions restricting eligibility, such as restrictions facing workers who quit for cause or are seeking part-time work. During the slack labor market of the Great Recession and its aftermath, they supported emergency extensions of UI, were skeptical of suggestions that these extensions might act as a disincentive to accept re-employment, and were critical of attempts to rein in the extensions (see the discussion in Woodbury and Simms 2011). Although directed at UI, these criticisms could be read as broad complaints about the lack of generous cash support for low-income households and the absence of Unemployment Assistance (reduced income support for the long-term unemployed, as exists in some European countries).

The alternative view is that UI is social insurance—that is, meant to replace the lost earnings of households whose earnings are normally adequate, rather than an income transfer program with the goal of bringing poor households out of poverty. Even with its flaws, the existing UI system can be defended as a reasonable interpretation of basic UI principles. Hansen and Byers (1990a) argued that reforming UI to better serve those with low earnings capacity and the long-term unemployed could lessen its already weak support among employers and limit its effectiveness by reducing funds available for regular UI benefits. In short, those who view UI as social insurance (for example, Blaustein 1993, chap. 3) believe that income maintenance for the poor and training for the long-term unemployed would be better handled by separate programs and funded by general revenues, not payroll taxes.

5.2 State Trust Fund Solvency

Unlike Social Security, UI is not a pay-as-you-go system, at least in principle. Rather, each state places its UI payroll taxes in a trust fund with the U.S. Treasury, from which benefits are paid. The intent is to "forward-fund" UI so that, in a recession, funds needed to pay benefits will be available and UI will serve as an automatic stabilizer (ACUC 1995, chap. 5).

The simplest measure of trust-fund solvency is the *reserve ratio*—net trust-fund reserves as a percentage of total payrolls—which can be calculated for each state individually or for all states aggregated. Figure 26.1 shows that the aggregate reserve ratio (darker line) has trended downward over the last 50 years; indeed, in the years preceding the Great Recession, the aggregate reserve ratio was lower than it had been before any other recent recession. Figure 26.1 also shows a key reason for this decline: The tax revenues collected for UI (as measured by the UI "cost ratio," or tax contributions as a percentage of total wages) trended down from between 1.0 and 1.3 percent during the 1980s, to between 0.5 and 0.8 percent during the 2000s (the lighter line).

Low and declining reserve ratios have important consequences. When unemployment rises in a recession, the trust funds of states with low reserves quickly become insolvent; these states must borrow (usually from the federal government) to pay UI benefits. For example, during and after the Great Recession, the trust funds of 31 states became insolvent, and these states borrowed in excess of $35 billion from the federal government (Vroman 2011). States that borrow must repay the federal loans, usually with interest, which creates a need to increase payroll taxes in a weak economy and a

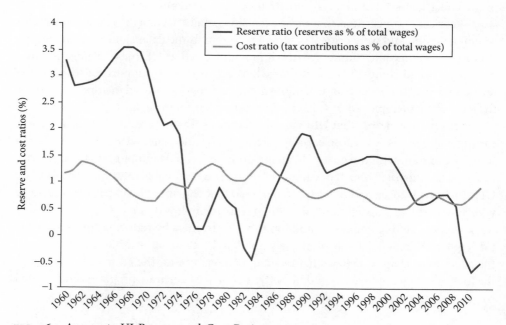

FIG. 26.1 Aggregate UI Reserve and Cost Ratios, 1960–2011

Note: The aggregate reserve ratio is the sum of all states' year-end trust-fund reserves as a percentage of all states' total payrolls in that year. The aggregate cost ratio is the sum of all states' regular UI tax contributions as a percentage of all states' total payrolls (both over the same year).

Source: U.S. Department of Labor, Employment and Training Administration, ET Financial Data Handbook 394 Report. http://workforcesecurity.doleta.gov/unemploy/hb394.asp

slack labor market. This places a drag on recovery and hampers the ability of UI to act as an automatic stabilizer. Further, states with insolvent trust funds often reduce benefits: during 2010 and 2011, eight states reduced benefit amounts or durations to limit UI payroll tax increases and reduce the burden of repaying their loans (Vroman 2011).

UI experts are virtually unanimous that the weak finances of most state UI systems have reduced the program's effectiveness as a counter-cyclical stabilizer and jeopardized its adequacy as an income replacement program (Woodbury and Simms 2011, 21–33). The most widely recommended way to improve the system's finances is to increase the payroll tax base and index it to the average weekly wage. This could be done by states individually or by Congressional action to increase and index the federal taxable wage base.

Raising the taxable wage base is necessary if earnings increase over time and the goal is to maintain a 50 percent replacement rate. Indexing the tax base to wage levels is an obvious way to accomplish this. Moreover, Vroman (2011) finds that whether a state indexes its tax base is a good predictor of its trust fund's solvency: Of the 16 states that indexed in 2008, only 5 (31 percent) had to borrow from the federal government during the Great Recession, but of the 35 that did not index, 29 (83 percent) needed to borrow.

5.3 Eligibility and "UI Modernization"

UI eligibility has received attention because UI recipiency has declined since the 1970s, potentially reducing the countercyclical effectiveness of UI (ACUC 1996, chap. 4). Also, research starting with Danziger and Gottschalk (1990) has emphasized that low-wage workers are more likely than others to be unemployed, and less likely to receive UI. The latter finding suggests that UI could do more to replace the lost earnings of low earners without abandoning its social insurance principles.

To address these concerns, the American Recovery and Reinvestment Act of 2009 included a "UI Modernization" package (based on a novel proposal from NELP) that offered incentive payments totaling $7 billion to states that included certain provisions in their UI law by September 30, 2011 (USDOL 2013, 88–89). A state received one-third of its incentive payment if it considered a claimant's earnings in the most recently completed quarter when determining monetary eligibility. The traditional base period excludes these recent earnings, making qualification difficult for recent labor-force entrants, re-entrants, and workers with sporadic work histories. Twenty-two states added such a provision in response to the UI Modernization incentives. A state received the remaining two-thirds of its incentive payment if its law included at least two of four additional provisions: allowing UI payments to claimants seeking part-time work (added by 26 states), qualifying claimants who quit for compelling family reasons (18 states), paying an additional 26 weeks of UI to exhaustees who enroll in approved training (16 states), and paying a dependents' allowance of at least $15 per dependent per week (3 states) (USDOL 2011).

5.4 Benefit Adequacy

The main UI wage-replacement issues concern where to set the weekly benefit amount and how long to set the duration of benefits. The early literature on benefit adequacy (see O'Leary 1998 for a review) has evolved into a literature on optimal UI. The literature is rather technical, and a comprehensive review is overdue (see Karni 1999 for a review of early developments), but the basic idea of optimal UI is straightforward. UI yields benefits to recipients in the form of consumption-smoothing (Gruber 1997), but it also entails social costs because it creates disincentives to work (for a review of empirical estimates, see Decker 1997). The generosity of UI should be increased as long as marginal consumption-smoothing benefits exceed the marginal cost of lost output due to reduced work effort.

The logic of optimal UI justifies increasing the potential duration of UI in a recession because the marginal cost of UI falls when the labor market is slack; that is, little or no output is lost when a worker remains unemployed for an additional week. It also justifies enforcing the work-search test and paying reduced benefits to workers with weak work histories; both reduce the marginal cost of UI and lead to higher benefits for eligible workers. Nevertheless, the implications of optimal UI analyses are sensitive to a range of assumptions: whether workers have savings or can borrow, how risk averse they are, how their job-search behavior responds to changes in weekly benefits and the potential duration of benefits, and the extent of worker heterogeneity. Analyses have quantified the optimal pattern, level, and duration of benefits by using empirical estimates to "calibrate" models of optimal UI (for example, Davidson and Woodbury 1997; Hopenhayn and Nicolini 1997; Wang and Williamson 2002; Chetty 2008; Shimer and Werning 2008), but inevitably, disagreement arises over the assumptions made and the estimates used to calibrate the models. As a result, the literature has yet to offer consensus on the optimal structure of UI benefits. Indeed, political and financial considerations have been more important than equity and efficiency criteria in contributing to recent benefit changes (see the earlier discussions of extended benefits and federal-state relations).

6 Conclusion

The downward trend in UI payroll taxes and the reluctance of states to broaden the UI taxable wage base suggest eroding support for the existing federal-state UI system. The most obvious outcome has been the insolvency of most states' UI trust funds. In short, a distaste for payroll taxes and concerns about the work disincentives associated with UI—the unemployment created by UI, as Feldstein (1976) called it—seem to dominate at the state level.

Federal UI policy, in contrast, has moved toward funding longer benefit durations in recessions (culminating in the 99-week durations under EUC08) and encouraging looser eligibility requirements (through the UI Modernization incentives). Recent reductions in regular state benefit durations in some states can be seen partly as a response to Congress's willingness to step in and finance emergency extended benefits whenever the labor market is weak. In effect, Congressional action has relieved the states of the need to finance UI benefits for as long as 26 weeks, which has been the norm since the early 1960s (Blaustein 1993, 302–306).

The endgame of this divergence between federal and state policy would seem to be abandonment of the federal-state arrangement, and its replacement by a national UI system. As Rubin (1990, 219) pointed out, "There are no 'states' rights' limitations on the authority of Congress to impose whatever provisions it wishes, or to substitute a national program for the present hybrid." Indeed, a national system has had advocates from the start and would have several advantages—a pooled national trust fund (hence, broader sharing of unemployment risk), uniform coverage, consistent treatment of employers with multistate operations, and potentially more efficient administration (West and Hildebrand 1997, 546–547).

But the federal-state system has proven remarkably durable and has its own advantages—decentralized policy authority and greater accountability of state administrators to a state's needs, a system that is potentially better suited and more responsive to a state's economic conditions, and the possibility for state-level experimentation. Moreover, the vested interests of the states in their systems and the near-certain aversion of Congress to another large federal bureaucracy would seem to make nationalization an unlikely prospect. However troubled the existing federal-state UI system may be, both financially and administratively, it seems likely to continue intact.

NOTES

1. Lesser requirements have been added over the years, pertaining for example to ensuring payment of interstate claims, covering state and local governments, paying extended benefits, short-time compensation (or work-sharing UI), and profiling workers into job-search assistance.
2. Throughout, specifics on state provisions come from USDOL (2012).
3. In the four slumps preceding the Great Recession, maximum potential durations (all three tiers) were 65 weeks (1975–1977), 55 weeks (1983), 72 weeks (1992), and 65 weeks (2002–2004).
4. Although their employees are potentially eligible for UI, nonprofit employers and state and local government employers do not pay FUTA taxes and usually reimburse the state for benefits paid to their former employees. Small farm employers and self-employed workers are wholly exempt from UI coverage.
5. Important federal-state issues also arise in the areas of federal benefit extensions, state trust-fund solvency (Whittaker 2012) and detection and reduction of fraud, abuse, and errors (Skrable 1997; Woodbury 2002), but space limitations preclude discussion of these issues.

REFERENCES

*Indicates recommended reading.

*ACUC (Advisory Council on Unemployment Compensation). 1994. *Report and Recommendations*. Washington, DC: ACUC.

*ACUC. 1995. *Unemployment Insurance in the United States: Benefits, Financing, and Coverage*. Washington, DC: ACUC.

*ACUC. 1996. *Defining Federal and State Roles in Unemployment Insurance*. Washington, DC: ACUC.

Anderson, Patricia. 1997. "Continuing Eligibility." In O'Leary and Wandner, eds., *Unemployment Insurance in the United States*, 125–161.

*Blaustein, Saul J. 1993. *Unemployment Insurance in the United States: The First Half-Century*. Kalamazoo, MI: W.E. Upjohn Institute.

Blaustein, Saul J., Christopher J. O'Leary, and Stephen A. Wandner. 1997. "Policy Issues." In O'Leary and Wandner, eds., *Unemployment Insurance in the United States*, 1–49.

Card, David, and Phillip B. Levine. 1994. "Unemployment Insurance Taxes and the Cyclical and Seasonal Properties of Unemployment." *Journal of Public Economics* 53 (January): 1–29.

Chetty, Raj. 2008. "Moral Hazard versus Liquidity and Optimal Unemployment Insurance." *Journal of Political Economy* 116 (March): 173–234.

Danziger, Sheldon, and Peter Gottschalk. 1990. "Unemployment Insurance and the Safety Net for the Unemployed." In Hansen and Byers, eds., *Unemployment Insurance*, 47–68.

Davidson, Carl, and Stephen A. Woodbury. 1997. "Optimal Unemployment Insurance." *Journal of Public Economics* 64 (June): 359–387.

Decker, Paul T. 1997. "Work Incentives and Disincentives." In O'Leary and Wandner, eds., *Unemployment Insurance in the United States*, 285–320.

Decker, Paul T., Cynthia K. Gustafson, and Phillip B. Levine. 2001. "Less-skilled Workers, Welfare Reform, and the Unemployment Insurance System." *Research in Labor Economics* 20: 395–432.

Deere, Donald R. 1991. "Unemployment Insurance and Employment." *Journal of Labor Economics* 9 (October): 307–324.

Fanning, Richard. W. 1995–1996. "The Federal-State Partnership of Unemployment Compensation." *University of Michigan Journal of Law Reform* 29 (1&2): 475–484.

Feldstein, Martin. 1976. "The Unemployment Caused by Unemployment Insurance." In *Proceedings of the Twenty-Eighth Annual Winter Meeting*. Madison, WI: Industrial Relations Research Association.

Gould-Werth, Alix, and H. Luke Shaefer. 2012. "Unemployment Insurance Participation by Education and by Race and Ethnicity." *Monthly Labor Review* 135 (October): 28–41.

Gray, John C., Jr., and Jane Greengold Stevens. 1995–1996. "The Law and Politics of the Enforcement of Federal Standards for the Administration of Unemployment Insurance Hearings." *University of Michigan Journal of Law Reform* 29: 509–526.

Gruber, Jonathan. 1997. "The Consumption Smoothing Benefits of Unemployment Insurance." *American Economic Review* 87 (1): 192–205.

Hansen, W. Lee, and James F. Byers. 1990a. "Unemployment Compensation and Retraining: Can a Closer Link Be Forged?" In Hansen and Byers, eds., *Unemployment Insurance*, 267–301.

Hansen, W. Lee, and James F. Byers. 1990b. *Unemployment Insurance: The Second Half-Century*. Madison: University of Wisconsin Press.

Hight, Joseph E. 1981–1982. "Unemployment Insurance: Changes in the Federal-State Balance." *University of Detroit Journal of Urban Law* 59: 615–629.

Hildebrand, Gerard. 1995–1996. "Federal Law Requirements for the Federal-State Unemployment Compensation System: Interpretation and Application." *University of Michigan Journal of Law Reform* 29 (1&2): 527–584.

Hopenhayn, Hugo A., and Juan Pablo Nicolini. 1997. "Optimal Unemployment Insurance." *Journal of Political Economy* 105 (2): 412–438.

Karni, Edi. 1999. "Optimal Unemployment Insurance: A Survey." *Southern Economic Journal* 66 (2): 442–465.

King, Miriam, Steven Ruggles, J. Trent Alexander, Sarah Flood, Katie Genadek, Matthew B. Schroeder, Brandon Trampe, and Rebecca Vick. 2010. *Integrated Public Use Microdata Series, Current Population Survey: Version 3.0 (machine-readable database)*. Minneapolis: University of Minnesota.

NASWA (National Association of State Workforce Agencies). 2012a. *A History of the National Association of State Workforce Agencies*. Washington, DC: NASWA. http://www.naswa.org/assets/utilities/serve.cfm?gid=bcdb456f-54c8-4570-b844-d02ce2c1cf58.

NASWA. 2012b. *Legislative Issue Update*. Washington, DC: NASWA. http://www.iawponline.org/imagevault/f1348513506.pdf.

NELP (National Employment Law Project). 2011. *2011 Annual Report*. http://www.nelp.org/page/-/Administrative/NELP_2011_Annual_Report.pdf?nocdn=12011.

Nicholson, Walter. 1997. "Initial Eligibility for Unemployment Insurance." In O'Leary and Wandner, eds., *Unemployment Insurance in the United States*, 91–123.

O'Leary, Christopher J. 1998. "The Adequacy of Unemployment Insurance Benefits." *Research in Employment Policy* 1: 63–110.

O'Leary, Christopher J. 2006. "State UI Job Search Rules and Reemployment Services." *Monthly Labor Review* 129 (June): 27–37.

O'Leary, Christopher J. 2013. "A Changing Federal-State Balance in Unemployment Insurance?" *Employment Research* 20 (January): 1–4.

*O'Leary, Christopher J., and Stephen A. Wandner, eds. 1997. *Unemployment Insurance in the United States: Analysis of Policy Issues*. Kalamazoo, MI: W.E. Upjohn Institute.

Rubin, Murray. 1983. *Federal-State Relations in Unemployment Insurance: A Balance of Power*. Kalamazoo, MI: W.E. Upjohn Institute.

Rubin, Murray. 1990. "Federal-State Relations in Unemployment Insurance." In Hansen and Byers, eds., *Unemployment Insurance*, 207–243.

Shaefer, H. Luke. 2010. "Identifying Key Barriers to Unemployment Insurance for Disadvantaged Workers in the United States." *Journal of Social Policy* 39 (3): 439–460.

Shimer, Robert, and Iván Werning. 2008. "Liquidity and Insurance for the Unemployed." *American Economic Review* 98 (5): 1922–1942.

Skrable, Burman. "Fraud, Abuse, and Errors in the Unemployment Insurance System." In O'Leary and Wandner, eds., *Unemployment Insurance in the United States*, 423–456.

Stettner, Andrew, Rebecca Smith, and Rick McHugh. 2004. *Changing Workforce, Changing Economy: State Unemployment Insurance Reforms for the 21st Century*. New York: National Employment Law Project. Update at http://www.nelp.org/site/issues/category/changing_workforce_changing_economy.

Topel, Robert H. 1984. "Experience Rating of Unemployment Insurance and the Incidence of Unemployment." *Journal of Law and Economics* 27 (April): 61–90.

Topel, Robert. 1990. "Financing Unemployment Insurance: History, Incentives, and Reform." In Hansen and Byers, eds., *Unemployment Insurance*, 108–135.

USDOL (U.S. Department of Labor). 2011. "*UI Modernization Incentive Payments—Approved Applications.*" Washington, DC: Employment and Training Administration, Office of Unemployment Insurance. http://workforcesecurity.doleta.gov/unemploy/laws.asp.

*USDOL. 2012. *Comparison of State Unemployment Insurance Laws 2012.* Washington, DC: Employment and Training Administration, Office of Unemployment Insurance.

USDOL. 2013. *Chronology of Federal Unemployment Compensation Laws.* Washington, DC: Employment and Training Administration, Office of Unemployment Insurance. http://www.oui.doleta.gov/unemploy/pdf/chronfedlaws.pdf.

UWC—Strategic Services on Unemployment and Workers' Compensation. 2012. Mission Statement. http://www.UWCstrategy.org/About-Us/Mission-Statement.

Vroman, Wayne. 2009. "Unemployment Insurance Recipients and Nonrecipients in the CPS." *Monthly Labor Review* 132 (October): 15–24.

Vroman, Wayne. 2010. "The Great Recession, Unemployment Insurance and Poverty." Paper Prepared for the Georgetown University and Urban Institute Conference on Reducing Poverty and Economic Distress after ARRA, April. http://www.urban.org/uploaded pdf/412072_great_recession.pdf.

Vroman, Wayne. 2011. "Unemployment Insurance and the Great Recession." Urban Institute Unemployment and Recovery Project Working Paper 2, November.

Wandner, Stephen A., and Thomas Stengle. 1997. "Unemployment Insurance: Measuring Who Receives It." *Monthly Labor Review* 120 (July): 15–24.

Wandner, Stephen A., and Andrew Stettner. 2000. "Why Are Many Jobless Workers Not Applying for Benefits?" *Monthly Labor Review* 123 (June): 21–32.

Wang, Cheng, and Stephen D. Williamson. 2002. "Moral Hazard, Optimal Unemployment Insurance, and Experience Rating." *Journal of Monetary Economics* 49: 1337–1371.

West, Thomas, and Gerard Hildebrand. 1997. "Federal-State Relations." In O'Leary and Wandner, eds., *Unemployment Insurance in the United States,* 545–598.

Whittaker, Julie M. 2012. "*The Unemployment Trust Fund (UTF): State Insolvency and Federal Loans to States.*" Report for Congress RS22954. Washington, DC: Congressional Research Service. Available at http://digitalcommons.ilr.cornell.edu/key_workplace/950/.

Woodbury, Stephen A. 2002. "Unemployment Insurance Overpayments and Underpayments." Testimony prepared for Hearings on Unemployment Fraud and Abuse, U.S. House Committee on Ways and Means, Human Resources Subcommittee, June 11.

Woodbury, Stephen A., and Murray Rubin. 1997. "The Duration of Benefits." In O'Leary and Wandner, eds., *Unemployment Insurance in the United States,* 211–283.

*Woodbury, Stephen A., and Margaret C. Simms. 2011. *Strengthening Unemployment Insurance for the 21st Century: A Roundtable Report.* Washington, DC: National Academy of Social Insurance. http://www.nasi.org/research/2011/report-strengthening-unemployment-insurance-2 1st-century-rou.

CHAPTER 27

....

CARE AND WORK-FAMILY POLICIES

....

SONYA MICHEL

1 INTRODUCTION

....

THE tension between caring responsibilities and wage-earning has existed as long as parents, especially mothers, have been working outside the home. In the United States, this occurred with the onset of the industrial revolution in the early 19th century. United States social policy has addressed the work-family issue more haltingly than other advanced market democracies, reflecting both the liberal or residual character of the American welfare state regime (Esping-Andersen 1990; Titmuss 1959), which dictates reliance on the market rather than the government for social provision, except for the most marginalized citizens; and the strength of conservative ideologies that uphold a male breadwinner/female caregiver division of social labor (Lewis 1992). This pattern also reflects class and racial divisions within American society. Until recently, policy has largely discouraged employment for white middle- and upper-class women, but has expected—and of late, mandated—poor and low-income mothers to work outside the home.

A review of policies toward wage-earning women with care responsibilities from the 1950s to the early 2010s shows how this pattern developed during a period when gender, racial, and class politics were in flux and debates over the nature of the welfare state became increasingly polarized. To fully understand American work and care policies, we must cast our net broadly to include not only measures that are so self-styled, but also those that implicitly affect work-family or work-care relations but are embedded in other categories of policy, such as public assistance and taxation. The focus in this essay will be on child care, after-school programs, and parental and family leave. The issue of elder care, which has increasingly affected employed women in the "sandwich generation," is discussed elsewhere in this publication.

2 THE EMERGENCE OF THE
WORK-FAMILY ISSUE

Work-family conflict was not conceptualized as such until mothers began entering the labor force in substantial numbers. From 1940 to 1980, the proportion of women who were employed nearly doubled, from 28.2 percent to 56 percent, and from the 1950s to the 1980s, the proportion of mothers working outside the home quadrupled. In 1950, only 15 percent of mothers with children under 18 were working, but by 1988, 60 percent of mothers with children aged three to five and half of those with children under one were in the labor force. Women composed the fastest-growing segment of the labor force, and 75 percent of them were of childbearing or childrearing age (15 to 60). By 1996, 70 percent of women with children under 18 were employed (Morgan 2006, 137–138).

Scholars and policy makers soon realized that it was difficult for wage-earning mothers to coordinate the demands of the workplace with responsibilities for their homes and families. One of the earliest voices calling attention to work-family conflict came from Catalyst, a New York-based organization begun in 1962 to encourage educated women, especially mothers, to consider pursuing careers. In 1980, Catalyst launched what it dubbed "the decade of fitting in family," calling on corporations to address issues such as parental leave. In 1989, the organization's founder, Felice Schwartz, created a ruckus in feminist circles by proposing in the *Harvard Business Review* what came to be called the "Mommy Track"—a career path designed to make it easier for women to balance work and family (Schwartz 1989). Schwartz claimed that such a path would allow firms to recruit and retain valuable female employees, but feminist Betty Friedan denounced it as a "Mommy Trap" that would deny women full equality in the labor force. The same year, UC Berkeley sociologist Arlie Hochschild (1989) published *The Second Shift*, a study that underscored Schwartz's concerns by demonstrating that wage-earning mothers actually had two jobs—one in the workplace, the other at home.

As rates of maternal employment continued to rise, progressive advocates and activists became more insistent in calling for work-family policies to ease women's burden. But this drew ire from New Right leaders like Phyllis Schlafly, who denounced feminist attempts to undermine "family values" and urged women to devote themselves to full-time at-home motherhood (Critchlow 2007, esp. chaps. 9–11). As a result, Congress was slow to respond to progressives' demands. In 1993, after seven years of wrangling, federal lawmakers finally passed the Family and Medical Leave Act (FMLA), which granted employees 12 weeks of unpaid leave to address family care needs, including childbirth and illness. But lawmakers repeatedly failed to pass other measures that would help women balance work and family, such as comprehensive child-care services for either preschool or school-age children, or family-friendly flexible work hours (so-called "flextime"). These difficulties gave rise to stories alleging that scores of highly educated professional women in the early 2000s were "opting-out" of the labor force when they became mothers, leaving well-paid jobs to stay home and raise their children (Belkin

2003).[1] According to sociologist Pamela Stone, the opt-out trend between 1984 and 2004 was not as pronounced as the popular media suggested (Stone 2008, 6–7). Nonetheless, work-family tensions—and public complaints—persisted (Warner 2006),[2] and in 2012, international relations specialist Anne-Marie Slaughter publicly declared that she had left her "dream job" as director of policy planning at the state department because she found that "juggling high-level government work with the needs of two teenage boys was not possible" (Slaughter 2012, 1; see also Sandberg 2010).

Poor and low-income women, however, do not have the option of choosing between work and family, not only because their wages are essential to their families' survival, but also because public policy has recently shifted from welfare to workfare. Starting in the 1960s, lawmakers in both parties came to believe that mothers receiving public assistance, particularly minorities, should be "rehabilitated" and integrated into the labor force (Mittelstadt 2005) and broke with the decades-long tradition of providing public assistance to lone mothers so that they could stay at home and care for their children. Rapidly abandoning encouragement for mandates, Congress passed a series of increasingly restrictive laws, starting with the Public Welfare Amendments of 1962 (PWA), then the Family Support Act of 1988 (FSA), and ultimately the Personal Responsibility and Work Opportunity Reconciliation Act of 1996 (PRWORA), which requires parents applying for public assistance to seek jobs or enter training programs, in some states as soon as six weeks after the birth of a child (Chappell 2009; see Weaver, this volume. Activists like the National Welfare Rights Organization and later the Women's Committee of 100 protested these actions (Kornbluh 2007; Mink 2002; Nadasen 2004), but it was difficult for them to make the case for allowing poor women to remain at home in light of growing rates of maternal employment across American society.

3 CHILD CARE

One of the chief pillars of maternal employment and work-family reconciliation is child care, but in the United States, child-care provision has developed sparsely and unevenly. From the early 19th through the early 20th century, the United States, like Canada and other industrializing countries in Europe, witnessed the rise of day nurseries—local, charitable institutions intended to care for children whose mothers, unable to depend on a male breadwinner (due to their absence, illness, disability or death), were compelled to work for wages outside the home. Clearly intended as emergency or stop-gap measures, nurseries offered only custodial services and served a clientele that was largely poor and working-class; their maternalist supporters had no intention of using child care to challenge the prevailing male-breadwinner ideal by enabling women to work outside the home on a regular basis.[3] Because of this self-limitation, nurseries failed to establish the basis for universal public services, though they eventually reached tens of thousands of families across the United States (Michel 1999).

In the early 20th century, day nurseries became increasingly stigmatized as professionalizing American social workers blamed maternal employment for weakening the mother-child bond and early childhood educators contrasted the meager services charities were able to muster with the vaunted developmental benefits of newly founded kindergartens and nursery schools. Although their schedules did not fit the needs of most wage-earning mothers (educators believed that young children could not effectively absorb instruction for more than a few hours per day), nursery schools soon became the darling of the voluntary sector and kindergartens found a niche in the public school system. Meanwhile, day nurseries languished as a kind of "policy orphan." Rather than promoting maternal employment, policy makers' preferred option for poor single mothers was, first, state-based mothers' or widows' pensions and later, federal Aid to Dependent Children—both measures designed to keep mothers in the home (Michel 1999, chap. 2).

World War II accelerated the development of child-care services across Western Europe and North America. In the United States, the war introduced federal financial support for child care for the first time, though local authorities had to initiate plans and apply for funding under the Community Facilities Act (also known as the Lanham Act). Despite the demand for women workers in defense industries, child-care advocates faced objections from social workers and other children's experts, who warned that breaking the "mother-child bond" would cause massive psychological damage (Michel 1999, chap. 4). When federal funding was abruptly withdrawn at war's end, wage-earning mothers clamored to keep child-care centers open, but government officials reminded them that public support had been intended to last "for the duration only." A few states and municipalities came up with new funding for services to low-income mothers, but the moment for federal support for universal child care had clearly passed (Fousekis 2011; Stoltzfus 2006).

Nevertheless, after the war, maternal employment did not disappear but, instead, after an initial dip, rose continuously (the baby boom notwithstanding). Neither voluntary nor commercial child care could keep pace with the need for services, but Congress offered little assistance, except for passing a limited income tax deduction for child care in 1954 (Michel 1999, 204–209). From the 1960s on, two countervailing forces buffeted U.S. child-care policy: second-wave feminism and the shift from welfare to workfare. Both called for child care as a means of promoting maternal employment, but with very different goals.

Starting in the 1960s, feminists of all stripes united to demand child care so that women could enter the labor force on an equal footing with men and achieve economic independence and gender equality. They differed, however, on tactics. Radical feminists, eschewing the idea of trying to find public support, set up experimental cooperative and "collective" centers in storefronts and women's centers around the country (Umansky 1996, 46–50; for a similar and even more radical movement in Germany, see Herzog 2005, chap. 4). Moderate organizations like the National Organization for Women (NOW), while pursuing a more conventional political path, nonetheless made strong demands, declaring that child care facilities should be established by law "on the same basis as parks, libraries and public schools, adequate to the needs of children from the preschool years through adolescence, as a community resource to be used by citizens from all income levels" (NOW Bill of Rights flyer, quoted in Umansky 1996,

46). In the 1960s, NOW joined early-childhood professionals, civil rights and welfare activists, labor and municipal officials to build a strong child-care coalition and found two staunch Congressional allies, Senator Walter Mondale (D-Minnesota) and Representative John Brademas (D-Indiana). In 1971 these two lawmakers introduced the Comprehensive Child Development Act (CCDA), which would have provided federal funding to expand the supply of child care, improve quality, and make it available to all families on a sliding scale. Despite strong public and Congressional support, President Richard M. Nixon vetoed the bill, denouncing public child care as a blow against family togetherness and a subversive form of "communal child rearing" (quoted in Michel 1999, 251; see also Karch 2013, chap. 3).

Meanwhile, Head Start, the program of compensatory early childhood education for low-income children initiated in 1965 as part of the Great Society, had become well established. In 1969, Nixon transferred the program from the Office of Economic Opportunity to the Office of Child Development in the Department of Health, Education, and Welfare, under the direction of Edward Zigler, a professor of psychology and director of the Child Study Center at Yale University, who was a long-time supporter of the program. Head Start enjoyed widespread popularity, but its limited hours and requirements for parental participation meant that it did not suit parents who needed full-time child care (Zigler and Styfco 2010).

After the failure of the CCDA, Congress did not again consider legislation for direct federal support to child-care services for nearly two decades. Throughout that time, however, lawmakers expanded and modified tax breaks for child-care expenses. The 1954 child-care tax deduction, initially limited to $600 per year, was increased to $900 in 1964, and to $1400 in 1971. In 1976 the deduction was converted to a tax credit of 20 percent of expenses up to $2000 a year for one child (for a credit of up to $400), or $4000 (an $800 credit) for two or more. In 1981, the maximums were raised to $4,000 and $8,000, respectively, but instead of a flat rate, the credit was calculated progressively, with greater benefits accruing to households with adjusted gross incomes of less than $28,000. That same year, Congress also exempted the value of employer-provided child care (up to $5000 per year) from taxation (Gabe, Lyke, and Spar 1999, 20–21).

Less visible than publicly supported child-care services, such benefits constitute part of what Howard (1999) has called the "hidden welfare state." In 1976, slightly over 2.6 million taxpayers received an average dependent care credit of $206; by 2009, more than 6.3 million taxpayers were doing so, at an average of $528.[4] Lower-income families have, since 1975, benefited from the Earned Income Tax Credit (EITC). Although these payments are not explicitly intended to pay for child care, they help cash-strapped families handle an expense that can take up to half of their total income (Glynn 2012; Misra and Moller's essay; Gitterman's essay).[5]

When Congress next considered direct support for child care, in the late 1980s, the nature of the opposition had shifted from antifeminism and anticommunism to general resistance to government expansion. Liberal Democrats sought to introduce several versions of an Act for Better Child Care Services (ABC), which would have widened public support for child care by basing fees on earnings rather that enrollment in welfare. The initiative enjoyed the support of some 135 national groups, but Congressional conserva-tives, backed by Presidents Reagan and George H.W. Bush, adamantly refused to create any new federal entitlements (Levy and Michel 2002, 244–245).

At the same time, however, efforts to provide targeted child care as a means of advanc-ing the nation's antipoverty policy were coming to the fore. Since the 1960s, a bipar-tisan consensus had been forming around the idea that welfare recipients should be required to work. Although lawmakers acknowledged that child care would be needed to implement such a policy, they had been reluctant to fund it adequately. As a result, the shift from welfare to "workfare" proceeded in fits and starts. The Public Welfare Amendments of 1962, intended to help welfare recipients achieve "self-sufficiency" by offering them "rehabilitation instead of relief" (Senator Abraham Ribicoff [D-Conn.], quoted in Michel 1999, 244), included grants-in-aid to state welfare agencies to promote the development of licensed child-care services, but few states drew down the funding (Levy and Michel 2002). With passage of the Family Support Act in 1988, targeted child care took on new life. This law mandated states to provide care for the children of AFDC recipients who were participating in approved educational or training programs or had accepted employment (AFDC-Child Care) and for those who were no longer eligible for AFDC benefits but still could not afford to pay full fees (Transitional Child Care or TCC). Federal mandates notwithstanding, just a few states managed to comply, and by 1995, the General Accounting Office found that only about 15 percent of eligible children were being served (Levy and Michel 2002, 243–244).

This problem was addressed to some extent in the 1990 Omnibus Budget Reconciliation Act, which provided additional funding for Head Start, offered child care to families "at risk" of needing public assistance (At-Risk Child Care, or ARCC), increased the Earned Income Tax Credit so that low-income families could pay for necessities like child care, and created a new program, the Child Care and Development Block Grant (CCDBG), to allow states to offer child care on a sliding scale to children under age 13 whose family income fell below 75 percent of the state's median. But the child-care component was poorly funded; although the original ABC bills had called for annual budgets of $2.5 billion, Congress appropriated less than $1 billion for CCDBG. As a result, 9.5 million of the 10 million children deemed eligible did not have access to child care (Levy 2000, 27).

With passage of Personal Responsibility and Work Opportunity Act (PRWORA) in 1996, work requirements tightened and funding for child care for poor and low-income children rose once again. PRWORA created the Child Care and Development Fund (CCDF), which consolidated AFDC-Child Care, ARCC, and TCC and added $4 bil-lion to the CCDBG appropriation. Despite attempts to coordinate the different pro-grams, the supply of child care remained inadequate and erratic, varying considerably among states. This created problems for the administration of PRWORA, which stipu-lated that parents who had no access to child care were to be exempt from the work requirement; in practice, however, many were still being penalized. Between 2002 and 2008, the Administration froze funding for the CCDF (Ewen and Matthews 2007), but the Economic Recovery Act of 2009 added a one-time supplement of $2 billion to its budget, over $250 million of which was to be used for "quality improvement." Between 1999 and 2010, only about 14 percent of eligible children were receiving services (Mezey, Greenberg, and Schumacher 2002; Smith and Gozjolko 2010, 3)—an improvement over CCDBG but still far from adequate.

Except during the "emergency" of World War II, the most successful rationales for direct federal support for child care in the United States, whether public or voluntary, have been associated with prevention of poverty. Congress has stepped in only when trying to advance its workfare agenda, leaving working-class and middle-class mothers to fend for themselves in the child-care market, using various forms of tax breaks to defray the cost of services. As maternal employment became the norm among women of all classes in the late 20th century, increasing demands for child care were met by an expansion of nonprofit and commercial centers, but given the lack of public subsidies, these services have had to rely on keeping staff wages low in order to survive (Morgan 2005).

Child-care facilities are not, as a rule, divided by class; in any given center, children may come from middle-class families who pay the full fee (which can range from hundreds to over a thousand dollars per month) or from low-income families paying on a sliding scale or using publicly funded vouchers. However, low-income families who earn too much to obtain subsidies can seldom afford center-based care and thus are often compelled to rely on informal, family-based services for toddlers, while leaving older children in "self care." In 2010, of the nearly 11 million children under five with employed mothers, just over 19 percent were in child care centers, whereas the rest received care from relatives or through a variety of other arrangements (U.S. Census Bureau 2010). In recent years, the high cost of center-based infant care and dissatisfaction with limited hours as well as the poor quality of public care has prompted parents with sufficient resources to hire live-in nannies—many of them low-paid female migrants from the developing world (Cheever 2002). The divided approach of lawmakers as well as the "divided constituency" of child-care consumers (Michel 1999, chap. 7) has largely kept universal child care off the federal agenda for the past few decades, and it is unlikely to gain traction in the current climate of fiscal austerity.

4 THE "PROBLEM" OF SCHOOL-AGE CHILDREN

While child-care advocates focused on children from zero to five, other policy makers were seeking ways to address the needs of school-age children of wage-earning mothers. The situation of this age group first captured public attention in the late 19th century, as compulsory school attendance displaced child labor (a practice that had served as a form of child care as well as a source of income for working-class families), leaving many children without supervision during "out-of-school hours" and long summer vacations.[6]

Early initiatives came from voluntary organizations like settlement houses, Boy Scouts and Girl Scouts, as well as police departments, and later Boys and Girls Clubs and the YMCA and YWCA, all of which initiated sports and recreational programs, classes in music and the arts, carpentry, sewing, and cooking. Designed to occupy children during the hours when schools were closed, these programs were primarily viewed not as a form of child care, but rather as a way to keep children off the streets; Americanize those who were immigrants; prepare working-class youth for their futures—gainful employment for boys, modern housewifery for girls; and discourage delinquency and maintain order, particularly in urban areas (Goodman 1979; Halpern 2003, chap. 1). By tacit mutual consent, public schools made no effort to absorb after-school programs but left them to run independently. Throughout the interwar years, they depended largely on private funding, though some support became available through New Deal agencies in the 1930s.

As it had with services for preschool children, World War II served as a catalyst for expanding school-age child care and increasing public funding. With millions of mothers being recruited for work in defense industries, the problem of "latchkey children" became headline news (Tuttle 1995). One journalist, after visiting factory towns across the country, declared that, "from Buffalo to Wichita it is the children who are suffering the most from mass migration, easy money, unaccustomed hours of work, and the fact that mama has become a welder on the graveyard shift" (Meyer 1944, 60; quoted in Halpern 2003, 55). In response, local Defense Day Care and Defense Recreational Committees pressured existing day nurseries and kindergartens to admit older children both before and after school hours, called for extended elementary school days, and initiated hundreds of new freestanding programs. Funding came from a mix of public and private sources, including school districts, civic organizations, and parent fees.

Wartime programs for school-age children proved to be less controversial than services for younger children; when it came to the older group, experts were less concerned about psychological health and mother-child bonding than about juvenile delinquency. In 1943, the federal government authorized the Office of Education and the Children's Bureau to set up "Extended-Day Services" (ESS), eventually serving some 320,000 children. But, like services for younger children, ESS lost federal funding as soon as the war ended, though many managed to continue into the postwar decades with state and municipal as well as voluntary funding (Michel 1999, 142; Tuttle 1995).

It was not until the 1970s that school-age child care, or after-school programs (ASP), as they came to be called, along with other work-family issues, once again came into focus, as rates of maternal employment shot up. In 1978 a community activist named Michelle Seligson began the School-Age Child Care Project (later the National Institute on Out-of-School Time, or NIOST) at the Wellesley College Centers for Women. Observing that ASP, like child care, had become a patchwork of public, voluntary, and commercial offerings of varying cost and quality, Seligson (1999) called on educators and policy makers to upgrade standards and tailor programs to meet the special needs of school-age children (136). While some policy makers emphasized the child-care benefits of school-age programs, others deplored what they saw as the further institu-tionalization of childhood, arguing that older children needed opportunities for more freedom and self-determination (Halpern 2003, chap. 3).

The fact that more middle-class women were now joining the labor force (Stone 2008, 6–7) gave the issue of school-age care new impetus, but, as before, concerns about social pathology among poor and low-income children would carry the day when it came to public support. Even so, federal funding was hard to come by. The unsuccessful 1971 Comprehensive Child Development Act would have provided services for children up to age 14, and in the 1980s, President Reagan approved a block grant for school-age resource and referral, but it was never funded. Not until the 1990s did states and then the federal government finally become involved in after-school programs. With passage of PRWORA in 1996, policy makers realized that moving welfare recipients into employ-ment would require care for school-age children as well as preschoolers. But such ser-vices could do double duty, addressing the problems of crime and poor educational achievement among low-income youth as well as needs for supervision. Several states, including California, Georgia, and Delaware, had already begun to use their own funds for targeted after-school programs, and in 1998 the federal government took over, with Congress, at the urging of President Clinton, approving a program called 21st Century Community Learning Centers (CCLC), to be run through public schools. Starting with an appropriation of just $200 million for the first year, the budget rapidly increased to $26 billion over a five-year period, and the number of public programs expanded accordingly (Afterschool Alliance n.d.).

The preventive rationale behind ASP gained fresh political impetus in 2002, when President George W. Bush included CCLC in the No Child Left Behind Act (NCLB). This legislation reauthorized funding for the program but, in keeping with Bush's emphasis on decentralization, transferred its administration from the U.S. Department of Education to individual state education agencies. The following year, the Bush admin-istration, citing "disappointing" findings from an evaluation of the programs, proposed a 40 percent reduction in funding. Strong bipartisan support in Congress blocked the most severe cuts, but Congressional appropriations fell nonetheless (McGuinn 2006).

Since 2002, Congress has appropriated an average of $1 billion per year for the Learning Centers through NCLB. Although still significant, this amount falls below the budget authorized by the original act. As a result, public school systems have opted to focus primarily on elementary-school-age children as opposed to those in middle and high school. Many of the children served are educationally as well as financially disad-vantaged; nearly two-thirds are low-income, and a disproportionate number have lim-ited English proficiency—over 16 percent, compared to 11 percent in the general student population (Gayl 2004). But perpetual underfunding has denied access to many eligible children. While serving approximately 1.6 million children in 2009, the program left another 18.5 million on wait lists. Moreover, as a result of budget cuts brought on by the recession, many programs have been forced to make cutbacks in size and offerings (Afterschool Alliance 2009).

Communities have attempted to make up for these shortfalls by using NCLB grants to leverage support and cooperation from state and local governments; voluntary, civic, and religious organizations; and large institutions such as universities, museums, and hospitals. Some 39 states have set up Statewide Afterschool Networks to ensure uniform standards and sustainability. Most notably, public schools have moved increasingly to incorporate ASPs; by 2008, 56 percent of the nation's estimated 49,700 public elementary schools had such programs located in their buildings. However, only 10 percent of these were designated as CCLCs, a status bringing in additional funding. But even those so designated reported in 2008 that they could not serve all eligible children because of lack of capacity (Parsad and Lewis 2009, 3).

Expense not only keeps down the capacity and quality of ASPs but limits participation by many of the children whom advocates seek to include. The annual cost of a quality full-year after-school program ranges from $1500 to $2500 per child, but public funding covers that cost only for the lowest-income children, leaving the bulk of families to pay fees themselves. For 38 percent of the parents in schools surveyed in one study in 2008, that barrier proved insurmountable. A lack of adequate transportation also deterred participation (Parsad and Lewis 2009, 3). Thus, despite the marked increase in funding for public after-school programs since 1998, many children are still left out—and many parents lack a key element of work-family reconciliation.

5 Parental and Family Leave

A third element of work-family policy is parental or family leave. The FMLA, which went into effect in August 1993, mandates that firms with 50 or more employees permit those who are eligible to take up to 12 weeks of unpaid leave per year to care for family members (a newborn, newly adopted or newly placed foster child; a child, spouse, or parent who has a serious health condition; or for the employee's own serious health condition, including maternity-related disability and prenatal care) and return to the same or an equivalent position. Employers must maintain employees' health insurance during the leave period if it was offered in the first place. To become eligible, employees must have worked for the firm for at least 12 months prior to taking leave (U.S. Department of Labor n.d.).

By mandating only unpaid leave, the United States stands apart from nearly every other advanced market society and most developing ones as well; only three other countries provide no paid time off for childbirth: Liberia, Papua New Guinea, and Swaziland (Fass 2009, 3). Moreover, at 12 weeks, U.S. leave time falls short of the International Labour Organization's (ILO) recommended 14 weeks and the OECD average of 18 weeks (OECD 2014b). In addition to leave for childbirth itself, many countries in the European Union offer liberal post-birth maternity, paternity, and parental leave. To be sure, some of these laws, particularly those allowing multiyear leaves, have been used to encourage women to stay at home and suppress unemployment levels (Morgan 2002, 155–157), but take-up rates in most countries by fathers as well as mothers have generally been high (Crampton and Mishra 1995, 284–285).

In the face of federal inaction, three American states have developed their own policies: in 2003, California passed a law granting employees contributing to the State Disability Insurance fund paid family leave of up to six weeks at 55 percent of their weekly wages, with a cap of $959; Washington State followed suit in 2007, providing 66 percent of wages, capped at $546; and New Jersey did so in 2008, offering a flat rate of $250 per week (Fass 2009, 8; cap figures are as of 2009).[7] Seven other states provide paid leave for new mothers through pregnancy disability, illness, or temporary disability programs (National Partnership for Women and Families 2012, 18). A number of employers also offer various forms of paid leave, and the proportion of women receiving paid maternity leave has slowly but steadily increased. Between 1981–1985 and 2006–2008, the proportion of working mothers receiving paid leave at the birth of their first child rose from 37.3 percent to 50.8 percent (Laughlin 2011).

The roots of job-protected family leave go back to 1919, when the newly formed International Labour Organization (ILO) urged its members to adopt maternity-leave policies. At that point, many European countries already had some form of leave in place, but the United States refused to follow the recommendation, despite the fact that its female labor force, including many women of childbearing age, was growing. American law makers did not address wage-earning mothers' need for job protection until 1978, when Congress passed the Pregnancy Discrimination Act (PDA), barring employment discrimination (i.e., transfer or dismissal) on the basis of pregnancy. Previously, pregnancy had frequently led to firing, and in most states, married women were barred from working as teachers in the first place. Although perceived as a bold step at the time, the PDA's impact was limited, since it did not cover federal employees or those who worked for small businesses (Crampton and Mishra 1995, 278). Moreover, it failed to adequately address the issue of work-family reconciliation since it made no provision for leave time.

This led Congress to embark on the torturous eight-year legislative process that started with a proposal for unpaid maternity leave in 1985 and eventually produced the FMLA. According to Anne Radigan (1988, 1), director of the Congressional Caucus for Women's Issues at the time, it reflected the "new prominence of family issues on the agenda of policymakers across the political spectrum." But feminists, particularly lawyers, were divided in their views of the initial proposal. Some believed that, however well intended, it involved "special treatment" for women and thus too closely resembled the protective labor legislation of the Progressive Era that had led to ongoing discrimination against women in the labor force. Others countered that women's unique childbearing capacity already put them at a disadvantage in the workplace, and thus they needed protection to make them competitive.

The conservative political environment of the Reagan era made this debate especially tricky but ultimately pushed supportive legislators to mobilize other constituencies, including seniors and people with disabilities in an effort to wrest the "profamily banner" from the right. Seeking to shift the equal treatment model "from the women's agenda to the family agenda" (Radigan, 1988, 8), these lawmakers called for extending job protection to all temporarily disabled employees and giving both parents leave for childbirth and adoption. By including fathers and framing the measure in terms of promoting healthy families, they hoped to overcome the bill's feminist associations. The final product enjoyed widespread support "from NOW to UMW [United Mineworkers of America] to the U.S. Catholic Conference" (Radigan 1988, 8), including advocates for seniors and people with disabilities.

But the measure still faced stiff opposition from business. The Chamber of Commerce declared that family leave constituted an "unwarranted government-mandated benefit that threatens the freedom and competitive edge of the American marketplace" (quoted in Radigan 1988, 3) and pointed out that many were already granting time off as a means of retaining skilled employees. While conceding that this was true, supporters noted several limitations: provisions varied, leave times were usually for only six to eight weeks, and few firms offered paid leave. This introduced "uncertainty" and placed "some workers at considerable risk" (National Council of Jewish Women, quoted in Radigan 1988, 8).

Congressional Republicans voiced more practical objections, arguing that employee leaves would lead to an increase in layoffs and cuts in other benefits and force fellow employees to work longer hours to compensate for those who were absent. Moreover, despite the fact that leaves would be unpaid, maintaining health insurance and hiring temporary workers would increase labor costs. Democrats countered that the FMLA would make the U.S. labor force more competitive by stabilizing jobs, lifting morale, reducing absenteeism, and increasing company loyalty. Firms could lower transitional costs by using cross-training to enable employees to fill in for one another, and permitting telecommuting (Crampton and Mishra 1995, 274–276).

While Congress debated and tweaked the various bills, states, localities, and individual firms took matters into their own hands. By 1990, 25 states and a number of cities had passed some sort of unpaid leave laws for periods ranging from 10 to 16 weeks, most including job protection and maintenance of health insurance. On the eve of FMLA's passage, 70 percent of employers were offering employees unpaid leave for birth, adoption, or the serious illness of a family member, and 60 percent to employees who were themselves seriously ill (Crampton and Mishra 1995, 282). But a federal law was still needed to establish standards.

In 1990 and again in 1992, Congress finally passed bills, only to draw vetoes from President George H.W. Bush. Although there was bi-partisan support in both houses of Congress, it was not sufficient to overturn the vetoes. As a candidate, Bill Clinton signaled his support for the FMLA, and the new Congress made it the first order of business when it convened in 1993. As soon as the bill passed, Clinton signed it into law.

In practice, the impact of the FMLA has defied expectations, negative and positive alike. Both liberal and conservative critics predicted that the impact of the law would be minimal because it exempted so many firms and provided only for unpaid leave. Conservatives claimed that it would end up penalizing those it was intended to protect (namely women) because it would discourage employers from hiring them (employment discrimination laws notwithstanding). Both predictions, according to policy scholar Jane Waldfogel (1999), have proven groundless. Analyzing data from a 1996 survey, she found that more firms were covered than before passage of FMLA and rates of leave taking had gone up, but the cost to firms was modest and likely to be offset by positive employment and earnings effects associated with the mandate (Waldfogel 1999, 299–300).

Supporters of the measure hoped that it would not only help relieve work-family tension but also lead to greater gender equality, but they, too, were disappointed. Sociologists Amy Armenia and Naomi Gerstel, analyzing data from the same 1996 survey, discovered marked racial as well as gender differences in patterns of uptake: white men were less likely to take parental leaves than white women or women and men of color; men were less likely to take leave for newborns but almost as likely as women to take it for seriously ill children and adult family members, particularly spouses; and men tended to take shorter leaves than women (Armenia and Gerstel 2006, 881–886).

Based on their findings, Armenia and Gerstel concluded that legislators' efforts to broaden the leave from mothers to parents in the interest of making it more gender-equal had failed to reduce gender inequality, partly because of deeply embedded social and cultural norms surrounding childbirth and family care, and partly because having only unpaid leave meant that in married-couple households, the higher-earning spouse—usually the man—would be less likely to take it (Armenia and Gerstel 2006, 886–889). Moreover, by treating all families the same, the law overlooked crucial differences that determined the likelihood of taking leave. For example, though lone parents were perhaps most in need of leave for practical purposes, they would be less likely to take it for financial reasons. Similarly, people of color might need more leave because of health problems but took less because they could not afford to lose wages (Armenia and Gerstel 2006, 874), and women with lower incomes took shorter maternity leaves than those who earned more.

A follow-up survey of employees and establishments conducted by the Department of Labor in 2000 (U.S. Department of Labor 2000), though less detailed than the earlier study, came up with similar results: In the six months prior to the survey, almost the same proportion of workers had taken leave as in 1995 (16 percent in 1995, compared to 16.5 percent in 2000), but there were increases in the percentage of leave-taking among older employees (ages 50–64), and those who were married, had children, and were earning between $50,000 and $75,000. Fewer employees were taking leave for personal health needs, more to care for children or parents. Over half noted that they had had financial concerns about taking unpaid leave. Two-thirds of leave-takers did receive some pay from their employers during these periods, but men were more likely to do so (70.4 percent) than women (62.5 percent). Over half said they would have taken longer leaves if they could afford to. Older, married, and more educated employees, as well as those earning over $20,000 per year, were more likely to have the benefit of paid leave than their younger, single, less-educated, and less well-paid counterparts. Overall, leave taking in 2000 was still greater among women than men (75.8 percent vs. 45.1 percent), but women and men with young children took leave at about the same rate—slightly over one-third—and nearly a third of women took leave for "maternity-disability." Unfortunately, the 2000 survey did not break down leave-taking patterns by race, so it is not possible to compare those trends with Armenia and Gerstel's findings on race in the 1995 data.

Since passage of the FMLA, numerous amendments have been proposed. Liberals have sought to extend coverage to smaller firms and for longer periods, and provide financial assistance so that low-income employees with care needs would be able to make full use of leave policy, whereas conservatives have pushed to narrow the definition of "serious health condition" and restrict the use of short, intermittent leaves to prevent frequent work interruptions. None of these efforts has gone very far, but several attempts were made, starting with President Clinton's proposed Family-Friendly Workplace Act of 1996, to extend to private-sector workers the flexible hours rules ("flextime") already enjoyed by federal employees. Despite some bi-partisan support, the bills have run into fierce Republican opposition; the last such attempt, supported by Senator Hillary Rodham Clinton, died in committee in 2009. One issue that the FMLA omitted, provisions for breastfeeding, was finally addressed in the Patient Protection and Affordable Care Act of 2010. This law requires employers to provide nursing mothers suitable spaces and adequate breaks from work to express milk for up to a year after childbirth (Drago, Hayes, and Lee 2010).

6 Conclusion

Overall, the U.S. record on work and care or work and family policies has been mixed. Although advocates and analysts have proposed dozens of specific measures that would allow all adults, but especially women, to balance work and care, Congressional support has tilted primarily toward direct policies targeted at poor and low-income workers and their families or toward indirect policies such as tax breaks that allow better-off families to navigate the care market more easily The FMLA, although theoretically universal, falls into the category of negative rights, protecting employees who take time off from work to care but offering them no compensation for doing so. In effect, the law implies that care is primarily an individual, not a social, responsibility, and those who cannot afford to take unpaid leave—mainly lower-paid women and minority workers—simply will not benefit from the law's protections. For a time in U.S. history, public assistance—first mothers' and widows' pensions, then AFDC—served as a kind of paid care leave for poor and low-income families, allowing mothers to stay at home and care for children (though making little accommodation for adults caring for those with chronic illnesses or disabilities or for the frail elderly). Now, however, those same caregivers must seek employment or enter job-training programs as a condition of receiving public assistance (Hill 2012). Many scholars (e.g. Wexler 1997; Mink 2002; Roberts 2003; Glenn 2010) have argued that U.S. work-family policies, taken to include laws such as PRWORA and CCLC as well as FMLA, implicitly value the caring labor of the wealthy and middle classes, which are largely white, while denigrating that of poor and low-income women and men, disproportionately people of color. The discourses deployed in Congressional debates over work-family policy as well as the outcomes of specific policies and programs largely confirm such a reading.

United States work-family policy stands in sharp contrast to that of other advanced market democracies, particularly those of Western Europe, Japan, and the Antipodes. All of these countries currently offer paid maternity if not parental leave, and many also provide high-quality child care (Morgan 2006). There is less difference in terms of care for school-age children, which, in these countries, as in the United States remains uneven (Elniff-Larsen, Dreyling, and Williams 2006). These differences partly reflect variations among welfare state regimes (Esping-Andersen 1990), partly pressures to improve work-family policies to reverse declining birth rates (on Japan see Peng 2002). Although employment rates for all women across these countries cluster between 50 and 60 percent, those for mothers are, with only a few exceptions, somewhat lower (OECD 2014a, Chart LMF1.2.A). The U.S. maternal employment rate falls between that of the Scandinavian countries, France, Germany, the UK, and several East European countries, at the high end, and Israel, Japan, Australia, Spain, and Italy at the lower. The relative strength of work-family policies explains some, if not all, of these differences.

NOTES

1. Here I am disagreeing with British sociologist Catherine Hakim (2002), who contends that mothers drop out of the labor force because of "lifestyle preferences," not inadequate social provision.
2. See also Warner's posts on the blog, 'Motherlode," in the *New York Times*: http://parenting.blogs.nytimes.com/author/judith-warner/.
3. Maternalism refers to an ideology that accepts traditional notions of "natural" gender difference but claims that women's proclivities toward morality, sympathy and care should be applied to society at large (Koven and Michel 1993).
4. The value of the 2009 credit has not kept pace with the changing value of the dollar; a credit of $206 in 1976 would be worth $776 in 2009 dollars. The cost of total tax expenditures (taxes foregone by the federal government) for the credit rose from $548 million in 1976 to $3346 billion in 2009.
5. In 2009, EITC tax expenditures totaled $58 billion; see Internal Revenue Service, EITC Statistics-at-a-Glance for Tax Year 2009.
6. Throughout the early phase of industrialization, families' need for children's income outweighed the perceived payoff of investment in their education; apprenticeships or on-the-job training were considered to be more valuable than additional years of schooling. This shifted as compulsory attendance laws were phased in, raising the average time for leaving school from fifth to eighth grade (Halpern 2003, 9).

7. Washington State has delayed implementation of its paid leave until 2015 owing to budgetary concerns.

REFERENCES

*Indicates recommended reading.

Afterschool Alliance. 2009. "Uncertain Times 2009: Recession Imperiling Afterschool Programs and the Children They Serve." http://www.afterschoolalliance.org/UncertainTimes2009.cfm.

Afterschool Alliance. [n.d.] "21st Century Community Learning Centers Federal Afterschool Initiative." http://www.afterschoolalliance.org/policy21stcclc.cfm.

*Armenia, Amy, and Naomi Gerstel. 2006. "Family Leaves, the FMLA and Gender Neutrality: The Intersection of Race and Gender." *Social Science Research* 35:871–891.

Belkin, Lisa. 2003. "The Opt-Out Revolution." *New York Times Magazine*, October 26. http://www.nytimes.com/2003/10/26/magazine/26WOMEN.html?pagewanted=all.

Chappell, Marisa. 2009. *The War on Welfare: Family, Poverty, and Politics in Modern America.* Philadelphia: University of Pennsylvania Press.

Cheever, Susan. 2002. "The Nanny Dilemma." In Barbara Ehrenreich and Arlie Hochschild, eds., *Global Woman: Nannies, Maids and Sex Workers in the New Economy.* New York: Holt, 31–38.

Commission on Family and Medical Leave. 1996. "A Workable Balance: Report to Congress on Family and Medical Leave Policies." Washington, DC: U.S. Department of Labor. http://www.dol.gov/whd/fmla/chapter1.htm.

Crampton, Suzanne M., and Jitendra M. Mishra. 1995. "Family and Medical Leave Legislation: Organizational Policies and Strategies." *Public Personnel Management* 24 (3):271–290.

Critchlow, Donald T. 2007. *Phyllis Schlafly and Grassroots Conservatism: A Woman's Crusade.* Princeton, NJ: Princeton University Press.

Drago, Robert, Jeffrey Hayes, and Youngmin Lee. 2010. *Better Health for Mothers and Children: Breastfeeding Accommodations Under the Affordable Care Act.* Washington, DC: Institute for Women's Policy Research. http://www.iwpr.org/publications/pubs/better-health-for-mothers-and-children-breastfeeding-accommodations-under-the-affordable-care-act.

Elniff-Larsen, Angela, Melissa Dreyling, and Jenny Williams. 2006. *Employment Developments in Childcare Services for School-Age Children.* Dublin: European Foundation for the Improvement of Living and Working Conditions. http://www.eurofound.europa.eu/pub docs/2006/32/en/1/ef0632en.pdf.

Esping-Andersen, Gøsta. 1990. *The Three Worlds of Welfare Capitalism.* Princeton, NJ: Princeton University Press.

Ewen, Danielle, and Hannah Matthews. 2007. *Families Forgotten: Administration's Priorities Put Child Care Low on the List.* Washington, DC: Center for Law and Social Policy (CLASP).

Fass, Sarah. 2009. *Paid Leave in the States: A Critical Support for Low-Wage Workers and Their Families.* New York: National Center for Children in Poverty, Mailman School of Public Policy, Columbia University.

Fousekis, Natalie. 2011. *Demanding Child Care: Women's Activism and the Politics of Welfare, 1940–1971.* Champaign: University of Illinois Press.

Gabe, Thomas, Bob Lyke, and Karen Spar. 1999. *"Child Care Subsidies: Federal Grants and Tax Benefits for Working Families."* Congressional Research Service RL 30081. March.

Gayl, Chrisanne L. 2004. "After-School Programs: Expanding Access and Ensuring Quality." Policy Report, Progressive Policy Institute. July. http://www.kidcareamerica.org/images/afterschool_0704.pdf.

Glenn, Evelyn Nakano. 2010. *Forced to Care: Coercion and Caregiving in America.* Cambridge, MA: Harvard University Press.

Glynn, Sarah Jane. 2012. "Fact Sheet: Child Care." Washington, DC: Center for American Progress. August 16. http://www.americanprogress.org/issues/2012/08/childcare_factsheet.html.

Goodman, Cary. 1979. *Choosing Sides: Playground and Street Life on the Lower East Side.* New York: Schocken.

Hakim, Catherine. 2002. "Lifestyle Preferences as Determinants of Women's Differentiated Labour Market Careers." *Work and Occupations* 29 (November):428–459.

*Halpern, Robert. 2003. *Making Play Work: The Promise of After-School Programs for Low-Income Children.* New York: Teachers College Press.

Herzog, Dagmar. 2005. *Sex After Fascism: Memory and Morality in Twentieth-Century Germany.* Princeton, NJ: Princeton University Press.

Hill, Heather D. 2012 "Welfare as Maternity Leave? Exemptions from Welfare Work Requirements and Maternal Employment. *Social Science Review* 86, no. 1 (March): 37–67.

Hochschild, Arlie. 1989. *The Second Shift: Working Families and the Revolution at Home.* New York: Viking.

Howard, Christopher. 1999. *The Hidden Welfare State: Tax Expenditures and Social Policy in the United States.* Princeton, NJ: Princeton University Press.

Karch, Andrew. 2013. *Early Start: Preschool Politics in the United States.* Ann Arbor: University of Michigan Press.

Kornbluh, Felicia. 2007. *The Battle for Welfare Rights: Politics and Poverty in Modern America.* Philadelphia: University of Pennsylvania Press.

Koven, Seth, and Sonya Michel eds. 1993. *Mothers of a New World: Maternalist Politics and the Origins of Welfare States.* New York: Routledge.

Laughlin, Lynda. 2011. "Maternity Leave and Employment Patterns of First-Time Mothers: 1961–2008." *Current Population Reports*: P70–128 (October). http://www.census.gov/prod/2011pubs/p70-128.pdf.

Levy, Denise Urias. 2000. "Child Care Policies in America: Interstate Differences and the Progress of Devolution." PhD diss., University of Illinois at Chicago.

Levy, Denise Urias, and Sonya Michel. 2002. "More Can Be Less: Child Care and Welfare Reform in the United States." In Michel and Rianne Mahon, eds., *Child Care Policy at the Crossroads: Gender and Welfare State Restructuring.* New York: Routledge, 239–263.

Lewis, J. 1992. "Gender and the Development of Welfare Regimes." *Journal of European Social Policy* 2 (3): 159–173.

McGuinn, Patrick. 2006. *No Child Left Behind and the Transformation of Federal Education Policy, 1965–2005.* Lawrence: University Press of Kansas.

Meyer, Agnes. 1944. *Journey Through Chaos.* New York: Harcourt, Brace.

Mezey, Jennifer, Mark Greenberg, and Rachel Schumacher. 2002. "The Southern Regional Initiative on Child Care. Analysis of Potential Barriers to Creating Coordinated Absence Policies for Collaborations Between Head Start And CCDF And TANF-Funded Programs." Center for Law and Social Policy. December http://www.policyarchive.org/handle/10207/bitstreams/13770.pdf.

*Michel, Sonya. 1999. *Children's Interests/Mothers' Rights: The Shaping of America's Child Care Policy.* New Haven, CT: Yale University Press.

Mink, Gwendolyn. 2002. *Welfare's End.* Ithaca, NY: Cornell University Press.

Mittelstadt, Jennifer. 2005. *From Welfare to Workfare: The Unintended Consequences of Liberal Reform, 1945–1965.* Chapel Hill: University of North Carolina Press.

Morgan, Kimberly J. 2002. "Does Anyone Have 'Libre Choix'? Subversive Liberalism and the Politics of French Child Care Policy." In Michel and Mahon, eds., *Child Care Policy at the Crossroads,* 143–170.

Morgan, Kimberly J. 2005. "The Production of Child Care: How Labor Markets Shape Social Policy and Vice Versa." *Social Politics: International Studies in Gender, State and Society* 12, no. 2 (Summer):243–263.

*Morgan, Kimberly J. 2006. *Working Mothers and the Welfare State: Religion and the Politics of Work-Family Policies in Western Europe and the United States.* Stanford, CA: Stanford University Press.

Nadasen, Premilla. 2004. *Welfare Warriors: The Welfare Rights Movement in the United States.* New York: Routledge.

National Partnership for Women and Families. 2012. "Expecting Better: A State-By-State Analysis of Laws That Help New Parents." May. http://npwf.convio.net/site/DocServer/ParentalLeaveReportMay05.pdf?docID=1052.

Nelson, Barbara. 1990. "The Gender, Race, and Class Origins of Early Welfare Policy and the Welfare State: A Comparison of Workmen's Compensation and Mother's Aid." In Louise Tilly and Pat Guerin eds., *Women, Policies, and Change.* New York: Sage, 413–435.

OECD. 2014a. OECD Family Database, LMF 1.2, "Maternal Employment." Paris: OECD. http://www.oecd.org/els/family/LMF1_2_Maternal_Employment_14May2014.pdf

OECD. 2014b. OECD Family Database, PF 2.1, "Key Characteristics of Parental Leave Systems." Paris: OECD. http://www.oecd.org/els/soc/PF2_1_Parental_leave_systems_1May2014.pdf

Parsad, B., and L. Lewis (2009). *After-School Programs in Public Elementary Schools.* NCES 2009-043. Washington, DC: National Center for Education Statistics, Institute of Education Sciences, U.S. Department of Education. http://www.naaweb.org/downloads/Publications/After-School%20Programs%20in%20Public%20Elementary%20Schools.pdf.

Peng, Ito. 2002. "Social Care in Crisis: Gender, Demography, and Welfare State Restructuring in Japan." *Social Politics* 9 (3): 411–443.

Radigan, Anne L. 1988. *Concept & Compromise: The Evolution of Family Leave Legislation in the U.S. Congress.* Washington, DC: Women's Research and Education Institute.

Roberts, Dorothy. 2003. *Shattered Bonds: The Color of Child Welfare.* New York: Basic Civitas Books.

Sandberg, Sheryl. 2010. "Why We Have Too Few Women Leaders." TED Lecture, December http://www.ted.com/talks/sheryl_sandberg_why_we_have_too_few_women_leaders.html.

Schwartz, Felice N. 1989. "Management Woman and the New Facts of Life." *Harvard Business Review* 69, no. 1 (January–February): 65–76.

Seligson, Michelle. 1999. "The Policy Climate for School-Age Child." *The Future of Children* 9, no. 2 (Autumn):135–139.

Slaughter, Anne-Marie. 2012. "Why Women Still Can't Have It All." The Atlantic, July–August http://www.theatlantic.com/magazine/archive/2012/07/why-women-still-can-8217-t-have-it-all/9020/.

Smith, Kristin and Kristi Gozjolko. 2010. "*Low Income and Impoverished Families Pay Disproportionately More For Child Care.*" Durham, N.H.: Carsey Institute, University of New Hampshire, Paper 93.

Stoltzfus, Emilie. 2006. *Citizen, Mother, Worker: Debating Public Responsibility for Child Care after the Second World War.* Chapel Hill: University of North Carolina Press.

Stone, Pamela. 2008. *Opting Out? Why Women Really Quit Careers And Head Home.* Berkeley: University of California Press.

Titmuss, Richard. 1959. *Essays on the Welfare State.* New Haven, CT: Yale University Press.

Tuttle, William M., Jr. 1995. "Rosie the Riveter and Her Latchkey Children: What Americans Can Learn About Child Day Care from the Second World War." *Child Welfare* 74, no.1 (January–February): 92–114.

Umansky, Lauri. 1996. *Motherhood Reconceived: Feminism and the Legacies of the Sixties.* New York: New York University Press.

U.S. Census Bureau. 2010. "Who's Minding the Kids?" Child Care Arrangements: Spring 2010. Table 3B. http://www.census.gov/hhes/childcare/data/sipp/2010/tables.html.

U.S. Department of Labor. 2000. "The 2000 Survey of Employees and Establishments." http://www.dol.gov/whd/fmla/chapter8.htm.

U.S. Department of Labor. [n.d.] *The Family and Medical Leave Act.* http://www.dol.gov/compliance/laws/comp-fmla.htm.

*Waldfogel, Jane. 1999. "The Impact of the Family and Medical Leave Act." *Journal of Policy Analysis and Management* 18:281–302.

Warner, Judith. 2006. *Perfect Madness: Motherhood in an Age of Anxiety.* New York: Riverhead Books.

*Wexler, Sherry. 1997. "Work/Family Policy Stratification: The Examples of Family Support And Family Leave." *Qualitative Sociology* 20 (2): 311–322.

Zigler, Edward, and Sally J. Styfco. 2010. *The Hidden History of Head Start.* New York: Oxford University Press.

CHAPTER 28

··

HOMEOWNERSHIP POLICY

··

PETER DREIER AND ALEX SCHWARTZ

1 INTRODUCTION

··

THE cover story on the September 6, 2010 issue of *Time* magazine, "The Case Against Homeownership," asked whether the American Dream of owning a home still made sense. "Buying a house is supposed to make us better citizens, better investors and better off," it began. "But that American Dream may well be a fantasy" (Kiviat 2010). It called the pursuit of homeownership a "cult" and a "fetish." It described the "dark side" of homeownership as "foreclosures and walkways, neighborhoods plagued by abandoned properties and plummeting home values, a nation in which families have $6 trillion less in housing wealth than they did just three years ago."

The article appeared three years after the nation's housing bubble had burst. The country was awash in "underwater" mortgages, an epidemic of millions of foreclosed homes, and a dramatic decline in the value of Americans' houses. *Time* and other publications wondered whether these stark realities would lead Americans to reconsider their love affair with homeownership. Polls revealed that the housing crash made Americans somewhat wary of homeownership as an investment and less optimistic about their likelihood of buying a home. Nevertheless, Americans still cherished the idea of owning a home and expected the government to help them achieve it. The belief in homeownership was so deeply ingrained in American culture that even the crisis of the nation's financial system and the dramatic loss of residential wealth over a few years period couldn't shake it.

The importance of culture will be a major theme of this chapter. Homeownership is supposed to bring freedom and security, two core values in American society. Homeownership may also facilitate racial segregation, a logic that was stronger in earlier eras than it is today. Understanding the links between culture and policy is complicated because U.S. housing policy is often indirect or unseen; unlike retirees or the disabled, homeowners do not receive monthly checks from the government. The federal government has long supported the goal of increasing homeownership through regulation and support of the financial system to strengthen credit for homeowners, tax subsidies for homeowners, as well as direct subsidies for consumers and developers (Carliner 1998; Collins 2002; Rapoport 2013). This chapter will briefly describe the history of these tools and explain how they work.

For most of human history, housing was viewed primarily as a form of shelter—protection against the elements. Since the mid-twentieth century, homeownership has also been seen as the most effective way for families to accumulate wealth. For most Americans, their home is their major asset and the principle source of their wealth (Mishel et al. 2012). That asset can provide a crucial buffer when individuals retire, face extraordinary medical bills, or lose their job. Thus housing policy intersects with many of the other social policies discussed in this volume.

2 HISTORICAL BACKGROUND

Before the Great Depression, the national government did little consciously to promote homeownership. Tenement reform laws passed in the early 1900s set the precedent that local government would set standards and regulate housing safety. During the 1930s, the public housing programs and banking reforms of the New Deal established the federal role in expanding homeownership and providing subsidies to the poor.[1] From that point on, public policy at all levels of government would favor owning over renting.

Until the Depression, the federal government played no significant role in housing finance.[2] Savings and loan associations and mutual savings banks dominated the housing market, but they had no protection if a borrower defaulted on a loan, making them extremely cautious. They required large down payments (up to 50 percent of the house value) and short time periods (often 10 years or less) for repayment. Even a household with a steady income, good credit record, and a down payment in hand might be rejected for a loan simply because local lenders lacked the funds (Jackson 1985, Schwartz 2010).

By the spring of 1933, more than half of all home mortgages were in default (Jackson, 1985: 193), undermining the solvency of many lending institutions. Fearing that banks were going under, many customers began to withdraw their savings, which made lending institutions even more strapped for cash and thus unable or unwilling to make loans (as portrayed in the James Stewart film, "It's a Wonderful Life"). In response, the federal government established the first home financing program to protect lending institutions, help homeowners at risk of losing their homes, stimulate employment in the building industry (and thus the wider economy), and expand homeownership.

The first new institutions included the Federal Home Loan Bank (1932, under President Herbert Hoover) and the Home Owners Loan Corporation (HOLC) (1933, under FDR). The former had little impact because the demand for mortgages was so low. The HOLC was more successful. It bought and refinanced mortgages in default and then rewrote them on terms that allowed owners to avoid foreclosure. It lengthened the terms of mortgages to 15 years, reducing the monthly payments for hard-pressed homeowners. About 40 percent of all eligible homeowners sought HOLC's help. Within two years, HOLC had acquired and refinanced more than one million mortgages, about 10 percent of all owner-occupied nonfarm properties, at a cost of about $3 billion (Jackson 1985, 196).

The Housing Act of 1934 created the Federal Savings and Loan Insurance Corporation (FSLIC), which insured individual depositors' accounts from bank failures, and the Federal Housing Administration (FHA), which guaranteed individual mortgages against default. Both agencies gave lenders the incentive to make more mortgage loans, at lower interest rates, with a much smaller down payment (closer to 20 percent than 50 percent), and for 25- and 30-year periods. This was a form of mortgage insurance for banks, not consumers. These laws were intended primarily to boost new housing construction, and thus employment. The FHA also required stricter design and construction standards for the homes it insured (Carliner 1998).

In 1944, Congress passed the Servicemen's Readjustment Act (aka the GI Bill of Rights) to reward military veterans and active-duty military personnel. This law is most famous for helping veterans afford college, but another provision provided low-cost mortgage loans, in many cases with no down payment required. Approximately 16 million veterans purchased homes through the VA (Veterans Administration) program.

The changes brought about by the FHA and VA soon extended to the rest of the housing industry. Lenders began to offer 30-year loans with low down payments on mortgages without federal insurance. Private insurance companies began to offer insurance on non-FHA mortgages. These changes made homeownership more affordable to working-class families. The FHA's requirements for appraisals, inspections, and construction standards soon became the industry yardstick.

After World War II, two federal agencies—the Department of Agriculture (USDA) and the Department of Housing and Urban Development (HUD), which was created in 1965 and absorbed the Federal Housing Administration—helped increase homeownership to families with modest incomes. In 1949 the Farmers Home Administration (a division of USDA) offered mortgages directly to farmers in areas where they could not get private loans. The program was extended to nonfarmers in rural areas in 1961. In 1968, the USDA started to provide subsidized mortgages to rural borrowers with modest incomes. The USDA made more than one million of these Section 502 loans between 1969 and 1993 (Carliner 1998).

In 1968, Congress enacted a similar program, HUD's Section 235, targeted to urban residents, hoping that subsidies to help low-income families become homeowners would improve their standard of living and quell the unrest that had led to several years of urban riots. By 1973, the program had helped about 400,000 low- and moderate-income families purchase homes. But Section 235 was mired in mismanagement and scandal; President Nixon and Congress ended it in 1973.

The federal government also shaped housing finance by expanding the availability of mortgage credit. In 1938, the Roosevelt administration created the Federal National Mortgage Association (Fannie Mae) to purchase, bundle, and resell FHA mortgages. In 1968, Congress changed Fannie Mae into a private "government-sponsored" corporation, with the mandate to purchase FHA and VA loans. At the same time, Congress created the Government National Mortgage Association to guarantee securities backed by pools of government-insured mortgages issued by private lenders. The Emergency Home Finance Act (1970) authorized Fannie Mae to buy conventional (not just government-insured) mortgages and also created the Federal Home Loan Mortgage Corporation (known as Freddie Mac). These organizations primarily dealt with single-family mortgages, which were easier to "pool" and sell to investors, and thus contributed to the expansion of homeownership.

Finally, the rapid expansion of the income tax during World War II had a profound effect. As more individuals owed income taxes, more could take advantage of deductions for home mortgage interest and property taxes. The effective cost of buying a home dropped. Initially, few people noticed this change. But when Brookings Institution economists began suggesting in the 1960s and 1970s that the homeowner deduction was inequitable and unnecessary (Aaron 1972), real-estate groups, especially the National Association of Home Builders and the National Association of Realtors, declared it sacrosanct and used their political influence to maintain it.

Collectively, these policies helped homeownership become the norm. In 1930, 48 percent of American households owned their own homes. Battered by the Depression, that figure dropped under 44 percent by 1940. It surged in the 1950s and 1960s, and by 1980 it reached almost 65 percent—the greatest increase in homeownership of the twentieth century (U.S. Census 2013).

2.1 State and Local Policies

State governments provide housing subsidies to developers through state revenues and through tax-exempt revenue bonds. Most states favor home ownership over rental housing (Katz et al. 2003). State housing finance agencies, for example, issue tax-exempt bonds to finance low-interest mortgages for first-time home buyers and for affordable rental housing. Cumulatively through 2010, these agencies had issued $260 billion in mortgage revenue bonds, compared to $95 billion in multifamily bonds for apartment buildings (National Council of State Housing Agencies 2012).

States and localities receive Community Development Block Grants (CDBG) from the federal government that can be used for an array of purposes. Rehabilitation of single-family housing accounts for about half of all housing-related CDBG expenditures, and direct homeowner assistance accounts for another 5 percent. In contrast, less than 7 percent of CDBG funds are used to rehabilitate multifamily housing (Schwartz 2010, 214).

The HOME Investment Partnership program, created in 1990, is another federal block grant for housing-related purposes. The program provides states and municipalities with funds that can be used for homebuyer activities, rehabilitation of owner-occupied properties, rental housing development, and tenant-based rental assistance. From 1992 through 2009, HOME allocated $21.7 billion. Homebuyer activities have accounted for

27 percent of total funding commitments (funding 373,866 units) and owner-occupied rehabilitation for another 17 percent (Schwartz 2010, 216).

Local governments have several ways to favor homeowners over renters. One is through their property taxes. Owner-occupied homes are frequently taxed at a lower effective rate than rental properties (Furman Center for Real Estate and Urban Policy 2012). Local zoning codes often favor single-family housing over multifamily housing (Danielson 1976). Tenant-landlord law remains biased against tenants—a remnant of its agrarian and feudal origins (Rose, 1973; Dreier 1982; Lebowitz 1981; Krueckeberg 1999). A 1967 federal government study, only slightly outdated by recent reforms, found that:

> The traditional legal interpretation of the tenants' obligation to pay rent as independent of the landlord's obligation means that no matter how badly the landlord fails in his obligations to the tenant, the tenant must continue to pay his full rent to the landlord on time, or be evicted (U.S. Dept. of Housing and Urban Development, 1967, 5).

Due to the influence of the real estate industry, only a few cities have adopted rent control, which limits rent increases. Since the 1970s, most states have adopted "warranty of habitability" laws, which impose certain duties on a landlord to maintain the premises in habitable condition. Failure to do so may be legal justification for a tenant to withhold rent until the problem is fixed. Except in New Jersey (which has a statewide "just cause" eviction law), landlords can evict tenants for almost any reason at all, not only failure to pay rent, and can use the power of the courts to back them up. Homeowners are more secure. Mortgage lenders can take possession of a home only if the homeowner fails to make payments. Even then, however, the process of foreclosure and eviction is relatively slow compared to the procedures available to a landlord to evict a tenant.

3 CLASS AND RACE

Homeownership is a vivid marker of inequality in American society, with some segments of the population far more likely than others to own their homes. Homeownership rates are highest among married couples, Whites, middle-aged and older household heads, and households in suburban and nonmetropolitan areas (See Table 28.1). Homeowners are increasingly more affluent than renters, and they are far wealthier. In 2011, the median annual income for homeowners was $62,500, nearly double renters' median income of $31,800. The gap between owners and renters is much greater in terms of net worth. In 2010, the median net worth of homeowners amounted to $174,600, compared to just $5,100 among renters. Homeownership can determine whether families amass any wealth at all: home equity accounts for a large proportion of total household wealth, and for all but the wealthiest households, it is the largest single asset (Bricker et al. 2012; Joint Center for Housing Studies 2012).

Table 28.1 Homeownership Rates for Selected Demographic and Geographic Groups

	1983	2004	2011
Total	64.9	69.0	66.2
Household Type			
Married Couple Families	78.3	84.0	81.4
Other Family Households	49.5	53.3	47.2
One-Person Households	46.2	55.8	56.1
Age of Householder			
Less than 25 Years	18.8	25.2	15.4
25 to 29 Years	38.3	40.2	35.9
30 to 34 Years	55.4	57.4	50.2
35 to 44 Years	69.3	69.2	62.8
45 to 54 Years	77.0	77.2	72.6
55 to 64 Years	79.9	81.7	78.8
65 Years and Older	75.0	81.1	80.8
Race and Ethnicity			
Non-Hispanic White	69.1	76.0	73.9
Non-Hispanic Black	45.6	49.1	45.9
Hispanic	41.2	48.1	47.2
Other	53.3	58.6	57.0
Metropolitan Status			
Central City	48.9	53.1	51.3
Suburban	70.2	75.7	72.1
Outside Metropolitan Area	73.5	76.3	73.4

Source: U.S. Census Bureau, American Housing Survey, 2011 and previous years.

Given that roughly two-thirds of Americans own their own homes, one might assume that the nation's housing policies are aimed broadly at the middle class. In fact, some of these policies are targeted at the lower and upper ends of the income distribution. For example, the FHA originally served borrowers with higher incomes, since less affluent families lacked the savings for a down payment and the monthly income for mortgage payments. But by 1970, the prices of FHA-insurance homes and the incomes of their owners were lower than those with conventional loans. By imposing limits on the prices of homes and the loan amounts covered by FHA insurance, Congress guaranteed that FHA-insured homes would be concentrated in inner-city and minority neighborhoods, disproportionately among low-income borrowers.

In contrast, the major tax expenditures have always benefited the more affluent. In 2012, three homeowner tax breaks cost the federal government $115 billion in lost revenues. The best known are the mortgage interest deduction ($68.5 billion) and the property tax deduction ($24.5 billion). Another provision of the tax code allows homeowners to exclude paying capital-gains taxes (on up to $250,000 in sales proceeds for singles and up to $500,000 for married homeowners) when they sell their homes. This cost the federal treasury $22.3 billion in 2012. Taken together, this spending dwarfs what the U.S. government does for poor renters via Section 8 vouchers or public housing.

Wealthy households are most likely to own homes, often expensive homes, and to itemize deductions on their tax returns. Their nominal tax rates are higher, which increases the benefits of any tax deduction. Thus, more than 76 percent of the mortgage interest and property tax subsidies went to the 19 percent of taxpayers with incomes over $100,000. One-third went to the wealthiest 4 percent of taxpayers with incomes over $200,000. Households with incomes above $200,000 averaged $6,641 from these two tax breaks. Only about 5 percent of households with incomes between $20,000 and $30,000 received any subsidy, averaging $679. Households between $30,000 and $75,000 do not fare much better (Dreier 2006; Howard 1997; U.S. Congress 2013).

The real-estate industry—homebuilders, realtors, and mortgage bankers—argues that the homeowner tax break is the linchpin of the American Dream, making home-ownership available to many families who could otherwise not afford to buy one. There is little evidence for this. These tax deductions help push up housing prices artificially, especially at the upper end, because homebuyers include the value of the tax subsidy in their purchase decision. And because tax breaks are so small for low-income and middle-income homeowners, they hardly make it more affordable to own a home rather than rent. A 2005 Congressional Research Service report noted that, "other homeown-ership subsidies, like down-payment assistance programs, are proven to be more effec-tive at increasing homeownership among lower-income families and are less expensive than the mortgage interest deduction" (Jackson 2005, i). Moreover, other countries with comparable homeownership rates (including Australia, England, and Canada) do not have these tax breaks.

These deductions also promote suburbanization and sprawl, encouraging homebuy-ers to buy larger homes in outlying areas rather than more modest homes in central cities and older suburbs. The tax code thus contributes to transportation gridlock, pol-lution, and costly infrastructure. In other words, the "cost" of these housing tax breaks is greater than the amount that appears in the federal budget each year. There are related "external" costs to the environment, public health, and other factors. By the same token, the promotion of owner-occupied housing—in cities as well as suburbs—affects access to other public goods and services. Compared with renters, homeowners tend to live in areas with better schools and amenities like parks and playgrounds (McClure and Schwartz 2013).

As illustrated in Figure 28.1, the homeownership rate among African American and Latino households is 10 to 20 percentage points lower than for whites and Asians at all income levels. Data on the incomes of African Americans, Hispanics, and whites show similar disparities in terms of banks' rejection of mortgage applications. Although some of the disparity reflects differences in income, assets, employment, credit history, and other factors, racial discrimination in the mortgage and housing markets prevents mil-lions of African Americans and Hispanics from becoming homeowners (Conley 2009; Katznelson 2006; Munnel et al. 1996; Shapiro and Oliver 1995). For example, national fair-housing audits show that African American and Hispanic home buyers face systemic discrimination in their interactions with real-estate agents, including their ability to inspect potential properties for purchase, receiving assistance in obtaining finance, in the amount and quality of encouragement provided. (Dewan 2013a). Above all, African Americans and Hispanics are often steered to predominantly minority neighborhoods, where, among other things, the prospects for price appreciation are lower than in other neighborhoods (Turner et al., 2002; Shapiro, Meschede, and Osoro 2013).

To some degree, these disparities are rooted in public policy. For instance, the 1934 federal law creating the FHA also required that homes with FHA insurance be located in "homogeneous" neighborhoods—which put the federal government's official stamp on residential segregation. In its 1935 *Underwriting Handbook,* the FHA stated that mortgage lenders should avoid making loans in areas with an "infiltration of inharmonious racial or nationality groups." The following year's edition of the *Handbook* noted that the presence of "incompatible racial and ethnic groups" or the possibility that a neighborhood could be "invaded by such groups" were sufficient reasons to deny making a mortgage loan in an area (quoted in Schwartz 2010, 55). The FHA preferred that this mandate be implemented through racially restrictive covenants on deeds, which prohibited property owners from selling their homes to minority (and in some cases Jewish) buyers. The FHA even supplied the forms for doing so.

This government-sponsored "redlining" had a significant impact on racial segregation and suburbanization. From 1934 to 1960, for example, the FHA insured more than five times as many mortgages in suburban St Louis County than in the city of St. Louis (Jackson 1985: 213). By 1966, the FHA hadn't insured even one home in Camden or Paterson, New Jersey, two declining industrial cities. Homeowners who wanted to

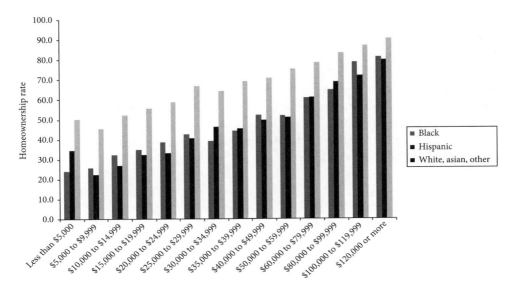

FIG. 28.1 Homeownership Rate by Income and Race Ethnicity in 2011.

remain in cities could not obtain FHA mortgages, whereas white homeowners who wanted to buy homes in suburbs had access to these affordable loans.

In 1948, the U.S. Supreme Court ruled in *Shelley v. Kraemer* that state and local governments could not enforce racially restrictive covenants. But FHA's policy of promoting "homogeneous" neighborhoods persisted until 1962, when President Kennedy issued an executive order requiring equal opportunity in both FHA and VA lending. This equal opportunity requirement was not extended to conventional mortgages until the 1968 Civil Rights Act.

In the 1970s, neighborhood groups and academic researchers discovered that local banks (primarily S&Ls) were taking their deposits but refusing to make loans (particularly for home repairs) in inner-city neighborhoods, thus contributing to a self-fulfilling prophecy of disinvestment and decline. Under pressure from community groups, and under the leadership of Senator William Proxmire (D-WI), Congress passed the Home Mortgage Disclosure Act in 1975, requiring lenders to make public the location of their loans, and the Community Reinvestment Act of 1977, requiring lenders to provide mortgages in all areas from which they draw deposits. Initially, federal bank regulators failed to significantly enforce either law, but community groups learned how to utilize the laws to embarrass lenders and pressure regulators. Eventually these laws were strengthened and banks began to voluntarily comply with their provisions, creating a stream of private investment into inner-city areas (Dreier 2003; Sidney, 2003). By 2007, the CRA had helped catalyze more than $4 trillion in private lending in inner-city areas. (Joint Center for Housing Studies 2002; National Community Reinvestment Coalition 2007; Immergluck 2011b). Complementing the CRA, Congress imposed "affordable housing goals" in 1992 on Fannie Mae and Freddie Mac, requiring them to purchase mortgages issued to low-income and minority borrowers and in inner-city and other disadvantaged communities.

Local zoning laws have also intersected with class and race. In 1926, the U.S. Supreme Court issued a landmark decision (*Village of Euclid v. Ambler Realty Company*) in defense of restrictive zoning, arguing that the presence of apartment buildings lowered the value of single-family dwellings. Zoning has often served to segregate residents by economic class, both within and between municipalities. It has also been used to segregate homeowners from tenants. Exclusionary zoning is directed primarily against the poor and racial minorities (who are disproportionately apartment dwellers). Many suburbs exclude apartments entirely (Babcock and Bosselman, 1973; Danielson 1976; Mandelker and Ellis 1998; McKibben 2004).

4 HOMEOWNERSHIP IN AMERICAN CULTURE

Americans have long cherished home ownership as a key element of the "American dream." They believe that owning a home means freedom and security, as homeowners have more freedom to decorate, renovate, and improve their dwellings than do renters (Rakoff 1977). Renters, in contrast, face restrictions on noise, pets, and how many people are permitted to live in the house. For many tenants, a major downside of renting is the constant risk of eviction. Especially when thinking about old age and retirement, homeowners are comforted by knowing they will always have a place to call their own.

The virtues attached to property ownership (and property owners), and their presumed absence among tenants who do not own property, have remained remarkably similar over the years. The earliest European settlers came in part to escape oppressive landlords (Kim 1978; Kraus 1939). As a colonial official observed in 1732, these people were "the better sort" who sought to "avoid the dependency on landlords" (Warner 1968, 16). The abundance of land created enthusiasm about the possibility of individual ownership and "nourished the first settlers' vision of land as a civil right, a right against the long-standing obligations of a crumbling feudal society" as well as "freedom for even the poorest family to win autonomy" (Warner 1972, 16).

The colonial era debate over whether tenants should be granted the vote hinged on these views. Among landowners, they argued, one could "always expect to find moderation, frugality, order, honesty, and a due sense of independence, liberty, and justice" (Carter and Stone 1821, 220). Those without property, in contrast, were considered "indolent and profligate" (Carter and Stone 1821, 221). Thomas Jefferson (1956, 37), who favored tenant suffrage, nevertheless held that "the small landholders are the precious part of a state." Only property owners were permitted to vote in federal elections until 1860 (Martin 1976). Referring to the Homestead Act of 1862, Abraham Lincoln said, "I am in favor of settling the wild lands into small parcels so that every poor man may have a home" (Robbins 1942).

Following the Civil War, tenancy became the lot of wage and salary workers, not just farmers. As more people came to the cities, the nation witnessed the first significant movement away from downtown neighborhoods near their industrial workplaces. At the time, thanks to the new trolleys, affluent middle-class families could afford to move to owner-occupied, one-or two-family houses in the "streetcar suburbs" (Warner 1962). Home ownership increasingly became not only a symbol of status and achievement, but also a goal that working-class families could strive for and attain.

After World War I and the Russian Revolution, the American real-estate industry promoted homeownership as a bulwark against socialism, as a way to promote more civic engagement and social stability, and even as a patriotic duty. Soon, the federal government adopted the same crusade. The campaign included "We Own Our Own Home" buttons distributed to schoolchildren, lectures at universities, newspaper editorials, model sermons, essay contests, and posters (distributed to two millions workplaces) about the benefits of homeownership (Vale 2007, 20–21). In their classic study of Middletown (pseudonym for Muncie, Indiana), Lynd and Lynd (1937, 411) found that even during the Depression, one of the most widely held values was "that home ownership is a good thing for the family and also makes for good citizenship."

During the twentieth century, every president and most other public figures have extolled the virtues of homeownership. President Calvin Coolidge observed that, "No greater contribution could be made to the stability of the nation, and the advancement of its ideals, than to make it a nation of homeowning families" (quoted in Dean 1945, 40). Facing a dramatic increase in home foreclosures and bank closures, President Herbert Hoover noted in 1931 that, "To possess one's own home is the hope and ambition of almost every individual in our country, whether he lives in hotel, apartment, or tenement" (Hoover 1931, 573). President Franklin Roosevelt echoed that, "A nation of home owners, of people who own a real share in their own land, is unconquerable" (quoted in Dean 1945: 40). President Lyndon B. Johnson said: "Owning a home can increase responsibility and stake out a man's place in his community...The man who owns a home has something to be proud of and a reason to protect and preserve it" (Johnson 1968). President George W. Bush, who made increasing homeownership a key aspect of his policy agenda, said: "We can put light where there's darkness, and hope where there's despondency in this country. And part of it is working together as a nation to encourage folks to own their own home" (Becker, Stolberg, and Labaton 2008). In a weekly address in May 2013, President Barack Obama said that "few things define what it is to be middle class in America more than owning your own cornerstone of the American Dream: a home" (Obama 2013).

Public opinion polls confirm the widespread appeal of homeownership (Fannie Mae 2014; Starobin 2011; Streitfeld and Thee-Brenan 2011). The U.S. Department of Housing and Urban Development (1978) found that 85 percent of people in the United States preferred owning a home to renting. Even in the midst of the 2007–2011 recession, with housing values declining, Americans' faith in homeownership remained robust. In 2011, 89 percent of existing homeowners said that they would choose to buy a home again (Edwards and Andrews 2011). Most renters (81 percent) said they would like to buy a home someday. Asked if they rented out of choice or because they couldn't afford to buy a home, only 24 percent of renters said they rented out of choice ("Home Sweet Home. Still." 2011). As the housing crisis persisted, however, Americans became more skeptical. In 2013, two-thirds of Americans said that the focus of national housing policy should be split fairly equally between rental and ownership, as opposed to promoting one over the other. In fact, 61 percent believed that renters can be just as successful as owners in achieving the American Dream (Hart Research Associates 2013).

5 HOMEOWNERSHIP AND THE RECENT HOUSING CRISIS

The U.S. housing market collapsed in 2007, triggering the worst financial crisis and economic recession since the 1930s. The crisis was precipitated by an unsustainable rise in house prices that started in the late 1990s and accelerated in the early and mid-2000s. The bubble was driven in part by the reckless, risky, and often illegal practices of banks and private mortgage companies, especially rapid increases in "subprime" and other forms of high-risk mortgage lending based on increasingly lax underwriting standards (Gramlich 2007; Immergluck 2009, 2011a, 2011b; Lewis 2010). Subprime loans made up 8.6 percent of all mortgages in 2001 but soared to 30.1 percent by 2006. After 2004, more than 90 percent of subprime mortgages came with adjustable interest rates that were initially low and then skyrocketed after several years (Joint Center for Housing Studies 2007).

Demand for mortgages was fueled by the proliferation of increasingly complex and risky mortgage-backed securities and their derivatives. These securities were in high demand among investors, hedge funds, and banks, and they were often incorporated into other securities. Banks made astounding profits while squeezing consumers. The growth of mortgage-backed securities was enabled by the major credit-rating agencies, which gave investment-grade ratings to most of the securities they assessed, even though the underlying mortgages were increasingly risky. As these events unfolded, federal regulators looked the other way (National Commission on the Causes of the Financial and Economic Crisis 2011; U.S. Dept. of Housing and Urban Development 2010; Zandi 2009; Suskind 2011; Dreier, Squires and Atlas 2008; McLean and Nocera 2010).

This crisis affected millions of Americans. The nation's homeownership rate peaked at 69 percent in 2004, before the bubble burst. By 2013, it had fallen to 65 percent, the first sustained drop since the Great Depression (U.S. Census 2013). More than 20 percent of all homeowners with a mortgage were "underwater" by 2012, with the balance of their mortgage exceeding the value of their home. In Nevada, Florida, and other areas hit hardest by the housing crisis, upward of 50 percent of all homeowners were underwater (Core Logic 2013). In 2011, total mortgage debt in the United States exceeded the total value of all residential real estate (Joint Center for Housing Studies 2011). More than five million households lost their homes to foreclosure from March 2009 through June 2011 (Immergluck 2012). Many others had to sell their homes to avoid foreclosure. As a result, the bursting of the housing bubble led to a decline not only in the homeownership *rate* but also in the *number* of homeowners.

Millions of low-income and middle-class families watched their major source of wealth stripped away, their neighborhoods decimated by falling property values, their cities devastated by dramatic declines in property tax revenues, and their economic security destroyed. The drop in housing values affected not only families facing foreclosure but also families in the surrounding community, because foreclosed homes in a neighborhood bring down the value of other houses in the area. The neighborhood blight was much worse in African American and Hispanic areas. African Americans and Hispanics were almost twice as likely as whites to lose their homes to foreclosures, in large part because they were more often the victims of predatory practices by lenders (Joint Center for Housing Studies 2007; Bocian, et. al, 2011).

In response, mortgage lenders imposed extremely stringent underwriting standards. Many borrowers who would have easily qualified for a mortgage before the crisis could, therefore, not obtain one afterwards—despite record-low interest rates. As of 2013, many lenders required down payments of at least 20 percent of the purchase price, and they rejected applicants without very strong credit ratings (Joint Center for Housing Studies 2012).

The Obama Administration launched its first foreclosure prevention programs in March 2009 with a goal of preventing seven to nine million foreclosures by helping owners refinance their mortgages on more favorable terms. As of March 2012, however, these programs had helped only 2.2 million homeowners avoid foreclosure. Its biggest shortcomings were relying on the voluntary participation of bank loan servicers and targeting only homeowners who were paying less than 31 percent of their income on their first mortgage, even if they were severely "underwater." Another proposal to assist homeowners—to reform the bankruptcy code to allow judges to restructure the terms of residential mortgages—was defeated in Congress by the banking industry lobby (Immergluck 2012; Schwartz 2012). Many economists argued that banks should reset mortgages to reduce borrowers' principal in order to help underwater homeowners, but lobbying by the financial industry made the Obama administration and Congress were reluctant to require banks to do so (Stiglitz and Zandi 2012). By 2013, however, a growing movement of community groups and labor unions was making headway at convincing the Obama administration and local governments to pressure banks to reset mortgages for underwater homeowners (Estevao 2012; Dewan 2013b and c; Dreier 2013a and b; Dreier 2013a; Kuttner 2013; Lowrey 2013).

6 Conclusion

Homeownership is often touted as beneficial for individuals and families, as well as for society in general. This is why government involvement is seen as essential (e.g., National Association of Realtors 2012). Nevertheless, a careful reading of the evidence indicates that homeownership entails sizable costs as well as benefits, leading many scholars and policy analysts to question the primacy of homeownership in American policy and culture. (Adams 2009; Belsky 2009; Coulson 2002; Krugman 2008; Rohe, Van Zandt, and McCarthy 2001; Rossi and Weber 1996; Shlay 2006).

Without a doubt, the home is the single most important asset for most Americans and a key source of economic security. However, the recent crisis demonstrated that many Americans are too invested in their homes. Principle residences account for about 10 percent of the wealth of the richest one percent of Americans, but 66.6 percent of the wealth of the middle three quintiles (Wolff 2013). Therefore, though the bursting of the housing bubble and resulting Great Recession affected households across the entire distribution, middle-class households and those below were hit particularly hard. From 2007 to 2010, the average wealth of the top 1 percent of households dropped 16 percent, but median wealth dropped an astounding 47 percent. The middle "fifth of households saw their housing equity drop 44.6 percent between 2007 and 2010, and in 2010 households in the bottom 40 percent of the wealth distribution had *negative* housing equity on average for the first time on record" (Mishel et al. 2012, 376). Many families who bought homes in the 2000s would have been better off renting their home and investing their money elsewhere (Li and Yang 2010). Given all the tax breaks and loan subsidies, it is understandable why they bet so heavily on homeownership.

Residential construction is also an important sector of the American economy. In 2005, 16 percent of all economic activity in America came from the housing sector. According to the National Association of Realtors (2012), the construction and sale of houses generates on average 2.5 million jobs annually. However, the construction of rental housing could provide the same economic impact and job creation stimulus as building single-family homes or condominiums. Homeownership may even have negative economic impacts. Many economists argue that government promotion of homeownership, through tax breaks and other policies, encourages people to buy bigger homes than they need and reduces savings needed for economic growth. (Aaron 1972; Gale, Gruber, and Stephens-Davidowitz 2007; Porter 2005; Lowenstein 2006; Poterba and Sinai 2011). Others argue that homeownership makes workers more rooted and less mobile. In the modern labor market, employees' mobility may be considered a positive factor in economic productivity and growth. The limited mobility of homeowners in a volatile and ever-changing job market may cause a mismatch in the location of work and available workers (Agnew 1981; Kemeny 1981; Oswald 2012; Branchflower and Oswald 2013; Norris 2013).

Finally, some advocates argue that homeownership enhances civic engagement (e.g., Dietz 2013). DiPasquale and Glaeser (1998), for example, found that homeowners are more likely to vote in local elections, know the name of their U.S. representative and school board members, and "work to solve local problems." But one can question whether homeownership directly causes people to become "good citizens" or whether those citizens are more likely to own homes. In fact, the evidence on homeowners' greater participation in civic life and organizations is mixed (Rohe and Stegman 1994). Glaeser and Sacerdote (2000) found that homeowners are much more likely than renters to vote for policies that will benefit themselves, even at the expense of community members or low-income residents, such as restricting new housing developments and voting in favor of strict zoning and land-use rules. (Again, this may simply be the result of homeowners having higher incomes.)

Housing tenure in the United States is almost always viewed as a choice between homeownership and renting. There are, however, alternative arrangements that encompass qualities, including the "bundle of rights" that are commonly associated with homeownership (Marcuse 1980 and 2008). These include "limited equity" and "cooperative" housing, and community land trusts, through which people purchase a home at a discount or receive a subsidy that imposes limits on the amount of profit they can make if they subsequently sell the property, but which confers many benefits of homeownership. By limiting the profits, these programs preserve the affordability of the housing for subsequent buyers. Alternatively, programs may allow properties to be sold at full market price but require the owner to share any profits with the government or a nonprofit organization so that the funds may be used to help subsidize homeownership for other families (Davis 1994; Jacobus 2010; Schwartz 2010; Temkin, Theodos, and Price 2010).

Clearly, it goes against the grain of American culture to suggest that homeownership should not be an essential part of the American Dream. But those values are powerful in part because they have been institutionalized by decades of public policies that privilege owning over renting—policies that effectively favor more affluent Americans and major industries. If the recent housing and financial crises do not lead policy makers to examine these policies more carefully, it is hard to imagine what else will.

Notes

1. Public housing is discussed in Chapter 5 in this volume.
2. Although deductions for home mortgage interest and property taxes date back to 1913, they helped very few people before the 1940s. One basic reason is that only the very rich paid income taxes during this era.

References

*Indicates recommended reading.

*Aaron, Henry. 1972. *Shelter and Subsidies: Who Benefits from Federal Housing Policies?* Washington, DC: Brookings Institution.

Adams, David. 2009. "Subprime Mortgages and Discriminatory Lending Homeownership: American Dream or Illusion of Empowerment?" *South Carolina Law Review* 60, no. 3 (Spring): 573–616.

Agnew, John A. 1981. "Home Ownership and the Capitalist Social Order." In Michael Dear and Allen J. Scott, eds., *Urbanization and Urban Planning in Capitalist Society*. New York: Methuen, 457–80.

Babcock, Richard F., and Fred P. Bosselman. 1973. *Exclusionary Zoning: Land Use Regulation and Housing in the 1970's*. New York: Praeger.

Becker, Jo, Sheryl Gay Stolberg, and Stephen Labaton. 2008. "Bush Drive for Home Ownership Fueled Housing Bubble." *New York Times*, December 21.

Belsky, Eric. 2009. "When Homeownership Is the Wrong Choice." *Los Angeles Times*, November 12.

Bocian, Debbie, Wei Li, Carolina Reid, and Roberto G. Quercia. 2011. *Lost Ground, 2011: Disparities in Mortgage Lending and Foreclosures*. November Durham, NC: Center for Responsible Lending.

Branchflower, David G., and Andrew J. Oswald. 2013. *Does High Home-Ownership Impair the Labor Market?* Washington, DC: Peterson Institute for International Economics.

Bricker, Jesse, Arthur B. Kennickell, Kevin B. Moore, and John Sabelhaus. 2012. "Changes in U.S. family finances from 2007 to 2010: Evidence from the Survey of Consumer Finances." *Federal Reserve Bulletin* 98, no. 2. (June): 1–80.

*Carliner, Michael. 1998. "Development of Federal Homeownership 'Policy.'" *Housing Policy Debate* 9 (2): 299–321.

Carter, Nathaniel H., and William L. Stone. 1821. *Reports of the Proceedings and Debates of the Convention of 1821*. Albany, NY: E and E. Hosford.

Collins, Michael. 2002. *"Pursuing the American Dream: Homeownership and the Role of Federal Housing Policy."* January Washington, DC: Millennial Housing Commission.

Conley, Dalton. 2009. *Being Black, Living in the Red: Race, Wealth, and Social Policy in America.* 10th Anniversary Edition. Berkeley, CA: University of California Press.

Coulson, N. Edward. 2002. "Housing Policy and the Social Benefits of Homeownership." *Business Review*, Q2: 1–16.

Core Logic. 2013. "Negative Equity Report, 3rd Quarter, 2012." (January 17). http://www.corelogic.com/research/negative-equity/corelogic-q3-2012-negative-equity-report.pdf.

Danielson, Michael. 1976. *The Politics of Exclusion.* New York: Columbia University Press.

Davis, John E. 1994. "Beyond the Market and the State: The Diverse Domain of Social Housing." In John E. Davis, ed., *The Affordable City: Towards a Third Sector Housing Policy.* Philadelphia: Temple University Press.

Dean, John. 1945. *Home Ownership: Is It Sound?* New York: Harper and Row.

Dewan, Shaila. 2013a. "Discrimination in Housing Against Nonwhites Persists Quietly, U.S. Study Finds." *New York Times*, June 11.

Dewan, Shaila. 2013b. "A City Invokes Seizure Laws to Save Homes." *New York Times*, July 29.

Dewan, Shaila. 2013c. "More Cities Consider Using Eminent Domain to Halt Foreclosures." *New York Times*, November 15.

Dietz, Robert. 2013. "Why Homeownership Still Matters." *U.S. News*, March 12.

DiPasquale, Denise, and Edward Glaeser. 1998. "Incentives and Social Capital: Are Homeowners Better Citizens?" *Chicago Working Paper in Law & Economics*, April.

Dreier, Peter. 1982. "The Status of Tenants in the United States." *Social Problems* 30 no. 2 (December): 179–198.

Dreier, Peter. 2003. "The Future of Community Reinvestment: Challenges and Opportunities." *Journal of the American Planning Association* 69 no. 4 (August): 341–353.

Dreier, Peter. 2006. "Federal Housing Subsidies: Who Benefits and Why?" In Rachel Bratt, Michael Stone, and Chester Hartman, eds., *A Right to Housing: Foundation for a New Social Agenda*. Philadelphia: Temple University Press, 105–138.

Dreier, Peter. 2013a. "Mobilizing to Hold Wall Street Accountable" *New Labor Forum.* 22 (Fall): 81–85.

Dreier, Peter. 2013b. "To Rescue Local Economies, Cities Seize Underwater Mortgages Through Eminent Domain." *The Nation*, July 12.

Dreier, Peter, Gregory Squires, and John Atlas. 2008. "Foreclosing on the Free Market: How to Remedy the Subprime Catastrophe." *New Labor Forum* 17 no. 3 (Fall): 18–30.

Edwards, Julia, and Edmund L. Andrews. 2011. "Why Some Americans Will Always Buy: Seven Reasons We're Buying and Four Reasons We're Not." *National Journal*, March 25.

Estevao, Jordan. 2012. "Activists Call for Firing of Federal Housing Finance Agency Head Over Role in Foreclosure Crisis." *Truthout*, June 5.

Fannie Mae. 2014. *"National Housing Market Survey Monthly Indicators."* (February) Washington, DC: Fannie Mae. http://www.fanniemae.com/resources/file/research/housingsurvey/pdf/nhs-monthly-data-031014.pdf.

Furman Center for Real Estate and Urban Policy Furman Center for Real Estate and Urban Policy. 2012. "Distribution of the Burden of New School York City's Property Tax." In *State of the New York City's Housing and Neighborhoods 2011*. New York, 8–28.

Gale, William, Jonathan Gruber, and Seth Stephens-Davidowitz. 2007. "Encouraging Homeownership Through the Tax Code." *Tax Notes*, June 18, 1171–1188.

Glaeser, Edward, and Bruce Sacerdote. 2000. "The Social Consequences of Housing." *Journal of Housing Economics* 9: 1–23.

Gramlich, Edward M. 2007. *Subprime Mortgages: America's Latest Boom and Bust.* Washington, DC: Urban Institute Press.

Hart Research Associations Hart Research Associations. 2013. *How Housing Matters: Americans' Attitudes Transformed by the Housing Crisis & Changing Lifestyles: A Report of Findings*, Chicago: John D. and Catherine T. MacArthur Foundation.

Hoover, Herbert. 1931. "Address to the White House Conference on Home Building and Home Ownership," December 2. In *Public Papers of the Presidents of the United States: Herbert Hoover, 1931*. Washington, DC: GPO, 1976, 572–576.

"Home Sweet Home. Still." 2011. Pew Research Center, April 12. http://www.pewsocialtrends.org/2011/04/12/home-sweet-home-still/.

Howard, Christopher. 1997. *The Hidden Welfare State: Tax Expenditures and Social Policy in the United States*. Princeton, NJ: Princeton University Press.

*Immergluck, Dan. 2009. *Foreclosed: High-Risk Lending, Deregulation, and the Undermining of America's Mortgage Market*. Ithaca, NY: Cornell University Press.

Immergluck, Dan. 2011a. "From Risk-Limited to Risk-Loving Mortgage Markets: Origins of the U.S. Subprime Crisis and Prospects for Reform," *Journal of Housing and the Built Environment* 26 (June): 245–262.

Immergluck, Dan. 2011b. "From Minor to Major Player: The Geography of FHA Lending During the U.S. Mortgage Crisis." *Journal of Urban Affairs* 33: 1–20.

Immergluck, Dan. 2012. "Too Little, Too Late, and Too Timid: The Federal Response to the Foreclosure Crisis at the Five Year Mark." *Housing Policy Debate* 23 (1): 199–232.

*Jackson, Kenneth. 1985. *Crabgrass Frontier: The Suburbanization of the United States*. New York: Oxford University Press.

Jackson, Pamela J. 2005. *Fundamental Tax Reform: Options for the Mortgage Interest Deduction*. August 8. Washington, DC: U.S. Congress, the Library of Congress, Congressional Research Service.

Jacobus, Rick. 2010. "Best of Both Worlds," *Shelterforce*, Winter.

Jefferson, Thomas. 1956. *A Jefferson Profile as Revealed in His Letters (Selected and Arranged by Saul Padover)*. New York: John Day.

Johnson, Lyndon B. 1968. Special Message to the Congress on Urban Problems: "The Crisis of the Cities." Message recorded in *Congressional Record*. 90th Congress, 2nd Session. February 22. http://www.presidency.ucsb.edu/ws/?pid=29386.

Joint Center for Housing Studies of Harvard University Joint Center for Housing Studies of Harvard University. 2002. *The 25th Anniversary of the Community Reinvestment Act: Access to Capital in an Evolving Financial Services System*. Cambridge, MA.

Joint Center for Housing Studies of Harvard University Joint Center for Housing Studies of Harvard University. 2007. *The State of the Nation's Housing 2007*. Cambridge, MA.

Joint Center for Housing Studies of Harvard University Joint Center for Housing Studies of Harvard University. 2011. *State of the Nation's Housing 2011*. Cambridge, MA.

Joint Center for Housing Studies of Harvard University Joint Center for Housing Studies of Harvard University. 2012. *State of the Nation's Housing 2012*. Cambridge, MA.

Katz, Bruce, Karen Brown, Margery Turner, Mary Cunningham, and Noah Sawyer. 2003. *Rethinking Local Affordable Housing Strategies: Lessons from 70 Years of Policy and Practice*. Washington, DC: Brookings Institution and Urban Institute. http://www.brookings.edu/research/reports/2003/12/metropolitanpolicy-katz.

Katznelson, Ira. 2006. *When Affirmative Action Was White: An Untold History of Racial Inequality in Twentieth-Century America*. New York: W. W. Norton.

Kemeny, Jim. 1981. *The Myth of Home Ownership*. Boston: Routledge and Kegan Paul.

Kim, Sung Bok. 1978. *Landlord and Tenant in Colonial New York*. Chapel Hill: University of North Carolina Press.

Kiviat, Barbara. 2010. "The Case Against Homeownership." *Time*, September 11.

Kraus, Michael. 1939. "America and the Irish Revolutionary Movement in the Eighteenth Century." In Richard B. Morris, ed., The Era of the American Revolution. Columbia University Press, NY (Gloucester, MA.: Peter Smith, 1971), 332–348.

*Krueckeberg, Donald A. 1999. "The Grapes of Rent: A History of Renting in a Country of Owners," *Housing Policy Debate* 10 (1): 9–30.

Krugman, Paul. 2008. "Home Not-So-Sweet Home." *New York Times*, June 23.

Kuttner, Robert. 2013. "Seize the Mortgages, Save the Neighborhood." *Los Angeles Times*, June 29.

Lebowitz, Neil H. 1981. "'Above party, class or creed': Rent Control in the United States, 1940–47." *Journal of Urban History* 7: 439–470.

*Lewis, Michael. 2010. *The Big Short: Inside the Doomsday Machine*. New York: W.W. Norton.

Li, Wenli, and Fang Yang. 2010. "American Dream or American Obsession? The Economic Benefits and Costs of Homeownership." *Federal Reserve Bank of Philadelphia Business Review*, Q 3: 20–30.

Lowenstein, Roger. 2006. "Who Needs the Mortgage Interest Deduction?" *New York Times Magazine*, March 5.

Lowrey, Annie. 2013. "White House Urged to Fire a Housing Regulator." *New York Times*, March 17.

Lynd, Robert, and Helen Lynd. 1937. *Middletown in Transition*. New York: Harcourt, Brace and World.

Mandelker, Daniel, and H. A. Ellis. 1998. "Exclusionary Zoning." In Willem van Vliet, ed., *The Encyclopedia of Housing*. Thousand Oaks, CA: Sage, 160–161.

Marcuse, Peter. 1980. "Ideology of Ownership and Property Rights." In Richard Plunz, ed., *Housing Form and Public Policy in the United States*. New York: Praeger, 39–50.

Marcuse, Peter. 2008. "The Housing Change We Need." *Shelterforce*, Winter.

Martin, Philip L. 1976. "The Supreme Courts' Quest for Voting Quality on Bond Referenda." *Baylor Law Review* 28: 25–37.

McKibben, Dave. 2004. "To Some, Affordable Housing Means Nightmare Neighbors: Mission Viejo Residents Denounce Plans for an Apartment Complex." *Los Angeles Times*, February 1.

McClure, Kirk, and Alex Schwartz. 2013. "*The Changing Geography of Rental Housing in the US and the Declining Potential of Rental Vouchers to Access Neighborhoods of 'Opportunity'* New York: New School University. Unpublished paper.

McLean, Bethany, and Joe Nocera. 2010. *All the Devils Are Here: The Hidden History of the Financial Crisis*. New York: Portfolio.

Mishel, Lawrence, Josh Bivens, Elise Gould, and Heidi Shierholz. 2012. *The State of Working America*. Ithaca, NY: Cornell University Press.

Munnell, Alicia H., Geoffrey M. B. Tootell, Lynn E. Browne, and James McEneaney. 1996. "Mortgage Lending in Boston: Interpreting HMDA Data." *The American Economic Review* 86 (1): 25–53.

National Association of Realtors National Association of Realtors. 2012. *Social Benefits of Homeownership and Stable Housing*. Washington, DC.

National Commission on the Causes of the Financial and Economic Crisis in the United States National Commission on the Causes of the Financial and Economic Crisis in the United States. 2011. *The Financial Crisis Inquiry Report*. New York: Public Affairs.

National Community Reinvestment Coalition National Community Reinvestment Coalition. 2007. *CRA Commitments*. Washington, DC.

National Council of State Housing Agencies National Council of State Housing Agencies. 2012. *State HFA Factbook: 2010 NCSHA Annual Survey Results*. Washington, D.C..

Norris, Floyd. 2013. "Challenge to Dogma on Owning a Home." *New York Times*, May 9.

Obama, Barack. 2013. "*Growing the Housing Market and Supporting our Homeowners*." Weekly Address. Washington, DC: The White House. May 11. http://www.whitehouse.gov/the-press-office/2013/05/11/weekly-address-growing-housing-market-and-supporting-our-homeowners.

Oswald, Andrew. 2012. "Home-ownership: Should Home-ownership Be Discouraged?" *The Economist*, September 19. http://www.economist.com/debate/days/view/882.

Porter, Eduardo. 2005. "Buy a Home, and Drag Society Down." *New York Times*, November 13.

Poterba, James, and Todd Sinai. 2011. "Revenue Cost and Incentive Effects of Income Tax Provisions for Owner-Occupied Housing," *National Tax Journal* 64 (2): 531–564.

Rakoff, Robert M. 1977. "Ideology in Everyday Life: The Meaning of the House." *Politics and Society* 7: 85–104.

Rapoport, Abby. 2013. "Vacation Homes for the Rich, Courtesy of Uncle Sam." *American Prospect*, January 16. http://prospect.org/article/vacation-homes-rich-courtesy-uncle-sam.

Robbins, Roy M. 1942. *Our Landed Heritage*. Princeton, NJ: Princeton University Press.

Rohe, William M., and Michael Stegman. 1994. "The Impact of Home Ownership on the Social and Political Involvement of Low-Income People." *Urban Affairs Quarterly* 30, no. 1 (September): 152–172.

Rohe, William M., Shannon Van Zandt, and George McCarthy. 2001. *The Social Benefits and Costs of Homeownership: A Critical Assessment of the Research*. October Cambridge, MA: Joint Center for Housing Studies of Harvard University.

Rohe, William M., and Harry L Watson, eds. 2007. *Chasing the American Dream: New Perspectives on Affordable Homeownership*. Ithaca, NY: Cornell University Press.

Rose, Jerome. 1973. *Landlords and Tenants*. New Brunswick, NJ: Transaction Books.

Rossi, Peter, and Eleanor Weber. 1996. "The Social Benefits of Homeownership: Empirical Evidence from National Surveys." *Housing Policy Debate* 7 (1): 1–35.

*Schwartz, Alex. 2010. *Housing Policy in the United States* 2nd ed. New York: Routledge, 227–240.

Schwartz, Alex. 2012. "U.S. Housing Policy in the Age of Obama: From Crisis to Statis." *International Journal of Housing Policy* 12 (2).

Shapiro, Thomas M., and Melvin L. Oliver. 1995. *Black Wealth/White Wealth: A New Perspective on Racial Inequality*. New York: Routledge.

Shapiro, Thomas, Tatjana Meschede, and Sam Osoro. 2013. "The Roots of the Widening Racial Wealth Gap: Explaining the Black-White Economic Divide." February Waltham, MA: Brandeis University Institute on Assets and Social Policy.

Shlay, Anne B. 2006. "Low Income Homeownership: American Dream or Delusion?" *Urban Studies* 43, no. 3 (March): 511–531.

*Sidney, Mara. 2003. *Unfair Housing: How National Policy Shapes Community Action*. Lawrence: University Press of Kansas.

Starobin, Paul. 2011. "A Dream Endangered. (Yeah, So?)" *The Next Economy: A Special Supplement to the National Journal*, Spring.

Stiglitz, Joseph, and Mark Zandi. 2012. "The One Housing Solution Left: Mass Mortgage Refinancing." *New York Times*, August 12.

Streitfeld, David, and Megan Thee-Brenan. 2011. "Despite Risks, Owning a Home Retains Its Allure, Poll Shows." *New York Times*, June 30.

Suskind, Ron. 2011. *Confidence Men: Wall Street, Washington, and the Education of a President.* New York: HarperCollins.

Temkin, Kenneth, Brad Theodos, and David Price. 2010. "*Balancing Affordability and Opportunity: An Evaluation of Affordable Homeownership Programs with Long-term Affordability Controls. Final Report.*" Washington, DC: Urban Institute.

Turner, M. A., S. L. Ross, G. C. Galster, and J. Yinger. 2002. *Discrimination in Metropolitan Housing Markets: National Results from Phase 1 HDS 2000 (Final report).* Washington, DC: U.S. Department of Housing and Urban Development.

U.S. Bureau of the Census. 2013. *Homeownership Rates for the US and Regions: 1965 to Present, Current Population Survey/Housing Vacancy Survey, Series H-111 Reports.* Washington, DC: GPO.

U.S. Congress. 2009. "*An Overview of Federal Support for Housing,*" November 3. Washington, DC: Congressional Budget Office.

U.S. Congress, Joint Committee on Taxation. 2013. *Estimates of Federal Tax Expenditures or Fiscal Years 2012–2017.* Washington DC: GPO.

U.S. Department of Housing and Urban Development U.S. Department of Housing and Urban Development. 1967. *Tenants' Rights: Legal Tools for Better Housing. Report on a National Conference on Legal Rights of Tenants.* Washington, DC.

U.S. Department of Housing and Urban Development U.S. Department of Housing and Urban Development. 1978. *The 1978 HUD Survey on the Quality of Community Life.* Washington, DC.

U.S. Department of Housing and Urban Development U.S. Department of Housing and Urban Development. 2010. *Report to Congress on the Root Causes of the Foreclosure Crisis.* Washington, DC: U.S. Department of Housing and Urban Development, Office of Policy Development and Research, January http://www.huduser.org/Publications/PDF/Foreclosure_09.pdf.

Vale, Lawrence. 2007. "The Ideological Origins of Affordable Homeownership Efforts." In William M. Rohe and Harry L Watson, eds., *Chasing the American Dream: New Perspectives on Affordable Homeownership.* Ithaca, NY: Cornell University Press, 15–40.

Ventry, Dennis. 2010. "The Accidental Deduction: A History and Critique of the Tax Subsidy for Mortgage Interest." *Law and Contemporary Problems* 73 (Winter), 233–284.

Village of Euclid v. Ambler Realty Company, 272 U.S. 365, 1926.

Warner, Sam Bass. 1962. *Streetcar Suburbs.* Cambridge, MA: Harvard University Press.

Warner, Sam Bass. 1968. *The Private City.* Philadelphia: University of Pennsylvania Press.

Warner, Sam Bass. 1972. *The Urban Wilderness.* New York: Harper and Row.

Williamson, Chilton. 1960. *American Suffrage from Property to Democracy: 1760–1860.* Princeton, NJ: Princeton University Press.

Wolff, Edward N. 2013. *The Asset Price Meltdown and the Wealth of the Middle Class.* Thousand Oaks, CA: Sage.

Zandi, Mark. 2009. *Financial Shock.* Saddle River, NJ: FT Press.

CHAPTER 29

....

PRIVATE HEALTH INSURANCE

Tax Breaks, Regulation, and Politics

....

JAMES A. MORONE

1 INTRODUCTION

....

BY the end of his administration, President Harry Truman (1945–1953) was baffled. "I just don't understand how anyone could be against my health program," he wrote. "We're trying to meet human needs, and not just to meet private greed" (quoted in Blumenthal and Morone 2009, 67). Universal health insurance coverage seemed, to President Truman, like an essential right of citizenship. Yet the U.S.—uniquely in the advanced industrial world—has never found a way to assure that all members of society have access to health insurance.

Three themes stand out in the long and conflicted history of American health insurance. First, the insurance system is highly fragmented—really, no system at all. Regulations vary by state, by insurer, and by insured population. Few rules apply to all insurers. Second, the American population falls into very different kinds of health-insurance risk pools. Large pools—where the risk is spread among many different people—mark government programs and large employers. Where risk is widely shared, health insurance is more affordable. On the other hand, small employers, small groups, and individuals face limited risk pools where cross-subsidization is more difficult, insurance is more expensive, and coverage is often difficult to buy at any price. The erosion of risk pools is embedded in the logic of unregulated competition between private insurance companies (Stone 2013). Finally, the fragmented health insurance nonsystem operates in tandem with a fragmented government biased against large-scale reforms. Powerful private interests find many nooks and crannies in the byzantine political process to check reforms they do not like. The result is a system biased toward narrow benefits to powerful groups (like tax breaks) and against systemic reform (like universal coverage).

In short, three forms of fragmentation mark American health care: unregulated payers, multiple risk pools, and inchoate government. The Affordable Care Act (the

ACA or Obama Care) finally imposes the first significant national rules across the health-insurance system.

2 CONSEQUENCES

Three consequences flow from the fragmented health-care regime: rising costs, limited access, and—despite constant rhetoric about the best care in the world—miserable outcomes by almost every comparative measure of population health. Health-care spending has risen inexorably in the United States: from 7.1 percent of the gross domestic product in 1970 to 12.2 percent in 1990 to almost 18 percent today. The growth in health expenditures seems so relentless that one health economist, Uwe Reinhardt, sarcastically builds forecast models predicting "when we'll have it all"—every penny in America spent on health care (current projection: 2072) (Reinhardt 1990, 47).

Moreover, although every nation feels cost pressures—from aging populations, new technology, and rising consumer expectations—no other country has seen the same kind of inflation in health costs as the United States. Industrial nations spend, on average, 10 percent of their gross domestic product on health care (see Table 29.1). And over the past 15 years, spending on health care across the industrial world has been flat as a percentage of the total economy. After the United States, the biggest spenders are

Table 29.1 Total Spending on Health as a Percent of GDP

	1970	1980	1990	2000	2010
Australia	4.1*	6.1	6.7	8.0	9.1*
Austria	5.2	7.4	8.4[b]	10.0	11.0
Belgium[1]	3.9	6.3	7.2	8.1d	10.5[d]
Canada	6.9	7.0	8.9	8.8	11.4
France	5.4	7.0	8.4	10.1	11.6
Germany	6.0	8.4	8.3	10.4	11.6
Italy	N/A	N/A	7.7	8.0	9.3
Japan	4.4	6.4	5.8	7.6	9.5*
Netherlands	N/A	7.4	8.0	8.0	12.0
Norway	4.4	7.0	7.6	8.4	9.4
Spain	3.5	5.3	6.5	7.2	9.6
Sweden	6.8	8.9	8.2	8.2	9.6
Switzerland	5.5	7.4	8.2	10.2	11.4
United Kingdom	4.5	5.6	5.9	7.0	9.6
U.S.	7.1	9.0	12.4	13.7	17.6
OECD AVERAGE					11.2

Source: OECD Health Data 2012 http://stats.oecd.org/Index.aspx?DataSetCode=SHA
[b]: break in series;
[d]: differences in methodology;
* estimate from prior calendar year.

Netherlands, France, and Germany—all spending about 25 percent *less* on health care relative to the rest of their economies.

A second number keeps going up: Americans without health insurance. The figure has increased from 34 million in 1990 to just under 50 million in 2012. Roughly 30 million more Americans have inadequate insurance. Half the people without insurance report putting off needed care. The U.S. Institute of Medicine estimates that at least 18,000 Americans a year die prematurely because they don't have health insurance; researchers suggest that mortality rates could be reduced by as much as 15 percent if the uninsured had "continuous health care coverage" (Kaiser Family Foundation 2004). The army of uninsured people is exacerbated by individuals who lose their coverage or cannot afford co-payments. Half of all personal bankruptcies result from health-care bills (Kaiser Family Foundation 2004).

Finally, American health outcomes are the worst in the industrial world. On most measures of population health—life expectancy, infant mortality, morbidity rates— the U.S. ranks lower than every other wealthy nation (and some developing ones). Depending on the study, the United States ranks somewhere around 35th in the world in life expectancy at birth—behind nations such as Croatia, Costa Rica, and the Sultancy of Brunei (Morone and Jacobs 2005, chap. 1). The problem of outcomes may be related to the problem of access to insurance. Older Americans, who enjoy universal coverage through Medicare, have the highest life expectancy in the world.

All three problems—rising costs, lack of insurance, and poor health outcomes— keep health insurance on the national agenda. Many reformers argue that American health-care problems stem from the same source: the chaotic nonsystem of insuring health care. Haphazard regulation leaves costs free to rise without the counterweight of a monopsony buyer, budget negotiations, effective markets, or system-wide regulations. Moreover, unregulated competition among private insurers creates a perverse incentive: insure only healthy people. The discipline of risk management makes it easy to shun those more likely to be sick (poor, minorities, people working for small companies, and anyone on economic margins). And with one in six uninsured, it is small wonder that health outcomes fall short of other wealthy nations.

3 THE AMERICAN DIFFERENCE

The American difference is often thought to be the difference between private and public health care. The United States, in this view, relies on private insurance companies rather than a public health-care system. This reading of America's exceptional public-private distinction is a myth. In the United States, the government pays for 44 percent of health care delivered each year—mainly through Medicare (which covers people over 65) and Medicaid (which covers some people with low incomes). For the population under 65, most (56 percent) get coverage through employers and just

5.5 percent through individual policies (Kaiser 2011). There is nothing unique about this: every nation mixes private and public health insurance, each in its own way (Béland and Gran 2008, 1–10).

In Britain, the National Health Service (or NHS) covers all citizens. Individuals have the option to top up their NHS coverage by buying private insurance, allowing them to bypass public service queues, cover gaps in the NHS (e.g., dental implants), and purchase amenities (such as a private room). Roughly 80 percent of the funding comes through the public tax-supported system and 20 percent from private insurance.

In Canada, private markets were originally restricted to services that were not covered by the public system, known as Medicare. In contrast to Britain, private companies could only offer insurance for ancillary services such as eyeglasses. "Extra billing"—special treatment for an additional fee—was banned for fear that it would subvert equality. In 2006, however, a court ruled (in *Chaoulli v. Quebec*) that when patients had to wait for life saving treatments, the government could not forbid "extra billing" or private insurance. By most accounts, the case has had limited impact on the Canadian system, which is still dominated by the single payer, public health-care model. In the mid-1960s, the federal government established guiding principles and provided funding (50 percent of Medicare spending at first, but that percentage declined starting in 1977). However, Medicare is organized, funded, and administered by the provinces (Boychuk and Banting 2008).

In Germany, most health care is paid for by private insurers (known as sickness funds), which operate under guidelines negotiated by peak associations within a regulatory framework. The sickness funds are private organizations that were originally tied to the workplace. It is an unusual model in that the government oversees an essentially private insurance system. German health-care analysts debate the advantages and disadvantages of market competition versus bureaucratic regulation, but always in the context of what they call the solidarity model: all Germans should be offered roughly equal health insurance based on a notion of shared risk (Morone 2000).

Every one of these national systems mixes public programs and private insurers. In some places (Canada, Britain), the government pays for most of the care; in others (Germany), the employers and employees pay through private insurers while the government oversees and regulates. All three nations—and most industrialized democracies—differ from the American case in two ways. First, all make a philosophical commitment to the solidarity principle that citizens are covered on relatively equal terms. Second, all have developed the institutional capacity and political will to regulate the entire health insurance system, although there are differences in how they do so. Authority can be set on the national (England, Scotland) or the provincial (Canada) level; it can be hammered out by a centralized budget authority (Britain) or through formal negotiations between payers and providers (Germany). In these three cases—and in almost every national health system—authority over health care rests in a clearly designated institutional locus. The lack of such institutional capacity—indeed, the antagonism to any such authority—is the most distinguishing feature of American health insurance.

In the United States each payer and insured group makes its own arrangements. Even fundamental questions are up for grabs: Who gets health insurance? From whom? Under what conditions? How will providers be overseen and reimbursed?

Many different actors throughout the public and private sectors shape U.S. health care. Important decisions are taken on the national level (for Medicare recipients), in the 50 state governments (Medicaid recipients, some employee plans, most individual insurance plans), by large employers (who negotiate the terms of worker coverage), and by private insurance companies (negotiating with employers or setting terms with individuals). We can multiply the categories further as private insurance companies face different rules and regulations if they are proprietary (for example, Anthem Blue Cross of California) or nonprofit (Anthem Blue Cross of Massachusetts).

4 The Rise of Private Health Insurance in America

Why does the U.S. health-care system operate as it does? The answer lies in the distinctive and ideologically charged way it developed over the past century. The modern U.S. health insurance system evolved thanks to chance, ideology, self-interest, and the fractured American state.

4.1 The Accidental Origins of Employer-Based Insurance

Medicine was cheap and ineffective at the start of the 20th century—the average consumer spent about $5 a year ($100 in today's terms). However, that soon changed. One celebrated estimate located "the great divide" in 1912: the random American patient going to the random American physician had a more than random chance of being helped by the encounter (Marmor 2000, 3). The medical establishment soon began to grow. It prospered through the 1920s only to be shaken by the Great Depression of the 1930s. In a single year, hospital receipts fell from $236 to $59 per patient. In 1931, hospitals filled only 62 percent of their beds (Anderson 1975; Starr 1982, 295–296).

In response, the medical establishment dropped its long-standing opposition to health insurance. In 1932, the American Hospital Association embraced an idea that Baylor University Hospitals pioneered in 1929 and underwrote Blue Cross hospital insurance plans. The American Medical Association followed with Blue Shield Plans (covering doctor's costs). The United States now had a nascent network of health-insurance plans. However, growth was slow and after a decade, less than 10 percent of the population had signed up (Blumenthal and Morone 2008, 81–83).

Then, an accidental event changed all the calculations. During World War II, the federal government capped wages in order to control inflation. In 1943, however, the Internal Revenue Service ruled that employer-based health plans did not count toward the cap and would not be taxed. It was a haphazard decision about a rare and little understood benefit but it would have far reaching consequences.

Employers, looking to attract employees in a tight wartime labor market, began offering fringe benefits like tax-free health insurance. Unions, newly legitimated by the New Deal and protected by the 1935 Wagner Act, eagerly negotiated health benefits after the Supreme Court declared that such benefits could be subject to collective bargaining (*Inland Steel v. National Labor Relations Board 1948*). The increasingly powerful unions developed a stake in the employer-based plans they negotiated and sometimes sponsored (Gottschalk 2001), and the Blue Cross-Blue Shield plans eagerly marketed to employer groups. The ingredients were now in place for the rapid rise of private insurance.

4.2 Challenge from the Government

At the same time, during the 1930s and 1940s, liberals in and out of government pressed for compulsory government health insurance. President Roosevelt refused to include health care in the Social Security Act of 1935 for fear that the entire bill might be lost. However, as victory in World War II came into sight, FDR tasked his long time aide, Sam Rosenman, with drafting a health plan. Roosevelt died before the plan was ready and it passed to President Truman, who seized it with a fervor that surprised his associates. Senate Minority leader Robert Taft (R-OH) set the terms of the debate when he dubbed it "the most socialistic measure that this congress has ever had before it, seriously" (quoted in Blumenthal and Morone 2008, 77).

In the run up to his long-shot 1948 reelection campaign, President Truman commissioned a blue ribbon panel on health care. The commission's report, *The Nation's Health—a Ten Year Program*, portrayed the failure of private health insurance with reams of data. In 20 states, less than 10 percent of the population had health insurance. The poorer the state, the more limited the coverage. Private health insurance, concluded the committee, covered a fraction of the population, offered them inadequate coverage, and was hardest to get where the need was the greatest (Blumenthal and Morone 2008, 81–83). The report became a liberal brief for public health insurance. "Every year," wrote the commission chair, "over 300,000 people die whom we have the knowledge and skill to save..." (Blumenthal and Morone 2008, 83). Note the ground on which liberals chose to fight the battle for national health insurance—a prediction that private insurance would not cover the population.

Truman ran for reelection in 1948 touting national health care as one of his central domestic issues. When he won, the American Medical Association taxed every physician and launched a ferocious (and brilliantly orchestrated) campaign against "socialist medicine." Representative John Dingell (D-MI), who had sponsored the administration's bill in the House, denounced the "20 million dollar...campaign of misrepresentation" (quoted in Blumenthal and Morone 2008, 91). The reality is that the interest group campaign did not matter much as Congress, dominated by conservative Southern Democrats, never intended to pass national health insurance. The media all reported that, as *Newsweek* put it, "the bill has no chance for approval at this session of Congress." The Ways and Means Committee did not even bother to consider the legislation (Steinmo and Watts 1995; Blumenthal and Morone 2008, 91).

Why did national health insurance fail in the United States, whereas it succeeded, at almost the same time, in Britain? The answer lies in the organization of Congress. Had the United States been operating under British (or German, or Canadian) parliamentary rules, Truman's election victory would have ensured passage. But American checks and balances made Truman's signature domestic issue on the hustings irrelevant in Washington. And that, in turn, created an opportunity for private-health-insurance markets.

4.3   Eisenhower's Chance—and the Rise of the Markets

In 1953, Republican Dwight Eisenhower succeeded Truman. President Eisenhower led Republicans to an accommodation with New Deal programs like Social Security, but he drew the line at new social-welfare programs. The most important contest was over health insurance. "We know that the American people will not long be denied access to adequate medical facilities," declared Eisenhower in 1954. What we needed, he concluded, was "a logical alternative to socialized medicine" (Eisenhower 1954).

Eisenhower tried to facilitate private coverage of vulnerable populations with a government reinsurance scheme that was voted down by Congress. However, the administration soon seized the IRS ruling from 1943 that exempted employee health plans from taxation. After the war, as employer health plans grew, the temporary policy remained in force but became increasingly chaotic as the IRS made ad hoc decisions about what qualified for the tax break. IRS officials began eyeing all the foregone revenues that, by the mid 1950s, were adding up.

In the most important health-care act of his presidency, Eisenhower sponsored the Revenue Act of 1954, which formalized and expanded the tax break so that health employer insurance premiums remained tax free. The administration went before Congress cheered on by a dream coalition of labor unions, the American Medical Association, the American Hospital Association, and the Chamber of Commerce. They all argued that this was the American way: a private sector solution to a public problem (Blumenthal and Morone 2008). Notice how the "American way" was subsidized by government tax policy. Today, that tax expenditure adds up to $131 billion a year. In effect, the government operates a "delegated welfare state"—delegating (and subsidizing) the task of providing insurance coverage to employers (Morgan and Campbell 2011; Mettler 2011; Hacker 2002).

Budget hawks in Congress immediately seized on the budget implications and complained about "a major loss of revenue," as Senator Russell Long (D-LA) put it. However, the IRS reform was already in place; Congress was being asked only to endorse and expand the status quo. Any other action would require stripping business and labor of a benefit they already enjoyed. The Revenue Act sailed easily through Congress and helped set employer health insurance into the bedrock of the American health insurance system. A little noticed revenue decision in 1943 proved to be the butterfly effect that led to an American health-insurance regime, which the Eisenhower administration—with a most uncharacteristic fiscal nonchalance—now formalized. Employee-based health insurance, which was already growing, took off.

The clash between liberals (touting a universal public system) and conservatives (relying on private health insurance markets) continued for another two decades. However, by the 1960s, liberals had lost the claim underlying Truman's crusade—that the private health-insurance system could not cover a large part of the population. The private system might be biased because it failed to cover people who fell outside the corporate sphere, but it insured 70 percent of the American public by the mid-1960s.

Competition among private health insurers soon injected a kind of instability into health care that was barely noticed at the time. Blue Cross, which was the first to provide hospital coverage, charged all enrollees the same rate, known as *community rating*. As a result, there were statewide risk pools in which the healthy subsidized the sick. As commercial carriers entered the market in each state, they employed *experience rating*, going after low-risk groups and offering them premiums tied to their own (lower) costs. In effect, they carved up the risk pool and disrupted the system of cross-subsidy that exists in community rating. As costs rose, and employment health insurance eroded, experience rating left individuals and small groups out of the insurance market. By 2000, only seven states required community rating.

The employee model was not well suited for populations outside the corporate work force, such as senior citizens and the poor. In 1965, the federal government partially filled those gaps in a way that fit the logic of the private insurance markets: government socialized the costs of the populations that were most difficult to cover. Indeed, from the very start, many liberals had opposed programs targeted to the poor because such programs undercut support for universal health insurance. And although some interests opposed Medicare as fiercely as they had opposed NHI (the American Medical Association, conservative Republicans), others (hospitals, conservative Democrats) understood that this was a way to protect private insurance markets by siphoning off the poor risks (Marmor 2000; Starr 1982)

Two very different government programs addressed senior citizens and the poor, and each program developed a distinctive relationship to private insurance markets. The program for the elderly, Medicare, was a version of Truman's health plan applied to almost all people over 65. Like the Canadian health-care system, this program operates in conjunction with private insurance, known colloquially as Medigap, which offers insurance policies that fill in many gaps and limits of the public program. Today, 81 percent of seniors have some kind of private insurance policy to supplement Medicare (Rowland and Lyons 1996, 78). Medicare is, for the most part, a national program with national regulations. However, Republicans are eager to inject private health insurance—and took a step in that direction when they added prescription drug coverage (in 2003).

The program for low-income individuals, Medicaid, is very different and features enormous state differences in eligibility and coverage. The program is administered by the states within federal guidelines and jointly funded, with states paying between 26 percent and 50 percent of the costs. The law mandated coverage of some groups such as children 6–18 years old in families with incomes at or below the poverty line. Eligibility for parents was tied to existing eligibility requirements for Aid to Families with Dependent Children (welfare), essentially leaving Medicaid eligibility up to the states. By 2012, the most generous Medicaid program (Connecticut) covered working parents with incomes up to 191 percent of poverty (about $38,000), while at the other end of the spectrum, Arkansas and Texas covered parents only up to 17 percent and 26 percent of poverty, respectively (Kaiser 2012). Only 8 state Medicaid programs cover childless adults—the program proscribes it unless states explicitly request the expanded coverage through a Medicaid waiver. Immigrants are not eligible until they have been in the country for five years.

The result is a patchwork of coverage that varies by state, by demographics, and by individual characteristics. Low-income Americans have an especially difficult time getting insurance coverage: low-wage jobs are unlikely to offer health insurance and Medicaid programs operate with byzantine rules, different eligibility criteria, and eternal fiscal crises because inexorably rising health-care costs squeeze every state's Medicaid budget.

By the late 1960s, the institutional structures of the contemporary American health-care regime were in place. Medicare, augmented by private insurance policies, covers people over 65. Fifty different Medicaid programs cover 44 million low-income individuals (and about one out of three children). Employers choose whether to offer coverage, subsidized by federal tax expenditures. Private insurers offer different risk-rated products to more affluent consumers. Small businesses, small groups, and individuals have an increasingly difficult time finding insurance coverage, and, as costs squeeze employers and state Medicaid budgets, the ranks of the uninsured grow (Kaiser 2011, Table 29.1).

4.4 The Clinton Reform and Managed Competition

The Clinton administration came to office in 1993 promising to address the health-care problem and devised an ambitious plan to control costs and expand coverage. The plan was to take existing programs (employer health care, Medicare, Medicaid), add insurance for those without it, and place them all within federally designed, state-run, regional pools. All health plans would offer standard benefit packages at a community rate. The Clinton reform squarely addressed the risk-pool problem: it aimed to place each region's population in one risk pool, regardless of who was paying. The carefully regulated competition among health plans was expected to hold down costs. At the heart of the proposal lay something called managed competition: Consumers would make choices among alternative health plans with population-based budgets (Hacker 1997; Starr 2011, ch. 3). For the first time, everybody in the complicated American system would play by the same regulatory rules.

The Clinton proposal ran into familiar charges of bureaucracy run amok; bloated, naïve, and arrogant government; the end of American medicine; and the return of socialism just three years after the collapse of communism. Shrewd political observers saw the real political problem: There were only 56 Democrats in the Senate, 4 shy of the number need to invoke cloture and end a filibuster.

Republicans in Congress defeated the plan and, in the backlash, took control of both chambers for the first time in 40 years. However, something funny happened to health policy. The managed-care revolution took off without the revolutionaries. A defeated proposal helped transform the health-care system—or perhaps simply sped up reforms that were already quietly under way (Morone 1999).

4.5 Managed care

The idea of system-wide rules collapsed with the Democratic reform effort, but many individual payers seized on a mechanism in the Clinton proposal—managed care—and used it to try to control their own costs. In managed care, payers use health-services research to determine which procedures were cost effective and should be authorized, thereby (in theory) improving care and reducing costs. No approval means no payment. In adopting this model, payers ranging from insurance companies to Medicare officials stopped deferring to providers and tried to seize control of medical practice—and with it, costs.

For a short time the managed-care hammer seemed to work as the relentless escalation in health-care costs abated. Health-care costs had stood at 13.3 percent of GDP in 1993 when Clinton organized his plan; five years later, with managed care widely in use, costs had slipped to 13.0 percent of GDP). This was one of the only periods in the past half-century when the health-care sector stopped its seemingly inexorable conquest of the American economy.

There was, however, a problem. The health-services research data never fully lived up to its promises; instead of guiding clinicians to the most effective treatments, it became a very blunt mechanism for controlling costs. Insurers refused to pay for treatments— often without much evidence to back their denials. Patients—often egged on by their health providers who were suddenly being told they could not order a procedure— began to howl. By one count, over 1,000 legislative proposals sprang up across the states, all designed to rein in managed care (Morone 1999).

After the brief pause in the mid 1990s, health costs leapt up, quickly making up for lost ground. In part, payers were not able to make their rigorous managed care regime stick against outraged premium payers; and, in part, providers shifted their costs from more effective cost cutters (inevitably the government programs) to less effective ones (Morone 1999).

5 Health Insurance Markets Before the Obama Health Reform

The story of the American health-care system over the past two decades can be put simply: In response to rising costs, governments pinch budgets and employers cut back their commitments, often shifting the burden to employees. For small groups, insurance coverage is increasingly difficult to find. And the health-insurance markets for individuals are near collapse.

5.1 Employer Health Insurance

Employer plans are the main source of health insurance for working adults. As noted earlier, 56.2 percent of the nonelderly population (149 million Americans) receives their coverage through employee benefit plans. These plans, however, are under stress. Three trends are clear over the past decade. First, costs have risen quickly; between 2001 and 2011, the premiums for employer plans rose 113 percent (from $7,061 $15,073 per employee). Second, employers have been shifting the costs to employees whose premium payments rose 133 percent in the same period. Third, employers are dropping out; about 10 percent stopped offering health insurance altogether (Kaiser, 2011). For all the erosion, the revenues lost to the federal treasury in foregone taxes kept rising, topping 130 million by 2010 (Blumenthal and Morone 2008).

The stress is especially visible on small employers. Less than half (41 percent) of all firms with fewer than 50 employees offer health insurance to their workers. Firms with 25 employees or fewer have an especially difficult time providing insurance coverage. The small group means high premiums, and firms that do manage to offer insurance may find they are one ill employee away from losing affordable coverage. Even innovative programs, such as subsidy programs funded by the Robert Wood Johnson Foundation to stimulate the health-insurance market for small business, soon run into a tough reality: Even heavily-subsidized insurance premiums are beyond the reach of most small employers. Jack Meyer, president of the Economic and Social Research Institute, summed it up: "For many [small businesses], any premium beyond zero dollars is too much" (Morone 2008, 31). A survey by the foundation added another discouraging word: Half the companies that did not provide health insurance for employees had no desire to do so (Morone 2008, 31).

Until the Obama Administration reforms, employer health plans were only lightly regulated. Responsibility for overseeing health insurance lies primarily at the state level and most state regulators focused on protecting insurance industry interests (Stone 1993). Moreover an obscure Congressional rule dramatically limited state regulatory authority. The Federal Employee Retirement Income Security Act of 1974—known as ERISA—received an unexpected reading in the courts, which found that employee-funded health plans are "preempted" from state regulations. This "ERISA preemption" means that large companies that "self-insure" by offering their own plans, are exempted from many state health-insurance regulations. States may not directly regulate, tax, or impose substantial costs on such plans, nor may they require employers to offer health insurance. For many years, the ERISA preemption made state-level health reform difficult because it removed most large employers from the reach of state health policy makers. The ERISA preemption does not apply to federal policy makers.

Even generous employer plans pose problems for beneficiaries. Many include a "stop loss" provision whereby individuals facing very expensive treatments may find their coverage suddenly come to an end. Federal law (ERISA) prevents states from interfering in the practice (Hall 2012). Another problem is job lock in which individuals are locked into their current jobs because it provides good health insurance coverage.

The Consolidated Budget Reconciliation Act of 1986 (COBRA) requires companies to maintain workers on their plans for up to 18 months; however, since the departed workers are responsible for up to 102 percent of the plan's costs (a family plan typically runs to $700 a month), only about 20 percent of workers take advantage of the program (Adams 2004).

5.2 Individual Health Insurance

By the time the Obama administration passed the Affordable Care Act, the market for individuals or families seeking insurance had almost disappeared. One survey reported that over 90 percent of the people who shopped for individual health insurance failed to make a purchase because they could not find an affordable plan or were rejected by the plans they sought to buy (Collins et al. 2006).

In most states, insurers will not cover *pre-existing conditions*. Individuals who lose their employee health insurance will not likely get coverage for chronic conditions or anything for which they have received treatment in the past. One study found that 92 percent of individuals with a self-reported "health problem" could not find insurance at any cost (Collins et al. 2006). Insurers may reject applications even if they simply suspect a pre-existing condition, or compute a statistical likelihood of high costs.

Moreover, insurers routinely include *lifetime caps* on health-insurance benefits. In one famous case, a North Dakota mother testified before Congress that her son had hemophilia that required expensive treatment. She had calculated when the family would reach its cap and the clock would run out on her son (McDonough 2011, 107). An especially controversial insurance practice is known as *rescission*—canceling a policy after individual claims are made, often over alleged errors in the original coverage application.

The result is a market that is very difficult to enter but easy to fall out of by getting sick. Insurers impose waiting periods, refuse to cover pre-existing (or even potentially pre-existing) conditions, cap benefits, cancel policies, rate applicants as statistical risks, charge extremely high prices, and, in general, follow the incentives generated by the market: Avoid insuring sick people.

5.3 Class, Race, and Ethnicity

The problems of health insurance can touch all Americans but they do not touch them equally. Poorer Americans have a harder time getting health insurance, suffer worse health, and, if they develop chronic diseases, have a difficult time coping with medical bills. However, poverty is only one part of the story. Race and ethnicity exacerbate the problems. Even among the poor, different demographic groups have very different experiences, with Hispanics, in particular, having a hard time getting health insurance.

Poor families struggle with health insurance. Studies that define low income as 138 percent of the federal poverty line (or about $32,000 for a family of four) find that almost half (45 percent) are uninsured; another 21 percent receive Medicaid. Even low-income individuals working full-time often do not have health insurance. We have already seen why: Small and marginal firms are not likely to offer health insurance. And the market for individual health policies is very difficult to access because the policies, when available, are far too expensive for low-income individuals.

Hispanics, in particular, have low levels of health insurance. A little more than a third (36.6 percent) get coverage through employers and, 32 percent are uninsured (Kaiser, 2011). The number of uninsured in the Hispanic community is high regardless of work status. Among full-time Hispanic workers making at least $46,000 (or twice the federal poverty line), 41 percent have no insurance; turn the focus on lower income workers (below 200 percent of the poverty line) and the number of uninsured rises to 80 percent.

The predictable result is that the Hispanic population is less likely to have a regular source of health care (a third do not) and is far less likely to receive preventive care or effective treatment. For example, among preschool children hospitalized for asthma, 21 percent of the white children, 7 percent of black, and just 2 percent of Hispanic children receive routine medications to prevent recurring asthma-related hospitalization (AHRQ 2000). Of course, the Hispanic community is extremely diverse—ranging from wealthy third-generation Cuban Americans to low-income, recent immigrants from El Salvador—but on average, they are unlikely to have medical insurance.

In 2004, the Institute of Medicine published a study that revealed a stunning litany of disparities in health and health care, especially as it affected the Hispanic and African

American communities (Smedley, Stith, and Nelson 2003). Black Americans face a long legacy of discrimination in the insurance markets. Risk-rating tables pioneered in the first decades of the twentieth century flatly ruled out African Americans as uninsurable risks. Although that kind of explicit discrimination is thankfully gone, African Americans still face difficulties getting insurance. They are 50 percent less likely to have employer health insurance than whites (42 percent of the black population is covered by employers) and half as likely to have individual insurance (it reaches just 3 percent of black families). One in five African Americans is uninsured, compared to 13.8 percent for whites and 32 percent for Hispanics (Kaiser 2011).

Partially as a consequence of poor insurance, the racial disparities in both health care and health outcomes remain, as the Secretary of Health and Human Services, Katherine Sebelius put it, "stunning and shocking" (Kaiser 2011). African Americans are one-third less likely to get coronary bypass surgery; they wait twice as long for follow-ups to abnormal mammograms; and they are less likely to get eyeglasses in nursing homes, antiretroviral therapy for HIV infection, and angioplasty during coronary episodes. They are more likely to have limbs amputated (AHRQ 2000; Kaiser 2011).

Researchers point to multiple explanations for such disparities, including physician decision-making, cultural barriers, and differences in where people get health care but every list of explanations prominently includes the lack of health insurance. Some scholars even argue that the market-based health insurance has an inherent racial bias. Deborah Stone traces out the long logical chain: Racial and ethnic minorities are disproportionately less healthy, making them less attractive to private insurers and thus disproportionately uninsured or underinsured. They, therefore, have erratic access to health care and, when they finally get care, they are sicker than other patients. At that point, "they are very unattractive (economically speaking) to providers." The conclusion: A long legacy of discrimination is—inadvertently, mechanically—reinforced by market-based health insurance (Stone 2005, 79).

America's fateful choice for private, experience-rated insurance reinforces ethnic and racial disparities in health care. The disparities were locked in by market incentives until the federal government, under the Affordable Care Act of 2010, finally promulgated regulations to rewrite insurance market rules.

6 REFORMING THE INSURANCE MARKETS: THE AFFORDABLE CARE ACT

Between 1992 and 2008, both Democrats and Republicans tried to reform health insurance markets in a pattern that political sociologist Paul Starr characterizes as "initiative, miscalculation, and defeat" (Starr 2011, 140–141). The Obama administration finally broke the logjam with an essentially conservative approach: Rather than replacing the insurance markets with a single payer system, as liberals hoped, the administration rewrote the rules and incentives for the insurance markets. Democrats in the administration and Congress tried to devise a fix for almost every insurance market twist and turn described earlier.

Critics have charged that the reform is numbingly complicated. This it is. An effort to patch up the insurance system is, inevitably, complex. It is the conservative nature of the plan—reform the private insurance system rather than replace it with a public system– that inevitably gives it so many complicated moving parts. However, the plan offers a conceptual (and a political) breakthrough: it imposes a regulatory regime on insurance markets, with national rules replacing the haphazard welter of state rules and regulations.

6.1 Regulating Insurance

The ACA has 10 parts or titles. Title 1 aims to fix the ground rules of the private-insurance market for both individuals and groups. To do so, the law overrules the ERISA preemption and includes self-insured corporations in the new rules. Provisions include:

- A prohibition on lifetime annual benefit caps.
- A prohibition on recissions (canceling a policy after an individual files a claim).
- Restrictions on annual limits and waiting periods before insurance takes effect.
- A requirement that insurers allow adult children to remain on parents' policy (until age 26).
- A requirement that insurers summarize benefits in four pages of 12-point font.
- A prohibition on discrimination on the basis of health status: no more preexisting conditions clauses, although some discrimination is permitted for tobacco use, age, and wellness program participation.
- A guarantee of availability and renewal of coverage—no more lost coverage following a large claim. The legislation also specifies minimum benefits.
- A requirement that insurers spend 80–85 percent of premiums on "medical related expenditures" or offer premium rebates.

The upshot is an end to "medical underwriting." When the ACA goes into full effect in 2014, individual medical histories will no longer govern the availability or price of health insurance.

6.2 Extending Coverage: Pools, Tax Credits, and Employers

Section 1 also attempts to fix the individual market by requiring states to create "insurance exchanges." These are large insurance pools open to anyone who wants to buy coverage from private companies offering plans. If a state does not create an exchange—and many states have been resisting—the federal government will create one. Individuals buying coverage on state exchanges receive tax subsidies to help them afford insurance, with subsidies expected to average about $6,000 a year per individual depending on income. Opponents of the law have seized on a drafting error to argue that exchanges organized by the federal government are not eligible for the subsidies, which means that the legal battles continue four years after the law was passed.

The subsidies for insurance exchanges are part of a broad tax credit. Families and individuals who purchase health insurance are eligible for a graduated federal government subsidy on their taxes if their income is below 400 percent of the federal poverty line ($92,200 for a family of four). For the first time, the federal tax credits extend beyond employer plans. Other tax measures include a new tax credit for small business to help pay for health insurance.

Moreover, the ACA will penalize businesses with more than 50 employees who do not offer health insurance ($2,000 per employee for firms with more than 30 employees). Many business leaders point out that the penalty is far lower than the costs of coverage, perhaps creating an inadvertent incentive to release employees to the state insurance exchange. Employers can be penalized for high-cost or low-value plans. The law also requires **employers** with more than 200 employees to automatically enroll employees, although individuals may opt out.

Finally, every uninsured individual must buy health insurance as long as a plan is available costing less than 8 percent of annual income (there are tax credits up to 400 percent of the poverty line). People who fail to buy health insurance face a tax penalty that amounts to 2 percent of annual income. This is the individual mandate that created controversy and litigation. Why is it in the law? The answer lies in the size of the insurance pool. If everyone has insurance, the risks are spread over a large population and the basic logic of shared (or pooled) risk comes into play: the lucky healthy subsidize the unlucky who get sick. The requirement reflects political and economic reality: insurers are now required to cover everyone, but they will be spreading the risk over a much broader population.

Proponents of the ACA sum up the insurance overhaul by describing a three-legged stool. First, the plan radically overhauls insurance markets. Second, it subsidizes individuals and small business, primarily through the tax code, to help them purchase insurance. Third, it requires that everyone carry health insurance (McDonough 2011, 107). As with any stool, all the legs—the different features of the program—are needed to support one another.

6.3 Medicaid Expansion

For the first time, the ACA systematized Medicaid such that everyone under 133 percent of poverty (about $30,000 a year for a family of four) would be covered, from Connecticut to Arkansas. The federal government, which normally covers between 50 percent and 74 percent of Medicaid costs, will fund 90 percent of the costs of newly mandated enrollees. For poor Americans without insurance, the Obama health reform offered a lifeline: expanding Medicaid to 133 percent of poverty would have swept most into the health program.

Unfortunately for these low-income Americans, the Supreme Court struck down this part of the law in June 2012. The Federal government may offer—but not require—the expanded coverage. Several Republican governors flatly declared they would not expand their programs in their states whereas others report leaning toward not participating. Analysts differ on whether politicians will be able to resist such generous terms—90 percent federal funding—for long. Slowly but surely, many predict, Medicaid will expand and, for the first time, cover all (or most) of America's poor (Morone 2013). However, for the short run at least, low-income individuals remain in health insurance limbo, negotiating their health care coverage state-by-state and individual-by-individual.

6.4 Who Is Left Out

There is much more to the plan. The ACA is a complicated matrix of newly regulated and subsidized private markets and an expanded Medicaid program. The Congressional Budget Office (CBO) originally estimated that both private market reforms and Medicaid expansion would each extend health insurance to 16 million Americans (32 million combined). By September 2012, the CBO revised the numbers downwards to 26 million Americans covered and an estimated 30 million still uninsured. Who will be uninsured?

Five large groups will lack coverage even in the most optimistic scenarios. First, undocumented immigrants are explicitly excluded. Second, many individuals eligible for Medicaid will not enroll in the program—often they simply do not know they are eligible; however, medical providers are permitted to enroll individuals if and when they show up for treatment, although these provisions will now vary from state to state. Third, even with subsidies and exchanges, some Americans will not be able to afford care yet be "too rich" to qualify for Medicaid. Fourth, many poor people will live in states that refuse to expand the Medicaid program. And, finally, the CBO estimates that some 6 million people will pay the penalty rather than seek insurance (CBO 2012).

7 What Next: The Future of Health Insurance

The politics of health-care reform will continue. Advocates of the ACA will press on; opponents continue to promise to "repeal and replace." After the Supreme Court upheld most of the legislation and President Obama won reelection, the chances of "repeal and replace" are extremely low. The central questions are how effectively the law can be implemented and whether it will prove popular. For now, the ACA remains a major achievement, providing insurance to as many as 26 million uninsured Americans.

We can measure the path ahead by returning to the three themes at the start of the essay. First, the ACA offers the most significant reforms of America's private-insurance system that the government has ever undertaken. The ACA speaks to the perverse incentives that had developed in insurance markets—shun the sickly. Second, the ACA clearly aims to construct large risk pools. Each state will have its own risk pool for individuals seeking insurance, and with generously subsidized premiums. Moreover, requiring everyone to carry health insurance and then proscribing risk management recreates the network of cross-subsidies last seen during the days of community rating.

However, the American political regime remains fragmented and easily stalemated. Even under the best scenarios, American health care will require further reforms. As many as 30 million people will remain uninsured. Costs will continue to rise. And an entrepreneurial and dynamic private health-insurance system will continue to evolve in unpredictable ways, posing new opportunities and new dilemmas. The passage of the ACA changes a great many things. Yet the most important question remains the same: Are American political institutions up to the challenge of managing health care?

REFERENCES

*Indicates recommended reading.

Adams, Scott. 2004. "Employer Provided Health Insurance and Job Change." *Contemporary Economic Policy* 22: 357–369.

Agency for Healthcare Research and Quality. 2000. *Addressing Racial and Ethnic Disparities in Health Care: Fact Sheet.* Pub. No. 00-P041, February Rockville, MD: Agency for Healthcare Research and Quality. http://www.ahrq.gov/research/disparit.htm.

Anderson, Odin W. 1975. *Blue Cross Since 1929: Accountability and the Public Trust.* Cambridge, MA: Ballinger.

*Béland, Daniel, and Brian Gran, eds. 2008. *Public and Private Social Policy Health and Pension Policies in a New Era.* London: Palgrave Macmillan.

*Blumenthal, David, and James A. Morone. 2008. "The Lessons of Success: Revisiting the Medicare Story." *New England Journal of Medicine* 359: 2384–2389.

Blumenthal, David, and James A. Morone. 2009. *The Heart of Power: Health and Politics in the Oval Office.* Berkeley: University of California Press.

Boychuk, Gerard, and Keith Banting. 2008. "The Ties that Bind: Social Diversity and Cohesion in Canada." In Daniel Béland and Brian Gran (eds.), *Public and Private Social Policy: Health and Pension Policies in a New Era.* Basingstoke: Palgrave: 561–600.

Collins, Sara R., Jennifer Kriss, Karen Davis, Michelle Doty, and Alyssa Holmgren. 2006. "Squeezed: Why Rising Exposure to Health Care Costs Threatens the Health and Financial Well Being of Families." *The Commonwealth Fund.* New York: Commonwealth Fund Pub. No. 953. September http://www.commonwealthfund.org/usr_doc/collins_squeezedrising-hltcarecosts_953.pdf.

CBO (Congressional Budget Office). 2012. *Payment of Penalties for Being Uninsured Under the Affordable Care Act.* September www.cbo.gov/sites/default/files/cbofiles/attach-ments/09-19-12-Indiv_Mandate_Penalty.pdf.

Eisenhower, Dwight David. 1954. "Address at the Alfred E. Smith Memorial Dinner." New York City. October 21. *The Public Papers of the Presidents: Dwight D. Eisenhower.* Eisenhower Library.

*Gottschalk, Marie. 2001. *The Shadow Welfare State.* Ithaca, NY: Cornell University Press.

Hacker. J. S. 1997. *The Road to Nowhere: The Genesis of President Clinton's Plan for Health Security*. Princeton, NJ: Princeton University Press.

*Hacker, Jacob S. 2002. *The Divided Welfare State*. New York: Cambridge University Press.

Hall, Mark. 2012. "Regulating Stop Loss Coverage May Be Needed to Deter Self-Insuring Small Employers from Undermining Market Reforms." *Health Affairs* 2 (February): 216–223.

Kaiser Family Foundation. 2004, "The Uninsured and Their Access to Health Care," http://www.kff.org/uninsured/upload/The-Uninsured-and-Their-Access-to-Health-Care-November-2004-Fact-Sheet.pdf.

Kaiser Family Foundation. 2011. *The Uninsured: A Primer*. Supplemental Data Tables: p. 3.

Kaiser Family Foundation. 2012. State Health Facts. http://www.statehealthfacts.org.

Marmor, Theodore. 2000. *The Politics of Medicare*. Rev. ed. New York: Aldine.

*McDonough, John. 2011. *Inside National Health Reform*. Berkeley: University of California Press.

*Mettler, Suzanne. 2011. *The Submerged State: How Invisible Policies Undermine American Democracy*. Chicago: University of Chicago Press.

*Morgan, Kimberly J., and Andrea Louise Campbell. 2011. *The Delegated Welfare State: Medicare, Markets, and the Governance of Social Policy*. New York: Oxford University Press.

Morone, James. 1999. "Populists in A Global Market: The Backlash Against Managed Care." *Journal of Health Politics, Policy and Law* 24: 887–895.

*Morone, James. 2000. "Citizens or Shoppers: Solidarity Under Siege." *Journal of Health Politics, Policy and Law* 25: 959–968.

Morone, James. 2013. "Bipartisan Health Reform? Obamacare in the States." *Issues in Governance Studies*. Washington DC: The Brookings Institution. http://www.brookings.edu/research/papers/2013/12/17-bipartisan-health-reform-obamacare-states.

Morone, James, and Lawrence Jacobs. 2005. *Healthy, Wealthy, and Fair: Health Care for the Good Society*. New York: Oxford University Press.

Reinhardt, Uwe. 1990. "Could Health Care Swallow Us All?" *Business & Health.*, January–February, 47–48.

Rowland, Diane, and Barbara Lyons 1996. "Medicare, Medicaid, and the Elderly Poor." *Health Care Finance Review* 18: 61–85.

Smedley, Brian, Adrienne Stith, and Alan Nelson. 2003. *Unequal Treatment: Confronting Racial and Ethnic Disparities in Health Care*. Washington DC: National Acadamies Press.

Starr, Paul. 1982. *The Social Transformation of American Medicine*. New York: Basic Books.

Starr, Paul. 2011. *Remedy and Reaction: The Peculiar American Struggle over Health Care Reform*. New Haven, CT: Yale University Press.

Steinmo, Sven, and Jon Watts. 1995. "It's the Institutions Stupid! Why Comprehensive National Health Insurance Always Fails in America." *Journal of Health Politics, Policy and Law* 20: 373–383.

Stone, Deborah. 1993. "The Struggle for the Soul of Health Insurance." *Journal of Health Politics, Policy and Law* 18: 287–318.

Stone, Deborah. 2005. "How Market Ideology Guarantees Racial Inequities." In James Morone and Lawrence Jacobs, eds., *Health, Wealthy and Fair: Health Care for a Good Society*. New York: Oxford University Press.

*Stone, Deborah. 2013. "Values in Health Policy: Understanding Fairness and Efficiency." In James Morone and Dan Ehlke. eds., *Health Politics and Policy*. Clifton Park, NY: Cengage. Ch. 1.

CHAPTER 30

....

PENSION AND HEALTH BENEFITS FOR PUBLIC-SECTOR WORKERS

....

LEE A. CRAIG

1 INTRODUCTION

....

IN addition to the benefits the welfare state provides for its citizens, governments also provide important comparable benefits to their own workers in the form of nonwage compensation. In the labor markets of modern developed economies, nonwage compensation—or, to use the more colloquial term "fringe benefits"—composes a substantial proportion of total compensation, roughly 30 percent of employer outlays in the United States (Ehrenberg and Smith 2009, 147). Retirement and health-insurance plans make up, by far, the largest share of fringe benefits, more than two-thirds of the total dollar value.[1] This chapter explains the basic characteristics of retirement and health plans for public-sector workers. It also briefly reviews the history of those plans, outlines their current structure, and discusses the future funding challenges faced by many of them. Because military pensions and social programs are discussed elsewhere in this publication, the focus here will be on benefits for civilian employees.

2 CHARACTERISTICS OF RETIREMENT AND HEALTH PLANS

....

Although today the term *pension* generally refers to cash payments received after the termination of one's working years, typically in the form of an annuity, historically, the term covered a wide range of benefits, including survivor's annuities and disability payments. In the United States, for example, the earliest public-sector pension systems, which were created even before the American Revolution, evolved from disability plans for members of colonial militia (Clark, Craig, and Wilson 2003). However, over time, disability came to be defined broadly, and eventually it included the inability to perform regular duties due to infirmities associated with old age more generally. Thus, what began as pension-disability plans evolved into pension-retirement plans.

Broadly speaking, there are two basic types of retirement plans: defined benefit plans and defined contribution plans.[2] Defined benefit plans promise workers a specified benefit at retirement, typically in the form of a life annuity paid in monthly installments. This annuity is commonly based on years of service (subject to a vesting requirement), annual earnings, and a "generosity factor" or "multiplier." For example, in the United States, the modal public-sector plan calculates a retiree's monthly pension annuity as follows: one-twelfth the number of years of service (subject to an initial five-year vesting period), times the average of the highest consecutive five years of salary, multiplied by 2.0 percent (Clark, Craig, and Sabelhaus 2011, 122–126). Thus, in retirement, a 30-year employee could expect to replace roughly 60 percent of her annual income, referred to as the "income replacement rate," during the final years of employment, which are typically the highest earning years. In contrast, in defined contribution plans, typically both the employer and the worker make periodic contributions to a retirement account. The retirement benefit is then based on the sum of these contributions and the investment returns they accrue prior to the worker's retirement.

A pension plan represents a contract between a public-sector employee and the organization for which he or she works. Each party receives something from the other. The worker obtains the promise of deferred compensation, which in turn receives favorable tax treatment. Under current U.S. tax law, pension wealth is generally not taxed until it is annuitized or otherwise accessed after retirement. Since the income replacement rate is typically less than one, and since personal income tax rates are progressive, workers who plan to save for retirement are financially better off if they do so through an employer-provided pension plan.

At the same time, public-sector employers use retirement plans to manage turnover. Hiring and training workers is costly, and because the value of a defined benefit pension typically becomes larger the longer the worker stays with his or her *current* employer, defined benefit plans provide incentives to reduce turnover relative to defined contribution plans. The discounted present value of the difference between the pension a worker receives if he or she remains with the current employer and the pension he or she receives if he or she quits (or is discharged) reflects the loss in pension wealth associated with changing jobs. The larger this difference, the less likely the worker is to quit (Allen, Clark, and McDermed 1993; Mitchell 1982). On average, public-sector workers have lower turnover rates than their private-sector counterparts, and a study of federal workers in the late-twentieth century concluded that their very low turnover rate was, at least partly, due to the unusually large pension penalties for leaving the civil service before retirement (Ippolito 1987).

Pension coverage is substantially higher in the public sector than it is in the private sector. Roughly 90 percent of public-sector workers are covered by an employer-provided pension plan, whereas only 55 percent of private sector workers are covered by a plan

(Clark et al. 2011, 162–166). Historically, most public-sector pension plans have been defined benefit plans, and this remains the case today. A sample of the largest state pension plans and state-run local pension plans shows that more than 90 percent of the plans are currently defined benefit plans (Wisconsin Legislative Council, 2009). In contrast, only 25 percent of private-sector plans are defined benefit plans (Clark et al. 2011, 166). On average, public-sector workers tend to be more risk-averse, less mobile, and more unionized than their private-sector counterparts, which accounts for the difference in the dominant plan type between the two sectors (Munnell, Haverstick, and Soto 2007). However, in the twenty-first century, a small but increasing number of public-sector employers are moving away from the defined benefit model (Clark et al. 2011, 195–213), a point explored in more detail later.

Health insurance is the second largest component, after pensions, of employer-provided fringe benefits. Currently, on average, public-sector employers pay for 86 percent of their employees' health insurance, and typically employers subsidize coverage for their employees' family members, paying, on average, 80 percent of the cost of that coverage (National Conference of State Legislatures 2011). However, the characteristics of these plans, and the generosity of the employer's subsidy, vary dramatically from employer to employer. A typical plan might offer employees and their families what is referred to as a "fee-for-service" benefit, in which, beyond some initial deductible cost, an employee is required to make a payment (called a "co-pay") to the health-care provider at the time of service and pay an additional percentage of any subsequent charges. Such plans often have a "managed–care" component, which limits the employee's choice of providers to those who are members of a "preferred provider organization" (PPO). In addition, some plans offer a single provider, referred to as a "health maintenance organization" (HMO). It is not uncommon for employers to offer employees a choice of plans—California, for example, offers its employees a choice of nine different plans (Clark and Morrill 2011). Typically, a primary difference between plans is the additional percentage of charges for which employees are responsible; the higher the percentage, the lower will be the employee's share of the monthly premium. Also, the higher the deductible and the more limited the choice of providers, the lower will be the employee's share of the premium.

Roughly 70 percent of public-sector employers also provide health insurance for their retired workers, a percentage nearly three times larger than that found in the private sector (U.S. Department of Labor 2009, 174 and 474). Because public-sector workers are more likely to have pensions than their private-sector counterparts, they tend to retire earlier, at age 58 versus age 61 (Munnell et al. 2011, 15). However, public-sector workers who retire without health benefits before they are eligible for Medicare at age 65 face the possibility of purchasing an individual or family health-insurance policy, the cost of which can be prohibitive. In the absence of employer-provided coverage, many public-sector workers would tend to stay on the job, even after they otherwise qualified for retirement, simply to maintain their health-insurance coverage until they qualify for Medicare (Munnell et al. 2007). Thus, as with pensions, public-sector employers typically offer health-care coverage as part of their human-resource-management policies.

3 HISTORY OF PUBLIC-SECTOR PLANS

Old-age pensions for civil servants date back centuries; however, pension *plans* were created much more recently. In the United States, the federal government did not adopt a universal pension plan for civilian employees until 1920. Before 1920, pensions were offered to some retiring federal civil servants, but Congress created them on a case-by-case basis (Clark et al. 2011, 17). In addition to being inefficient, this system was subject to abuse, and ending it became a key objective of Congressional reformers. The movement to create public-sector pension plans reflected the broader growth of the welfare state. By the early twentieth century, 32 countries around the world, including most European nations, had some type of old-age pension for their nonmilitary public employees. In the United States, prior to the late-nineteenth century, the vast majority of federal employees (in fact the vast majority of all government employees) were patronage employees, who served at the leisure of an elected or appointed official. The key to the creation of a civil-service pension plan was the replacement of patronage workers with a civil service.

The conversion from patronage to a civil service resulted from three related forces. One of these was the progressive movement. Patronage was blamed for the "[s]candals and charges of fraud and inefficiency" in government, and thus the civil service became an objective of the "good government" movement at the local, state, and federal levels. A second force, which focused on federal employment, was a collection of businesses and trade groups, which "since the growing commercialization of the economy in the post-Civil War period depended on the smooth functioning of the postal system for shipments and billing receipts and of the customhouses for the import of intermediate and final goods." The final force was the politicians who administered the patronage appointments. With the dramatic growth in government employment following the Civil War (five percent per annum through 1911), managing the patronage process became cumbersome and time-consuming. As a result, elected officials and public-sector managers agreed that the one-time gains from converting the public-sector labor force to a civil service outweighed whatever benefits they might have hoped to reap from maintaining the patronage system. Interestingly, this process began before public-sector labor unions exerted much influence on wages, benefits, or working conditions (Johnson and Libecap 1994, 19–20 and 77).

In response to these forces at the federal level, in 1883, Congress passed the Pendleton Act, which created the federal civil service. Henceforth, federal workers were protected from the harshest effects of the labor market and the political spoils system, and because many civil servants simply did not want to retire from their federal sinecures, the conversion from patronage to civil service led to an abundance of superannuated federal employees. The inefficiency of these workers tended to defeat one of the purposes of civil service reform. In response to the aging of the federal work force, Congress passed the Federal Employees Retirement Act in 1920, which created a defined benefit pension plan for federal civil servants (Craig 1995).

The spoils system also dominated hiring at the state and local level. Thus, as it did at the federal level, the United States tended to lag behind other countries in the establishment of pensions for state and local workers. Municipal workers in Austria-Hungary, Belgium, France, Germany, the Netherlands, Spain, Sweden, and the United Kingdom were covered by retirement plans by 1910 (Squier 1912). By that date, only a few large American cities had established plans for their employees, although the forces that led to the creation of the federal civil service were also at work at the local and state levels (Johnson and Libecap 1994, 21). Until the first decades of the twentieth century, however, these plans were generally limited to three groups: police officers, firefighters, and teachers. New York City established the first such plan for its police officers in 1857. Like the colonial militia plans, the New York City police pension plan served as a disability plan until a retirement feature was added in 1878 (Mitchell et al. 2001).

Despite the relatively late start, the subsequent growth of municipal plans was rapid. By 1916, there were 159 U.S. cities that had plans for police officers, firefighters, or school teachers, and 21 of those cities included other municipal employees in some type of pension coverage (*Monthly Labor Review* 1916). By 1928, the *Monthly Labor Review* could characterize police and fire plans as "practically universal." At that time, all cities with populations over 400,000 had a pension plan for either police officers or firefighters or both. Several of those cities also had plans for their other municipal employees, and several cities maintained pension plans for city school teachers separately from state-managed teachers' plans.

As for state governments, they lagged **behind** the larger municipalities in providing pensions for their civil servants, though New York, New Jersey, Rhode Island, and Virginia had established plans for their public school teachers before Massachusetts established the first retirement pension plan for civil servants in 1911. As late as 1929, only six states had pension plans for their civil servants, that is, nonteaching employees (Millis and Montgomery 1938). However, after individual municipalities and local school districts began adopting plans for their teachers, the states moved fairly aggressively in the 1910s and 1920s to create or consolidate plans for teachers. By the late 1920s, 21 states had formal retirement plans for their public school teachers, and 31 states had some type of plan by 1940 (Clark et al. 2011, Tables 2.1 and 3.1), and at the time, 40 percent of *all* state and local employees were schoolteachers. All these developments occurred years before Social Security was enacted in 1935.

Employer-provided health insurance is a much more recent phenomenon than employer-provided pensions. In the late-nineteenth century, railroads and other large industrial firms typically kept physicians on staff to care for employees injured on the job, and by the 1920s "physicians were common in the larger companies" across the country (Starr 1982, 201). With the notable exception of the U.S. Army and Navy, this practice was limited to the private sector; however, in 1929 two sets of public-sector workers were part of the first large-scale, employee-group health-insurance plans. In Dallas, the Baylor University Hospital contracted with 1,500 school teachers to offer what would become the first Blue Cross hospitalization plan. The teachers paid $6 a year for up to 21 days of hospital care. Over the next decade, 38 other Blue Cross plans opened across the country. Also in 1929, the Los Angeles public works department hired two physicians to provide medical care for 2,000 employees and their families. The initial premium was $2 per month. The success of these plans, especially the Blue Cross model, induced private insurers to enter the market, and by 1940 roughly 10 million workers were covered by a hospitalization plan (Starr 1982, 295–299).

In the face of price and wage controls during World War II, both pension and health care benefits expanded dramatically. The War Labor Board ruled that increases in fringe benefits were not inflationary and, therefore, not subject to federal wage controls; thus, in the tight war-time labor market, employers tried to reward and retain workers through more generous fringe benefits. The practice continued after the war, as the federal courts deemed fringe benefits a mandatory bargaining issue in union contracts, and the Internal Revenue Service did not consider them income for tax purposes. As a result, by the mid-1950s roughly 60 percent of the labor force was covered by an employer-provided health plan (Starr 1982, 313).

Despite the early start in the public sector, the subsequent growth of employer-provided health plans was heavily concentrated in the unionized private sector, but this progress eventually impacted the public sector. At the local, state, and federal levels, the conversion of government employees from patronage workers to civil servants began before public-sector unions had obtained much power, and the early pension plans were largely a response to the aging of the government work force that resulted from the job protections that civil servants enjoyed. The same was not true of the advent and expansion of health-care plans for public-sector employees. Once these plans started to spread through the private sector, public-sector unions, which had grown in size and power over the course of the twentieth century, demanded similar benefits for their members. For their part, public-sector employers had to compete with the private sector for workers, so, they generally agreed to offer such plans with relatively little labor strife (Johnson and Libecap 1994, 76–92 and 112). As a result of these forces, most of today's public-sector health plans emerged in the 1960s and 1970s (Clark and Morrill 2011).

4 Funding Public-Sector Plans

A pension is a contract between the worker and the employer, with the employer promising to pay a benefit in the future in return for the employee's work today. However, to an extent, workers pay for their benefits through lower wages. One estimate puts the share of pension benefits paid through lower wages of public-sector workers at roughly 40 percent of the total value of the benefit (Craig 1995, 318). The remainder is paid by the employer in the future, and how that future payment is funded is an important economic and political question.

A "pay-as-you-go" pension plan is one with no "fund" set aside to pay future pension liabilities. The employer relies on current revenues to meet current liabilities. The term "funded pension" is typically used to describe a pension plan that has a specific source of revenues dedicated to pay for the plan's liabilities. Typically, at least some of these revenues would be generated from the returns on a pool of assets—a fund. The term "actuarially sound" characterizes a pension plan in which the present value of the assets in the pension fund is equal to or greater than the present value of expected future liabilities. The funding ratio, a key indicator of the soundness of a pension fund, is the ratio of assets to liabilities. Thus a ratio of one or greater would characterize an actuarially sound or "fully funded" plan.[3]

The revenues to create the fund come from the contributions of employees and taxpayers. The fund can also derive income from the returns to the assets it holds. Most public-sector plans require a contribution from employees covered by the plan. A recent sample of state and state-run local plans shows that 93 percent require an employee contribution (Wisconsin Legislative Council 2009, 19). In a sense, all public-sector pension plans are implicitly funded and actuarially sound to the extent that they are backed by the coercive powers of the state. Through its monopoly of taxation, the government can collect (at least in theory) whatever revenues are required to meet its liabilities, and so the public-sector employer's promise of future benefits is based ultimately on the government's taxing power. Of course, in practice, a public-sector employer's ability to extract revenues from taxpayers is constrained by the political process, through which taxpayers can be expected to place limits on the generosity of public-sector workers' compensation.

One way in which both employees and taxpayers typically attempt to reduce their contributions to public-sector plans is by taking on investment risk. Plans do this by investing in a portfolio that includes stocks, corporate securities, and other risky assets. Historically, that strategy has lowered the average cost of funding benefit promises, though it has also created wide swings in the funding ratio as a result of fluctuations in the market value of the assets held by the fund.[4] It follows that a pension plan that is currently fully funded is not necessarily a plan that will be able to pay all promised benefits with certainty. Large declines in asset values for many types of investments do occur on occasion, and they negatively impact a pension-plan's funding status.

The funding of public-sector retirement plans has become a major policy issue and concern, especially for state and local governments. The perception that public-sector jobs pay substantially more than comparable private-sector jobs, combined with the recent financial crisis and resulting economic downturn, have led to calls to reform public-sector benefits in general and retirement plans in particular. Depending on which methodology one chooses, as of 2010, state and local retirement plans were collectively underfunded by between $1 and $5 trillion (Biggs 2010; Novy-Marx and Rauh 2009; Pew Center on the States 2010), and federal pensions may be underfunded by comparable amounts. These estimates are based on complex calculations that involve many variables and a number of crucial assumptions.

Currently, the overall average funding ratio for state and local pension plans is roughly 85 percent, and about two-thirds of plans report being less than 90 percent funded (Clark et al. 2011, 180–194). Debates associated with estimating the "true" ratio primarily revolve around three assumptions: (a) the measurement of *future liabilities*; (b) the "*smoothing*" of changes in asset values when market values fluctuate; and (c) the *interest rate* employed to discount future liabilities.

Generally speaking, there are two approaches to estimating the present value of *future pension liabilities*, that is, the promises public-sector employers have made to their employees. One, referred to as the "accrued benefit obligation" or ABO, which can be described as a narrow measure, includes only benefits accrued to date for current and past employees. The other approach, which yields a broader measure, is referred to as the "projected benefit obligation" or PBO; it includes expected future benefit accruals associated with future employees. Current actuarial practice in public-sector pension accounting uses the PBO measure, which proponents of the ABO measure argue over-states liabilities. Novy-Marx and Rauh (2009) estimate that aggregate PBO liabilities in a sample of public-sector pension plans were $2.98 trillion, as of the end of 2008, and shift-ing from PBO to ABO lowers estimated liabilities by $0.11 trillion, or about 4 percent.

Although market prices are readily available for most regularly traded financial assets, standard actuarial practice allows state and local pension plans to "*smooth*" investment gains and losses over a period of time (usually five years). This smoothing approach, which lengthens the period over which state and local governments can delay making the contributions needed to restore full funding, contrasts with using current prices to "mark (assets) to market." Critics of smoothing argue that declines in asset values, such as pension funds experienced during the financial crisis of 2008–2009, and which will not be fully accounted for in funding ratios until 2014, create situations in which stated asset values are much higher than the "true" value of the assets in the plans' port-folios. Of course, smoothing works in both directions; large gains in asset values do not immediately contribute to improved funding status, which would lower required con-tributions by plan sponsors. The practice of smoothing has an additional benefit during economic downturns. Specifically, when state and local governments are struggling to meet payrolls and avoid layoffs as a result of a decrease in tax revenues, a sharp increase in required pension contributions would worsen fiscal pressures.

The most fundamental and vociferously debated assumption that affects funding ratio calculations is the *interest rate* at which future liabilities are discounted. Standard actuarial practice allows pension plans to discount future liabilities by the expected return on their investment portfolios, which, for public-sector plans, has tended to aver-age around 8 percent annually. Critics of this approach argue that public-sector benefit payments should be discounted at a lower interest rate—one that would be based, for example, on the historical returns on government bonds, and, thus, one that is roughly half the expected rate of return on the typical pension portfolio. The choice between the two discount rates has a large impact on funding ratios. Novy-Marx and Rauh (2009, 199) estimate that aggregate liabilities of state-managed plans increase by nearly 75 per-cent, rising from $2.98 trillion to $5.17 trillion, when a U.S. Treasury interest rate is sub-stituted for the long-run market rate of return. This adjustment would reduce the overall mean funding ratio from 85 percent to less than 50 percent and would represent a dra-matic increase in the collective unfunded liability of public-sector pension plans.

Today, there are 2,670 "retirement systems that are sponsored by a government entity" in the United States (Munnell, Haverstick, Soto, et al. 2008, 1), the vast majority of which are plans for local public employees. By any reasonable standard, many of these plans are grossly underfunded. Recent estimates put the collective value of the unfunded liabilities of these local plans at $600 billion (Novy-Marx and Rauh 2010). As recently as 2000, state-run pension plans (including those for local public-sector employees) were running a $56 billion pension surplus, and more than half the states were managing plans that were fully funded. However, by 2006, only six states maintained fully funded plans, and by 2008 only four did (Pew Center 2010, 16).[5]

Although the debates concerning the details of pension funding tend to be conducted among academics and actuaries, it is important to understand that there exists a key political dimension to the outcome of these clashes. Currently, Republican politicians are more likely than their Democratic opponents to emphasize the expense to taxpayers of public-sector pensions, and Republicans tend to advocate cuts in pension benefits or increases in worker contributions. Conversely, Democratic politicians, who tend to be more supportive of the current generosity of public-sector plans, are more likely to advocate an increase in taxpayer contributions as the source of funding when plans clearly need to be better funded (Munnell, Golub-Sass, et al. 2008).

Recent examples of the differences between political parties can be found in Wisconsin and Illinois. The Wisconsin state employees' pension fund is well funded (at 100 percent, one of the highest ratios in the country); however, a Republican legislature and governor recently forced state workers to dramatically increase their contributions to the state plan. In contrast, in Illinois, which has among the lowest public-sector funding ratios in the country at 41 percent (the average for its three main state-employees' plans), a Democratic-controlled legislature dramatically increased state income taxes to cover, among other things, the state's unfunded pension liabilities (Munnell et al. 2012, 10–13).

The local plans, many of which are quite small, often suffer from two economic conditions. One is that the taxpayers' share of contributions is usually derived from a relatively small and undiversified tax base. Thus, during economic downturns, the plans are forced to confront political constraints on the revenues taxpayers are willing to contribute (Munnell, Aubry, and Havertick 2008). The second condition is that many plans were created during a period in which local urban growth was quite rapid. In a sense, there never was a golden age of public-sector pension funding. The funds were often constructed, and future promises made to workers, based on the assumption of continuing growth in the municipal labor force.[6] This was especially true in the Northeast and Midwest. As long as municipal employment was growing, the pension fund contributions of younger workers could be counted on to subsidize the retirement of (a smaller number of) older workers. Once that growth slowed and then stopped, however, the funds came under financial stress. The best way to see this is in the "dependency ratio," that is, the ratio of pension-plan beneficiaries to workers. As this ratio increases, it puts pressure on the actuarial soundness of the plan. If the plan is fully funded and the ratio increases, then—holding benefits constant—there are three possibilities: contributions (from taxpayers or current employees) must increase, the returns on pension assets must increase, or benefits must decrease. In the United States, a sample of state and local plans shows that, between 1990 and 2008, the dependency ratio increased by nearly 50 percent, from 0.33 to 0.49 (Cheng 2011, Table 7), which, collectively, strained the actuarial soundness of the plans.

In contrast to pension plans, health-care provisions for public-sector workers tend to be treated, for both legal and accounting purposes, as current compensation rather than a contract for future benefits, and thus they are funded on a pay-as-you-go basis. In practice, this means current health care liabilities are paid from current tax revenues, and realized or expected shortfalls in funding are covered by either additional appropriations or a reduction in employee benefits, which in practice means employees pay a larger share of their coverage. In recent decades, shortfalls have been disproportionately covered by tax revenues. Expenditures per capita, as measured by health-insurance premiums, have risen at an average annual compounded rate of 5.9 percent since 1960, whereas the share of coverage paid by employees has actually declined over time (U.S. Department of Labor, 1992, 2; 2011a, 10; and Gruber and Levy 2009, 28). However, these trends are unlikely to continue. Indeed, regardless of which political party is in power, state and local governments have tended to cut health-care benefits in recent years, increasing deductibles and co-pays and reducing access to fee-for service plans (EBRI 2009).

The practice of funding current employee health-care liabilities from current appropriations obscures the costs of future liabilities. Recently adopted accounting standards require public-sector employers to calculate and report the present value of the future liabilities of the health-care plans for their current employees and their retirees. As a result, several states are currently considering establishing funds to meet the future health-care liabilities of their current employees (Community Care of North Carolina 2012). However, the funding issues they face with respect to current employees are minor compared to those incurred on behalf of retirees. Partly, this is simply the difference between the average cost of care for employees, who tend to be relatively younger, and retirees. The current funding shortfall of public-sector retiree health benefits could exceed $1 trillion; however, as of 2010, only 10 states explicitly funded their retiree health benefits, and the mean funding ratio of those plans is only 26 percent (Clark and Morrill 2010, 2–3 and 86–87).

5 CURRENT FEDERAL CIVIL SERVICE PLANS

The federal Civil Service Retirement System (CSRS), created in 1920, remains one of the two main civil service pension plans in the United States.[7] Currently, the benefit formula is a step function in which the generosity multiplier is: 1.50 percent of pay for the first five years of service; 1.75 for the next five years; and 2.00 percent for years of service beyond ten. Thus, a federal employee with 25 years of service would have a multiplier of

1.85 percent and an income replacement rate of 46.25 percent. Similar to other defined benefit plans, the annual annuity is the product of the multiplier, years of service, and highest three years average salary. Federal employees contribute 7.0 percent of their salaries to the plan, and they are not part of the Social Security system.

The other federal civil service plan, the Federal Employees Retirement System (FERS) established in 1983, is a hybrid plan, with a traditional defined-benefit component, a defined-contribution component, and a Social Security component. The defined-benefit component of the plan pays an annual annuity upon retirement equal to one percent of the average of the highest three years of salary times the number of years of service.[8] Employees contribute 0.8 percent of their salary to the defined benefit plan. The defined contribution component of the plan allows employees to contribute up to the Internal Revenue Service's maximum contribution rate, and the federal government will match these contributions up to 5 percent of salary as follows: 1 percent regardless of the employee's contribution; 3 percent to match dollar-for-dollar the employee's contribution; and 0.5 of 1 percent for the employee's next 2 percent.

Currently, there are 2.7 million nonuniformed federal employees. Roughly 85 percent are in FERS (U.S. Department of Labor, 2011b), and this figure is growing, because no employees have been added to CSRS since the early 1980s. FERS is fully funded, but CSRS is not. Recent estimates of the CSRS underfunding put the figure in the range of $700 billion (Losey 2011, 1). Under the current funding regimes, in the long run, the underfunding issue will diminish as the workers (and their beneficiaries) hired before 1984 die out. In the intermediate term, however, underfunding will remain an issue. After a worker retires, neither the worker nor the federal agency that employed the worker continues to make a contribution to the fund. With no new revenues entering the fund, its actuarial condition will only worsen in the absence of an increase in employee or federal taxpayer contributions or a cut in benefits.

The health care benefits for federal employees differ between military personnel and their families and nonuniformed civil servants and their families.[9] Uniformed military personnel are covered by the Defense Department's Military Health System, which is a comprehensive medical care system provided directly by the department. Retirees and dependents are covered by a separate system, though it too is administered by the Military Health System. The plan offers several options, which vary, as many public-sector plans do, from a fee-for-service plan to an HMO plan (U.S. DoD, 2006).

In addition to the military plans, all permanent federal employees and temporary employees whose appointments extend beyond one year are covered under the Federal Employees Health Benefits plan (FEHB). Broadly speaking, the FEHB includes the option of choosing between a fee-for-service plan, with a PPO component, and an HMO plan. On average, the federal government pays for 75 percent of the total costs of these plans, which is substantially less than the share paid by state and local governments for their workers. Coverage is extended to family members and continues in retirement. It is difficult to assess the unfunded liabilities of these federal plans because of the manner in which the federal government accounts for them, which is less straightforward than pension accounting.[10]

In general, with respect to support for benefits for federal workers, the political parties in Congress align similarly to their state and local counterparts. During the period in which Democrats controlled Congress (1955–1981), the long-run trend in the value of benefits was positive, but in the past three decades, during which Republicans controlled one or both houses for substantial periods of time, the expansion of benefits slowed or their value was eroded, and this process continues. Recently, the Republican-controlled U.S. House proposed to increase the annual contributions federal workers make to their pension plans by 5.0 percentage points (phased in over five years). In addition, to maintain the current federal subsidies to student loans, which are supported by Democrats, the House proposed to further increase federal employee pension contributions by 1.2 percentage points.[11]

6 CURRENT STATE AND LOCAL PLANS

State and local workers were initially excluded from participating in the Social Security system, because, when the act was passed, there were constitutional concerns about the federal government forcing the states, as employers, to pay their share of the payroll tax.[12] However, in 1950 Congress passed legislation that permitted the states to enroll in the Social Security system those public-sector employees not otherwise covered by a retirement plan, and, in 1954, state and local governments could add to the system employees who were covered by a pension plan. Prior to 1983, these governments could withdraw from the system if they chose to do so; however, the comprehensive Social Security reform legislation of that year subsequently prohibited withdrawal once a state or local government entered its employees in the system. In 1991, Congress mandated coverage for all state and local employees who were not otherwise covered by an employer-provided pension plan.

The vast majority of the more than 2,500 public-sector plans in the United States are defined-benefit plans. As a result of the underfunding of many of these plans, several states, including those that oversee local plans, have reconsidered the generosity of their plans. Four states no longer offer defined-benefit plans to new employees; six states offer their workers a choice between a defined-benefit and defined-contribution plan; and six states have developed combination plans, that is, plans that have a defined benefit and a defined contribution component. In addition, 17 states have increased the number of years used to calculate the employee's final average salary in the pension benefit formula; two states have decreased the generosity factor in the benefit formula; 24 states have increased the retirement age or otherwise changed the rules for normal retirement; 15 states have increased the number of years required for vesting; and over the past two years, 26 states have increased required employee contributions (Clark and Craig 2011).

Collectively, these changes will reduce the unfunded liabilities of state and local public pension plans, but they will also make public-sector employment relatively less appealing to workers. The average value of pension wealth accumulated by public-sector workers exceeds that of the average private-sector worker (Munnell et al. 2011). These changes will move the value of public-sector pension plans closer to those offered by the private sector. The factors that might explain why some state and local governments have moved toward substantially revising or eliminating their defined-benefit plans include the current actuarial status of the plan (less sound plans might be more likely to be revised); the employees' contributions to the plan (the more employees contribute, the less likely the plan is to be revised); the role of unions among the workers covered by the plan (the weaker the union influence, the more likely the plan is to be revised); and the impact of political parties (Republican majorities in legislative bodies are more likely to be associated with revisions to the plan). Recent scholarly work suggests that, of these factors, Republican control has the largest impact on the probability that a substantial revision will be made to the plan (Munnell, Golub-Sass, et al. 2008). To the extent that the Tea Party's influence within the Republican Party continues to rise, one would expect the shift from defined-benefit to defined-contribution plans, along with the other changes described earlier, to continue in the public sector.

It is difficult to summarize the current status of health plans for state and local employees. A recent summary of such plans reports that, on average, current employees have more than five options from which to choose, and these options vary from state to state. (The variation among municipalities and counties is too great to concisely summarize.) Most states offer various types of fee-for-service plans, usually with a PPO component, or an HMO plan, or a choice between the two, and every state offers coverage of some type for its retired workers (Clark and Morrill 2010, 84). Although the Patient Protection and Affordable Care Act has passed legal muster, it is difficult to predict the impact the act's myriad regulatory components will have on the character and generosity of employer-provided health insurance.

7 CONCLUSION

Pensions and health care make up the largest component of fringe benefits paid to workers by public-sector employers in the United States. Arguably, the most striking feature of public-sector pension plans is the divergence between the value of the promises governments have made to their workers and the funds that have been set aside to meet those promises. State and local pensions funded by state governments are collectively underfunded by between $1 and $5 trillion; local pensions not funded by state governments are collectively underfunded by roughly $600 billion; and federal civil service pensions are underfunded by roughly $700 billion. (In addition, U.S. military pensions, which are discussed elsewhere in this publication, are underfunded by roughly $1 trillion.) Even if one accepts the most conservative of these estimates, it follows that, in the future, either workers will be forced to contribute more to their pension funds, taxpayers will be asked to contribute more, or benefits will be cut. If the recent experiences of the states are indicative of the direction of the system as a whole, then the difference between public-sector pension-fund assets and liabilities will be narrowed by increases in worker contributions and cuts in benefits. In the long-run, the private-sector trend toward substituting defined contribution plans for defined benefit plans, a process that has already begun in the public sector, is likely to accelerate.

In contrast to pension liabilities, which (with some limitations) have historically been recognized as legally binding contracts, employer-provided health-care benefits are viewed as current compensation. As a result, public-sector employers have not typically funded the health-care liabilities of their employees; rather, they have organized their health plans on a pay-as-you-go basis. In practice, lawmakers have responded to realized or projected shortfalls in funding by simply increasing taxpayer contributions to the plans and cutting benefits, but in the future, reducing the generosity of the plans is likely to be the more frequently employed option (Clark and Morrill 2011, 1). For accounting and funding purposes, health benefits for retirees have been treated differently than those for current employees. All states currently provide some type of health plan for their public-sector retirees. As of 2010, ten states explicitly funded their retiree health benefits. Still, the current funding shortfall of public-sector retiree health benefits probably exceeds $1 trillion.

NOTES

1. The other major component is "paid vacations, holidays, and sick leave."
2. In addition, there are so-called "hybrid" plans that possess characteristics of both defined benefit and defined contribution plans.
3. Some scholars argue that 100 percent funding is suboptimal. See, for example, D'Arcy, Dulebohn, and Oh (1999).
4. The only public-sector retirement plans of any size that do not explicitly take on some market risk are Social Security and the plan for federal civil servants, in which returns are tied to nonmarketable, special-issue U.S. Treasury bonds.
5. Although local plans display tremendous variance in their funding status, on average, they are comparable to the state-managed plans (Munnell, Haverstick, Aubry, et al., 2008).
6. Clark et al. note that the sources of public contributions to early municipal pension funds included permits for dancing schools and boxing contests, as well as fees for dog licenses, arguably not the revenue sources most likely to lead to actuarial soundness (2003, 175).
7. The current federal plans are described in Hustead and Hustead (2001).
8. For employees who have reached age 62, with 20 or more years of service, the generosity factor is 1.1 percent.
9. For an overview of U.S. military plans, see U.S. DoD (2006). The civil service health-care plans are summarized in U.S. Office of Personnel Management (2001).
10. See U.S. Department of Commerce (2012) for an example of the complexity of the issues involved.
11. For a summary, see [http://www.washingtonpost.com/blogs/federal-eye/post/gop-raise-retirement-costs-to-pay-for-student-loans/2012/06/01/gJQAw3w86U_blog.html]. Accessed June 20, 2012.
12. For a concise summary of the Social Security system and its relationship to public-sector pension plans, see Clark et al. (2011, 50–65 and 73–81).

REFERENCES

*Indicates recommended reading.

Allen, Steven G., Robert L. Clark, and Elizabeth Ann McDermed, 1993. "Pension Bonding and Lifetime Jobs." *Journal of Human Resources* 28: 463–481.

Biggs, Andrew. 2010. "An Options Pricing Method for Calculating the Market Price of Public Sector Pension Liabilities." AEI Working Paper, second version.

Cheng, Yijing. 2011. "Underfunding of State and Local Pension Plans in the United States: The Role of the Dependency Ratio." Unpublished manuscript.

Clark, Robert L., and Lee A. Craig. 2011. "State Pension Plans Step Up Efforts to Adapt to 21st Century Financial Pressures." *Pension and Benefits Daily*, August, 1–5. Arlington, VA: Bureau of National Affairs.

*Clark, Robert L., Lee A. Craig, and Jack W. Wilson. 2003. *A History of Public Sector Pensions in the United States*. Philadelphia: University of Pennsylvania Press.

*Clark, Robert L., Lee A. Craig, and John Sabelhaus. 2011. *State and Local Retirement Plans in the United States*. Cheltenham, UK: Edward Elgar.

*Clark, Robert L., and Melinda Morrill. 2010. *Retiree Health Plans in the Public Sector: Is There a Funding Crisis?* Cheltenham, UK: Edward Elgar.

Clark, Robert L. and Melinda Morrill. 2011. "Containing Health Insurance Costs of Active and Retired Public Sector Employees." Poole College of Management Working Paper, North Carolina State University, Raleigh.

Community Care of North Carolina. 2012. *Proceedings of State Symposium: State Health Plans During Times of Fiscal Austerity*, March, Raleigh, NC.

Craig, Lee A. 1995. "The Political Economy of Public-Private Compensation Differentials: The Case of Federal Pensions." *Journal of Economic History* 55: 304–320.

D'Arcy, Stephen P., James H. Dulebohn, and Pyungsuk Oh. 1999. "Optimal Funding of State Employee Pension Systems." *Journal of Risk and Insurance* 66: 345–380.

Employee Benefits Research Institute. 2009. *Fundamentals of Employee Benefit Programs*. 6th ed. http://www.ebri.org/publications/books/?fa=fundamentals.

Ehrenberg, R. G., and R. S. Smith. 2009. *Modern Labor Economics: Theory and Public Policy*. 10th ed. Boston: Pearson.

Gruber, Jonathan, and Helen Levy. 2009. "The Evolution of Medical Spending Risk." *Journal of Economic Perspectives* 23: 25–48.

Hustead, Edwin C., and Toni Hustead. 2001. "Federal Civilian and Military Retirement Systems." In Olivia S. Mitchell and Edwin C. Hustead, eds., *Pensions in the Public Sector*, 66–104. Philadelphia: University of Pennsylvania Press.

Ippolito, Richard. 1987. "Why Federal Workers Don't Quit." *Journal of Human Resources* 22: 281–299.

Johnson, Ronald, and Gary Libecap. 1994. *The Federal Civil Service System and the Problem of Bureaucracy*. Chicago: University of Chicago Press.

Losey, Stephen. 2011. "Fed Pensions Underfunded by $673 Billion." *Federal Times*. http://www.federaltimes.com/article/20111016/BENEFITS02/110160303/1001.

Millis, Harry A., and Royal E. Montgomery. 1938. *Labor's Risk and Social Insurance*. New York: McGraw-Hill.

Mitchell, Olivia S. 1982. "Fringe Benefits and Labor Mobility." *Journal of Human Resources* 17: 286–298.

*Mitchell, Olivia S., David McCarthy, Stanley C. Wisniewski, and Paul Zorn. 2001. "Developments in State and Local Pension Plans." In Olivia S. Mitchell and Edwin C. Hustead, eds., *Pensions in the Public Sector*. Philadelphia: University of Pennsylvania Press. *Monthly Labor Review*, various issues.

Munnell Alicia, Jean-Pierre Aubry, and Kelly Haverstick. 2008. "*Why Don't Some States and Localities Pay Their Required Pension Contributions?*" Issue Brief No. 7, May. Center for Retirement Research, Boston College, Boston. (Hereafter CRR.)

*Munnell Alicia, Juan-Pierre Aubry, Josh Hurwitz, Madeline Medenica, and Laura Quinby. 2012. "*The Funding of State and Local Pensions: 2011–2015.*" Issue Brief No. 24. May. CRR.

*Munnell Alicia, Juan-Pierre Aubry, Josh Hurwitz, and Laura Quinby. 2011. "*Comparing Wealth in Retirement: State-Local versus Private Sector Workers.*" Issue Brief No. 21, October CRR.

Munnell Alicia, Alex Golub-Sass, Kelly Haverstick, Mauricio Soto, and Gregory Wiles. 2008. "*Why Have Some States Introduced Defined Contribution Plans?*" Issue Brief No. 3, January CRR.

Munnell Alicia, Kelly Haverstick, Jean-Pierre Aubry, and Alex Golub-Sass. 2008. "*The Funding Status of Locally Administered Penison Plans?*" Issue Brief No. 8, October CRR.

*Munnell Alicia, Kelly Haverstick and Mauricio Soto. 2007. "*Why Have Defined Benefit Plans Survived in the Public Sector?*" Issue Brief No. 2, December CRR.

Munnell Alicia, Kelly Haverstick, Mauricio Soto, and Jean-Pierre Aubry. 2008. "*What Do We Know about the Universe of State and Local Plans?*" Issue Brief No. 4, March. CRR.

National Conference of State Legislatures. 2011. *2011 State Employee Health Benefits: Monthly Premium Costs (Family and Individual Coverage)*.

*Novy-Marx, Robert, and Joshua D. Rauh. 2009. "The Liabilities and Risks of State-Sponsored Pension Plans." *Journal of Economic Perspectives* 23: 191–210.

Novy-Marx, Robert, and Joshua D. Rauh. 2010. "The Crisis in Local Government Pensions in the United States." Unpublished manuscript.

Pew Center on the States. 2010. *The Trillion Dollar Gap*. Washington, DC: Pew Charitable Trusts.

Squier, Lee Welling. 1912. *Old Age Dependency in the United States*. New York: Macmillan.

Starr, Paul. 1982. *The Social Transformation of American Medicine: The Rise of a Sovereign Profession and the Making of a Vast Industry*. New York: Basic Books.

U.S. Department of Commerce, Bureau of Economic Analysis. 2012. "What Is Included in Federal Government Employee Compensation?" http://www.bea.gov/faq/index.cfm?faq_id=553&searchQuery=&start=0&cat_id=0.

U.S. Department of Defense. 2006. "Military Health System Overview Statement." http://armed-services.senate.gov/statemnt/2006/April/Chu-Winkenwerder%2004-04-06.pdf.

U.S. Department of Labor, Bureau of Labor Statistics. 1992. "Expenditures for Health Care Plans by Employers and Employees." http://www.bls.gov/news.release/hce.toc.htm.

U.S. Department of Labor, Bureau of Labor Statistics. 2009. "Employee Benefits in the United States." http://www.bls.gov/ncs/ebs/benefits/2009/ebbl0044.pdf.

U.S. Department of Labor, Bureau of Labor Statistics. 2011a. "Employee Benefits in the United States." http://www.bls.gov/news.release/pdf/ebs2.pdf.

U.S. Department of Labor, Bureau of Labor Statistics. 2011b. *Federal Government Civilian Employment*. http://www.bls.gov/oco/cg/cgs041.htm.

U.S. Office of Personnel Management. 2001. *Federal Employees Health Benefits*. Washington, DC: GPO.

Wisconsin Legislative Council. 2009. *Comparative Study of Major Public Employee Retirement Systems, 2008*. Madison: Wisconsin Legislative Council.

CHAPTER 31

··

SOCIAL PROGRAMS FOR SOLDIERS AND VETERANS

··

MEREDITH KLEYKAMP AND CROSBY HIPES

1 INTRODUCTION

··

BEING poor and working for pay are the two classic ways to become eligible for social benefits. Nevertheless, some scholars (Gifford 2006a; Skocpol 1992) argue that governments also reward military service and child-rearing with sizable benefits. Military benefits have sometimes been characterized as a "camouflaged" welfare state because they are often ignored in discussions of the U.S. welfare state, both as a single case and in comparison with other industrialized nations (e.g., Gifford 2006a; Gifford 2006b). Others contend that military benefits are part of the compensation package for those who serve, and differ in important ways from other social welfare programs: military and veterans' benefits are received in exchange for services rendered, not as entitlements. Regardless of whether they are characterized as compensation or entitlements, the scope of the military welfare state is more expansive than many assume, and far more generous than most other private or public-sector employment benefits packages or public sector entitlements (Congressional Budget Office 2011).

In 2010, there were an estimated 22.7 million veterans and 1.4 million active duty military personnel in the United States (U.S. Department of Veterans Affairs 2010b; U.S. Department of Defense 2010). This group comprises nearly 8 percent of the total U.S. population, and the group's relatively high voter turnout relative to other social categories—especially among pre-Vietnam veterans—makes them a significant political interest group (Teigen 2006). Many, but not all, veterans receive some benefits or services from the Department of Veterans Affairs (VA). In 2009, total VA expenditures stood at approximately $100 billion, with nearly $45 billion covering pensions and direct compensation payments, and another $40 billion covering medical care expenses (U.S. Department of Veterans Affairs 2010a). Although only a fraction of spending on Social Security or Medicare, these are nontrivial expenditures. In the Department of Defense, active duty health-care and retiree pensions and health care top $100 billion, nearly 15 percent of the overall defense budget. Because of the generous pension military retirees receive, the Pentagon spends $1.36 on pensions for every $1 spent on active duty pay, but fewer than 20 percent of those who ever serve stay in the military long enough to earn this pension (Dao and Walsh 2011). Although pensions, direct compensation payments, and medical care account for the majority of the benefits provided to service members and veterans, there are additional programs and benefits. Some programs are well known, such as the G.I. Bill or the VA mortgage-guaranty program, whereas other programs may be less familiar outside military populations.

In this essay, we briefly review the historical contours of military and veterans' benefits. We discuss the major programs for both current and former military members through the Department of Defense (DoD) and Department of Veterans Affairs (VA), and the program requirements. We highlight the near-universality of this integrated web of institutional supports for military populations, which stands in stark contrast to the fragmented, conditional nature of the civilian welfare state. We discuss in detail two key features of the military benefit system: the camouflaged nature of these generous benefits as part of the American welfare state, and inequality in access to these benefit programs. We conclude by discussing future challenges to the military welfare system, including the ability to maintain generous health-care coverage and pensions for military retirees and the challenge of caring for a generation of wartime veterans, more of whom have survived catastrophic injuries requiring a lifetime of care than in previous generations.

2 THE EVOLUTION OF A MILITARY WELFARE STATE

Social programs for soldiers and veterans have long been a substantial component of the American welfare state, often preceding and dwarfing programs for civilians. The provision of military welfare programs is justified by the perceived deservingness of soldiers and veterans, who have demonstrated tremendous citizenship through their sacrifices (Segal 1989). Furthermore, since the transition to an all-volunteer force (AVF), military welfare programs have served as tools for recruitment and retention, similar to benefits offered to civilian government employees. This section provides a brief overview of the historical development of military welfare programs, highlighting the importance of military programs in the evolution of the broader U.S. welfare state. It is organized both sequentially and by theme, because different programs have ushered in new eras in the system of military compensation.

2.1 Veterans' Pensions

Debates over policies for Revolutionary War veterans represent the first government consideration of entitlements for a specific population, even as there was bipartisan support for *some level* of benefits (Jensen 2005). Arguments centered on the principle of targeting one group for benefits at the exclusion of other citizens in need. Eventually Congress agreed to provide benefits only to those veterans who had sacrificed their lives for the nation. In 1794, the federal government gave cash payments to widows and orphans of deceased Revolutionary War officers, and in 1802 extended payments to noncommissioned officers' families as well (Albano 1994). The Pension Act of 1818 was a larger-scale bill, granting a lifetime pension to Revolutionary War veterans who were unable to maintain a living (Jensen 2005). In 1832, Congress extended pensions to all veterans of the war, regardless of need. The cost of these pensions was ultimately $75 million, greater than the total cost of fighting the war (Resch 2000). Entitlements for the nation's earliest veterans set a precedent of providing for military personnel no matter the cost, and eventually, no matter the need, even when equivalent programs for civilians were nonexistent.

Costly provisions for military personnel continued after the Civil War, and their distribution began to reflect increasing politicization of veterans' interests. Pensions were typically reserved for northern, Union veterans despite funding for pensions coming from nationwide tariffs that disproportionately affected Southern merchants (Quadagno 1988; Skocpol 1992). Pension policy making often pitted political parties and competing business interests against each other. The 1879 Arrears Act—which passed Congress with almost unanimous political support—awarded past pensions to Civil War veterans who demonstrated a newly discovered disability related to wartime service, leaving government officials the power to determine worthiness. As a result, the distribution of pension benefits became intertwined with political support (Skocpol 1992). Civil War pensions swelled to 42 percent of government expenditures by 1893, with the value of these pensions constituting a more significant form of government welfare than pensions available in Germany or Britain at the time (Skocpol 1992).

Pensions for World War I veterans were also relatively generous, in effect providing insurance for veterans even if they did not have service-related disabilities. By 1933, there were 412,000 veterans receiving pensions for disabilities unrelated to service, more than the amount receiving pensions for service-connected disabilities (Campbell 2004). By the start of World War II, the provision of old-age benefits to civilian society through Social Security made veterans' pensions superfluous, and they were significantly restricted (Campbell 2004). However, the historic provision of pensions had rendered large-scale military benefits a permanent feature of the expanding U.S. welfare state.

Due in part to their displays of citizenship, and in part to their importance as a voting bloc, programs for soldiers and veterans have evolved to constitute a substantial portion of the U.S. welfare state (Segal 1989; Skocpol 1992). Reflective of the status of military personnel, some of the most prominent and substantial benefit packages for soldiers and veterans have passed Congress with bipartisan support, namely the Arrears Act expanding post-Civil War pensions (Skocpol 1992) and the original post-WWII G.I. Bill (Canaday 2003; Military.com 2006). For both the Revolutionary War and post-WWII G.I. Bill benefits, debate hinged on the *extent* of benefits rather than a need for them (Jensen 2005; Military.com 2006; Conrad 2005).

2.2 Health Care

The military also pioneered programs in health care. The National Home for Disabled Volunteer Soldiers was one of the first facilities designed to provide care to veterans (Skocpol 1992; Kelly 1997). Originally intended for veterans with disabilities directly linked to service, by 1884 the Home transitioned to provide a safety net for all elderly veterans (Kelly 1997). The World War Veterans Act of 1924 further extended health benefits originally designed as workmen's compensation to veterans with non-service-connected health issues (Campbell 2004; Stevens 1991). This program represents one of the earliest forms of subsidized health care covering a substantial portion of the population. In the 36 years before Medicare and Medicaid, 40–60 percent of federal spending on health care was for veterans with disabilities not related to military service (Campbell 2004).

In 1956, the Dependents Medical Care Act expanded subsidized health care for soldiers and veterans, allowing the Department of Defense to contract with civilian health-care providers, since the military alone was unable to meet the needs of veterans and their families (Van Dyke and Elliott 1969). The Civilian Health and Medical Program of the Uniformed Services (CHAMPUS), created in 1966, consolidated health-care policy for soldiers, veterans, and their dependents. CHAMPUS represented an expansion of health care for military personnel, but also the extension of military welfare to include military families.

The United States is the rare industrialized nation without universal health insurance (see the World Health Organization 2000 for a comparison of health-care systems). However, U.S. military personnel and their families have long received free or low-cost health care through both military and civilian medical providers. Those receiving health care in Department of Defense (DoD) or VA facilities are part of a national medical system served by salaried public doctors, nurses, aides, and administrators (Stevens 1991). This care has been evaluated as some of the highest quality care in the U.S. system, public or private (Asch et al. 2004). In nations with national health insurance, military personnel, their families, and veterans may be eligible for some special treatment such as faster access to health care (in the UK), or additional benefits (in Canada), but the sharp divisions between access to quality care between military and civilian populations is much less stark.

2.3 Helping Soldiers Transition to the Civilian Labor Force

Military welfare provisions were initially linked to injury or old age, but evolved to include programs for younger soldiers transitioning into civilian society. One such program is veterans' historic privilege in applying for civil-service jobs. Although this hiring prefer-ence began after the Civil War, it expanded greatly following WWI (Campbell 2004). In 1919, veterans scoring a 65 on the civil-service exam were given a greater hiring prefer-ence than civilians with a perfect score. Not surprisingly, the percentage of veterans in the civil service increased dramatically, and by 1953 half of all federal employees were vet-erans (Campbell 2004). Currently, veteran civil- service applicants are entitled to either 5 or 10 additional points added to a passing examination based on their level of disability, among other factors (U.S. Office of Personnel Management, n.d.).

The G.I. Bill of 1944 also helped ease veterans' transition back to civilian society, pro-viding education and training for WWII veterans re-entering the labor force. There was much political support for WWII veteran benefits, partially as a reaction to the per-ceived mistreatment of WWI veterans, who had marched on Washington to demand bonuses (Canaday 2003). After some debate over the extent of benefits, Congress even-tually passed the G.I. Bill unanimously (Conrad 2005; Military.com 2006). The G.I. Bill impacted a generation of veterans, and by 1947 veterans made up 49 percent of students enrolled in college, with many also using the G.I. Bill for job training (Mettler 2005). Following the Korean War, the Veterans' Readjustment Assistance Act provided ben-efits comparable to those granted under the 1944 G.I. Bill, and 42 percent of Korean War veterans used these benefits to attend college (Levy 2004). The noncontributory provision of benefits was replaced by a contributory system in 1977, under the Veterans Educational Assistance Program, and again with the Montgomery G.I. Bill in 1985 (Angrist 1993). Rather than reflecting a reduction in educational benefits for military personnel, these policies were a response to the steep increase in U.S. education costs. Even rising educational costs have not tempered the expansion of veterans' educational benefits in recent years.

2.4 Expanding Benefits to Families

Over time, the goal of military social welfare provisions has shifted from providing entitlements to a deserving group of people to furthering recruitment and retention. Included in this shift is an increasing focus on providing for military families. Family policies for military personnel were long ignored by policymakers, because many sol-diers historically were unmarried and childless. Historically, housing policies only entitled soldiers to live in military barracks, although officers could be granted larger housing (Segal 1989). Health care was also provided directly through the military on a space-available basis (Van Dyke and Elliott 1969).

The extension of military welfare benefits to dependents has increased greatly since the end of WWII, and more recently with the beginning of the AVF. Since WWII, more married personnel have joined the military, and the military has provided them with benefits such as home loans, health care, and family housing (Howard 1997; Van Dyke and Elliott 1969; Twiss and Martin 1999). Approximately 40 percent of WWII veterans received a VA-insured home loan through which they were able to borrow at below-market rates, benefiting many American families (Howard 1997).

3 MILITARY AND VETERAN BENEFIT
PROGRAMS TODAY

Military service members and veterans have access to a wide variety of programs ranging from free health care to recreation facilities. Indeed, the military base might be considered the contemporary "company town" because of the extensive supports available.
The most distinguishing feature of military welfare programs is their near universality
in the military population, compared with the fragmented and nonuniversalistic programs for the civilian population. Whereas European nations and Canada have universal, citizenship-based programs, civilian benefits in the United States are a mix of
social insurance and means-tested programs. But military benefit programs, in mixing
elements of social insurance and assistance for all, more closely resemble the welfare
regimes of Western Europe (cf. Esping-Andersen 1990; Hacker 1998). Because currently
serving members of the armed forces have access to a different set of programs than do
veterans, we distinguish these two military populations in the following discussion.

3.1 Current service members[1]

Active duty service members and their families have access to a host of very generous
benefit programs, the majority of which are available irrespective of need, income, or
other criteria. Rank or pay grade, and dependency status serve as the primary differen-
tiators in the military welfare state when benefits are stratified. The cost of sustaining a
volunteer military force with such provisions is not cheap. As much as one-third of the
regular defense budget (not including supplements for the wars in Iraq and Afghanistan)
goes to military pay, health-care, and retiree pensions (Dao and Walsh 2011).

The most generous of these military benefits is the free or very low cost health care
for service members and dependents. Tricare (formerly CHAMPUS) is the military's
managed health-care program for active duty, activated guard and reserve members,
and their families.[2] Tricare oversees health care in Military Treatment Facilities (MTFs
are DoD hospitals and outpatient clinics located on military installations) and by civilian providers. There is no cost to active-duty members or dependents for enrollment
fees, deductibles, or copays for Tricare Prime enrollees (who rely on MTFs as their
main source of care in an HMO-like option), and both Extra and Standard (a Preferred
Provider Organization and traditional fee-for-service program, respectively) enrollees
incur low annual deductibles ($150 per individual, or $300 per family maximum) and
co-pays (15–20 percent of fees). These costs are a fraction of what a typical civilian with
good health-care coverage would pay, and lower than what other federal employees
pay. They also do not come as a trade-off for higher wages; the Congressional Budget
Office recently concluded that military cash compensation exceeded that of comparable

federal civilian workers (Congressional Budget Office 2011). These benefits are available to all active service members and the spouses and unmarried children of active-duty members.

Military housing is another important benefit. The military Basic Allowance for Housing (BAH) is meant to provide equitable housing allowances and compensation across the wide range of housing markets in civilian communities. BAH rates differ by duty location, pay grade, and dependency status. BAH is only payable when government housing is not provided on a military installation (i.e., a barracks room, or on-post/base houses or apartments). BAH rates are frequently adjusted and pegged to local average rental, utility, and insurance costs for dwellings of a particular size, based on pay grade and family status. As an example, under the latest 2012 rates, a married E-4 (a junior enlisted person typically in their early 20s) with one child stationed in Washington DC would receive $1902 per month for BAH (on top of their base pay). An O-4 (an officer with around 10 years of service) in the same situation would receive $3030[3]. The fair market rents for a 3-bedroom residence in the DC area are just over $1700 per month (Arlington Partnership for Affordable Housing 2012). BAH can be used to cover a mortgage, and potentially contributes to wealth accumulation for homeowners, although the frequent moves to different duty stations preclude home ownership for many military members.

Military benefits also come through the hidden welfare state of tax expenditures (Howard 1997). Military compensation is untaxed during service in a combat zone, providing a substantial tax break over the past decade. Military personnel also benefit from the ability to maintain permanent state residency in the face of repeated cross-country moves, often in a state without state income tax. Personnel must declare their permanent state of residence as the location in which they intend to live upon completion of their service. They must have compelling evidence to support their choice (prior residence, family, property ownership) and cannot declare for the simple purposes of tax evasion.

The defined-benefits pension provided to military retirees now seems like a vestige of an earlier era. Individuals who serve on active duty (regardless of their experience in combat) for 20 years are eligible to retire with a military pension amounting to half of one's salary at retirement, for life. Given that many enlist at age 18, a retiree might draw a pension beginning as early as age 38. The retirement pension amounts to a retainer, paid to ensure availability in the future if needed. In practice, the program remains probably the most generous employer-provided, defined-benefit retirement plan available. And retirees are free to draw on this pension while continuing in another career in the public or private sector, in which they ultimately might earn a second pension.

A final, often overlooked benefit of service is the Servicemembers' Group Life Insurance (SGLI) program that automatically provides active-duty members with $400,000 coverage, and the Servicemembers' Group Life Insurance Traumatic Injury Protection (TSGLI) program for traumatic injury. Given the dangerous nature of military service, this is a nontrivial benefit protecting the survivors of military personnel killed or injured while serving.

3.2 Veterans[4]

The Veterans Administration, now the Department of Veterans Affairs (VA), administers a wide variety of programs grouped under nine main headings: health care; service-connected disability compensation; pensions; education and training; home-loan guaranty; life insurance; burial and memorial benefits; transition assistance, including vocational rehabilitation and employment; and dependent and survivors benefits. Not all of these programs parallel social welfare programs in the nonmilitary sector (such as transition assistance or memorial benefits), and many originate from the unique needs of caring and providing for those injured or disabled during service.

Veterans discharged with anything other than a dishonorable discharge (the vast majority of veterans) are eligible for most VA benefits, with a more recent requirement that veterans serve for 24 continuous months on active duty. Unlike the programs for active-duty members, many VA benefits are not universally available, with access stratified based on level of service-connected disability, wartime service, or a means test. Access to VA health care in particular is prioritized based on level of service-connected disability and income. In most years, only the highest priority veterans have been able to enroll in VA health care, leaving veterans without a compelling need for care ineligible. Only a minority of veterans utilize VA programs: in 2008, only 35 percent of all veterans used any VA programs or services in that year (U.S. Department of Veterans Affairs 2009).

Veterans seeking VA health care must first apply for enrollment. Applicants are assigned a priority group (1–8) based on a mix of level and source of disability, valorous service, and income. All recent combat veterans can enroll in VA health care, regardless of disability or income, for a limited post-service window (2–5 years have been the cutoffs in recent years, although the policies are often changing). In 2010, approximately 8.5 million veterans were enrolled in the VA health-care system (U.S. Department of Veterans Affairs 2011a). Veterans who are not enrolled in the system receive no health-care benefits from the VA.

In addition to VA health care, the Tricare for Life (TFL) program provides military retirees and their families continuing access to the same Tricare programs as those for active-duty members and their families. This retiree health plan is paid for by DoD, not the VA. Retirees and family members under age 65 can continue their care for a small annual enrollment fee of $260 per individual, or $520 per family per year (as of October 1, 2011 when fees increased for the first time since 1995).

Many retirees continue on with long civilian careers, and are eligible for coverage under their civilian employer's health-care plan. But retirees often elect to use their inexpensive Tricare benefits rather than their employer-provided plan. Prior to 2001, Tricare benefits expired at age 65, when retirees and family members could be covered by Medicare. Now, Tricare for Life covers beneficiaries as a secondary payer to Medicare. The low cost to retirees, and high cost to the DoD of covering retiree health care, has prompted lawmakers, led by John McCain (R-AZ) to consider raising fees for retiree health care further, or to require enrollment in employer-provided plans first when available. This proposal was dropped after it met with sharp opposition from retirees and their political advocates in organizations like the Military Officers Association of America (MOAA), the Veterans of Foreign Wars (VFW), and American Legion. Given the rising cost of retiree health care, it will continue to be a point of debate as military budgets are swamped by health-care and pension costs, and as the National Security Strategy re-emphasizes hardware procurement over personnel.

The VA also provides direct compensation for veterans with a service-connected disability, and pensions for low-income veterans with 90 days of service, at least one of which was during a period of war. In 2010, approximately 3.7 million veterans received either a VA pension or disability compensation (U.S. Department of Veterans Affairs 2011a). Based on disability rating, veterans may receive anywhere from $123 per month in disability payment (for a 10 percent disability rating) up to $2,673 per month (for a 100 percent disability rating) for life. In comparison, the average SSDI benefit for a disabled worker was $1064 per month (Szymendera 2010).

Probably the most familiar veterans' benefit was the Montgomery G.I. Bill for post-WWII veterans. The VA has provided educational and transitional assistance benefits to soldiers ever since, although the scope and generosity of those benefit programs have varied over time. The current educational and vocational rehabilitation benefits under the Post-9/11 G.I. Bill went into effect in August 2009, and, in 2010, the VA spent around $4.5 billion on programs used by roughly 1 million beneficiaries that year (U.S. Department of Veterans Affairs 2011a). Under the new program, individuals with at least 90 days of service on or after September 11, 2001, or individuals discharged with a service-connected disability after 30 days of service who receive an honorable discharge, are eligible for educational benefits. The program provides 36 months of education, along with a stipend for housing and books, generally payable for up to 15 years after release from active duty. Rising public tuition levels will likely have an impact on the future cost of the Post-9/11 G.I. Bill program.

Although military benefits have expanded to cover families in recent decades, veterans' benefits have rarely extended to family members. Since 2009, however, and for the first time in history, some veterans can transfer their G.I. Bill benefits to a spouse or child. Transferability requires longer service from the veteran, with complex rules around additional service meant to ensure 10 years of post-9/11 service for those wishing to transfer G.I. Bill benefits to dependents. Notably, the transfer must be requested and approved while the service member is still in the armed forces, which may limit the full use of available G.I. Bill benefits by dependents. However, with many eligible veterans not using their educational benefits, any increases due to transfers will increase costs to the VA, on top of the cost increases due to the more generous post-9/11 program.

The VA also helps veterans purchase homes and refinance home loans. This VA guaranty protects lenders from loss if the borrower fails to repay the loan. The VA loan guaranty program is complex, with numerous variations, limits, and exceptions to the program. In general, eligibility is based on period of service (during wartime), or on having 24 months of continuous active duty service, with an "other than dishonorable" discharge. In a tightening credit market, this loan guaranty provides a substantial benefit aiding veterans' wealth accumulation, with 1.3 million active home loans guaranteed through the program in 2009 (Reserve Officers Association 2010). This benefit can be used while still on active duty.

Taken together, the benefit programs available to military members and veterans are notable for their limited upfront cost to the beneficiary, generosity of benefit levels, their wide scope of coverage, and their near universality. Benefits have grown more generous in real and relative terms compared with provisions available to civilian employees, although civilian government employee benefits tend to parallel trends in military benefit changes. Military pensions and health care in particular look like the comprehensive packages available to earlier generations of public- and private-sector workers, who have seen those packages dismantled in recent years. Whether military benefits will face a similar fate in the coming years remains an open question.

4 The Hidden U.S. Military Welfare State

Welfare provisions for current and former military personnel are often ignored by researchers when discussing the U.S. welfare state as a whole, leading some to see military benefits as an "invisible" or "camouflaged" welfare system (Campbell 2004; Gifford 2006a, 2006b). Civilians increasingly benefit from a "hidden" or "submerged" welfare state (Howard 1997; Mettler 2011) that takes the form of tax deductions or exemptions, disguising the role of the government in aiding Americans across the political, economic, and demographic spectrum. Similarly, the constellation of military benefits may not be recognized as an important component of the American welfare state. Unlike the hidden civilian welfare state, however, military benefits are provided through in-kind services and universalistic programs to care for a wide variety of needs, rather than through taxation or other obscured fiscal policies. The generous benefits have led some to compare the military with socialist democracies; Wesley Clark, former presidential candidate and NATO commander, suggested that the military is "the purest application of socialism there is" (Kristoff 2011). In this European-style welfare regime, military welfare also structures stratification within military populations, reducing inequality by granting benefits equitably within the population (Esping-Andersen 1990; Hacker 1998). But veterans' benefits are less universalistic than those for active-duty service members. They are more often stratified by need, income, or other criteria, perhaps reflecting the interstitial status that veterans hold between civilian and military worlds.

Gifford (2006a; 2006b) sees military welfare as a fundamental yet misunderstood component of the larger U.S. welfare state. He argues that, without considering military benefits, one may falsely conclude that the U.S. welfare state only supports families who demonstrate extreme need, when, in fact, the military has long provided generous benefits such as health care and child care for a substantial portion of U.S. families (Gifford

2006a; 2006b). Campbell (2004) also sees military welfare as substantial yet "invisible," often predating and influencing the creation of similar civilian welfare programs. For example, the early pension system for war veterans existed long before Social Security, serving as a form of old-age insurance for many. And before Medicare or Medicaid came into being, the military was already providing health care to soldiers, veterans, and—by 1956—their dependents. In short, the vestiges of early programs for soldiers and veterans undergird the bulk of current civilian programs.

The invisibility of the military welfare state may contribute to an underlying sense that provisions for soldiers and veterans are inevitable. That is, the American public takes for granted that soldiers and veterans deserve benefits, whereas those for other social groups are more controversial and subject to debate. Since the deservingness of military personnel is rarely questioned, programs for soldiers and veterans appear more as earned privileges than government handouts. Even referring to military pensions, health care, and other benefits as entitlements or social welfare programs raises the ire of military populations who see these programs as recruiting or retention tools, general compensation, or deferred compensation.

Segal (1989) also argues that military service in the peacetime volunteer force provides jobs and opportunities for those who are disadvantaged in the civilian labor force. "The peacetime deterrent force... is articulated with the welfare system as well, providing job training, employment, income, and security to those who are disadvantaged in the civilian labor force and financial assistance to those who are seeking higher education in an era of rapidly escalating college costs. These welfare functions are received in exchange for service, not as entitlements" (Segal 1989, 100). During wartime, however, these benefits come at a higher price, disproportionately putting the least fortunate in harm's way. Past policy has experimented with treating military service as a jobs program for so-called "low-aptitude" men who scored below the 30th percentile on the Armed Forces Qualification Test (AFQT), allowing men who otherwise would not have met entrance standards to serve in the military (Laurence and Ramsberger 1991). "Project 100,000" was engineered by Secretary of Defense Robert McNamara with the stated goal of providing a means of economic mobility to the disadvantaged through military service. The program was not successful; these men had higher rates of occupational reassignment, remedial training, and dying in combat than their regular-standards peers (mostly because low-aptitude scores pushed them into low-skill military roles in the infantry.) After their service, these men fared worse in civilian life than nonveterans of comparable aptitude levels (Laurence and Ramsberger 1991). In recent years, some policy analysts have re-invigorated the notion of military (or military-like) service and education as a kind of workfare or training program for low-income men (cf. Mead 2007; Price 2010). Gifford (2006b) sees broad implications of the military for labor markets, suggesting that military "employment" is a central part of the social safety net by providing employment opportunities that draw away surplus labor, thereby reducing competition and driving up wages in the open labor market.

Gifford (2005) has also noted how the generous provision of benefits for military personnel and their families has spillover consequences for the availability of private-sector health insurance or a safety net in communities. "As both potent political symbols and members of a well-positioned interest group, armed forces not only absorb finite resources, but also create discursive obstacles to other groups seeking benefits from the state." (Gifford 2006b, 478–479). Rather than military programs paving the way for generous civilian welfare programs, as the historical record might suggest, military health care crowds out the availability of private health insurance and a private health-care safety net for civilians. For example, higher medical uninsurance rates are associated with lower rates of employer-offered health benefits in areas of higher military presence. This stems from two processes. First, military communities attract civilian employment sectors noted for their low wages and lack of benefits (e.g., retail and personal services such as tailoring or barbering), which drive down civilian rates of insurance coverage in the community. Additionally, the generous health-care coverage provided by the government to military members and their families may crowd out the need for employers to offer subsidized health care for their employees when many of them may be military family members or retirees. Finally, the widespread use of MTFs by military-community members shifts the pool of insured patients away from civilian providers, reducing the risk pool available to offset potential charity care that providers in the community might offer.

5 Inequality and Military Welfare

Welfare programs for soldiers and veterans represent a nontrivial portion of the U.S. welfare state, and we argue this reflects the perceived deservingness and entitlement of military personnel. Nonetheless, the distribution of military welfare is the subject of controversy, centering on who profits and who loses from those generous benefits as well as who has access to high-status military positions and military service in the first place. Inequality in military welfare reflects some of the same social characteristics that alter access to privileges in the civilian world: gender, sexual orientation, race, and class.

As Gifford (2006a, 388) notes, military welfare provisions "actively structure the social relations of recipients, primarily in ways that promote the reproduction of dominant gender and familial forms." Because most soldiers and veterans are men, they are much more likely to benefit, whereas women—who have historically served in more limited or marginalized roles in the military—may struggle without a social safety net (Campbell 2004; Ritter 2002). Historically, women were not allowed to serve in many military roles except in times of extreme need, and, thus, were only entitled to benefits via relationships with male soldiers or veterans (Segal 1995). In the wake of the Vietnam War, veteran hiring preferences in the public sector were seen by some as systematically disadvantaging women because few veterans were women (Thompson 1973). Although women's participation began to rise under the AVF, women currently only make up approximately 14 percent of the active-duty forces (U.S. Department of Defense 2009).

Even women who do choose to serve may face differential access to benefits due to rank, because women are less likely to achieve officer status compared to men (Segal and Segal 2004). Furthermore, the timing of family formation and childbearing makes maintaining a military career challenging. Although the military provides high-quality child care, the demand far exceeds the supply, and women are more likely than men to opt out of a 20-year military career (Military Leadership Diversity Commission 2010). As a consequence of being less likely to serve until retirement, proportionately fewer women are eligible for lifetime benefit programs such as retirement pensions.

Research suggests the enforcement of rules as a mechanism by which gender inequality persists in the military. Some of the military's formal rules may disproportionately affect women, which may cost them the achievement of higher rank and may even lead to early discharges or other-than-honorable discharges. For example, Pershing (2001) found that women received proportionally higher numbers of honor-code violations at the U.S. Naval Academy compared to men. At the intersection of gender and sexual orientation, the military discharged proportionally more women under the recently repealed Don't Ask, Don't Tell policy, which provided for the discharge of personnel identified as homosexual. Although this policy is no longer in effect, many questions remain about how legally married same-sex couples will be integrated into the military's family-benefits system. Current policy is in flux with the recent Supreme Court decision to repeal the federal Defense of Marriage Act (DOMA) that prohibited providing same-sex married couples the benefits available to those in heterogamous marriages.

Access to and distribution of military benefits has been structured as well by race and class, either by policy or practice. Although African Americans, American Indians, and Asians have served in every war since the creation of the United States, official integration of the military did not take place until after World War II (Moskos 1966; Segal and Segal 2004). Following integration, African Americans in particular have served in large numbers relative to their share of the general population, accounting for 20 percent of the U.S. Army active component in 2010 (compared to 13 percent of the general population) (U.S. Army 2010). Just as women often face a "glass ceiling" in obtaining high-status positions, African Americans are less likely to attain officer status, and among officers, they are less likely to attain a flag rank than whites. In 2010, only 13 percent of U.S. Army officers were African American, compared to 21 percent of enlisted forces (U.S. Army 2010). Although blacks are less likely to attain the highest officer ranks, many attain high enlisted ranks as non-commissioned officers (NCO) and serve for 20 or more years. Thus, because of their representation among NCOs, African Americans still gain substantial benefits through their military service.

Although the all-volunteer force has been referred to as a "poverty draft," enlisting only those with the least opportunity, the military does not draw heavily from the lowest socioeconomic groups, many of whom fail to meet eligibility standards due to poor educational outcomes, poor health, or criminal history (Segal and Segal 2004). Most recruits come from middle and lower middle class backgrounds, and the generous military benefits provided exceed those likely to be found in the jobs available to them in the civilian labor market. In the military labor market, all military jobs are relatively good jobs in that pay is mostly consistent given a common rank or time in grade, and most jobs in the military have a path for upward mobility. This structure reduces inequality within the military, mostly due to differences based on rank, whereas differential occupational sorting strongly influences income and other inequalities in the civilian labor market. But given the fairly low proportion of Americans who serve, the reductions to class-based inequality are limited to the time while serving, when pay and benefits are relatively good and equitable.

6 MAJOR CHALLENGES FACING MILITARY AND VETERANS' BENEFITS PROGRAMS

6.1 Pension and Health-Care Costs

The military and veterans' benefit systems will face fiscal challenges in the near and long-term future as a result of the generous benefits promised to past and current service members and their families. Because the VA provides lifetime health care for enrolled veterans and the DoD provides generous health care for service members, retirees and their families, and pensions for military retirees, both the DoD and the VA face rapidly escalating costs. Lifetime support does not just cover service-connected problems, and, over time, the general costs of an aging veteran population will strain VA and DoD budgets, already stretched thin by a decade at war. In addition, the military has increasingly moved toward a career-oriented force, with a greater emphasis on remaining in the military until retirement, implying larger fractions of military members who wish to stay in to earn a pension and lifetime access to low-cost health insurance. In the words of a Defense Business Board member, "Today, we're on the path in the Department of Defense to turn it into a benefits company that may occasionally kill a terrorist" (Keith 2011). Military health-care costs account for $52.5 billion in the next proposed budget, and retirees' pensions represents another approximately $50 billion a year (Keith 2011).

Civilian employees have found that promises can be broken, as numerous pension programs have collapsed under current demographic and fiscal realities. Civilian pension programs have struggled under the costs of maintaining defined benefits over a postretirement lifetime (when retirement typically comes in the early to mid-sixties, rather than two decades earlier for military retirees), because costs are not spread across a wide base. The cost of military benefits is spread over a national tax base, which facilitates their maintenance. These costs have been supported not only because they are socially constructed as deserved compensation for sacrifice, but also because the burden for their provision is spread broadly across the polity. After a decade of war fought with one of the smallest militaries in the nation's history—one staffed exclusively by volunteers—the politics and economics of unshared sacrifice likely temper resistance to

paying the costs of programs for soldiers and veterans. Lawmakers, backed by their constituents, have resisted not only cutting spending on these programs, but even reducing
the pace of their growth. President Obama drew on this bipartisan support for veterans
by including them as a key component of his 2012 State of the Union address, saying "As
[veterans] come home, we must serve them as well as they've served us. That includes
giving them the care and the benefits they have earned—which is why we've increased
annual VA spending every year I've been President" (Obama 2012).

   We are also winding down a decade at war during which a much higher proportion
of wounded servicepersons survived traumatic injuries with lasting mental and physical disabilities. About one-third of servicepersons returning from Iraq or Afghanistan
report symptoms of a mental health or other cognitive condition such as posttraumatic
stress disorder (PTSD), depression, or traumatic brain injury (TBI). These conditions
may lead to full disability ratings for life, and the estimated societal cost of treating
PTSD and depression alone—not including any associated disability pension—ranges
from $4.0 to $6.2 billion for only the first two years postdeployment (Tanielian and
Jaycox 2008). The cost of caring for this generation of service-disabled veterans is
already tremendous, and costs are projected to increase for at least the next 30 years
(Edwards 2010). Both the DoD and VA budgets will likely be strained for the next several decades. It is not unthinkable that the unchecked costs of the current benefit system
could impede military capability in the near future, as benefit costs compete with military procurement in the budgetary process.

NOTES

1. Information on benefits available to military members and their families is available at
   http://www.military.com/benefits, and much of the following discussion comes from this
   website and its associated links.
2. The majority of this section draws from web-based information available at the following
   webpage and associated links: http://www.tricare.mil/Welcome/Plans.aspx.
3. Figures computed using the Department of Defense BAH calculator at http://www.
   defensetravel.dod.mil/site/bahCalc.cfm.
4. This section draws extensively from U.S. Department of Veterans Affairs 2011b.

REFERENCES

*Indicates recommended reading.

Albano, Sondra. 1994. "Military Recognition of Family Concerns: Revolutionary War to 1993."
   Armed Forces and Society 20 (2):283–302.
Angrist, Joshua D. 1993. "The Effect of Veterans Benefits on Education and Earnings." *Industrial
   and Labor Relations Review* 46 (4):637–652.
Arlington Partnership for Affordable Housing. 2012. http://www.apah.org/facts/index.html.

Asch S. M., E. A. McGlynn, M. M. Hogan, R. A. Hayward, P. Shekelle, L. Rubenstein, J. Keesey, J. Adams, and E. A. Kerr. 2004. "Comparison of Quality of Care for Patients in the Veterans Health Administration and Patients in a National Sample." *Annals of Internal Medicine* 141 (12): 938–945.

*Campbell, Alec. 2004. "The Invisible Welfare State: Establishing the Phenomenon of Twentieth Century Veterans' Benefits." *Journal of Political and Military Sociology* 32 (2):249–267.

Canaday, Margot. 2003. "Building a Straight State: Sexuality and Social Citizenship Under the 1944 G.I. Bill." *Journal of American History* 90 (3): 935–957.

Congressional Budget Office. 2011. "Analysis of Federal Civilian and Military Compensation." http://www.cbo.gov/sites/default/files/cbofiles/ftpdocs/120xx/doc12042/01-20-compensation.pdf.

Conrad, Peter R. 2005. "The Servicemen's Readjustment Act of 1944: The History, People, and Effects on Minorities." Honors Thesis. http://opensiuc.lib.siu.edu/cgi/viewcontent.cgi?article=1342&context=uhp_theses.

Dao, James, and Mary Williams Walsh. 2011. "Retiree Benefits for the Military Could Face Cuts." *New York Times*. September 18. http://www.nytimes.com/2011/09/19/us/retiree-benefits-for-the-military-could-face-cuts.html.

Edwards, Ryan D. 2010. "U.S. War Costs: Two Parts Temporary, One Part Permanent." NBER Working Paper 16108. http://www.nber.org/papers/w16108.

Esping-Andersen, Gøsta. 1990. *The Three Worlds of Welfare Capitalism*. Princeton, NJ: Princeton University Press.

Gifford, Brian. 2005. "The Spillover Effects of Military Communities on the Need for Health Care Safety-Net Services." RAND Working Paper WR-299. http://www.rand.org/content/dam/rand/pubs/working_papers/2005/RAND_WR299.pdf.

*Gifford, Brian. 2006a. "The Camouflaged Safety Net: The U.S. Armed Forces as Welfare State Institution." *Social Politics* 13 (3): 372–399.

Gifford, Brian. 2006b. "Why No Trade-Off Between Guns and Butter? Armed Forces and Social Spending in the Advanced Industrial Democracies, 1960–1993." *American Journal of Sociology* 112 (2): 473–509.

Hacker, Jacob S. 1998. "The Historical Logic of National Health Insurance: Structure and Sequence in the Development of British, Canadian, and U.S. Medical Policy." *Studies in American Political Development* 12 (1): 57–130.

Howard, Christopher. 1997. *The Hidden Welfare State: Tax Expenditures and Social Policy in the United States*. Princeton, NJ: Princeton University Press.

Jensen, Laura S. 2005. "Constructing and Entitling America's Original Veterans." In Anne L. Schneider and Helen M. Ingram, eds., *Deserving and Entitled: Social Constructions and Public Policy*, 35–36. Albany: State University of New York Press.

Keith, Tamara. 2011. "Health Care Costs New Threat to U.S. Military." NPR, Morning Edition, June 7. http://www.npr.org/2011/06/07/137009416/u-s-military-has-new-threat-health-care-costs.

Kelly, Patrick J. 1997. *Creating a National Home: Building the Veterans' Welfare State 1860–1900*. Cambridge, MA: Harvard University Press.

Kristoff, Nicholas. 2011. "Our Lefty Military." *New York Times*, June 15. http://www.nytimes.com/2011/06/16/opinion/16kristof.html.

Laurence, Janice H., and Peter F. Ramsberger. 1991. *Low Aptitude Men in the Military: Who Profits, Who Pays?* New York: Praeger.

Levy, Richard E. 2004. "Of Two Minds: Charitable and Social Insurance Models in the Veterans' Benefits System." *Kansas Journal of Law & Public Policy* 13:303–337.

Mead, Lawrence. 2007. "Toward a Mandatory Work Policy for Men." *Future of Children* 17 (2): 43–72.

*Mettler, Suzanne. 2005. *Soldiers to Citizens: The G.I. Bill and the Making of the Greatest Generation*. New York: Oxford University Press.

Mettler, Suzanne. 2011. *The Submerged State: How Invisible Government Policies Undermine American Democracy* Chicago: University of Chicago Press.

*Military.com. 2006. "GI Bill turns 62 Today." http://www.military.com/NewsContent/0,13319,102383,00.html.

Military Leadership Diversity Commission. 2010. *Reenlistment Rates Across the Services by Gender and Race/Ethnicity*. Issue Paper 31. http://mldc.whs.mil/download/documents/Issue%20Papers/31_Enlisted_Retention.pdf.

Moskos, Charles C., Jr. 1966. "Racial Integration in the Armed Forces." *American Journal of Sociology* 72 (2): 132–148.

Obama, Barack. 2012. *"Remarks by the President in the State of the Union Address."* http://www.nytimes.com/interactive/2012/01/24/us/politics/state-of-the-union-2012-video-transcript.html.

Pershing, Jana L. 2001. "Gender Disparities in Enforcing the Honor Concept at the U.S. Naval Academy." *Armed Forces & Society* 23:419–442.

Price, Hugh B. 2010. "Using Military Education and Training Methods to Help Struggling Students and Schools." *State Education Standard*, 9–13, 60. Available at http://www.brookings.edu/~/media/Files/rc/articles/2010/0714_military_education_price/0714_military_education_price.pdf.

Quadagno, Jill. 1988. *The Transformation of Old Age Security: Class and Politics in the American Welfare State*. Chicago: University of Chicago Press.

Resch, John. 2000. *Suffering Soldiers: Revolutionary War Veterans, Moral Sentiment, and Political Culture in the Early Republic*. Amherst: University of Massachusetts Press.

Reserve Officers Association of the United States. 2010. "Statement on V.A. Home Loan Guaranty Program Reserve Officers Association of the United States and Reserve Enlisted Association before the Subcommittee on Economic Opportunity House Veterans Affairs Committee United States House." May 20. http://www.roa.org/site/DocServer/HVAC_Testimony_VA_Home_Loan_Guaranty_Program_5-20-10.pdf?docID=27844&AddInterest=1622.

Ritter, Gretchen. 2002. "Of War and Virtue: Gender, American Citizenship and Veterans' Benefits After World War II." In Lars Mjoset and Steven van Holde, eds., *Comparative Social Research: Comparative Study of Conscription in the Armed Forces*, 20:201–226. JAI Press.

Segal, David R. 1989. *Recruiting for Uncle Sam: Citizenship and Military Manpower Policy*. Lawrence: University Press of Kansas.

Segal, David. R., and Mady Wechsler Segal. 2004. "America's Military Population." *Population Research Bulletin* 59 (4).

Segal, Mady Wechsler. 1995. "Womens' Military Roles Cross-Nationally: Past, Present, and Future." *Gender and Society* 9 (6):757–775.

*Skocpol, Theda. 1992. *Protecting Soldiers and Mothers: The Political Origins of Social Policy in the United States*. Cambridge, MA: Harvard University Press.

Stevens, Rosemary. 1991. "Can the Government Govern? Lessons from the Formation of the Veterans Administration." *Journal of Health, Politics, Policy and Law* 16 (2): 281–305.

Szymendera, Scott. 2010. "Primer on Disability Benefits: Social Security Disability Insurance (SSDI) and Supplemental Security Income (SSI)." U.S. Senate, Special Committee on Aging. http://aging.senate.gov/crs/ss27.pdf.

Tanielian Terri, and Lisa H. Jaycox. 2008. *Invisible Wounds of War: Psychological and Cognitive Injuries, Their Consequences, and Services to Assist Recovery*. Santa Monica, CA: RAND Corporation. http://www.rand.org/pubs/monographs/MG720.html.

Teigen, Jeremy M. 2006. "Enduring Effects of the Uniform: Previous Military Experience and Voting Turnout." *Political Research Quarterly* 59 (4): 601–607.

Thompson, Judith Jarvis. 1973. "Preferential Hiring." *Philosophy and Public Affairs*. 2 (4): 364–384.

Twiss, Pamela, and James A. Martin. 1999. "Conventional and Military Public Housing for Families." *Social Service Review* 73 (2): 240–260.

U.S. Army. 2010. "Active-duty Profile FY 2010." http://www.armyg1.army.mil/hr/docs/demographics/FY10_Army_Profile.pdf.

U.S. Department of Defense. 2009. "Active Duty Military Personnel by Rank/Grade." http://siadapp.dmdc.osd.mil/personnel/MILITARY/rg0909f.pdf.

U.S. Department of Defense. 2010. "Population Representation in the Military Services." http://prhome.defense.gov/MPP/ACCESSION%20POLICY/PopRep2010/.

U.S. Department of Veterans Affairs. 2009. *Analysis of Unique Veterans Utilization of VA Benefits & Services*. http://www.va.gov/VETDATA/docs/SpecialReports/uniqueveteransMay.pdf.

U.S. Department of Veterans Affairs. 2010a. *Trends in the Geographic Distribution of VA Expenditures: FY2000 to FY2009*. http://www.va.gov/vetdata/docs/QuickFacts/Gdx-trends.pdf.

U.S. Department of Veterans Affairs. 2010b. *Veteran Population Projections: FY2000 to FY2036*. http://www.va.gov/vetdata/docs/quickfacts/Population-slideshow.pdf.

U.S. Department of Veterans Affairs. 2011a. *Department of Veterans Affairs Statistics at a Glance*. http://www.va.gov/vetdata/docs/Quickfacts/Homepage_slideshow_FINAL.pdf.

U.S. Department of Veterans Affairs. 2011b. *Federal Benefits for Veterans, Dependents and Survivors*. 2011 ed. http://www.va.gov/opa/publications/benefits_book.asp.

U.S. Office of Personnel Management. "Vet Guide." http://www.opm.gov/staffingPortal/Vetguide.asp#2Types.

Van Dyke, Frank, and Robin Elliott. 1969. *Military Medicare: The Physician-Service Component of the Civilian Health and Medical Program of the Uniformed Services (CHAMPUS)*. U.S. Department of Defense Report.

World Health Organization. 2000. *The World Health Report. Health Systems: Improving Performance*. http://www.who.int/whr/2000/en/index.html.

PART VIII

POLICY OUTCOMES

CHAPTER 32

....

POVERTY

....

DAVID BRADY AND LANE M. DESTRO

1 INTRODUCTION

....

THE noted historian Michael Katz (2001, 9–10) writes:

> The American welfare state resembles a massive watch that fails to keep very accurate time. Some of its components are rusty and outmoded; others were poorly designed; some work very well. They were fabricated by different craftsmen who usually did not consult with one another; they interact imperfectly; and at times they work at cross-purposes.

Indeed, American social policy does have many clumsy qualities and is quite underdeveloped. One of the consequences of this is that the United States has very high levels of poverty, especially relative to other affluent democracies (Rainwater and Smeeding 2004; Brady 2009). This strikingly high poverty and its seeming intractability have often led to a fatalistic view that social policy cannot or never will be able to reduce poverty.

In contrast to such fatalism, this essay contends that several U.S. social policies effectively reduce poverty. To advance this argument, we review the recent social science literature on U.S. social policy and poverty. We concentrate attention on recent articles in journals of public policy, economics, social work, demography, and sociology. We discuss the effectiveness of the most relevant and salient social programs. Finally, we conclude by discussing the limitations of the literature's exclusive focus on the U.S. case. We argue that the field would benefit from greater incorporation of the comparative social policy literature. Before proceeding, we describe the patterns of poverty in the United States. In the process, we explain the problems with the official U.S. measure of poverty.

2. THE OFFICIAL U.S. MEASURE OF POVERTY

According to the official U.S. measure of poverty, about 12.5 percent of the population was poor in 2007 (see Table 32.1).[1] Poverty also varies considerably across demographic groups. Only 10.5 percent of whites and 10.2 percent of Asians were poor, whereas 24.5 percent of blacks and 21.5 percent of Hispanics were poor. As has been well documented, a large share of U.S. children is poor. In 2007, 18.0 percent of children fell below the official threshold. By contrast, only 9.7 percent of elderly adults (over 64 years old) were poor.

Such patterns inform a great deal of poverty scholarship and debates. The key problem is that these numbers are based on the flawed official U.S. measure. Experts have known since at least the 1980s that the official U.S. measure has serious limitations (Citro and Michael 1995; Brady 2003; Blank 2008). Indeed, the problems have worsened over time such that the official measure is even less reliable and less valid today than it was a decade or two ago (Brady 2009). Nevertheless, the official measure continues to be widely used, prominently discussed in the media and in policy debates, and entrenched in the federal government (Brady 2003). The Obama administration recently approved the dissemination of a supplemental poverty measure, but this measure does not actually replace the problematic official measure.

There are at least four major problems with the official measure (see Brady 2003, 2009). First, the official measure is out of date. The measure was established in the late 1960s, but was actually based on data from the mid-1950s. As a result, the official measure fails to consider many needs of contemporary families, such as paid child care and health care. The official measure was originally based on the assumption that families needed income for an emergency food budget multiplied by three. This assumption

Table 32.1 Patterns in 2007 U.S. Poverty with Official U.S. Measure and Relative Measure

	% Poor Official U.S. Measure	% Below Half of Median Equivalized HH Income (Luxembourg Income Study)
Overall	12.5	16.0
White	10.5	n/a
Black	24.5	n/a
Asian	10.2	n/a
Hispanic (any race)	21.5	n/a
>64 Years Old	9.7	24.7
<18 Years Old	18.0	17.7

Sources: U.S. Census Bureau and Luxembourg Income Study.
Note: 2007 is the most recent available data for the United States in the LIS.

was never tested, and because the thresholds have only been updated for inflation, this anchoring no longer exists. Plus, it is clear that food is a smaller share of family expenses today. Second, the measure's thresholds are simply too low relative to the needs of contemporary families. Convincing historical evidence shows that the measure was intentionally set low to ease the political goal of "winning the war on poverty" (Katz 1989; O'Connor 2001). Further, the value of the threshold has declined precipitously in recent decades. Third, the official measure is not informed by leading theoretical conceptualizations of poverty, such as social exclusion (Silver 1994) and capability deprivation (Sen 1999). Fourth, the official measure is based on a crude definition of income that ignores taxes and inconsistently counts transfers. For example, even though many elderly pay taxes on Social Security benefits and all working families pay payroll taxes, the official measure is based on pretax income. Many working families receive the Earned Income Tax Credit (EITC) and since the 1990s, the EITC has grown into the largest assistance program for families with children—much larger than Temporary Assistance to Needy Families (TANF) (Danziger 2010). Yet, the official measure ignores the EITC. Additionally, some transfers are counted and others ignored. For example, Social Security pensions count as income for the official measure, but Food Stamps, housing subsidies, and child-care vouchers do not. The official measure also neglects states' taxes and transfers, which further compounds its reliability and validity problems. Because of the inconsistent counting of taxes and transfers, comparisons over time periods have become increasingly problematic. Altogether, poverty is probably higher than the official measure reports.

As a result, it seems appropriate to be cautious with any research—including the literature reviewed in what follows—based solely on the official measure. This point is demonstrated by the fact that when the new supplemental poverty measure is used, the proportion poor increases for almost all groups and the rate of elderly poverty nearly doubles (Short 2011).

One way for the field to advance would be to incorporate measurement lessons from international poverty research (Rainwater and Smeeding 2004). The simplest defensible alternative would be a relative measure grounded in a comprehensive definition of economic resources (Brady 2009). It is especially important that poverty measurement be based on disposable income after accounting for taxes and transfers. Another promising alternative would refocus poverty scholars' attention on material deprivation or social exclusion. Though the conceptualizations have limitations (see Béland 2007), European scholars are far ahead of American poverty researchers in studying consumption, material deprivation, and social exclusion (Marlier and Atkinson 2010; Nolan and Whelan 2010). Incorporating consumption and deprivation or shifting our focus to social exclusion would also partly address calls to broaden the outcomes studied in welfare and poverty research (Lichter and Jayakody 2002).

Such advances in poverty measurement can be illustrated by returning to Table 32.1. The Luxembourg Income Study (LIS) has become the leader in the international social sciences of income and poverty. The LIS harmonizes income data that comprehensively incorporate taxes and transfers. Using the LIS and a relative measure of poverty defined as 50 percent of the median equivalized income, poverty patterns look quite different. Instead of 12.5 percent, fully 16 percent of the United States would be poor with this more defensible measure. Even though they are still much more likely to be poor than working-aged adults, poverty among children is slightly lower. By contrast, poverty among the elderly is significantly higher (Brady 2004). In sum, poverty in the United States would be much higher and demographic variations may look quite different if a more valid and reliable measure of poverty is used.

3   THE ELEPHANT IN THE ROOM: SOCIAL INSURANCE

For the most part, American poverty research devotes much more attention to social assistance programs targeted at the poor. By contrast, the largest and arguably most important social policies affecting poverty tend to be neglected. Social insurance programs like old age and survivor's insurance (OASI), unemployment insurance (UI), and disability insurance attract much less attention. Yet, as some poverty researchers acknowledge (e.g., Blank 1997), these programs actually have a huge impact on poverty (Scholz, Moffitt, and Cowan 2009). As noted earlier, better measures of poverty reveal that elderly poverty is much more common than the official measure suggests (Citro and Michael 1995; Brady 2004). Still, OASI obviously reduces elder poverty. As Katz (2001, 236–237) writes, "Without a doubt, Social Security has reduced poverty among the elderly... Without Social Security, by one estimate, 56 percent of the elderly would have lived in [official] poverty by 1992."

Although vulnerable single-mother families historically relied on Aid to Families with Dependent Children (AFDC), this population now relies more on UI than on TANF (Shaefer and Wu 2011). Unemployment Insurance also reduces the likelihood and depth of poverty for millions of others (Levine 2006). Further, many would be more economically insecure without disability insurance (Parish, Rose, and Andrews 2009). If one were to weigh the impact of various social policies on poverty, it is plausible that OASI is the most important antipoverty program in the United States. Social insurance like OASI and Medicare are certainly much more expensive, and reach more people, than welfare programs targeted at the poor (Katz 2001).

OASI and other social-insurance programs are broader and more inclusive than means-tested social-assistance programs targeted at the poor. Several such social-insurance programs necessitate employment, but they still reach a much broader cross-section of the population. Thus, the effectiveness of OASI in fighting poverty and the broad popularity and politics surrounding it suggest that relatively more inclusive social-insurance programs may be a more effective strategy for reducing poverty (Brady and Burroway 2012).[2]

4 WELFARE REFORM

One of the major U.S. social-policy changes of the past several decades was the end of AFDC. This policy-making episode, popularly known as "welfare reform," replaced AFDC with TANF. The reform set time limits on benefits and established qualifying conditions that often required employment or training. Welfare reform was also a massive experiment in federalism. States differed in the rules, funding, benefits, additional services (e.g., child care), enforcement, and overall zealousness of welfare reform. Whereas AFDC was a federal benefit almost guaranteed for all low-income single mothers, TANF runs through a system of block grants distributed to states. Though significant interstate differences existed under AFDC, these differences were exacerbated after reform. As Danziger (2010, 527) remarks, "The wide discretion allowed by the federal legislation has led some analysts to suggest that welfare is now more state than federal policy and that there are now 50 different welfare programs."

United States poverty scholars jumped to evaluate the many variations in welfare reform across states. Indeed, the late 1990s was a period of substantial investment in poverty research by government agencies, private foundations, think tanks, and advocacy organizations. In some ways, this investment and the enthusiasm to evaluate welfare reform may have had a legitimating effect on the reform. Indeed, this period is notable for the relative dearth of big picture debates about whether more imaginative and ambitious social policies would have had better effects. Indeed, the literature lacked critiques of the Clinton administration, which had conceded when the Republican Congress discarded the proposals of poverty experts in the White House. Nevertheless, welfare reform did provide real opportunities for poverty research. Massive datasets, like "Welfare, Children and Families: A Three City Study," were collected, and scholars used private and local funds and access to administrative records to study state-specific changes (e.g. Reingold, Pirog, and Brady 2007).

If nothing else, one major trend emerged during this period: the number of AFDC/TANF recipients plummeted (Lichter and Jayakody 2002; Danziger 2010). President Clinton and conservatives often proclaimed this was proof that welfare reform was a success. Yet, it is essential to recall that this massive decline was partly coincidental to welfare reform. AFDC rolls peaked at 14.2 million recipients in 1994, fully three years before welfare reform went into effect nationally in 1997. Danziger (2010) shows that, by 1996, rolls had already dropped to 12.6 million. Although welfare reform probably played some role, it also appears that there were preemptive changes by welfare recipients and welfare bureaucrats in anticipation of the reform and its time limits. Also fueling the decline were the economic prosperity of the mid-1990s and the expansion of the EITC (Ziliak et al. 2000).

Regardless, single-mother employment rose in the late 1990s. The literature suggests that interstate differences in welfare reforms and related policies cannot explain interstate differences in welfare exits or maternal employment (Danielson and Klerman

2008; Danziger 2010; Moffitt 2008). For example, Lim, Coulton, and Lalich (2009) provide nuanced results showing that states' TANF work requirements encouraged employment for "later welfare leavers" but had no effect on "early welfare leavers." They also show that more lenient work requirements helped early leavers obtain jobs with health insurance. Herbst (2008) shows that work rules have larger effects when the economy is strong. Danielson and Klerman (2008) conclude, based on a rigorous comparison of pre- and postreform periods, that a confluence of welfare reform, other social policies (e.g., EITC) and the growing economy contributed to the decline of recipiency. Despite this positive news, most conclude that the employment of former welfare recipients remains quite uneven, unstable, and insecure (Wood, Moore, and Rangarajan 2008). Even more troubling, a much higher share of single mothers neither works nor receives welfare now than ever before (Danziger 2010).

Evidence that welfare reform actually improved the well-being of low-income single mother families is harder to come by. According to the LIS, poverty rates among children in single-mother families declined from 54.2 percent in 1994 to 52.2 percent in 1997, 47.7 percent in 2000, 46.6 in 2004, and 40.5 in 2007. At the same time, the poorest families experienced a significant decline in economic resources after welfare reform (Katz 2001, 338). Altogether, the literature seems to conclude that welfare reform should only get partial credit for positive outcomes and even then it was only responsible for modest improvements (Danziger 2010; Lichter and Jayakody 2002; Kaestner and Tarlov 2006). A few studies offer fine-grained information on the daily lives of former welfare recipients that allows for a deep understanding of well-being after reform (e.g. Seefeldt 2008). Further, recent evidence suggests that welfare reform did little to increase marriage. In a convincing study, Graefe and Lichter (2008) use difference-in-difference models to show that welfare reform was not strongly associated with changes in marriage among unmarried mothers, even among the most disadvantaged mothers. In a telling contrast, Gassman-Pines and Yoshikawa (2006) show that the much more generous New Hope program—which provided ample income subsidies and support services— led to a significant increase in marriage for never-married mothers.[3]

Last, welfare reform demonstrated the importance of implementation and enforcement for social policy. Welfare reform was supposed to turn welfare offices into employment agencies and brokers for social services like child care. Yet, many social workers and welfare managers treated TANF recipients just as they had during AFDC (Danziger 2010). If anything, recipients may have experienced an increase in hassles and hurdles (Watkins-Hayes 2009). There is convincing evidence that welfare reform, and the greater discretion it brought states, administrators, and social workers, facilitated the racially unequal treatment of recipients (Fording, Soss, and Schram 2011). For example, Schram and colleagues (2009) provide compelling experimental and administrative evidence to show that case managers are more likely to recommend sanctions against Black recipients. Further, the administration of welfare reform has contributed to a "new paternalism" and a disciplinary turn in social policy that appears to have undermined the political and civic rights of welfare recipients (Bruch, Feree, and Soss 2010).

5 Employment-Related Policies

Among antipoverty policies, perhaps the biggest success story of the past few decades has been the EITC. The EITC is a refundable tax credit that workers can claim at the end of the year if their earnings are below a certain level. The EITC was expanded in the late 1980s, and then expanded even more in the early 1990s (Myles and Pierson 1997). The EITC has since become the largest cash public assistance program for poor families (Scholz et al. 2009). Katz (2001, 13) explains how significant, and in some ways surprising, this policy change was: "With virtually no opposition, the Clinton administration engineered a massive increase in an income transfer program at a time when other forms of social welfare faced only real or proposed cutbacks." It is worth noting that the EITC subsequently attracted criticism from Republican politicians for alleged fraud. Nevertheless, it may be reasonable to say that the EITC is the principal antipoverty program for working families in the U.S. (Waldfogel 2009). Katz (2001, 296) claims, "It lifted more children out of poverty than had any other safety net program." The number of people claiming the EITC grew considerably in the 1990s and quickly surpassed the number of AFDC/TANF recipients (Blank 1997; Scholz et al. 2009). Still, it appears that the full benefits remain unrealized because many low-income families face barriers to receiving the EITC (Hirasuna and Stinson 2007).

The EITC also complements labor market regulations like the minimum wage. For example, Neumark and Wascher (2011) find that the interaction of the EITC and higher minimum wages produces significant, positive labor-market responses for very poor families, the poorly educated, and minority mothers. They claim that minimum wages by themselves do not facilitate mother's workforce engagement, and the interaction may even have adverse effects on low-skilled adults and teenagers. Still, Neumark and Wascher find that the EITC by itself raises the employment and earnings of single mothers. The beneficial interactions of the EITC with minimum wages is especially notable given that some economic research suggests that the minimum wage is not terribly effective at reducing poverty, especially for single mothers (Sabia 2008). These results are also notable as some favor expanding the EITC as an alternative to the minimum wage. This is partly because most working single mothers already earned wages above state and federal minimum wages.

Beyond the EITC, scholars have studied welfare-to-work programs and welfare reform's effects on employment (e.g., Autor and Houseman 2006). One of the emphases of welfare reform was to force low-income single mothers into the workforce. Of course, low-income single mothers were already working in large numbers (Blank 1997). Yet, welfare reform added incentives, required employment and training, and occasionally offered supportive social services. What were the effects of these changes? There is some evidence that welfare reform encouraged employment (Autor and Houseman 2006; Cheng 2007). However, in contrast to the rhetoric of proponents of welfare reform, the results were modest. Other factors, like the expansion of EITC and the booming

1990s economy, were much more important than welfare reform to single-mother employment (Noonan, Smith, and Corcoran 2007). Although it appears that the employer-subsidies of welfare reform contributed to short-term improvements in labor market outcomes, there is little evidence of sustained benefits (Hamersma 2008). Moreover, the restrictive aspects of TANF probably increased working poverty (Cheng 2007). Even though employment might have increased, it was often low-wage jobs that failed to pay sustainable wages. Further, though employment-based programs were most successful in encouraging employment for the most disadvantaged families, those families also suffered from worse mental health and well-being (Alderson et al. 2008).

6 CHILD POLICY

As noted in Table 32.1, with both the official and LIS measures of poverty, children are much more likely to be poor than working-aged adults. For the most part, the literature on child-centered social policies related to poverty breaks down into two areas: child care and child support. We begin with child support. A number of scholars have argued that child support is a key and increasingly important source of income for low-income families (Cancian and Meyer 2006; Waldfogel 2009). Beginning in the 1980s, scholars and policy makers began to pay more attention to the financial support provided by noncustodial parents. The timing of this partly reflected a cultural shift that problematized the frequent absence of support from noncustodial fathers. However, interest in enforcing child-support orders and collecting child-support payments also reflected the increasing attention of governors and states to share the costs of supporting low-income families (Katz 2001). The attention to child support grew even further as it was often linked to states' TANF programs after welfare reform. Most states required that child support paid on behalf of TANF participants be used to offset their TANF benefits and child social services (Cancian, Meyer, and Caspar 2008). Overall, child support seems to somewhat reduce poverty, particularly when it is strictly enforced. Benefits of the increased enforcement of child support and its link to TANF include more quickly established paternity, the increased likelihood of payment by noncustodial fathers, and the receipt of child support by custodial families (Cancian et al. 2008).

Of course, not all aspects of the emphasis on child support have reduced child poverty. Once child support is established, noncustodial fathers' support tends to remain fixed even when fathers' earnings improve (Ha, Cancian, and Meyer 2010). Mothers often have very little knowledge about the rules regarding the interaction of child support, TANF, and other programs (Meyer, Caspian, and Nam 2007). If participants' knowledge had been greater, program impacts likely would have been larger (Meyer et al. 2007). Finally, one counterproductive unanticipated consequence has been that parents of children on TANF have an incentive to avoid formal child support (Roff 2010). States typically limit the amount of formal child support they will disregard before families' TANF benefits are reduced. Although policies vary by state, any child support paid above a certain limit to families also receiving TANF can be retained by the state to recoup program costs. As a result, stricter enforcement of child support has probably encouraged custodial and noncustodial parents into informal arrangements, which do not seem to be as reliable or beneficial for children (Roff 2010).

Beyond child support, there has been less literature on child care, child-care subsidies, and early childhood education. These programs have become increasingly important for poverty since the 1996 welfare reform. This is because mothers' employment is taken for granted and even required for many programs, especially TANF. It is clear that there remains a gap between the need/demand for work-family policies and the private provision of such policies, and this is especially consequential to low-wage workers and single mothers (Waldfogel 2009). For instance, marginal workers—especially those with less education and in smaller firms—are less likely to have access to parental leave, dependent-care benefits, and child care. It seems quite clear that publicly-provided child care would support employment and make a sizable difference to low-income families (Waldfogel 2009). For instance, Ha (2009) provides convincing evidence that child-care subsidies raise mothers' earnings (also Tekin 2007). Perhaps one of the more successful programs to curb poverty and its consequences on children is Head Start. Head Start benefits children's learning, but it also functions as a form of partial child care for some low-income preschool children (Conley 2010). Therefore, substantial expansions of child care and early child education would enhance many aspects of low-income families' well-being.

7 "Moving to Opportunity" and Housing

Since at least Wilson (1987), neighborhood effects have been one of the most widely studied aspects of poverty. The theory was that concentrated inner-city poverty triggered a host of social ills. Even net of individual characteristics, children exposed to such neighborhood effects were more likely to drop out of high school, commit crimes, have a teen pregnancy, and generally have worse life chances. Inspired by the scholarship on neighborhood effects, scholars and the federal government led a major experimental study on housing and neighborhoods called "Moving to Opportunity" (MTO).

If the U.S. social policy and poverty literature in the 1990s and early 2000s was led by studies of welfare reform, the subsequent period was led by MTO. Moving to Opportunity was a bold, innovative, and extremely expensive policy intervention designed to assess the consequences of neighborhood poverty (e.g. Katz, King, and Liebman 2001). Moving to Opportunity was based in Baltimore, Boston, Chicago, Los Angeles, and New York, and focused on low-income families with children who lived in concentrated poor neighborhoods. Families volunteered for a program and were then randomly assigned to one of three groups. Some were given Section 8 vouchers, others were provided with a more elaborate treatment involving housing-search assistance and life-skills counseling, and a third group served as the control group. Families receiving Section 8 vouchers and the stronger treatment were required to move to neighborhoods with less than 10 percent poverty. Evaluations of MTO demonstrate that neighborhood poverty has sizable effects on adolescent violent criminal behavior and mental health (e.g. Ludwig, Duncan, and Hirschfield 2001).

Nevertheless, some read the MTO literature as failing to provide compelling evidence of neighborhood effects on life chances, especially adult economic outcomes (Lundquist-Clampet and Massey 2008; Wilson 2009). Such critics note that the treatment was rather weak, because families typically moved to racially segregated neighborhoods that were only modestly less poor than the neighborhoods they left. Additionally, there was considerable selectivity in volunteering, the compliance rates were not ideal, and many families were transient in the new neighborhoods. Among African Americans, there was no statistically significant difference in the racial composition or poverty of neighborhoods for treatment and Section 8 groups (Clark 2008). Thus, one might ask whether the very high costs of the demonstration were justified given questions about design and execution. Proponents of MTO counter that it was not a weak intervention because it produced significant changes in neighborhood environments, and it resulted in significant and positive effects on some outcomes, such as improving the mental health and reducing the arrests of young females (Ludwig et al. 2008). Finally, Ludwig and colleagues (2008) argue that MTO still provides more convincing evidence than observational studies.

In our judgment, there are legitimate concerns with the quality of evidence produced by MTO. It seems most appropriate to read the evidence as lacking definitiveness for evaluating neighborhood effects (Wilson 2009). Further, MTO cannot speak to the intergenerational and long-term effects of spells of residence in concentrated poor neighborhoods (Sharkey 2008). Still, MTO provides appropriate moderation to the enormous attention that neighborhood effects have received in the poverty literature. MTO should encourage scholars to move beyond neighborhood effects and explore a broader variety of sources and consequences of poverty.

Beyond MTO, scholars have studied various housing programs for the poor. Public housing has often been criticized in the United States and, on balance, low-income public housing residents sometimes have worse outcomes than similar low-income private housing residents (e.g. Aratani 2005; Fertig and Reingold 2007). Yet, the adverse consequences of public housing appear to be fairly small (e.g. Reingold, Van Ryzin, and Ronda 2001). Identifying the causal effects of public housing is quite difficult because there are selection effects into public housing. It could be that people with certain personal characteristics (e.g., depression) are more likely to end up in public housing, and it could be that such personal characteristics—rather than public housing itself—that explain the adverse consequences. Some seeking to rigorously identify the causal effect of public housing have concluded that public housing has no effect on employment outcomes (Newman, Holupka, and Harkness 2009). Others find that public housing effectively reduces hardship for the poor (Berger et al. 2008). For instance, Carlson and colleagues

(2011) evaluate a broad set of outcomes (e.g., children's health, education, and criminal behaviors) of the Section 8 program and conclude that the program is both effective and efficient. Further, there is convincing evidence that low-income housing assistance does reduce the odds that low-income families become homeless (Fertig and Reingold 2008).

8 Food and Health Programs

Two of the key outcomes of poverty are food insecurity and poor health. When family income declines, worse health and insufficient food and nutrition often result (see, e.g., Duncan et al. 1998; Korenman and Miller 1997; McLeod and Shanahan 1993). As a result, scholars have studied programs designed to improve the health and nutrition of the poor. Arguably, food and health programs have become even more important as traditional cash-assistance programs like TANF have declined. Even though TANF rolls declined after welfare reform, food-stamp rolls spiked upward and reached a historic high in 2009 (Danziger 2010). In addition, food security and health most likely cause and are caused by poverty (e.g., through employment).

A number of scholars have investigated whether programs like Food Stamps and Women, Infants and Children (WIC) improve food security. For some time, there has been concern with the apparent finding that families receiving Food Stamps tend to be more food insecure than families not receiving Food Stamps. However, recent, more rigorous comparisons show that this "food insecurity paradox hinges on assumptions about the data that are not supported by the previous food stamp participation literature" (Gundersen and Kreider 2008, 352). Rather, recent studies show that the receipt of Food Stamps makes a difference and improves the well-being of low-income families. For instance, Bartfield and Dunifon (2006) find that interstate variation in food security can partly be explained by the availability and accessibility of federal nutrition assistance programs.

Since 1996, scholars have debated whether welfare reform led to worse health and health behaviors for the poor. The evidence is mixed, as some show that welfare reform did not alter health behaviors (Kaestner and Tarlov 2006), whereas others emphasize the precarious health of the poor and the limited access to health care of poor and near-poor families (Seccombe and Hoffman 2007). For instance, the poor are less likely to have sufficient health insurance, to be able to afford health care (including preventative health care), and to reside proximate to health care providers. Nevertheless, more pronounced is that the poverty and welfare literatures have tended to neglect health outcomes. As mentioned earlier, the poverty literature emerged from the 1990s with a consensus that poverty worsened health. Yet, since then, there have been important innovations in social policy, including the extension of the State Children's Health Insurance Program (SCHIP). Unfortunately, few have studied whether and how such policies affect the well-being of low-income families. Moreover, there has not been nearly as much research on Medicaid as there has been on TANF and welfare reform. Arguably, health programs deserve more attention, and more scrutiny of health would appropriately shift poverty scholarship toward well-being instead of welfare rolls (Lichter and Jayakody 2002). Finally, there are strong reasons to argue that reducing poverty could help reduce health-care costs in the long run. With greater economic resources, more families could afford preventative health care that would reduce the need for more expensive health-care interventions later on.

9 CONCLUSION

The literature shows that many social policies effectively reduce poverty. Social insurance has powerful, albeit underappreciated, impacts on poverty. The 1996 welfare reform and the decline of AFDC rolls received much attention. The EITC is a clear success, reducing working poverty and improving the economic resources of low-income families. Child support and child care have expanded as public programs and have at least somewhat improved child well-being. Food and health programs do make a difference, though remain relatively understudied. As noted at the beginning, the major problem is not that social policies have been counterproductive or have failed. Rather, the real problem is that social policies for the poor remain underdeveloped and incomplete. The enormity of the social problem of widespread and deep U.S. poverty swamps the federal and state government attempts to address the problem.

As noted earlier, the literature still relies on the flawed official U.S. measure of poverty. Thus, one simple way for U.S. poverty scholarship to improve would be to move away from the official measure. Relative measures of poverty, material deprivation, well-being, and social exclusion would be productive directions for future research.

Despite the problems of the official measure, the main limitation of the literature is that it concentrates exclusively on the United States. For the most part, the literature examines only the United States and rarely even cites studies about or from other countries. As Smeeding and colleagues (2001, 162) remark, the U.S. poverty literature, "rests on an inherently parochial foundation, for it is based on the experiences of only one nation." The focus on the United States would be reasonable if the United States were representative of all affluent democracies. However, the United States is actually quite unrepresentative for questions of social policy and poverty. The United States has dramatically higher poverty, and its social policies are much weaker than other affluent democracies (Brady 2009; Brady, Fullerton, and Moren-Cross 2009; Rainwater and Smeeding 2004).

There are at least three problems with this reliance on the U.S. case. First, the U.S. literature samples on the dependent variable. This is a selection bias that occurs when unusual or rare cases are used to make theoretical generalizations. The classic version is when a study examines only cases in which the outcome is present. One cannot discern why some countries have low poverty if one only observes a country with high poverty. The United States is arguably an outlier in poverty, and since at least the 1970s, poverty has always been high (Brady 2009). Partly because the U.S. poverty literature only studies the United States, the literature cannot really explain how or why the United States is unusual.

To illustrate this point, imagine that an individual was randomly assigned to be born in one of 18 affluent democracies circa 2000 (see Brady 2009 for a list of countries). The probability of the poverty rate in the society would be the cross-national mean: 9.6 percent. The United States is an outlier in this distribution with a poverty rate greater than 17 percent. Many affluent democracies accomplish poverty rates near 5 percent, and all other affluent democracies with available data exhibit poverty levels below the United States. Therefore, when we study the United States, we are already choosing an extreme outlier. Much of the literature focuses on groups in the United States that are particularly vulnerable to poverty, for example the unemployed or single mothers. By doing so, the problem of sampling on the dependent variable may be even worse. If one only studies groups with a high likelihood of being poor, one cannot discern how they differ from groups that have a low likelihood of poverty.

Second, focusing on the United States leads to what we call "the fallacy of intractability." As mentioned in the introduction, because poverty has consistently been high in United States, policy makers, the public, and even scholars often presume that antipoverty policies have been unable to overcome this intractable social problem. The conventional wisdom is often pessimistic about what social policy can accomplish. Despite the effectiveness of more generous U.S. states at raising incomes at the bottom of the distribution (Moller 2008), the over-time and cross-state variation in U.S. social policy for the poor is quite small compared to variation among affluent democracies. Incorporating the much larger variation across countries reveals that social policy is very effective in reducing poverty (Brady 2009; Brady et al. 2009). Further, a rich comparative literature shows us that the underdevelopment and incompleteness of U.S. social policy is largely due to political factors like the absence of genuine Leftist parties, the weakness of organized labor, and cultural values favoring free markets and individualism. Therefore, the problem of high U.S. poverty is better understood as due to politics, not policy (Brady 2009; Brady et al. 2010).

Third, by concentrating exclusively on the United States, poverty scholars are unable to contextualize how vulnerabilities are related to poverty. For example, single motherhood is perhaps the most well studied correlate of poverty. The implicit presumption is that this characteristic has a consistent relationship with poverty across space and time. The policy solution obviously is to reduce single motherhood, not weaken the relationship between single motherhood and poverty. Yet as Brady and Burroway (2012) show, single mothers are much more likely to be poor in the United States than in other affluent democracies, and their particularly high poverty should be viewed as unusual, not the norm. Unfortunately, American poverty scholars have inappropriately presumed that single-mother poverty is universal and thus intractable when, in reality, it is quite malleable. To exemplify this problem, American policy scholars have exercised considerable worry over whether AFDC/TANF encourages unmarried births and how to encourage the marriage of low-income unmarried mothers. In contrast, comparative research shows that it would be more effective simply to raise the incomes of single-mother families (Brady and Burroway 2012).

In conclusion, the U.S. social policy and poverty literature has made significant contributions. We have learned a lot about the effectiveness of different social policies and, more broadly, the causes and consequences of poverty. The literature has kept pace with important changes and trends in poverty. What have been lacking are a comparative perspective and a better appreciation of how unusual and unrepresentative the U.S. case is. For poverty and social policy scholarship in the United States to advance, there is a significant need for greater integration of the comparative social policy and international poverty/inequality literatures.

NOTES

1. We report 2007 rates because that is the most recent year for which Luxembourg Income Study data are available for the United States. The official U.S. measure is calculated based on various thresholds for pretax income, while factoring in household size and composition. For example, for a family of four, the threshold in 2007 was $21,100–$21,736 and for a family of two, it was $12,550-$14,291.
2. Of course, this raises concerns about efficiency. Encompassing social insurance programs are quite expensive—and increasingly so with growing elderly populations and declining fertility. There is some literature on the trade-offs between efficiency and equality, however much of that literature remains quite descriptive. There is a need for further research on how egalitarianism affects efficiency and economic performance across affluent democracies, which often have quite different market institutions along with more generous social policies than the United States.
3. New Hope was a demonstration project conducted in two inner-city Milwaukee areas from 1994 through 1998. The project offered low-income people who were willing to work full-time a variety of benefits (e.g., an earnings supplement, subsidized health insurance and child care, etc.) for three years.

REFERENCES

* Indicates recommended reading.

Alderson, D. P., Lisa A. Gennetian, Chantelle J. Dowsett, Amy Imes, and Aletha C. Huston. 2008. "Effects of Employment-Based Programs on Families by Prior Levels of Disadvantage." *Social Service Review* 82:361–394.

Aratani, Yumiko. 2005. "Public Housing Revisited: Racial Differences, Housing Assistance, and Socioeconomic Attainment Among Low-Income Families." *Social Science Research* 39:1108–1125.

Autor, David, and Susan Houseman. 2006. "Temporary Agency Employment: A Way Out of Poverty?" In Rebecca M. Blank, Sheldon H. Danziger, and Robert F. Schoeni, eds., *Working and Poor*. New York: Sage, 312–337.

Bartfield, Judi, and Rachel Dunifon. 2006. "State-Level Predictors of Food Insecurity Among Households with Children." *Journal of Policy Analysis and Management* 25:921–942.

Béland, Daniel. 2007. "The Social Exclusion Discourse: Ideas and Policy Change." *Policy & Politics* 35:123–139.

Berger, Lawrence M., Theresa Heintze, Wendy B. Naidich and Marcia K. Meyers. 2008. "Subsidized Housing and Household Hardship Among Low-Income Single Mother Households." *Journal of Marriage and Family* 70:934–949.

Blank, Rebecca M. 2008. "Presidential Address: How to Improve Poverty Measurement in the United States." *Journal of Policy Analysis and Management* 27:233–254.

Blank, Rebecca M. 1997. *It Takes a Nation.* Princeton, NJ: Princeton University Press.

Brady, David. 2003. "Rethinking the Sociological Measurement of Poverty." *Social Forces* 81:715–752.

Brady, David. 2004. "Reconsidering the Divergence Between Elderly, Child and Overall Poverty." *Research on Aging* 26:487–510.

*Brady, David. 2009. *Rich Democracies, Poor People: How Politics Explain Poverty.* New York: Oxford University Press.

Brady, David, and Rebekah Burroway. 2012. "Targeting, Universalism and Single Mother Poverty: A Multi-Level Analysis Across 18 Affluent Democracies." *Demography* 49:719–746.

Brady, David, Andrew Fullerton, and Jennifer Moren-Cross. 2009. "Putting Poverty in Political Context: A Multi-Level Analysis of Adult Poverty Across 18 Affluent Western Democracies." *Social Forces* 88:271–300.

Bruch, Sarah K., Myra Marx Feree, and Joe Soss. 2010. "From Policy to Polity: Democracy, Paternalism, and the Incorporation of Disadvantaged Citizens." *American Sociological Review* 75:205–226.

Cancian, Maria, and Daniel R. Meyer. 2006. "Child Support and the Economy". In Rebecca M. Blank, Sheldon H. Danziger, and Robert F. Schoeni, eds., *Working and Poor* 338–365. New York: Sage.

Cancian, Maria, Daniel R. Meyer, and Emma Caspar. 2008. "Welfare and Child Support: Complements, Not Substitutes." *Journal of Policy Analysis and Management* 27:354–375.

Carlson, Deven, Robert Haveman, Thomas Kaplan, and Barbara Wolfe. 2011. "The Benefits and Costs of the Section 8 Housing Subsidy Program: A Framework and Estimates of First-Year Effects." *Journal of Policy Analysis and Management* 30:233–255.

Cheng, Tyrone. 2007. "How Is "Welfare-to-Work" Shaped by Contingencies of Economy, Welfare Policy and Human Capital?" *International Journal Social Welfare* 16:212–219.

Citro, Constance, and Robert T. Michael. 1995. *Measuring Poverty: A New Approach* Washington, DC: National Academy Press.

Clark, William A.V. 2008. "Reimagining the Moving to Opportunity Study and Its Contribution to Changing the Distribution of Poverty and Ethnic Concentration." *Demography* 45:515–535.

Conley, Amy. 2010. "Childcare: Welfare or Investment?" *International Journal of Social Welfare* 19:173–181.

Danielson, Caroline, and Jacob Alex Klerman. 2008. "Did Welfare Reform Cause the Caseload Decline?" *Social Service Review* 82:703–730.

*Danziger, Sandra K. 2010. "The Decline of Cash Welfare and Implications for Social Policy and Poverty." *Annual Review of Sociology* 36:523–545.

Duncan, Greg J., W. Jean Yeung, Jeane Brooks-Gunn, and Judith R. Smith. 1998. "How Much Does Childhood Poverty Affect the Life Chances of Children?" *American Sociological Review* 63:406–423.

600 DAVID BRADY AND LANE M. DESTRO

Fertig, Angela R., and David A. Reingold. 2008. "Homelessness Among At-Risk Families with Children in Twenty American Cities." *Social Service Review* 82: 485–510.

Fertig, Angela R., and David A. Reingold. 2007. "Public Housing, Health, and Health Behaviors: Is There a Connection?" *Journal of Policy Analysis and Management* 26:831–860.

Fording, Richard, Joe Soss, and Sanford Schram. 2011. "Race and the Local Politics of Punishment in the New World of Welfare." *American Journal of Sociology* 116:1610–1657.

Gassman-Pines, Anna, and Hirokazu Yoshikawa. 2006. "Five-Year Effects of an Anti-Poverty Program on Marriage among Never-Married Mothers." *Journal of Policy Analysis and Management* 25:11–30.

Graefe, Deborah Roempke, and Daniel T. Lichter. 2008. "Marriage Patterns among Unwed Mothers: Before and After PRWORA." *Journal of Policy Analysis and Management* 27:479–497.

Gundersen, Craig, and Brent Kreider. 2008. "Food Stamps and Food Insecurity: What Can Be Learned in the Presence of Nonclassical Measurement Error?" *Journal of Human Resources* 43:352–382.

Ha, Yoonsook. 2009. "Stability of Child-Care Subsidy Use and Earnings of Low-Income Families." *Social Service Review* 83:495–525.

Ha, Yoonsook, Maria Cancian, and Daniel R. Meyer. 2010. "Unchanging Child Support Orders in the Face of Unstable Earnings." *Journal of Policy Analysis and Management* 29:799–820.

Hamersma, Sarah. 2008. "The Effects of an Employer Subsidy on Employment Outcomes: A Study of the Work Opportunity and Welfare-to-Work Tax Credits." *Journal of Policy Analysis and Management* 27:498–520.

Herbst, Chris M. 2008. "Do Social Policy Reforms Have Different Impacts on Employment and Welfare Use as Economic Conditions Change?" *Journal of Policy Analysis and Management* 27:867–894.

Hirasuna, Donald P., and Thomas F. Stinson. 2007. "Earned Income Credit Utilization by Welfare Recipients: A Case Study of Minnesota's Earned Income Credit Program." *Journal of Policy Analysis and Management* 26:125–148.

Kaestner, Robert, and Elizabeth Tarlov. 2006. "Changes in the Welfare Caseload and the Health of Low-Educated Mothers." *Journal of Policy Analysis and Management* 25:623–643.

Katz, Lawrence F., Jeffrey Kling, and Jeffrey Liebman. 2001. "Moving to Opportunity in Boston: Early Results of a Randomized Mobility Experiment." *Quarterly Journal of Economics* 116: 607–654.

Katz, Michael B. 1989. *The Undeserving Poor.* New York: Pantheon.

*Katz, Michael B. 2001. *The Price of Citizenship* New York: Henry Holt.

Korenman, Sanders, and Jane E. Miller. 1997. "Effects of Long-Term Poverty on Physical Health of Children in the National Longitudinal Survey of Youth". In G. J. Duncan and J. Brooks-Gunn, eds., *Consequences of Growing Up Poor.* New York: Sage, 70–99.

Levine, Phillip B. 2006. "Unemployment Insurance Over the Business Cycle: Does It Meet the Needs of Less-Skilled Workers." In Rebecca M. Blank, Sheldon H. Danziger, and Robert F. Schoeni, eds., *Working and Poor.* New York: Sage, 366–395.

*Lichter, Daniel T., and Rukamalie Jayakody. 2002. "Welfare Reform: How Do We Measure Success?" *Annual Review of Sociology* 28:117–141.

Lim, Younghee, Claudia J. Coulton, and Nina Lalich. 2009. "State TANF Policies and Employment Outcomes Among Welfare Leavers." *Social Service Review* 83:525–555.

*Ludwig, Jens, Greg J. Duncan, and Paul Hirschfield. 2001. "Urban Poverty and Juvenile Crime: Evidence from a Randomized Housing-Mobility Experiment." *Quarterly Journal of Economics* 116:655–679.

Ludwig, Jens, Jeffrey Liebman, Jeffrey Kling, Greg Duncan, Lawrence Katz, Ronald, Kessler, and Lisa Sanbonmatsu. 2008. "What Can We Learn about Neighborhood Effects from the Moving to Opportunity Experiment?" *American Journal of Sociology* 114:144–188.

Lundquist-Clampet, Susan, and Douglas Massey. 2008. "Neighborhood Effects on Economic Self-Sufficiency: A Reconsideration of the Moving to Opportunity Experiment". *American Journal of Sociology* 114:107–143. Luxembourg Income Study (LIS) Database, http://www.lisdatacenter.org. Luxembourg: LIS.

Marlier, Eric, and A. B. Atkinson. 2010. "Indicators of Poverty and Social Exclusion in a Global Context." *Journal of Policy Analysis and Management* 29:285–304.

Meyer, Daniel R., Maria Caspian, and Kisun Nam. 2007. "Welfare and Child Support Program Knowledge Gaps Reduce Program Effectiveness." *Journal of Policy Analysis and Management* 26:575–597.

McLeod, Jane D., and Michael Shanahan. 1993. "Poverty, Parenting, and Children's Mental Health." *American Sociological Review* 58:351–366.

Moffitt, Robert. 2008. "A Primer on Welfare Reform." *Focus* 26:15–25.

Moller, Stephanie. 2008. "The State and Structural Vulnerability: Policy Egalitarianism and Household Income." *Research in Social Stratification and Mobility* 26:323–340.

Myles, John, and Paul Pierson. 1997. "Friedman's Revenge: The Reform of 'Liberal' Welfare States in Canada and the United States." *Politics & Society* 25:443–472.

Neumark, David, and William Wascher. 2011. "Does a Higher Minimum Wage Enhance the Effectiveness of the Earned Income Tax Credit?" *Industrial and Labor Relations Review* 64:712–746.

Newman, Sandra, C. Scott Holupka, and Joseph Harkness. 2009. "The Long-Term Effects of Housing Assistance on Work and Welfare." *Journal of Policy Analysis and Management* 28:81–101.

Nolan, Brian, and Christopher T. Whelan. 2010. "Using Non-Monetary Deprivation Indicators to Analyze Poverty and Social Exclusion: Lessons from Europe?" *Journal of Policy Analysis and Management* 29:305–325.

Noonan, Mary, Sandra Smith, and Mary Corcoran. 2007. "Examining the Impact of Welfare Reform, Labor Market Conditions, and the Earned Income Tax Credit on the Employment of Black and White Single Mothers." *Social Science Research* 36:95–130.

*O'Connor, Alice. 2001. *Poverty Knowledge* Princeton, NJ: Princeton University Press.

Parish, Susan L., Roderick A. Rose, and Megan E. Andrews. 2009. "Income Poverty and Material Hardship Among U.S. Women with Disabilities." *Social Service Review* 83:33–52.

*Rainwater, Lee, and Timothy M. Smeeding. 2004. *Poor Kids in a Rich Country: America's Children in Comparative Perspective*, New York: Sage.

Reingold, David, Maureen Pirog, and David Brady. 2007. "Empirical Evidence on Faith Based Organizations in an Era of Welfare Reform." *Social Service Review* 81:245–283.

Reingold, David, Gregg G. Van Ryzin, and Michelle Ronda. 2001. "Does Urban Public Housing Diminish the Social Capital and Labor Force Activity of Its Tenants?" *Journal of Policy Analysis and Management* 20:485–504.

Roff, Jennifer. 2010. "Welfare, Child Support, and Strategic Behavior: Do High Orders and Low Disregards Discourage Child Support Awards?" *Journal of Human Resources* 45:59–86.

Sabia, Joseph J. 2008. "Minimum Wages and the Economic Well-Being of Single Mothers." *Journal of Policy Analysis and Management* 27:848–866.

Shaefer, H. Luke, and Liyun Wu. 2011. "Unemployment Insurance and Low-Educated, Single, Working Mothers Before and After Welfare Reform." *Social Service Review* 85:205–228.

Scholz, John Karl, Robert Moffitt, and Benjamin Cowan. 2009. "Trends in Income Support." In M. Cancian and S. Danziger, eds., *Changing Poverty, Changing Policies*. New York: Sage, 203–241.

*Schram, Sanford F., Joe Soss, Richard C. Fording, and Linda Houser. 2009. "Deciding to Discipline: Race, Choice, and Punishment at the Frontlines of Welfare Reform." *American Sociological Review* 74:398–422.

Seccombe, Karen, and Kim A. Hoffman. 2007. *Just Don't Get Sick: Access to Health Care in the Aftermath of Welfare Reform*. New Brunswick, NJ: Rutgers University Press.

Seefeldt, Kristin. 2008. *Working After Welfare: How Women Balance Jobs and Family in the Wake of Welfare Reform*. Kalamazoo, MI.: W.E. Upjohn Institute for Employment Research.

Sen, Amartya. 1999. *Development as Freedom*. New York: Anchor Books.

Sharkey, Patrick. 2008. "The Intergenerational Transmission of Context." *American Journal of Sociology* 113:931–969.

Short, Kathleen S. 2011. "The Supplemental Poverty Measure: Examining the Incidence and Depth of Poverty in the U.S. Taking Account of Taxes and Transfers." Paper presented at the 86th Annual Conference of the Western Economic Association.

Silver, Hilary. 1994. "Social Exclusion and Social Solidarity: Three Paradigms." *International Labour Review* 133:531–578.

Smeeding, Timothy M., Lee Rainwater, and Gary Burtless. 2001. "U.S. Poverty in Cross-National Context." In S. Danziger and R. Haveman, eds., *Understanding Poverty*. New York and Cambridge, MA: Sage and Harvard University Press, 162–189.

Tekin, Erdal. 2007. "Child Care Subsidies, Wages and the Employment of Single Mothers." *Journal of Human Resources* 42:453–487.

U.S. Census Bureau. *Current Population Survey, 2007 and 2008 Annual Social and Economic Supplements*. http://www.census.gov/cps/.

Waldfogel, Jane. 2009. "The Role of Family Policies in Antipoverty Policy." In M. Cancian and S. Danziger, eds., *Changing Poverty, Changing Policies*. New York: Russell Sage, 242–265.

Watkins-Hayes, Celeste. 2009 *The New Welfare Bureaucrats*. Chicago: University of Chicago Press.

Wilson, William Julius. 1987. *The Truly Disadvantaged*. Chicago: University of Chicago Press.

Wilson, William Julius. 2009. *More Than Just Race*. New York: W.W. Norton.

Wood, Robert G., Quinn Moore, and Anu Rangarajan. 2008. "Two Steps Forward, One Step Back: The Uneven Economic Progress of TANF Recipients." *Social Service Review* 82:3–28.

Ziliak, James P., David N. Figlio, Elizabeth E. Davis, and Laura S. Connolly. 2000. "Accounting for the Decline in AFDC Caseloads: Welfare Reform or the Economy?" *Journal of Human Resources* 35:570–586.

CHAPTER 33

....

INEQUALITY

....

STEPHANIE MOLLER AND JOYA MISRA

1 INTRODUCTION

....

INEQUALITY reflects disparities in the income and assets held by members of society. A society with high levels of equality would be one in which all members have similar opportunities to achieve preferred outcomes. Yet, in most countries, life chances and outcomes vary by the class status in which one is born, by gender, by race, ethnicity, or nationality, as well as by other statuses such as age, ability, and sexuality. Via the mechanism of social policy, the state plays a central role in redistributing resources to ensure greater equality or at least increased opportunities for members of disadvantaged groups. Yet, as Gøsta Esping-Andersen (1990, 23) cogently argues, "The welfare state is not just a mechanism that intervenes in, and possibly corrects, the structure of inequality; it is, in its own right, a system of stratification. It is an active force in the structuring of social relations."

This chapter considers how the U.S. welfare state redistributes incomes through social policies. These policies may not only correct inequality, but reinforce stratification, as suggested by Esping-Andersen. Social policies reflect and reinforce existing ideas about the nature of inequality, and the potential for state intervention to correct it. For example, the foundation of the U.S. welfare state is economic liberalism, because policies are designed to complement free-market capitalism. In this context, individuals are expected to be independent workers, and most social-welfare programs are designed to complement labor force participation and discourage dependency. Since the U.S. welfare state is built on a liberal economic foundation, the universal social programs tied to citizenship found in many advanced industrialized countries are nearly nonexistent in the United States, with the exception of public education. Instead, eligibility and benefits in most programs are conditioned by employment and wages. As a result, inequities found in the labor market, including employment opportunities and wage inequalities, are not only corrected but may also be reinforced by the U.S. welfare state. Furthermore, the United States directs less toward public social spending, with even means-tested programs providing less generous benefits than those found in other countries, which has important implications for inequality (Gordon 1994; Lieberman 2001; Mink 1995; Quadagno 1990, 1994, 2000).

Given the importance of cross-national research to understanding inequality in the United States, we will begin by comparing inequality in the United States to other advanced industrialized countries. We will then present data on inequality in the United States by race and gender. Finally, we will discuss how specific policies alter levels of inequality by redistributing income or institutionalizing sources of income inequality.

2 U.S. INCOME INEQUALITY IN CROSS-NATIONAL CONTEXT

It is well-established that the United States has higher income inequality than other advanced industrialized nations. Our focus is on inequality at the household level, so we examine welfare-state interventions that target households. This is illustrated in Figure 33.1, which presents—in U.S. dollars—market-based income (including wages and salaries, interest and dividends, and income from properties) and post-tax-and-transfer income (including welfare-state interventions such as taxes and social policy transfers to individuals and families) across countries. For every country, light grey reflects market income and dark grey represents post-tax-and-transfer income. The upper and lower dots reflect income for the 95th and 5th percentiles of each country's income distribution, whereas the shaded region represents the range between the 25th percentile and the 75th percentile (the interquartile range).

Focusing on the interquartile range, market income (the light grey box) is more unevenly distributed in all countries than post-tax-and-transfer income (the dark gray box). It is interesting to consider how many economies generate earnings inequalities. Yet, most economies do a better job of reducing inequality through their tax-and-transfer policies. The United States exhibits the highest levels of inequality in both market income and post-tax-and-transfer income, but what is exceptional about the United States is truly how much less redistributive the welfare state is. English-speaking countries have the greatest dispersion of post-tax-and-transfer income, whereas Scandinavian countries have the smallest dispersion. Additionally, comparing the change in income at the 5th percentile (the bottom dot) from market income to post-tax-and-transfer income reveals that the U.S. welfare state is less successful at buttressing the incomes of the lowest segment of the income distribution through taxes and transfers than most other countries.

Focusing solely on post-tax-and-transfer income (the dark gray bar), median income is slightly higher in the United States than most other countries. Yet, individuals in the 25th percentile of the income distribution in the United States are worse off than individuals in the 25th percentiles in Norway, Austria, and Switzerland; their income is nearly identical to their equivalents in Denmark and Canada. The 75th percentile in the United States, however, has much higher income than the 75th percentile in every other

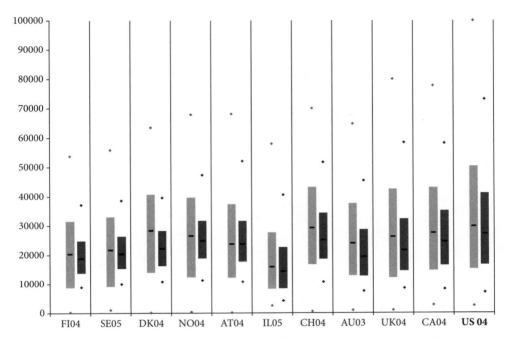

FIG. 33.1 Cross-National Distribution in Market and Disposable Income

Source: LIS Web Tabulator.

country. In fact, individuals in the 75th percentile of the post-tax-and-transfer income distribution in the United States have higher incomes than individuals in the 95th percentile in Finland, Sweden, Denmark, and Israel. Inequality is relatively high in the United States, with individuals in the bottom segment of the U.S. income distribution worse off compared to other advanced industrialized countries presented in Figure 33.1, whereas those at the top are substantially better off.

When considering changes in income inequality over time, the United States has followed the same trend as most advanced industrialized countries, experiencing a decline in income inequality in the early part of the 20th century due to WWI and the Great Depression. These events dramatically reduced the income share of top income earners, resulting in lower inequality across countries (Atkinson, Piketty, and Saez 2009). Since the 1970s, many countries have seen a rise in income inequality (Alderson and Nielsen 2002), but the United States is distinctive in the sharpness of its rise. Figure 33.2 presents income inequality, measured through the Gini index,[1] since the 1980s. United States values are compared to the average levels of inequality in Canada, Denmark, France, Germany, Italy, Netherlands, Spain, Sweden, and the United Kingdom. This figure presents both pre-tax-and-transfer and post-tax-and-transfer inequality. The United States has certainly experienced a sharper increase in post-tax-and-transfer inequality, compared to these other countries (for more detailed comparisons across countries, see Atkinson, Piketty, and Saez 2009; OECD 2012). This sharp rise is partially attributable to limited efforts by the state to redistribute income. Indeed, levels of pre-tax-and-transfer

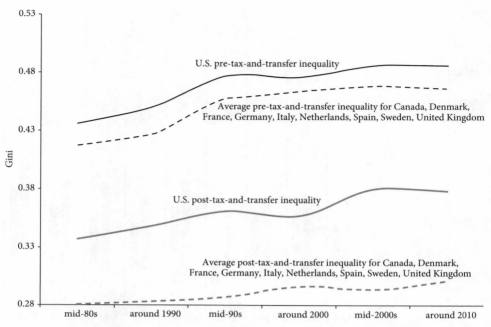

FIG. 33.2 Income Inequality over Time; A Comparison of the United States to Select Advanced Industrialized Countries

Source: OECD 2012.

income inequality in the United States are comparable to other countries over time; it is not until governments intervene with policies and redistributive programs that the United States looks exceptional.

3 INCOME INEQUALITY ACROSS RACE AND GENDER

Although most stratification researchers focus on class inequality, a burgeoning literature examines simultaneously class, race, and gender inequality (Cotter, Hermsen, Vanneman 1999; Acker 2000; McCall 2001; Browne and Misra 2003). Gender inequality is, of course, complicated insofar as women's experiences of inequality are often shaped by the opportunities of the men around them (this is particularly true for heterosexual women, but may also reflect women's relationships with fathers, sons, and other family members). Women, and mothers in particular, face more obstacles to sustained labor force participation because they have more extensive care-work responsibilities, relative to men (Folbre 2002). Social policies play an important role in moderating—or

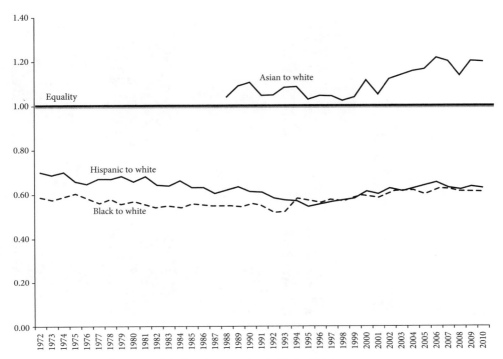

FIG. 33.3 Historic Ratios of Median Income in theUnited States

Source: U.S. Bureau of the Census 2012.

entrenching—gender inequalities, as they may increase opportunities for women workers, ease the burdens of work-family conflicts, or reinforce the male-breadwinner model, which disadvantages many women.

Race, ethnicity, and nationality further intersect with gender and class to shape equality. Some countries, including the United Kingdom and United States, have a long history of discriminatory labor markets and social policies that tend to exclude minority groups (Lewis 2000; Lieberman 2001). Although both men and women of color have been disadvantaged with regards to employment, women of color have historically earned less than men of color (Branch 2011), though currently, U.S. men of color's earnings may be artificially high, because so many men are incarcerated, and, therefore, not included in measures of men's earnings (Western and Pettit 2005). Relative to white women, inequalities may be particularly intense for women of color, who often earn less and have had less access to social welfare benefits (Browne and Misra 2003; Mink 1995; Moller 2002).

When examining inequality within the United States by race and ethnicity, clear patterns emerge. Figure 33.3 presents ratios of median income for Asian to white, Hispanic to white, and black to white families. A value of 1 represents pure equality. This figure illustrates that Asian families have higher median income than white families (falling above 1.0), although this is not true for all Asian families; for example, immigrants

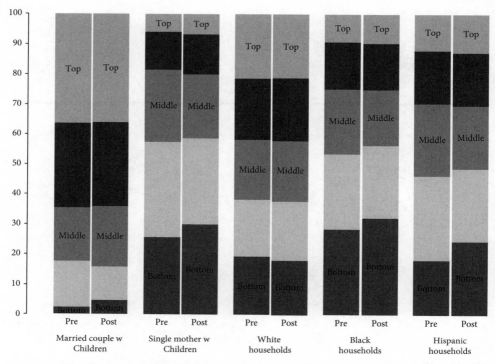

FIG. 33.4 Distribution of Households across Quintiles of the Income Distribution for Pre-Tax-and-Transfer Income and Post-Tax-and-Transfer Income by Family Structure and Income.

Source: U.S. Dept. of Labor 2009.

from Southeast Asia experience high unemployment, lower incomes, and high rates of poverty (Segal et al. 2002). In contrast, Hispanic and black families have lower median income relative to white families, and there has been little change over time. Median income for black families is consistently about 60 percent of median income for white families.

To further illustrate the effectiveness of U.S. social policy by race, class, gender, and family type, Figure 33.4 presents the extent to which taxes and transfers in the United States alter income inequality. This figure presents the percentage of households that fall in each quintile of the income distribution when considering pre-tax-and-transfer income (pre) and post-tax-and-transfer income (post). For married couple households with children, there is little difference between their distribution in the pre-tax-and-transfer and post-tax-and-transfer income distributions. Median post-tax-and-transfer income is slightly higher than median pre-tax-and-transfer income (at $50,536 versus $42,855, data not shown); yet the distribution around the median is comparable. When considering gender inequality, scholars have argued that a clear indication of gender equality is the ability of women to form and maintain autonomous households (Orloff 1993). Yet, single mothers have limited ability to maintain economically stable autonomous households in the United States. Sixty percent of single-mother households fall in the bottom two quintiles of the income distribution and close to 30 percent fall in the bottom quintile. In addition, *after* taxes and transfers are added to income, a larger percentage of single mother households fall at the bottom of the income distribution and a smaller percentage fall in the middle of the income distribution—suggesting that taxes and transfers exacerbate gender inequality.

A similar trend is found when examining racial inequality. White households have slightly lower inequality post-tax-and-transfer (compared to pre-tax-and-transfer), because they are less likely to fall in the bottom quintile and more likely to fall in the middle quintile once taxes and transfers are added to income. In contrast, both black and Hispanic households are more likely to fall in the bottom quintile of the income distribution (and less likely to fall in the middle) once taxes and transfers are incorporated in income. Clearly, the U.S. welfare state exacerbates racial and ethnic inequalities. Although transfer programs including TANF, Food Stamps, Medicaid, and other programs are targeted to poor families, inequality by family structure and race are actually worse once the full complement of tax and transfer programs are included.

4 Social Policy Strategies and Inequality

Are these differences in inequality across demographic groups explained by differences in policy strategies? Figures 33.1, 33.2, and 33.4 suggest that policy strategies do matter, since there are recognizable differences across countries and demographic groups in the extent to which governments redistribute income. This is most visible by examining the change in the distribution of income between market income and post-tax-and-transfer income.

How policy strategies matter has generated an extensive amount of research. Indeed, researchers have found that there are multiple paths through which welfare states can alter inequality. Tax and transfer policies, such as family allowances, pensions, and unemployment benefits, define the minimal economic standard of living for particular groups in a country. Work-family policies such as family leave and child care help parents, and mothers in particular, have children while also maintaining economic security through labor-force participation. Finally, health-care policies offer citizens access to health care and insurance, helping to lessen the economic implications of poor health.

The United States trails most countries on the availability or generosity of these policies. Table 33.1 presents country rankings on policies that are associated with lower levels of inequality cross-nationally. Beginning with social transfers, extensive research has found that taxes and transfers reduce inequality (Bradley et al. 2003; Hicks and

Table 33.1 Country Rankings on Generosity of Various Policy Measures and on the Gini Index, Circa 2004

	Family Allowances[a]	Pensions[b]	Unemployment Benefits[c]	Parental Leave Weeks	Parental Leave Generosity[e]	Public Child Care, 0.2[f]	Public Child Care, 3.6[f]	Health Care[d]	h
Sweden	9	13	14	8	2	1	7	3	1 (.23)
Finland	8	5	12	13	7	3	10	10	2 (.25)
Luxembourg	3	1	1	15	4	6	13	1	3 (.26)
Austria	2	2	5	7	9	11	6	8	4 (.27)
Czech Republic	15	6	10	1	5	15	4	2	4 (.27)
Netherlands	12	14	4	17	11	2	3	16	6 (.28)
France	6	8	5	3	3	4	1	5	7 (.29)
Germany	6	9	2	1	8	13	7	6	7 (.29)
Hungary	5	6	7	6	1	10	5	11	7 (.29)
Ireland	4	16	15	16	11	7	14	6	10 (.31)
Australia	1	18	17	9	11	7	18	15	11 (.32)
Canada	12	10	7	10	6	9	12	13	11 (.32)
Spain	17	3	3	4	11	15	10	12	11 (.32)
UK	9	12	18	14	11	17	9	4	14 (.33)
Italy	15	4	11	12	10	12	2	8	15 (.35)
Poland	14	14	16	5	11	18	17	14	15 (.35)
Israel	9	17	9	10	11	5	4	17	17 (.38)
United States	18	11	13	18	11	14	14	18	17 (.38)

[a] Family allowances as a percentage of GDP (OECD 2012)

[b] Public pension net replacement rate, 2011 (OECD 2011)

[c] Net replacement rates for average worker in two – worker family with children in initial stage of unemployment, 2008 (OECD 2012)

[d] Public expenditure on health as a percentage of total expenditures on health (Misra et al. 2012)

[e] Weeks of parental leave multiplied by the wage replacement rate (Misra et al. 2012)

[f] Percent of children (0–2) in public childcare (Misra et al. 2012) g: Percent of children (3–6) in public childcare (Misra et al. 2012)

[h] Gini coefficient in parentheses (OECD 2012)

Kenworthy 2003; Korpi and Palme 1998; Mahler and Jesuit 2006; Wang, Caminada, and Goudswaard 2012)—a 33 percent reduction, on average, across countries (Brandolini and Smeeding 2009). Additionally, countries with generous social spending and progressive tax structures have the largest middle class (Pressman 2009).

The United States falls behind all other wealthy countries on the generosity of transfers (see Table 33.1), in part because the United States primarily relies on taxes and targeted programs, yet even these targeted programs are minimally funded. Temporary Assistance to Needy Families (TANF) is a prime example of the United States' focus on targeted assistance. Rather than providing universal allowances (i.e., cash assistance) to all families with children, the United States provides targeted assistance through TANF that offers limited support to families in poverty who meet certain criteria. If we consider TANF comparable to family allowances, the United States trails all other countries on the generosity of family allowances (See Table 33.1) although the Earned Income Tax Credit, discussed later, also operates as a type of family allowance. TANF replaced an earlier, also targeted assistance program, Aid to Families with Dependent Children (AFDC). Although programs such as AFDC and TANF are not as effective as universal family allowances in reducing poverty (Kenworthy 1999; Christopher 2002; Christopher et al. 2002; Smeeding 2005; Misra et al. 2007a; Misra et al. 2012), they do help to reduce inequality, if only minimally (Danziger, Haveman, and Plotnick 1986; Lobao and Hooks 2003; Moller, Alderson, and Nielsen 2009).

In addition to targeting assistance, the United States relies heavily on taxes, as opposed to transfers, to redistribute income. In fact, in 2007, the United States spent 1.2 percent of its GDP on public benefits to families. Less than 10 percent of this spending was in the form of cash benefits, whereas 45 percent was in the form of tax breaks and another 45 percent was in-kind benefits (e.g., health care). This is a remarkably different composition of spending than found in other countries. For example, Sweden spent 3.1 percent of GDP on public benefits to families in 2007. Of this spending, 40 percent was in the form of cash benefits to families; 60 percent was in-kind benefits; none was in the form of tax breaks to families (OECD 2011b).

One example of the U.S. emphasis on tax breaks is found in the Earned Income Tax Credit (EITC), one of the largest antipoverty cash-assistance programs in the United States. Spending on the EITC outpaces spending on TANF as well as Food Stamps (Hotz and Scholz 2003); some scholars refer to the EITC as the United States' version of family allowances (Kamerman 1998). The EITC was adopted in 1975 and consistently expanded. It provides tax credits to low income and lower-middle-income working families, primarily those with children. The EITC is most supportive of working parents whose jobs withhold taxes and, despite working, are poor. The EITC is less supportive of very poor families, since members of these families often work in jobs that do not withhold taxes; some of the poorest families are also nonworkers and do not qualify for the EITC (Hotz and Scholz 2003). Although some researchers have generally found that cash transfer systems are more redistributive than tax systems (Wang et al. 2012); Meyer and Rosenbaum (2001) suggest that not only is the EITC an effective antipoverty program, but that it has been more successful at stimulating maternal employment than welfare reform (TANF) has been. The EITC is also politically popular, because it only provides benefits for working families (Hotz and Scholz 2003).

The U.S. reliance on tax programs such as the EITC is part of a larger strategy in which cash assistance and other direct forms of social support are eschewed in favor of indirect or hidden programs (Garfinkel, Rainwater, and Smeeding 2006; Mettler 2011). Americans take over $1 trillion in tax credits and tax deductions, including the home mortgage interest deduction, subsidized student loans, tax-exempt health benefits, employer pensions, and other deductions (Howard 1997; Koch and Mettler 2012). The value of these credits is larger than spending on Social Security or Medicare, and they mostly benefit middle class families (Howard 1997; Koch and Mettler 2012). The Child and Dependent Care Tax Credit (CDCTC) and flexible-spending accounts are designed to help families afford child care while working. Yet, these programs, unlike the Earned Income Tax Credit, primarily advantage middle and upper income families (Maag, Rennane, and Steuerle 2011). For example, lower income families should presumably reap the greatest benefits from the CDCTC, because the credit begins phasing out at $15,000, changing from 35 percent of eligible child-care expenses to 20 percent of eligible child-care expenses for families with adjusted gross income above $43,000 (IRS 2011). However, the CDCTC actually benefits individuals in the upper 40 percent of the income distribution the most because these families have the largest child-care expenses. Indeed, the top 40 percent of the income distribution takes 54 percent of CDCTC benefits, compared to 17 percent of individuals in the bottom 40 percent of the income distribution (Maag et al. 2011). Importantly, though, families in the top decile claim less than 1 percent of this benefit. This heavy reliance on hidden programs is one of the reasons inequality is high in the United States (Howard 1997).

Although the United States relies heavily on targeting and taxes to redistribute income, it does offer two fairly generous programs to support the temporarily unemployed and the aged. Unemployment insurance programs aim to protect workers and their families from the vagaries of the labor market and thus help preserve lower levels of inequality. Indeed, although eligibility criteria have tightened across countries in recent years and the extent to which benefits replace wages has become less generous, unemployment insurance continues to play an important role in reducing inequality by buttressing the incomes of the unemployed (Immervoll and Richardson 2011; Kenworthy and Pontusson 2005). Yet, the United States trails most other countries, except the United Kingdom, Ireland, Australia, and Poland, on the generosity of unemployment benefits.

In the United States, to be eligible for unemployment insurance, one must have sufficient work history, yet groups of individuals—by race, ethnicity, and immigration status—have unequal access to employment. In 2011, 7.5 percent of white men and 8.3 percent of white women were unemployed, compared to much higher rates for black and Latino/a men and women—at 14.1 percent and 17.8 percent for black women and men and 11.8 percent and 11.2 percent for Latinas and Latinos (U.S. Dept. of Labor 2012). These numbers may underestimate differences across groups of discouraged workers, those who are no longer actively seeking employment. Indeed, Schmitt and Jones (2012,

3) show that when workers who are "discouraged, marginally attached, or part-time due to economic reasons" are included in the unemployment rate, these rates are much higher. For example, 12.4 percent and 12.8 percent of white women and men, 21.9 percent and 25.5 percent of black women and men and 21.1 percent and 19.8 percent of Latinas and Latinos would be considered unemployed using these measures. These discouraged workers do not receive unemployment benefits.

One of the most generous social insurance benefits in the United States is distributed through Social Security, a program primarily for the aged and retired. Pensions, such as Social Security, are highly redistributive. In fact, they are the most effective policy at redistributing income in many advanced industrialized countries (Wang et al. 2012). Although the United States is not a policy laggard when considering pensions, it is also not at the top of the list (see Table 33.1). The United States is in 11th place (out of 18) on public-pension net replacement rates for average earners, defined as "the individual net pension entitlement divided by net preretirement earnings, taking account of personal income taxes and social security contributions paid by workers and pensioners" (OECD 2011, 124). The U.S. provides a higher net replacement rate than the UK, Sweden, Poland, the Netherlands, Ireland, Israel, and Australia. Indeed, Social Security is the largest social insurance program in the United States, reflecting the fact that it is not viewed as a government handout, but instead as a reimbursement of the payroll taxes citizens have contributed to the system.

There are two components of Social Security, contributory benefits and noncontributory benefits, with the former paid to workers and the latter paid to spouses and dependents (for example, the survivors benefit). Historically, both forms of benefits institutionalized race and gender inequality because occupations employing large numbers of women and black workers, including domestic and agricultural occupations, were excluded from eligibility (Harrington Meyer 1996; Lieberman 1995; Sainsbury 1994; Quadagno 1994). These exclusions have since been overturned, and, as a result, Social Security is more redistributive today than it was in the past. In fact, many researchers have found that Social Security, notably the contributory portion, redistributes income across class, race, and gender; yet scholars continue to suggest that eligibility is tied to male patterns of work because individuals with uninterrupted work, that is, women who leave employment to care for children and sick parents or low-income workers who have bouts of unemployment, are less likely to qualify for contributory benefits (Harrington Meyer 1996; Herd 2005).

Researchers have also criticized the noncontributory portion of Social Security for rewarding an increasingly archaic male breadwinner model. Fewer women are marrying and fewer marriages are lasting long enough for a spouse to qualify for noncontributory benefits. This is particularly true for black families. As a result, women, and black women in particular, (as well as same-sex partners) are increasingly ineligible for this benefit (Harrington Meyer 1996; Herd 2005; Tamborini, Iams, and Whitman 2009). Instead, these women are more likely to rely on targeted TANF assistance, which is less generous and requires a considerably more onerous process to receive benefits. Yet, although there are undeniable benefits to providing targeted assistance to those in need, when the welfare state relegates certain segments of the population to targeted assistance (i.e., single mothers) and other segments to more effective universal assistance, the result is institutionalized inequality. This is a problem in the U.S. welfare state, particularly when examining historical benefits. Mothers and racial and ethnic minorities are less likely to be beneficiaries of social insurance, but they are more likely to be beneficiaries of less generous, and more burdensome public assistance programs (Brown 1999; Mettler 1998; Quadagno 1990, 1994).

Two other broad types of policies that can alter levels of inequality are work-family policy and health-care policy, yet the United States offers paltry support in both of these areas. Work-family policies, including subsidized child care and paid parental leaves, have major consequences for gender and class inequality (Gornick and Meyers 2003; Gauthier 2011; Pettit and Hook 2005, 2009; Misra et al. 2011a, 2011b; Morgan and Zippel 2003). Work-family policies relieve some of the pressures families face in balancing care and employment, and are strongly associated with higher levels of women's employment and wages (Gornick and Meyers 2003; Misra et al. 2011a, 2011b; Pettit and Hook 2009). These policies are important for reducing inequality because child-bearing increases vulnerability, and single mothers have some of the highest poverty rates across countries (Misra et al. 2012).

The United States does not provide paid maternity leave, although it does now offer unpaid leave to some workers, and California, New Jersey, and Washington state do provide limited paid leave (Fass 2009; Milkman and Appelbaum 2004). The Family and Medical Leave Act, implemented in 1993, requires that employers with more than 50 employees provide up to 12 weeks of unpaid leave for various family obligations, including childbirth, adoption, and care for a sick spouse, child, or parent (Moore 1997). The policy does not cover many workers, such as those who work for companies with less than 50 employees, and does not provide wage replacement, which is crucial to many workers' economic stability. Yet even with these limitations, laws such as the Family and Medical Leave Act help to reduce gender inequality. Indeed, there is evidence of lower occupational sex segregation in U.S. states with a history of family-leave policies. However, there is an important caveat—family leave is only associated with lower inequality when also accompanied by antidiscrimination legislation (Moller and Li 2009). However, FMLA would be much more effective at reducing gender and class inequality if it incorporated wage replacement and covered the full population of workers (Misra et al. 2012; Selmi 1999)

Family leave would also be more effective if it were utilized by both women and men. During the leave period when women exit the labor force, men continue to acquire human capital in the form of job-specific skills and experience that may generate faster upward mobility (Estévez-Abe 2005). There is some evidence that family-leave legislation has resulted in more leave time and slightly lower work attachment among women (Blau and Ehrenberg 1997; Klerman and Leibowitz 1997). Furthermore, Mandel and Semyonov (2006) find in cross-national research that women who live in countries with longer family leaves are more likely to work, but they are less likely to enter traditionally male-dominated occupations, including managerial occupations. Yet in countries with moderate, well-paid family leaves, mothers appear to be more successful at maintaining employment and earning good wages (Misra et al. 2011b; Budig, Misra, and Boeckmann 2012).

Like family leave, child care helps parents balance the competing demands of caretaking and employment (Kamerman and Kahn 1991; Gornick and Meyers 2003; Morgan 2006). Early childhood education programs, usually targeted at preschool children and with varying hours, support parental employment and foster children's development, whereas child-care programs targeted toward infants and toddlers with hours that cover the average workday may be more likely to emphasize employment support (Morgan 2006). Gender inequality appears to be lower in countries with more publicly provided child care because it enhances women's labor-market participation and wages (Pettit and Hook 2005; Misra et al. 2011b; Budig et al. 2010, 2012), although this may differ by how the programs are structured (for example, early-childhood programs with limited hours) (Lewis 2009). Child care also reduces the risk of poverty for families with children, particularly those headed by single mothers (Misra et al. 2007a, 2007b, 2012). Given that child care is a policy tool that can enhance labor-force participation, increasing reliance on the market, and since early childhood education fosters child development, it is notable that the United States does not devote more resources to child care and early childhood education. Indeed, cross-nationally the United States ranks toward the bottom in publicly provided child care for ages 0–2 or ages 3–6 (see Table 33.1). As previously noted, rather than offering widespread public child care, the United States offers Child and Dependent Care Tax Credits and flexible spending accounts, but these benefits are only weakly redistributive.

Although this chapter has focused primarily on income inequality, it is also important to note that social policies have important implications for health inequality. Kennedy, Kawachi, and Prothrow-Stith (1996) show that, controlling for poverty, the U.S. states that are more redistributive have better health outcomes, including health outcomes for African Americans vis-à-vis whites. Maintaining a reasonably healthy population is important for income inequality because poor health can impede labor-market entry and job retention, potentially plummeting individuals and families into poverty and thus inflating the bottom of the income distribution (Conley and Springer 2001; Mullahy and Wolfe 2002; Brady 2005; Garfinkel et al. 2006; Schuring et al. 2007). Therefore, income inequality and health are deeply interrelated, and redistributive social policies can generate lower inequality in both income and health.

Health-care policies also have important implications for income inequality since health and income are intricately related. Health insurance coverage in the United States trails that of other advanced industrialized nation, yet the United States spends far more than any other nation on health (Anderson and Frogner 2008; Hacker 1998; Woolhandler, Campbell, and Himmelstein 2003). Although most wealthy countries have a system of national health insurance, the United States is somewhat exceptional in only having public health care for the elderly (Medicare) and the poor (Medicaid) (Hacker 1998). This leads to an interesting contradiction: very high levels of health-care spending, combined with higher levels of uninsured and underinsured families.

Although about 30 percent of American families are covered by Medicare or Medicaid, both racial and ethnic minorities and poor families are least likely to be insured (DeNavas-Walt, Proctor, and Smith 2011 p. 29). As a result, Americans spend more on health care than most other countries, with life expectancies that are much lower than in other countries (Anderson and Frogner 2008). Research also shows that poor families spend more of their income on health care (Ketsche et al. 2011).

5 CONCLUSION

U.S. social policies help to reduce inequality, but they have limited effectiveness, particularly in comparison to other advanced industrialized countries, in reducing inequality by race, class, gender, and family structure. This is evident in the fact that labor market inequalities have been incorporated into the provisions of the U.S. welfare state. As a result, the U.S. welfare state helps, minimally, to reduce inequality among white individuals and dual parent couples, but it fails to reduce and to some extent exacerbates inequality among single-mother households and racial and ethnic minorities.

Social policy further plays a role in both challenging and entrenching gendered assumptions about what men and women should be doing. White women and women of color have faced discrimination in the labor market, so that many women do not have the same opportunities to depend on the social insurance programs that might help reduce inequality. Although historically and cross-nationally, social policies have supported a heterosexual male-breadwinner female-caregiver model of families, policies that emphasize men's parental leave, for example, can challenge these notions. Yet, the United States has an unusual mix of social policies aimed at gender: There are very few work-family policies, such as widespread publicly subsidized child care, or paid parental leaves. However, public assistance benefits for families with children like TANF are premised on the notion that mothers should be working and they should be married. Therefore, the United States promotes, in some senses, a notion of men and women both being engaged in the paid labor market—yet without state support for the caregiving that must occur in families with children. As a result, many families find it exceptionally difficult to balance paid employment with care, leading to an inflation of the lower tail of the income distribution through higher levels of poverty for families with children in the U.S., relative to most other wealthy countries.

Of course, more broadly, to understand how U.S. social policy shapes inequality, it is crucial to recognize that U.S. social policy has been created in ways that reflect the intertwining of class, race, and gender inequalities. Gwendolyn Mink (1995) persuasively argues that U.S. social policy entrenches class, gender, and racial discrimination in its entitlements, rewarding certain kinds of white mothers, disregarding or punishing mothers of color, and only rewarding those minority men whose occupations and incomes were similar to those of white men. For example, U.S. social policy may reflect a certain notion of what it means to be a white, middle class mother, who has access to health insurance through employment and earnings that allow her to pay for childcare. Yet, a working-class mother in a low-wage job that does not include benefits experiences a much different reality. U.S. social policy has also been increasingly unable to address the inequalities created by the criminal justice system, which imprisons a very large number of low-income men of color, creating long-term employment disadvantages, the disenfranchisement of men of color, and an even more deeply racialized opportunity structure (Wakefield and Uggen 2010; Western and Beckett 1999).

There is still a tremendous amount of work to be done to clarify how the United States can minimize inequality within the context of economic liberalism. Cross-national research on policies such as family leave and child care, policies that arguably align with U.S. cultural values, have not adequately addressed the intersection of race/ethnicity, class, and gender. This type of analysis is necessary to help U.S. scholars better understand the implications of these policies in a diverse society. Furthermore, given that wealth is much more unequally distributed by race and gender than income, and given that components of the hidden welfare state provide tax breaks that help individuals acquire assets, such as homeownership, future research should more fully address wealth inequality within the United States and cross-nationally (Conley 1999; Keister 2000). Additionally, cross-national research on policy outcomes should devote more attention to tax policies. Researchers have a much clearer understanding of the implications of social transfers for income inequality than tax policies, in part because Western European countries rely more heavily on transfers than taxes to redistribute income. A more thorough analysis of transfers and taxes would inform U.S. policy development. Researchers have started down this path, but there are opportunities for further research in this area (Wang et al. 2012).

NOTE

1. The Gini index measures the degree to which the income distribution among households differs from a perfectly equal income distribution. A Gini index of 0 represents perfect equality (where all households of the same size have comparable income), while an index of 100 implies perfect inequality (imagine a scenario where 1 household earns all of the income in a country).

REFERENCES

*Indicates recommended reading.

Acker, Joan. 2000. "Revisiting Class: Thinking from Gender, Race and Organizations." *Social Politics* 7 (2):192–214.

Alderson, Arthur S., and François Nielsen. 2002. "Globalization and the Great U-Turn: Income Inequality Trends in 16 OECD Countries." *American Journal of Sociology* 107:1244–1299.

Anderson, Gerard F., and Bianca K. Frogner. 2008. "Health Spending in OECD Countries: Obtaining Value Per Dollar." *Health Affairs* 27 (6): 1718–1727.

Atkinson, Anthony B., Thomas Piketty, and Emmanuel Saez. 2009. "Top Incomes in the Long Run of History." Working Paper 15408, National Bureau of Economic Research. http://www.nber.org/.

Blau, Francine D., and Ronald G. Ehrenberg, eds. 1997. *Gender and Family Issues in the Workplace*. New York: Sage.

Bradley, David, Evelyne Huber, Stephanie Moller, François Nielsen, and John Stephens. 2003. "Distribution and Redistribution in Post-Industrial Democracies." *World Politics* 55:193–228.

Brady, David. 2005. "The Welfare State and Relative Poverty in Rich Western Democracies, 1967–1997." *Social Forces* 83:1329–1364.

Branch, Enobong. 2011. *Opportunity Denied: Limiting Black Women to Devalued Work*. Newark, NJ: Rutgers University Press.

Brandolini, Andrea, and Timothy Smeeding. 2009. "Income Inequality in Richer and OECD Countries." In Wiermer Salverda, Brian Nolan, and Tim Smeeding, eds., *Oxford Handbook of Economic Inequality*. Oxford: Oxford University Press, 71–100.

Brown, Michael K. 1999. *Race, Money and the American Welfare State*. Ithaca, NY: Cornell University Press.

Browne, Irene, and Joya Misra. 2003. "The Intersection of Gender and Race in the Labor Market." *Annual Review of Sociology* 29:487–513.

Budig, Michelle J., Joya Misra, and Irene Boeckmann. 2010. "The Wage Penalty for Motherhood in Cross-National Perspective: The Importance of Work-Family Policies and Cultural Attitudes." Paper presented at the Population Association of America, Dallas, April.

*Budig, Michelle J., Joya Misra, and Irene Boeckmann. 2012. "The Motherhood Wage Penalty in Cross-National Perspective: Do Work-Family Policies Matter?" *Social Politics* 19:163–193.

Christopher, Karen. 2002. "Welfare State Regimes and Mothers' Poverty." *Social Politics* 9:60–86.

Christopher, Karen, Paula England, Tim M. Smeeding, and K. R. Phillips. 2002. "The Gender Gap in Poverty in Modern Nations: Single Motherhood, the Market, and the State." *Sociological Perspectives* 45:219–242.

Conley, Dalton. 1999. *Being Black, Living in the Red: Race, Wealth, and Social Policy in America*. Berkeley: University of California Press.

Conley, Dalton, and Kristin. W. Springer. 2001. "Welfare State and Infant Mortality." *American Journal of Sociology* 107:768–807.

Cotter, David A., Joan M. Hermsen, and Reeve Vanneman. 1999. "Systems of Gender, Race, and Class Inequality: Multilevel Analyses." *Social Forces* 78:433–460.

Danziger, Sheldon, Robert Haveman, and Robert Plotnick. 1986. "Antipoverty Policy: Effects on the Poor and Nonpoor." In Sheldon H. Danziger and Daniel H. Weinberg, eds., *Fighting Poverty: What Works and What Doesn't*. Cambridge, MA: Harvard University Press, 50–77.

DeNavas-Walt, Carmen, Bernadette Proctor, and Jennifer Smith. 2011. "Income, Poverty, and Health Insurance Coverage in the United States, 2010." U.S. Bureau of the Census. http://www.census.gov/prod/2011pubs/p60-239.pdf.

*Esping-Andersen, Gøsta. 1990. *The Three Worlds of Welfare Capitalism*. Princeton, NJ: Princeton University Press.

Estevéz-Abe, Margarita. 2005. "Gender Bias in Skills and Social Policies: The Varieties of Capitalism Perspective on Sex Segregation." *Social Politics* 12 (2): 180–215.

Fass, Sarah. 2009. "Paid Leave in the States: A Critical Support for Low Wage Workers and Their Families." National Center for Children in Poverty. http://www.nccp.org/publications/pub_864.html.

Folbre, Nancy. 2002. *The Invisible Heart: Economics and Family Values*. New York: Free Press.

Garfinkel, Irwin, Lee Rainwater, and Timothy M. Smeeding. 2006. "A Re-examination of Welfare States and Inequality in Rich Nations: How In-Kind Transfers and Indirect Taxes Change the Story." *Journal of Policy Analysis and Management* 25:897–919.

Gauthier, Anne. H. 2011. "Comparative Family Policy Database." Version 3 [computer file]. Available through Netherlands Interdisciplinary Demographic Institute and Max Planck Institute for Demographic Research. http://www.demogr.mpg.de/cgi-bin/databases/FamPolDB/index.plx.

Gordon, Linda. 1994. *Pitied but Not Entitled: Single Mothers and the History of Welfare*. Cambridge, MA: Harvard University Press.

Gornick, Janet C., and Marcia K. Meyers. 2003. *Families That Work: Policies for Reconciling Parenthood and Employment*. New York: Sage.

Hacker, Jacob. 1998. "The Historical Logic of National Health Insurance: Structure and Sequence in the Development of British, Canadian, and U.S. Medical Policy." *Studies in American Political Development* 12:57–130.

Harrington Meyer, Madonna. 1996. "Making Claims as Workers or Wives: The Distribution of Social Security Benefits." *American Sociological Review* 61:449–465.

Herd, Pamela. 2005. "Reforming a Breadwinner Welfare State: Gender, Race, Class, and Social Security Reform." *Social Forces* 83:1365–1394.

Hicks, Alexander, and Lane Kenworthy. 2003. "Varieties of Welfare Capitalism." *Socio-Economic Review* 1:27–61.

Hotz, V. Joseph, and John Karl Scholz. 2003. "The Earned Income Tax Credit." In R. Moffitt, ed., *Means-Tested Transfer Programs in the U.S.* Chicago: University of Chicago Press, 141–197.

Howard, Christopher 1997. *The Hidden Welfare State: Tax Expenditures and Social Policy in the United States*. Princeton, NJ: Princeton University Press.

Immervoll, Herwig, and Linda Richardson. 2011. "Redistribution Policy and Inequality Reduction in OECD Countries: What Has Changed in Two Decades?" LIS Working Papers Series, No. 571. http://www.lisdatacenter.org/working-papers/.

IRS. 2011. Publication 503: "Child and Dependent Care Expenses." http://www.irs.gov/pub/irs-pdf/p503.pdf.

Kamerman, Sheila B. 1998. "Does Global Restructuring and Retrenchment Doom the Children's Cause?" University lecture, Columbia University. http://www.columbia.edu/cu/ssw/faculty/sbklecture.html.

Kamerman, Sheila B., and Alfred J. Kahn. 1991. *Childcare, Parental Leave, and the Under 3s*. Westport, CT: Greenwood.

Keister, Lisa A. 2000. *Wealth in America*. Cambridge: Cambridge University Press.

Kennedy, Bruce P., Ichiro Kawachi, and Deborah Prothrow-Stith. 1996. "Income Distribution and Mortality: Cross-Sectional Ecological Study of the Robin Hook Index in the United States." *BMJ* 312: 1004.

Kenworthy, Lane. 1999. "Do Social-Welfare Policies Reduce Poverty? A Cross-National Assessment." *Social Forces* 77:1119–1139.

Kenworthy, Lane, and Jonas Pontusson. 2005. "Rising Inequality and the Politics of Redistribution in Affluent Countries." *Perspectives on Politics* 3:449–471.

Ketsche, Patricia, E. Kathleen Adams, Sally Wallace, Viji Diane Kannan, and Harini Kannan. 2011. "Lower-Income Families Pay a Higher Share of Income Toward National Health Care Spending Than Higher-Income Families Do." *Health Affairs* 30:1637–1646.

Koch, Julianna, and Suzanne Mettler. 2012. "Who Perceives Government's Role in Their Lives? Assessing the Impact of Social Policy on Visibility." Working paper. Available at http://www.ash.harvard.edu/extension/ash/docs/mettler.pdf.

Korpi, Walter, and Joakim Palme. 1998. "The Paradox of Redistribution and Strategies of Equality: Welfare State Institutions, Inequality, and Poverty in the Western Countries." *American Sociological Review* 63:661–687.

Klerman, Jacob Alex, and Arleen Leibowitz. 1997. "Labor Supply Effects of State Maternity Leave Legislation." In Francine D. Blau and Ronald G. Ehrenberg, eds., *Gender and Family Issues in the Workplace*. New York: Sage, 65–91.

Lewis, Gail. 2000. *"Race," Gender, Welfare: Encounters in a Postcolonial Society*. Cambridge: Polity Press.

Lewis, Jane 2009. *Work-Family Balance, Gender and Policy*. Cheltenham, UK: Elgar.

Lieberman, Robert C. 1995. "Race, Institutions, and the Administration of Social Policy." *Social Science History* 19:511–542.

Lieberman, Robert C. 2001 [1998]. *Shifting the Color Line: Race and the American Welfare State*. Cambridge, MA: Harvard University Press.

LIS Web Tabulator. Accessed June 2012–December 2013. www.lisdatacenter.org. Luxembourg: LIS.

*Lobao, Linda, and Gregory Hooks. 2003. "Public Employment, Welfare Transfers, and Economic Well-Being Across Local Populations: Does a Lean and Mean Government Benefit the Masses?" *Social Forces* 82:519–556.

Maag, Elaine, Stephanie Rennane, and C. Eugene Steuerle. 2011. *A Reference Manual for Child Tax Benefits*. Washington, DC: Urban Institute.

Mahler, Vincent A., and David K. Jesuit. 2006. "Fiscal Redistribution in the Developed Countries: New Insights from the Luxembourg Income Study." *Socio-Economic Review* 4:483–511.

Mandel, Hadas, and Moshe Semyonov. 2005. "Family Policies, Wage Structures, and Gender Gaps: Sources of Earnings Inequality." *American Sociological Review* 70:949–967.

Mandel, Hadas, and Moshe Semyonov. 2006. "A Welfare State Paradox: State Interventions and Women's Employment Opportunities in 22 Countries." *American Journal of Sociology* 111:1910–1949.

McCall, Leslie. 2001. *Complex Inequality: Gender, Class, and Race in the New Economy*. New York: Routledge.

Mettler, Suzanne. 1998. *Dividing Citizens: Gender and Federalism in New Deal Public Policy*. Ithaca, NY: Cornell University Press.

*Mettler, Suzanne. 2011. *The Submerged State: How Invisible Government Policies Undermine American Democracy*. Chicago: University of Chicago Press.

Meyer, Bruce D., and Dan T. Rosenbaum. 2001. "Welfare, the Earned Income Tax Credit, and the Labor Supply of Single Mothers." *Quarterly Journal of Economics* 116 (3): 1063–1114.

Meyer, Robert H., and David A. Wise. 1983. "The Effects of the Minimum Wage on the Employment and Earnings of Youth." *Journal of Labor Economics* 8:66–100.

Milkman, Ruth, and Eileen Appelbaum. 2004. "Paid Family Leave in California: New Research Findings." *The State of California Labor* 4:45–67.

*Mink, Gwendolyn. 1995. *The Wages of Motherhood: Inequality in the Welfare State, 1917–1942.* Ithaca, NY: Cornell University Press.

Misra, Joya, Michelle J. Budig, and Irene Boeckmann. 2011a. "Cross-National Patterns in Individual and Household Employment and Work Hours by Gender and Parenthood." *Research in Sociology of Work* 22:169–207.

Misra, Joya, Michelle Budig, and Irene Boeckmann. 2011b. "Work-Family Policies and the Effects of Children on Women's Employment Hours and Wages." *Community, Work, and Family* 14:139–147.

Misra, Joya, Michelle J. Budig, and Stephanie Moller. 2007a. "Reconciliation Policies and the Effects of Motherhood on Employment, Earnings, and Poverty." *Journal of Comparative Policy Analysis* 9:35–155.

Misra, Joya, Stephanie Moller, and Michelle J. Budig. 2007b. "Work-Family Policies and Poverty for Partnered and Single Women in Europe and North America." *Gender & Society* 21:804–827.

Misra, Joya, Stephanie Moller, Eiko Strader, and Elizabeth Wemlinger. 2012. "Family Policies, Employment and Poverty Among Partnered and Single Mothers." *Research in Social Stratification and Mobility* 30:113–128.

Moller, Stephanie. 2002. "Supporting Poor Single Mothers: Gender and Race in the US Welfare State." *Gender & Society* 16 (4): 465–484.

Moller, Stephanie, Arthur Alderson, and François Nielsen. 2009. "Changing Patterns of Income Inequality in U.S. Counties." *American Journal of Sociology* 114:1037–1101.

Moller, Stephanie, and Huiping Li. 2009. "Parties, Unions, Policies, and Occupational Segregation in the United States." *Social Forces:* 87 (3): 1529–1560.

Moore, Maureen F. 1997. *Family and Medical Leave.* CA: Lexis Law.

Morgan, Kimberly. 2006. *Working Mothers and the Welfare State: Religion and the Politics of Work-Family Policies in Western Europe and the United States.* Stanford, CA: Stanford University Press.

Morgan, Kimberly J., and Kathrin Zippel. 2003. "Paid to Care: The Origins and Effects of Care Leave Policies in Western Europe." *Social Politics* 10:49–85.

Mullahy, John, and B. Wolfe. 2002. "Health Policies for the Nonelderly Poor." In Sheldon H. Danziger and Robert H. Haveman, eds., *Understanding Poverty.* Cambridge, MA: Harvard, 278–313.

OECD. 2011. Pensions at a Glance 2011 Retirement-income Systems in OECD and G20 Countries: Retirement-income Systems in OECD and G20 Countries. OECD Publishing. Available at http://www.oecd-ilibrary.org.

OECD. 2012. "Income Distribution and Poverty: Data, Figures, Methods and Concepts." http://www.oecd.org/.

Orloff, Ann. 1993. "Gender and the Social Rights of Citizenship." *American Sociological Review* 58:303–328.

Pettit, Becky, and Jennifer L. Hook. 2005. "The Structure of Women's Employment in Comparative Perspective." *Social Forces* 84:779–801.

*Pettit, Becky, and Jennifer L. Hook. 2009. *Gendered Tradeoffs: Family, Social Policy, and Economic Inequality in Twenty-One Countries.* New York: Sage.

Pressman, Steven. 2009. "Public Policies and the Middle Class Throughout the World in the Mid-2000s." LIS Working Paper Series, No. 517. http://www.lisdatacenter.org/working-papers/.

Quadagno, Jill. 1990. "Race, Class and Gender in the U.S. Welfare State: Nixon's Failed Family Assistance Plan." *American Sociological Review* 55:11–28.

*Quadagno, Jill. 1994. *The Color of Welfare*. New York: Oxford University Press.

Quadagno, Jill. 2000. "Another Face of Inequality: Racial and Ethnic Exclusion in the Welfare State." *Social Politics* 7 (2): 229–237.

Sainsbury, Diane, ed. 1994. *Gendering Welfare States*. Thousand Oaks, CA: Sage.

Schmitt, John, and Janelle Jones. 2012. "Long-Term Hardship in the Labor Market." Washington, DC: Center for Economic Policy Research. http://www.cepr.net/documents/publications/long-term-hardship-2012-03.pdf.

Schuring, Merel, Lex Burdorf, Anton Kunst, and Johan Mackenbach. 2007. "The Effect of Ill Health on Entering and Maintaining Paid Employment: Evidence in European Countries." *Journal of Epidemiology and Community Health* 61:597–604.

Segal, Elizabeth A., Keith M. Kilty, and Rebecca Y. Kim. 2002. "Social and Economic Inequality and Asian Americans in the United States." *Journal of Poverty* 6 (4): 5–21.

Selmi, Michael. 1999. Family Leave and the Gender Wage Gap. *N.C. Law Review* 707:770–773.

Smeeding, Timothy. 2005. "Public Policy, Economic Inequality, and Poverty: The United States in Comparative Perspective." *Social Science Quarterly* 86:955–983.

Tamborini, Christopher, Howard M. Iams, and Kevin Whitman. 2009. "Marital History, Race, and Social Security Spouse and Widow Benefit Eligibility in the United States." *Research on Aging* 31:577–605.

U.S. Bureau of the Census. 2012. "Race and Hispanic Origin of Householder—Families by Median and Mean Income." Table F-5. http://www.census.gov/hhes/www/income/data/historical/families.

U.S. Department of Labor. Bureau of Labor Statistics. 2009. "Effect of Benefits and Taxes on Income and Poverty." http://www.census.gov/hhes/www/cpstables/032010/rdcall/toc.htm.

U.S. Department of Labor. Bureau of Labor Statistics. 2012. "Unemployed Persons by Marital Status, Race, Hispanic or Latino Ethnicity, Age, and Sex." http://www.bls.gov/cps/cpsaat24.htm.

Wakefield, Sara, and Christopher Uggen. 2010. "Incarceration and Stratification." *Annual Review of Sociology* 36:387–406.

Wang, Chen, Koen Caminada, and K. P. Goudswaard. 2012. "The Redistributive Effect of Social Transfer Programmes and Taxes: A Decomposition Across Countries." *International Social Security Review* 65:27–48.

Western, Bruce, and Katherine Beckett. 1999. "How Unregulated Is the U.S. Labor Market? The Penal System as a Labor Market Institution." *American Journal of Sociology* 104 (4): 1030–1060.

*Western, Bruce, and Becky Pettit. 2005. "Black-White Wage Inequality, Employment Rates, and Incarceration." *American Journal of Sociology*. 111:553–578.

Woolhandler, Steffie, Terry Campbell, and David U. Himmelstein, 2003. "Costs of Health Care Administration in the United States and Canada." *New England Journal of Medicine* 349:768–775.

CHAPTER 34

....

CITIZENSHIP

....

SUZANNE METTLER AND ALEXIS N. WALKER

1 INTRODUCTION

....

IN American public discourse, the concept of citizenship typically evokes images such as people casting their votes at the ballot box, immigrants being sworn in as citizens by a judge, soldiers serving their country, or members of civic associations performing good works in their communities. Social policy may seem irrelevant to citizenship when it is portrayed in these ways, yet the earliest forms of American social provision were rooted in rationales pertaining to citizenship. Late 18th century and 19th century lawmakers sought to reward those who served the nation in the military and to promote and nurture "good citizenship" through education. Major 20th century expansions of the welfare state were deeply consequential for citizenship, influencing the status and integration of social groups and the extent to which they participated in public affairs. Amid changing conceptions of the role of the public and private sectors in the early 21st century, the design of social policies influences how Americans think about and relate to government, how they view its appropriate role in society, and how they perceive their own social status and that of others. Welfare states are usually judged by the extent to which they alleviate or exacerbate poverty and economic inequality, with quantitative measures offering comparisons across welfare states. But social policy bears crucial significance for citizenship as well, often in ways that are not as easily quantified. Historical research on American political development has revealed that ideas about citizenship played a central role in the development of social policy. Throughout U.S. history, policymakers have often justified social policies on the basis that they would develop Americans' civic capacity and inculcate participatory norms. In addition, research spanning the realms of political behavior and public policy, including both quantitative and qualitative methods, have found that U.S. social policy has shaped citizens' experiences of government and their political participation and attitudes. Established social policies have influenced citizens' ability to practice their political rights, the extent of solidarity or division in society, and people's inclination to engage in civic life. In sum, American civil and political rights cannot be fully understood apart from their interaction with social rights and provision.

This essay offers an introduction to thinking about the relationship between citizenship and social policy. First we consider the place of social policy in different theoretical understandings of citizenship in social science research. The body of the chapter explores the mechanisms through which social policies can influence citizenship, tracing their impact on membership, identity, and belonging; political attitudes; and political participation and other forms of civic involvement. The final sections consider the contemporary relationship between social policy and citizenship and offer directions for future research.

2 CONCEPTUALIZING CITIZENSHIP AND SOCIAL POLICY

In American scholarship on citizenship, social policy is typically more conspicuous by its absence than by how it is considered. Citizenship has usually been conceptualized as: (1) specific civil and political rights, and (2) the practice of exercising those rights. Using these traditional lenses, the concept has been used as a tool for assessing and measuring the quality of U.S. democracy. Social scientists to a large degree have reinforced these understandings of citizenship through their efforts to categorize and track over time the expansion or retraction of civil and political rights and to measure the extent and effectiveness of civic engagement as a means of assessing the quality of our democracy.

Researchers who focus on law and public policy have concentrated on citizenship as it is conveyed by the state through civil and political rights, and they have examined the history of expansion and denial of these rights. At its most basic, citizenship is a legal status bestowed by the state. Thus, immigration scholars have tracked the history of immigration laws that denied or admitted new citizens (Motomura 2006; Tichenor 2002). Others, like Rogers Smith (1997), have explored how the civil and political rights attendant with the legal status of citizenship have been bestowed and denied over the course of American history. In these works, citizenship is a formal status that is gained through the granting of rights by the state.

Alternately, scholars of political participation and public opinion have viewed citizenship and democracy through the lens of civic engagement. The position held by Sidney Verba, Kay Lehman Schlozman, and Henry E. Brady (1995, 1) that "[c]itizen participation is at the heart of democracy" is a guiding belief among many of the political scientists studying these topics. Civic engagement is thought to be the glue that holds democracy together by connecting citizens to their government. Americans take part as full citizens when they formulate opinions on political matters; interact and connect with their fellow citizens; and exercise their voice through voting and other forms of participation. Thus, public opinion scholars try to assess the degree of political knowledge Americans possess (Converse 1964; Delli Carpini and Keeter 1996; Lupia and McCubbins 1998; Zaller 1992), sociologists and others study the form and vibrancy of American civic organizations (Putnam 2000, Skocpol 2003), and political participation scholars seek to understand what motivates Americans to participate and to explain variation in rates of doing so (Rosenstone and Hansen 1993; Skocpol 2003; Verba and Nie 1972; Verba, Schlozman, and Brady 1995; Wolfinger and Rosenstone 1980). Citizenship, in this view, is developed in practice through active engagement in our polity.

These two currents of citizenship research in American political science fit the distinction, noted by Kymlicka and Norman (1995, 284), between "citizenship-as-legal-status, that is, as full membership in a particular political community; and citizenship-as-desirable-activity, where the extent and quality of one's citizenship is a function of one's participation in that community". Both understandings of citizenship offer a valuable foundation for exploring the concept, but they come up short for several reasons. First, neither current gives attention to social rights, without which civil and political rights can be meaningless, and citizens may remain incapable of practicing active civic engagement. As Robert Dahl writes, "In order to exercise the fundamental rights to which citizens in a democratic order are entitled—to vote, speak, publish, protest, assemble, organize, among others—citizens must also possess the minimal resources that are necessary in order to take advantage of the opportunities and to exercise their rights" (Dahl 2003, 152). Considering the availability of such resources requires attention to social policy. Second, whether citizenship is regarded as either rights or practice, neither of these conceptions pays attention to how people experience government, whether they perceive themselves to be excluded or included as citizens, and the implications for their civic status and identity. Finally, these two types of citizenship suggest two separate and unrelated processes, failing to examine how legal rights, political practice, and experience may be interrelated. Indeed, being a legal member of a community does not guarantee that one is treated as a fully incorporated citizen. For example, even today, long after civil and political rights have been extended to African Americans, severe racial inequalities persist as evidenced by numerous social and economic indicators (King and Smith 2011). Social policies have failed to close these gaps, and thus many African Americans likely have yet to experience full inclusion as citizens.

The concepts of citizenship-as-legal-status and citizenship-as-desirable-activity have overshadowed a third strain of thought examining citizenship and social rights. In this third strain, political theorists have been equally active as more empirical social scientists in discussing social policy. As is evident in T. H. Marshall's 1950 seminal essay "Citizenship and Social Class," a longstanding European intellectual tradition links social rights to full citizenship. For Marshall, social rights are an expansive concept from "the right to a modicum of economic security and welfare to the right to share to the full in the social heritage and to live the life of a civilized being according to the standards prevailing in the society" (1998, 94). By envisioning financial stability and inclusion in a community as a right of full citizenship, Marshall was conceptualizing citizenship as much more than just legal inclusion and political participation.

Marshall's work was groundbreaking because he identified social rights as equally important to full citizenship as civil and political rights. Civil rights ensured individual freedom, political rights enabled one to participate in the political process, but for Marshall it was through social rights that one could exercise one's political and civil rights on equal footing with one's fellow citizens. In other words, social citizenship is "the right to defend and assert all one's rights on terms of equality with others" (Marshall 1998, 94). For Marshall, the substance of political and civil rights was diminished by gross inequalities in society, particularly divisions along class lines, and, thus, he believed nations, in the forward march of progress, would advance beyond the stage of extreme inequality. He considered advanced nations to develop through predictable stages, extending first civil rights, then political rights, and finally social rights to all citizens.

More recent scholarship has developed the concept of social citizenship further, first in elucidating variation in ways that different nations incorporate citizens. Gøsta Esping-Andersen (1990) criticized Marshall's assumption that universalism is the norm in advanced welfare states. He pointed out that, in fact, nations vary considerably in the ways that they structure social citizenship: "One may cultivate hierarchy and status, another dualisms, and a third universalism" (Esping-Andersen 1990, 58). He proceeded to identify three ideal types of stratification pursued by different nations: conservative, liberal, and social democratic. Each one, through its public policies, promotes a different approach to what he terms decommodification, meaning "when a person can maintain a livelihood without reliance on the market" because they are somewhat insulated from market forces and, in times of need, like illness or old age, not forced to sell their labor on the market (Esping-Andersen 1990, 21–22).

Even within a single nation, furthermore, different groups of citizens are often incorporated on different terms and at different points in time. Ann Orloff (1993) observed such variation pertaining to gender. She argued that, for many women, full decommodification comes not only from the ability to leave the labor market to fulfill parenting responsibilities without repercussions, but also through the ability to enter the labor market by having choice and support for "private-sphere" responsibilities like child care. Nations vary considerably in these respects.

Scholars of the American welfare state have shown that in the United States, the relationship between social policy and citizenship has developed in a far different way than Marshall expected to be the norm. Nancy Fraser and Linda Gordon (1992) argued that civil and political rights have not necessarily led to social rights: rather, the property- and contract-centered understanding of civil rights has contributed to an aversion by the American public to the very term *social rights* and to a preference for social policies based on those who have earned such benefits versus the underserving who only receive charity.

Nor did the development of rights in the United States follow such a straightforward trajectory as Marshall would have expected. On one hand, most white male Americans—regardless of whether they owned property—gained political rights in advance of their European counterparts, yet gained social rights well after them. Furthermore, other groups of Americans gained rights far later on, and sometimes through a different sequence than Marshall anticipated (Quadagno 1994, 8). Social rights were not only extended more slowly and sporadically than Marshall anticipated but also in ways that defied classification into any of the three major types of stratification identified by Esping-Andersen, those pertaining to work, status, or universal principles (Mettler 1998). For example, during the first century-and-a-half of American history, most social policies were extended on the basis of republican ideals: either citizens were to be rewarded for their fulfillment of civic duties, as in the case of benefits for military veterans; or good citizens should be cultivated through social provision, as in the case of educational policy (Skocpol 1992; Orloff 1991; Macedo 2003).

In recent decades, scholars have begun exploring the relationship between social policy and citizenship in the United States. Some examine the relationship between social rights and membership, status, and civic identity in the political community. Political rights may serve as the formal basis for full citizenship, but it is often through social rights that an individual becomes meaningfully incorporated as such. Other scholars investigate the links between social policy and civic engagement or political participation—for instance, the ways in which social programs can provide citizens with the capacity for the full exercise of political rights by promoting education, health, and community. Still others look at how social policy influences citizens' knowledge of and views about government and of their responsibilities in relation to it.

Thus, the incorporation of social policies into our understanding of citizenship helps further develop the two currents of citizenship that have dominated American social science to date. This new area of research has pushed us to consider citizenship as composed not only of civil and political rights but also of social rights. Moreover, status is formally composed of not only possessing rights but also of lived experiences of government that shape one's identity, sense of membership in a community, and willingness and ability to participate in politics. Formal rights, status, experience, and practice interact to create citizenship, and, as emerging scholarship is finding, social policies play a unique role in shaping each of these elements of citizenship in the United States.

3 How Social Policy Influences Citizenship

Over the past quarter-century, a pair of analytical approaches emerged that have provided scholars with tools for thinking more systematically about how social policy may influence citizenship. First, policy scholars Anne Schneider and Helen Ingram argued that policy makers inscribe social constructions of target populations in policy design, favoring different tools for different groups. These policies, in turn, convey messages to citizens about "what government is supposed to do, which citizens are deserving (and which not), and what kinds of attitudes and participatory patterns are appropriate in a democratic society" (Schneider and Ingram 1993, 334). Citizens shape their orientation to government and the style and frequency of their participation in response to policy messages. Advantaged groups receive positive messages that convey to them that government is responsive and that encourage them to engage in conventional forms of political participation. Groups construed as dependents or deviants, by contrast, receive negative messages that prompt withdrawal from participation.

Separately, several historical institutionalists developed the theory of policy feedback, of how policies established at an earlier period of time may shape subsequent politics. Skocpol (1992) observed how policies can affect the capacity, identity, and goals of social groups, as Civil War veterans' benefits did for veterans, and the achievement of maternalist policies did for the federated women's associations that mobilized on their behalf. Building on this approach, Paul Pierson (1993) argued that policies may generate both resource effects, generating resources and incentives that promote some political strategies over others, and interpretive effects, acting as sources of information and meaning.

This approach has been adapted to studying effects on citizenship through a synthesis of Pierson's conceptual apparatus with Sidney Verba, Kay Schlozman, and Henry Brady's Civic Voluntarism model and also aspects of Schneider and Ingram's approach (Mettler 2002). The resulting framework features two distinct pathways. First, through the payments, goods, and services they offer, policies may have resource effects on individuals that enhance or diminish their civic capacity. Second, the rules and procedures of policy design may bestow messages on citizens, conveying interpretive effect that shape their civic predisposition or inclination for involvement and attitudes about government and politics. Both may ultimately affect their likelihood of civic engagement.

Through these sorts of mechanisms and other related ones, social policies may have a wide array of effects on citizenship. In the following section, we offer a brief overview of the dynamic and emergent scholarship in this area. A more comprehensive inventory appears in Mettler and Soss, 2004.

3.1 Membership, Identity, and Belonging

Social policies define, first and foremost, who is and who is not included as a member of the political community. They operate through cognitive mechanisms, by conveying what Ingram and Schneider have called "messages" or what Pierson has called "interpretive effects" to beneficiaries and possibly to other citizens, as well (Schneider and Ingram 1993; Pierson 1993).

The political philosopher Judith Shklar examined how a wide array of policies, including those shaping the right to work, affect citizens' "standing" in the political community, whether they enjoy public respect, and thus whether they experience full inclusion (Shklar 1991). For Shklar, Americans lose their standing when they cannot work and thus the right to work—and the social policies that promote the ability to work like job training programs, educational policies that foster employability, labor regulations, public works programs, and incentives to businesses to create jobs—influence citizenship (Shklar 1991, 99–102). In the United States, employment status has long been associated with independence and freedom (Schlozman and Tierney 1986; Foner 1995). Employment is the basis on which individuals acquire eligibility for a wide array of other social benefits, ranging from unemployment insurance to the Earned Income Tax Credit and Social Security.

In addition, social policies can influence citizens' sense of their own or others' civic status, conveying notions of deservingness (Schneider and Ingram 1993). Some policies, such as the World War II G.I. Bill, have treated recipients as honored citizens, bestowing generous benefits on them and delivering them in a manner that conveys dignity and respect (Mettler 2005b). Other policies, such as public assistance, have stigmatized beneficiaries and conveyed the message that government is not responsive to people like them (Soss 1999a, 1999b). Through programs like Old Age Insurance (Social Security), New Deal social policies incorporated men, particularly whites, into benefits administered by the national government in a uniform manner and according to bureaucratic norms, whereas most women and men of color were left to the highly variable policies at the state level, for which eligibility more often depended on local social and cultural norms. This differentiation in policies fostered different forms of civic status (Mettler 1998).

Some social roles are sanctioned by social policies that endow them with the legitimacy of the state and indicate that they constitute acceptable and valued identities with public worth. The long history of veterans' benefits in the United States, beginning well in advance of other social-welfare policies, helped to enshrine the role of the citizen soldier in American political culture. Questions about deservingness have loomed over many other types of social provision, but the established connection between social benefits and veteran status places their legitimacy—and the honor of beneficiaries—beyond reproach (Mettler 2005a). Policies ranging from spouse and survivors' benefits in Social Security to advantages in the tax code for married couples who file jointly have bestowed legitimacy on heterosexual marriage and particularly on the role of women within it. In addition, in many ways they have treated women who remained outside of the paid workforce more preferably than those who work intermittently and/or for low wages (Canaday 2009; Harrington Meyer 1996; Nelson 1990; Sainsbury 1999).

Social policies may also, by extension, influence how some citizens view other groups of citizens—whether they consider them to be deserving of government benefits. Being associated with a stigmatized policy can promote a marginalized status for a particular social group (Soss 1999b). Women on public assistance, particularly African Americans, became subject to such dynamics during the mid-20th century, as the policy they utilized fell from its respected status in 1935 to a disparaged one within the space of about 20 years (Mettler 1998, chap. 6) and then retained that negative image over subsequent decades (Gilens 1999). Conversely, recipients of the Earned Income Tax Credit, though drawn from much of the same demographic group as those on welfare, benefit from a positive social perception (Jacobs and Page 2009, 63).

These dynamics, in combination, influence how social policies affect stratification within a society. Some policies may foster solidarity, a sense of social cohesiveness, and shared interests across class and other divisions, whereas other policies may reinforce or exacerbate differences and inequality (Esping-Anderson 1990, chap. 3.) Universal policies may help incorporate less advantaged citizens as full members, and prompt others to view them as such, whereas targeted policies may reinforce their separateness (Skocpol 1991; Wilson 1991).

3.2 Political Participation and Other Forms of Civic Involvement

The vast literature on political behavior pertains directly to matters of participatory citizenship, and yet it proceeded for decades without probing how social policy might influence involvement. In part, this likely emanated from the lack of survey data that includes both indicators of individuals' rates of participation, on the one hand, and their usage of social programs, on the other. Finally, Verba, Schlozman, and Brady included both types of questions in their comprehensive Civic Participation Study of 1990, and they investigated the relationship in their classic book, *Voice and Equality*. They found that beneficiaries of more inclusive programs, such as Social Security and Medicare, were much more likely to get involved in advocating on behalf of their programs than were beneficiaries of means-tested programs such as Food Stamps, AFDC, Medicaid, and subsidized housing (1995, 208–210). An exception was the Welfare Rights Movement of the 1960s and 1970s, which was spurred by the activism of poor mothers receiving welfare that briefly defied research predictions and became vocal proponent for the poor (Nadasen 2005). Verba, Schlozman, and Brady also found that beneficiaries of the means-tested programs, like parents of school-aged children, did become significantly more active in political activity pertaining to the particular policy issues that benefited their families, but this heightened issue activity was still not enough to make up for their overall lower levels of participation relative to the rest of the public (1995, 394–398). In other words, experiences of social policy bore a relationship to how much and toward what end beneficiaries took part as citizens.

Subsequent analyses, primarily involving case studies, have delved into explaining the mechanisms through which social policy usage influences political participation or other forms of civic involvement. Some emphasize how citizenship is shaped through interpretive or cognitive messages. Soss found that controlling for several factors, recipients of Aid to Families with Dependent Children (AFDC) were significantly less likely to vote than recipients of a social insurance program, Social Security Disability Insurance (SSDI). He hypothesized that policy experiences engendered political learning, as individuals gained distinct experiences of government and took away unique messages about the value of political action. His in-depth interviews with program respondents revealed that SSDI recipients encountered a responsive agency and thus developed a greater sense of external political efficacy, which could explain their higher voter turnout. Conversely, AFDC recipients found the agencies they dealt with to be unresponsive or even hostile to their claims, thereby diminishing their sense of external efficacy (Soss 1999a). Such inhibiting effects can be mitigated, however. In the same study, Soss found that AFDC recipients whose children were enrolled in Head Start—a program that encourages parental involvement and assertiveness—were more willing to voice grievances at the welfare office and displayed higher levels of external political efficacy. The exception of Head Start lends credence to Soss's claim that it is not just poverty and education levels that are stifling turnout, and it further illustrates the role social policies can play in reinforcing or challenging participatory inequalities.

Similarly, in a study of the World War II G.I. Bill's education and training benefits, Mettler found that beneficiaries later participated as members of a greater number of civic organizations and political activities than veterans with similar characteristics who did not use the benefits. The results were not attributable to veterans' level of education, and thus were not primarily a resource effect; rather, they emanated from the interpretive effects of the experience of program usage that helped fund veterans' education. Through survey and interview data, Mettler found that those who experienced the G.I. Bill perceived themselves to be treated with dignity and respect through the course of program delivery. They also gained a level of education most could not have afforded and some would not even have considered (Mettler 2005a). The impact on civic involvement endured for the first 15 years after program usage, and disappeared after that, suggesting that the effects of social policy on citizenship through cognitive effects may be time-limited (Mettler and Welch 2004).

Examinations of other social policies have suggested a more prominent role for resource effects on civic engagement. Andrea Campbell's study of Social Security and Medicare showed that seniors have not always been as active in politics as they came to be by the latter 20th century; rather, as program beneficiaries they acquired a more tangible sense of their interests and took action to protect the benefits on which they relied. Lower-income beneficiaries, who depended more heavily on the benefits, experienced the strongest boost in their civic engagement. Besides isolating resource effects, Campbell also found that program beneficiaries were more likely than others to be mobilized by parties and groups. Looking across a wider array of programs, she observed that recipients of means-tested programs were deprived of the policy experiences that could have helped to propel their greater involvement (Campbell 2003).

In a study that showcases the impact of social policy on citizenship, Deondra Rose examined the effect of federal student aid programs on social and participatory citizenship. She found that usage of the policies enabled Americans—especially women—to acquire higher levels of education than they would have otherwise, enhancing their social citizenship. Then, in turn, those with more education participated at higher levels in politics. The experience of program usage itself, controlling for educational level, did not affect participation, suggesting that the resources following from heightened educational attainment, rather than cognitive responses to program usage, were primarily responsible for the higher rates of subsequent political involvement (Rose 2012).

Recent studies have further expanded our understanding of how social policy influences participatory citizenship. Some of the advances come as responses to methodological criticisms, namely the charge of endogeneity: that there is something distinctive that leads some populations to utilize a program and it is this unique trait, rather than program usage, that accounts for different rates of participation (Mead 2004). Scholars have made a variety of efforts to grapple with this charge, including a two-stage model approach (Mettler and Welch 2004) and more recently, longitudinal panel data that include a wide array of control variables (Bruch, Ferree, and Soss 2010; Morgan and Campbell 2011, chap. 7). Some newer studies have also made substantive advances, incorporating analysis of a larger number of polices (Mettler and Stonecash 2008) or by exploring new and different policy areas, such as contemporary welfare to work programs (Soss, Fording, and Schram 2011) and Medicare prescription-drug coverage (Morgan and Campbell 2011). Much work remains to be done, but scholars have made headway in developing analytical frameworks and testing hypotheses.

3.3   Effect on Attitudes

Compared to the scholarship on participatory outcomes, less research to date has probed how social policies influence attitudes associated with citizenship. In a few instances, attitudes receive some attention in studies that focus more directly on participation. For instance, in work described earlier, Soss finds that heightened external efficacy results from positive experiences of policy usage, and Campbell and Rose each discern an impact on political interest (Soss 1999a, Campbell 2003, Rose 2012).

Examining how social policy influences civic attitudes offers a promising direction for understanding more about the effects of the American welfare state, particularly in its contemporary form. Howard and Hacker have observed that U.S. social policy, compared to that of other nations, features a much greater proportion of provision that is either hidden in the tax code or are administered by private organizations, such as employers (Howard 1997; Hacker 2002). This phenomenon raises fundamental questions about how such policies, compared to more direct and visible ones, may influence citizens' views of government and their roles and responsibilities in relation to it. Studies focusing on the creation and subsequent development of these hidden forms of social policy indicate that, although interest groups appear to have been mobilized by them, ordinary citizens have not been (Howard 1997; Hacker 2002).

Recent survey research has permitted empirical investigation of the impact of policies on civic attitudes. Controlling for several factors such as income and education, Mettler found that the greater the number of direct visible social programs individuals had used, including Social Security, Medicare, the G.I. Bill, public assistance, and others, the more likely they were to agree both that government had helped them in times of need and that it had provided opportunities for them. Conversely, usage of greater numbers of tax expenditures and other hidden programs had no impact on perceptions that government had helped and even made beneficiaries significantly more likely to disagree that it had provided opportunities for them. Recipients of hidden policies were also much less likely to take action to influence them than were those who used the more visible policies. Such policies can be said to constitute a "submerged state" because of their immense size and scope paired with most citizens' lack of awareness of them (Mettler 2011).

Experimental analysis has revealed that providing citizens with a very small amount of information about social policies in the tax code enabled them to formulate opinions about them at much higher rates and to do so in ways that made sense, given their values and interests. Once informed about the distributive effects of policies, individuals became less supportive of those that favored more affluent Americans and more supportive of those favoring the less well-off (Mettler 2011, chap. 3). As it stands, however, the vast and growing submerged state undermines democratic citizenship because it hinders' citizens' ability to recognize the actual role of government and to take meaningful positions on its actions. Such attitudinal effects are ripe for further study, particularly because the presence of the federal government in citizens' lives has varied greatly over time (Mettler and Milstein 2007).

4 CONTEMPORARY ISSUES AND DEVELOPMENTS

The United States has a tradition of welfare state development based on particular notions of citizenship, especially adopting social policy to reward good citizens and to promote virtuous citizenship in others. This history has often led the nation to adopt policies designed differently than those in other nations. For instance, Skocpol (1992) has documented how, after the Civil War, at a time when European nations were developing social provision targeted to workers and their families, the United States singled out Union soldiers and their families for assistance. By rewarding veterans for their service, these pension programs offered a fuller and more inclusive social citizenship to their beneficiaries than the rest of the public. Veterans' benefits after World War II further promoted veterans' political identity and subsequent political involvement as a unified, mobilized constituency (Mettler 2005b). Other policies, such as K-12 education, were developed for the purpose of promoting the development of good citizens.

A full analysis of the different conceptions of citizenship incorporated into social policies over the course of American history lies beyond the scope of this analysis. Instead, we offer some reflections on the relationship between these matters in the contemporary period.

Since the 1970s, the United States—like many other nations—has experienced growing market-based inequality in incomes. The majority of Americans in this period have seen their wages stagnate, after-tax incomes that have failed to keep up with the rising cost of living, and increasing economic insecurity. For those in the highest income brackets, the last 40 years has enabled the acquisition of a staggering amount of wealth: "In short, the United States now possesses a small class of very rich Americans who are much richer than other Americans, than the affluent of other nations, and than American elites in historical perspective" (Soss, Hacker, and Mettler 2007, 7).

Over this same time period of rising income inequality, compared to many other western nations, the United States has done less to try to mitigate such disparities. The distinctive social policies of the U.S. welfare state have been fairly ineffective in alleviating the rise in economic inequality and the accompanying increase in political inequality. In fact, government deregulation, tax policy and other policy decisions have exacerbated both trends (Hacker and Pierson 2010).

Although senior citizens continue to enjoy access to programs that extend social citizenship—Social Security and Medicare, which have maintained their real value—working-age Americans have, in many ways, seen their social rights atrophy, as the value of many benefits have deteriorated in real terms. Benefits in policies such as Temporary Assistance to Needy Families and Pell Grants have deteriorated in real terms. Aside from the policies for the elderly and Medicaid, the main social policies that have increased in real value are those channeled largely through the tax code or other mechanisms. Examples of tax expenditures include the Earned Income Tax Credit, home mortgage interest deduction, and employer-provided health benefits, which are excluded from taxable income (Mettler and Milstein 2007). Many of these policies were created in the distant past, but they can increase automatically as market conditions or other factors change, and unlike regular spending programs, they are not subject to scrutiny as part of the annual budget process. In addition, as presidents from Bill Clinton to Barack Obama have sought to create new social policies or to expand existing ones, tax expenditures have provided their vehicle of choice, presumed to offer the best chance of winning bipartisan support.

These trends, in combination, have several effects on Americans' relationship to government and how they experience citizenship. Just as economic inequalities have increased, many of the social programs that could help to mitigate its effects—and fostered political engagement—have deteriorated. Meanwhile, the policies that have become more commonly utilized are those that obscure government's role, tend to shower their largest benefits on the affluent, and make the role of the market appear to be more prominent—even if it is heavily subsidized by government.

The consequences for citizenship in the contemporary period are troubling because, as Marshall feared, rising inequality is proving to be a growing threat to civil, political, and social citizenship. The extreme amount of wealth held by a small group of elites threatens American citizens' ability to have a meaningful voice in government. As Marshall emphasized over half a century ago, a modicum of economic equality helps promote civic and political engagement and vibrant democracy (1998, 94). Moreover, the turn to more submerged policies has fostered a growing sense of alienation, as citizens no longer see the state as a beneficial presence in their lives (Mettler 2011). The success of the Tea Party movement, which vilifies the welfare state even as many of its members are receiving or close to receiving Social Security (Skocpol and Williamson 2012), and the approval rating of Congress sinking into the single digits are better understood in light of these developments. Rising inequality combined with the prevalence of submerged policies creates resentment toward the state while obfuscating who or what policies to hold responsible, thus threatening democratic accountability.

American social policies have promoted full citizenship and active and engaged citizens in the past—resulting in redistribution not just of wealth but also an equalization of political voice. Lawmakers can look back in American history to find inspiration for addressing contemporary economic and political inequality. American social policy has defined deservingness in a multitude of ways and, although using the concept of citizenship to animate social policy making has not traditionally promoted universal policies; it has promoted welfare-state expansions and could do so again in the future.

For social-policy researchers, the task of understanding the links between social policy and citizenship are crucial in the face of rising economic and political inequality. We cannot understand the role social policy has played in creating the current economic situation without understanding how citizenship ideals have animated social-policy making and led to such distinctive policy choices. Nor can we fully understand how to tackle the current situation without appreciating how the American welfare state not only influences poverty rates and inequality, but also the meaning and measure of citizenship.

5 Conclusion—A Social Science Research Agenda on Social Policy and Citizenship

Traditional social-science scholarship has underexplored the relationship between social policy and citizenship in American politics. Emergent scholarship is shedding new light on the subject and the area is ripe for further inquiry. Building on the work of early trailblazers, there are several new and exciting directions researchers should pursue in exploring the links between social policy and citizenship. One direction for further research is to expand which policies we examine. Extending the scope of policies that fall under the social-policy rubric to include a broader range of policies—especially regulatory, education, and labor policies like minimum wage laws and laws pertaining to labor unions—will further enrich our understanding of the government's role in citizen's lives.

The second direction for further research is expanding which groups we study and the ways we understand group effects. Past research has identified the ways social policy can have distinct effects for specific classes, races, and genders. Other identities have received less attention including age cohorts, geographic distinctions, and sexual orientation. For instance, Canaday (2009) explores how enforcement of heterosexual norms and the creation of the category of homosexuality shaped U.S. social policy and, in turn, homosexual identity. Likewise, future research should be attentive to the possibility of intersectional relationships as group identities can overlap creating effects that are different or greater than any single-group identity (for example, Hancock 2007, Weldon 2008).

The third direction for further research is to move beyond individual policies. Given the findings by several scholars that policies like the G.I. Bill, Social Security, and AFDC can have important consequences for recipients' participation, the next step is to start thinking more cumulatively about how these experiences with programs may overlap, cancel each other out, or otherwise interact. For example, Mettler and Stonecash (2008) find that the larger the number of programs individuals used, the stronger the policy feedback effect. Another way research should try to move beyond examining individual policies is to explore mass political behavior rather than just recipient populations (see Mettler and Soss 2004 for a research agenda). Social policies can have consequential effects not just for those who are included but also for those who are excluded, or for mass publics generally (e.g. Flavin and Griffin 2009).

Finally, as has been noted in this essay, the linkages between social policy and citizenship in the United States diverge from those found in other advanced industrial nations. Understanding the relationship between social policy and citizenship in the United States could be improved by more comparative analysis. The processes existing research has uncovered, like the cognitive and resource effects identified by policy feedback scholars, are likely occurring in other nations. Comparative work, like O'Connor, Orloff, and Shaver's (1999) examination of how liberalism and gender play out differently in four similar nations, can help us better identify similar processes as well as the consequences of distinctive policy choices across nations.

These new avenues of research should enrich what is already an exciting area of social science research. By pushing us to rethink our traditional understanding of social policy as simply an output in the political process, and citizenship as constituted solely by civil and political rights, this research offers us a new lens for understanding the effects of the state in citizens' lives. For social scientists, exploring the ways citizenship and social policy interact is proving crucial to helping us better understand what binds citizens and the state and the ways these binds are constituted and reconstituted every day through Americans' experiences with the U.S. welfare state.

REFERENCES

*Indicates recommending reading.

Bruch, Sarah K., Myra Marx Ferree, and Joe Soss. 2010. "From Policy to Polity: Democracy, Paternalism, and the Incorporation of Disadvantaged Citizens." *American Sociological Review* 75 (2): 205–226.

*Campbell, Andrea Louise. 2003. *How Policies Make Citizens: Senior Political Activism and the American Welfare State*. Princeton, NJ: Princeton University Press.

Canaday, Margot. 2009. *The Straight State: Sexuality and Citizenship in Twentieth-Century America*. Princeton, NJ: Princeton University Press.

Converse, Phillip E. 1964. "The Nature of Belief Systems in Mass Publics." In David E. Apter, ed., *Ideology and discontent*. New York: Free Press. 212–242.

Dahl, Robert A. 2003. *How Democratic Is the American Constitution?* New Haven, CT: Yale University Press.

Delli Carpini, Michael X., and Scott Keeter. 1996. *What Americans Know About Politics and Why It Matters*. New Haven: Yale University Press.

*Esping-Andersen, Gøsta. 1990. *The Three Worlds of Welfare Capitalism*. Princeton, NJ: Princeton University Press.

Flavin, Patrick, and John D. Griffin. 2009. "Policy, Preferences, and Participation: Government's Impact on Democratic Citizenship." *Journal of Politics* 71 (2): 544–559.

Foner, Eric. 1995. *Free Soil, Free Labor, Free Men: The Ideology of the Republican Party Before The Civil War*. Oxford: Oxford University Press.

Fraser, Nancy, and Linda Gordon. 1992. "Contract Versus Charity: Why Is There No Social Citizenship in the United States?" *Socialist Review* 22 (July–September): 45–68.

Gilens, Martin. 1999. *Why Americans Hate Welfare: Race, Media, and the Politics*. Chicago: University of Chicago Press.

Hacker, Jacob S. 2002. *The Divided Welfare State: The Battle Over Public and Private Social Benefits in the United States*. New York: Cambridge University Press.

Hacker, Jacob S. and Paul Pierson. 2010. *Winner-Take-All Politics: How Washington Made the Rich Richer—and Turned Its Back on the Middle Class*. New York: Simon & Schuster.

Hancock, Ange-Marie. 2007. "Intersectionality as a Normative and Empirical Paradigm." *Politics & Gender* 3 (2): 248.

Harrington Meyer, Madonna. 1996. "Making Claims as Workers or Wives: The Distribution of Social Security Benefits." *American Sociological Review* 61 (June): 449–465.

Howard, Christopher. 1997. *The Hidden Welfare State: Tax Expenditures and Social Policy in the United States*. Princeton, NJ: Princeton University Press.

Jacobs, Lawrence R. and Benjamin I. Page. 2009. *Class War? What Americans Really Think About Inequality*. Chicago: University of Chicago Press.

King, Desmond, and Rogers Smith. 2011. *Still a House Divided: Race and Politics in Obama's America*. Princeton, NJ: Princeton University Press.

Kymlicka, Will, and Wayne Norman. 1995. "Return of the Citizen: A Survey of Recent Work on Citizenship Theory." In Ronald Beiner, ed., *Theorizing Citizenship*. Albany: State University of New York. 283–323.

Lupia, Arthur, and Mathew D. McCubbins. 1998. *The Democratic Dilemma: Can Citizens Learn What They Need to Know?* Cambridge: Cambridge University Press.

Macedo, Stephen. 2003. *Diversity and Distrust: Civic Education in a Multicultural Democracy*. Cambridge, MA: Harvard University Press.

*Marshall, T. H. 1998 [1950]. "Citizenship and Social Class." In Gershon Shafir, ed., *The Citizenship Debates: A Reader*. Minneapolis: University of Minnesota Press. 93–112.

Mead, Lawrence M. 2004. "The Great Passivity." *Perspectives on Politics* 2:671–675.

Mettler, Suzanne. 1998. *Dividing Citizens: Gender and Federalism in New Deal Public Policy*. Ithaca, NY: Cornell University Press.

Mettler, Suzanne. 2002. "Social Citizens of Separate Sovereignties: Governance in the New Deal Welfare State." In Sidney M. Milkis and Jerome M. Mileur, eds., *The New Deal and the Triumph of Liberalism*. Amherst: University of Massachusetts Press. 231–271.

Mettler, Suzanne. 2005a. *Soldiers to Citizens: The G.I. Bill and the Making of the Greatest Generation*. Oxford: Oxford University Press.

Mettler, Suzanne. 2005b. "Policy Feedback Effects for Collective Action: Lessons From Veterans' Programs." In Helen Ingram, Valerie Jenness, and David Meyer, eds., *Routing the Opposition: Social Movements, Public Policy, and Democracy in America*. Minneapolis: University of Minnesota Press. 211–235.

Mettler, Suzanne. 2011. *The Submerged State: How Invisible Government Programs Undermine American Democracy.* Chicago: University of Chicago Press.

Mettler, Suzanne, and Andrew Milstein. 2007. "American Political Development from Citizens' Perspective: Tracking Federal Government's Presence in Individual Lives Over Time." *Studies in American Political Development* 21, no. 1 (Spring):110–130.

Mettler, Suzanne, and Joe Soss. 2004. "The Consequences of Public Policy for Democratic Citizenship: Bridging Policy Studies and Mass Politics." *Perspectives on Politics* 2, no. 1 (March): 55–73.

Mettler, Suzanne, and Jeffrey M Stonecash. 2008. "Government Program Usage and Political Voice." *Social Science Quarterly* 89, no. 2 (June):273.

Mettler, Suzanne, and Eric Welch. 2004. "Civic Generation: Policy Feedback Effects of the G.I. Bill on Political Involvement Over the Life Course." *British Journal of Political Science* 34, no. 3 (July): 497–518.

Morgan, Kimberly J., and Andrea Louise Campbell. 2011. *The Delegated Welfare State: Medicare, Markets, and the Governance of Social Policy.* New York: Oxford University Press.

Motomura, Hiroshi. 2006. *Americans in Waiting: The Lost Story of Immigration and Citizenship in the United States.* Oxford: Oxford University Press.

Nadasen, Premilla. 2005 *Welfare Warriors: The Welfare Rights Movement in the United States.* New York: Routledge.

Nelson, Barbara J. 1990. "The Origins of the Two-Channel Welfare State: Workmen's Compensation and Mother's Aid." In Linda Gordon, ed., *Women, the State, and Welfare.* Madison: University of Wisconsin Press. 123–151.

O'Connor, Julia S., Ann Shola Orloff, and Sheila Shaver, eds. 1999. *States, Markets, Families: Gender, Liberalism, and Social United States.* Cambridge: Cambridge University Press.

Orloff, Ann. 1991. "Gender in Early U.S. Social Policy." *Journal of Policy History* 3:249–281.

*Orloff, Ann. 1993. "Gender and the Social Rights of Citizenship: The Comparative Analysis of Gender Relations and Welfare States." *American Sociological Review* 58, no. 3 (June): 303–328.

Pierson, Paul. 1993. "When Effect Becomes Cause: Policy Feedback and Political Change." *World Politics* 45, no.4 (July): 595.

Putnam, Robert D. 2000. *Bowling Alone: The Collapse and Revival of American Community.* New York: Simon & Schuster.

Quadagno, Jill S. 1994. *The Color of Welfare: How Racism Undermined the War on Poverty.* New York: Oxford University Press.

Rose, Deondra Eunique. 2012. "The Development of U.S. Higher Education Policy and Its Impact on the Gender Dynamics of American Citizenship." PhD diss. Cornell University.

Rosenstone, Steven J., and John Mark Hansen. 1993. *Mobilization, Participation, and Democracy in America.* New York: Macmillan.

Sainsbury, Diane. 1999. "Gender, Policy Regimes, and Politics." In Diane Sainsbury, ed., *Gender and Welfare State Regimes.* Oxford: Oxford University Press. 245–275.

Schlozman, Kay Lehman, and John T Tierney. 1986. *Organized Interest and American Democracy.* New York: Harper & Row.

*Schneider, Anne L., and Helen M Ingram. 1993. "Social Construction of Target Populations: Implications for Politics and Policy." *American Political Science Review* 87, no. 2 (June): 334.

*Shklar, Judith N. 1991. *American Citizenship: The Quest for Inclusion.* Cambridge, MA: Harvard University Press.

Skocpol, Theda. 1991. "Targeting Within Universalism: Politically Viable Policies to Combat Poverty in the United States." In Christopher Jencks and Paul E. Peterson, eds., *The Urban Underclass*. Washington, DC: Brookings Institution. 411–436.

Skocpol, Theda. 1992. *Protecting Soldiers and Mothers: The Political Origins of Social Policy in the United States*. Cambridge, MA: Belknap Press of Harvard University Press.

Skocpol, Theda. 2003. *Diminished Democracy: From Membership to Management in American Civic Life*. Norman: University of Oklahoma Press.

Skocpol, Theda, and Vanessa Williamson. 2012. *The Tea Party and the Remaking of Republican Conservatism*. Oxford: Oxford University Press.

Smith, Rogers M. 1997. *Civic Ideals: Conflicting Visions of Citizenship in U.S. History*. New Haven, CT: Yale University Press.

*Soss, Joe. 1999a. "Lessons of Welfare: Policy Design, Political Learning, and Political Action." *American Political Science Review* 93, no. 2 (June): 363.

Soss, Joe. 1999b. "Spoiled Identity and Collective Action: Political Consequences of Welfare Stigma." Paper delivered at the 1999 Annual Meeting of the International Society for Political Psychology.

Soss, Joe, Richard C., Fording, and Sanford Schram. 2011. *Disciplining the Poor: Neoliberal Paternalism and the Persistent Power of Race*. Chicago: University of Chicago Press.

Soss, Joe, Jacob S., Hacker, and Suzanne Mettler, eds. 2007. "The New Politics of Inequality: A Policy-Centered Perspective." In Joe Soss, Jacob S. Hacker, and Suzanne Mettler, eds., *Remaking America: Democracy and Public Policy in an Age of Inequality*. New York: Sage. 3–23.

Tichenor, Daniel. 2002. *Dividing Lines: The Politics of Immigration Control in the United States*. Princeton, NJ: Princeton University Press.

Verba, Sidney, and Norman H. Nie. 1972. *Participation in America: Political Democracy and Social Equality*. New York: Harper & Row.

Verba, Sidney, Kay Lehman Schlozman, and Henry E. Brady, 1995. *Voice and Equality: Civic Voluntarism in American Politics*. Cambridge, MA: Harvard University Press.

Weldon, S. Laurel. 2008. Intersectionality. In Gary Mazur Goertz, Amy Cambridge eds., *Politics, Gender, and Concepts: Theory and Methodology*. New York: Cambridge University Press. 193–218.

Wilson, William Julius. 1991. "Public Policy Research and the Truly Disadvantaged." In Christopher Jencks and Paul E. Peterson, eds., *The Urban Underclass*. Washington, DC: Brookings Institution. 411–436.

Wolfinger, Raymond E., and Steven J. Rosenstone. 1980. *Who Votes?* New Haven, CT: Yale University Press.

Zaller, John. 1992. *The Nature and Origins of Mass Opinion*. Cambridge, MA: Cambridge University Press.

INDEX

....

Figures, notes, and tables are indicated by "f," "n," and "t" following page numbers.